EMPIRE OF SECRETS

EMPIRE OF SECRETS

BRITISH INTELLIGENCE, THE COLD WAR

AND THE TWILIGHT OF EMPIRE

CALDER WALTON

THE OVERLOOK PRESS
NEW YORK, NY

This edition first published in hardcover in the United States in 2013 by
The Overlook Press, Peter Mayer Publishers Inc.

141 Wooster Street
New York, NY 10012
www.overlookpress.com
For bulk and special sales, please contact sales@overlookny.com,
or write us at the address above.

Cataloging-in-Publication Data is available from the Library of Congress.

Manufactured in the United States of Americas
ISBN 978-1-4683-0715-3

2 4 6 8 10 9 7 5 3 1

TO JENNIFER

Contents

Illustrations

Sir Vernon Kell, the founding father of MI5. *(Getty Images)*
The original 'C', Sir Mansfield Cumming. *(Imperial War Museum)*
T.E. Lawrence. *(Imperial War Museum)*
RFC plane with aerial reconnaissance camera, 1916. *(Imperial War Museum)*
The 'Colossus' at Bletchley Park. *(Topfoto)*
Jasper Maskelyne. *(Mary Evans Picture Library)*
Dummy tank, Middle East, 1941–42. *(The National Archives, ref. W0201–2022)*
Dummy Spitfire. *(The National Archives, ref. AIR20/4349)*
Dudley Clarke. *(Courtesy of Churchill Archives Centre)*
László Almásy. *(akg-images/Ullstein Bild)*
Long Range Desert Group, North Africa. *(Getty Images)*
Sir Percy Sillitoe. *(Popperfoto/Getty Images)*
Police use tear gas during a riot in Calcutta, 1947. *(Getty Images)*
The bombing of the King David Hotel, Jerusalem, 22 July 1946. *(Getty Images)*
Menachem Begin wanted poster. *(Getty Images)*
Sir John Shaw. *(The Bodleian Libraries, the University of Oxford)*
MI5 report on Jewish terrorism in the Middle East. *(The National Archives, ref. CO 733/457/14)*
British soldiers question a group of schoolboys in Jerusalem, 1947. *(Getty Images)*
Major Roy Farran at his brother's grave, 1948. *(PA/PA Archive/Press Association Images)*
British paratrooper in the Malayan jungle, 1952. *(Getty Images)*
Ghana's independence ceremony, 1957. *(Time & Life Pictures/Getty Images)*
Jomo Kenyatta. *(Popperfoto/Getty Images)*

Suspected Mau Mau victim. *(Getty Images)*

Mau Mau prisoners in Kenya. *(Gamma-Keystone via Getty Images)*

The arrival of the *Empire Windrush* at Tilbury, 22 June 1948. *(Topfoto)*

The Petrov affair, 1954. *(National Archives of Australia)*

British paratroopers embarking for Suez, 1956. *(Popperfoto/Getty Images)*

Cheddi Jagan with ousted ministers, British Guiana, 1953. *(Bettmann/Corbis)*

Archbishop Makarios visiting a British Army camp in Cyprus, 1960. *(Topfoto)*

British soldiers in Cyprus, c.1956. *(Getty Images)*

British soldier threatening Arab demonstrators, Aden, 1967. *(Getty Images)*

Chris Patten, Hong Kong, July 1997. *(Eric Draper/AP/Press Association Images)*

The US base on Diego Garcia. *(Corbis)*

Abbreviations and Glossary

Abwehr – German espionage service

ASIO Australian Security Intelligence Organisation – Australian domestic intelligence service

ASIS Australian Secret Intelligence Service – Australian foreign intelligence service

CIA Central Intelligence Agency – American foreign-intelligence-gathering agency

CID Criminal Investigation Department – Department of regular police force

CPGB Communist Party of Great Britain

DIB Delhi Intelligence Bureau – Pre-independence Indian intelligence agency

DSO Defence Security Officer – MI5 liaison officer in a colonial or Commonwealth country

FBI Federal Bureau of Investigation – US law-enforcement agency

GC&CS Government Code & Cypher School – Pre-war and wartime British SIGINT service

GCHQ Government Communications Headquarters – Renamed post-war British SIGINT service

HOW Home Office Warrant – MI5's mechanism for mail and telephone interception

HUMINT Human intelligence

IB Intelligence Bureau – Indian intelligence service, another name for DIB

IPI Indian Political Intelligence – Pre-independence agency in London responsible for intelligence on Indian affairs

JIC Joint Intelligence Committee – 'High table' of British intelligence community

KGB Committee for State Security – Soviet foreign intelligence-gathering agency

LIC Local Intelligence Committee – Regional colonial intelligence set up in colonies on MI5's advice in early Cold War

MI5 – British intelligence service responsible for counter-espionage, counter-subversion and counter-sabotage in British territory

MI6 – Secret intelligence service responsible for gathering HUMINT from non-British territories

NSA National Security Agency – US SIGINT agency

RCMP Royal Canadian Mounted Police – Canadian law-enforcement agency

SAS Special Air Service – British special forces

Security Service – MI5

SIFE Security Intelligence Far East – MI5 inter-service intelligence outfit in the Far East

SIGINT Signals intelligence

SIME Security Intelligence Middle East – MI5 inter-service intelligence outfit in the Middle East

SIS Secret Intelligence Service – British foreign-intelligence-gathering service

SLO Security Liaison Officer – MI5 liaison officer in a colonial or Commonwealth country

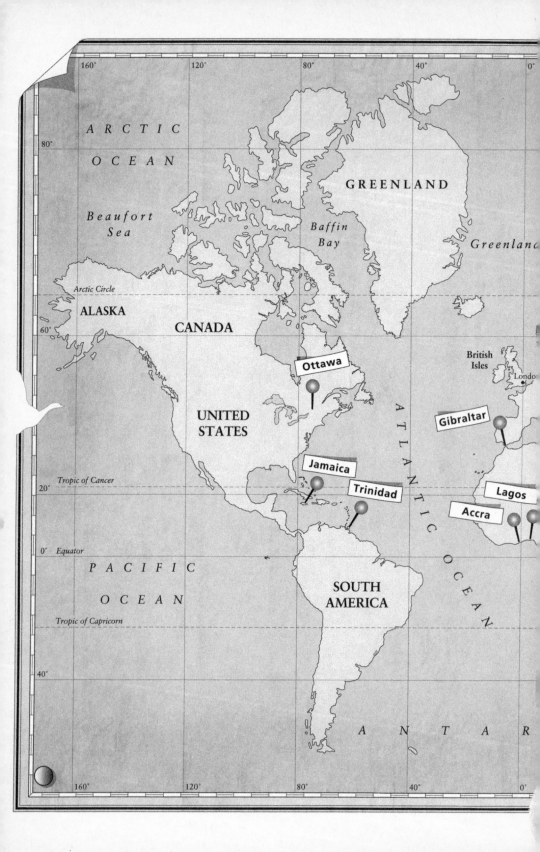

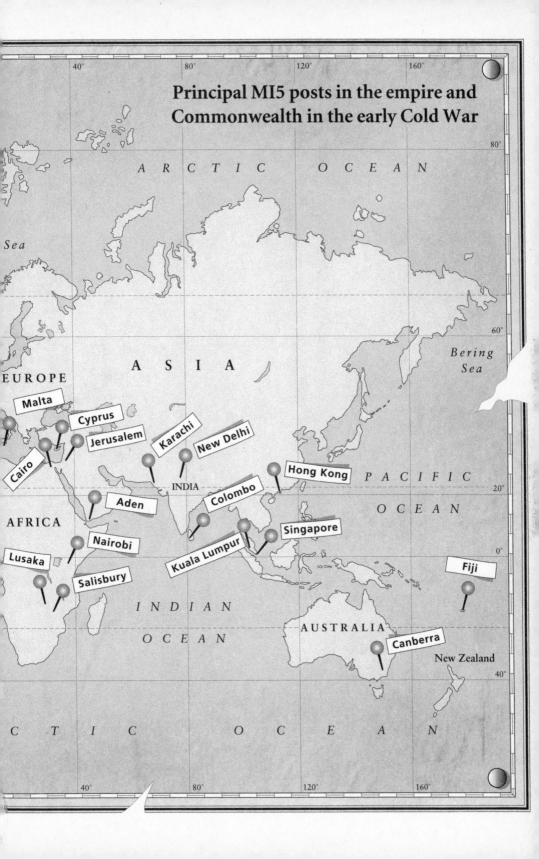

Principal MI5 posts in the empire and Commonwealth in the early Cold War

We are quite impartial; we keep an eye on all people.
HERBERT MORRISON, *Home Secretary (February 1941)*

Introduction

In times of travail, Britain's tendency was to rely more, not less, on spies.
Her entire empire history urged her to do so. The thinner her trade routes,
the more elaborate her clandestine efforts to protect them. The more
feeble her colonial grip, the more desperate her subversion of those who
sought to loosen it.

JOHN LE CARRÉ, *The Honourable Schoolboy*[1]

*On a cold morning in April 1947, a female terrorist slipped into the main
headquarters of the Colonial Office in London. After politely asking a security
guard if she could shelter from the chill indoors, she placed an enormous
bomb, consisting of twenty-four sticks of dynamite, wrapped in newspaper,
in the downstairs toilet, then calmly walked back out into the busy street and
disappeared into the crowd. Her identity was not known at the time to either
the police or MI5, but she worked for a terrorist 'cell' in Britain belonging to
the Stern Gang, one of the two main paramilitary organisations fighting the
British in Palestine. The explosives used for the bomb had been given to her
by another Stern Gang agent, a wounded Franco-Jewish war veteran, known
as the 'dynamite man', who had avoided detection by smuggling the dynamite
into Britain in his artificial leg. The aim of these agents, and of other Stern
Gang cells operating in Britain, was to use violence to force the British government into establishing an independent Jewish state in Palestine.*

*Even before this incident, MI5 had already been placed on high alert for
possible terrorist outrages to be conducted in Britain. In the light of increasingly alarming reports from its sources in the Middle East, warning that
Jewish paramilitaries planned to extend their 'war' against the British from
Palestine to Britain itself, MI5 mounted intensive surveillance operations on
known radical Jewish and Zionist groups in Britain. MI5's investigations
revealed a number of terrorist cells operating in London, whose members*

were planning bombing campaigns and assassinations of leading British politicians. In 1946 the head of MI5 briefed the Prime Minister that he and cabinet ministers were targets. That same year, another terrorist cell launched a letter-bomb campaign directed at every member of the British cabinet. All of the bombs, found to be potentially lethal, were successfully intercepted.

The bomb left in the Colonial Office was only detected after, by sheer luck, it had failed to go off because its timer broke. If it had successfully detonated, it would have caused carnage and chaos at the centre of Whitehall, probably on a similar scale to an attack that the other main militant group fighting the British in Palestine, the Irgun, had carried out in Jerusalem in July 1946, blowing up the King David Hotel and killing ninety-one people.

When the bomb at the Colonial Office was discovered, it led to an immediate Europe-wide search for the female Stern Gang agent, headed by MI5, SIS (MI6) and the London Special Branch. She was eventually apprehended in Belgium. MI5 also identified Irgun members operating in Britain, who were kept under surveillance or arrested. The head of the Irgun, however, remained at large, and continued to plan attacks against the British, in both Palestine and Europe. His name was Menachem Begin. He went on to become the sixth Prime Minister of the state of Israel, and the joint winner of the Nobel Peace Prize.[2]

This episode is just one among a vast number of remarkable, and mostly undisclosed, security operations that Britain's intelligence services were involved in during the period immediately after the Second World War, when Britain began to lose its empire. It has only recently been revealed through declassified intelligence records, and it not only adds a new chapter to the history of the early Cold War, but also has a chilling contemporary resonance. In a striking parallel with the world today, it reveals that the infiltration and radicalisation of a terrorist minority from the Middle East was experienced in Britain more than half a century ago. In fact, as this book reveals, in the aftermath of the Second World War the main threat to British national security did not come from the Soviet Union, as we might expect, but from Middle Eastern terrorism. However, the terrorists then did not come from Palestinian and Islamist groups, as they would do in the late twentieth century, and do today, but from Jewish (or 'Zionist') extremists. As Niall Ferguson has argued, terrorism is the original sin of the Middle East.[3]

*   *   *

This book tells the secret, largely untold, history of Britain's end of empire – the largest empire in world history – and is the first study devoted to examining the involvement of British intelligence in that story. Like Britain's secret services themselves, it offers a global perspective: the agency responsible for imperial security intelligence, MI5, was involved everywhere in the empire where British national security was threatened – which in the early Cold War included almost all of Britain's territorial holdings. It provides a panoramic tour of Britain's declining empire after 1945, and the clandestine activities of the British government as this occurred. Its subject matter ranges from wartime espionage campaigns waged in the deserts of North Africa to shady back-channel communications with African dictators; from violent counter-insurgencies (or 'Emergencies') in the jungles of Malaya and Kenya, and the hills of Cyprus, to urban warfare campaigns in Palestine and the Arabian Peninsula. It reveals CIA plots and covert activities in British colonies, KGB assassinations, and failed coups sponsored by the British and US governments in the Middle East, primarily intended to secure oil and other natural resources.

Intelligence is the 'missing dimension' of the history of Britain's end of empire (or 'decolonisation', as it is known to historians), which took place largely in the two decades after 1945. The activities of Britain's intelligence services are conspicuously missing from almost all histories of that period. Part of the reason for this is perfectly understandable. During Britain's rapid retreat from empire, the British government only tacitly avowed the existence of MI5, but did not officially recognise that of SIS or GCHQ. This meant that there were no officially-released intelligence records for historians to study – it was obviously impossible for government departments to release records if the departments themselves did not officially exist. Intelligence was, therefore, quietly and subtly airbrushed out of the history books.[4]

But while historians in the past were crippled by a lack of official records relating to British intelligence and the end of empire, the same is not true today. Britain's intelligence services have at last come in from the cold. In the late 1980s, the British government finally gave up its practice of denying the existence of its intelligence services, and placed them, for the first time, on a statutory basis – MI5 in 1989, and SIS and GCHQ in 1994. One of the consequences of this was that the intelligence services have, in recent years, at last removed themselves from the historical never-never land they previously occupied, and begun to acknowledge that they do actually have a past. In 1992 Whitehall departments began the so-called Waldegrave Initiative on Open Government, which for the first time brought independent historians into the review and declassification process of government records, including intelligence records. Since then, Britain's intelligence services have begun to declassify records in earnest. This has meant that this book, and others like it, can finally place Britain's secret departments in the historical position they deserve. In fact, the result of the government's declassification process is that there are now almost too many intelligence records relating to the British empire to study.[5]

Despite the unprecedented volume of records that have been crashing into archives in recent years, the overwhelming majority of historians of Britain's end of empire have continued to ignore the role of Britain's intelligence services. Even the best, and most recently published, histories of the period have a yawning gap when it comes to the role of the intelligence services. In the few books that do mention them, they usually appear as little more than an afterthought, in the footnotes of history. This omission is even more bizarre considering that almost every history of the Second World War now mentions the successes of Allied code-breakers at Bletchley Park in cracking the German Enigma code, known to the British as the 'Ultra' secret. However, hardly any history of Britain's end of empire (or for that matter of British activities in the Cold War) yet mentions Bletchley Park's post-war successor, GCHQ. We are supposed to believe that British code-breakers abruptly stopped operating in 1945. Unsurprisingly, this was not the case. Far from being a mere footnote to post-war history, in reality Britain's intelligence services were as active in the years after 1945 as they were during wartime. In fact, since the early twentieth century they had been actively working behind the scenes, removed from public gaze, just as they continue to be today in many of the countries that formerly comprised the British empire. With this in mind, the basic proposition of this book can be summarised concisely: it argues that the current state of the history of Britain's end of empire is in the same position that the history of the Second World War was in before the disclosure of the Ultra secret. By ignoring the role of intelligence, our understanding of the demise of the British empire is at best incomplete, and at worst fundamentally flawed.[6]

It is impossible to understand how and why British intelligence was involved in Britain's often violent retreat from empire after 1945 without first understanding the root causes of why Britain relinquished that empire. Readers should be warned that this is an enormous subject, with as many different interpretations as there are historians. Pinpointing an exact moment for the beginning of the end of the British empire is an archetypal brain-teaser, which historians are unable to agree on – some have argued that it began in the early twentieth century with the Second Boer War in South Africa, between 1899 and 1902, when it took Britain much longer than predicted, and 45,000 troops, to defeat rebellious farmers in the colony. Others date it to the Second World War, particularly with the Atlantic Charter in August 1941 and then the Lend Lease programme, by which the United States provided Britain with urgently needed war supplies, both of which meant that Washington could largely dictate the future of Britain and its empire after the war. Others believe the decisive moment was the advent of the new Labour government in 1945, committed to the reform of local government in British colonies. Still others believe that it occurred much later, with the disastrous Suez crisis in 1956. The reality is that it is probably impossible to pin down a single event that conclusively represents the end of Britain's imperial power, though if I were forced to choose one, it would perhaps be the Suez crisis, which, for reasons we shall see in this book, represented a humiliating failure for Britain and revealed that it was no longer a major world power.[7]

Nevertheless, out of all the ink devoted over the years to understanding why Britain 'scuttled' out of its empire in the post-war years, it is possible to divide the explanations given by historians into four distinct categories. One is that given by nationalist historians, who argue (unsurprisingly) that anti-colonial 'freedom fighters' were responsible for forcibly ejecting the British from their colonies. A second explanation is economic necessity: Britain emerged from the Second World War essentially as a bankrupt state, facing a credit crunch of epic proportions, and was forced to slash its defence budget in the two decades after 1945, at precisely the time that its military commitments in its colonies abroad increased. As the historian Paul Kennedy has put it, Britain was overstretched in its imperial commitments in 1945, and was forced to relinquish control of its colonies because it could not afford to keep them on. A third interpretation is a failure of will: Britain won the war in 1945, but then proceeded to lose the peace, no longer desiring to maintain a colonial empire. A fourth interpretation is that of external pressures: after 1945, the British government was attacked on the international stage for its colonial empire, a repugnant anachronism in the post-war world, which was widely criticised by the United States and the Soviet Union alike.[8]

It is tempting to suppose that there was a linear decline in Britain's status in the post-war years, from a leading world power to a second-rate nation, but this was not the case. Even labelling British decolonisation a 'process' is misleading, because it implies that it was a planned programme. However, it only seems like a process when viewed in retrospect. The liquidation of the empire was never written down as a deliberate policy, by the Colonial Office or any other government department. It would be reading history backwards to suppose that Britain somehow marched triumphantly towards an enlightened, post-colonial future in the years after 1945. The fact is that few, if any, official British records dealing with anti-colonial movements in the late 1940s and early 1950s actually discuss 'independence'. Instead, they refer to 'self-government', which meant that colonies would begin to take control of their own affairs, but with Britain usually retaining control over their security, defence and foreign affairs.

Self-government for colonies was not the same as full independence. When Clement Attlee's Labour government came to power in 1945 it revised Britain's former policies in the Middle East, largely to combat the encroachment of the Soviet Union in the region, away from military bases and autocracies to a commitment to more broadly-based popular regimes. As Foreign Secretary Ernest Bevin memorably put it, Britain would throw its support behind peasants, not pashas. At first glance, this looks like a commitment to broadly-based democratic rule in the empire, which would inevitably mean eventual independence for colonies. However, Britain's transfer of power in India in 1947 and its evacuation from Palestine in 1948 did not herald the empire falling apart under a tidal wave of democratic nationalism. Attlee's government actually put the brakes on colonial emancipation whenever it could. Between 1948 and 1959 only three colonies gained independence from Britain – the Sudan (in 1956), the Gold Coast and Malaya (both in 1957) – and some British officials were dismissive of the idea of relinquishing greater control to colonies for much longer than we might imagine. The wartime Home Secretary, Herbert Morrison, claimed that giving colonies self-government, let alone independence, would be like giving a ten-year-old child 'a latch key, a bank account and a shot gun', while others spoke, albeit rhetorically, of a *revival* and *resurgence* of empire, if only as a strategy for winning the Cold War. The great imperial historian Jack Gallagher pointed out that recruitment to the Colonial Office doubled in the decade after 1945. In this respect, in the post-war years the British empire was being reshaped and refurbished, not abandoned. MI5 approached its Cold War imperial responsibilities in a similar vein, vastly expanding them after 1945. It was only as events progressed that it became clear that its reforms to enhance imperial security were actually taking place as Britain was losing its empire.

Rather than following a planned programme, Britain's exit from empire was actually a pragmatic response to events, in which the Colonial Office, assisted by MI5, attempted to negotiate the best possible outcome for the British government to events that were often beyond their control. Harold Macmillan, under whose Conservative premiership from 1957 to 1963 Britain rapidly withdrew from empire, famously quipped that political decisions were taken because of 'Events, dear boy, events.' As historians like to point out, there were two great periods during which events overtook Britain and accelerated its withdrawal from empire: from 1945 to 1948 and from 1959 to 1964. The main pressures on the British government in both periods were from the USA, the UN and the great anti-colonial empire in the East, the Soviet Union.[9]

The pace of British decolonisation sped up when Macmillan appointed Iain Macleod as Colonial Secretary in October 1959, with a remit to 'get on with it'. Within two years of taking his post, Macleod had effectively worked himself out of a job. Between 1960 and 1964 a total of seventeen British colonies gained independence, and as we shall see, MI5 was involved in many of these transfers of power. Macleod stated that he deliberately hastened the pace of withdrawal from colonies to avoid protracted violence and large-scale bloodshed of the kind seen in the Belgian Congo. The disintegration of Belgian rule in the Congo in 1960, with its ensuing chaos and carnage, was a visible warning for British policy-makers of how not to manage an exit from empire. One of Macleod's successors as Colonial Secretary, Duncan Sandys, who between 1962 and 1964 became another great liquidator of empire, to borrow the phrase of the historian David Cannadine, stated in July 1964 that 'we have no desire to prolong our colonial obligations for a day longer than is necessary'. This is the closest we can come to finding an official declaration by Macmillan's government of the 'end of empire'.

In the opinion of one of the most eminent historians of Britain's end of empire, Ronald Hyam, it was the external pressures imposed on the British government by the United States, the United Nations and the Soviet Union, more than any other reason, that explain how and why Britain relinquished its empire. As Hyam and several others have shown, the geopolitical concerns of the Cold War formed the context, and dictated the manner, in which Britain scrambled out of its empire. It was also the

Cold War context that lies at the heart of the involvement of British intelligence in British decolonisation. As almost every history of the period has shown, the Cold War was primarily an intelligence conflict, in which the intelligence services of Western governments and Eastern Bloc countries were pitted against each other, and fought at the front line. One veteran Whitehall intelligence official, Michael Herman, has rightly said that during the Cold War, Western and Eastern Bloc countries relied on intelligence assessments (of each other) to an extent that was unprecedented in peacetime. Given the connection that existed between Britain's end of empire and the Cold War on the one hand, and the Cold War and intelligence on the other, it should come as little surprise to learn that Britain's intelligence services played a significant role in British decolonisation. [10]

This book offers a new chapter to the existing history of Britain's last days of empire, as well as to our understanding of the Cold War and the history of international relations after 1945. Against the background of the Cold War, that is to say the rapid breakdown in relations between Western governments and the Soviet Union after 1945, and with the looming spectre of Soviet KGB-sponsored subversion in Britain's dwindling colonial empire, British intelligence played a crucial role in the way that post-war British governments pulled out of the empire and passed power to independent national states across the globe. Britain's clandestine services had to deal with a succession of insurgencies (or 'Emergencies') across the empire, but at the same time tried to maintain close links with the very groups that were often violently rejecting British rule. Given the geopolitical concerns of the Cold War, a main requirement for Britain and its allies was to prevent former British colonies being absorbed by the Soviet Union as satellite states. British colonial intelligence thus lay at the forefront of the Cold War, both for Britain and its main Western ally, the United States. The sequence of colonial insurgencies that Britain experienced in the death throes of its empire threatened at times to turn the Cold War into a hot war. In this context, the so-called 'special relationship' between Britain and the United States – much discussed, particularly on this side of the Atlantic, but also much misunderstood – was the linchpin and driving force for an enormous overhaul of colonial intelligence that Britain embarked on in the early Cold War. As successive spy scandals broke out in Britain, particularly the revelation of the 'Cambridge spies' in 1951, pressure from Washington forced London to enhance security standards not only at home, but across its colonial empire.

*   *   *

Before proceeding any further, it would be useful to say a few words on terminology. One of the difficulties in studying intelligence history is that, like the study of government departments more generally, sometimes ideas can get lost in an alphabet soup of acronyms, so getting some of the basic terminology that will appear in this book sorted out at this stage will be helpful. There are three main services that comprise the British intelligence community: MI5, GCHQ and SIS. The Security Service, also known as MI5, plays a central role in this book. It was not simply a 'domestic' intelligence service, as is sometimes thought, but was Britain's imperial intelligence service, responsible for security intelligence matters (counter-espionage, counter-subversion and counter-sabotage) in all territories across Britain's global empire. Then there is Britain's largest, best-funded, and most secretive intelligence service: the Government Code and Cypher School (GC&CS), which after 1945 was renamed the Government Communications Headquarters (GCHQ). GC&CS was, and GCHQ remains, responsible for intercepting and decoding communications, known as signals intelligence (or SIGINT). Thirdly there is Britain's foreign intelligence service, the Secret Intelligence Service (SIS), also known as MI6, which was, and remains, responsible for gathering human-based intelligence (known as 'HUMINT') from non-British territories all over the world. From the little information that can be discerned from publicly available sources, it appears that SIS's espionage operations took place in a world less like that of James Bond, its most famous fictional officer, than like that from the pages of a John le Carré novel – less to do with licences to kill and high-tech gadgets, and more to do with grey-haired men in pipe-smoke-filled rooms, hunched over stacks of yellowing files, with matron-like women regularly bringing the tea trolley around.

The most senior body within the British intelligence community, then as now, was the Joint Intelligence Committee (or JIC). It was responsible for collating intelligence from all the different intelligence services (MI5, SIS and GCHQ), as well as military intelligence (army, navy and air force), assessing it and distributing it to high levels of the British government. The JIC was not an intelligence *collection* body, but an intelligence *assessment* outfit. In the first years after its establishment before the Second World War, it came solely under the control of the military Chiefs of Staff. However, as the Cold War set in after 1945, and particularly after the Suez crisis in 1956, the JIC moved out of the control of the military and became directly responsible to civilian cabinet ministers. As well as sitting at the peak of the domestic British intelligence community, the JIC was also positioned at the centre of a complicated web of imperial intelligence agencies and assessment bodies stretching across the empire. Reading some reports on how British imperial intelligence operated in the Cold War, one gets the impression that it was a finely-turned, well-oiled machine. In reality, however, it evolved haphazardly, and looked better on paper than it performed in reality. This was revealed by the repeated intelligence failures in British colonies after 1945, as intelligence chiefs spectacularly failed to detect outbreaks of anti-colonial insurgencies in Palestine, Malaya, Kenya, Cyprus and Aden.

In theory, at least, the British intelligence community formed a web across the empire through MI5. MI5's representatives stationed in empire and Commonwealth countries were called Security Liason Officers (SLOs). Until recently their activities have been shrouded in secrecy, with their actions leaving hardly any traces in official British records. With the recent release of MI5 records, we can now see that SLOs operated from official British residencies in colonial and Commonwealth countries, sometimes openly and sometimes under cover, disguising their MI5 postings under titles such as 'Second Secretary' or 'Cultural Attaché'. According to MI5's Director-General's charter, an SLO's job with a colonial government was to provide 'liaison, supply of external intelligence, training [and] operational advice'. They reported directly to MI5's headquarters in London, and from there their reports, if deemed sufficiently serious, could be passed by MI5 all the way up to the JIC. SLOs also reported to regional MI5 liaison outfits, such as Security Intelligence Middle East (SIME), headquartered in Cairo, and Security Intelligence Far East (SIFE), headquartered in Singapore, whose function was to pool regional intelligence reports from MI5 as well as GCHQ and SIS, and pass the most important information back to the JIC in London. As the Cold War set in, MI5's SLOs were also responsible for reporting to and liaising with Local Intelligence Committees (LICs), which sprung up (largely at MI5's instigation) in a number of colonial territories and Commonwealth countries. High-ranking local officials sat on the LICs, and their meetings were often chaired by the colonial Governor himself, which meant that MI5's SLOs had a direct channel of communication to all of the most important officials in British colonies. Again, reports from LICs were passed on to the JIC in London if deemed sufficiently serious. The problem was that often reports were not deemed sufficiently serious, and were merely passed up the hierarchy of the colonial intelligence apparatus, rather than to London.

This lay at the heart of many of the failures that British intelligence experienced in successive colonies after 1945. Finally, it should be noted that the actual groundwork of intelligence-gathering in the British empire in the Cold War was performed by special branches established within colonial police forces. MI5 overhauled colonial special branches as the Cold War escalated after 1945.

This book is based on a wealth of previously classified intelligence records which have only recently been released to the public. The research for it, which took the best part of ten years to complete, is predominantly based on MI5 records, which makes sense considering that MI5 was Britain's imperial intelligence service. This has involved reading literally hundreds of MI5 records and dossiers, many of them multi-volume, spanning thousands of pages. As well as MI5 records, JIC records have helped to provide an overview of what the British intelligence community considered as threats to Britain and its empire during the post-war years. These have proved particularly useful as, at present, SIS does not release records from its own archives, although Keith Jeffery's recent official history of the first forty years of SIS, like Christopher Andrew's official centenary history of MI5, does provide an insight into areas still hidden away from historians. In addition to drawing on intelligence records that until recently were still classified, kept under lock and key in secret Whitehall departments, I have consulted a range of private collections of papers from a number of archives. Together with interviews conducted with former intelligence officials, it has thus been possible to weave together a narrative of the history of British intelligence, the Cold War, and Britain's twilight of empire.

During my doctorate at Cambridge, and then as a post-doctorate research Fellow also at Cambridge, I was given the exciting opportunity to be a research assistant on Christopher Andrew's unprecedented official history of MI5. This position gave me privileged access to MI5 records, before their release. It was during my doctorate, and also in the research for Andrew's authorised history of MI5, that I realised that the role of British intelligence was missing from the overwhelming majority of books on Britain's end of empire. All of the records that this book is based on are now declassified, and are available at the National Archives in London. There are overlaps between this book and Andrew's official history of MI5, but this book is more than a history of a single intelligence service, whether MI5, SIS or GCHQ. It is the first history, based on intelligence records, of the involvement of British intelligence as a whole, meaning all three of those services, in Britain's twilight of empire during the Cold War.

This book also draws on a tranche of previously 'lost' Colonial Office records which were only made available to the public in April 2012, after a high-level court case forced the British government into admitting their existence. These supposedly 'rediscovered' records are said to contain some of the grimmest paperwork on the history of Britain's end of empire, and the story of how they finally came to see the light of day is a shameful chapter in the history of British colonial rule, a cover-up of massive proportions.

In 2009 a group of elderly Kenyans instigated legal proceedings at the High Court in London against the British government for gross abuses allegedly committed on them while they were detained as Mau Mau suspects fifty years previously, during the colonial 'Emergency' in Kenya. As part of the proceedings of the case, the Foreign and Commonwealth Office (the successor to the Colonial Office) was forced to reveal the existence of 8,800 files that colonial officials had secretly spirited away from thirty-seven different British colonies across the world, including Kenya, Cyprus, Aden, Palestine, Nigeria and Malaya, as the sun set on the empire. The official explanation for why these records were deliberately removed was that they might 'embarrass' Her Majesty's government. In reality, it was because they contained some of the darkest secrets of the last days of empire.

The first cache of the previously 'lost' records, only made publicly available in April 2012, revealed that the British government deliberately set about destroying, culling and then removing incriminating records from colonies as they approached independence in order to prevent them falling into the hands of post-independence governments. By destroying and removing these records, Britain was then able to inculcate a fictional history of its colonial benevolence, in which occasional abuses and violence may have been inflicted on local populations, but these were the exception, not the rule. The 'lost' Colonial Office records revealed such a claim to be nonsense. Burying the British empire was a far more bloody affair than has previously been acknowledged or supposed.[11]

The records that were not deliberately destroyed by colonial officials in the last days of empire were transferred back to Britain, and were eventually housed at a top-secret Foreign Office facility at Hanslope Park, near Milton Keynes in Buckinghamshire, where they remained hidden for fifty years, until the High Court (assisted by a few Foreign Office officials determined that they should see the light of day) forced their release. Hanslope Park's official title is curiously neutral-sounding: 'Her Majesty's Communications Centre'. To local inhabitants, however, it is known as 'spook central'. The secret facility has a long history of involvement with Britain's intelligence services: during the Second World War it was home to the Radio Security Service, a SIGINT outfit known as MI8 that was responsible for detecting German agents operating in Britain. The idea that the government could have 'mislaid' or 'lost' this archive is as shameful as it is preposterous. The records at Hanslope Park referring to Kenya alone were housed in three hundred boxes, occupying 110 feet of shelving. Thanks to the Kenyan case that went before the High Court, we can now see that Hanslope Park acted as a depository for records detailing the most shameful acts and crimes committed in the last days of the British empire.[12] In June 2013 the British government settled the Kenyan case out of court. Speaking on behalf of the government, the foreign secretary, William Hague, issued a public apology, for the first time admitting that "Kenyans were subject to torture and other forms of ill-treatment at the hands of the colonial administration". By settling the case before it went to full trial, the British government was probably attempting to avoid establishing what for it would be an unwanted legal precedent, which could be used by claimants in other former British colonies alleging torture and mistreatment at the hands of British forces. The result, however, may be precisely the opposite: the British government's apology, and the £20 million compensation it gave to Kenyan victims, may open the flood gates to other claimants.

This is the first book to draw on that secret archive. At the time of writing, only the first wave of records has been released to the public, but more are to follow. This book is therefore necessarily the first word, not the final word, on the secrets contained at Hanslope Park. Even though only the first tranche of these records, amounting to about 1,200 files, is available at the time of writing, they still reveal a number of previously unknown horrific stories. They show that the 'elimination of ranking terrorists' was a repeated theme in secret monthly reports circulated by the director of intelligence in British-controlled Malaya in the 1950s, suggesting that Britain effectively operated a shoot-to-kill policy there. They also show that successive British governments hoodwinked Parliament and the public over the decision to give the US a military base on the small island in the Indian Ocean, Diego Garcia, and that in order to pave the way (literally) for this, Britain forcibly removed islanders from their homes. This sad story has a resonance closer to our own times: the same base on Diego Garcia has apparently been used as a transfer site by the US as part of its policy of 'extraordinary rendition' in the so-called 'war on terror'.

As well as adding a new dimension to our understanding of both Britain's last days of empire and the Cold War, this book reveals clear – and often alarming – parallels with the world today. Among other matters, it reveals how Western governments have both used and abused intelligence; it describes the practical limitations that were faced by under-resourced intelligence services, as well as the fine line that existed between safeguarding security and upholding civil liberties, a line that in some instances was crossed; it reveals a number of dramatic, unpublicised spy scandals; it shows that just over half a century ago the British government conspired with its allies to bring about 'regime change' in the Middle East, and 'sexed up' intelligence reports in order to do so; it demonstrates the difficulty of tracking down terrorist cells that are determined to cause death and destruction; and the central role that intelligence played in combating brutal guerrilla insurgencies. It also offers a new history of 'rendition', revealing that during the Second World War, German agents were captured in various parts of the British empire and then transported to top-secret interrogation facilities in Britain, despite MI5's recognition of the dubious legality of doing so. It provides a haunting testimony to the fact that, in several post-war colonial 'Emergencies', British soldiers tortured detainees during interrogations – despite the belief of British intelligence that doing so was counter-productive and would not produce reliable intelligence. A central theme of this book is that a repetition of such catastrophic failures can only be avoided if we understand those that occurred previously; or as Winston Churchill put it, in order to understand the present, let alone the future, we must first look back at the past.

1

Victoria's Secrets:
British Intelligence and Empire
Before the Second World War

One advantage of the secret service is that it has no worrying audit. The service is ludicrously starved, of course, but the funds are administered by a few men who do not call for vouchers or present itemised accounts ...

He considered the years to come when Kim would have been entered and made to the Great Game that never ceases day and night, throughout India.

RUDYARD KIPLING, *Kim*[1]

Governments have conducted espionage and intelligence-gathering efforts for centuries. Indeed, intelligence-gathering – often said to be the world's second oldest profession – is as old as governments themselves. In Britain, there was a 'secret service' operating at least since the reign of Queen Elizabeth I in the sixteenth century, which under Sir Francis Walsingham was tasked to gather intelligence on the Spanish Armada and to uncover various Catholic intrigues and plots. However, it was not until the nineteenth century, and more importantly the early twentieth century, that the British government began to devote significant resources to intelligence, and turn it into a professional, bureaucratic enterprise. Despite Britain's long history of clandestine espionage work, in fact it was not in the 'domestic' realm that its intelligence-gathering was to develop most rapidly. Instead, it was in the British empire, which in the course of the nineteenth and twentieth centuries grew to become the greatest empire in world history, that intelligence found a particularly important role.[2]

From the earliest days of the British intelligence community, which was established in the early twentieth century, there was a close connection between intelligence-gathering and empire. It is not an exaggeration to say that in its early years British intelligence was British *imperial* intelligence. This is not surprising when it is considered that intelligence played an essential role in the administration of the empire, which by the 1920s had grown to encompass one-quarter of the world's territory and population. After 1918, as one geographer proudly commented, the empire reached its widest extent, covering 'one continent, a hundred peninsulas, five hundred promontories, a thousand lakes, two thousand rivers, ten thousand islands'. The empire had four kinds of dependent territories: colonies, protectorates, protected states and trust territories. At one end of the spectrum, colonies were those territories, like Kenya, where the monarch of the United Kingdom had absolute sovereignty, while trust territories, at the other end of the spectrum, were those assigned to Great Britain for administration under a special mandate, like Palestine. There was often little practical difference between colonies and protectorates. The Colonial Office usually referred to territories under 'traditional' rulers, with a British resident, as 'protected states'. The typology of these dependent states was incredibly confusing (sometimes even to the Colonial Office itself).

One reason for the importance of intelligence in the empire was the lack of sheer manpower required to cover such enormous territories. Even at its height, British rule in India was maintained through an incredibly small number of administrative officials, with the renowned Indian Civil Service in the Raj boasting a total of just 1,200 posts, at a time when the population of India was probably around 280 million. Before 1939 the Indian army of 200,000 men, together with a British garrison of 60,000, was responsible for keeping the peace on land from Egypt to Hong Kong – British territories 'East of Suez', to use the phrase from the time. With such meagre resources at its disposal, British rule in India required up-to-date and reliable information on its enemies, both imagined and real. This was acquired through networks of informants and agents, and from intercepted communications. It is little wonder that, as one study has termed it, the British empire in the nineteenth century was an 'empire of information'.[3]

Intelligence-gathering also came to the forefront in Britain's imperial military campaigns in the late nineteenth and early twentieth centuries. One of the most exhilarating theatres for intelligence operations, or spying, lay in India's North-West Frontier – now the tribal borderlands of Pakistan – where Victorian Britain fought the 'Great Game' with Russia, a conflict memorably portrayed by Rudyard Kipling in *Kim*, arguably one of the greatest espionage novels of all time. In *Kim*, Kipling described the 'Great Game' as essentially an intelligence conflict, which 'never ceases day or night', with both Britain and Russia running spies and informants to discover the other's intentions. However, the reality was that it was often not difficult for Russia to spot British imperial intelligence agents: they were often extremely amateurish and deployed flimsy covers, variously posing as butterfly collectors, archaeologists and ethnographers. That said, it was in the 'Great Game' that some distinctly more professional forms of intelligence-gathering were born, particularly in a process that would later become known as signals intelligence (SIGINT), the interception and decryption of communications, or 'signals'. In 1844 the Indian army pioneered one of the first permanent code-breaking bureaus in the world, which gained notable successes in reading Russian communications long before any similar European SIGINT agency had done so. The British military also made innovative use of intelligence during its campaigns in Egypt in the 1880s, successfully deploying a series of agents and scouts to reconnoitre the location of Egyptian forces in the desert.[4]

The very process of Britain's colonial expansion in the Victorian period, especially during the so-called 'scramble for Africa' beginning in the 1880s, necessitated new forms of systematic intelligence-gathering, such as mapping and census-taking. In undertaking such activities, Britain was not acting differently from its imperial rivals at the time – France, Russia, Germany and Italy. Before any colonial power could dominate, control and exploit colonial populations, in Africa or elsewhere, it first had to map them. In practice, however, the process of mapping an empire often ignored its realities. Maps imposed European geometrical patterns on amorphous landscapes, drawing frontiers that cut through tribal communities as well as ethnic and linguistic groups. To this day, it is not difficult to spot the borders of those countries, particularly in Africa, which were drawn by European cartographers: many are arranged at right angles and slice through geographical features and ethnographic groupings. Sometimes European powers displaced and resettled colonial populations in order to make *them* reflect the ethnographic colonial maps. In the 'white man's burden' of colonial rule, subtle realities did not matter.[5]

Given all that, it is no coincidence that Britain's first Directorate of Military Intelligence, established in 1887, grew from the Topographical and Statistical Department in the War Office, which was responsible for mapping much of the British empire. Moreover, it was a violent colonial 'small war' in an outpost of the British empire, the Second Anglo-Boer War in southern Africa, waged between 1899 and 1902, which first alerted the British government to the need for establishing a permanent intelligence service. The so-called Boer War exposed to Britain's military leaders, the Chiefs of Staff in London, how fragile the nation's colonial holdings were. It took the British military much longer than expected, three years, and also the deployment of some 45,000 troops, to defeat a group of rebellious Dutch Boer farmers in the Cape Colony (now South Africa) who harried the British Army through guerrilla warfare. In fighting the insurgency there, it has to be noted that the British military developed some ominous strategies, not least the establishment of 'concentration camps', or detention camps, where suspected insurgents were 'concentrated'. This type of warfare, in which the distinction between combatants and non-combatant civilians was blurred, was to have horrific echoes in the twentieth century. As far as intelligence was concerned, the kind of irregular warfare that Britain faced in the Boer War, like that experienced by other European powers in their own colonial 'small wars' – literally *guerrilla* in Spanish – revealed the paramount need for effective intelligence-gathering. In fact, it was during the Boer War that a British officer, Lt. Col. David Henderson, wrote an influential paper for the War Office in London, 'Field Intelligence: its principles and practice', which became the basis of a manual, 'Regulations for intelligence duties in the field', published by the War Office in 1904. This manual became the inspiration for the British Army's intelligence corps, founded ten years later, on the outbreak of the First World War.[6]

Despite Britain's long history of intelligence-gathering, a watershed occurred in the early twentieth century. Partly in response to fears of Britain's colonial frailty, as revealed by the Boer War, but more specifically as a result of fears about the growing threat posed by the German empire, in October 1909 the British government took the momentous decision to establish a permanent, peacetime intelligence department. This decision was taken by the Committee of Imperial Defence – significantly, it was *imperial* defence that led to the setting up of Britain's spook agencies. The department, known as the 'Secret Service Bureau', was divided into two branches. The 'domestic' branch, MO5(g), was responsible for security intelligence – counter-espionage, counter-sabotage and counter-subversion. During the First World War MO5(g) was renamed Military Intelligence 5, or 'MI5', and after the war it was again rechristened the Security Service – twin designations (the Security Service, MI5) that it keeps to the present day. Sir Vernon Kell, a retired officer from the South Staffordshire Regiment, served as Director-General of MI5 from 1909 to 1940, roughly one-third of its history to date, making him the longest-ever serving head of any British government department.[7]

Meanwhile, the 'foreign' branch of the Secret Service Bureau, first known as MI1C, was renamed Military Intelligence 6, or 'MI6', during the First World War. Thereafter it became known as MI6 or the Secret Intelligence Service (SIS) – again, twin designations that it retains to the present day. Its first head was Sir Mansfield Cumming, a Royal Navy officer who had taken early retirement due to ill-health. By all accounts he was a remarkable character. In the early stages of the First World War he lost a leg in a road traffic accident in France – as the story goes, he hacked his own leg off with a pocket penknife in order to drag himself to safety from the wreckage of his car. This accident caused him to use a wheelchair, and colleagues later recalled that he would terrorise the corridors of power in Whitehall, spinning at high speeds around corners.[8]

In taking the decision to establish a professional intelligence department in 1909, the British government actually came late to the 'intelligence game' when compared to other European powers, most of which had already set up such bodies by the turn of the twentieth century. France had established code-breaking 'black chambers' (*cabinets noirs*) in the middle of the nineteenth century, while tsarist Russia had an infamous intelligence service (the *Okhrana*), and Germany had a specialised intelligence service (*Nachrichtendienst*) operating at least since the time of the Franco-Prussian war in 1870. The reason for Britain's late arrival into the world of espionage was due to strong opposition from some Victorian and Edwardian politicians, who decried 'intelligence' as an inherently un-English pursuit: gentlemen 'did not read each other's mail', went the phrase, and 'espionage' was not even an English word, as some liked to point out. It was better to leave such sordid exploits to the Continental powers, where they belonged.[9]

The formation of the two services that would later become known as MI5 and SIS represented a fundamental break with all British intelligence-gathering efforts up to that point. For the first time, the government had professional, dedicated peacetime intelligence services at its disposal. Operational distinctions between MI5 and SIS, particularly jurisdictional disputes over what constituted 'domestic' and 'foreign' territory, proved a thorny subject that would only be resolved over subsequent decades. Nevertheless, the crucial point is that, unlike all British intelligence-gathering efforts up to that point, after 1909 the government was equipped with independent intelligence bureaucracies, furnished with card-catalogue index registries, which brought together information from all available sources. Whereas previously the British military and various government departments, such as the India Office, had gathered intelligence and conducted espionage for their own purposes, often on an *ad hoc* basis, the services established in 1909 had two specific combined purposes: to gather and assess intelligence. They were also inter-departmental, that is to say they were meant to 'service' all British government departments with the intelligence they needed. Although MI5 and SIS grew out of Britain's military intelligence department (MO5), they were different from the intelligence departments of the armed forces, which were not inter-departmental. All three of the armed services, the army, Royal Navy and Royal Air Force, would go on to maintain their own intelligence departments, but it is MI5 and SIS (and later GC&CS) that are usually understood to be Britain's intelligence services, or, more amorphously, 'British intelligence'. The establishment of MI5 and SIS also witnessed for the first time a distinction between various grades of classified information (or 'intelligence'), such as 'secret' and 'top secret'. Thus, while British government departments before 1909 had *gathered intelligence*, and would continue to do so thereafter, the breakthrough for the government was that after 1909 it had for the first time its own *intelligence services*.

To this day, MI5 and SIS retain many of the practices established in their earliest days. The Chiefs of SIS retain the designation 'C', a title that was first used by Sir Mansfield Cumming, which is variously understood to stand either for 'Cumming' or for 'Chief'. Other SIS rituals established in its earliest times which continue to the present include a green light outside C's room (indicating that C is busy), special green ink that is reserved for him alone to use, and the ubiquitous and sometimes pointless use of codenames. SIS reports are still referred to as 'CX reports', apparently meaning 'C Exclusively'. Similar continuities also exist in MI5. The terms 'Put Away' ('P/A') and 'Look Up' ('L/U'), for example, can be seen on the front of countless declassified MI5 records, indicating when a file has been looked up and then put away in a secure cabinet – both of which were terms used by Kell soon after his 'Bureau' was established. The same is true of 'Nothing Recorded Against' ('NRA'), which refers to one of the most important, but least glamorous, activities that MI5 officers have undertaken since Kell's time: when an MI5 officer has looked up an individual in the service's central archive, but has found nothing incriminating.

Eccentric rituals and designations apart, MI5 and SIS also retain much more important legacies from their early history. From the outset of their operations it was established that neither would have any executive powers. In contrast to law-enforcement agencies such as London's Special Branch at Scotland Yard, or the US Federal Bureau of Investigation (FBI), neither MI5 nor SIS has ever had any powers of arrest. Readers may be disappointed to learn that SIS officers have never had 'licences to kill'. Instead, MI5 and SIS have always relied on police authorities in Britain, particularly Special Branch, to carry out arrests for them. This was a calculated strategy on the part of the Chiefs of Staff and the British government. By decoupling intelligence-gathering from law enforcement, policing, and executive action more generally, they hoped to avoid the establishment of a 'police state', which they feared would be created by providing the secret services with powers of arrest. They also seem to have concluded that policing is a very different activity from intelligence work, which is not necessarily concerned with either arrests or law enforcement. Intelligence-gathering involves acquiring information in an anticipatory, prophylactic manner – fragments of information from here or there which may or may not become important one day. This distinction between intelligence and policing continues to the present day, and in fact is one of the reasons why the FBI at the start of the twenty-first century is considered to be ill-equipped to deal with the threat of terrorism, which requires anticipatory intelligence, not policing.[10]

Despite the notable continuities in MI5 and SIS's history from 1909 onwards, it would be erroneous to suppose that in the years immediately after their foundation they were anything like the services they would later become. It is a myth that ever since the sixteenth century 'British intelligence', like the British empire itself, grew steadily in size and influence, spreading its tentacles across the world. This myth was mostly derived from Edwardian spy novelists like Erskine Childers, whose writings, such as *Riddle of the Sands*, depicted a powerful British intelligence service actively thwarting its enemies both at home and abroad. The reality could not have been further from such fictions. For years after their establishment, both MI5 and SIS remained desperately short of resources. The diary of MI5's first and longest-serving head, Sir Vernon Kell, reveals how perilous the organisation's existence was in its early days. In the years before the First World War, MI5 and SIS were both run on shoestring budgets. At the outbreak of war in 1914, MI5 had an entire staff of just fifteen – including the office's caretaker. Staff numbers in SIS were similarly meagre. During his first week on the job in 1909, the first Chief of SIS, Sir Mansfield Cumming, noted rather miserably in his diary that he sat alone in his new office, without the telephone ringing, and with no one visiting him because the Bureau was too secret to be listed in a Whitehall telephone directory. This was very much a one-man-and-a-dog operation.[11]

The First World War led to the massive expansion of the machinery of Britain's secret state – just as it did in all other major belligerent European powers. In fact, it is fair to say that the war was the event that created the modern national security state. Every fighting nation built up unprecedented surveillance systems, and the strains of 'total war', in which all of a country's resources were mobilised towards the war effort, necessitated an enormous increase in security and surveillance, both in Britain and across its empire. Total war required total surveillance. All of the warring governments were equipped with vastly increased new powers of detention and investigation, particularly through mail interception. MI5's staff expanded dramatically after 1914, growing from a handful on the outbreak of war to reach 844 in 1918, of whom 133 were officers, as opposed to other ranks, while its central registry of people and organisations grew from 17,500 card indexes in 1914 to over 250,000 cards and 27,000 personal files in 1918. The Defence of the Realm Act (DORA), passed soon after the outbreak of hostilities in 1914, provided MI5 and other departments of the British secret state with enormously increased powers of surveillance. This is illustrated by the fact that at the start of the war the Post Office employed a single censor to intercept, open and analyse mail, but by its end the Censor's Office had grown to employ over 2,000 officials, each of whom opened on average over 150 letters per day. It was also during the First World War that MI5 became more than just a 'domestic' intelligence service, as it is sometimes still mistakenly understood to be, and made a claim to be an imperial service, responsible for security intelligence in all British territories across the globe.[12]

The First World War is often regarded as a European war, a view that is reinforced by the famous war poetry of the Western Front, which vividly captures the horrific realities of trench warfare, with thousands of men being sent to their deaths in conditions akin to hell on earth. In reality, however, from the outset it was a worldwide war. Contrary to what we might expect, the first shots fired by British forces on land in the war did not take place in Europe, but were fired on 12 August 1914 at a German wireless station in Togoland, and soon after the outbreak of hostilities it became a deliberate policy of the Prusso-German General Staff to incite revolution and subversion (termed *Revolutionspolitik*) in the colonial empires and 'weak points' of its enemies. In September 1914 the German Chancellor, Theobold von Bethmann Hollweg, told his Foreign Ministry:

'England appears determined to wage war until the bitter end ... Thus one of our main tasks is gradually to wear England down through unrest in India and Egypt.' It is revealing that while the British used the term 'Great War', from the start the German military spoke of a 'World War' (*Weltkrieg*).[13]

In 1914 the German General Staff established a new department, the Intelligence Bureau for the East (*Nachrichtenstelle für den Orient*), attached to the Foreign Ministry, which was led by an aristocratic Prussian archaeologist and explorer, Max von Oppenheim. The exploits of Oppenheim's Bureau read much like the fantastic accounts of dastardly German plots to stir up unrest in India found in John Buchan's classic wartime espionage novel *Greenmantle* (1916). Buchan describes a fiendish plan by the Central Powers to incite revolt in the Middle East and India, which it falls to his heroes, Major Richard Hannay and his friend Sandy Arbuthnot, a master of foreign tongues and exotic disguises, to thwart. In fact, Buchan's story was not as absurd as the author purposefully made it appear. Buchan served as a war correspondent and briefly as a military intelligence officer at British headquarters in France, where he would have had access to intelligence records. His novel was fictional in degree, but not in essence.[14]

The reality was that before the war, Germany had been carefully cultivating links with Turkey and other Middle Eastern countries, which acted as the gateway to British India. Beginning in the 1890s, the German emperor, Kaiser Wilhelm II, had sponsored the construction of the Berlin–Baghdad railway, and during a trip to Damascus in 1898 he went so far as to declare himself the 'protector' of all Muslims – though it is unclear what reaction this received. Oppenheim's new intelligence Bureau was responsible for inciting revolt among Germany's enemies, and at various times during the war it sponsored French pacifists and Mexican nationalists, and most famously – or infamously, depending on one's perspective – it helped a Russian émigré called Vladimir Ilyich Ulyanov, more popularly known by his pseudonym, Lenin, to return to Russia in April 1917 in a sealed bomb-proof train, with ample funds, shortly after which he successfully instigated a revolution against the temporary Russian government. There is no evidence that Lenin was a German agent *per se*, but he was certainly sponsored by Oppenheim's Bureau – though presumably Lenin himself would have argued that it was he who was playing the German intelligence services, not the other way around. Nevertheless, in many ways the Bolshevik revolution *was* the greatest success of the wartime German intelligence services. Meanwhile, the main targets of Oppenheim's Bureau in the British empire were Indian and Bengali nationals, Irish republicans and Arab *jihadists*.[15]

On 5 November 1914, soon after the outbreak of hostilities, the Ottoman empire entered the war on Germany's side, and largely as a result of pressure from the German government, the Turkish Caliphate issued *fatwas* ordering all Muslims to wage a holy war (*jihad*) against Britain and its allies. British War Office records reveal the extent to which the Chiefs of Staff in London were concerned about subversion in the Indian army, one-third of whose soldiers were Muslims. It was also not lost on the Chiefs of Staff, nor on MI5, that approximately half of the world's then 270 million Muslims lived under either British, Russian or French rule.[16]

At the beginning of the war, India was the only part of the British empire that MI5 was in direct contact with, communicating with the Director of Criminal Intelligence (DCI) in Delhi, Maj. John Wallinger. Previously, the main responsibility for dealing with Indian 'seditionists' or 'revolutionaries' (members of the *Ghadr* 'revolt' party) had fallen to the London Special Branch, but in the course of the war MI5 increasingly took a lead in dealing with Indian revolutionaries in Britain. After 1914 the German Foreign Ministry established an 'Indian Committee' in Berlin, which revolved around the exiled Indian academic and lawyer Virendaranath Chattopadhyaya, who had become a revolutionary while studying law at Middle Temple in London, and was a close confidant of the man who would later become the first leader of independent India, Jawaharlal Nehru. One of the agents being run by Chattopadhyaya in wartime Britain, Harish Chandra, was identified by MI5 through intercepted communications and interrogated by MI5 officers in October 1915. They persuaded him to act as a double agent, and he duly passed over considerable amounts of information on German plots in India. Reassuringly for MI5 and the Chiefs of Staff, the intelligence produced by Chandra revealed that the German Foreign Ministry was making increasingly unrealistic and far-fetched plans for subversion in India. The intensive interception of the mail of 138,000 Indian troops serving on the Western Front likewise convinced MI5 and the War Office that there was no widespread support for revolutionaries or for pan-Islamism among those soldiers – though one censor did report a worrying trend among them to write poetry, which he considered 'an ominous sign of mental disquietude'. It was judged that the best strategy was to let the German Foreign Ministry continue wasting time, money and energy on fruitless plans for subversion in India.[17]

MI5's main wartime expert on Indian affairs was Robert Nathan, who joined the organisation in November 1914, having spent twenty-six years in the Indian Civil Service and also serving as Vice Chancellor of Calcutta University before he was forced to resign due to ill-health. Within MI5, Nathan surrounded himself with a number of veterans of the Indian army, police and civil service. By 1917, MI5's G-Branch, which was responsible for investigations, had a total of twenty-eight officers, eight of whom had previously served in India. This was an unusually large collection of Indian veterans for any British government department outside India itself. One of Nathan's continual wartime concerns was possible political assassinations on British soil. In July 1909 an Indian *Ghadr* revolutionary had assassinated Sir William Curzon Wyllie, a former Indian Army officer and aide to the Secretary of State for India, on the steps of the India Office in London. Based in part on information provided by its double agent Chandra, MI5 feared that similar attempts might be made during the war. No such plot ever materialised, but MI5 continued to intercept and scrutinise the correspondence of known revolutionaries in London. In the spring of 1916 Nathan travelled to the USA, where his intelligence provided the US authorities with much of the evidence used at two major trials of the *Ghadr* movement, the first of which was held in Chicago in October 1916 and ended with the conviction of three militants. The second trial, held in San Francisco, came to a dramatic climax in April 1918 when one of the accused, Ram Singh, shot the *Ghadr* leader Ram Chandra Peshawari dead in the middle of the courtroom. The head of Special Branch in London, Basil Thomson, commented:

In the Western [United] States such incidents do not disturb the presence of mind of Assize Court officials: the deputy sheriff whipped an automatic from his pocket, and from his elevated place at the back of the court, aiming above and between intervening heads, shot the murderer dead.[18]

The Indian National Congress – the political body that would later become the main vehicle for anti-colonial nationalism in India – does not seem to have attracted any significant attention from MI5 or any other section of the British intelligence community during the First World War. This was partly because Congress had no significant wartime German connection, but also because before 1914 it was little more than a middle-class debating society that met only sporadically. There was nothing to suggest that it would emerge from the war as a mass movement that would become a focus for resistance to the British Raj. The main transformation of Congress's fortunes would be due to Mohandas Karamchand 'Mahatma' Gandhi, an English-educated barrister of Inner Temple, who more than anyone else would set in process the downfall of the British empire in India a generation later. Nevertheless, in retrospect it is clear that in the pre-war and wartime years, MI5 and British intelligence authorities in India showed a remarkable lack of interest in Gandhi. When he returned in 1915 to India from South Africa, where he developed the technique of *satyagraha*, or passive resistance, which he later used against the Raj, the Department of Criminal Intelligence in Delhi described him as 'neither an anarchist nor a revolutionary', but just as a 'troublesome agitator whose enthusiasm had led him frequently to overstep the limits of South African laws relating to Asiatics'.[19]

Reflecting the worldwide nature of the war, that same year, 1915, the British Chiefs of Staff instructed MI5 to establish a department to deal with German-sponsored subversion in the British empire. This new department, D-Branch in MI5, led by an officer called Frank Hall, expanded rapidly, so that by 1917 it had nineteen full-time officers. For cover, D-Branch used the name 'Special Central Intelligence Bureau' when communicating with colonial and Commonwealth governments. According to a post-war report compiled on D-Branch, its responsibilities included undertaking visa checks on individuals travelling in the empire and providing colonial governments with information on known and suspected German agents. By 1916 D-Branch was in touch with 'the authorities responsible for counter-espionage in almost every one of the colonies'. However, during the war MI5 did not actually station officers in British colonies or other dependent territories overseas. Instead, it operated as a 'clearing house' for security intelligence on German espionage and subversion by maintaining direct personal contacts with a number of colonial police forces, known as its 'links', and consolidating all the information it received from those links across the empire into a single registry, which contained around 45,000 records in 1917. By the end of the war MI5 could justifiably boast that it presided over a unique, empire-wide index of security intelligence information. One of the clearest manifestations of its dramatically increased responsibilities was its famous 'Black Lists' of German agents, which it circulated to all colonial and Commonwealth governments. These grew from a single volume in 1914 to a weighty twenty-one volumes in 1918, which included 13,524 names.[20]

The most famous example of German attempts to sponsor subversion in the British empire involved British counter-measures orchestrated by the now-legendary figure T.E. Lawrence, 'Lawrence of Arabia' – Oxford historian, archaeologist, cartographer, linguist, intelligence officer and expert guerrilla fighter. Lawrence and his colleagues, a group of self-proclaimed 'intrusives', established the so-called Arab Bureau in Cairo in 1914, which pioneered the use of guerrilla warfare against Turkish forces fighting on the side of Germany and the Central Powers in Arabia. In many ways the efforts of Lawrence and British forces in the Middle East during the First World War represent the first modern intelligence war: Lawrence's forces combined intelligence gained from human agents with intelligence from signals radio intercepts, processes which are now known as human intelligence (HUMINT) and signals intelligence (SIGINT) respectively. The use of aerial reconnaissance, now known as image intelligence (IMINT), was also pioneered by the Royal Flying Corps in the clear skies over Arabia.[21]

The most important success of the Arab Bureau in its four-year wartime existence was to convince the War Office in London not to send an expeditionary force to Arabia. Lawrence and others in the Arab Bureau argued that a permanent British force landed in the Hejaz, the rocky province bordering the Red Sea, would inevitably be regarded by Arabs as an invading Christian, 'crusader' force – with disastrous consequences. Instead, the Arab Bureau insisted that the British should forge an alliance with the local Hashemite dynasty, who could take primary responsibility for fighting the Central Powers in Arabia, with the British providing assistance through intelligence and irregular warfare. This is precisely what occurred. British forces, led by Lawrence, collaborated with the Sharif of Mecca, Hussein bin Ali – who claimed to trace his descent back to Mohammed and Adam – and waged a series of spectacularly successful guerrilla attacks on Turkish and German forces in the Sinai Peninsula, conducting diversionary raids on railways and assaults on isolated garrisons in the Hejaz, through Aqaba to Amman and Damascus. In his famous self-dramatising account of his wartime exploits, *Seven Pillars of Wisdom*, Lawrence emphasised that intelligence-gathering was the key to successful irregular warfare: 'The first line of guerrilla warfare,' he wrote, 'is accurate intelligence.' Lawrence's wartime mission was to divert Turkish forces from Palestine to protect the Hejaz railway. Assisted by Lawrence's diversionary actions in the Hejaz, the leader of the Egyptian Expeditionary Force, General Edmund Allenby, won successive victories in Gaza and Beersheba, which ultimately led to the capture of the city of Jerusalem in December 1917. Allenby was joined by Lawrence in triumphantly entering the Holy City on foot – the first Christian soldiers to capture the city since the time of the Crusades.[22]

As well as attempting to incite subversion against the British in India and the Middle East, the German military also sponsored unrest in one of Britain's closest imperial possessions: Ireland. In fact, one of the most notorious cases that British intelligence was involved with in the entire First World War related to German attempts to forge an alliance with dissident Irish republicans. During the war, the signals department of the British Admiralty, codenamed 'Room 40', led by Reginald 'Blinker' Hall, grew in importance and size, and successfully intercepted and read many German communications. As with the rest of the British intelligence community, the war transformed the scale and nature of the British SIGINT, institutionalising code-breaking in ways that had not previously existed in Britain. One of the most notorious wartime German communications intercepted and circulated by Room 40 was the so-called 'Zimmermann telegram' of January 1917, in which the German Foreign Minister, Arthur Zimmermann, offered the Mexican government the chance to retake lost territories in the United States, including land in Texas, Arizona and New Mexico, if it declared war on the United States. Although the Zimmermann telegram is commonly known to be one of the causes of the US government's entry into the war, the role that Room 40 played in the episode is still generally not properly appreciated in most histories of the First World War, despite having been discussed by intelligence historians for over thirty years: Room 40 intercepted the notorious telegram and passed it on to US authorities, who then publicly exposed it, while keeping secret the role of British code-breakers.[23]

In the two years after outbreak of war in 1914, Room 40 code-breakers decrypted at least thirty-two German cables relating to Irish nationalists. The most important related to the 'Easter Rising' of April 1916, and Germany's support of an exiled Irish nationalist, Sir Roger Casement, to help carry out the uprising in Dublin. Room 40's decryption efforts gave the British government foreknowledge of the uprising, and provided exact knowledge of Germany's arms supplies to Ireland. On information provided by Room 40, in April 1916 the Royal Navy intercepted the U-boat carrying Casement to Ireland before he could carry out his mission. Casement was ultimately executed by the British in Dublin in August 1916. During his incarceration he begged the British authorities to allow him to communicate with the leaders of the uprising, and warn them to abandon their plans. However, it seems doubtful that even if he had made such an intervention it would have prevented the council of the Irish Republican Brotherhood from proceeding. Furthermore, we now know that the controversial 'Casement Diaries' – lurid details of which, including graphic descriptions of Casement's homosexual exploits, were deliberately released by Blinker Hall to blacken Casement's name during his trial – were not forgeries concocted by the British, as many Irish nationalists at the time and since have maintained, but were in fact genuine. The attempts by the German government to incite an anti-British 'fifth column' in Ireland, the 'back door to England', was a strategy that would be repeated by Hitler a generation later, in the Second World War.[24]

While the British secret state expanded rapidly during the First World War, the years after the war saw an equally quick deterioration of its resources. MI5 and SIS both had their budgets slashed, and MI5's staff shrunk from 844 in 1918 to just twenty-five officers in 1925. It should be stressed that the dwindling resources of the British secret state after 1918 lay in sharp contrast to many states in post-war Europe, which turned to various forms of bloody authoritarian rule. In Soviet Russia, Fascist Italy and Nazi Germany, secret police forces expanded rapidly, and their leaders applied security practices forged during the First World War, such as mass registration and detention, to their populations even in times of peace. While the British government had interned at least 32,000 'enemy aliens' on security grounds, largely on MI5's advice, between 1914 and 1918, such drastic methods were taken only as wartime 'emergency measures' in Britain. The 'totalitarian' states of Nazi Germany and Soviet Russia, however, which were effectively at war all the time, and mobilised their populations along wartime lines, applied wartime security practices even while at peace. The head of Germany's intelligence service in the First World War, Walter Nicolai, summarised this view when he wrote that for Germany to become a world power again it had to behave as though it was at 'war in peace', and would have to gather intelligence on all its enemies, at home and abroad. By contrast, the resources of the British secret state were cut so dramatically in the post-war years that by 1925 MI5 had a total of only twenty-four mail and telephone interceptions operating in the whole of Britain. Its staff consisted of just sixteen officers by 1929, and as MI5's in-house history noted, its resources were so inadequate in the 1920s that its operations 'reduced to a minimum'. Between 1919 and 1931, MI5 was relegated to investigating subversion in the British armed forces.[25]

Despite the dwindling of its resources, throughout the 1920s and 1930s MI5 continued to pride itself on its imperial responsibilities established during the First World War. During the interwar years the overwhelming thrust of MI5's duties was focused on the threat posed by the Soviet Union. With hindsight, we can see that MI5 and SIS both miscalculated, and were slow to react to, the growing threat posed by Nazi Germany after Hitler came to power in 1933. That said, MI5's focus on the Soviet Union was hardly irrational. Soon after the Bolshevik revolution in 1917, the Soviet Union became just as much of an empire as the former Russian tsarist empire which it replaced – and posed a similar threat to the British empire. Immediately upon coming to power, Lenin pledged his support for a worldwide revolution against imperialism, which he famously described as the 'highest form of capitalism'. The threat posed by the Soviet Union to the British empire was exposed by the head of the Intelligence Bureau in Delhi, Sir David Petrie, who went on to become the Director-General of MI5 from 1941 to 1946. In the late 1920s he wrote a classified official history, *Communism in India, 1924–27*, the circulation of which was limited to a small number of senior British officials in London and Delhi. Petrie warned that the Soviet Union posed a double threat for the British empire, especially in India: Soviet expansion was a strategic threat along the traditional lines of the 'Great Game' with Russia, but it also posed a subversive threat, with Moscow supporting anti-colonial movements inside the British empire. As it turned out, Petrie's forecast was remarkably accurate: for over seven decades following the Bolshevik seizure of power in 1917, interrupted only by the Second World War, the Soviet Union became the main supporter of anti-colonial movements in the British empire and other European colonial empires. The reality was therefore that throughout the 1920s and 1930s the British government was engaged in a low-level 'cold war' with the Soviet Union, long before the real Cold War set in after 1945.[26]

During the interwar years, Britain's armed forces (the army, Royal Navy and RAF) all maintained intelligence departments that focused on the empire and Commonwealth. However, it was MI5 that was responsible for overall imperial security intelligence, maintaining direct contact with British intelligence authorities in India, the Delhi Intelligence Bureau (DIB), or Intelligence Bureau (IB) as it was also known, through a small London-based outfit known as Indian Political Intelligence (IPI). IPI was officially part of the India Office, which paid its budget, but from 1925 onwards it was housed in MI5's headquarters at 25 Cromwell Road in

London, opposite the Natural History Museum. The office space that MI5 rented to IPI (at rates that IPI often considered exorbitant) was by any standards pitiful: it consisted of three small, low-ceilinged, poorly-lit, dingy rooms in the attic of MI5's headquarters. According to IPI's head, Sir Philip Vickery (London Club: 'East India'), these quarters were of such poor quality, with a 'minimum amount of light and airspace' and with half the main room 'in darkness', as to be almost 'uninhabitable'. IPI was run on such a minuscule budget from the India Office that in 1926 it had only a handful of officers in London, equipped with three secretaries, one clerk and one typist, and apart from a few liaison officers in India, it had only two officers stationed elsewhere abroad, in Paris and Geneva. These few personnel formed the entire official security intelligence liaison channel between British intelligence and authorities in the subcontinent of India. Just how ill-equipped IPI was can be seen from a report in 1927: Vickery had to campaign hard for the purchase of 'one extra hanging lamp' for IPI's attic office – for which the Department of Works ultimately seems to have refused to pay. When MI5 moved to its new headquarters, 'Thames House', Millbank, near Lambeth Bridge, IPI came with it, though its new accommodation was no better than before.[27]

Despite the scanty resources at its disposal, sharing an office with MI5 allowed IPI to collaborate closely with other sections of British intelligence. Throughout the 1920s and 1930s, MI5 and IPI continued to monitor the activities of Indian revolutionaries in Britain. Their main subject matter increasingly became communist agents travelling between Britain and India on behalf of the Communist International (Comintern), an underground network that Moscow had established in March 1919 to act as a vehicle to export the 'workers revolution' from the Soviet Union to countries abroad. MI5 and IPI's investigations were focused on detecting agents acting as secret couriers for the Comintern, passing information between the British Communist Party and communist cells in India. The main investigative mechanism they relied on was a Home Office Warrant (HOW), which allowed for the interception of telephone and postal communications. Unlike SIS, which operated abroad and collected intelligence from foreign countries illegally, MI5 and IPI's area of operations, domestically in Britain and also in the empire, were constrained by law in ways that did not apply to SIS. This was the case even though at the time MI5 (and IPI) did not have any powers at its disposal, either in statute or in common law, which allowed it to intercept mail. Despite existing in a shadowy legal netherworld, MI5 records reveal that it worked hard to operate hard within a legalistic framework, even if not a legal one.

In order to impose a HOW, MI5 had to apply to the Home Office, with a written explanation of why a warrant was sought, and the Home Secretary then had to sign off on it. HOWs were extremely resource intensive – hence the small number that were operating in the 1920s. The actual interception of communications was carried out by a small, secretive section of the General Post Office (GPO), known as the 'special censor section', whose workers had all signed the Official Secrets Act. This section's work was laborious and far from glamorous: its office was equipped with a row of kettles, kept almost continually boiling, which were used to steam open letters, after which their contents were photographed, resealed and sent on their way. Some of these intercepted communications, still found in MI5 records today, contain information about the private lives of MI5 targets and their broader social history that cannot be found in any other archive. Telephone calls were likewise intercepted ('tapped') by the GPO, which employed a small team of transcribers at the main telephone exchange in Paddington, London. The team included foreign-language speakers, especially 'White' (anti-Bolshevik) Russian émigrés, who translated telephone conversations in Russian and other Eastern European languages. Later, MI5 and the GPO developed an innovative device, based on a modified gramophone machine, which was used to record telephone conversations. This machine allowed record discs to be mechanically added and taken off the recording device, or 'pooled', thus eliminating the hitherto tedious task of GPO workers having to switch them manually.[28]

The first agent identified by MI5 as acting as a Comintern courier was Percy Glading, a member of the British Communist Party who in 1925 travelled to India under the alias 'R. Cochrane'. Glading's covert trip was revealed to MI5 and IPI by intercepted communications through a HOW. Over the following years he also used his secretary, a pretty twenty-five-year-old blonde named Olga Gray, to deliver funds to communists in India. However, unknown to Glading or anyone else in the British Communist Party, Olga Gray was in reality an undercover MI5 agent, who had been recruited and planted into the British Communist Party in 1931 by MI5's legendary agent runner, Maxwell Knight, one of MI5's most successful counter-espionage officers in the twentieth century. After retiring from MI5 as a spymaster in 1946, Knight embarked on a highly successful broadcasting career, becoming known as 'Uncle Max', a colourful presenter of children's radio nature programmes. According to a later

report on Knight's agent-running section, 'M Section', the six-year penetration of Gray into the British Communist Party had been so successful
that she had achieved 'the enviable position where an agent becomes a
piece of furniture, so to speak: that is, when persons visiting an office do
not consciously notice whether the agent is there or not'.[29]

Olga Gray's courier mission in 1935 to India for the British Communist
Party provided MI5 and IPI with an extraordinary insight into how
Comintern agents were run, and also revealed the identities of communist
agents in India. However, her trip was an extremely delicate task for MI5,
which had to go to remarkable lengths not to blow her cover. As Maxwell
Knight later recalled, it was so badly organised by the British Communist
Party that without MI5's help it is unlikely that she would ever have got to
India. Knight helped her devise a suitable cover story – that she was a
prostitute – without making it appear that she had received help in
concocting it. He also feared that if her passport and other paperwork for
travel to India were approved too quickly, her superiors in the Communist
Party might become suspicious. Her MI5 handlers therefore ensured that
it was delayed sufficiently not to arouse any suspicion. After her trip, Gray
revealed to MI5 the existence of a substantial Soviet espionage network
operating in Britain. Its ringleader was none other than Percy Glading,
and it was based at the Woolwich Arsenal in London, where Glading
worked as a mechanic, and where he and his agents gained access to sensitive information on British armaments.

The strain of acting as a double agent began to take a toll on Olga Gray
– she appears to have had at least one nervous breakdown – so in 1937
MI5 decided to wind up the Soviet network at the Woolwich Arsenal and
have its agents arrested. Gray testified at Glading's trial for espionage at the
Old Bailey in February 1938, appearing anonymously behind a screen as
'Miss X'. Her evidence helped to convict him of spying for Soviet intelligence, for which he was imprisoned for six years. The trial judge congratulated her for her 'extraordinary courage' and 'great service to her country'.
Soon afterwards, she left for Canada under a new name.[30]

As well as providing intelligence on Soviet networks in India and
Britain, Olga Gray's position in the British Communist Party – unassuming
but central – provided her, and thus MI5, with unique access to codes used
by the Party to send radio messages to Comintern networks in Europe.
Her information helped the Government Code and Cypher School
(GC&CS), Britain's first official peacetime SIGINT agency, established in
1921, to break radio traffic messages passing between the headquarters of

the Comintern in Moscow and its numerous representatives abroad, in countries as far apart as China, Austria and the United States. GC&CS gave this radio traffic the codename 'Mask'. The Mask traffic revealed to the British government that Moscow provided secret subsidies to the British Communist Party and also to its newspaper, the *Daily Worker*. In January 1935 Mask revealed the existence of a secret radio transmitter, based in Wimbledon, in south-west London, which was being operated by a member of the British Communist Party's underground cell to send messages to Moscow. MI5 closely monitored the activities of those agents identified.[31]

MI5 and IPI identified other Comintern couriers, such as British Communist Party member George Allison, alias 'Donald Campbell', who, following a tip-off from MI5, was arrested in India in 1927 for travelling on a forged passport. However, the most important direct involvement of British intelligence in the empire at this time was with the so-called 'Meerut conspiracy case', a long-drawn-out trial that opened in India in 1929. Although their involvement was not publicised, both MI5 and IPI provided crucial evidence of the Comintern's attempts to use communist agents in India to incite labour unrest there. In August 1929 the Deputy Director of MI5, Sir Eric Holt-Wilson, led a delegation of British officials to India to provide evidence at the trial and to testify to the authenticity of the intercepted documents – thus overcoming any objections the defence counsel might raise that the documents were unreliable 'hearsay' evidence, and should be inadmissible. The delegation, travelling First Class by ship and train, included five London Metropolitan Police Special Branch officers, as well as the head of the special censor section of the GPO, Frederick Booth, and the official in charge of the team in the GPO that actually photographed the documents, H. Burgess. They liaised closely with Sir David Petrie at the IB in Delhi, and judging from existing IPI records, it also appears that GC&CS provided intercepted communications passing between Moscow and a communist cell operating in India.[32]

After providing evidence at the Meerut trial, Sir Eric Holt-Wilson embarked on an enormous worldwide tour, visiting and liaising with security officials from Hong Kong to New York. Holt-Wilson's extensive trip was all the more remarkable given that it was made in an age before long-distance air travel, when the journey from Britain to India took weeks. More than any other MI5 officer in the first half of the twentieth century, Holt-Wilson – nicknamed 'Holy Willy' on account of his strong Anglican beliefs and because he was a rector's son – was responsible for promoting the idea that MI5 was an imperial agency. In fact, he often referred to it as the 'Imperial Security Service'. Holt-Wilson returned to India in 1933, at the conclusion of the Meerut trial, which led to the prosecution of a number of communist agents. Upon his return to London the next year he gave a closed lecture to the London Special Branch, at which he emphasised MI5's imperial responsibilities:

> Our Security Service is more than national; it is Imperial. We have official agencies cooperating with us, under the direct instructions of the Dominions and Colonial Offices and the supervision of local Governors, and their chiefs of police, for enforcing security laws in every British Community overseas.
>
> These all act under our guidance for security duties. It is our duty to advise them, when necessary, on all security measures necessary for defence and civil purposes; and to exchange information regarding the movement within the Empire of individuals who are likely to be hostile to its interests from a security point of view.[33]

Holt-Wilson went on another extensive overseas journey in 1938. The main purpose of this trip was to review local security and intelligence services in India and a number of other colonies and Dominions, and ensure that their security standards were adequate to meet the needs of the looming war with the Axis Powers. However, during the trip he himself displayed a remarkable disregard for basic security procedures – certainly far less care than he was attempting to instil in the colonial authorities he visited. In a series of soppy love letters that he sent by open, unsecured post back to his wife – a vicar's daughter twenty years his junior – in England, Holt-Wilson described in detail the local intelligence officials he met, and also lamely attempted to glamorise for her benefit the nature of his 'cloak and dagger' work. If these letters, found in his personal papers now held in Cambridge, had been intercepted by the Axis Powers, they would have revealed a range of sensitive information on British imperial security and intelligence matters. The fact was that Holt-Wilson, a keen huntsman and one-time President of the Ski Club of Great Britain, was not one for modesty – which is surprising for someone whose career necessitated working in the shadows. In his own words he was 'a champion shot', and in the official description he penned for himself in *Who's Who*, he stated that he was the Director-General of the 'Imperial Security Intelligence Service', and also accurately but pompously noted that he was 'author of all pre-war official papers and manuals on Security Intelligence Police Duties in Peace and War'. Not very subtly for one of Britain's senior intelligence officials, Holt-Wilson also listed his home address in his *Who's Who* entry. [34]

In March 1938 Holt-Wilson arrived in India, where he met the new head of the IB in Delhi, Sir John Ewart, whom he referred to as the 'K ['Kell'] of India'. He next travelled to Singapore and Hong Kong, where as he reported to his wife, he was spotted by local press reporters as being involved with 'hush-hush' work. In Singapore he liaised with a local MI5 officer stationed there, Col. F. Hayley Bell, in Holt-Wilson's unflattering opinion a 'deaf madman', whose deafness made hushed conversations difficult. He also met Hayley Bell's daughter, Mary Hayley Bell (later Lady Mills), who in 1942 would write a popular wartime play, *Men in Shadow*, about resistance groups in France, which would attract the attention of MI5 for revealing sensitive details of escape routes from occupied France. MI5 only allowed the play to be performed after the passages in question were removed. At a dinner held in his honour during Holt-Wilson's visit to Hong Kong in April 1938, which was officially described as an 'inspection of the colony's defences' so as not to attract too much press attention, the Governor proposed a toast to 'good old Thames House' (MI5's headquarters), which was lost on all the guests except for himself and Holt-Wilson. [35]

Ireland was a particularly important recruiting ground for colonial police officers, many of whom would deal with intelligence matters across the empire. After the Irish Free State was granted a form of Dominion status in 1921, a stream of former officers of the disbanded Royal Irish Constabulary (RIC) moved into the Indian and other colonial police forces, particularly in Palestine, where they gained a reputation for stern discipline and 'backbone'. Ireland was also the theatre that provided a model for policing and counter-insurgency operations that persisted in British military thinking for several decades. In 1934 Major General Sir Charles Gwynn published an influential book, *Imperial Policing*, on low-intensity conflicts or 'small wars'. Drawing on lessons from Ireland, and the tactics the British used to crush the Indian Mutiny in the 1850s and other Indian revolts at Dinshawai (1906) and Amritsar (1919), Gwynn recommended that to be effective, colonial policing required the use of minimum necessary force, with the aim of restoring civilian government as soon as possible, and tactics such as troops moving in sweeping column formations against enemies. While Gwynn's recommendations were undoubtedly applicable to Palestine in the 1930s, they left their mark for much longer than they should have on British military authorities, who continued to apply these tactics to anti-colonial insurgencies in the post-war years, when they were largely irrelevant because Britain's enemies in those conflicts did not fight in open, regular and identifiable formations. Thanks in large part to Gwynn, there was a direct continuum between the way the British military crushed colonial revolts in India in the 1860s, and how it tackled post-war insurgencies in places like Palestine, Malaya, Kenya and Cyprus.[36]

THE THREE-MILE RULE

In 1931 the British government finally drew an official distinction between MI5 and SIS's responsibilities. Ever since the establishment of the two services in 1909, when MI5 was made responsible for 'domestic' security intelligence and SIS for 'foreign' intelligence-gathering, there had been confusion over whether the empire and the Commonwealth counted as domestic or foreign territory. The issue was finally resolved following a fierce turf war within Whitehall over intelligence matters. In 1931 the London Special Branch, led by its eccentric head Sir Basil Thomson, essentially attempted to take over MI5. Although the bid was unsuccessful, it led to a major review of intelligence matters within Whitehall, led by the top-secret committee responsible for them, the Secret Service Committee, chaired by Sir John Anderson, the Permanent Undersecretary at the Home Office. One of the recommendations of the Committee in June 1931 was that MI5 should have increased responsibilities. From that point on MI5 was given responsibility for all forms of counter-espionage, military and civilian – previously it had been limited to detecting espionage in the British armed forces – and a number of skilled officers were transferred from the London Special Branch to MI5, including Guy Liddell (a future Deputy Director-General of MI5) and Milicent Bagot (who had an ency-clopaedic knowledge of Comintern activities, and is thought to have been the inspiration for John le Carré's character, the eccentric Sovietologist Connie Sachs). One of the other major decisions taken by the Secret Service Committee was that MI5 would assume responsibility for security intelligence in all British territories, including the empire and Commonwealth, while SIS would confine itself to operating at least three miles outside British territories. In other words, from 1931 onwards a three-mile demarcation line was drawn around all British territories worldwide, at the time covering roughly one-quarter of the globe, which acted as the official boundary between MI5 and SIS.[37]

With this operational border established, MI5 was given more of a free rein to concentrate on imperial security matters – hence Holt-Wilson's numerous trips overseas and his attempts to promote the view that MI5 was an imperial service. Throughout the 1930s MI5 collaborated with IPI and the Delhi IB to keep a close watch on the main anti-colonial political leaders in India, such as Nehru, whom IPI considered – accurately – to be, next to Gandhi, the 'second most powerful man in India'. Whenever Nehru travelled to Britain in the 1930s, which he did on several occasions, MI5 monitored his activities, often imposing HOWs to intercept his post and telephone conversations, and instructed Scotland Yard to send undercover officers to his speaking engagements. Judging from IPI records, it also seems that IPI acquired a source close to Nehru himself: it obtained sensitive information relating to the death of his wife from tuberculosis in 1936 at a hospital in Switzerland following a trip Nehru made to Britain. The information reaching IPI included private arrangements that Nehru's family was considering for the funeral, which most likely came from an informant within Nehru's close entourage. MI5 and IPI also attempted to track the activities of the Comintern agent Narendra Nath Bhattacharya, also known as M.N. Roy – but were not always successful: on at least one occasion Roy was able to travel to Britain without being discovered. At the same time, MI5 and IPI also scrutinised the activities of the British Communist Party's leading theoretician and anti-colonial Indian campaigner, Rajani Palme Dutt, who acted as a Comintern agent on at least one trip to India. They likewise kept a close eye on Dutt's younger brother Clemens, who led the 'Indian section' of the British Communist Party, and even discovered the cover address that Clemens used to communicate secretly with underground communist sympathisers. Furthermore, although no specific file has yet been declassified, it is likely that MI5 also worked in conjunction with SIS to track the movements of the notorious German Comintern agent Willi Münzenberg, who moved widely around Europe and even further afield, and in 1927 organised a conference in Brussels against imperialism.[38]

However, MI5's claim in the 1930s that it was an imperial service was more aspiration than reality, more chest-puffing than fact. Throughout the decade it had such limited resources at its disposal that there was no way it could have a meaningful supervisory role over imperial security intelligence as a whole. As late as 1938 it had a total staff of just thirty officers, only two of whom worked in its counter-espionage section, B-Division, in London – that is, a grand total of two officers formed the front line of detecting Axis espionage in Britain, to say nothing of the empire. However, a turning point for the involvement of British intelligence in the empire occurred in the late 1930s, when MI5 broke with its past practices and, instead of merely receiving intelligence from colonies abroad, began to post officers to British territories overseas for the first time. These officers were known as Defence Security Officers (DSOs) and were attached to British military general headquarters (GHQs) in British colonies and other dependencies. Their responsibilities were focused on coordinating security intelligence on Comintern activities, and as the Second World War approached, increasingly on the threat posed by the Axis Powers.[39]

The first DSO stationed abroad was posted to Egypt. Egypt had gained independence from Britain in 1935, but in a manner that would be replicated over subsequent decades in other British territories – as we shall see – the British government had negotiated a series of favourable treaties for itself, which allowed for a continued British presence in Egypt. From 1935 onwards British military headquarters for the Middle East was based in Cairo, and London continued to have control over the Suez Canal, the strategic gateway to India – which would become a hotly contentious subject after the war, and the focus of one of Britain's greatest ever foreign policy disasters, signifying the final eclipse of Britain's imperial power in the Middle East. MI5's first DSO in Egypt was Brig. Raymund Maunsell, an old India hand whose appointment in 1937 was followed by those of other DSOs in Palestine and Gibraltar in 1938. These officers would form the basis of MI5's wartime security liaison outfit run throughout the Middle East, known as Security Intelligence Middle East (SIME), which would form the vanguard of countering wartime Axis espionage in the region. On the outbreak of war in 1939, MI5 increased the number of its DSOs permanently stationed abroad to six: in Cairo, Gibraltar, Malta, Aden, Singapore and Hong Kong.[40]

Although the establishment of MI5's DSOs was a watershed in the history of British intelligence, with just six officers stationed overseas, MI5 was still clearly not the imperial service that it claimed to be. As the official history of British intelligence in the Second World War noted, in 1939 MI5 was just a 'skeleton' of an imperial security service. It took the war for it to become truly the imperial service that it claimed to be. It was also the war that transformed the involvement of Britain's largest and most secret intelligence services, GC&CS, in the British empire.[41]

In the pre-war years, MI5 claimed to be – but had not yet actually become – a service *for* the empire. Even at this stage, however, it was a service *of* the empire. This was most clearly shown by the high proportion of senior MI5 officers in the pre-war years who began their careers in the empire. Its first head, Sir Vernon Kell, and his deputy who served him for twenty-eight years, Sir Eric Holt-Wilson, had both previously served in British colonial campaigns. Its Director-General during the Second World War, Sir David Petrie, was similarly an old colonial sweat, having served as the head of IB in Delhi from 1924 to 1931, and carried scars of his service (literally) on his legs with wounds from a bomb attack inflicted by an Indian revolutionary in 1914. The sources that Petrie used for his classified official history, *Communism in India*, included intercepted correspondence of both Indian communists and the Comintern. The post-Second World War head of MI5, Sir Percy Sillitoe, likewise had a former colonial police career, having served in the British South Africa Police. One of the few pre-war British counter-espionage desk officers, John Curry, had served with the Indian police for a quarter of a century before joining MI5 in 1933. Curry was among the limited number of people in British intelligence, and in Whitehall generally, who recognised and warned about the threat posed by Nazi Germany after 1933. He had previously written a history of the Indian police, which attracted the attention of Sir David Petrie, and in 1945 was the author of MI5's in-house history, which has now been declassified. MI5's most successful wartime interrogator, Robin 'Tin Eye' Stephens (discussed in the next chapter), was also a former Indian policeman, as was MI5's semi-senile septuagenarian wartime Deputy Director-General, Brigadier O.A. 'Jasper' Harker, later described by the notorious KGB spy Kim Philby as filling his position in MI5 with handsome grace, but little else. With such strong colonial connections in the pre-war years, MI5's working culture and outlook undoubtedly also had a colonial feel. An examination of the CVs of MI5 officers before the Second World War reveals that several of them included 'pig sticking' among their hobbies, a hangover from colonial service in India of the pink-gin-and-polo type. Moreover, because pay in MI5 at the time was so poor, many of its senior staff, doubtless burnt out from too much sun, came from independently wealthy backgrounds.[42]

These connections with the British empire did not only exist in MI5: they were also prominent in the rest of the pre-war British intelligence community. In fact, a remarkable number of Britain's leading spooks in those years had previously served in the empire. In SIS, for example, the two most important counter-espionage desk officers st the time were both former Indian policemen. The first was Valentine Vivian, known to his friends as 'Vee Vee', the son of a Victorian portrait painter, who entered SIS in 1925 after serving in the Indian police and in an IPI station in Constantinople. Vivian had a glass eye, which he tried to shield by awkwardly standing at right angles to those he met. Philby – who had a vested interest in making his former SIS colleagues look as incompetent as possible – depicted him in his KGB-sponsored memoirs as being afraid of his subordinates in SIS, and acidly described him as 'long past his best – if, indeed, he ever had one'. Vivian's subordinate in SIS's pre-war section dealing with counter-espionage, Section V, was Felix Cowgill, the son of a missionary, who had served as a personal assistant to Petrie in the Delhi IB. Cowgill's colonial past gave him, as one of his wartime colleagues described, a 'sallow face and withdrawn tired air that came of long years of service in India'. Philby poisonously described him as tempestuous and incompetent: 'His intellectual endowment was slender. As an intelligence officer, he was inhibited by a lack of imagination, inattention to detail and a sheer ignorance of the world we were fighting in,' but even Philby conceded that Cowgill had 'a fiendish capacity for work', sometimes toiling through the night, knocking an array of pipes into wreckage on a stone ashtray on his desk. Whether this was the case or not, he was certainly spectacularly outmanoeuvred by Philby for wartime promotion within SIS – with disastrous consequences for British intelligence, as we shall see.[43]

There were similar colonial connections within GC&CS, the first Director of which, Alistair Denniston, began his career in India, where he successfully intercepted and decrypted Russian traffic. Likewise, the department in GC&CS that successfully broke Comintern radio traffic in the 1930s was led by a brilliant major from the Indian army, John Tiltman, who had been running a small but successful interception outfit in north-west India before being brought back to London in 1929. There were also colonial connections in Special Branch at Scotland Yard. Its pre-war head, Basil Thomson, had an eccentric colonial career: after being educated at Eton and dropping out of Oxford he joined the Colonial Office, and at the age of twenty-eight became the Prime Minister of Tonga, where – as he vividly noted in his memoirs – his first true friends were cannibals. He also went on to become private tutor to the Crown Prince of Siam and Governor of Dartmoor Prison.[44]

Officers in Britain's intelligence services brought to their new roles many of the practices they had acquired in their colonial postings. In

GC&CS, Tiltman wholeheartedly incorporated decryption techniques pioneered in India. The Special Branch adopted the technique of finger-printing, which became the most basic form of police and security inves-tigations in the modern world, from India, where it had been invented. MI5 also embraced techniques pioneered in the empire. When its Registry collapsed during the Battle of Britain in the summer of 1940 – essentially giving up under the strain imposed on it during an apparently imminent Nazi invasion – Petrie advised reforming it on lines that he had devised for card-cataloguing 'revolutionaries and terrorist suspects' in India.[45]

The intelligence services of other major European powers had similar colonial hangovers, both in terms of staff and practices. Some influential French intelligence officers during the Second World War started their careers in the French colonial empire. More ominously, there were also colonial connections with the secret police and intelligence services of Europe's murderous 'totalitarian' regimes before 1945. This was first iden-tified by the philosopher Hannah Arendt, who in her book *The Origins of Totalitarianism* (1951) argued that twentieth-century totalitarianism had its roots in European colonial rule in the late nineteenth century. Arendt believed that the type of savagery that European powers inflicted upon colonial populations, as graphically depicted in Joseph Conrad's novel *Heart of Darkness*, modelled on Belgian rule in the Congo, was in the first half of the twentieth century brought back to its heartland: Europe. Although Arendt's thesis was at first largely discounted by scholars, more recently it has been re-examined, and is now regarded by historians as having in many ways been proved correct.[46]

The Soviet secret police, the NKVD – subsequently renamed the KGB – imposed security practices such as mass detention which had been forged by the British in India, the French in Algeria, and by the Russians in their own empire. In Spain, Franco's 1936 rebellion against the demo-cratic government was waged predominantly by former *Africanista* gener-als, who, as one study has noted, were steeped in a 'colonial mentality' and embarked on a 'colonial clearing-up', namely institutionalised repression, of a working class deemed to be 'hardly human'. These colonial connec-tions with authoritarian regimes are hardly surprising when it is consid-ered that the nature of European colonial rule allowed for the development of new forms of bureaucratic domination of 'inferior' races, which involved the registration of entire populations, mass deportation and the forced separation of races. These were all hallmarks of mass murder in Europe in the twentieth century: cataloguing, controlling and massacring.

Colonies also provided a testing ground for new forms of warfare, which could be freely deployed against expendable, lesser, races. Europe's colonial 'small wars' gave rise to, or allowed for the first testing of, concentration camps, barbed wire and machine guns – which were all then re-imported for use in Europe itself. The genocidal war that the Prusso-German army waged in the German colony of South-West Africa (present-day Namibia) foreshadowed the extermination policies conducted by the Nazis on the Eastern Front a generation later. It is no coincidence that it was in German South-West Africa that one of the founders of Nazi pseudo-scientific ideas of 'racial hygiene', Eugen Fischer, conducted his first research experiments supposedly proving the 'inferiority' of certain races. Later Fischer led forced sterilisation programmes against racial 'degenerates' in Nazi Germany, which paved the way for and legitimised mass-murder programmes – Fischer was a teacher of the so-called 'Angel of Death' at Auschwitz, Joseph Mengele.[47]

In the years before 1945, then, both in Britain and in a number of other European imperial powers, both democratic and non-democratic, there was a continuum between empire and 'domestic' intelligence services. However, as we shall see, in Britain in the second half of the twentieth century precisely the opposite occurred. In the two decades after 1945, Britain's intelligence services posted a succession of intelligence officers out to the empire and Commonwealth. Recruits to MI5 at this time spent on average between a quarter and a half of their careers stationed in colonial or Commonwealth countries. It was the cataclysmic event of the Second World War that permanently transformed the imperial responsibilities of the British secret state. Ironically, the importance of MI5's colonial responsibilities would increase after 1945, precisely when Britain's imperial power began to decline.[48]

2

Strategic Deception:
British Intelligence, Special Operations
and Empire in the Second World War

'You were a spy then?'
  'Not quite ... Really I was still a thief. No great patriot. No great hero. They just made my skills official.'

MICHAEL ONDAATJE, *The English Patient*[1]

Towards the end of the Second World War, Sir David Petrie, the wartime Director-General of MI5, wrote to the Foreign Secretary, Sir Anthony Eden, outlining some of the notable successes that MI5 and British intelligence more generally had gained during the war. As Petrie explained, the successes of Britain's wartime intelligence services had necessarily not been disclosed to the public, and it was likely that they would have to remain under a veil of secrecy for the foreseeable future: 'The full story can perhaps never be told but if it could be, it could perhaps claim acceptance as truth mainly on the grounds that it seems stranger than fiction.' In many ways the story of Britain's wartime intelligence successes still seems stranger than fiction, but luckily for us it can now be told. Put simply, the story is that during the war Britain's intelligence services gained unprecedented successes: they learned more about their enemies than any power had ever learned about another in the history of warfare. At the end of the war, the Supreme Allied Commander in Europe, General Dwight D. Eisenhower, personally congratulated them for the role they had played, which in his opinion was 'decisive' in bringing the conflict to a successful conclusion for the Allies.[2]

Britain's intelligence services achieved their wartime successes both in Britain itself and across the empire and British-occupied territories – from the deserts of North Africa to the hilltops of India and the steamy jungles of Malaya. The Second World War was the event that revolutionised Britain's imperial intelligence responsibilities, with MI5, SIS and GCHQ being directly involved in colonial affairs in earnest for the first time. However, before we can turn in detail to the wartime operations of British intelligence, it is necessary to understand their context. It is only by appreciating how the intelligence services operated domestically, from their headquarters in London, that their activities in distant outposts of the empire can be understood.

NAZI NEMESIS: INTELLIGENCE FAILURE
– INTELLIGENCE SUCCESS

The unprecedented successes of British intelligence during the Second World War are all the more remarkable when it is considered how weak the collective position of MI5, SIS and GC&CS was in 1939. The British secret state began the war with pitiful intelligence on its enemies, the Axis Powers. GC&CS had failed to make any significant headway in reading German communications, which relied on the famous Enigma code. The situation was similarly bleak for MI5 and SIS: they had such a dearth of intelligence that in 1939 they barely knew the name of the German military intelligence service (the Abwehr) or of its head (Admiral Wilhelm Canaris). MI5's official in-house wartime historian, John 'Jack' Curry, who had worked as a counter-espionage officer before the war, and was therefore well placed to comment on what Britain knew at the time about Nazi intelligence, described MI5 as entering the war in a state of 'confusion' that often amounted to 'chaos':

> In 1939 we had no adequate knowledge of the German organisations which it was the function of the Security Service [MI5] to guard against either in this wider field of the 'Fifth Column' or in the narrower one of military espionage and purely material sabotage. We had in fact no definite knowledge whether there was any organised connection between the German Secret Service and Nazi sympathisers in this country, whether of British or alien nationality.[3]

A similarly bleak picture was given by one of MI5's principal wartime counter-espionage desk officers, Dick White, who went on to become the only ever head of both MI5 and SIS. He later recalled that MI5 started the war 'without any real documentation on the subject we were supposed to tackle. We had a very vague idea of how the German system worked, and what its objectives were in time of war.'[4]

Much of the reason why the British secret state had so little information on Nazi Germany at the beginning of the war was that, for most of the 1930s, its intelligence services had been starved of resources. In 1934 Whitehall's Defence Requirements Committee had predicted that Nazi Germany would be the 'ultimate enemy' for Britain and its empire, but in the years that followed, MI5 and SIS failed to obtain any significant increase in funding or staff. Some minority voices, such as John Curry in MI5, warned from an early stage that Britain's intelligence machinery needed to gear up to face the threat of Nazi Germany. From 1934 onwards Curry was advising that it would be dangerous simply to dismiss *Mein Kampf*, in which Hitler essentially outlined his vision for world domination, as the writings of a crazed lunatic – which of course it was, but it was also much more. As Curry argued, the problem for Britain (and the rest of the world) was that this crazed lunatic was now in power, so his diatribe in *Mein Kampf* had to be taken seriously. However, Curry was a voice in the wilderness within Whitehall, and neither MI5 nor SIS managed to secure any major expansion of resources in the pre-war years. While both agencies failed to make their warnings about Hitler sufficiently loud to be heard, Whitehall bureaucrats and bean-counters were only too willing to disregard the warnings they did hear as merely the perennial cry for more resources from intelligence services – after all, armies always ask for more tanks. As late as 1939, SIS was so underfunded that it could not even afford wireless sets for its agents.[5]

MI5's lack of reliable intelligence on Nazi German intelligence was made worse by the frenzied 'spy scares' that broke out in Britain in the early stages of the war, just as they had in 1914. During the so-called 'phoney war', the period after September 1939 when war had been declared but proper fighting had not yet commenced, hysterical reports from the British public bombarded MI5's London headquarters about German 'agents' – and even 'suspicious'-looking pigeons, which led MI5 to establish a falconry unit, appropriately led by a retired RAF wing-commander, to track down and 'neutralise' enemy pigeons. Its efforts were unsuccessful: all of the pigeons killed by MI5's falcons turned out to be innocent British birds – a new twist on the term friendly fire.[6]

More seriously than rogue pigeons, the paucity of intelligence on the Axis Powers essentially led to MI5's near total collapse. In July 1940, amid the Battle of Britain and the so-called 'fifth column' crisis, MI5's internal bureaucracy completely broke down under the strain of checking reports on supposed enemy agents and other 'suspicious' activities, ranging from the plausible to the preposterous. So many reports of 'enemy spies' bombarded MI5 that its central Registry, the nerve centre of its operations, which in 1940 contained two million cards and 170,000 'personal files' or dossiers, ground to a halt and then collapsed. The chaos that these reports caused – those on 'enemy light signalling' alone reached a stack five feet high in MI5's office – was made worse by the spectre of events on the Continent. Between May and June 1940 Hitler launched an unprecedented 'lightning war' (*Blitzkrieg*) in Europe, which led to the surrender of European countries from the Netherlands to Norway in quick succession. Hitler's *Blitzkrieg* was facilitated by 'fifth column' saboteurs and agents planted and parachuted into the invaded countries. With their conventional armies obliterated, the Dutch gave up after just five days of fighting; the Belgians after seventeen. At the end of May the entire British Expeditionary Force (BEF) was evacuated from the Continent at Dunkirk, and by mid-June Britain's greatest ally in Europe, France, had ignominiously surrendered. Britain was standing alone in Europe, fighting for its survival, with only its empire and Commonwealth to support it. The Joint Intelligence Committee, Britain's highest overall intelligence assessment body, sombrely planned for its own evacuation from London, and speculated on how it could survive (by hiding in bunkers) after the Nazi invasion of Britain that appeared imminent. The JIC was not fantasising: the German leadership had drawn up detailed plans for an invasion of Britain (codenamed Operation *Sealion*), which included the arrest and likely execution of a number of senior MI5 and SIS officers, whose names the Gestapo had probably found in London telephone directories and entries in *Who's Who*, which in many cases, as we have seen with Sir Eric Holt-Wilson, gave their home addresses.[7]

The situation for Britain was actually even worse than this suggested. Due to the Nazi–Soviet Pact of August 1939, the Soviet Union and Nazi Germany entered the war as allies. It is often forgotten that the invasion of Poland in September 1939, which brought Britain into the war, was carried out by German and Soviet forces together. For a nightmare period between the outbreak of war in September 1939 and Nazi Germany's invasion of Russia in June 1941, it appeared that Germany, Italy, Japan and the Soviet Union would act in uneasy concert and divide the spoils of the world between themselves. Britain nearly went to war with the Soviet Union when the Red Army invaded Finland in November 1939, and as papers of the British Chiefs of Staff reveal, in April 1940 the RAF was planning a devastating bombing attack on the Soviet Union, codenamed Operation *Pike*.[8]

In these circumstances, with Britain standing alone against Nazi and Soviet forces, in the summer of 1940 MI5 concluded – inaccurately, as it turned out – that large-scale German sabotage and espionage networks were operating in Britain, as they had done in Europe. The truth would only be revealed later: unbeknownst to MI5 at the time, code-breakers at Bletchley Park had in fact identified virtually all German agents operating in Britain. Unaware of this, in June 1940 MI5 took one of the most controversial decisions it would ever take, recommending the mass internment of all 'enemy aliens' in Britain. In total over 27,000 foreign nationals were interned in Britain during the war on MI5's orders. In Britain, as with the wartime internment of Japanese Americans in the United States, this was a lamentable low point in the history of civil liberties.[9]

Due to its lack of reliable information on Nazi Germany, British intelligence started the Second World War effectively fighting in the dark. To make matters worse, it was chronically under-resourced: in 1939 MI5 had a total staff of only thirty-six officers. The bungling efforts of British intelligence in the early days of the war were symbolised by a catastrophic incident that befell SIS in October 1939, soon after the outbreak of hostilities. Two SIS officers stationed in the Netherlands, Richard Stevens and Sigismund Payne Best, were lured to the town of Venlo on the Dutch–German border on the pretext of meeting a group of anti-Hitler German officers. In reality, the 'resistance' group was controlled by the Gestapo. The two SIS officers were immediately arrested, dragged from neutral Dutch territory across the German border, and imprisoned for the rest of the war. Inexplicably, they had come to the rendezvous with a complete list of their agents in Germany, all of whom were promptly arrested and neutralised (with many executed) by the Nazi authorities. In one fatal swoop, Britain's network of agents in the Third Reich was dismantled.[10]

The 'Venlo incident' seems to have cast a long shadow. Although little information is currently available in British records, it does not seem that after Venlo SIS assisted or sponsored any significant anti-Hitler resistance groups within Germany. This may have been caused by anxiety after Venlo, or it may have been due to fears within Whitehall that killing Hitler would simply create a martyr and unleash further demons. None of the various wartime attempts made on Hitler's life by German officers, the most famous of which was the 'July Bomb Plot' of 1944, appears to have been sponsored by SIS or any other part of British intelligence. Armchair assassins and 'critical historians' today rarely comprehend the genuine bravery shown by these plotters, but even with that concession, contrary to what has been suggested in a recent Hollywood film, Operation *Valkyrie* in July 1944 was not intended to oust Hitler and establish democratic government in Germany. Instead, it was an attempt by a group of German officers to replace the Third Reich with a non-democratic military dictatorship.[11]

One of the reasons the British secret state had such poor intelligence on Nazi Germany at the start of the war was the extreme difficulty of gaining reliable information on a closed police state like the Third Reich. To this day, understanding its power structures is still one of the most controversial, and voluminous, subjects in modern history. Historians today, equipped with German records, which British intelligence at the time was not, are unable to agree on such basic questions as who was ultimately in charge of Nazi Germany and whether Hitler was a 'strong dictator' or a 'weak dictator'. That said, in the pre-war years British intelligence as a whole failed catastrophically to understand the mindset of the Nazi leadership. There were a few pre-war officers, in particular MI5's John Curry and Dick White, who grasped the true nature of the strategic threat posed by the Third Reich, but their attempts to convince the rest of Whitehall of this came to little. The Oxford historian and wartime recruit to SIS Hugh Trevor-Roper was shocked to find that none of his colleagues had bothered to read the 'sacred texts' of those they were fighting, such as *Mein Kampf*. To make matters worse, MI5 and SIS had given an overwhelming priority in the pre-war years to Soviet and Comintern activities, and had largely neglected the growing threat of Nazi Germany. This also meant that they viewed the Nazi threat through the paradigm of the Comintern, and erroneously concluded that fascist organisations such as Oswald Mosley's British Union of Fascists (BUF) were run along similar lines to the British Communist Party, which was controlled by Moscow. In fact the black-shirted members of the BUF were above all British, and contrary to what MI5 believed, were not willing to bow to instructions from Berlin or Rome in the way that the 'internationalised' British Communist Party followed instructions from 'the centre', Moscow. That said, it is impossible to know exactly how the BUF would have reacted if there had been a Nazi invasion of Britain.[12]

The remarkable failures of Britain's intelligence services before the war led them in some astonishing directions during it. By 1942 the intelligence chiefs in Whitehall had become so desperate in their bid to understand the mindset of the Nazi leadership that they employed a water-diviner, nicknamed 'Smokey Joe', and a Dutch astrologer, Louis de Wohl, who both claimed that they could predict Adolf Hitler's behaviour from his star sign (Libra rising). It was only after de Wohl had been employed for several months that MI5 and SIS realised he was nothing more than a con artist.[13]

One of the main reasons why, despite the meagre intelligence Britain had at the start of hostilities, its intelligence machinery achieved such phenomenal wartime successes was because of Winston Churchill, who, as the world's leading intelligence historian Christopher Andrew has pointed out, more than any British political leader before or since was an enthusiastic believer in intelligence matters. Churchill had probably first become interested in 'cloak and dagger' activities while serving as a reporter in the Boer War from 1899 to 1900, but his interest blossomed after he became Home Secretary in 1910. As Home Secretary he helped the fledgling Secret Service Bureau in its early days – he was a contemporary of Sir Vernon Kell's at Sandhurst – providing it with increased powers to intercept letters (HOWs) and steering a revised Official Secrets Act through Parliament in 1911, which made it easier to bring prosecutions for espionage. Churchill's fascination with intelligence continued after he became Prime Minister in May 1940, Britain's 'darkest hour', which under Churchill became its finest. As Prime Minister he was an avid consumer of intelligence reports, and allowed for vastly more resources to be given to the intelligence services. Under Churchill, the Joint Intelligence Committee (JIC), which had been established in 1936, came into its own, operating as a streamlined assessment body for all of Britain's intelligence services, and producing concise weekly reports for Churchill and his cabinet on threats to British national security – a legacy that lasts down to the present day. Britain's separate intelligence services began to collaborate in ways they previously had not, thus effectively becoming the British intelligence community.[14]

It was in the realm of signals intelligence (SIGINT) that Churchill's support of the intelligence services paid the biggest dividends. The unprecedented successes gained by British intelligence during the war were caused largely by the herculean efforts of the code-breakers at GC&CS, based at Bletchley Park. In the course of the war, Bletchley Park would come to preside over mass-espionage on an industrial scale. In May 1941 Churchill received a top-secret request from Bletchley Park begging for more resources. He was so perturbed that he demanded 'Action this Day', and instructed his military assistant, General Hastings 'Pug' Ismay, to give GC&CS all the resources it needed and to report that this had been done. In December 1940 Bletchley Park had managed, with the assistance of

Polish code-breakers, to crack the first of the famous German Enigma codes. With the resources that Churchill now threw behind it, GC&CS expanded rapidly: by 1943 its code-breakers were reading on average 3,000 German communications per day. These decrypts were codenamed Ultra, but were also known as ISOS, standing for 'Intelligence Services Oliver Strachey' (ISOS), named after a high-ranking official at GC&CS, and more generally were termed 'Most Secret Sources' (or MSS for short). The Ultra decrypts were passed by SIS, which had formal control over GC&CS during the war, directly to Churchill himself on an almost daily basis. Ultra provided such accurate and rapid 'live' intelligence that some German communications from the Eastern Front or the deserts of North Africa actually arrived on Churchill's desk in London before they reached Hitler in Berlin. Bletchley Park code-breakers also acquired chilling 'real time' messages about the Holocaust. As early as 1941, intercepts of low-grade German traffic from the Eastern Front were revealing to Bletchley Park what, with hindsight, we can see was the evolution of the Nazi 'Final Solution' – the mass murder of European Jews and other supposed racial subhumans (*Untermenschen*). There is some existing but disputed evidence that the British and US governments refused to release what Bletchley Park had discovered about the Holocaust because to do so would have jeopardised the Ultra secret. On present evidence, it is impossible to state whether this was the case or not.[15]

Over 12,000 people are thought to have worked at Bletchley Park, and their voluminous Ultra decrypts contributed to Allied military successes in a number of areas. The leader of British forces in North Africa in 1942, General Sir Bernard Montgomery, was provided with a stream of high-grade Ultra decrypts that revealed the location of his opponent Erwin Rommel's Afrika Korps. The decrypts flowing to Montgomery were so accurate that after the war the JIC worried that when the history of the North African campaigns came to be written, historians would realise that he had some kind of foreknowledge of Rommel's movements, and would be able to piece the puzzle together. As it turned out, the JIC gave historians far too much credit – the Ultra secret remained hidden for years after the war. We now know that the decrypts assisted Montgomery's Eighth Army in its famous victory in the summer of 1942 at El Alamein, once an obscure port on the edge of the Egyptian desert, which was a major turning point in the Allied campaign in North Africa. By May 1943 Montgomery's 'desert rats' had effectively driven Rommel's Afrika Korps into the sea in Tunisia. Bletchley Park's Ultra decrypts also produced direct benefits for the Allies in the Battle of the North Atlantic: they revealed the locations of German U-boats, allowing the Admiralty to manoeuvre supply convoys away from danger, bring shipping losses down to bearable levels, and contributed to Allied victories in the Battle of Cape Matapan (March 1941) and the Battle of the North Cape (December 1943).[16]

Ultra decrypts likewise made possible MI5's now-legendary 'Double Cross System', the process by which every German agent in Britain was identified, and many of them turned into double agents. It was only after Ultra came on-line in December 1940 that MI5 could establish conclusively whether any unidentified German agents were operating in Britain, and also, crucially, whether the disinformation that MI5's double agents were passing back to Germany was being believed by the German High Command. The MI5 officer T.A. 'Tar' Robertson, who was in charge of Section B1a within MI5, responsible for running double agents, would later describe how Ultra decrypts allowed MI5 to see whether the files of its enemies were being stocked with the exact information that MI5 desired. In several cases, MI5 watched with pride as its disinformation was passed by the Nazi intelligence services across Europe and beyond. The magnitude of these successes was later summarised by Sir John Masterman, the head of MI5's wartime deception committee, who noted that during the war Britain 'actively ran and controlled the German espionage system in this country'.[17]

Churchill later reflected on the value of the intelligence produced by Bletchley Park and the secrecy of its operations, describing its code-breakers as 'the geese that laid the golden eggs but never cackled'. Some historians, including F.H. 'Harry' Hinsley, who worked as a junior official at Bletchley Park and who later became the editor of the magisterial official history of British intelligence in the Second World War, have suggested that the intelligence produced by Bletchley Park was so valuable that it shortened the war by up to two years, saving countless lives on both sides. More recently, doubt has been cast on this claim, with historians arguing that the Second World War was really a war of matériel production, and that once the Soviet Union and the United States entered the war, in June 1941 and December 1941 respectively, victory for the Allies was assured. Although counter-factual 'what if' postulations can produce endless debates, the reality was that, if the war in Europe had not ended in May 1945, the Allies would have dropped an atomic bomb on Germany – which was the original target for the bombs dropped on Japan in August 1945.

A-FORCE: THE BIRTH OF BRITISH STRATEGIC DECEPTION

The idea of strategic deception – that is, providing false information to misguide an enemy's strategy – was put to best use by Allied forces in Europe, but it was not originally conceived there. During the so-called phoney war, between the outbreak of war in September 1939 and the Battle of Britain in the summer of 1940, the Middle East was the only theatre where British forces were directly fighting Axis forces, and it was there that innovative uses of intelligence for modern military affairs were born. Before either MI5 or SIS had begun to envisage the idea of strategic deception, it was being pioneered by a small, crack intelligence outfit attached to the Cairo-based staff of the British commander in the Middle East, General Archibald Wavell. Wavell was one of the best-educated generals in British military history, a quiet, scholarly type who liked to write poetry in his spare time and had lost an eye in the Great War. He knew the history of Lawrence of Arabia well, and valued the use of intelligence in war. The unit he established was known as 'A-Force', and the man he placed in charge of it was a brilliant military intelligence officer, Lt. Col. Dudley Clarke, who came up with a number of ingenious deception ploys. In Clarke's view, it was possible to do more than prevent secrets reaching an enemy's intelligence service (counter-espionage): secrets obtained through counter-espionage could also be used to deceive an enemy's strategy (strategic deception).[18]

In 1940 Clarke recruited a young officer, Jasper Maskelyne, who came from a long succession of famous stage magicians and conjurors, to help him build an entire false city out of plywood in the Egyptian desert, three miles from the port of Alexandria. The 'city' built by Maskelyne's group, the so-called 'Magic Gang', was apparently so realistic-looking from the air – complete with a false lighthouse and anti-aircraft batteries – that it deceived German bombers, which destroyed it instead of the actual city of Alexandria. To misdirect German bombers, the Magic Gang also used a series of elaborate mirrors to create optical illusions over the Suez Canal in order to obscure intended targets there. A-Force also assisted with deception campaigns before the strategically key Second Battle of El Alamein, fought in the Western Desert of Egypt from October to November 1942. It built 2,000 false tanks to the south of El Alamein, complete with convincing pyrotechnics, which deceived Rommel into thinking that the main Allied attack under Montgomery would come from the south, when in reality it came from the north. Maskelyne had a vested interest in exaggerating his trickery heroics in the post-war account he penned, *Magic–Top Secret*, because he felt his wartime exploits had not been recognised. Some historians have doubted his tales, but it does seem that he deserves more credit than he has been given. The authors of the official history of British intelligence in the Second World War, who had access to classified records, note Maskelyne's 'numerous and valuable contributions' to Allied visual deception in the Middle East. Thanks to A-Force and the Magic Gang's trickery, the Germans at El Alamein believed that British forces were 40 per cent larger than they actually were.[19]

In October 1941 Clarke travelled to London, where he briefed the War Office on his ideas of strategic deception. The War Office was so impressed that soon afterwards it established a top-secret outfit known as the 'London Controlling Section' (LCS). Although its name does not feature in most histories, it was one of the most important – if not *the* most important – Allied intelligence agencies in the entire Second World War. The LCS only had non-executive powers – to plan, coordinate and supervise – but this did not mean its influence was limited. In the opinion of M.R.D. Foot, the esteemed late official historian of Britain's wartime sabotage organisation, the Special Operations Executive, the LCS was more important than either MI5, SIS or GC&CS during the war. Headed from May 1942 by Lt. Col. J.H. Bevan, its purpose was to 'prepare deception plans on a worldwide basis with the object of causing the enemy to waste his military resources'. The actual running of double agents and other deception ploys was carried out by MI5 and the other services, but it was the LCS that had overall responsibility for coordinating all the disinformation sent to Germany and Britain's other enemies. A-Force's pioneering efforts in strategic deception in the Middle East therefore inspired the LCS, which then took it to new heights. As the official history of British intelligence in the Second World War noted, a small acorn planted in the deserts of North Africa by Dudley Clarke grew during the war into an enormous tree, spreading across Europe and the British empire.[20]

The first significant use of strategic deception by the LCS was with Operation *Torch*, the Allied landings in North Africa in November 1942. In the run-up to the landings, one of MI5's prize double agents, a Spanish national, Juan Pujol García, codenamed 'Garbo', sent letters to his German handlers with misinformation about the timings of the landings. One of Garbo's letters gave information from a fictional sub-agent supposedly operating in Britain stating that Allied ships had set sail from Scotland, apparently destined for North Africa. Although the letter contained accurate information, MI5 deliberately delayed it so that it would not arrive until after the actual landings had occurred. The plan worked perfectly: Garbo's German handlers were thankful for his accurate information, which had unfortunately arrived too late for them. Similar deception material on the *Torch* landings was passed to Nazi intelligence by the double agent 'Cheese', an Italian of Jewish parentage who had been recruited by SIS before the war, but was then also recruited by the Abwehr in France in 1940, and thereafter served as a British double agent. In February 1941 the Abwehr sent Cheese to Egypt, where he secretly worked under the control of MI5's regional outfit, SIME. He and his MI5 case officers created a fictional sub-agent whom they called 'Paul Nicosoff', in reality a British signals officer, who passed over strategic deception material to Nazi intelligence. By the autumn of 1942 Cheese was providing an almost daily service of reports from 'Paul Nicosoff', and in the period leading up to Operation *Torch* was in direct communication with Rommel's headquarters, furnishing false information on the mobilisation of British forces in the Middle East. By the end of the war Cheese and 'Paul Nicosoff' had transmitted 432 messages to the Abwehr station in Cairo, and Ultra decrypts revealed that the Abwehr classified them as reliable. The success of strategic deception in Operation *Torch* was clear: General Alfred Jodl, Hitler's closest military adviser, Chief of the Operations Staff of the German High Command (OKW), told Allied interrogators after the war that the landings in North Africa had come as 'a complete surprise'.[21]

The next major use of strategic deception by the LCS was with Operation *Mincemeat*, which involved the Allied invasion of Europe from North Africa, opening up a 'second front' to relieve pressure on the Soviet forces in the east. *Mincemeat* deceived the German High Command into thinking that the Allied invasion of Italy, the 'soft underbelly of Europe', as Churchill termed it, would not take place in Sicily, as was actually intended, but instead in Sardinia and Greece. Operation *Mincemeat*, begun in early 1943, was the brainchild of an MI5 officer, Charles Cholmondeley, and a brilliant wartime naval intelligence recruit, Ewen Montagu, who was assisted by another naval intelligence officer, Ian Fleming (the future creator of James Bond). Together they devised an outstanding ruse: to drop a dead body over the side of a ship, carrying supposedly top-secret Allied plans for the invasion of Sardinia. The deceivers were so meticulous in their preparations that they created a complete false persona for the dead body, known as 'Major Martin', even putting a photograph of his fictional fiancée (in reality an MI5 staff member) in his wallet and obtaining the stub of a cinema ticket from a showing in London a few nights before his 'death'. 'Major Martin', who in reality had been found in a London morgue, a deceased homeless man without any known relatives, achieved more in death than he apparently ever did in life. After his body was found off the Spanish coast, the German High Command was deceived by the documents in his briefcase that outlined the supposed Allied plans for the invasion of Sardinia, and on Hitler's personal orders troops were diverted there – even though it would have been perfectly obvious to any child with a school atlas that the Allies' intended destination from their base in North Africa was Sicily, not Sardinia.[22]

The climax of Britain's wartime deception campaigns was Operation *Fortitude*, the deception operation paving the way for the Allied cross-Channel invasion of Fortress Europe on D-Day, 6 June 1944 – the largest seaborne invasion in naval history. In preparation for D-Day, MI5's star double agent Garbo and his MI5 handler, Tomás Harris, passed over voluminous amounts of false strategic intelligence to Germany about non-existent Allied forces stationed in Britain. Garbo helped to fabricate an entire false US army group, 'the First United States Army Group' (FUSAG), which was never more than a collection of balsawood tanks and inflatable ships, but just like Dudley Clarke's previous deceptions in the Egyptian desert, nevertheless looked realistic from the air. The most important misinformation that Garbo supplied to his German spy-masters was a radio message on 5 June 1944 which convinced the German High Command into thinking that the main Allied landings would not be in Normandy, but in the area around Calais. Based on this information, crucial SS Panzer divisions were diverted to Calais, where they awaited an invasion force that would never arrive. Garbo's deception information, which diverted Nazi forces and allowed the Allies to establish a crucial bridgehead, undoubtedly saved Allied lives. A measure of the value that the Nazi leadership attached to him was that Hitler personally awarded him an Iron Cross, making him the only person ever to have received both a Nazi Iron Cross and a British MBE.[23]

SPY VS SPY: AMATEURS VS PROFESSIONALS

In the years after the war, some MI5 officers such as Tar Robertson would criticise the deception tricks of Dudley Clarke and A-Force in the Egyptian desert as 'amateur'. A-Force was certainly not a professional intelligence service in the way that MI5 or SIS were. It was also the case that Clarke was a highly eccentric individual. In a truly bizarre episode, in 1943 he was arrested in Madrid dressed as a woman. At first he told the Spanish police that he was conducting research for a news report on people's reactions to men dressed as women, but he then changed his story and stated that he had been bringing the clothes to a friend, and decided to try them on as 'a prank' – but as one official in the British embassy in Madrid noted, this did not explain why the women's shoes and brassière he was wearing fitted him.[24]

For all of Clarke's undoubted eccentricities, it was unfair for Robertson to suggest that he and A-Force were 'amateur'. The root of the tension between MI5 and outfits such as A-Force was that MI5 was concerned with counter-espionage for its own sake – to prevent an enemy from gaining British secrets – and viewed strategic deception as an extreme form of counter-espionage, whereas agencies like A-Force tended to view strategic deception as the ultimate goal. A-Force's disinclination to regard counter-espionage as an end in itself seems to be the reason Robertson played down its efforts.[25]

Robertson was one of MI5's best agent handlers in the first half of the twentieth century. He was a professional intelligence officer who joined the service in the early 1930s, having served in the Seaforth Highlanders regiment of the British Army – his tendency to persist in wearing the regiment's uniform of Scottish trews earned him the affectionate nickname 'passion-pants' within MI5. During the war he led Section B1a of MI5, which was responsible for running all double-cross agents – 120 in total. Robertson's success had much to do with his affable manner, which could put even tough enemy agents at ease. Nevertheless, as a professional intelligence officer, he naturally regarded those who saw matters differently from himself and MI5, particularly over the use of strategic deception, as novice upstarts.[26]

In labelling A-Force 'amateur', Robertson overlooked a crucial point: MI5, like the rest of the British intelligence community, actually owed much of its wartime success to the influx of amateur outsiders into its ranks. A flood of outstanding, if eccentric, individuals equipped Britain's wartime intelligence services with a degree of ingenuity and creativeness hitherto missing. They included a number of high-powered intellectuals from Britain's leading universities, with Bletchley Park in particular becoming a bastion of such brainpower. Among its most notable recruits were the brilliant mathematicians Alan Turing, Alfred 'Dilly' Knox and Gordon Welchman, all from Cambridge University. Two-thirds of the

Fellowship of King's College, Cambridge, worked at Bletchley Park at some point during the war. Turing was essentially responsible for devising an entirely new system of mechanised 'bombes' to power decryption efforts against the Enigma code – for this reason he has justifiably been termed the father of modern computer science. Recruits into SIS included high-calibre Oxford academics such as the historian Hugh Trevor-Roper and the philosophers Stuart Hampshire and Gilbert Ryle. Some notable literary figures also entered SIS's wartime ranks, sometimes with humorous results: when Malcolm Muggeridge and Graham Greene were given training by SIS on the use of secret inks, which included instructions on how to obtain raw material for an ink codenamed 'BS' (birdshit), their reactions were understandably bemused. Intellectual heavyweights who joined MI5 during the war included Victor Rothschild from Cambridge, who became MI5's in-house expert on sabotage, and from Oxford the academic lawyer H.L.A. Hart and the historian John Masterman. Masterman, a brilliant academic, a bachelor and one of the best spin bowlers in English cricket at the time, became the chairman of MI5's 'Twenty Committee', which oversaw all the double-cross agents that MI5 ran during the war. In a typical example of the wordplay used by its academically-minded members, the Twenty Committee was so called because a double cross, 'XX', is the Roman numeral for twenty.[27]

Alongside this kind of intellectual firepower, less academic professions also produced some outstanding wartime officers for British intelligence. One of MI5's best agent handlers, Cyril Mills, came from an unlikely family background: he was the son of the famous circus-owner Bertram Mills. Probably the best working relationship that developed during the war between an agent and an intelligence case officer was that of the 'amateur' MI5 wartime recruit Tomás Harris and his double agent Garbo. Harris joined MI5 from the unlikely background of an antiquarian art dealership in London. His fluency in Spanish made him the obvious handler for Garbo, and the two worked brilliantly together, building up an extremely detailed but entirely fictional espionage network, consisting of twenty-eight sub-agents in various parts of Britain, who in reality were 'nothing more than a figment of the imagination'. Garbo had to make use of a guidebook when describing the locations of these bogus agents to his German handlers, because he had not travelled widely in Britain. As Harris later commented, Garbo's imagination was worthy of Milton.[28]

Another benefit of 'amateur' wartime recruits like Harris was that they were less concerned with careerism, and staying within the corridors of power of the secret state, than their professional colleagues, which meant they were more free to come up with creative ideas and less worried if those ideas did not work. That said, it should be noted that ingenuity and creativity only go so far in the mechanics of agent-running: there comes a point when it has to involve tiresome, but necessary, methodical research. One former SIS officer who worked closely with MI5's Section B1a recalled that his day-to-day business involved such mind-numbing tasks as reading a Madrid telephone directory backwards in order to find an agent's name from an intercepted telephone number.[29]

BRITAIN'S INTELLIGENCE EMPIRE

During the Second World War Britain's intelligence services essentially faced the same kind of threats as they had in the First World War. The intelligence services of the Axis Powers attempted to incite revolt and unrest across the British empire just as the Central Powers had done. To counter these threats, Britain's secret state built up unprecedented imperial intelligence capabilities. The Second World War was when Britain's imperial intelligence came of age, and MI5's pre-war vision of being an imperial security service became a reality. It increased the number of officers (DSOs) posted to colonial and Commonwealth countries from six at the start of the war to twenty-seven by its end, supported by twenty-one secretarial staff, stationed across the globe, from Trinidad to Aden to Kuala Lumpur. DSOs communicated with the 'Overseas Control' section in MI5's headquarters in London, run by an officer named Col. Bertram Ede, using secure cyphers and under the cover address 'Subsided'. During the war several senior MI5 officers made trips to British territories overseas to oversee and help reform local security. Both Dick White and Tar Robertson visited the Middle East, and recommended ways in which MI5's inter-service outfit there, known as Security Intelligence Middle East (SIME), could function more efficiently, particularly in running double agents. MI5 also maintained highly secret laboratories in two outposts of empire, Bermuda and Singapore, run by specially recruited scientists – real-life James Bond Q-types – whose responsibilities included testing intercepted letters for secret inks.[30]

Along with MI5's expanded imperial role, the war also revolutionised SIGINT operations in British territories overseas, and led to GC&CS's direct involvement in colonial and Commonwealth countries. GC&CS's regional hub in India, the so-called 'Wireless Experimental Centre' in

Delhi, dramatically increased the amount and quality of traffic it intercepted, obtaining volumes of enemy communications once the Enigma
code had been cracked. GC&CS did the same in other parts of the empire,
in Hong Kong, Cyprus, Malta and the British Army's wireless station at
Sarafand in Palestine, which acted as a local collection point for GC&CS
in the Middle East. A similar surge in intercepted traffic occurred in the
largely civilian outfit that GC&CS ran at Heliopolis, in Egypt, and in the
SIGINT station that the RAF ran for GC&CS in Iraq, which was occupied
by Britain and the Allies during the war. The massive expansion of
GC&CS's overseas wartime operations led to some ingenious developments. When a tall antenna was needed to intercept radio communications in Egypt, workers at the Radio Security Service (RSS), the outfit
under MI5's control responsible for intercepting illicit radio communications sent to and from agents, came up with the idea of sticking one on top
of the Great Pyramid – effectively making this wonder of the ancient
world the largest wireless receiver on the planet.[31]

As in the First World War, during the Second World War it became a
strategy of Britain's enemies to forge alliances with anti-colonial groups
campaigning for independence within the British empire. Once again,
Ireland was an obvious target for Germany to incite anti-British revolt,
and the Abwehr attempted unsuccessfully to forge links with the Irish
Republican Army in a plan codenamed Operation *Kathleen*. The IRA took
full advantage of Britain's weakened domestic security during the war,
launching a bombing campaign in 1939 in which London's Hammersmith
Bridge was among the targets attacked – which increased MI5's fears of a
'fifth column' operating in Britain. At the time, security threats posed by
the IRA were not the responsibility of MI5, but fell squarely on the shoulders of the Special Branch at Scotland Yard – which had originally been
established in the 1880s as the 'Special Fenian Branch'. In the immediate
pre-war years, MI5 did have a link with the police in Dublin and Belfast,
and also maintained a liaison with military intelligence (G2) in the Irish
Free State (or Eire as it was called after 1937). During the war it opened a
desk devoted to Irish affairs, led by Cecil Liddell, brother of the wartime
Director of MI5's B-Division, Guy Liddell. However, MI5 only really
became involved in dealing with the IRA during the war if there was a
clear German connection. Luckily for MI5, all of the German agents sent
to Ireland to link with the IRA proved to be spectacularly inept. They were
either identified by other agents already in MI5's custody, tracked down
by the Irish police, or identified in Ultra decrypts provided by Bletchley

Park. One agent, Herman Görtz, was parachuted into Ireland in the summer of 1940 wearing full Luftwaffe uniform and regalia. His wireless set was destroyed on landing, he nearly drowned while crossing the river Boyne, which also claimed the bottle of invisible ink he was supposed to communicate with, and he was totally unsuccessful in contacting the IRA's leadership. Although he was not tracked down by the Irish police until November 1941, while he remained at liberty his mission was a complete failure. After his arrest he was imprisoned in Dublin for the rest of the war, and when told that he would be repatriated back to Germany he committed suicide in a Dublin police station.[32]

THE FAILURE OF AXIS INTELLIGENCE

It is easy to romanticise the story of the wartime successes of British intelligence, and to forget a fundamental point: for all of Britain's wartime intelligence achievements, its secret services were fortunate to face opponents who were generally ineffective, in some cases spectacularly so. The failures of the Nazi intelligence services were ultimately due to the authoritarian nature of the Third Reich itself. Like the intelligence services of all one-party authoritarian regimes, they were extremely good at intelligence *collection*: keeping detailed records on their enemies, conducting surveillance and using the fear of denunciation to terrorise populations into submission. They enforced the racial conspiracy theories of the Nazi leadership with ruthless zeal, orchestrating the 'Final Solution' with a cold, bureaucratic efficiency. They also mounted some successful operations against the British: the notorious Venlo incident was followed by the 'Cicero' spy affair, by which classified information was obtained from the British consulate-general in Istanbul from 1943 to 1944. In the Netherlands they identified and overran resistance groups working for the British Special Operations Executive, and recruited double agents from among their members. However, these successes were the exceptions, not the rule.

Just like the Soviet Union's NKVD operating at the same time, the Nazi intelligence services were astonishingly poor at intelligence *assessment*: their activities were more concerned with furthering the racial conspiracies of the leadership than with gathering critical information. The Nazi *Sicherheitsdienst* ('Security Service' – SD), for instance, had an entire division devoted to researching church records to identify Jewish and Slavic ancestry, while the SS, Hitler's murderous elite corps, devoted its resources to researching bizarre subjects like the significance of top hats and Gothic pinnacles at Eton, the suppression of harps in Ulster and the activities of Freemasons.[33]

This type of warped activity was accentuated by the fact that there were a number of inbuilt reasons preventing the objective collection of intelligence by Nazi officials: they were often afraid of reprisals against themselves or their families if they produced 'wrong' reports, and this inevitably created a large degree of sycophancy among their ranks, with junior staff wary of voicing dissenting opinions. There is some evidence to suggest that, due to their fear of admitting failures to their superiors, some Abwehr officers continued to run agents even when they suspected that their cover had been blown. The head of the Abwehr, Admiral Wilhelm Canaris, is known to have been strongly anti-Hitler, and was eventually executed for treason in April 1945 on the Führer's personal orders. However, contrary to what has been alleged, there is no evidence that Canaris was secretly in communication with SIS during the war to negotiate a peace settlement.[34]

One of the main Abwehr officers conducting operations against Britain and its empire, Dr Nikolaus Ritter, who also went by the alias 'Clark Gable' because, he said, of his resemblance to the Hollywood actor, later unconvincingly claimed to have known that the cover of some of the agents he sent to England was blown, and that he was really running a triple-cross against Britain. By the middle of the war, after a series of failed intelligence missions, Ritter's Abwehr career was over. He went on to be in charge of civil air defence in Hanover, and was responsible for coordinating the city's defences on the evening of a devastating Allied raid in October 1944, when his powers of prediction spectacularly failed him. Believing that a diversionary raid was the main thrust of the attack, Ritter stood Hanover's air defences down. Precisely six minutes after he gave his order, 1,500 Allied bombers arrived overhead. Ritter was immediately retired. One of the last reports we find on him in MI5 records is from 1945, after his capture by the Allies, which notes that he is in charge of sweeping out the canteen in a British interrogation facility in occupied Germany, and that he has one subordinate under him in his sweeping duties – Kurt Zeitzler, the former Chief of the German General Staff.[35]

AXIS PLOTS IN THE BRITISH EMPIRE

One of the most harebrained schemes devised by the Abwehr in the entire war – and it devised many – occurred in the spring of 1941, when Ernst Paul Fackenheim, a Palestine-born Jewish prisoner in a German concentration camp, was recruited and sent on a mission to Palestine to learn what he could of the British efforts to stop Rommel taking the Suez Canal. Unsurprisingly, Fackenheim gave himself up to the Allies after he was dropped into Palestine by parachute. The German intelligence services devised similarly ill-conceived plots elsewhere in the Middle East. Operation *Atlas* was planned by the Abwehr together with Hitler's Arab protégé, the virulent anti-Semite Grand Mufti of Jerusalem, Haj Amin el Husseini, who from 1940 was exiled in Berlin, installed at the splendid Bellevue Palace where he set himself up as a kind of Lawrence of Arabia figure, and was known as Hitler's guest in the red fez. The gist of Operation *Atlas* was that in September 1944 two Arab fighters and three Abwehr agents would be dropped from a Heinkel 111 over Jericho with banknotes and ten cylinders of poison with which to poison the wells in Tel Aviv – apparently in a perverse reversal of the old conspiracy theory that Jews were responsible for poisoning wells in Europe. The Abwehr agents would then help fund anti-British revolts in Palestine and neighbouring countries. Although the Abwehr did not know it, details of the mission had been disclosed to the Allies by Ultra decrypts obtained by Bletchley Park, and its agents were tracked down and arrested. One of the Arab agents, Ali Hassan Salameh, known as 'the cut-throat', was wounded in a skirmish with the Palestine police, but limped off to fight another day, waging violent campaigns against Jews in Palestine and, after 1948, against Israelis. Salameh's son inherited his father's implacable anti-Semitism. Born in 1940, he was known as 'the red prince', and would become notorious as the chief of operations of Black September, the Palestinian terrorist organisation responsible for the massacre of Israeli athletes and officials at the 1972 Munich Olympics. Nothing better illustrates how animosities and hatred can be passed down through the generations in the modern history of the Middle East.[36]

Another, equally unsuccessful, Nazi espionage network in the Middle East was the so-called 'Pyramid' organisation in Egypt, led by Count László Almásy, a Hungarian explorer and the real-life original of 'the English Patient'. In the award-winning novel of that name by Michael Ondaatje and film by Anthony Minghella, Almásy is depicted as a handsome airman and hero. In reality he was neither handsome nor a hero, but an unsuccessful Nazi intelligence officer, according to his MI5 file a 'hunchback … shabbily dressed, with a fat and pendulous nose, drooping shoulders and a nervous tic'. In the novel and the film, Almásy is depicted as dying from a morphine overdose, with his heart broken. In reality, he died of amoebic dysentery in 1951. After his recruitment by Nazi intelligence in Paris sometime in the immediate pre-war years, Almásy was sent to Egypt to report on British troop and shipping movements. His mission was a total failure. In 1942 he was supposed to infiltrate two agents into British-occupied Egypt, who would report directly to Rommel's headquarters in the Middle East by wireless. For this task he recruited an Egyptian, Mohsen Fadl, who was working for the Egyptian tourist board in Paris, and a former cotton trader named Hans Eppler, the illegitimate son of a German woman who had married an Egyptian judge. Both proved unqualified disasters.

In May 1942 Almásy began Operation *Condor*, an epic but ultimately unsuccessful mission to smuggle his two agents into Egypt. It involved a hellish journey of about 3,000 miles, in two stolen US trucks and two Chevrolets, from Libya across the Egyptian desert. The first attempt was a failure, with the vehicles becoming stuck in quicksand and the drivers falling desperately ill. The second, however, was a success. After dropping his agents in the town of Asyut, Almásy made the return journey to Libya. His agents travelled on to Cairo, where they went underground in the city's red-light district, and blew the £3,000 he had given them on cheap champagne, cabarets, prostitutes and nightclubs. Their mission produced no important intelligence, but they did manage to recruit one of the best belly-dancers in Egypt, described in MI5 records as 'an exponent of the *dance de ventre*', who installed them on a houseboat on the Nile, in the cocktail bar of which they hid their radio transmitters. Their attempts to make wireless communication with Rommel's headquarters were unsuccessful: unknown to them, the Abwehr unit with which they were supposed to communicate had been captured by the Allies. In a desperate bid to get messages to the German forces they recruited a young signals officer in the Egyptian army named Anwar Sadat – the future President of Egypt. In fact, Almásy's entire mission had been compromised from the outset: Bletchley Park and MI5's inter-service agency, SIME, had been closely monitoring it as it took one inept turn after another. Almásy was identified in Ultra decrypts as operating under the codename 'Salam', an anagram of the first five letters of his surname. After three months watching its every move, SIME finally decided to put an end to the network, and in July 1942 Almásy and all of his agents, including the young Sadat, were arrested.[37]

One of the most complicated counter-espionage and deception agents run anywhere in the British empire in the Second World War was 'Silver', who was skilfully handled by British and Allied intelligence services in

India. Silver is revealed by IPI records, now held at the British Library in London, to have been Bhagat Ram, an Afghani who was the right-hand man of the great Indian-Bengali nationalist leader Subhas Chandra Bose. In the course of the war Ram, who also went by the alias of 'Ramat Khan', actually became a triple agent, working at various times for Germany, the Soviet Union and Britain, and there is some evidence to suggest that he was also in communication with Chinese intelligence.[38]

Ram was a fiercely anti-British Indian nationalist, whose twin allegiances lay with India and the cause of communism. When war in Europe was declared in 1939, he and Bose threw in their lot with the Axis Powers – Nazi Germany and the Soviet Union started the war as allies through the Nazi–Soviet Pact of 1939. Bose, who regarded the war as India's great opportunity, helped to lead the 'Quit India Movement', whose aim was to eject the British from India, and also assisted with the formation of the Indian National Army (INA), which collaborated with the Japanese and fought bloodily against the Allies. Indeed, some of the writings of the Burmese wartime nationalist leader Ba Maw, who also collaborated with the Japanese, show an affinity with many of the tenets of National Socialism. As a corollary to the wartime 'Jewish Brigade' of the British Army, during the war some 3,000 Indians joined a special division of the German army (the Wehrmacht), which was later absorbed into the notorious Waffen-SS. Facing a 'fifth column' threat, the British authorities in Delhi arrested and detained its supposed ringleaders. Bose was imprisoned in late 1940, as was his main rival in India's Congress Party, Jawaharlal Nehru. However, in January 1941 Bose escaped incarceration in Calcutta and fled to Afghanistan, where he made contact with German forces, including the Abwehr.[39]

Bose and Ram's fortunes were transformed by Nazi Germany's surprise attack on the Soviet Union, codenamed Operation *Barbarossa*, on 22 June 1941. Hitler's disastrous decision was the result of his desire to establish a slave empire and 'living space' (*Lebensraum*) in the east for 'pure' Germanic races. One of its results was that previous diplomatic alliances were instantly overturned, with the Soviet Union and Britain becoming allies overnight. While Bose, India's so-called 'man of destiny', remained a supporter of Nazi Germany, Ram held his allegiance to communism and the Soviet Union even higher, which led him to side with the Soviet Union's new ally: his old foe, Britain. Ram started to work as an agent for British and Soviet intelligence – one of the few double agents shared by the two nations during the war. He presented himself to the Abwehr station in Kabul as a kind of modern-day Rudyard Kipling or Lawrence of Arabia figure, and started passing misinformation to them in October 1942.[40]

As in other parts of the British empire, local security agencies in India looked to Britain's homeland intelligence services, particularly MI5, for guidance on how to run double-cross agents. Early in 1943 a senior MI5 officer, John Marriott, who was secretary to the 'Twenty Committee', travelled to India – with the honorary rank of Major, in order to afford him 'better treatment' than a civilian – to help coordinate the running of double agents, particularly Silver. Marriott was given a warm welcome by the IB in Delhi, but as his reports back to MI5 in London reveal, he was far from impressed with the IB. Between bouts of dysentery and suffering from the extreme heat in India – there are still apparently sweat marks on some of the pages of his reports – he noted that the IB had only fifty officers in total, stationed across the various provinces of India. With just twelve officers at its headquarters in Delhi, the IB was, according to Marriott, 'understaffed and overworked'. Moreover, apart from Silver, it lacked any other meaningful double-cross agents. However, as Marriott conceded, part of the problem was that he often found it difficult to understand the details of cases in India – a former London solicitor, he undoubtedly had an English 'home counties' outlook. As he explained in one report to MI5 in March 1943:

> I quite honestly find myself unable to recall the name of the man whose file I am reading sometimes, and anything like association of ideas or even being able to recall a name which appears on the previous page is for the moment beyond me. Place names are even worse. I don't pretend to be awfully good at the geography of western Europe so you can imagine the lack of response I feel when I read that a man has travelled from Monywa to Kalewa and thence has followed the Tamu Road.[41]

Despite the meagre resources the IB in Delhi had at its disposal, together with MI5, it ran the Silver case – perhaps so named because one of the IPI officials working on it in London was a Mr Silver – remarkably successfully. Overall control came under the military intelligence unit led by Lt. Col. Peter Fleming, attached to the staff of the Commander in Chief in India, Wavell, who showed as much appreciation for intelligence there as he had in the Middle East. However, the day-to-day running of the case was carried out by William 'Bill' Magan, then a British Army officer attached to the IB, who would go on to play an important role in MI5's involvement with anti-colonial movements, and broader issues of British decolonisation, in the post-war years. Magan had begun his career as an Indian cavalry officer, and was described to his wife before their marriage in New Delhi in 1940 as 'a cavalry officer who has actually read a book'. With Magan's assistance, Ram successfully portrayed himself to the Abwehr in Kabul as the head of a totally fictitious 'All India Revolutionary Committee', and depicted India as on the brink of disintegration due to Axis subversion and propaganda. In reality, the 'All India Revolutionary Committee' was nothing more than a figment of Ram and Magan's imagination, and the wireless communications despatched to the Abwehr every night actually originated from Magan and Ram in the garden of the British High Commission in Delhi. As a subsequent MI5 report noted, through Ram British intelligence established a 'direct line' to Berlin. The disinformation provided by Ram, portraying India as on its last knees, helped to persuade the German High Command not to transfer more military divisions to India. Ram also made contact by wireless with Japanese intelligence in Burma. Documents captured after the war revealed that, thanks in part to the deception information he provided, the Japanese military judged that Allied troops in South-East Asia numbered fifty-two divisions, a staggering 72 per cent higher than reality. Subhas Chandra Bose died in an air crash in August 1945, never aware that Ram was secretly working for British and Soviet intelligence. In his posthumously published memoirs he misguidedly described Ram as his trusted comrade, 'who secretly passed messages to comrades in India' against the British.[42]

FORCE 136: THE SPECIAL OPERATIONS EXECUTIVE

At the same time that Britain's intelligence services were running double-cross agents like Silver in India, its special forces were also actively thwarting Axis plots in the empire. British territories in the Middle East, particularly Egypt, occupy as important a place in the history of British irregular warfare as they do in that of British strategic deception. As with modern strategic deception, the Middle East was the birthplace of Britain's modern special forces. Dudley Clarke, the founding father of strategic deception, was also one of the founders of the modern British special forces. In 1940 he was instrumental in setting up a self-sufficient and highly mobile new unit which he termed the commandos, and in July 1941 he helped to establish one of the most famous of all special forces units:

the Special Air Service (SAS). The SAS was founded in Egypt by Colonel David Stirling, under the British Commander in Chief of the Middle East, General Claude Auchinleck, but Clarke provided valuable input to the new regiment: he explained to its leaders the benefits of strategic deception, as he had done to the LCS, and he even helped to create its emblem, featuring the sword of Damocles, which it retains to the present day. During the war the SAS successfully used groups of men and jeeps, known as Long Range Desert Groups, to harry German forces, and after the war it would perform a valuable role in anti-colonial revolts, or 'Emergencies' as they were termed, in various parts of the globe.

Along with the commandos and the SAS, the Special Operations Executive (SOE) also conducted sabotage operations against the Axis Powers in various parts of the British empire. SOE is commonly associated with Europe, but in fact it was an empire-wide service, operating in the Middle East, Africa and the Far East. It was very much the stuff of 'Boy's Own' adventure stories. Strictly speaking, in the British tradition at least, it was not an intelligence agency at all, but a paramilitary organisation, established in July 1940 with the aim of waging a supposedly 'new' type of irregular warfare against the Axis Powers – apparently the lessons of guerrilla warfare that existed from Lawrence of Arabia's days had been forgotten by the Chiefs of Staff in London. SOE picked up where Lawrence had left off. Its remit was, to use Churchill's famous phrase, 'to set Europe ablaze'. Its headquarters in Electra House, Baker Street – earning its personnel the nickname 'the Baker Street Irregulars' – were inconspicuously identified by a brass plate on the front door that merely read 'Inter-Services Research Bureau'. From there SOE organised paramilitary and sabotage operations in enemy-occupied territories in Europe and further afield, as well as establishing communications networks in those countries and arranging escape routes from them. In total, during the war it probably employed close to 10,000 men and 3,000 women across the globe.[43]

At first SOE's operations in the Far East were run out of Singapore, but with the Japanese advance in late 1941 and early 1942, its headquarters were moved first to India, where it was known as the 'India Mission'. From mid-1942 onwards overall control for its operations in Malaya and Burma was switched to new headquarters in Ceylon, where SOE adopted the cover name 'Force 136'. Force 136 was led throughout the war by Colin Mackenzie, a former Scots Guards officer with a razor-sharp intellect (he was a student of John Maynard Keynes at Cambridge) who had been badly injured during the First World War. Its operations in the Far East, like broader British interests there, were totally transformed by the rapid advance of Japanese forces through British territories: Hong Kong fell on Christmas Day 1941, Malaya and Burma in early 1942, followed by the catastrophic surrender of the city of Singapore on 15 February. The capitulation of Singapore has rightly earned a place among the worst defeats in modern British military history, and we can now see that it was the result of a massive intelligence failure on the part of the British. Although it is a myth that the enormous guns protecting the city were facing the wrong way when the Japanese attacked, British forces were supplied with the wrong type of ammunition, and they had also been provided with little accurate intelligence from MI5 or SIS warning when and from which direction the Japanese forces would arrive – in fact, they unexpectedly came by land, hiking through the thick Malayan jungles, and not by sea, as expected.

In the immediate pre-war years SIS's operations in the Far East had been centred on a single officer, Harry Steptoe. No matter how good Steptoe might have been – and many commentators have followed Kim Philby in considering him totally incompetent, a 'near mental case' who cooked his own goose – clearly the task of gathering intelligence on imperial Japan was greater than the resources that SIS devoted to it. Once Japanese forces had captured Malaya and Singapore there followed a mass evacuation of Force 136 and other service personnel from the city, with some Force 136 officers, such as Eric Battersby, only reaching safety after a gruelling hike from Malaya to Siam (Thailand). Other Force 136 members, such as John Davis and Richard Broome, escaped from Singapore on Mackenzie's personal orders in a small vessel from Malaya to Ceylon, where they arrived after a horrendous thirty-two-day journey, with only a tiny amount of food and clean water. An even smaller minority, including Lt. Col. Freddie Spencer Chapman of Force 136 and Captain (known as 'Major') Louis Cauvin of SIS, remained in Malaya to fight an extremely lonely war, operating deep in the jungle, where they suffered from malaria and were often near to starvation while they waited for supplies and reinforcements to arrive, and for broken communications to be reinstalled with Force 136's headquarters in Ceylon. Only forty or so of the stay-behind forces in Malaya avoided death or capture by the Japanese.[44]

Help eventually arrived when John Davis smuggled a group of Chinese agents into Malaya by submarine in May 1943. Thereafter he dramatically zig-zagged around the Indian Ocean by submarine, landing in the Malacca

Straits in August 1943. He was soon joined by Richard Broome, and together they set about trying to track down any survivors of the stay-behind forces. They finally located Chapman, who had been training Malayan guerrilla fighters deep in the jungle, on Christmas Day 1943. On 31 December at Blantan Davis signed an agreement (written on a page torn from an exercise book) on behalf of the Allied Supreme Commander for South-East Asia, Lord Louis Mountbatten, with the leader of the guerrillas fighting the Japanese in Malaya, the so-called 'Malayan People's Anti-Japanese Army', a communist named Chin Peng. Davis was empowered by Mountbatten to 'aid and strengthen' the guerrilla forces in Malaya, and Force 136 provided arms, supplies and money in return for Chin Peng's guerrillas stirring up labour disputes against the Japanese occupiers and sabotaging Japanese shipping.[45]

Force 136 supplied Chin Peng's fighters with large amounts of equipment, or 'toys', to use the vernacular of Force 136's Quartermaster of Operations (Q-Ops), who was responsible for them. These 'weapons of minor destruction', as one MI5 report described them, included Chinese stone carvings with hidden compartments for explosives; Balinese carvings made of high explosives, finished to look like wood, sandstone or porcelain; tins of kerosene disguised as soya sauce; ammunition hidden in cigarette packs; sten guns; and wireless transmitters. Despite the best efforts of Q-Ops to make such 'toys' safe, there were inevitable risks. One SOE operator, David Smiley, was injured (in Europe, not the Far East) when a briefcase loaded with explosives went off prematurely. Largely in response to the difficulties of hauling unwieldy wireless transmitter sets ('W/T' for short) weighing up to four hundred pounds through the jungles of Malaya, by 1942 SOE had developed lighter and more portable models, codenamed BI and BII – but at fifty pounds they were still heavy, and could not be fitted easily into a suitcase. The RAF also dropped food supplies and ammunition to guerrilla forces in the jungle.[46]

As well as its paramilitary activities, SOE, including Force 136, seems to have been involved in undercover political activities in the empire. It is known that it was responsible for distributing funds to bribe political groups in the Middle East to buy support for the British war effort, and the same appears to have occurred in the Far East. Force 136's operations expanded so rapidly that by 1943 it had a total staff of 680 in Ceylon, the India Mission deployed 450 agents throughout South-East Asia, and by 15 August 1945 there were 308 SOE personnel, five Gurkha support groups and forty-six W/T sets in the field in Malaya – by any standards, a significant number. As the war progressed, Force 136 developed more elaborate strategies. By 1944, with wireless communications with its headquarters in Ceylon reinstalled, it was developing a plan with the Malayan guerrilla fighters, codenamed Operation *Zipper*, for the Allied reinvasion and recapture of Malaya and Singapore. However, events were to overtake these plans: the war ended with the dropping of atomic bombs on Japan in August 1945, before Operation *Zipper* could become a reality.[47]

Over the years, much ink has been devoted to analysing the successes and failures of SOE, both in the Far East and in Europe. One way of measuring its effectiveness is by considering the goals it set itself. From 1943 onwards, Force 136's aims were essentially to establish a submarine link between Ceylon and Malaya, to create an intelligence system within Malaya, contact and support guerrilla fighters, and find any survivors of left-behind forces. Given these aims, it seems fair to say that it was largely successful. In other ways, however, Force 136 was a failure. It never really adopted the sabotage role that it was intended to have in Malaya – which was, after all, the main purpose of SOE. Instead, it developed into much more of an intelligence agency than was originally planned, and thereby trod squarely on the toes of SIS. Unsurprisingly, the result was a fierce turf war, with SIS regarding SOE as a maverick organisation full of cowboys.[48]

The encroachment of SOE's activities into SIS's realm in the Far East raises an obvious question: would it have been better to combine intelligence collection and covert operations into a single organisation, as happened with the US Office of Strategic Services (OSS), and later with the CIA, which was in many ways its successor? The British tradition shunned this idea: a single agency, ran the argument, would be unable both to collect impartial intelligence and to carry out actions based on it. But, given the fierce resentment between some SOE and SIS officers, it is likely that Britain's wartime intelligence activities in the Far East would have been more effective had they been formally combined into a single service.[49]

The confusion over what Force 136's charter entailed in the Far East is part of a much broader picture relating to SOE's failures during the war. Critics have pointed out that far from 'setting Europe ablaze', as it was tasked to do by Churchill, in fact its operations in Europe barely produced a smoulder. It certainly had some notable failures, the most notorious of which were its operations in the Netherlands, where from 1942 onwards the Abwehr totally compromised its operations, capturing its main agents and using their remarkably ineffective wireless codes to fool SOE into thinking they were still operational, and to continue to provide them with information and supplies – the Abwehr's famous 'England game' (*Englandspiel*). However, it should be remembered that what the Abwehr did to SOE in the Netherlands for eighteen months – SOE finally realised in 1944 that its agents there had been blown – the British did to the Germans through the Double Cross System for six years.[50]

Furthermore, there were instances when SOE's operations produced significant successes for the Allies. Its sabotage of heavy-water supplies at Vermork, in Norway, probably frustrated Nazi Germany's attempt to build an atomic bomb. Its guerrilla operations at Montbéliard, in occupied France, showed how a small group of men could take out a machine-gun turret where successive bombing raids had failed. Finally, and probably more importantly than anything else it achieved, as M.R.D. Foot has noted, SOE gave a sense of self-respect back to countries, in Europe and the Far East, whose conventional armies had been totally overpowered by the Axis Powers. Many of the agents it dropped into occupied territories to assist local resistance groups displayed remarkable bravery. Wing Cmmdr. Forrest Frederick Edward Yeo-Thomas (codenamed 'the White Rabbit') forged valiant links with the French resistance and managed to escape Nazi captivity. Others, such as Violette Szabo, did not live to tell their tale, succumbing to Nazi interrogation, torture and execution. In total, SOE sent fifty-five female agents into occupied Europe, thirteen of whom were either killed in action or executed.[51]

BRITISH INTELLIGENCE AND WARTIME 'RENDITION'

During the Second World War British intelligence developed imperial responsibilities in ways that it simply hitherto had not. MI5 posted more officers to British colonial and Commonwealth countries than it ever had previously, and GC&CS dramatically expanded its capabilities, hoovering up enemy traffic from its regional collection stations across the empire. Meanwhile, SOE armed guerrilla fighters against the Axis Powers. However, there is one chapter in the story of Britain's wartime imperial intelligence responsibilities that is apparently so sensitive it has only recently been disclosed. It has some remarkable parallels with controversial intelligence and security practices in the present day.

As part of its counter-espionage efforts, during the Second World War British intelligence ran a top-secret process of detaining, interrogating and transporting enemy agents between various parts of the British empire. At times this came close to being a form of state-sponsored kidnapping – closely resembling the process of 'extraordinary rendition' employed by the US government in the so-called 'war on terror' closer to our own time. After December 1940, Ultra decrypts revealed a number of German agents operating throughout the British empire and Commonwealth. In the first six months of 1942, six high-level agents were identified (but not arrested) in different British colonies, and in June 1942 one of them operating in Mombasa, in Kenya, was detained by local police. His detention sparked a debate within MI5 about what should be done with him and other such agents. MI5 wanted them, as well as any other agents who may have been working in different parts of the empire, to be interrogated, and if possible turned into double agents as part of its Double Cross System. However, MI5's officers in Section B1a, responsible for counter-espionage, were reluctant to have them interrogated in the distant outposts of empire, where effective methods could not be guaranteed. Furthermore, MI5 feared that if the identified agents were interrogated locally, it would have to release the most closely guarded secret of the war, Ultra, to colonial authorities who could not necessarily be trusted – interrogators invariably used information derived from Ultra to trick enemy agents into thinking that British intelligence knew everything about their missions. Instead, MI5 wanted the agents to be brought to its own top-secret interrogation facility, Camp 020, located in a former lunatic asylum, Latchmere House, in Ham Common, a suburb of South London.

Camp 020, which probably derives its name from the 'Twenty Committee' responsible for overseeing the Double Cross System, operated outside the control of any British government department except for MI5, and was without legal oversight. Its aim was to isolate and 'break' enemy agents, who were held without trial, in some cases for years, with the intention of turning them into double agents. Because its detainees were non-combatant enemy agents, international regulations concerning the treatment of prisoners of war did not apply to Camp 020. Nor was it inspected or listed by the Red Cross. In short, its detainees were placed in a legal void. The question that MI5 needed answering was whether it was legally justifiable to detain foreign nationals, and transport them from British territories overseas for interrogation in Britain. One of the leading figures in B-Division, Dick White, put it in the following terms to MI5's legal adviser Toby Pilcher (a future High Court judge):

... we shall find ourselves in a particularly serious position if it is ruled that the legal machinery for detaining an enemy agent in a Colony and subsequently bringing him to the U.K. is found to be faulty in law ... I am afraid that this is a case in which we cannot leave the matter in doubt, for were the detention of an enemy agent brought here under this proposal to be tested by Habeas Corpus [the legal process by which a prisoner can demand to be brought before a court], in all probability it would be a moment when he was already installed in Camp 020. Subsequent publicity attendant upon a test of Habeas Corpus would be extremely detrimental to Camp 020 and might jeopardise our whole position with regard to it.[52]

Under the draconian Defence Regulations that had been enacted in Britain on the outbreak of war, it was impossible for the overwhelming majority of those detained to bring *habeas corpus* proceedings against the responsible authorities – which was invariably MI5, acting behind the cover of the 'War Office'. That said, in at least one case a detainee did demand to be brought before a court, though unsurprisingly, given how expansive the British state's powers of detention were under the Defence Regulations, his case was ultimately unsuccessful.[53]

There is also some evidence to suggest that there was more going on behind the scenes in the famous wartime legal case of *Liversidge v Anderson* in 1942 than appears in the recorded judgement of the House of Lords. The case has gone down in the annals of legal history as a low point in the story of civil liberties and the rule of law in Britain, with the judiciary cowing before the power of the executive. It involved a Polish-born naturalised British citizen, Jack Perlzweig, who went by the name of Liversidge, who was detained in 1940 under Regulation 18b of the Defence (General) Regulations 1939. This regulation allowed the Home Secretary (Sir John Anderson) to detain persons of hostile origin if he had 'reasonable grounds' to suspect them of being involved in acts contrary to the defence of the realm. Put simply, Mr Liversidge asked to see what evidence the Home Secretary had against him, and asked the court to consider whether it constituted 'reasonable grounds' for his detention without trial, which he argued was false imprisonment. The majority verdict of the Law Lords – who heard the case in an annexe to the House of Lords because their usual chamber had been bombed out in the Blitz – stated that in times of national emergency courts had no authority to question whether the Home Secretary's evidence against an individual constituted reasonable grounds for his detention. It is likely that the 'reasonable grounds' for Liversidge's detention were really derived from adverse intelligence on him provided by MI5. The case of *Liversidge v Anderson* was really, it seems, to do with how intelligence could be introduced into court, which was difficult, if not impossible, because the British government only tacitly recognised the existence of MI5. The use of intelligence as evidence is an issue that courts in England, and in the Western world more generally, are still grappling with to the present day.

There was a significant problem for MI5 when it came to the detention and transportation of enemy agents from overseas territories to Britain. By a curious omission in the colonial legislation passed by Parliament on the outbreak of war, Colonial Order 12(5)a, there was no equivalent to Defence Regulation 18b, which meant that it was legally permissible for aliens detained in British colonies to bring *habeas corpus* proceedings. This brought a stark warning from MI5's legal adviser Toby Pilcher, who stated that in his opinion, under the existing legislation it was 'undesirable, and probably illegal, to remove an alien from a ship and detain him in a colony'. Following a high-powered meeting in June 1942 between Dick White, Pilcher and the Colonial Office's legal adviser, it was decided that the only way to resolve the problem was to introduce 'ad hoc legislation' under the Defence Regulations 'specifically empowering the Governor [of a colony] to remove a suspect alien from a ship or aircraft visiting the colony, and to detain him pending his removal from the colony'. Before long MI5 and the Colonial Office had formulated a written codicil, or warrant, which could be quickly signed by colonial governors allowing enemy aliens to be detained on British territory and then rendered to Britain for interrogation. This was precisely what occurred during the rest of the war – confirming the axiom that laws are silent during wars (*silent leges inter arma*).[54]

The willingness of MI5 to go along with this process of detaining and transporting – kidnapping, in all but name – individuals, despite its original lack of legal authority to do so, is all the more striking when the heavyweight legal brains it employed during the war are considered. One of the B-Division officers centrally involved in detaining and transporting enemy agents to Camp 020 was H.L.A. (Herbert) Hart, an Oxford academic lawyer who went on to become one of the most eminent legal philosophers of the second half of the twentieth century. On one level, it is surprising that ideas of 'natural justice' and 'fairness' did not prevent lawyers working in MI5 – a large number of whom were wartime recruits from the Law Society – from supporting such legally dubious practices as detention without trial. On another level, however, it is less surprising than it may seem. H.L.A. Hart is most famous for his ideas of legal positivism, which, put crudely, argue that there is not necessarily an inherent association between the validity of laws and ethics or morality, and that laws are made by human beings. The thrust of legal positivism is therefore that laws are essentially malleable.[55]

One cannot help concluding that MI5's wartime lawyers (in both its legal section and its counter-espionage division) were willing to overlook the weighty ethical and moral issues raised by detaining and transporting enemy agents, so long as the formality of 'ad hoc' emergency legislation was in place and all the other legal niceties were fulfilled. This narrow focus on formality, rather than substance, is a characteristic as common among some lawyers today as it apparently was then. Furthermore, it is notable that prior to the passing of 'ad hoc' emergency legislation, neither H.L.A. Hart nor MI5's legal advisers, including several future High Court judges, nor the Colonial or Foreign Offices' legal advisers, could find any legal justification for the detention and transportation of foreign nationals without due process – which is striking given the allegations of 'extraordinary rendition' today, because it allegedly involves exactly the same matters, but the law requiring due process is no different now from what it was during the Second World War.

It is impossible to state with certainty how many enemy agents were transported from British colonies to Camp 020 for interrogation during the war. At least twenty-three such agents can be identified in declassified MI5 records, though the true number may be considerably more. Whatever it was, many of the cases were highly dramatic, while others bordered on farce. One of the most important involved an Argentinean national of German descent, Osmar Hellmuth, who worked in the Argentine consulate in Barcelona, and who in September 1943 was identified as acting as a courier between the officially neutral Argentine government and the Third Reich. Working under diplomatic cover, Hellmuth's mission was to travel to Germany, where he was to meet the head of the SS, Heinrich Himmler, and possibly even Hitler, and purchase arms and other equipment for the Argentine government, which from June 1943 was ruled by a military junta led by General Pedro Pablo Ramírez. Hellmuth's high-level mission made a mockery of the claims by General Ramírez that the Argentine government remained neutral in the war.

The tip-off about Hellmuth's mission to Nazi Germany came from the SIS head of station in Buenos Aires, who forwarded it to SIS's headquarters at the Broadway Buildings in London, where it was received by none other than Kim Philby, then working on the Iberian desk of Section V (counter-espionage), based in St Albans, just outside London. Philby passed the information on to MI5 – as he probably also did to his KGB masters. SIS and MI5 together orchestrated a detailed plan for Hellmuth's detention and transfer to Britain, which was put into effect the following month, October 1943, when Hellmuth set sail from South America to Spain. As soon as his ship touched British soil en route, at Trinidad in the West Indies, MI5's DSO there arranged for him to be arrested by local police. This was authorised at the highest level, by the British Governor of Trinidad, who signed Hellmuth's arrest and detention order under the newly enacted 'ad hoc' legislation – though in fact it was clearly in violation of Hellmuth's diplomatic status. Hellmuth was put on a waiting British seaplane that flew him to Bermuda, and from there he was transported on board a Royal Navy cruiser, the *Ajax*, to England, where he arrived in early November.

After his installation at Camp 020, MI5 interrogators set to work on him, and he was quickly broken. He revealed an array of highly explosive diplomatic information, producing letters written with secret ink, giving up the identities of senior Nazi intelligence officials, such as Siegfried (or Sigmund) Becker, the head of the *Sicherheitsdienst* mission in Argentina, and disclosing that the Argentine Minister of War, the future President Juan Perón, was involved in the Nazi arms deal. Hellmuth also confessed that part of his mission to Germany had been to contact the notorious Nazi espionage chief Walter Schellenberg, the head of the SS's foreign intelligence department and later head of Section VI (foreign espionage) of the Reich Security Main Office (*Reichssicherheitshauptamt*, RSHA). With duelling scars on his cheeks, a signet ring stashed with cyanide, and a desk in his Berlin office mounted with machine guns which could spray the room with bullets at the flick of a switch, Schellenberg was very much the stereotype of an arch villain.[56]

The information produced by MI5's interrogation of Hellmuth at Camp 020 was of such massive diplomatic importance that the British government decided to go public with it and expose the duplicity of the Argentine government. This caused a sensation, with General Ramírez being forced publicly to disavow Hellmuth. As the post-war history of Camp 020 noted, the Hellmuth case forced Argentina to sever diplomatic relations with the Third Reich, and helped to precipitate the collapse of the Ramírez government. It also had repercussions in Nazi Germany itself, with Himmler blaming the head of the Abwehr, Canaris, for the chaos it caused and demanding Canaris's resignation.

Other Axis agents were also arrested when they landed in Trinidad, and transported to Camp 020. This happened with the German agent Juan Lecube – a former footballer, greyhound-owner and ex-Spanish civil servant – and also with Leopold Hirsch, who was arrested on board the *Cabo de Hornos* in Trinidad harbour after his identity was revealed when his name was given *en clair* in a German telegram intercepted by Bletchley Park. The case of Gastão de Freitas Ferraz is a striking example of how seizing an agent at sea saved Allied lives. De Freitas was a wireless operator on a Portuguese fishing depot ship, who was recruited by the Abwehr to provide maritime intelligence under the neutral cover provided by his Portuguese employment. However, while his ship was en route from Newfoundland to Lisbon in October 1942, he was arrested and removed first to Gibraltar then to Camp 020. At the point when he was arrested on the high seas, his ship was on the tail of a convoy taking part in Operation *Torch*, the Allied landings in North Africa. De Freitas was interrogated at Camp 020, confessed and was detained for the duration of the war. If he had not been kidnapped, it is almost certain that he would have seen the invasion convoy taking part in *Torch* and reported it by radio, which would have had disastrous consequences for the Allies. His arrest seems to have saved the Allied invasion of North Africa.[57]

Perhaps the most bizarre wartime rendition case was that of Alfredo Manna, an Italian agent operating in the neutral territory of Portuguese South Africa (present-day Mozambique). Manna was one of a number of agents run by the Italian Consul, Umberto Campini, in Lourenço Marques (today the city of Maputo), whose mission was primarily to report on Allied shipping movements off the coast of East Africa. It is unclear how British intelligence identified Manna: it may have been from an Ultra decrypt, or it may have been the result of good old-fashioned detective work on the part of the local SIS representative stationed in Lourenço Marques, the journalist Malcolm Muggeridge. Nevertheless, by early 1943, MI5 and SIS, sensing that he was far from loyal to his Italian masters, hoped to turn Manna into a double agent. Muggeridge worked closely with a local SOE team to devise an elaborate plan, 'along the best Hollywood lines', as he later put it, to detain Manna and transport him to Britain for interrogation. According to Muggeridge, a devout Catholic and future biographer of Mother Teresa, the plan was essentially to 'kidnap' him. Knowing that Manna's great weakness was women, Muggeridge hired an exotic casino dancer named Anna Levy to lure him to the border of British territory in Swaziland. As the later history of Camp 020 noted: 'There he was seized, gagged and bound by British agents, who took care to leave him on the right side of the border.' Manna was promptly arrested by local police and transported, via South Africa, to Britain. Thus an Italian agent, enticed by an exotic dancer to a border and dragged across it by British agents, came to be interrogated at Camp 020. Although Manna's interrogation at Camp 020 did not result in him becoming a double agent, it did yield valuable intelligence on Axis espionage in southern Africa, particularly on local ship-watching operations.[58]

One of the reasons MI5 was determined to have Axis agents brought to Camp 020 for interrogation was to avoid disclosing the Ultra secret. It also wanted them to be interrogated in the most effective manner possible – which for MI5 meant not resorting to physical violence. Contrary to what we might assume, and contrary to its ominous first appearances, Camp 020 did not permit the use of physical coercion during interrogations. This is confirmed by contemporary records, such as the diary of Guy Liddell, the wartime head of MI5's B-Division, which was written without the intention of ever being made public, and by the subsequent testimonials of Axis agents who were detained at the camp, and who had no reason to lie about their treatment. The MI5 officer who ran Camp 020, Lt. Col. Robin Stephens, enforced a strict policy of no physical violence, or 'third degree' measures, in the facility. 'Tin Eye' Stephens, so called because of his thick monocle, believed that the aim of interrogation should be to draw out all information possible from an agent, and not simply to obtain quick answers to specific questions. The only way to do that, he judged, was to refrain from physical coercion. 'Violence is taboo,' he wrote in his in-house post-war history of Camp 020, entitled A Digest of Ham after the camp's location at Ham Common, 'for not only does it produce an answer to please, but it lowers the standard of information.' He wrote in another post-war report:

> Never strike a man. In the first place it is an act of cowardice. In the second place, it is not intelligent. A prisoner will lie to avoid further punishment and everything he says thereafter will be based on a false premise. Through stupidity, therefore, an investigation becomes valueless.[59]

None of this should give the impression that Camp 020 was a soft place. Its tactics for 'breaking' agents included every conceivable trick of what

Stephens termed 'mental pressure': newly arrived prisoners were usually stripped, humiliated and disorientated; they were terrified by rows of barking dogs; confined to small solitary cells; threatened with court-martial and execution. Microphones were installed in their cells to over-hear conversations; guards disguised as prisoners (known as 'stool pigeons') were sent into cells to get them talking; false newspapers were printed to trick them into thinking their friends and family at home had been killed; and Ultra decrypts were used to convince them that all the details of their missions had already been discovered. Stephens noted that every man has a price, and every man is capable of being broken – it is simply a question of applying the right mental pressure to do so.

The way in which MI5 interrogators broke Osmar Hellmuth is instruc-tive. As soon as he arrived at Camp 020 in November 1943, Hellmuth was marched into a room where he was faced by a number of high-ranking British officers sitting behind a desk, in what looked like a military court. He was then subjected to a barrage of shouts from 'the Commandant' (Stephens), who told him that the Argentine government and his German spymasters had abandoned him, and that he would be executed as a spy. As a final touch, the Commandant added that he hated all spies with a passion. The bad-cop show was now over, and the good cops were free to go to work. Hellmuth was taken into another room, where a different group of officers plied him with soft words, telling him that they under-stood the difficult position he was in, and wanted to help. It did not take long for Hellmuth to break.[60]

Stephens's rule against the use of physical coercion is all the more strik-ing given that in the summer of 1940, Camp 020 interrogators were desperately questioning enemy agents amid an invasion crisis – undoubt-edly the greatest threat to British national security in the twentieth century. Many of the techniques that they employed, such as sleep deprivation and humiliation, would today constitute forms of 'torture' under international law. However, for Stephens there was a clear distinction between 'physical pressure' and 'mental pressure'. It should be stressed that he did not reject physical 'third degree' measures because he was a humanitarian at heart – fourteen German agents held at Camp 020 were executed, and Stephens later declared that he wished more had been. Rather, he rejected them because in his opinion they produced unreliable intelligence. Stephens was one of the most successful Allied wartime interrogators. His interroga-tions at Camp 020 played a significant role in the Double Cross System, producing about twelve double agents run by MI5 during the war (out of about 120 in total). They also helped to build up a unique card-catalogue index on the German intelligence services.[61]

Although it was not termed 'rendition' at the time, the process devised by British intelligence during the Second World War resembles the US government's recent policy of 'extraordinary rendition', which is claimed by its proponents to be a necessary tactic in the 'war on terror'. However, there is a fundamental difference between the two. During the Second World War, German and Axis agents were brought from British territories abroad to Britain specifically in order to safeguard their effective interrogation – which at Camp 020 meant every method short of physical coercion. In sharp contrast, 'extraordinary rendition' policies instigated after 11 September 2001 involve exactly the opposite: the US government and its allies deliberately sending suspects to third-party countries with poor track records on human rights, where they have allegedly been tortured to gain intelligence. The assumption behind recent 'extraordinary rendition' policies is that torture can produce intelligence. Given MI5's experiences during the Second World War, and the observations of its most successful interrogator, Stephens, it seems doubtful whether this is so. An inescapable conclusion is the dictum given by William Pitt the Younger: 'Necessity is the plea for every infringement of human freedom.'

ALLIES AND ENEMIES: BRITAIN AND THE USSR

If the greatest wartime successes of the British secret state were against its enemies, the Axis Powers, its greatest failure was its inadequate surveillance of its ally, the Soviet Union. Britain's intelligence services – MI5, SIS and GC&CS – were not blind to the Soviet threat during the war, even after June 1941, when the two countries became allies. As early as 1942, Guy Liddell, the chain-smoking wartime head of MI5's B-Division, was sombrely noting in his diary, which he dictated to his secretary at the end of every working day:

> There is no doubt that the Russians are far better in the matter of espionage than any country in the world. I am perfectly certain that they are well-bedded down here and that we should be making more active enquiries. They will be a great source of trouble for us when the war is over.[62]

The problem for the British intelligence community was that investigating an ally was an extremely delicate matter. Liddell noted in his diary in 1943 that if MI5 did try to investigate the Soviet threat, which he increasingly felt was necessary, but got found out, there would be 'an appalling stink'. As soon as the Soviet Union entered the war in June 1941, the Foreign Office placed an embargo on all British intelligence-gathering efforts on it. Apparently allies do not spy on allies – an honourable, but totally naïve, assumption when it came to the Soviet Union. We now know from Soviet archives that Moscow devoted as many resources to gathering intelligence on its wartime allies, Britain and the United States, as it did on its enemies, the Axis Powers.[63]

Despite Britain's intelligence services effectively having their hands tied by the Foreign Office in terms of spying on Moscow after June 1941, they tried to devise ways around the embargo. GC&CS concocted an ingenious method of sidestepping the ban, using intercepted German communications that discussed Soviet matters to gain information. MI5 also undertook measures to continue investigating the Soviet threat, opening a new department, F-Division, to investigate 'subversive activities' – the main focus of which was communism and Soviet activities. F-Division was led by Roger Hollis, a pre-war entrant to MI5 recruited from a tobacco firm in the Far East, who had left Oxford before taking his degree – he was described by Evelyn Waugh as a 'good bottle man' at Oxford. As we shall see, Hollis went on to become a Director-General of MI5, and was falsely accused of being a Soviet agent. In reality, he, arguably more than anyone else in the British intelligence community, took seriously and attempted to investigate wartime Soviet espionage, arguing that the leopard had not changed its spots. Rather than the Soviet embassy in London, which was now a forbidden fruit, the main priority for Hollis's F-Division was surveillance of the British Communist Party. This was never going to be sufficient to detect Soviet espionage, for Soviet agents knew to distance themselves from overt communist organisations, but given the restrictions imposed on F-Division, it was the only legitimate avenue left open to it. One of Hollis's personal triumphs was in 1942, when he organised the installation of bugging equipment in the headquarters of the British Communist Party in King Street, London. These eavesdropping microphones, codenamed source 'Table' or 'special facilities' in MI5 records, were almost certainly telephone receivers modified so as to be always switched on, thus picking up ambient conversations. As we shall see, they would provide MI5 with crucial intelligence in the post-war years about various anti-colonial 'liberation' leaders who communicated with the British Communist Party.[64]

Towards the end of the war, SIS also started to focus on the Soviet threat. In 1944 it set up a new department, Section IX, the precise remit of which was the 'collection and interpretation of information concerning Soviet and communist espionage and subversion in all parts of the world outside of British territory'. Unfortunately, the second head of Section IX (after John 'Jack' Curry) was none other than the high-level Soviet penetration agent Kim Philby. Philby was arguably the most successful of the five so-called 'Cambridge spies' – the others were Guy Burgess, Donald Maclean, Anthony Blunt and John Cairncross – who had been recruited by Soviet intelligence before the war and then manoeuvred themselves into sensitive positions in the British wartime administration, including its intelligence services, by portraying themselves as trustworthy members of the Establishment – four of the five went to Trinity College, Cambridge. In fact, because so few pre-war MI5 and SIS officers had university degrees – most had military backgrounds, often with colonial experience – the perverse situation was that at the start of the war Soviet intelligence actually had more recruits from British universities working for it than Britain's own intelligence services did. Coupled with their respectable backgrounds, another reason Philby and the other members of the 'Cambridge Five' were able to penetrate to the heart of wartime Britain was that MI5's background checks at the time were totally inadequate: they were based on a process called 'negative vetting', meaning that they depended on whatever information MI5 had in its Registry. It did not carry out its own active background checks. This process overlooked a simple fact: that it was possible for agents to make themselves invisible to MI5 by deliberately distancing themselves from organisations whose membership would lead to their names being filed in its Registry – which is exactly what the five Cambridge spies did.[65]

The story of how Philby got himself appointed as the head of Section IX is the epitome of deception and subterfuge. By a process of skilfully outmanoeuvring his rivals, particularly his immediate superior, Felix Cowgill, and playing one faction in SIS off against another, he made himself the most obvious candidate for the post. As one of Philby's wartime colleagues in SIS, Robert Cecil, later recalled of his appointment, 'the history of espionage contains few, if any, comparable achievements'. From his position as the head of Section IX, Philby was able to betray all of the most important British efforts to counter Soviet espionage in the immediate post-war years to Moscow. In the years to come he would establish himself as Whitehall's leading expert on Soviet espionage. Before his eventual exposure in the early 1950s, he was even being tipped as a future Chief of SIS – the consequences of which for Western intelligence in the Cold War can scarcely be imagined. The post-war diaries of MI5's Guy Liddell, only declassified in October 2012, show that he struggled to come to terms with the defection of Burgess and Maclean, and the suspicion cast upon Philby, whom he trusted. Philby has justifiably been described as the greatest spy in history.[66]

HORIZON SCANNING

As Britain's wartime intelligence machine began to refocus on the Soviet threat, one area provided more information than anywhere else about the operational methods used by Soviet intelligence. From 1940 onwards, the two states of Iraq and Persia (Iran) were jointly occupied by British and Soviet forces, and this led to exceptionally close collaboration between the two Allied intelligence services. Iran's capital Tehran was also the setting in November 1943 of the famous meeting of the 'Big Three', Churchill, Roosevelt and Stalin, which symbolised, at least outwardly, the collaboration between the Allies. However, as Churchill later claimed, it was in Tehran that he realised for the first time how small the British nation was:

> There I sat with the great Russian bear on one side of me, with paws outstretched, and on the other side the great American buffalo, and between the two sat the poor little English donkey ...[67]

From late 1944 onwards the British collaborated with Soviet intelligence in running a double agent, codenamed 'Kiss' – one of only two double agents run by British and Soviet intelligence together during the war, the other being Silver (see pp.50–3). Kiss, an Iranian national recruited by the Abwehr in pre-war Hamburg, was run from the inter-service British intelligence centre based in Baghdad, Combined Intelligence Centre Iraq (CICI). Under the guidance of his British and Soviet controllers, he radioed false information on British and Soviet troop movements in Iraq and Iran to the Abwehr. However, the real importance of the Kiss case, as is revealed by his MI5 file, was the proximity it gave British officials to their Soviet counterparts, allowing them to study their methods at close quarters – as the Soviets doubtless did to the British too. MI5's DSOs in Tehran and Baghdad used the opportunity to gather as much information as they could on their Soviet opposite numbers, particularly the names and backgrounds of intelligence officers, and passed this information back to

F-Division in London. MI5's DSO in Tehran, Alan Roger, explained in one report in December 1944 that although gathering information on Soviet intelligence was not part of his official mission – the Foreign Office ban still outlawed it – he nevertheless thought that it might one day become useful. He was more right than he could have known. The Kiss case collapsed in March 1945, apparently due to bitter mutual mistrust between Soviet and British officials – a forewarning of events that were to follow with the onset of the Cold War.[68]

Occupied Iraq and Iran gave an early indication of the kinds of problems Britain would repeatedly face in the post-war years, as relations between Western countries and the 'great bear' to the east deteriorated. Towards the end of the war, the head of CICI in Baghdad despatched back to London a series of stark warnings about the consequences of Britain pulling out of Iraq and Iran too quickly at the end of hostilities. If it did so, he predicted, both countries would soon be overrun by Soviet intelligence officials, who would seek to turn them into Soviet satellite states. As we shall see, this fear would greatly colour London's reaction to colonial 'liberation' movements in the post-war years, as the Cold War set in.[69]

As the war in Europe wound down, MI5 and SIS began to address the problem of the Soviet Union in earnest. In December 1944 Sir David Petrie noted that for a long time he had been 'a complete convert to the view that the role of F. Division will appreciate in importance after the war'. After the end of hostilities in Europe in May 1945, as Petrie was preparing to leave his position as MI5's Director-General, he circulated a long memorandum 'on the shape of things to come', in which he forecast – pessimistically but accurately – that one form of totalitarianism in Europe would be replaced by another. In August 1945 he held a high-level meeting with the Chief of SIS, Sir Stewart Menzies, about the problem of crypto-communists employed on secret work – on which Philby in SIS would certainly have been briefed – and on 5 September 1945 he, Hollis and other F-Division officers discussed at length, the 'leakage of information through members of the Communist Party'. Their meeting was more significant than either Petrie or Hollis realised. Later that same day, a cypher clerk working at the Soviet embassy in Ottawa, Igor Gouzenko, defected to the West, bringing with him alarming and dramatic evidence of wartime Soviet espionage. It confirmed Britain's worst fears. The Cold War had begun. However, before MI5 could deal properly with the new situation, it first had to deal with a different and even more urgent threat: international terrorism.[70]

'The Red Light is Definitely Showing': MI5, the British Mandate of Palestine and Zionist Terrorism

A bomb outrage to have any influence on public opinion now must go beyond the intention of vengeance or terrorism. It must be purely destructive.

JOSEPH CONRAD, *The Secret Agent*[1]

I have always been clear that the best method of dealing with terrorists is to kill them.

GENERAL SIR ALAN CUNNINGHAM,
High Commissioner for Palestine and Transjordan[2]

Despite all of its wartime successes, the British secret state did not emerge from the Second World War in a strong position. Reports from the 'high table' of the British intelligence community, the Joint Intelligence Committee (JIC), stated frankly that it had little available intelligence on its 'new' enemy, the Soviet Union. The JIC's immediate post-war reports are revealing as much for what they do not say as what they do. Although it seems incredible with hindsight, between December 1944 and March 1946 – that is, at precisely the time when we would imagine that the JIC would have been focusing on the re-emerging Soviet threat – the JIC was totally silent on the Soviet Union. Taken as a whole, JIC reports from this period do, however, shed light on the origins of the conflict that would shape the whole second half of the twentieth century: the Cold War. We can now see that in the immediate post-war period, during the transition between World War and Cold War, the JIC was relatively optimistic about Britain's future relations with Moscow. It was certainly not expecting a war to break out between Britain or its allies and the Soviet Union.[3]

However, by 1946 JIC reports, which were circulated to Britain's leading military figures, a small circle of cabinet ministers and top civil servants, had begun to take a much more pessimistic and hard-line approach, and were warning that a war with the Soviet Union could erupt as the result of a series of mutual miscalculations between Western governments and Moscow. This supports the most recent research on the origins of the Cold War, offered by historians such as John Lewis Gaddis and former intelligence practitioners such as Gordon Barrass, which suggests that it arose essentially because of conflicting signals given by the West and the East, and a range of mutual misinterpretations.[4]

WINNING THE WAR, LOSING THE PEACE

The essential problem for the JIC was that between 1944 and 1946 it lacked any useful intelligence on the Soviet Union, either from SIS, GCHQ (the new name given to GC&CS at Bletchley Park after 1945) and MI5, or from their counterparts in US intelligence. This is not entirely surprising, given how difficult it was to gather any objective intelligence on the Soviet Union. As with the Third Reich, British and US intelligence found it virtually impossible to penetrate the heavy police and surveillance presence in the Soviet Union, run as a police state, and London and Washington also found it virtually impossible to understand the mindset of the post-war Soviet leadership. Churchill was close to the mark when he famously remarked in October 1939 that the Soviet Union was 'a riddle wrapped in a mystery inside an enigma'. At the end of the war, MI5's in-house historian John Curry lamented that the position in which MI5 found itself regarding the Soviet Union in 1945 was the same as it had been regarding Nazi Germany in 1939: it faced a complete dearth of intelligence. In reality, the situation was even worse than Curry and MI5 assumed. From his position as head of Soviet counter-intelligence in Section IX within SIS, Kim Philby almost certainly helped to prepare some of the post-war JIC papers on the Soviet threat. Through the Cambridge spies and other well-placed agents in the West, the Soviet Union was able to obtain the most sensitive secrets of Britain and other Western governments in the post-war years.[5]

One of the priorities for British and Allied intelligence in 1945 was dismantling Axis intelligence networks. As the end of the war approached, a stream of apparently reliable reports stated that the Nazi leadership was making megalomaniacal plans to rise again if Germany were defeated. These schemes focused on Hitler's so-called 'Werewolf' organisation, through which SS officers planned to orchestrate guerrilla warfare against the victorious Allies. Meanwhile, the German security service (*Sicherheitsdienst*) was apparently planning to disperse sabotage sleeper agents across Europe and the rest of the world to help create a Fourth Reich out of the rubble of the Third 'Thousand Year' Reich. The first alarming reports along those lines came to MI5 in March 1945, when a four-man team of German sabotage agents was captured and interrogated in Allied France. They had been flown in a German-captured US B-17 Flying Fortress deep behind Allied lines in France, from which they parachuted in with instructions and equipment to organise sabotage networks. The agents revealed that their sabotage colleagues had been equipped with a number of poisons, 'not the usual ampoules of hydrocyanic acid, with which agents have been equipped in recent months to commit suicide after arrest'. Instead, they were planning to kill Allied officers with poisons infused in everyday commodities such as sausages, chocolate, Nescafé, schnapps, whisky and Bayer aspirin. They had also been instructed on how to leave arsenic and acids on books, desks and door handles.[6]

Alarm was heightened when the Supreme Headquarters of the Allied Expeditionary Force (SHAEF) discovered sabotage plots involving secret weapons such as poisonous cigarette lighters which would kill the smoker; a belt buckle with a silver swastika that concealed a double-barrelled .32 pistol; and germ warfare 'microbes' that were to be hidden in female agents' compact mirrors. SHAEF also obtained some mysterious pellets and brown capsules that would emit fatal vapours when placed in an ashtray and heated by a cigarette. These were forwarded to MI5 in London, where they were tested by the service's expert on counter-sabotage, Lord Rothschild, and its in-house scientist, Professor H.V.A. Briscoe of Imperial College London. Although SHAEF was sceptical about some of the supposed sabotage plots, the conclusion of one of its reports in March 1945, entitled 'German terrorist methods', was that Allied personnel should be forbidden from eating any German foods or smoking German cigarettes, 'under pain of severe penalties'.[7]

However, contrary to all of the warnings and intelligence assessments made in London and Washington, the Nazi threat – and that of imperial Japan – disintegrated far more quickly than predicted. As it turned out, neither Nazi Germany nor the Japanese secret police (the *Kempeitai*) organised any effective stay-behind networks after the Allied victory. British intelligence nevertheless devoted significant resources to hunting down and capturing Nazi war criminals on the run. The Oxford historian and wartime SIS officer Hugh Trevor-Roper was sent by SIS to Berlin to make a detailed report on the final days of Hitler and the attempted escapes of Nazi leaders. His report eventually became a best-selling book, *The Last Days of Hitler*. One of the leading figures in the 'Final Solution', Ernst Kaltenbrunner, for example, was captured in Austria disguised as a huntsman and was then secretly transported to Britain. Though it has not been acknowledged in historical accounts to date, Kaltenbrunner's interrogation by MI5 at Camp 020 played a significant role in his successful prosecution and execution at Nuremberg. Likewise, the notorious leader of the SS and architect of Nazi mass murder in Europe, Heinrich Himmler, was captured by the Allies as he attempted to flee across the German border in disguise. However, Himmler committed suicide in British detention, by biting into a cyanide pellet hidden in one of his teeth, before he could be brought to trial.[8]

The political situation in post-war Britain did not create an easy atmosphere for its secret services. The new Labour government of Clement Attlee, elected in July 1945, made an election promise to keep them on a tight leash. The Labour Party had experienced difficult relations with Britain's intelligence services ever since the scandalous 'Zinoviev affair' in 1924, which had led to the downfall of Britain's first Labour government under Ramsay MacDonald. The affair involved a letter supposedly sent by one of the Soviet leaders, Grigory Zinoviev, to the British Communist Party, in which Moscow apparently implored communist fellow travellers to spread revolution to Britain and its colonies. MacDonald's government suspected that the letter was a forgery, concocted by conservative elements in British intelligence, but the Conservative Party pounced on the scandal, and implicated the Labour Party in the affair. It is now known that the letter was indeed a fake, but it was not devised by MI5 or any other part of British intelligence: it was forged by anti-Bolshevik White Russians, probably in one of the Baltic countries.[9]

Meanwhile, Churchill's parting shot before he left office as Prime Minister in 1945 was to warn that a 'socialist' government in Britain would inevitably establish a 'Gestapo' and a 'police state'. To nip Churchill's prediction in the bud, when MI5's wartime Director-General Sir David Petrie retired in 1946, Attlee attempted to keep MI5 under his control as much as possible, choosing a former policeman, Sir Percy Sillitoe, as Petrie's successor. Many within MI5, probably with good reason, regarded Attlee's choice of an outsider as a vote of no confidence. The fact was that MI5 emerged from the war judged not for its triumphs, like the Double

Cross System, which remained secret, but instead on claustrophobic wartime security measures, including the temporary curtailment of civil liberties and, perhaps most notoriously, mass internment in Britain.[10]

For Britain's intelligence services, as for many other departments in Whitehall, the transition from war to peace witnessed a rapid wind-down. Just as after the First World War, in the years after 1945, in 'Austerity Britain', funding of the nation's intelligence services was slashed, their emergency wartime powers removed, and their staff numbers drastically reduced. Many of the brilliant amateur outsiders who had joined the ranks of the intelligence services during the war returned to their pre-war professions. MI5's staff numbers were reduced from 350 officers at its height in 1943, to just a hundred in 1946. Its administrative records reveal that it was forced to start buying cheaper ink and paper, and its officers were instructed to type reports on both sides of paper to save money. Combined with all this, MI5 also soon became demoralised. The officer who had been responsible for skilfully running its double agents section during the war, Tar Robertson, was so disheartened with the service after the war that in 1947 he took early retirement and went off to become a sheep farmer in Gloucestershire, hardly ever speaking publicly of his secret wartime exploits. There were some serious discussions within Whitehall, as there had been after the First World War, about shutting MI5 down altogether. Unfortunately for MI5, in the post-war years it faced the worst possible combination of circumstances: reduced resources, but increased responsibilities. After the war Britain had more territories under its control than at any point in its history, and because MI5 was responsible for security intelligence in all British territories, it acquired unprecedented overseas obligations.[11]

A D-DAY FOR TERRORISM

If the British intelligence community faced an uneasy situation in the post-war period, with reduced funding, greater responsibilities, awkward relations with the Labour government and scanty intelligence on their new Soviet enemy, MI5 was confronted with an even more urgent threat. Recently declassified intelligence records reveal that at the end of the war the main priority for MI5 was the threat of terrorism emanating from the Middle East, specifically from the two main Jewish (or Zionist) terrorist groups operating in the Mandate of Palestine, which had been placed under British control in 1921. They were called the Irgun Zevai Leumi

('National Military Organisation', or the Irgun for short) and the Lehi (an acronym in Hebrew for 'Freedom Fighters of Israel'), which the British also termed the 'Stern Gang', after its founding leader, Avraham Stern. The Irgun and the Stern Gang believed that British policies in Palestine in the post-war years, blocking the creation of an independent Jewish state, legitimised the use of violence against British targets.

As the Second World War came to a close, MI5 received a stream of intelligence reports warning that the Irgun and the Stern Gang were not just planning violence in the Mandate of Palestine, but were also plotting to launch attacks inside Britain. In April 1945 an urgent cable from SIME warned that Victory in Europe (VE-Day) would be a D-Day for Jewish terrorists in the Middle East. Then, in the spring and summer of 1946, coinciding with a sharp escalation of anti-British violence in Palestine, MI5 received apparently reliable reports from SIME that the Irgun and the Stern Gang were planning to send five terrorist 'cells' to London, 'to work on IRA lines'. To use their own words, the terrorists intended to 'beat the dog in his own kennel'. The SIME reports were derived from the interrogation of captured Irgun and Stern Gang fighters, from local police agents in Palestine, and from liaisons with official Zionist political groups like the Jewish Agency. They stated that among the targets for assassination were Britain's Foreign Secretary, Ernest Bevin, who was regarded as the main obstacle to the establishment of a Jewish state in the Middle East, and the Prime Minister himself. Before his retirement as MI5's Director-General, Sir David Petrie warned that the spike of violence against the British in Palestine, and the planned extension of Irgun and Stern Gang operations to Britain, meant that the 'red light is definitely showing'. MI5's new Director-General, Sir Percy Sillitoe, was so alarmed that in August 1946 he personally briefed the Prime Minister on the situation, warning him that an assassination campaign in Britain had to be considered a real possibility, and that his own name was known to be on a Stern Gang hit-list.[12]

The Irgun and the Stern Gang's wartime track record ensured that MI5 took these warnings seriously. In November 1944 the Stern Gang assassinated the British Minister for the Middle East, Lord Moyne, while he was returning to his rented villa after a luncheon engagement in Cairo. Moyne, an heir to the Guinness dynasty, was a wealthy and well-connected figure, and his assassination prompted a furious reaction from Churchill. The wartime leader had been a long-time supporter of the Zionist cause, having known the Zionist political leader Chaim Weizmann (who later became the first President of Israel) since the early 1900s, when he was an

MP and Weizmann a lecturer at Manchester University, but despite his private outrage with the Stern Gang 'gangsters', he urged moderation. However, Moyne's murder was followed by an escalation of violence in Palestine, with incidents against the British and Irgun and Stern Gang fighters being followed by bloody reprisals. In mid-June 1946, after the Irgun launched a wave of attacks, bombing five trains and ten of the eleven bridges connecting Palestine to neighbouring states, London's restraint finally broke. British forces conducted mass arrests across Palestine (code-named Operation *Agatha*), culminating on 29 June – a day known as 'Black Sabbath' because it was a Saturday – with the detention of over 2,700 Zionist leaders and minor officials, as well as officers of the official Jewish defence force (Haganah) and its crack commandos (Palmach). None of the important Irgun or Stern Gang leaders was caught in the dragnet, and its result was merely to goad them into even more violent counter-actions. On 22 July the Irgun dealt a devastating blow, codenamed Operation *Chick*, to the heart of British rule in Palestine, bombing the King David Hotel in Jerusalem, which housed the offices of British official-dom in the Mandate, as well as serving as the headquarters of the British Army in Palestine and all the British intelligence services operating there.[13]

The bombing was planned by the leader of the Irgun, Menachem Begin, later to be the sixth Prime Minister of Israel and the joint winner of the Nobel Peace Prize. On the morning of 22 July, six young Irgun members entered the hotel disguised as Arabs, carrying milk churns packed with five hundred pounds of explosives. At 12.37 p.m. the bombs exploded, ripping the façade from the south-west corner of the building, which caused the collapse of several floors in the hotel, resulting in the death of ninety-one people, including British civilians, Arabs and Jews, some of whom were maimed beyond recognition, and causing a further forty-five casualties. Begin later claimed that he had given adequate warnings about the bomb, which were ignored by the British authorities: a young Irgun courier, Adina Hay-Nissan, had made three telephone calls to the hotel's switchboard, as well as to the French consulate and the *Palestine Post* before the explosion. However, the reality was that, as her terrorist bosses knew well, the Irgun issued so many warnings that the British police had become blasé, and the bomb went off just fifteen minutes after the warn-ings, leaving little time for evacuation.[14]

The Chief Secretary of the Palestine Mandate, Sir John Shaw, who narrowly escaped being killed in the explosion, and who went on to work for MI5, was adamant that he never received a warning about the bomb

– he privately recorded in MI5 files that he was contemplating suing Begin for libel following Begin's assertion in his book *The Revolt* (1951) that Shaw had ignored the warning. Shaw graphically described to Labour MP Richard Crossman how he lost nearly a hundred of his 'best officers and old friends' in the bombing, and in its aftermath helped to dig lacerated bodies from the rubble, attending thirteen funerals in just three days. The explosion was so powerful that the body of the Postmaster General was hurled across the street from the hotel into the YMCA, where his remains had to be literally scraped off a wall. One clerk in the hotel had his face cut almost entirely in half by shards of flying glass. A photograph from the scene shows a typewriter sitting on top of a pile of rubble, with dismembered fingers still attached to its keys. The post-war diaries of Guy Liddell reveal that in the aftermath of the bombing, Shaw made an urgent trip to London, where he briefed the JIC:

> He [Shaw] was obviously considerably moved by his recent experience. The principal point of his statement [to the JIC] was his conviction that Palestinian Arabs would prove entirely intransigent. He thought that we were lucky to have got over the funerals of the Arab victims in the King David Hotel without any serious incident. He thought that it was quite on the cards that, although the Arabs knew that in a street fight with the Jews they could not hope to win, they might at any moment commit some outrage which would cause things to flare up. It might even lead to a Holy War.

In terms of fatalities, the King David Hotel bombing was one of the worst terrorist atrocities inflicted on the British in the twentieth century. It was also a direct attack on British intelligence and counter-terrorist efforts in Palestine: both MI5 and SIS had stations in the hotel.[15]

In the wake of the bombing, the Irgun and the Stern Gang launched a series of operations outside Palestine, just as the reports coming into MI5 had warned. At the end of October 1946 an Irgun cell operating in Italy bombed the British embassy in Rome, and followed this in late 1946 and early 1947 with a series of sabotage attacks on British military transportation routes in occupied Germany. In March 1947 an Irgun operative left a bomb at the Colonial Club, near St Martin's Lane in the heart of London, which blew out the club's windows and doors, injuring several servicemen. The following month a female Irgun agent left an enormous bomb, consisting of twenty-four sticks of explosives, at the Colonial Office in

London. The bomb failed to detonate because its timer broke. The head of Special Branch, Leonard Burt, estimated that if it had gone off it would have caused fatalities on a comparable scale to the King David Hotel bombing – but this time at the heart of Whitehall. At about the same time, several prominent British politicians and public figures connected with Palestine received death threats from the Stern Gang at their homes and offices. Finally, in June 1947 the Stern Gang launched a letter-bomb campaign in Britain, consisting of twenty-one bombs in total, which targeted every prominent member of the cabinet. The two waves of bombs were posted from an underground cell in Italy. Some of those in the first wave reached their targets, but they did not result in any casualties. Sir Stafford Cripps was only saved by the quick thinking of his secretary, who became suspicious of a package whose contents seemed to fizz, and placed it in a bucket of water. The Deputy Leader of the Conservative Party, Sir Anthony Eden, carried a letter bomb around with him for a whole day in his briefcase, thinking it was a Whitehall circular that could wait till the evening to be read, and only realised what it was when he was warned by the police of the planned attack, on information provided by MI5. General Evelyn Barker, the former head of British land forces in Palestine, was saved when his wife smelt something strange – gunpowder – as she was opening the morning post, and called the police. None of the other letter bombs in the second wave got through to their targets, but ballistics experts at the Home Office found that all the bombs were potentially lethal.[16]

MI5's involvement in dealing with Zionist terrorism offers a striking new interpretation of the history of the early Cold War. For the entire duration of the Cold War, the overwhelming priority for the intelligence services of Britain and other Western powers would lie with counter-espionage, but as we can now see, in the crucial transition period from World War to Cold War, MI5 was instead primarily concerned with counter-terrorism. This sensitive chapter in the history of the Cold War and Britain's end of empire was not publicly revealed until the recent declassification of MI5 records. It also provides a remarkable new chapter in the history of modern international (trans-national) terrorism. Most studies on the subject suggest that this began in earnest in July 1968, with the hijacking of an Israeli El Al flight by Palestinian terrorists. In fact, as we can now see from MI5 records, it began over twenty years earlier. In the years after 1945, Jewish-led terrorist groups in Palestine deliberately sought to internationalise their conflict with the British. The infiltration and radicalisation of a terrorist minority from the Middle East – so prevalent among terrorist groups today – was experienced in Britain half a century ago.[17]

THE BRITISH MANDATE OF PALESTINE

Britain became the uneasy patron of Zionism when it was granted Mandatory Power over Palestine by the League of Nations in 1921. The doctrine of Zionism, the political movement seeking to establish a Jewish national homeland in Palestine, was largely derived from the writings of Theodor Herzl, in particular his book *Der Judenstaat* (1896). However, it was the famous (and fateful) Declaration framed by the British Foreign Secretary, Arthur James Balfour, in November 1917 that set the agenda for British policies in Palestine for the next twenty years. The Balfour Declaration provided Zionist groups with a moral, and they argued also a legal, right for Jews to settle in Palestine. Made public on the same day as the Bolshevik coup in St Petersburg, the Declaration was designed to be a rallying point for the Allies, a kind of Christmas present for beleaguered troops and governments which was also intended to whip up further support for Britain in Russia and the United States. The Declaration stated that Britain aimed to establish a 'National Home for the Jewish People' in Palestine, but went on to state, 'it being clearly understood that nothing shall be done which may prejudice the civil and religious rights existing of non-Jewish communities in Palestine'. Balfour was a man of deep intellect, who in his youth had published a book defending philosophic doubt. Unfortunately, his Declaration left a good deal of doubt, failing to explain what the nature of the Jewish homeland in Palestine would be, leading to the joke that Palestine was the twice promised land.[18]

Despite the British government's clear wording in the Balfour Declaration of its intention to create a 'National Home for Jewish People', it was subsequently interpreted by many Zionists as a pledge to create a *Jewish* state, not just a state *for Jews*. The description of Palestine by the Zionist writer Israel Zangwill as 'a land without people for a people without land' apparently overlooked the fact that Arabs and Christians had been living there for generations. At the time of the Balfour Declaration, the Jewish community in Palestine (the *Yishuv*) numbered 85,000, while the Arab population was 750,000, but over subsequent years Jewish immigration steadily increased, so that by 1946 the Jewish population totalled 600,000. Growing levels of Jewish immigration to Palestine soon sparked off major Arab disturbances in response. In 1933 the Syrian Wahhabist

preacher Izz al-Din al-Qassam launched pro-*intifada* attacks on Jews and
the British police in Palestine – for which he is commemorated to this day
by teams of Palestinian suicide bombers, who remember him as the leader
of the first Palestinian armed nationalist grouping.

It was largely in response to increased levels of Jewish immigration that
in 1936 a major Arab revolt erupted, lasting until 1939. The so-called 'Arab
Revolt' was only put down by a tough response from the British military
and police, who, backed up by the RAF, fought Arab forces in pitched
battles. The British military and the Palestine police inflicted brutal interrogations on Arab insurgents, a practice that was known as 'duffing up'
after one especially robust police officer, Douglas Duff, who before serving
in the Palestine Police had been one of the Black and Tans in Ireland.
British forces also collaborated with Haganah, which had been formed in
1921 in response to anti-Jewish violence in Palestine. Applying the military doctrine that the best form of defence is offence, the British military
leader Captain (subsequently Major General) Orde Wingate – whose
Christian beliefs made him a natural Zionist supporter – established
'Special Night Squads', whose ranks consisted of Haganah and British
volunteers, and included legendary future Israeli military leaders such as
Moshe Dayan. Wingate would later be famed for creating the Chindits, a
special-forces airborne deep-penetration unit, who were trained to operate far behind enemy lines in Japanese-occupied territories in the Far East
during the Second World War.[19]

The British government generally favoured the position of Arabs in
Palestine, despite the anti-British violence unleashed there during the
Arab Revolt. This was because the Chiefs of Staff in London, their views
coloured by nostalgic memories of Lawrence of Arabia, feared doing
anything that could destabilise Palestine, which was a crucial strategic base
from which to guard the eastern Mediterranean, the gateway to the Suez
Canal, and the vital supply route to the subcontinent of India. The Arab
Revolt revealed to London that an orgy of violence between Jews and
Arabs would arise if Jewish immigration to Palestine were not restricted.
Military and Colonial Office mandarins were also worried about provok-
ing the sixty million Muslims living in India. As a result, in 1939 the British
government published a White Paper limiting the number of Jewish
immigrants to Palestine to a total of 75,000 over the next five years, which
effectively meant a quota of 1,250 immigrants per month.[20]

When the war in Europe broke out, the majority of the *Yishuv* remained
strongly opposed to the White Paper, but nevertheless supported Britain

in the conflict. The Zionist leader David Ben-Gurion said that Jews had to fight the war as if there were no White Paper, and the White Paper as if there were no war. The British Army quickly found recruits for a special unit it formed, the Jewish Brigade, which acted as a counterpart to the Nazi SS Division of Muslims that fought in the Balkans. However, matters soon became more complicated. In 1941 the Haganah established a special 'commando' unit, the Palmach, one of the aims of which was to fight anyone, including the British, who opposed increased levels of Jewish immigration to Palestine. It was during a Palmach operation that Moshe Dayan lost an eye. Furthermore, for a minority of so-called 'Revisionist' Zionists, even the Palmach's 'resistance' against the British was not enough. Revisionists were so-called because they purported to revise the ideas of Zionism. They pursued a fanatical right-wing agenda, taking inspiration from the extremist writings of the Polish Zionist politician Vladimir Jabotinsky. Their beliefs lay in sharp contrast to the broadly left-wing politics of the majority of the *Yishuv*, who followed a generally socialist agenda tinged with Marxism – reflective of which is the fact that Israel did not elect a right-wing government until the 1970s. Revisionists dispensed with traditional Jewish doctrine of restraint (*havlagah*), rejected mainstream Zionist aspirations derived from Herzl's writings in the 1880s, and instead believed that it was necessary to fight for the establishment of an independent and predominantly Jewish state in Palestine (*eretz Israel*) on both sides of the river Jordan. The cornerstones of Revisionist Zionism were a belief that the Haganah's reliance on defence was inadequate given the wartime threat, and more offensive action was needed; that the British must be compelled to fulfil their pledges to protect and defend the *Yishuv*; that neither Britain nor Jews would ever placate the Arabs with political concessions or buy them off with economic development; and that an 'iron wall' had to be erected to separate the two peoples in Palestine.

The main Revisionist fighters were the Irgun and the Stern Gang. The Irgun had been established in 1931 in opposition to the 'moderate' policies pursued by the Haganah, and was led first by David Raziel and then, after 1944, by Menachem Begin, a future Prime Minister of Israel. One of the reasons Begin was chosen as the Irgun leader was that he was invisible to British intelligence and the Palestine Police. After fleeing his native Poland to escape invading Nazi forces, he was arrested by the Soviet NKVD and sent to a Gulag, from which he escaped, it seems with the assistance of Soviet intelligence, to Palestine. The Irgun guessed rightly that because of his itinerant background, Begin would not appear on Britain's wartime intelligence's radar. Under Begin's command, the Irgun specialised in bombing buildings and other infrastructure, and by 1945 was estimated by British intelligence to have between 5,000 and 6,000 members – figures that were exaggerated, perhaps by as much as three times, due to the difficulties in penetrating the Irgun with agents.

The Stern Gang was an even smaller and more extremist group than the Irgun, from which it split in 1940 because the Irgun was too 'moderate'. It was led by Avraham Stern, a romantic poet, former philosopher and gunman, whom the British eventually eliminated in 1942. The circumstances of Stern's death were controversial. It appears that a Palestine police officer, Geoffrey Morton, shot him dead while he was unarmed and un-handcuffed, apparently as he was attempting to jump out of a window. Thereafter the Stern Gang's leadership included the future seventh Israeli Prime Minister, Yitzhak Shamir, who was the architect of Lord Moyne's assassination and who adopted the *nom de guerre* 'Michael' in honour of Sinn Féin's Michael Collins. The Stern Gang's speciality was political assassinations, and by 1945 it was estimated to have between three hundred and five hundred members – again an inflated estimate, but about the same number of trigger-pulling members as there then were in the IRA.[21]

After the Stern Gang's assassination of Moyne in 1944, the Haganah helped the British to track down Stern Gang members – a period known as the 'hunting season', or *Sezon*. Zionist political leaders initially hoped that the 1945 election victory in Britain of the Labour Party, traditionally a supporter of the Zionist cause, would help to ease British restrictions on Jewish immigration to Palestine. However, their hopes were soon dashed. The new British Foreign Secretary, Ernest Bevin, came to office with a background as a tough trade union negotiator, and had formerly been a supporter of the creation of a Jewish state, but within days of coming to power he changed his mind – and thus became public enemy number one for Zionist Revisionists, who regarded him as the main impediment to *eretz Israel*. Bevin's policy over Palestine was not shaped by closet 'anti-Semitism', a claim that has often been made, but instead by his belief that a civil war would break out between Jews and Arabs if unrestricted Jewish immigration were permitted in Palestine. That said, he often displayed shocking insensitivity, joking that the US government supported mass immigration to Palestine 'because they did not want too many Jews in New York', and when power cuts threw one set of Anglo–Jewish negotiations in 1947 into literal darkness, he ponderously joked that 'there was no need for candles because they had Israe*lites*'.[22]

The Holocaust transformed British policies on Palestine. As details of Nazi mass-murder programmes in Europe appeared in the world's media after 1945, it became increasingly unacceptable to world opinion for Britain to block the entry of Jewish refugees into Palestine. The new US President, Harry Truman, repeatedly demanded that the British government should allow 100,000 Jewish refugees immediate entry into Palestine, even though his demand was not supported by the US State Department, which advised that Jewish immigration to Palestine should be controlled. Despite the pressure on it, the British government refused to increase substantially the Jewish immigration quota. With their hopes of securing greater Jewish immigration now sunk, all of the Zionist militias in Palestine – the Haganah, the Irgun and the Stern Gang – came together in late 1945 to fight the British in what was termed the Hebrew or United Resistance Movement.

At this stage the British were faced with what appeared to be a hopelessly irreconcilable situation. By the end of the war, some British officials were already pessimistically forecasting that Britain would be unable to square the circle in the Palestine triangle between themselves, Jews and Arabs. In 1945 the Special Commissioner in Palestine, Sir Douglas Harris, said that Britain was doing little more than ploughing sand. Not long after, the British Chancellor of the Exchequer, Hugh Dalton, complained to Attlee that it was impossible to build a firm base on a wasps' nest.[23]

Before 1948 several leading politicians of the future state of Israel were involved in fighting the British. Menachem Begin, one of the great pillars of Israeli politics, was denounced by the British as a terrorist, as was another future Israeli Prime Minister, Yitzhak Shamir, and at least one future Israeli Supreme Court Judge (Meir Shamgar) as well as a future Minister of Justice (Shamuel Tamir). Avraham Stern himself was subsequently commemorated on an Israeli postage stamp, and today the Israeli town of Stern is home to a number of the country's leading political and intellectual elites. All of this leads one to ask whether it is legitimate to call these fighters 'terrorists'. After the state of Israel was established in May 1948, the overwhelming majority of those who had fought the British refused to admit that they were ever 'terrorists', instead labelling themselves 'freedom fighters'. However, the fact of the matter is that, at the time, Stern Gang operatives openly admitted to using 'terrorist' tactics. The Stern Gang is thought to have been one of the last groups in the world to call itself a 'terrorist' organisation. Some of its members apparently used the term 'terrorism' as a badge of honour, romanticising the role of violence. Deceitful mythologies still insist that the Irgun and the Stern Gang acted as 'soldiers' and were 'freedom fighters of the highest moral standards'. As recently as July 2006 a group of right-wing Israelis, including Benjamin Netanyahu, attended a commemoration organised by the 'Menachem Begin Heritage Centre' for the sixtieth anniversary of the bombing of the King David Hotel, which they insisted on labelling an act of 'freedom fighting'. A plaque commemorating the attack attracted an official response from the British ambassador in Tel Aviv, who urged that it was offensive to celebrate an act of terrorism. In reality, the Irgun and the Stern Gang targeted and killed innocent civilians. The victims of over half of the forty-two assassinations carried out by the Stern Gang and the Irgun were Jewish, supposedly acting as 'collaborators' with the British.

The extent to which the Irgun and the Stern Gang lacked legitimacy was seen in the fact that, after the state of Israel was created in May 1948, the new Israeli government was itself forced to deal with their threat. When David Ben-Gurion became Israel's first Prime Minister, the firm stance he had always taken against the Stern Gang and the Irgun led to some dramatic confrontations. In June 1948 he ordered Jewish troops to fire on a boat moored off the coast of Tel Aviv, the *Altalena*, named after Vladimir Jabotinsky's old *nom de plume*, which was bringing Jewish sympathisers and arms to the Irgun. At this point the fragile young Israeli state came closer to civil war than it would in its entire history. The episode has echoes closer to our own time. In 1995 Israel's Prime Minister, Yitzhak Rabin, was assassinated by an ultra-Zionist Jewish extremist in a 'revenge attack' for proposed Israeli withdrawals from the Gaza Strip and for the fact that Rabin had been one of the troops responsible for shelling the *Altalena* in 1948.[24]

MI5 AND COUNTER-TERRORISM

In the post-war years MI5 did not have a specific department dedicated to counter-terrorism, but dealt with it under the rubric of 'counter-subversion', the concern of F-Division. The F-Division officers most concerned with Zionist activities were Alex Kellar and his assistant James Robertson. Kellar was a flamboyant Scot who held law degrees from Edinburgh and Columbia Universities, and was probably the inspiration for the 'man in cream cuffs' depicted by John le Carré in his first novel *Call for the Dead* (1961), played in the 1966 film (retitled *The Deadly Affair*) by Max Adrian wearing a dragon-patterned silk dressing gown with a purple handkerchief and a rose in his buttonhole. During the war Kellar had served as head of SIME, travelling frequently between London and the various stations MI5 maintained in the Middle East. Later, while stationed in the Far East, Kellar would memorably put in expense requests to MI5 HQ for tropical kit, including 'two Palm Beach and one Saigon linen suitings, white shirts, drill, sharkskin dinner jackets'. Kellar's homosexuality was widely known within MI5, a remarkable fact given that at the time homosexual practices were still illegal in Britain, and as such were regarded within Whitehall vetting circles as a potential source for blackmail. Vetters also apparently overlooked the homosexuality of the Cambridge spy Anthony Blunt. Despite his sometimes unserious appearance – he had a penchant for wearing purple socks – in the course of his thirty-five-year career in MI5 Kellar served in the front line during the last days of the British empire and the Cold War, acting as a roaming troubleshooter in successive Emergencies that broke out in Britain's holdings across the globe.[25]

Even though Kellar had covert dealings at the highest level with colonial administrations throughout the empire, brokering deals with national leaders behind closed doors as they were preparing to gain independence, until now there has been almost no trace of his activities in official declassified British records. One collection of essays on British policing and decolonisation, edited by the historian David Anderson and published in 1992, noted that a 'shadowy' person named Kellar was present in a British colony on the eve of independence, but otherwise, until now his career has been shrouded in secrecy. Like many leading British intelligence officials, he did not publicly discuss his clandestine work after his retirement. At the end of his long MI5 career he went to work quietly – and appropriately – for the English Tourist Board.[26]

MI5 maintained a presence in the Middle East through SIME, which by 1946 had twenty-six DSOs stationed from Gibraltar to Baghdad, including in the main cities of Palestine – Jerusalem, Tel Aviv, Jaffa, Haifa, Gaza and Nablus. In their reports on Zionist matters, which they never thought would be declassified and read by outsiders, some MI5 officers showed a degree of the mild anti-Semitism that infected much of Britain's ruling classes at the time. Despite some comments by officers which today would be regarded as politically unacceptable, MI5 as a whole was always careful to separate the activities of the overwhelming majority of Jews and Zionists from the tiny minority who posed a security threat to Britain, as was stressed by the new Director-General, Percy Sillitoe, in a confidential lecture to the London Special Branch in March 1948:

M.I.5 are not of course concerned with the activities of Jews as such. Nor does M.I.5. devote time to studying Zionist activities as a whole, except where these are definitely of a subversive nature or prejudicial to the defence plans of the British Empire. There is nothing illegal in Zionism as a political creed. It only comes within our province when some of the activities of its extremist supporters qualify beyond doubt to be described as secret, subversive or illegal, and thus a danger to the security of the Empire and of this country.[27]

Sillitoe further explained MI5's overall approach to national security threats in his later memoirs, recalling that when he joined the service:

Among the points that were called especially to my attention was the ruling that the work of M.I.5 is unconnected with political matters, and that it must never be thought or suggested that the politics of those who seek to subvert our realm or institutions have a bearing on M.I.5's activities to frustrate their efforts. It must be borne in mind that the function of M.I.5 is a purely defensive one; it is charged solely with detecting activities liable to undermine the national security of this country; the creed, politics, or nationalities of those responsible for such activities is immaterial.[28]

MI5 used the term 'Zionist terrorism' rather than 'Jewish terrorism' because its investigations did not just target Jews, but were much broader in scope, spreading out to include non-Jewish supporters of 'Revisionist' terrorism, including arms dealers and people-traffickers. That said, MI5 records reveal that from the start of its investigations, it acknowledged how delicate its inquiries into Zionist extremism would have to be. For instance, one target for investigation was the celebrated Jewish writer and Zionist sympathiser Arthur Koestler – a fact that if it had become public knowledge would have been extremely awkward for MI5 and the British government generally. As Koestler's MI5 file makes clear, the reason he was investigated was that he was extremely well connected in Zionist circles in London, Europe and Palestine, and it was hoped that his connections might reveal undercover Irgun and Stern Gang operatives. Koestler was certainly well versed in the aims of the Irgun and the Stern Gang. His novel *Thieves in the Night* (1946) perfectly encapsulated how Jewish youths could be radicalised to violence over the issue of Palestine. Its fictional protagonist, Joseph, turns from a quiet life in academia to violence because he believes that a nation state of pacifists could never survive. MI5 also made enquiries into a tireless humanitarian and Zionist supporter, Joel Brandt. Brandt had worked in anti-Nazi resistance movements throughout Europe, and in spring 1944 had brokered the failed 'lorries for lives' deal, by which Jews would be released by the Nazis in exchange for trucks. However, as MI5's file on him reveals, he was also involved in the clandestine migration of Jews from Europe to Palestine, and as MI5 argued, whatever the humanitarian basis of his actions, they had security implications in Palestine. Still, the inescapable fact was that in its covert enquiries into Brandt, MI5 was targeting a heroic figure of anti-Nazi resistance and a well-known human rights campaigner.[29]

It was against the background of escalating violence in Palestine in 1946, particularly following the bombing of the King David Hotel in Jerusalem and the British embassy in Rome, that MI5 received a number of reports from SIME warning that the Irgun and the Stern Gang were planning to extend their operations to Britain itself. Percy Sillitoe described these alarming reports in a lecture to Special Branch at Scotland Yard in September that year:

> Reports that the IRGUN ZVAI LEUMI or STERN Group may attempt the assassination of a prominent British figure outside the Middle East have in fact been growing in number since the beginning of this year and culminated a few days ago in a report that the IRGUN and STERN, in the event of the death sentence of the 18 STERN Group members now in custody in Palestine [for the bombing of the King David Hotel], intended jointly to set up representative 'cells' in London ... Should such plans for extending their activities abroad be realised by the IRGUN and STERN, we might be faced with a real danger of assassinations or the sabotage of important buildings in this country, and particularly in London.[30]

In December 1946 MI5 received a report from its DSO in Jerusalem:

> It is reported that a group of IZL [Irgun] agents are now in England. Their numbers are said to be between 8 and 10 persons who originate not only from Palestine, but also from America and Europe.[31]

The problem for MI5 in London, and local security forces in Palestine, was the extremely difficult nature of detecting and countering the Irgun and the Stern Gang. Both groups were organised vertically into cells, whose members were unknown to those in other cells, and whose extreme loyalty meant they were nearly impossible to penetrate. As Alex Kellar noted in one MI5 report, 'these terrorists are hard nuts to crack, and it is by no means easy to get them to talk'. To complicate matters further, they also frequently made use of false identities and disguises. Female agents used hair dye or wigs to alter their appearance, while male agents were known to dress as women to elude security patrols.[32]

Menachem Begin, whose hatred of the British was implacable, was known to travel under several aliases, and in the wake of the King David Hotel bombing he managed to elude the Palestine police and the £2,000 bounty on his head by a series of clever disguises. In November 1946 the Palestine police produced alarming reports that he might be travelling incognito to Britain. Then, in early 1947, the alarm reached fever pitch when SIS sent a report to MI5 warning that Begin was thought to have undergone plastic surgery to alter his appearance, though as the report dryly concluded, 'we have no description of the new face'. The story soon leaked to the press, with the *News Chronicle* running the headline 'Palestine Hunting a New Face', and sarcastically noting that although Begin might have changed his appearance, it was 'likely that the flat feet and bad teeth have remained'. As it turned out, the reports of Begin's plastic surgery were inaccurate: they were caused by confusion within the Palestine CID when comparing photos of him. Begin had not actually left Palestine, but had grown a beard and disguised himself as a rabbi, evading the local police by concealing himself in a secret compartment in a friend's house in Jerusalem. When he agreed to give a secret interview to Arthur Koestler, he did so in a darkened room: Koestler vainly attempted to counter this by drawing heavily on his cigarettes, hoping to generate enough of a glow to catch a glimpse of Begin's appearance.[33]

The situation was made all the more alarming for MI5 by the fact that members of the Irgun and the Stern Gang were known to have served in British forces during the war. With bitter irony, some of them had been trained by SOE and SIS while serving in the elite Palmach commando unit of the Jewish paramilitary organisation the Haganah. Just like the former members of a number of other guerrilla groups the British armed during the war, such as communist forces in Malaya, the Irgun and the Stern Gang used their training in explosives and other paramilitary warfare against their former masters. Reports landing on MI5's desks throughout the summer of 1946 warned that Irgun and Stern Gang fighters were likely to be still serving within British military ranks, and were planning to use that as a cover to travel to Britain. MI5 was thus faced with the real possibility that terrorists could arrive in Britain wearing British military uniforms.[34]

MI5'S COUNTER-TERRORIST MEASURES

With these startling reports coming into its London headquarters, MI5 devised a range of measures to prevent the extension of Zionist terrorism from Palestine to Britain. These have left few traces within records previously in the public domain, but as we can now see from MI5's own records, they were often extremely elaborate. The front line of its counter-terrorist defence was what was termed 'personnel security', which involved making background checks and scrutinising visa applications for entry into Britain. On MI5's recommendation, all visa applications made by Jewish individuals from the Middle East were immediately telephoned through to MI5 for checking against its records before the applicants were permitted entry. MI5 also conducted a series of background vetting checks against its records on approximately 7,000 Jewish servicemen known to be in the British armed forces. This led to the identification of forty individuals with suspected extremist sympathies, twenty-five of whom were discharged from the armed forces, while the other fifteen were posted to areas in the Middle East where they posed minimal security threat. MI5's security measures also involved heightened inspections at ports and other points of entry to the United Kingdom, to each of which an MI5-compiled 'Index of Terrorists' was distributed, while on MI5's advice Scotland Yard ratcheted up its protection of many leading political and public figures, and increased the number of officers detailed to guard Buckingham Palace. In October 1947 a senior Palestine police CID officer, Major John O'Sullivan, travelled to London and provided MI5 with microfilm photographs of terrorist suspects that were added to the Index. Some of these mug-shots are today held with unconcealed pride by former Irgun and Stern Gang members.[35]

At the same time as these 'personnel security' measures, which were designed to frustrate the entry of terrorists or terrorist sympathisers into Britain, MI5 embarked on the intensive surveillance of extremist Zionist political groups and individuals who were already there. Its assumption in doing this was that Irgun or Stern Gang operatives who succeeded in gaining entry to Britain would at some point make contact with these organisations or individuals, and therefore scrutinising their activities could provide crucial leads to tracking them down. MI5 also assumed that agents would make contact with elements of the diaspora Jewish community in Britain. These assumptions would prove correct.

To investigate Zionist groups and individuals in Britain, MI5 used the full repertoire of investigative techniques at its disposal. At the heart of its investigations were Home Office Warrants, which allowed for mail interception and telephone taps. In the post-war years MI5 imposed HOWs on all the main Zionist political bodies in Britain: the Jewish Agency for Palestine, the Jewish Legion, the Jewish-Arab Legion, the Zionist Federation of Jewish Labour and the United Zionist 'Revisionist' Youth Organisation. The last of these, in particular, caused a good deal of alarm within MI5. Some of its members addressed local Jewish clubs in North London with firebrand speeches against the British, fusing religion with politics. Another source of concern was the *Jewish Struggle*, a Revisionist publication based in London that frequently reprinted extremist Irgun propaganda from Palestine, typically denouncing the British as 'Nazis' and advocating the use of violence. MI5's fear was that the *Jewish Struggle* would act as a recruiting platform for future terrorists in Britain. In December 1946 Alex Kellar and MI5's legal adviser, Bernard Hill, met the Director of Public Prosecutions, and decided that, although there was insufficient evidence to prosecute, they would officially warn the editors of the *Jewish Struggle* that if they continued to publish Irgun material, their periodical would be shut down. The *Jewish Struggle* appears to have ceased publication soon after. MI5 could legitimately claim to have helped close down a hate-mongering publication fuelling terrorism in Britain.[36]

One of the extremist Zionist organisations that MI5 was most concerned about was a Jewish youth group based in Stoke Newington in North London affiliated with the United Zionist Revisionist Movement and known by its acronym in Hebrew, 'Betar'. MI5 placed a HOW on its headquarters, which revealed a number of visitors who were involved with illegal arms purchases. It also showed that the Betar was much more than the educational organisation it claimed to be. While it did have a legitimate educational role, schooling its members in the history, geography and languages of the Middle East, they were also subjected to Irgun and Stern Gang propaganda, and in some cases even trained in hand-to-hand combat. As one MI5 report noted, the Betar was really concerned with nothing short of ideological indoctrination, by which Jewish youths were brainwashed to fight for the establishment of a sovereign Jewish state in Palestine. Another in-house report went so far as to state that the group bore 'a striking resemblance both in general character and structure to the Hitler Youth Movement'.[37]

The parallel was not as outlandish as it might at first appear. Recent scholarship has shown that some of the early leaders of the Irgun and the Stern Gang were highly influenced by non-democratic ideologies – both fascist and communist – in Eastern Europe, from where many of them originated. The ideology of Betarim youth groups in Britain and Poland stemmed from Józef Piłsudski's extremist government in interwar Poland, which strove for an ethnically pure Polish nation. Betarim groups in Poland are known to have modelled themselves on the Balilla youth movement of Italian fascism, with red-brown uniforms rather than the Italian black shirts. The journalist Aba Achimeir, who was scorched by experiences in the Bolshevik revolution, wrote a Hebrew column called 'From a Fascist Notebook': 'We need a Mussolini,' he argued, although he would also accept something like Sinn Féin/IRA. Before the war, some German 'Revisionist' Zionists had openly described themselves as 'Jewish black shirts' who aimed to establish a 'Jewish fascist' state in Palestine. During the war, the Stern Gang even sought an alliance with the Axis Powers. At the end of 1940, as Britain was fighting for its survival in the Battle of Britain, it offered to cooperate with the Nazis, naïvely concluding that Britain, not Hitler's Germany, was the main enemy of the Jewish people. As Italian and German forces were advancing through Egypt, and Axis victory seemed assured, Stern made a similar offer of support to Mussolini. These offers came to nothing, but they show the extent of Stern's hatred of the British.[38]

MI5 was also correct about the indoctrinating nature of the Betarim. One Stern Gang recruit, Geula Cohen, who went on to become a member of the Israeli parliament (Knesset), wrote in her memoirs that she was first radicalised to violence ('evil' in her words) as a young woman in a Betar group in Palestine. Although the Betar in London was not shut down, as MI5 advised, its members were kept under close surveillance.[39]

In early 1947 MI5 uncovered a group in North London whom it believed 'to have been planning terrorist outrages in this country'. The group centred on a stateless company director of Russian origin, Joel 'Leo' Bella, and his main accomplice, Harry Isaac Pressman, a British national, also of Russian origin, who ran a firm of chemical manufacturers in Stoke Newington. MI5 detected them through telephone checks and intercepted correspondence, obtained through a HOW imposed on the United Zionist 'Revisionist' Youth Organisation. On MI5's advice, in July 1947 the Special

Branch raided Pressman's flat in North London, where they discovered a quantity of terrorist literature, twenty-four hand grenades and twenty-four detonators in his lock-up garage. Despite the strong evidence against him, MI5 was unable to bring a successful prosecution against Pressman. The major problem was that its information was derived from a HOW, which meant that, in a manner that is still all too familiar today, it was inadmissible as evidence in an English court. Pressman claimed that he had hired his garage to an unidentified third party, and that he knew nothing about the arms found there. Ultimately neither Bella nor Pressman was prosecuted, but another member of their group, Eric Prinz, was threatened with deportation to Russia, and MI5 and Special Branch kept their activities under close observation.[40]

MI5's surveillance of extremist 'Revisionist' organisations in Britain revealed that some of their members exaggerated their own importance and their capabilities of carrying out acts of terrorism. However, as internal MI5 reports noted, the most dangerous threat did not necessarily come from mainstream Revisionists, but from renegade individuals loosely affiliated with them. As Alex Kellar suggested, the problem was that 'there is always the possibility that some unpredictable act of violence might be committed by one of their more hotheaded members'.[41]

An 'unpredictable act of violence' was precisely what occurred. In August 1948, after Britain had in fact withdrawn from the Mandate of Palestine, a twenty-three-year-old Jewish grocer from Aldgate, East London, Monte Harris, an Irgun sympathiser associated with the Hebrew Legion, took it upon himself to carry out an act of terrorism in Britain by blowing up British trucks and tanks that were returning from Palestine. MI5 seems to have first discovered Harris's name when it appeared in a package containing explosives, disguised as a food parcel, sent from the United States to Irgun sympathisers in Britain. His lock-up shop in Aldgate was raided by Special Branch in August 1948, following three weeks' intensive surveillance, which at one point involved officers disguising themselves in tennis clothes while following Harris to a tennis match. The search of his shop unearthed twelve primers, forty-eight feet of fuse wire, two dozen detonators and sufficient ingredients to make a substantial number of thermite incendiary explosives. In Special Branch's opinion there would have been 'a wave of incendiarism and sabotage in England' if Harris had not been caught. In October 1948 he was sentenced at London's central criminal court to seven years' imprisonment, which the judge hoped would act as a deterrent against future acts of terrorism and

political violence in Britain. Harris was released early, in 1950, and immediately moved to Israel. However, finding himself persecuted there for his
previous activities, he eventually settled in Ireland.[42]

DANGEROUS LIAISONS

As part of its counter-terrorist operations, MI5 obtained valuable intelligence from Britain's other intelligence services, as well as from local
police and security agencies in Palestine. It worked closely with its sister
agency, SIS, which in the wartime and immediate post-war years ran a
regional outfit throughout the Middle East under a cover name, the Inter-
Service Liaison Department (ISLD). MI5 also liaised with Britain's
SIGINT agency, GC&CS, which, although documentary evidence is
scarce, seems to have provided it with valuable counter-terrorist intelligence. The British Army had maintained an intercept station at Sarafand
in Palestine since 1923, and in 1944 the head of GC&CS paid tribute to
the 'close liaison between GC&CS and Sarafand'. MI5's Middle Eastern
section found the wartime SIGINT derived from Zionist communications to be of 'considerable assistance', and judging from MI5 records, in
the post-war years GCHQ (the renamed GC&CS) successfully broke
most of the major Zionist diplomatic communications – codenamed
sources 'Cream', 'Fog' and 'Buttercup'. It also seems likely that GCHQ
provided intelligence on the location of Irgun and Stern Gang radio
transmitters. One undercover Stern Gang radio broadcaster, Geula
Cohen, later described how the Palestine police caught her totally by
surprise and arrested her while she was transmitting messages. Her location was probably discovered from information provided by GCHQ
which allowed it to be triangulated from her broadcasts, a process known
as direction-finding ('D/F' in colloquial intelligence terms).[43]

Another major source of MI5's counter-terrorist intelligence in the
post-war years was moderate Jewish and Zionist groups, both in Palestine
and Britain. It forged close links with the body officially responsible for
representing Zionist wishes to the British government, the Jewish Agency.
In fact, MI5's policy towards the Jewish Agency was duplicitous: it cooperated with it, but at the same time kept it under close surveillance, running
telephone and letter checks on its London headquarters even while it was
liaising with its officers. The reason for this was that although MI5 trusted
the Agency's security officials, it suspected that its broader staff and
membership might contain Irgun and Stern Gang supporters. The

willingness of the Agency to provide the British with intelligence on the Irgun and the Stern Gang reveals the extent to which those groups' activities were not supported by the majority of the Jewish population in Palestine – and this, it should be noted, has no parallel in contemporary Arab and Islamist terrorism. The bombing of the King David Hotel brought the coordinated Hebrew Resistance Movement, between the Haganah, the Irgun and the Stern Gang, to an end. The Irgun's bombing operation was not approved by the Haganah, and after July 1946 it therefore provided the British with intelligence on the Irgun and the Stern Gang, and helped British security personnel to hunt them down.[44]

In Palestine itself, MI5's DSO stationed in Jerusalem in the post-war years, Henry Hunloke, a former Conservative MP, maintained close liaison with Jewish Agency officials, and acquired valuable intelligence from them, for example on suspected terrorists clandestinely entering or leaving Palestine. One of the Agency officials from whom both MI5 and SIS received counter-terrorist intelligence was Reuven Zislani, who worked in the foreign intelligence department of the Agency. After 1948 Zislani changed his name to Reuven Shiloah and became the first head of Israel's foreign intelligence service, the Mossad.[45]

In its efforts to establish contacts with Jewish Agency officials in Britain, MI5 at first proposed using one of its long-standing agents, codenamed 'U35': this was 'Klop' Ustinov, father of the playwright Sir Peter Ustinov. After some deliberation, however, it decided to establish different people as go-betweens, or 'cut-outs', to use intelligence terminology, to liaise between it and the Agency. The first informal contact was made through one of MI5's own officers, Anthony Simkins, later one of the authors of F.H. Hinsley's official history of British intelligence in the Second World War, and then a more permanent channel was established through an unnamed individual from British military intelligence codenamed 'Scorpion'. Although the declassified documentation is presently incomplete, it seems likely that the Jewish Agency representative who met MI5's cut-out in London was Teddy Kollek, later a long-standing and celebrated mayor of Jerusalem, who during the war had become the deputy head of the Jewish Agency's intelligence department. From January 1945 to May 1946, Kollek was the Agency's chief external officer in Jerusalem, and was in regular touch with MI5's DSO Palestine, Henry Hunloke, and SIME, to whom he gave intelligence on 'intended terrorist activities'. Kollek is known to have provided MI5 with counter-terrorist intelligence in Palestine: for example, in August 1945 he revealed the location of a secret

Irgun training camp near Binyamina, and told an MI5 officer that 'it would be a great idea to raid the place'. The information he provided led to the arrest of twenty-seven Irgun fighters, including the father of a later Israeli cabinet minister.[46]

Some of the meetings held in March 1947 between the Jewish Agency official – probably Kollek – and MI5's cut-out, Scorpion, took place in London's finest restaurants. One was over a lavish meal of 'oysters, duck and petit pots de crème au chocolat', while another featured gin and 'rich red roast beef'. The meetings did produce some intelligence on Irgun and Stern Gang fighters suspected of being about to leave Palestine, whose names MI5 placed on 'watch lists' at British ports and airports. Despite the value of this information, one MI5 officer could not help noting that his mouth started to water when he read Scorpion's reports. After all, this was a time when, in Austerity Britain, bread rationing was in place.[47]

THE DYNAMITE MAN

Despite all of MI5's counter-terrorist efforts, it failed to detect some Irgun and Stern Gang operatives in Britain. The Stern Gang cell primarily targeting Britain was based in France, and was led by Yaacov Eliav, who was born in Russia, arrived in Palestine in 1917 and joined the Stern Gang in 1935. Eliav was responsible, in his own words, for having 'invented the letter bomb', and was later known as the 'Dynamite Man' on account of his skill at handling explosives. It was he who was responsible for posting the waves of letter bombs from Italy, whose targets were members of the British cabinet and other figures closely associated with Palestine. Eliav would later deny that he was ever a terrorist, and after the creation of Israel in 1948 would put his knowledge of explosives to use within the Israeli Defence Force, rising high in one of its counter-terrorist units. In the process, he showed a spectacular inability to comprehend that those underground groups that he labelled terrorist organisations, such as the Palestine Liberation Organisation, regarded themselves as freedom fighters just as he had before 1948.[48]

From his base in Paris in 1946, working under the *nom de guerre* 'Yashka', Eliav recruited at least two operatives to smuggle explosives into Britain. The first of them, Jacques Martinsky, a former member of the French resistance who had lost a leg in the war, devised a brilliant ploy to smuggle explosives into Britain, concealing a cache of gelignite inside his artificial leg. However, when he attempted to get through London airport on 6 March 1947 he was turned back on account of not being able to show good reason for entry into Britain. With this plan thwarted, Eliav dreamt up another plot. He used another of his agents, Robert Misrahi, a student at the Sorbonne and a protégé of Jean-Paul Sartre, to smuggle explosives into Britain in what Eliav termed an 'explosive coat' with dynamite hidden in its shoulder pads and other compartments. Misrahi slipped through British customs sometime in the spring of 1947, and it does not appear that MI5 ever detected his presence. It was Misrahi who left the bomb that exploded at the Colonial Club on 8 March, and he may also have contributed dynamite to the enormous bomb left at the Colonial Office on 17 April 1947.[49]

The bomb deposited at the Colonial Office, which failed to go off because its timer broke, was the climax of a terrorist operation conducted by a young female Irgun operative, Betty Knout (or Knouth). She was the daughter of a well-known Jewish writer in Paris, David Knout, an ardent 'Revisionist' Zionist and disciple of Vladimir Jabotinsky, the founding father of 'Revisionist' Zionism. Eliav selected and recruited her for his main operation in Britain, correctly guessing that women were less likely to attract attention and be searched at British border inspections than men. Knout successfully slipped through British customs on 14 or 15 April 1947, and began surveillance on her target from a small hotel room she rented in Paddington. Early on the morning of 17 April she checked out of her hotel wearing a smart suit and an expensive coat, and went to Victoria station, where she deposited her belongings. Her plan was to get out of the country as soon as she left the bomb. She then went to the Colonial Office in Whitehall, where, as planned, she politely asked the security guard at the front desk if she could use the toilet. At first he refused, but she won him over and proceeded to a downstairs toilet, where she left the bomb, consisting of twenty-four sticks of explosives wrapped in copies of the *Evening Standard* and *Daily Telegraph*. She then calmly walked out of the building, politely thanking the security guard on her way, and slipped into the crowds outside. She headed straight to Victoria station, took a train to the south coast, from where she caught a ferry to Belgium, where she met another operative, Jaakov Elias, at a prearranged rendezvous.[50]

The bomb at the Colonial Office was found by a cleaner, leading to a Europe-wide hunt for the culprit. To start with, it appears that neither Special Branch, nor MI5 or SIS, had any significant leads. However, their luck changed on 2 June 1947 when Belgian police, who had been placed on alert by MI5, detained Knout and Elias for acting suspiciously at a border checkpoint while attempting to cross from Belgium into France. A search of their possessions revealed envelopes addressed to a number of British officials, including Sir John Shaw, as well as detonators, batteries and a time fuse. The head of Special Branch, Commander Leonard Burt, travelled to Belgium and sent Knout's fingerprints back to London, where they were quickly found to match those on the bomb at the Colonial Office. When she was arrested in Belgium, Knout was wearing the same expensive suit and carrying a distinctive handbag that matched the description of the young woman who left the bomb in London. 'Elias's' fingerprints identified him as Yaacov Levstein, a well-known fighter in Palestine, who had been sentenced to life imprisonment in 1942 but had escaped. The Belgian authorities, working closely with MI5 and Special Branch, sentenced Knout to a year's imprisonment and Elias to eight months. Later, at a press conference in Tel Aviv, Knout expressed regret that she had been unable to fulfil her mission of posting the letter bombs in her possession.[51]

Another operative run by Eliav was Yaakov Heruti, whose mission in 1947 was to use his cover of studying at London University to open a 'second front' in Britain. As with Betty Knout, Elias provided Heruti with logistical support and the names of local sympathisers in London, and it appears that he was undetected by MI5 as a Stern Gang operative for the duration of his time in Britain, from October 1947 until May 1948. Heruti, who went on to become a lawyer and right-wing activist in Israel, describes in detail in his recently-published Hebrew-language memoirs how he recruited a number of Jewish sympathisers in Britain to his 'cell'. His base of operations was a small basement flat in a Yiddish-speaking area in Whitechapel, East London. He received funds from a wealthy Jewish individual in North London, whose name he does not reveal, but who reportedly lost many relatives in the Holocaust and was a fanatical 'Revisionist', with a bust of Jabotinsky in his front hall.

The process by which Heruti met his wealthy sponsor was elaborate: through an intermediary, he placed a password on a selected page of the Stern Gang newsletter *Ha-ma'as*, which both men then quoted to each other: 'Thus we reduced the risk of attracting secret agents and those working for the British secret police.' Stern Gang supporters in New York provided Heruti and his cell with explosives, on one occasion smuggling them into Britain inside modified transistor radios. In May 1948, as Britain was pulling out of Palestine, Heruti delivered a deadly book bomb to the family home near Birmingham of a former special forces officer, Major Roy Farran, who had been involved with British covert paramilitary operations in Palestine, where he was controversially acquitted of murdering a young Stern Gang sympathiser in 1947. The bomb, hidden in a copy of Shakespeare's works, was opened by Farran's brother Rex, wholly unconnected with Palestine, who was killed in the explosion. It was so powerful that the loose change in the victim's pockets was blown into the house's garden – though incredibly, the family cat, which was also in the room, somehow survived. Heruti later showed little remorse, noting that the killing 'was a frustrating failure, we were looking for the murderer, not his brother'. In an attempt to escape from possible further attacks by the Stern Gang, Roy Farran moved to Canada, where he hoped to live an anonymous life.However, his old enemies soon discovered his location. Every year for the rest of his life he received a Christmas card from the Stern Gang.[52]

There is strong evidence to suggest that, besides Heruti, other undetected Stern Gang fighters were also operating in Britain. A former Stern Gang member has described how, from 1946 onwards, he ran a 'sleeper cell' in Britain that would be activated if political deadlock occurred over the creation of the state of Israel in 1948. His cell had instructions from its leaders in Palestine to carry out a series of high-level assassinations, targeting the Foreign Secretary, Ernest Bevin, as well as bombing electricity and water supplies. The leaders of this and other cells were Jews from Palestine, but the operatives who would actually carry out the attacks would be local British nationals with Jewish backgrounds who had no connection with extremist Zionist groups, which would have alerted the police and MI5. They were 'clean skins', to use subsequent counter-terrorist terminology. This former Stern Gang member has stated that some of the members of his cell went on to have successful careers in Britain, and no action was ever taken against them. This suggests that they remained unidentified, unless MI5 was playing the 'long game', keeping them in place but under surveillance for as long as possible in order to gain intelligence on them – which is a possibility.[53]

In addition to sleeper cells, there is some evidence that an undetected Stern Gang cell really was planning to assassinate Bevin, just as MI5 feared, in circumstances that could be straight from the pages of Frederick Forsyth's The Day of the Jackal. At least two former members of the Stern Gang operating in London have said that they came extremely close to assassinating Bevin, with their operations only being called off at the last moment in May 1948 by their bosses in Palestine when Britain began withdrawing from the Mandate. Their first plan was simply to shoot Bevin as he was travelling on his usual route to work, 'in a big black car, easily visible from afar, without any escort'. Failing this, they planned to leave explosives along his route. One of the agents even claimed to have planted a bomb disguised as a book under Bevin's seat in the House of Commons while posing as a tourist, but it failed to go off. There is no corroboration of this story in any other source, and on balance it seems that some of the alleged plots against Bevin are spurious, with supposed would-be assassins subsequently romanticising their roles. However, both of the accounts by former Stern Gang agents contain facts that can be substantiated, such as the Gang's robbery of Barclays Bank in Jerusalem in 1947, and therefore they cannot be completely discounted. The reality is that the Irgun and the Stern Gang almost certainly had undetected agents operating in Britain, planning acts of terrorism at the heartland of the empire.[54]

INTERNATIONAL SPONSORS OF TERRORISM

As the terrorist threat intensified, MI5 became increasingly worried about the support shown by foreign groups, and even foreign powers, to the Irgun and the Stern Gang. It did not take much detective work for MI5 to discover that the two groups were receiving technical support from the IRA. One Jewish IRA leader, Robert Briscoe, who was also a member of the Irish parliament, a 'Revisionist' Zionist and a future mayor of Dublin, was known by MI5 to support the Irgun, and in his memoirs he recalled that he assisted them in every way he could. Briscoe, who in his own words 'would do business with Hitler if it was in Ireland's good', made several trips to Britain before the war and met Irgun representatives there. He wrote in his memoirs that he elected himself 'to a full Professorship with the Chair of Subversive Activities against England', and helped the Irgun to organise themselves on 'IRA lines'. In order to enhance the intelligence cooperation on IRA–Irgun–Stern Gang links, in October 1947 MI5 despatched an officer and a Palestine police officer, Major J. O'Sullivan, temporarily in London to brief MI5 on Zionist terrorism, to Dublin. They liaised with the Irish CID, which kept Briscoe under surveillance and passed its findings on to MI5.[55]

The former Chief Rabbi of Ireland, Isaac Herzog, was also an open supporter of both Irish Republican and Zionist terrorism. After his emigration to Palestine in 1936, Herzog rose to arguably the most important position in the Jewish religious world, the Chief Rabbinate of Palestine. MI5's DSO in Palestine and the Palestine police both apparently kept a close watch on Rabbi Herzog's activities. In a manner that encapsulates the tensions that existed between moderates and extremists in both Palestine and Ireland, one of Herzog's sons, Chaim, disapproved of his father's collusion with terrorism. Chaim Herzog served in British military intelligence on D-Day, went on to help establish the Israeli intelligence community, and eventually became President of Israel.[56]

The stance taken by the US government over Palestine, and in particular the position of Jewish Americans, sometimes made it difficult for MI5 to obtain cooperation from US authorities on issues of Zionist terrorism. At the twenty-second Zionist Congress, held in 1943, Chaim Weizmann had castigated American Zionists for advocating 'resistance' in Tel Aviv from the comfort and safety of New York. The growing sense of animosity that many Jewish Americans felt towards Britain after the war was portrayed in a successful play by Ben Hecht, *A Flag is Born*, which opened on Broadway in September 1946. The play was virulently anti-British, and featured an A-list cast, including Paul Muni and the young Marlon Brando. Hecht later wrote an open 'Letter to the Terrorists of Palestine', published in the *New York Times*, in which he claimed:

> Every time you blow up a British arsenal, or wreck a British jail, or send a British railroad sky high, or rob a British bank, or let go with your guns and bombs at British betrayers and invaders of your homeland, the Jews of America make a little holiday in their hearts.[57]

The unambiguous support shown by the US administration towards Zionist aspirations was one of the main factors which led in February 1947 to the British government's decision to hand the entire matter of Palestine over to the United Nations. More specifically, MI5 knew that some extremist Zionist groups operating in the United States, such as the 'Bergson Group' and the 'Hebrew Committee for the Liberation of Palestine', were raising funds and logistical support for the Irgun and the Stern Gang, with explosives and ammunition sometimes being sent in food packages to Britain. MI5 established a useful working relationship with American military (G-2) intelligence in occupied zones of Europe over clandestine Jewish migration to Palestine and Zionist terrorism, but in general the relationship between British and US intelligence over Zionism was difficult. In March 1948 the JIC noted that, although it did not believe there was a significant Zionist element within the recently established CIA, the JIC's reports on Palestine would inevitably be controversial in Washington, and should only be given to the head of the CIA in person, and not left with him. It also advised that other British intelligence reports on Zionist matters should be censored before they were passed on to US authorities. Meanwhile, Operation *Gold*, run by US Navy intelligence, was intercepting cable traffic with Jewish gun-runners, but this was not shared with Britain, nor was it acted upon by Washington.[58]

One of the few ways in which MI5 was able to receive cooperation from the FBI on Zionist matters was by stressing many prominent Zionists' connections with communism and the Soviet Union. MI5 believed that several members of the Irgun and the Stern Gang had made their way to Palestine with the aid of Soviet intelligence. Menachem Begin and Nathan Friedman-Yellin, a leader of the Stern Gang, were both of Polish origin, and MI5 rightly suspected that the Soviets had helped them 'escape' to Palestine during the war. Several Zionist leaders advocated cooperation with the Soviet Union, including the head of 'security' for the Jewish Agency in Palestine, Moshe Sneh, who was aware of if not actively involved with planning the King David Hotel bombing. MI5's suspicions have been confirmed by subsequent research, which shows that on several occasions the Stern Gang appealed to Moscow for aid.[59]

This makes the involvement of Kim Philby in SIS's investigations into Zionist terrorism all the more interesting. Philby's position as head of Section IX in SIS, Soviet counter-intelligence, afforded him a legitimate interest in the Middle East – an interest that he probably also inherited from his father, the noted Arabist Harry St John Philby. During the war St John Philby had unsuccessfully attempted to broker a deal for the partition of Palestine, the so-called 'Philby Plan'. Kim Philby's manipulative agenda in SIS's Zionist investigations is difficult to determine. On 9 July 1946 SIS circulated a report throughout Whitehall advising that the Irgun was planning to take 'murderous action' against the British Legation in Beirut. Almost certainly this was an inaccurate warning of the King David Hotel bombing, which occurred two weeks later. It was Philby who circulated the report. Philby had less motivation for sabotaging British investigations into Zionist terrorism, however, than he did in other fields. He undoubtedly would have secretly welcomed the terrorist campaign waged in the British Mandate of Palestine as undermining the British empire, but when he was working on Zionist affairs for SIS – and by extension for the KGB – immediately after the war, the Soviet Union's policy towards

Palestine had not yet crystallised. Moscow initially supported the creation of the state of Israel, hoping that it would be a thorn in the side of the 'imperialist' West, and the Soviet Union was the first country in the world to recognise Israel when it was established in May 1948. However, Stalin miscalculated: over the coming years, Israel built up a special relationship with the USA, not with the Soviet Union, and Stalin spent the final years before his death in 1953 consumed with anti-Semitic conspiracy theories. By this time Philby was no longer working on Zionist matters for SIS, and therefore not for the KGB either. In the absence of still-closed KGB archives, Philby's precise role in Zionist matters must remain a matter for speculation. Nevertheless, Moscow certainly would have been interested to learn, through him, that London suspected Soviet involvement in Zionist terrorism.[60]

JEWISH 'ILLEGAL' IMMIGRATION

Together with its counter-terrorist operations in Britain, in the immediate post-war years Britain's intelligence services were also assessing and countering Jewish 'illegal' immigration to Palestine. In fact, MI5 and SIS helped to shape the British government's overall response to this immigration. In 1939 a quota system was established which limited the number of Jewish immigrants to Palestine to 7,500 per year. Immigration above that number was termed 'illegal' by the British government. Then as now, 'illegal immigration' was a term fraught with controversy, and a fierce debate about it raged between Zionist politicians and the British government. MI5's role in it was not to debate the moral and legal aspects of Jewish immigration into Palestine, but to produce dispassionate assessments for Whitehall about its security implications. Despite MI5's attempts to formulate cold-hearted and objective judgements, the urgent humanitarian dimensions were inescapable – as reading the reports today, they still are. Reports coming to MI5 from SIME described in detail the desperate condition of Jewish refugees arriving in Palestine, many of whom were survivors of the Holocaust. Britain's attempts to prevent these refugees from entering Palestine led to some horrendous incidents. One of the most notorious occurred in July 1947, when a converted ferry, the *President Warfield*, renamed *Exodus 1947*, which was bringing Jewish refugees to Palestine from France, was boarded by the Royal Navy. This was fiercely resisted by the passengers and crew, leading to three fatalities. The British authorities then controversially transferred the passengers to three deportation ships, and sent many of them back to the British Zone in Germany. When they eventually arrived at the port of Hamburg, some were so weak they had to be carried ashore. The Jewish Agency was quick to spot the propaganda that could be gained from the *Exodus* affair, which soon came to symbolise the overall struggle for Jewish immigration to Palestine (*Aliyah Bet*): the world's press labelled the vessel a 'floating Auschwitz'.[61]

In making its assessments of Jewish 'illegal' immigration to Palestine MI5 worked closely with a range of British and foreign government departments, including the Palestine police and Allied authorities in occupied zones in Europe. In September 1946 it despatched a liaison officer to Europe to impress on local security and police officials the security implications for Britain posed by the clandestine migration of Jewish refugees from Europe to Palestine. MI5 argued that as long as Jewish migration from Europe to Palestine remained unregulated and clandestine, there would be risks of accidents or even fatalities. In a horrendous incident in 1940, elite Palmach commandos of the Haganah had attempted to disable a French liner, the *Patria*, which had carried Jewish refugees to Palestine, but whom the British wished to deport to Mauritius. However, they used too many explosives, with the result that the ship went down in just fifteen minutes, and 250 people drowned.

Based on information provided by Allied authorities in Europe, in August 1946 MI5 estimated that there were probably 350,000 Jewish refugees scattered across Europe as 'Displaced Persons' (DPs). Many of those who had survived the Nazi onslaught, some of whom subsequently faced the Soviet imposition of communism in Eastern Europe, desired to set off to Palestine. MI5 found that while 'illegal' immigration was being organised primarily by the intelligence department of the Haganah (*Mossad le Aliyah Bet*), Allied humanitarian relief agencies, such as the United Nations Relief and Reconstruction Agency, were providing passive support, if not active assistance.[62]

MI5's overall assessment was that mass Jewish immigration to Palestine would almost certainly cause civil war between Jews and Arabs, as it had threatened to do during the 'Arab Revolt' in the 1930s. SIGINT provided by GCHQ revealed the violent opposition in neighbouring Arab states, especially Egypt, to increased Jewish immigration to Palestine – and that those states were prepared to use force to prevent it. The main policy devised by the British authorities to prevent 'illegal' immigration was to intercept refugee ships. Detention centres were established in Cyprus to house intercepted refugees, who were then permitted to enter Palestine through the quota system. This was, however, another public relations disaster for the British government, whose critics accused it of establishing 'Nazi-style concentration camps'. The British also deported some Irgun and Stern fighters to detention centres in Eritrea, which again attracted claims that they were no better than the Nazis. Such criticism sometimes came from surprising quarters, not least from the Assistant Secretary at the Colonial Office, Trafford Smith, who privately minuted his despair:

> The plain truth to which we so firmly shut our eyes is that in this emergency Detention business we are taking a leaf out of the Nazi book, following the familiar error that the end justifies the means (especially when the means serve current expediency). We are out to suppress terrorism, and because we can find no better means we order measures which are intrinsically wrong, and which, since their consequence is evident to the whole world, let us in for a lot of justifiable and unanswerable criticism.[63]

Rather than pursuing the ill-conceived and counter-productive measures of deporting and detaining Jewish refugees, MI5 advised the cabinet and the Chiefs of Staff to concentrate their efforts on preventing 'illegal' immigration 'at source'. With the assistance of SIS, MI5 identified a number of South American and Greek shipping companies that chartered vessels to Jewish refugees, and the Foreign Office was able to exert pressure on these governments to prevent companies registered in their countries from carrying out this practice. In the summer of 1947 the JIC, which had examined the issue of illegal immigration on several occasions in 1946 and 1947, concluded that the measures to stop immigration 'at source' appeared to be having an impact. The overall success of British counter-measures was noted in an MI5 report, which stated that by 1948 'only 1 out of some 30 ships carrying illegal immigrants reached their destination'.[64]

While MI5 made assessments and was involved in defensive measures to counter unrestricted Jewish migration to Palestine, Britain's other intelligence services attempted actively to subvert the flow of migrants. Soon after the end of the war in 1945 the deception planning agency, the LCS (discussed in Chapter 2), now renamed the 'Hollis Committee', devised plans to misdirect ships carrying Jewish refugees bound for Palestine. These plans do not seem to have progressed far, but soon SIS was plotting more elaborate, and violent, operations. In February 1947 it carried out an operation, appropriately codenamed *Embarrass*, for 'direction action'. A small team, mostly comprised of former SOE personnel, was recruited to attach limpet mines to refugee ships and disable them before they could set sail. In the summer of 1947 the team mined five ships in Italian ports – having first checked that no one was on board. Nevertheless, if Operation *Embarrass* had been made public, the fact that its agents were mining boats containing Holocaust survivors would have been disastrous for the British government. In fact, SIS planned to mine the *Exodus 1947*, but was blocked at the last moment. Some SIS officers later remarked that if they had been permitted to carry out 'direct action' on the *Exodus 1947*, the government would have been spared much of the embarrassment of the ensuing incident.[65]

Operation *Embarrass* did not stop there. When some of the mines were discovered, SIS blamed them first on a fictitious Arab opposition group, the 'Defenders of Arab Palestine', and then on the Soviet government. It obtained typewriters that were known to be used by dissident Arab groups and Soviet authorities, and used them to type letters implicating both groups, which it then carefully leaked around Whitehall. In a further twist, SIS made it appear that the British government was using the traffic of Jewish refugees to get its own agents out of Europe, hoping thereby to get the Soviets to block the flow of migrants to Palestine. SIS therefore attempted to deceive not only Jewish refugees, Arab opposition groups and the Soviet government, but the British government itself. This was truly the stuff of smoke and mirrors.[66]

Britain's policy of limiting Jewish immigration to Palestine, both overt and covert, was beset with controversy and resentment. It was, however, symptomatic of a much deeper problem that undermined British rule in Palestine: Britain was faced with a range of contradictory demands regarding the future of the Mandate – from Jews, Arabs and world opinion at large. In early 1946 an Anglo-American committee of inquiry was appointed to find a settlement in Palestine, but despite the best efforts of its members, who in April 1946 recommended that a compromise be found so that Jews should not dominate Arabs in Palestine, nor Arabs dominate Jews, the committee's findings were not accepted by either party. By September 1947 the JIC in London was painting a gloomy picture for the British government of the future of the Mandate, concluding that any settlement would be unacceptable either to Jews or Arabs. Britain found itself in a situation that was rapidly becoming ungovernable. In 1947 100,000 troops – one-tenth of the military manpower of the entire British empire – were tied down in Palestine, a financial burden that London could not afford.[67]

BRITAIN'S INTELLIGENCE FAILURE IN PALESTINE

MI5 had considerably more success in dealing with Zionist terrorism in Britain than either the British military or police achieved in Palestine itself. Palestine was the intelligence war that Britain lost. Scholars such as Bruce Hoffman and David Charters have shown that, despite Britain's overwhelming security presence in Palestine, with effectively one police officer on every street corner in the Mandate, its forces were unable to keep the peace there. The British military had a superiority of about 20:1 over its enemies in Palestine, which was considerably better than in other counter-insurgencies (in Malaya the ratio was 5:1), but nevertheless it was unsuccessful in Palestine and successful in Malaya. This was largely because the British Army in Palestine relied on outmoded counter-insurgency tactics. At the time, the army's counter-insurgency effort – still described as 'imperial policing' – was hardly a doctrine at all, and involved tactics such as sweeping column formations of troops to engage enemies, together with cordons and searches. Such tactics had proved effective in the Arab Revolt before the Second World War, but that had been a predominantly rural insurgency, supported by the majority of the population, in which insurgent troops fought in obvious and clearly distinguishable formations. This was diametrically opposite to the post-war struggle fought by the Irgun and the Stern Gang, who waged their war mainly as an urban insurgency, refusing to fight British forces in open formations, and often disguising themselves and blending into crowds. Unlike the pre-war Arab Revolt, the Irgun and the Stern Gang's insurgency was not supported by the majority of the local population.

The British Chiefs of Staff responded in May 1945, as the war in Europe ended, by sending the tough 6th Airborne Division to Palestine, but their use of outdated, obsolete tactics had disastrous results. Collective punishments, curfews, cordons, searches and martial law had all been effective in the Arab Revolt, which was a mass uprising, but in the post-war years (martial law was declared in Tel Aviv and the Jewish quarter in Jerusalem in March 1947) they caused unnecessary hardship and had the effect of alienating the Jewish population – precisely those people whom the British needed to provide intelligence. Britain's counter-terrorist policy in Palestine thus quickly became counter-productive.[68]

The root cause of the intelligence failure in Palestine was a staggering inability to coordinate intelligence efforts. There was a myriad of British intelligence-gathering agencies operating in the Mandate, from MI5, SIS and GCHQ to the Palestine police and its CID, as well as the British Army's own intelligence department. This large number of outfits, all attempting to gather information, produced little worthwhile intelligence, and were bad at sharing what they did discover. None of them apparently succeeded in penetrating the Irgun or the Stern Gang with well-placed agents. On the one hand this was due to the tightly controlled 'cell' structure of the two groups, but on the other it was caused by poor levels of training and recruitment on the part of British agencies. Neither the Palestine police nor MI5, nor any other British agency, made any significant effort to recruit Hebrew-speakers. The only policeman who succeeded in being integrated into the Stern Gang was identified and executed by them in 1944. Thereafter, it became a policy of the Irgun and the Stern Gang to identify and eliminate counter-terrorist officers in the Palestine CID, MI5 and SIS. Five agents employed locally by MI5 were killed in the King David Hotel, and in September 1946 Stern Gang assailants killed an SIS officer stationed in Palestine, Major Doran, by throwing a grenade onto his balcony. Years later, Menachem Begin could legitimately gloat that he had won the 'clash of brains' against the British in Palestine.[69]

With poor levels of operational intelligence, British forces increasingly turned to violence. Some officials subjected Irgun and Stern Gang prisoners to physical and psychological torture during interrogations. However, there is no substantiated evidence for the allegation that Maurice Oldfield, a future Chief of SIS, then working in British military (army) intelligence, 'talked cheerfully about beating them up and pushing people's heads under buckets of water' – a picture that certainly does not fit with Oldfield's well-documented character as a quiet, ascetic type, a skilled medieval scholar more at home in an Oxford library than in a violent shooting war, who was probably the model for John le Carré's famous character George Smiley. While some of the 'third degree' measures that British officials inflicted on Irgun and Stern Gang prisoners may have been a result of poor training, revenge for attacks on colleagues or sheer vindictiveness, there was a much more structural and systemic problem in Britain's counter-insurgency effort in Palestine that bred uncontrolled violence. This was the operation of undercover British paramilitary forces.

In February 1947, Brigadier Bernard Fergusson, a senior police officer in Palestine, who had served with General Orde Wingate behind enemy lines in Burma, pioneered a new type of paramilitary unit to fight the Irgun and the Stern Gang on their own terms. The unit was largely comprised of former SAS and SOE personnel, and their tactic was to pose as members of the Irgun and the Stern Gang, gather intelligence on them, and then arrest or eliminate them. The unit referred to their operations as 'Q-Patrols', derived from the name given to disguised merchant ships that had sunk German U-boats in the First World War. One of the undercover squads was led by Major Roy Farran, who selected men 'with Jewish looks', who after sunbathing for several weeks to darken their skin could pose as members of the terrorist organisations.[70]

Many of the operations of Farran's undercover unit remain murky. However, in May 1947 he was implicated in the murder of a sixteen-year-old Jewish Stern Gang supporter, Alexander Rubowitz, who was abducted in a taxi and never seen again. There was a large amount of circumstantial evidence that Farran was involved – his hat was found at the scene – and he subsequently even signed a confession that he had committed the crime. Despite the evidence against him, a local court acquitted him on all counts. When the verdict was announced, there was an outcry in Palestine. The Stern Gang vowed to hunt Farran down and kill him, eventually sending the letter bomb to his home in England that killed his brother. The case was a public-relations disaster for the British administration in Palestine, with many people unsurprisingly believing there had been a cover-up. A recent study has reached the same conclusion. The case certainly stank of a cover-up, but in fact on a narrow point of law there were grounds for Farran's acquittal: the confession he signed was not administered under oath, and it was not clear what pressure he was under when he signed it; and Rubowitz's body was never found, which made it difficult, if not impossible, to prove that he had been murdered. Such narrow points, however, did little to impress the Jewish community in Palestine. The verdict fuelled their discontent with the British administration.[71]

The Rubowitz case had implications that went far beyond the personal tragedies of the murder of a Jewish youth in Palestine and the revenge killing of Farran's brother in England. The types of paramilitary operations that Farran was engaged in were actually a catalyst for escalating violence. Paramilitary units like his were a recipe for disaster in terms of feuds, revenge attacks and extra-judicial killings of insurgents and suspects who almost certainly could have been dealt with through conventional military operations or in the courts. As we shall see, British forces deployed similar types of 'pseudo-gangs' and 'snatch squads' to fight dirty end-of-empire wars in a number of other insurgencies, in Malaya, Kenya and Cyprus. Supporters of such paramilitary units argue that they provided a crucial way of fighting insurgencies, but the reality was that, cut off from centralised oversight, they had unrestricted power to abuse prisoners and administer extra-judicial 'justice'. Undercover squads led to uncontrolled violence.[72]

Terrorism was one of the reasons the British government decided in September 1947 to relinquish control of Palestine – though it was not the only reason, as some Irgun and Stern Gang members subsequently claimed. The uncomfortable lesson that other later militant groups drew from the story of Palestine was that terrorism could force governments to change their policies. Public opinion in Britain towards the Mandate was undermined by events such as the Irgun's brutal revenge killing of two British sergeants, Cliff Martin and Mervyn Paice, near Nathanya in July 1947. Their bodies, which were found hanging from a tree in a eucalyptus grove, had been booby-trapped, and another soldier was badly injured as they were recovered. British anger at the execution of the two sergeants soon boiled over: a grenade was thrown from a police armoured car into a crowded café in Tel Aviv, killing four Jews; another police armoured car was driven through a Jewish funeral procession; and the police opened fire on a crowded bus and taxi rank.

Palestine thus became embroiled in a depressing circle of violence and counter-violence: when British soldiers flogged Jews, the Irgun captured British officials and repaid them in kind; when the British Army were faced with booby traps and electronically detonated roadside mines they evacuated civilians, only to be mocked for cowardice. Some British officials knew it was time to leave when they found their animosity towards Zionist terrorists was extending to Jews in general – just as many Israelis would later suspect all Arabs of terrorism. As one colonial official, Ivan Lloyd Phillips, noted: 'It's quite time I left Palestine. I never had any sympathy with Zionist aspirations, but now I'm fast becoming anti-Jewish in my whole approach to this difficult problem & view matters objectively with a growing (and very real feeling) of personal antipathy.'[73]

In February 1947 the British government decided to hand the entire matter of Palestine over to the UN, and on 14 May 1948 Britain formally began to withdraw from the Mandate. At a press conference on the final day of British rule, the Chief Secretary of the British Administration, Sir Henry Gurney, was asked: 'And to whom do you intend to leave the keys to your office?', to which he replied, 'To nobody. I shall leave them under the mat.' Although the story is probably apocryphal, it perfectly encapsulates Britain's ignominious retreat from Palestine. The final British High Commissioner in Palestine, Sir Alan Cunningham, made an undignified exit amid scenes of escalating violence, driving from Jerusalem in an armour-plated Rolls-Royce Daimler equipped with inch-thick bulletproof glass, which had originally been built for King George VI in the Blitz.[74]

Even as British officials were withdrawing, MI5's worst fears about security in Palestine were realised: spurred on by unrestricted Jewish immigration, open warfare broke out between Jews and Arabs. The 1948 Arab–Israeli war, known to Israelis as the 'War of Independence' and to Arabs as *al-Nakbah*, the disaster, led to an enormous refugee crisis. In the words of Menachem Begin: 'The British officials prophesied that on their departure there would be war between Arabs and Jews. They guessed rightly.' Arab fighters mutilated Jewish bodies, exhibiting handfuls of severed fingers and parading decapitated bodies around the Holy City. In the village of Deir Yassin on 9 April 1948 the Irgun and the Stern Gang murdered more than 250 Arab civilians. Even Israel's first Prime Minister, David Ben-Gurion, spoke of an 'ethnic clean-out'. Towards the end of 1948 the UN voted for the partition of Palestine. The result was that Israel, strongly supported by the US government, became a Jewish state and not just a homeland for Jews. The consequences haunt Palestinians to the present day. All told, some 750,000 Arabs fled or were expelled from the new state of Israel.[75]

Contrary to expectations, Irgun and Stern Gang activities against the British did not cease when Britain formally withdrew from Palestine. The Stern Gang bomb directed at Roy Farran in England, which killed his innocent brother, occurred in early May 1948, as Britain was preparing to leave the Mandate. In October that year MI5 received reliable intelligence that following the Stern Gang's assassination of the UN envoy in Palestine, Count Folke Bernadotte, it was planning to send assassination squads to Paris to murder members of the UN General Assembly whom they considered to have 'sold out' for minimalist Zionist aspirations. As late as 1952, Menachem Begin was involved in a plot to assassinate West Germany's first post-war Chancellor, Konrad Adenauer, with a book bomb, over German reparations for Nazi war crimes. Ultimately, it was left to Israel to deal with the Irgun and the Stern Gang. After 1948 the Israeli state inherited many of the security concerns, and adopted many of the same security procedures, which the British had previously faced and devised in Palestine. Some of the British 'emergency regulations' have remained unchanged on the Israeli statute books, and have frequently been invoked as a basis for Israeli destruction of property, collective punishment, and the confiscation of land on the Gaza Strip and the West Bank.[76]

4

The Empire Strikes Back:
The British Secret State and Imperial
Security in the Early Cold War

The road to victory of the Revolution in the West lies through revolutionary alliance with the liberation movements of the colonies and dependent territories against Imperialism.

JOSEPH STALIN[1]

British decolonisation, unlike that of its main imperial rival, France, began in time for an orderly withdrawal from empire. One of the most important ways in which British governments prepared for, and smoothed, the end of colonial rule was with intelligence. In the years immediately after 1945, as Western relations with the Soviet Union deteriorated, the British secret state, particularly MI5, embarked on an enormous project to reform British colonial security to meet the needs of the growing Cold War. Over the next two decades MI5 officers helped to reform local security, train colonial intelligence officials, and posted Security Liaison Officers (SLOs) to every major British colony and dependency that gained independence in the post-war years. Without significant exception, these SLOs were asked by new national governments to remain in place after independence, and liaised closely with those new governments. In several cases, intelligence matters actually shaped the politics of decolonisation.

To appreciate the relationship between the escalation of the Cold War, on the one hand, and the decline of Britain's empire on the other, it is crucial to understand how pivotal the years 1947 and 1948 were for geopolitical strategic considerations. These two years witnessed the rapid development of the Cold War struggle between the West and the Soviet Union, and also the first significant erosion of Britain's imperial power, as its empire in Asia fell apart. 1947 saw the breakdown of a meeting of Western and Soviet Foreign Ministers held in Moscow, an event that clearly revealed a chill in relations between Moscow and the West. The same year also witnessed Britain's decision to build its own nuclear weapon ('with a bloody Union Jack on top of it', as Foreign Secretary Ernest Bevin thundered); Stalin's decision to establish a new Communist International, Cominform, to replace the Comintern, which he had nominally disbanded during the war; and the development of the US doctrine of 'containing' worldwide communism, if necessary by force, first enunciated by the US ambassador in Moscow, George Kennan, and subsequently put into practice by Washington's twin policies for containment and the reconstruction of post-war Europe, the Truman Doctrine and the Marshall Plan. In 1948 came the communist takeover of Czechoslovakia; the famous airlift conducted by British, French and US forces to the Soviet-blockaded city of Berlin; and the development of collective security treaties in Europe and the Soviet Union that would divide the world into two armed camps, enforced in 1949 through the Warsaw Pact and the North Atlantic Treaty Organisation (NATO).

At the same time, 1947 and 1948 saw a momentous decline in Britain's standing as an imperial power, as it lost the jewel in its imperial crown, India – including Burma and Ceylon. This, combined with the decision to evacuate Palestine, was without precedent: there had never before been a devolution of power to an entire subcontinent. Three-quarters of all of the British empire's subjects were removed with the loss of the Raj, which took place at midnight on 14–15 August 1947, with 'the stroke of a pen in the twinkling of an eye', as the secret Indian intelligence outfit in London, IPI, phrased it. Churchill termed Britain's disorganised evacuation from India 'Operation Scuttle'.

Although it is tempting to view Indian independence as heralding 'the end of the British empire', it would be inaccurate to do so: at the time, even the most fierce anti-colonial movements, for example in colonies like the Gold Coast (present-day Ghana), were not campaigning for total independence from Britain, but for 'self-government', meaning greater control over their own affairs. It is crucial to appreciate that the British government never formulated an overall plan for how to relinquish control of its colonies: it was not a predetermined policy, conducted as a kind of inevitable march towards decline, with Britain destined to have the status of a small nation. Instead, in the two decades after 1945, the British Colonial Office – particularly under the two great 'liquidators of empire', Iain Macleod and Duncan Sandys – and colonial governments themselves formed pragmatic responses to events that were often totally outside their control. Far from being a process carefully worked out in Whitehall and the capitals of British colonies, decolonisation was actually a story of crisis management for British officials. Britain's secret agencies were able to provide policy-makers, lurching from one anti-colonial crisis to another, with valuable information on the situations they faced.

One issue more than any other coloured Whitehall's discussions on these momentous events: the fear that if Britain withdrew too rapidly from its colonies a power vacuum would be created, into which the Soviet Union would rapidly move. Britain and other Western governments feared that as the Cold War deepened, the Soviet Union would exert influence over those countries gaining independence from Britain, and the red on British imperial maps would be replaced by the red of communism – a fear that was enhanced with the communist takeover of China in 1949 and the outbreak of the Korean War in 1950. This fear was articulated by the British Chiefs of Staff in the summer of 1946, as they discussed the impending relinquishment of power in India. Thereafter, it became a recurring theme.[2]

Ever since the Bolshevik Revolution in 1917, the Soviet Union had posed a strategic threat to the British empire. As we have seen, Lenin famously declared that imperialism was the highest form of capitalism. It was therefore logical that communists would attempt to smite British colonial rule, one of the most obvious manifestations of Western 'capitalism' and 'imperialism', and Stalin proclaimed that the Soviet Union's road to victory in the West lay in undermining and attacking colonial rule. Lenin and Stalin regarded colonies as the soft underbelly of imperialism, an easy target and an ideal base from which to export the worldwide workers' revolution.

Britain's fears were undoubtedly heightened by the background of the members of its intelligence services, which as we saw in Chapter 1 were largely comprised of officers who had begun their careers in the empire, particularly in India, where notions of the nineteenth-century 'Great Game' with Russia died hard. In fact, there had effectively been a 'cold war' between Britain and the Soviet Union in the decades after 1917. When seen from this perspective, Britain's post-war struggle with Soviet Russia was part of a much longer-term conflict in the twentieth century, which was interrupted by the Second World War. In many ways, the Cold War was thus a return to pre-war concerns for Britain. After 1945 the task facing the British government and its allies was to fight 'new' forms of Soviet subversion by strengthening vulnerable vestiges of old colonialism. The broad strategic fears about the threat posed to Britain by the Soviet Union were confirmed in 1939, when one of the main NKVD (KGB) officers in Europe, Walter Krivitsky, defected to the West. In a series of top-secret meetings held with MI5 and SIS in London in early 1940, Krivitsky explained that it was Moscow's deliberate policy to target and support anti-colonial 'liberation' movements in the British empire, and that the KGB, to use its own terminology, pursued 'active measures' to free colonial peoples from the shackles of Western imperial rule. It was in this context, within an escalating Cold War, that Britain's intelligence services played a major role in Britain's withdrawal from its colonial holdings: they were better placed than any other government department to assess the threat posed by communism in colonies seeking independence from Britain.[3]

SPY SCANDALS: THE COLD WAR SETS IN FOR BRITAIN

In Britain itself, the onset of the Cold War was revealed through a series of spy scares. These scandals, which exposed Soviet agents at the heart of the British secret establishment, had a dramatic impact on domestic security arrangements, as well as those across the empire. As we saw in Chapter 2, the event that really started the Cold War was the defection of the Soviet cypher clerk Igor Gouzenko in Canada in September 1945. The information he provided revealed that the British atomic scientist Dr Alan Nunn May, who had worked on the Manhattan Project, the top-secret Allied wartime project to build the world's first nuclear weapon at Los Alamos, New Mexico, had spied for Soviet intelligence. The revelation dropped like a bombshell on Western governments and their intelligence agencies, and on MI5 in particular, which had been responsible for vetting Nunn May during the war.[4]

Following Nunn May's identification, MI5 launched an intensive investigation into him, which at one point in October 1945 involved officers waiting for him to appear at a scheduled rendezvous with his Soviet controller outside the British Museum. However, Nunn May never appeared, almost certainly because Kim Philby, who knew of MI5's surveillance because of his position in Section IX in SIS, had warned him not to proceed with the meeting. As a last resort, in February 1950 MI5 sent in its ace interrogator and spy-catcher, William 'Jim' Skardon, a former Special Branch officer and handwriting expert, who had a remarkable ability to get even the most recalcitrant subject to talk. His tactics with Nunn May were a mixture of befriending the scientist, gaining his trust and confidence, and bluffing, telling him that the evidence against him was overwhelming and that he should 'make a clean breast' and confess his guilt. In reality, as Skardon knew, without a confession from Nunn May, MI5 lacked sufficient evidence to prosecute him. On 20 February 1946 Nunn May made a full confession of his Soviet espionage, and was later prosecuted and sentenced to ten years' imprisonment for breaking the Official Secrets Act (1921).[5]

Much worse was to follow for British intelligence. Towards the end of the war, US military code-breakers (assisted by their colleagues at GC&CS) had begun to break a series of high-grade Soviet communications passing between North America and Moscow, which the US and British governments codenamed 'Venona'. The Venona decrypts, in total nearly 3,000 Soviet diplomatic communications, revealed shocking levels of Soviet penetration on both sides of the Atlantic. They disclosed that over two hundred Americans had worked for Soviet intelligence during the war and after it, and that every department of Franklin D. Roosevelt's wartime administration had been penetrated by Soviet agents. Venona was probably the greatest single source of information for Western governments on Soviet espionage in the entire Cold War – so sensitive that its existence was only made public in 1995, after the fall of the Soviet Union. Some of the Soviet agents referred to in the Venona decrypts have never been identified.[6]

In the United States, information provided by Venona was sometimes used in highly controversial ways, as in the notorious case led by the FBI against Julius and Ethel Rosenberg, who were tried, prosecuted and executed for Soviet espionage in 1953. Although the FBI could not reveal it at the time, much of its information against the Rosenbergs came from Venona, which provided conclusive evidence of their espionage – but did not justify their execution by electric chair at Sing Sing prison. Some eyewitnesses reported that Ethel Rosenberg only died after repeated electric shocks, with smoke rising from her head.[7]

One of the most important Soviet agents revealed by Venona was codenamed 'Charles'. He was identified in September 1949 as having worked on the Manhattan Project. Just like the British spy Alan Nunn May, he had passed vital intelligence to his Soviet controllers on how to build a nuclear bomb, including 'complete technical drawings' and calculations. By a process of carefully compiling circumstantial evidence about agent Charles within the Venona decrypts, MI5 identified him as a German émigré scientist, Dr Klaus Fuchs. Fuchs had been responsible for many of the theoretical calculations on the Manhattan Project concerning atomic fission and the 'implosion method' used in a plutonium bomb. Unfortunately for MI5, it had given him a clean bill of health during the war, vetting and clearing him before he gained access to Britain's atomic project, codenamed the Tube Alloys Project, and then for the much more substantial Manhattan Project. Contemporary MI5 records reveal that some of the officers responsible for vetting Fuchs, in MI5's C-Division, had been sceptical about his loyalties, but that the evidence they had on file against him was fragmentary – testimony to the insufficiency of its process of 'negative vetting' for Soviet counter-espionage. To make matters worse, after the war MI5 had again cleared Fuchs for top-secret work, this time at Britain's nuclear research establishment at Harwell in Oxfordshire, where he was working when Venona exposed him. Although it is probably an exaggeration to call Fuchs 'the man who gave the bomb to the Soviet Union', as did the head of the FBI, J. Edgar Hoover, and some of the British press when the case went public, it was undoubtedly true that Soviet atomic scientists made great use of technical information provided by him, chiefly by using it to corroborate their own ongoing research.[8]

The problem for MI5 was that it could not produce Venona as evidence against Fuchs in court. As is still the case today, SIGINT intercept material was not permissible evidence in English courts, which meant that MI5 had either to catch Fuchs in the act of espionage, or gain a confession from him. B-Division within MI5 launched an intensive investigation into him, which revealed little more than a possible affair with the wife of another leading scientist at Harwell, Herbert Skinner, and the fact that Fuchs was a bad driver. The reason MI5's surveillance failed to produce any evidence of espionage was, as Fuchs later admitted, that by this time he had given up his espionage activities for Soviet intelligence. With a growing sense of despair, in December 1949 MI5 once again decided to send in its ace interrogator, Jim Skardon. He skilfully befriended Fuchs in a series of informal interviews at Harwell, sometimes conducted over lunch in nearby pubs, during the course of which he tricked the scientist into confessing his guilt. Skardon let Fuchs believe that if he confessed he would still be able to hold a teaching post at a university, even though Skardon knew this was not the case.[9]

Fuchs signed a full confession on 24 January 1950, 'under considerable mental pressure', and was prosecuted for breaking the Official Secrets Act 1921. In proceedings that took just ninety minutes, the judge hearing the case in camera at the Old Bailey, Lord Goddard, sentenced him to the maximum possible term of imprisonment, fourteen years. The atmosphere of paranoia in Britain surrounding the Fuchs case was captured in a contemporary film by the Boulting brothers, *Seven Days to Noon* (1950), which depicted a Special Branch officer, loosely modelled on Skardon, frantically attempting to hunt down a crazed nuclear scientist. Fuchs was released from prison for good behaviour in 1959, and moved to East Germany, where he received the Order of Merit of the Fatherland and continued his nuclear research until his death in 1988.[10]

The Fuchs case was not the last to expose the shortcomings of British intelligence. In the late 1940s Venona revealed a Soviet agent, codenamed 'Homer', operating in the upper echelons of the British government. By a process of careful elimination based on details provided by Venona, in April 1951 MI5 eventually identified 'Homer' as Donald Maclean, a high-flying Cambridge graduate working in the Foreign Office. This was the first step that eventually led to the exposure of the ring of five 'Cambridge spies' who had penetrated the British secret state during the war. The year 1951 became an *annus horribilis* for British intelligence, during which Whitehall faced the worst cases of Soviet penetration into Britain in the entire twentieth century. In May of that year, Maclean and his fellow Cambridge agent Guy Burgess dramatically defected to the Soviet Union, leaving behind them a trail of destruction, and clues pointing to their fellow spies. Suspicion was soon cast on their close Cambridge friend Anthony Blunt, who had served in MI5 during the war, working for a time as assistant to the Director of MI5's B-Division, Guy Liddell, whose diary often features Blunt 'popping in' and out of his office, doubtless obtaining information that he relayed to his Soviet controllers.

Blunt was the epitome of the English Establishment: a Fellow of Trinity College, Cambridge, a brilliant art historian, Director of the Courtauld Art Institute in London, and the Surveyor of the King's Pictures. Beginning in 1951 MI5 conducted a long investigation into him, but he refused to confess, which meant that MI5 once again lacked sufficient evidence to prosecute. In 1963 MI5's suspicions against Blunt were confirmed by an American communist, Michael Straight, who had known him while studying at Trinity College, and the following year Blunt – by then Sir Anthony – confessed his guilt. He was given immunity from prosecution in return for his cooperation with MI5's further counter-espionage investigations. Over a decade later, the journalist Andrew Boyle publicly exposed him as a Soviet agent in his book *Climate of Treason* (1979), a fact that was subsequently confirmed by Margaret Thatcher in the House of Commons, whereupon Blunt was stripped of his honours. In his memoir, which was only publicly released in July 2009, twenty-six years after his death, Blunt described his espionage for the Soviet Union as the 'biggest mistake' of his life, and said that after his exposure he considered suicide on several occasions.[11]

Following Burgess and Maclean's defection, suspicion was soon cast on their close Cambridge friend, Kim Philby. At that time Philby was the SIS head of station in Washington DC, responsible for liaising with the CIA, and was being widely tipped within SIS as a future Chief of the service. Philby was immediately recalled to London and interrogated by SIS and MI5, but knowing that he could not be prosecuted without a self-incriminating confession, he declined to provide one. He also used his speech impediment, a stammer, to break up the tempo of his interrogations and unsettle his interrogators, who included MI5's legal adviser, Helenus 'Buster' Milmo, a barrister who acquired his nickname from his ability to 'bust' a confession from those he cross-examined. Philby resigned from SIS in 1951, and took up a career as a journalist in the Middle East, writing for the *Economist* and the *Observer*, though it is possible that he continued to work informally for the service. He eventually defected to the Soviet Union from Beirut in 1963, leaving another trail of destruction and suspicion in his wake.

The identity of the suspected missing 'fifth man' in the Cambridge spy network confused, and at times tormented, British intelligence for over three decades after Maclean and Burgess's defection. In 1987, in the so-called '*Spycatcher* affair', a group of disruptive conspiracy theorists, led by the renegade former MI5 officer Peter Wright and the journalist Chapman Pincher, would accuse – among others – a Director-General of MI5, Roger Hollis, of being the missing 'fifth man'. However, there is no evidence to support this claim in Soviet archives viewed without restriction by two KGB defectors to the West, Oleg Gordievsky and Vasili Mitrokhin, or in those seen by Soviet military intelligence (GRU) defectors. The true identity of the fifth Cambridge agent was in fact revealed in 1990 by Gordievsky to be John Cairncross, another graduate of Trinity College, who had been recruited by the KGB in the 1930s. Cairncross joined the Foreign Office before the war, and during it he worked in SIS and at Bletchley Park. From there he betrayed voluminous amounts of top-secret information to the Soviet Union, including the Ultra secret, as well as the Allies' greatest wartime secret, the Manhattan Project. Cairncross, the least publicised of the Cambridge spies, was actually one of the most damaging agents in the Soviet network.[12]

THE 'SPECIAL RELATIONSHIP'

These dramatic spy scandals had a profound impact on international relations, leading not only to a chill in those between Western governments and the Soviet Union, but also producing a serious deterioration in those between Western governments themselves, especially between London and Washington. The exposure of the Cambridge spies was a low point in the history of British intelligence, and the 1950s was a period known as 'the horrors' within SIS. The so-called 'special relationship' between the British and US governments, which involved an unprecedented sharing of intelligence in peacetime, was stretched to breaking point.

One of the areas of closest collaboration between London and Washington was SIGINT. After the establishment in 1952 of the US government's SIGINT agency, the National Security Agency (NSA), Britain's SIGINT agency, GCHQ, as GC&CS was renamed after 1945, received significant funding from it. The close cooperation between the NSA and GCHQ allegedly arose in part because it was illegal for the NSA to intercept the communications of US citizens and businesses, but no such prohibition existed for GCHQ, which meant that the NSA could receive intercepted US communications from GCHQ without breaking US law. The NSA established its own stations in Britain, for example at Chicksands in Bedfordshire, and by the early 1950s all of the British and American intelligence services were swapping liaison officers. Some former GCHQ officers recalled that in the Cold War (and apparently still today) there was a special section within NSA's headquarters in Maryland, Virginia, which housed GCHQ staff, something unique within intelligence liaison between Western allies in the Cold War – it was even furnished with a royal emblem over its doorway, a small bit of Britain at the heart of US intelligence. The intelligence relationship between Washington and London was reinforced by the fact that many leading American intelligence officers had begun their careers serving in the wartime OSS, and spoke of their British colleagues from those days with a degree of reverence. The OSS officer posted in London to liaise with British intelligence, Ernest Cuneo, later candidly remarked: 'The British taught us everything we knew but not everything *they* knew.' Despite the extraordinarily close cooperation that would develop between London and Washington in the years just after 1945, as the Cold War set in, the intelligence relationship between the two capitals started out as far less close, or special, than its subsequent promoters portrayed. Significantly, in 1946 the first permanent MI5 liaison officer stationed in Washington, Richard 'Thistle' Thistlethwaite, and his successor Geoffrey Patterson, did not have unrestricted access to the FBI, as their opposite numbers did to MI5 in London.[13]

The idea of the special relationship was constructed in the 1950s, most importantly by Churchill after his election as Prime Minister in October 1951, largely to cover over the cracks that had occurred in Washington and London's relationship in the immediate post-war years. Churchill also developed the notion in order to enhance Britain's standing in the world, which was declining by the mid-1950s. Far from being close partners in the immediate post-war years, actually the intelligence link between London and Washington almost completely broke down. In the wake of the Gouzenko defection in September 1945, and the subsequent revelation that Alan Nunn May had been involved in espionage, the United States took the dramatic step, with the McMahon Act of 1946, of making it illegal for any US government department to share atomic intelligence with any foreign power. The McMahon Act caused panic in Whitehall, and the US administration explained to British intelligence officials in no uncertain terms that the sharing of atomic intelligence would not be resumed until Britain had enhanced security standards in its most sensitive departments. The British government embarked on a process of overhauling its entire security apparatus, the onus for doing which fell squarely on the shoulders of MI5.[14]

In May 1947, as a direct result of pressure from Washington, Prime Minister Clement Attlee established a top-secret 'committee on subversive activities', known simply as GEN-183 after its Cabinet Office designation. The committee, comprised of a select number of cabinet ministers, top civil servants, and MI5's new Director-General, Sir Percy Sillitoe, was designed to deal with the issue of the penetration of subversives into sensitive departments within the British government – the committee always referred to 'subversives', even though its sights were in fact focused squarely on communists, not on subversives generally. One of the primary concerns of the committee was whether 'positive vetting' (meaning active investigation into an individual) should be introduced into background checks for posts in secret departments, as Washington recommended. Contrary to what we might assume, the main opposition to the introduction of positive vetting came from MI5, not from the committee itself: Attlee's Labour government showed itself to be far more hawkish about expanded security checks than MI5. A curious situation thus arose whereby a socialist Labour government, which was traditionally hostile to the idea of a 'police state', was advocating increased and intrusive surveillance, while a clandestine service was arguing against it.

The reason for MI5's resistance to positive vetting was purely down to practicalities: it lacked the resources to carry it out. As Sillitoe told the GEN-183 committee, in a perfect world MI5 would be the first to recommend positive vetting for all applicants to sensitive government posts as the most effective way of safeguarding national secrets. However, the reality was that MI5 had so few staff and such meagre resources at its disposal – it had under a hundred officers in 1947 – that if positive vetting were enacted, all of its other investigations would simply grind to a halt, and it would become little more than a vetting agency.

As a result of MI5's resistance, the GEN-183 committee decided that the only option was to stumble forward with negative vetting, and hope that MI5's records were sufficient to detect Soviet agents. In the post-war years MI5's Registry contained 250,000 cards on individuals with communist connections – meaning that it had information relating to communist activities for roughly one in every two hundred people in the British population. The committee hoped that MI5's net would be cast wide enough to catch Soviet agents.

The entire security architecture within Whitehall, however, was once again overhauled following the exposure of Klaus Fuchs in 1949 and the Cambridge spy network in 1951, which painfully revealed the inadequacy of 'negative vetting'. As a result of even greater pressure from Washington in the wake of these scandals, Attlee and then Churchill's new government finally decided to introduce positive vetting, and provided MI5 with additional staff to carry it out. Thereafter, the use of positive vetting dramatically increased, so that three decades after its introduction a staggering 68,000 civil servants were being positively vetted (or 'pv'd', to use the colloquial Whitehall term). As the political commentator and historian Peter Hennessy has shown, the success of the GEN-183 committee was that, despite extreme political pressure being placed on it at times, it never resorted to overreactions like those experienced in the United States under Senator Joseph McCarthy. Instead of publicly naming and shaming suspected communists in government departments, MI5 and the committee tended instead to move them quietly away from areas where they posed dangers, to less sensitive posts within government.

The introduction of positive vetting had far-reaching consequences, which permanently changed the nature of work in Whitehall. MI5's stringent new background checks meant that it was no longer possible for civil service jobs to be given to applicants simply because they came from the 'right' social circle. The Cambridge spies had exploded the myth that it was impossible for gentlemen educated at the finest schools and universities to be traitors. From the 1950s onwards, all applicants to sensitive posts in the British government, irrespective of their backgrounds, had to pass the same vetting tests.[15]

The special intelligence relationship between London and Washington had dramatic consequences for domestic security arrangements not only in Britain, but across the empire. Britain's colonial empire placed London in an extremely awkward position with its closest ally, Washington. It desperately needed to retain the United States' support – for financial and military reasons, as well as for atomic research – but at the same time, Whitehall departments were acutely aware of American public criticism over 'colonialism'. A central tenet of the 'Atlantic Charter', signed between Roosevelt and Churchill in August 1941, which set out the Allies' goals in the Second World War, had been that the USA would not support the British empire or other forms of colonial rule after the war. The post-war economic settlement, in which Washington essentially bailed out British wartime debts through massive loans amounting to $3.75 billion, meant that the US government was able, to a considerable extent, to dictate the fate of the British empire. Although Churchill famously claimed in November 1942 in a speech at Mansion House in London that he had not become the King's First Minister to preside over the liquidation of the British empire, the reality was that by signing up to US loans he was not only the architect of Britain's wartime victory, but also largely the author of its imperial decline. The British government had effectively mortgaged the empire; the problem was that, in the post-war period, its creditors in Washington demanded a new kind of contract.[16]

COLONIAL SECURITY: THE FRONT LINE OF THE COLD WAR

It was the special intelligence relationship between London and Washington that guided British colonial security in the early Cold War. Just as pressure from Washington kick-started London into action to review and overhaul security within Britain itself, so US pressure caused Whitehall to orchestrate a massive reform of colonial security across the empire. MI5 was quick to appreciate that colonial security would play an integral role, and form a front line, in the Cold War. Sir Percy Sillitoe recalled in his memoirs that the defection in Canada in September 1945 of Igor Gouzenko spurred on MI5 to look at the question of the Soviet Union's subversive involvement in the British empire:

> The disclosing of the spy ring in Canada which immediately preceded my appointment made the Department [MI5] much more conscious than it has previously been of the possibility of security leakages in the Commonwealth countries which share our secrets. And we were becoming ever more aware that among peoples under British rule which were gradually becoming politically mature and groping towards self-government, the firebrands and malcontents – as well as men who sincerely felt that Britain was pursuing an overbearing policy towards them – were being stirred wherever possible to rebellion and trouble-making by Communists.[17]

In the five years after 1946, Sillitoe made twelve substantial trips to British territories overseas, liaising with and helping to reform intelligence authorities as far afield as Canada, Palestine, Egypt, Kenya, Rhodesia, South Africa, Singapore, Hong Kong, Malaya, Australia and New Zealand. These trips made him one of the most widely travelled heads of any contemporary British government department. Impressive as they were for that time, they nevertheless sometimes had a comic air to them. The fact that Sillitoe had previously had a fairly public career as a policeman before he entered MI5 meant that he was quite well-known to the British press, and consequently his appointment as head of MI5 was an open secret on Fleet Street – making him, bizarrely, the publicly known head of a secret service that was not publicly avowed. On several occasions when leaving on a trip overseas he attempted to avoid press attention by disguising himself with sunglasses, though as he later recalled, such attempts probably attracted more attention than they deflected.

Sillitoe's travels set a precedent that was followed by successive heads of MI5, particularly Sir Roger Hollis (Director-General from 1956 to 1965) and Sir Martin Furnival-Jones (Director-General from 1965 to 1972). In fact, as Director-General at a time when Britain rapidly accelerated decolonisation, Hollis was more concerned about imperial and Commonwealth security than he was about security in Britain itself.[18]

In 1948 MI5 opened a new department in its London headquarters to deal with colonial concerns. In January 1950 Sillitoe brought in Sir John Shaw, an old colonial hand, to head this 'Overseas', or 'OS' Section. Shaw had served in West Africa in the 1920s, as Chief Secretary in Palestine, where he narrowly escaped being killed in the bombing of the King David Hotel, and then as Governor of Trinidad. As the head of OS Section he conducted a series of lengthy tours of the Middle East, Far East and Africa. Due to his six-foot-five-inch frame and his frequent trips overseas, he earned the nickname within MI5 'the flying pencil'. Other officers in OS Section included Alex Kellar and James Robertson, both of whom played prominent roles in dealing with Zionist terrorism. In 1953 the responsibilities of OS Section were taken over by another department in MI5, E-Division, led by Bill Magan.[19]

British intelligence records reveal that London had several overriding, and related, fears about colonial security in the early Cold War. The first concerned what seemed to be the very real threat of a Third World War. After Moscow's successful detonation of its first atomic weapon in August 1949 – which both British and US intelligence failed to predict – both the Soviet Union and Western governments were in the position of being able to launch a nuclear Armageddon against each other. The fear of a nuclear holocaust permeated contemporary JIC assessments, many of which essentially became Doomsday planning, projecting catastrophic numbers of casualties and the obliteration of essential infrastructure in major cities in Britain and the empire. Some of the JIC's most chilling reports related to the detonation of 'dirty' atomic bombs, or 'weapons of mass destruction', the term used in one report. Planning for nuclear Armageddon also had a clear colonial agenda. The British intelligence community reasoned that if such a war erupted Britain, or more likely what remained of it, would have to rely on the empire and Commonwealth for support, as it had done in both previous world wars, and would not need to fear a Soviet 'fifth column' in those countries. This required building up local security services sufficiently robust to prevent Soviet intrusion in those states seeking independence from Britain.[20]

Another prevailing fear within the corridors of Whitehall related to the circulation of intelligence, in particular US intelligence, to empire and Commonwealth countries, some of whose governments the JIC considered dangerously 'insecure'. There was one part of the empire, more than any other, which caused alarm in Whitehall about 'leakage' of intelligence in the early Cold War: Britain's greatest imperial possession, India.[21]

BRITISH INTELLIGENCE AND THE TRANSFER
OF POWER IN INDIA

Britain's transfer of power in India, the jewel in its imperial crown, is a story of gross mismanagement. Although the story of how and why Britain lost control of its Asian empire, and entered into its last chukka of rule in the Raj, is complex, one of the central reasons was that towards the end of the Second World War it became clear that the British administration was powerless to stem the tide of Indian nationalism – and had effectively already lost control of its Asian empire. The spiritual leader of India, Mahatma Gandhi, described Britain's wartime promise to guarantee Indian independence as a post-dated cheque written by a failing bank. This was shown at the end of the war, when, in the face of intense pressure from Indian nationalist politicians, the British administration decided not to prosecute the most treacherous of those who had joined the Indian National Army, which had fought with the Japanese against the British during the war, and were already in British jails. After the end of the war, communal violence between India's 255 million Hindus and its ninety-two million Muslims spiralled bloodily out of control, especially after the leader of the Indian League, Muhammad Ali Jinnah, called for a 'day of action' on 16 August 1946. Some of the worst atrocities between Hindus and Muslims occurred in Bihar, in eastern India, where in 1946 approximately 7,000 Muslims were slain, and local British military officials launched what they appropriately termed Operation *Grisly*, which involved picking putrefied bodies up from the streets.[22]

Following the massive electoral victory of India's Congress Party in March 1946 for domestic party leadership in India, Clement Attlee's Labour government sent a high-profile delegation to India to discuss constitutional advancement towards independence, which included Sir Stafford Cripps ('Stifford Crapps', as Churchill nicknamed him), the First Lord of Admiralty, A.V. Alexander (known for singing and playing the piano), and Attlee's elderly Secretary of State for India, Lord Pethick-Lawrence ('Pathetic Lawrence'). Suffering from bouts of diarrhoea, the cabinet mission failed to produce any significant results. At one point, its talks faltered because Gandhi was observing a day of silence.

After the stalemate of this mission, in the last months of 1946 Attlee's cabinet in London took the monumental decision to relinquish power in India altogether. The cabinet minutes are typical of Attlee's laconic style, listing just five bullet points as the reasons for withdrawing from India, including that Britain could not maintain military control there in light of its commitments elsewhere, such as Palestine, even if it wanted to do so. By December 1946 there were only 608 Europeans left in the entire famed Indian Civil Service. Attlee also acknowledged that world public opinion was against Britain remaining in India. The original timetable for withdrawal was set for June 1948, which was to be implemented by a new Viceroy, Lord Louis Mountbatten. Within just four and a half months, however, he completed the transfer of power and buried the British Raj. With hindsight, it is clear that Mountbatten should have stuck to Attlee's original timetable for withdrawal, and rebuilt the Indian army, which could have kept order in the Punjab, which became a bitterly contested border region between India and Pakistan. As it was, Britain's accelerated evacuation from India, and its partition of the subcontinent into the states of India, and East and West Pakistan, was a process drenched in bloodshed, accompanied by ethnic cleansing, mass population displacement and communal slaughter, often on sadistic levels.

Despite all of the chaos surrounding Britain's transfer of power to India in 1947, and the bloodshed and civil war that followed Partition, the British government was nevertheless able to maintain relatively close diplomatic relations with both the new Indian and Pakistani governments. Both states remained in the Commonwealth – from which the word 'British' was politely dropped after their governments objected. One of the reasons the British and Indian governments were able to maintain better relations than many expected was the close personal bonds between the Mountbattens and the first Prime Minister of independent India, Nehru – with some suggesting that the relationship between Nehru and Mountbatten's wife was even closer. In an act that symbolised the continued relationship between the two countries after independence, the new Indian government asked Mountbatten to stay on after 1947 as its first 'Governor General'. The framework of the civil service of the British Raj was also largely preserved in independent India.

Although it was not publicised at the time, and has been largely airbrushed out of history books since, there was another way in which Britain maintained close relations with the newly independent Indian government: through intelligence liaisons. The activities of MI5, SIS and GCHQ are conspicuously missing from the twelve-volume *Transfer of Power in India* series of published records, although it is likely that because it was an officially commissioned British government publication, its editors had access to intelligence records, and knew more about intelligence in the last days of the Raj than they could disclose in print. Some British officials later made throwaway comments that hinted at the role of intelligence in the demise of Britain's Indian empire. The academic and journalist H.V. Hodson, who had personal knowledge of the workings of the British administration in India during the Second World War, wrote in his celebrated book on its end, *The Great Divide*: 'A regime such as that which ruled India depends more upon secret intelligence than does one rooted in popular support and national patriotism.' Recently available MI5, IPI and JIC records show that Hodson was correct. British intelligence played a critical, but covert, role in Britain's transfer of power in India, and London's relationship thereafter with the new Indian government.[23]

The first major Whitehall discussion about the future of intelligence in India occurred towards the end of the Second World War, after the failure of a mission led by Stafford Cripps to broker a deal for constitutional advancement in the subcontinent. In December 1944, Britain's Director of Military Intelligence, Major Francis Davidson, and the head of the IB in Delhi, Sir Denys Pilditch, began to address the question of intelligence liaison with Indian authorities if Britain were to withdraw from India. In consultation with MI5, they concluded that IPI and the IB in Delhi would have to be disbanded. It would be impossible, they argued, for organs of the British government to be answerable to Indian ministers.[24]

In April 1945, as the war in Europe was ending and India's national government began to take shape, the IB and IPI once again urged Whitehall to address the future of intelligence in India. They argued that it should be kept away from Indian ministers for as long as possible, but recognised that it would be futile to try to conceal the existence of the IB in Delhi from them altogether.[25]

The real breakthrough came on the eve of Indian independence, when Britain's senior spy chiefs held a number of key meetings in Whitehall to hammer out the intelligence relationship with the new government. The most important meetings were held on 24–25 April 1946, following cabinet discussions over the devolution of power in India, but these were followed by further meetings in November, after the establishment of the interim government in India. Those in April were attended by Britain's highest-ranking intelligence officials concerned with India: the Director-General of MI5 (Sir David Petrie) and one of its senior officers (Dick White), the Chief of SIS (Sir Stewart Menzies, a debonair former head of the Eton Beagles), as well as the heads of IPI (Sir Philip Vickery) and the IB in Delhi (Norman Smith, who was in London on a 'flying visit'), and a

senior official in the Indian Office (D.T. Monteath). It was concluded at
the meeting that IPI and the IB would only be able to exist for as long as
they were headed by 'Europeans'. As soon as an Indian head was appointed
to either, they would have to be closed down. It would be impossible,
Britain's intelligence chiefs predicted, for them to function as effective
British intelligence services if they were headed by Indians, whose loyalties
would obviously lie with their own government.[26]

The meetings also concluded that in preparation for Britain's departure, the IB in Delhi would need to destroy all 'sensitive' records in its
possession. That is exactly what happened. The IB set about destroying
and sanitising 'compromising' records on the nationalist leaders coming
into government, as well as on the network of agents and informers who
had kept them under surveillance before then. One GCHQ officer
stationed in Delhi, Alan Stripp, later recalled that he became the chief
'burning officer', with piles of intelligence records being burnt night and
day in the central square of the Red Fort before the handover of power. In
September 1946 the penultimate Viceroy of India, Lord Wavell, even joked
with Nehru that on his instructions the IB had destroyed all 'compromising papers' on him and other Congress leaders – at which both men
laughed. The issues that British intelligence confronted in India before
1947 regarding the sharing of intelligence and the destruction of sensitive
records would be repeated over the subsequent decades as Britain relinquished power in other colonies and territories.[27]

The diaries of MI5's Guy Liddell show that the issue of establishing a
robust intelligence liaison with the independent Indian state was a subject
of frequent discussion among Britain's senior intelligence chiefs in the
spring of 1947. The watershed moment for the history of British intelligence in India occurred in April that year, as Britain accelerated the pace
of its withdrawal, and the head of the IB in Delhi, Norman Smith, a former
police commissioner in Bombay, retired and returned to England. At this
point, Britain's intelligence chiefs in London made the groundbreaking
decision that, for the first time, the position of head of the IB would be
given to an Indian. The man chosen for the job by Nehru's caretaker
government was T.G. Sanjeevi Pillai, a forty-nine-year-old district super-
intendent from Madras. Sanjeevi seems to have been chosen because he
was loyal and was not from either the Indian Civil Service or the IB. As
with many subsequent nationalist leaders in other British colonies, the
scars of Nehru's various jail sentences – totalling seven years – had left him
deeply suspicious of anything to do with British police. For Nehru, the

words 'police' and 'intelligence' were synonymous. After all, political surveillance was an open secret in the Raj. As Nehru explained in his book *The Discovery of India*, which he wrote in prison in 1944, and which would become a celebrated tract for anti-colonial leaders worldwide:

> During the last quarter of a century or more I have not written a single letter, which has been posted in India, either to an Indian or a foreign address, without realising that it would have been seen, and possibly copied, by some secret service censor. Nor have I spoken on the phone without remembering that my conversation was likely to be tapped.[28]

Nehru was not wrong. During the period of caretaker government in India, before full independence, the man who effectively served as Interior Minister, Sardr Patel, took over day-to-day control of intelligence matters, and showed himself to have a far less emotional and more pragmatic approach to them than Nehru. Like Nehru, Patel realised that the IB had probably compiled records on himself and most of the leaders of Congress. However, unlike Nehru, he did not allow this to colour his judgement about the crucial role that intelligence would play for the young Indian nation. Since the 1930s the IB in Delhi and its counterpart in London, IPI, as well as MI5, had built up files on many Congress and Muslim League leaders, including Motilal Nehru and his son Jawaharlal, and Mahatma Gandhi – often called the Father, Son and Holy Ghost of India. This was not because the intelligence agencies viewed Congress and the Muslim League as 'subversive' – they were legitimate and legal political bodies – but because some of their members were known or suspected to be closely affiliated with communism.[29]

The remarkable twist in the story of the final days of British rule in India was that, contrary to all British intelligence predictions, in the end it was not necessary for the IB and IPI to be shut down once control for them had passed to an Indian head, Sanjeevi, and an Indian minister, Patel. Far from being suspicious of intelligence matters, Patel was in fact an enthusiastic believer in the activities of the IB, especially in countering communism. In November 1946, before his departure as head of the IB, Norman Smith met Patel and briefed him on the IB's functions. The meeting was an extraordinary success: Patel not only allowed the continued existence of the IB, but, amazingly, also sanctioned the continued surveillance of extremist elements within his own Congress Party. As Smith's report of the meeting reveals, Patel was adamant that the IB should 'discontinue the collection of intelligence on orthodox Congress and Muslim League activity', but at the same time he authorised it to continue observing 'extremist organisations'. Patel was particularly concerned about the Congress Socialist Party, many of whose members were communist sympathisers. The stance taken by Patel, who was sailing very close to the wind with regard to Congress and the Muslim League, was not lost on the IB: as Smith noted, the Congress Socialist Party was, after all, a 'Congress organisation and subject to Congress discipline'. Smith's report of his meeting with Patel concluded:

> ... it may be expected that they [Patel and the interim Indian government] will want to keep at least as close a watch on movements liable to subvert Congress/Muslim League authority as the previous official governments have kept on movements calculated to undermine British authority.[30]

It is hard to imagine a clearer expression of *Realpolitik*. The reason Patel was so amenable to continued surveillance of some of his fellow Indian politicians (keeping tabs on his own supporters, as one IPI report put it) was his fear of communism. In the words of another IPI report, Patel was 'rabidly anti-communist'. His fears were well-founded. Communism was the bogey that most threatened the young state of India in the years immediately after 1947. It was not the case that the British Raj was transformed overnight into an equally dominant Indian state. Communist riots broke out in Bengal in 1947, and after the transfer of power in neighbouring Burma, the Burmese government was forced to wage a violent guerrilla war against communist insurgents, which Congress in New Delhi viewed with alarm. Its fears were accentuated by events further afield, with the aggressive rise of communism in China, and the Soviet Union's expansion into Eastern Europe, taking over Czechoslovakia in 1948. Soviet archives confirm that after 1947 the KGB pursued 'active measures' to court a number of Congress politicians and other Indian leaders.[31]

Nehru's inherent distrust of the British police did not prevent his government-in-waiting, under the guidance of Patel, from negotiating a close liaison with British intelligence. In March 1947, on the eve of independence, MI5's Deputy Director-General, Guy Liddell, travelled to India and obtained agreement from Nehru's government-in-waiting for an MI5 officer to be stationed in New Delhi after the end of British rule. At midnight on 14–15 August 1947, India achieved its 'tryst with destiny', and

Nehru proudly broadcast to the newly independent nation that as the world slept India awoke, and the world's largest democracy was born. However, behind all of the public diplomatic arrangements surrounding the birth of the new nation, MI5 quietly maintained liaison officers in New Delhi, who worked hard behind closed doors to build a close relationship with India's security and intelligence agencies. MI5's first Security Liaison Officer in New Delhi, Kenneth Bourne, found close allies in Patel and Sanjeevi, as did the next SLO, Bill U'ren, who had previously served in the Indian police for twenty-two years. Sanjeevi continued as head of a reborn Delhi Intelligence Bureau, DIB, which retained the name of its predecessor in the Raj – one suspects in honour of it. Although it was not apparent at the time, the deal that MI5 brokered to maintain an SLO in New Delhi after independence set an important precedent. In every other major British colony or dependency, the continued presence of an MI5 SLO became a significant, though usually undisclosed, part of Britain's transfer of power. India, as we have seen the birthplace of much of British intelligence, was also the testing ground for much of the way that the British secret state would handle Britain's end of empire.[32]

For almost a quarter of a century after Indian independence, relations between MI5 and its Indian counterpart, the DIB, were closer than those between any other departments of the British and Indian governments. MI5's SLO in New Delhi in 1948, Eric Kitchen, reported that the head of the DIB, Sanjeevi, lost 'no opportunity of stressing the value which he places on maintaining our relationship on a professional and personal level'. That same year, Sanjeevi was sent by Nehru's government to London for 'exhaustive talks' with MI5 on its 'methods for purging the Civil Service of suspected elements and about security arrangements generally'. In July 1950 Nehru replaced Sanjeevi as head of the DIB with B.N. Mullik, who had previously served as Sanjeevi's deputy, and before that as a police officer in Saran District, which in 1946 had witnessed some of the worst scenes of communal violence. For the next fourteen years Mullik served as Director of the DIB, becoming one of Nehru's most trusted advisers. However, Nehru's abhorrence of anything to do with the British police placed Mullik in an awkward position, and in order to allay his master's fears, he deliberately shielded Nehru from the details of the DIB's liaison with British intelligence. In his memoirs, Mullik noted that Nehru was 'only vaguely aware of how and to what extent Intelligence functioned', and subtly commented that the DIB turned to a 'friendly nation' for training in foreign intelligence. MI5 records reveal that the 'friendly nation' was Britain.

Like his predecessor as head of the DIB, Sanjeevi, Mullik was an enthusiastic supporter of liaison with MI5. He represented India at the Commonwealth Security Conference held in London in 1953, and the relationship he established with MI5's SLO in New Delhi, Walter Bell, was so close that he encouraged Bell to visit DIB outstations as well as its headquarters. It is striking that MI5's SLO in New Delhi, unlike its other SLOs stationed overseas, conducted his business undercover, concealing his identity by using an alias, and was not publicly avowed by either the British or Indian governments. As one Colonial Office report explained, this was done at Mullik's personal request and was due to 'political reasons' – doubtless Nehru's deep suspicion of the British police, and also the increasingly turbulent Anglo–Indian diplomatic relations in the 1950s.[33]

The deal MI5 obtained from Nehru's government to maintain an SLO in New Delhi after independence had implications for British intelligence that stretched far beyond India. In the period immediately after independence, SIS had a station operating in New Delhi, as well as MI5. This contradicted the operational agreement reached between the two services in 1931 (discussed in Chapter 1), by which SIS limited its activities to non-British territories, while MI5 was responsible for security intelligence in all colonial and Commonwealth countries. In light of increasing SIS activities in India, and what MI5 felt was SIS's encroachment into its jurisdiction, in March 1948 the new British High Commissioner, Sir Archibald Nye, who had been briefed by MI5 before taking up office, turned the entire matter over to London. The result was that the Prime Minister issued what became known as the 'Attlee Directive', made orally and never in writing, which prevented SIS from conducting clandestine operations in Commonwealth countries. The Attlee Directive set the operational agenda for MI5–SIS relations in colonial territories for the next two decades – the period of British decolonisation. It was not until the 1960s that MI5 surrendered the lead to SIS in India and other Commonwealth countries. Some SIS officers have criticised the Attlee Directive as greatly undermining the agency's ability to gather intelligence in those countries once it eventually took over responsibility for them from MI5.

Meanwhile, back in London, soon after independence MI5 became the sole channel by which Britain could communicate security intelligence to the Indian authorities. IPI was formally closed down in August 1947 and its responsibilities were taken over by MI5's OS Section – a natural move, considering how close the two services were. Some 7,200 files and 106,000 cards were transferred from IPI to MI5's Central Registry, and several IPI officers also moved across to MI5, including its final head, Sir Philip Vickery.[34]

A particular source of concern for MI5 and the DIB, running like a sore through Anglo–Indian diplomatic relations in the early Cold War, revolved around the person of V.N. Krishna Menon, the Congress Party's leading left-wing firebrand. Menon was one of Nehru's closest confidants, serving as the first Indian High Commissioner in London after independence, and later effectively became Nehru's Foreign Minister, as the Indian representative at the United Nations. MI5 and the DIB were united in their deep distrust of Menon, described as 'smooth and false' by Harold Macmillan. MI5 knew Menon well: he had spent most of his career before Indian independence in London, where he worked as a barrister and in 1932 helped to set up the 'India League', the unofficial mouthpiece of the Congress Party in Britain, later also becoming a Labour councillor in St Pancras. His activities in London in the 1930s were closely followed by both IPI and MI5. MI5 opened a file on him in 1929, and because of his suspected connections with the British Communist Party, imposed a HOW on him in December 1933, which allowed for his mail to be intercepted. The application for the HOW identified him as 'an important worker in the Indian Revolutionary Movement', and MI5's subsequent investigations quickly confirmed that he moved in communist circles – during the war he was expelled from the Labour Party because of his communist links. Long before Indian independence, MI5 had thus built up a detailed picture of Menon's activities, filling several thick files.[35]

Menon's appointment as Indian High Commissioner in London immediately after independence caused MI5 severe anxiety. Although it stopped short of labelling him an outright communist, MI5's assessment was that his politics were 'pink' and 'fairly far to the left'. More alarming than Menon's politics, however, were those of the people with whom he associated and some of his other activities. MI5's investigations revealed that he was having an affair with a known communist sympathiser; had a drug problem; corruptly obtained contracts, including lucrative arms deals, for Indian firms; and personally profited from his official positions. MI5 noted that his personal bank account and those of the India League were so closely mixed that it would be surprising if any audit could ever untangle them. MI5's Deputy Director-General, Guy Liddell, put on file his opinion about Menon's continued position as High Commissioner in London:

Whatever his politics may be, and they appear to go fairly far to the Left, MENON is clearly dishonest, immoral, an opportunist and an intriguer ... whether or not MENON's retention as High Commissioner is the lesser of two evils, the relations between him and Miss TUNNARD [his lover], who is at least a fellow traveler, are of considerable importance. As long as those relations continue, it is reasonable to suppose that anything of interest that MENON hears about will be passed to the Communist party through her.

In my view, if it were at all possible, it would be far better to cut our losses and get rid of MENON. I should doubt whether he could tell the Communist Party anything more than they already know. As long as he remains the security position vis a vis India, whether it be the passing of documents or the attendance of Indians at courses, remains bad. MENON's presence here really vitiates the whole position.[36]

As soon as Menon was appointed High Commissioner, MI5 warned the JIC that his position presented a serious risk to British security. At an urgent meeting of the JIC in August 1947, which was not recorded in the JIC's official minutes, MI5's Director-General (Sillitoe) and its Deputy Director-General (Liddell) warned that Menon was 'a first class intriguer with a bad moral record' who would probably pass information on to his close communist associates in London, from where it was likely to find its way to Moscow. MI5 identified at least twelve communist sympathisers and fellow travellers employed on the staff of India House in London, and warned the JIC that, given these associations and Menon's other links with communists, it was not possible to safeguard intelligence shared with the Indian High Commission, as the British government would inevitably have to do after 1947.[37]

As a result of pressure exerted by MI5, the JIC agreed that sensitive information passed to the Indian High Commission would have to be carefully screened, and British ministers whom Menon met would have to be warned about his associations. In order to bypass him, MI5 began to act as a channel for passing information securely, via the DIB in India, directly to the Indian government. The DIB India shared MI5's concern about Menon: Mullik refused to post a DIB liaison officer to India House while Menon was there for fear of sensitive information finding its way through him to the British Communist Party.[38]

Although MI5 and apparently the DIB India did not fully appreciate it, Menon's long period in London had made him extremely anglicised. By the time he became High Commissioner in London in 1947, the only language he spoke was English, having forgotten much of his native Hindi, and he also preferred English food and tweed suits to curries and traditional Indian dress. However, MI5's fears of Menon's pro-communist and Soviet sympathies were not fanciful. On at least one occasion in his later political career in India, the KGB paid his election expenses.[39]

The year 1955 witnessed the dawn of a new era in Indian–Soviet relations, and consequently in Western relations with India. Nehru and the Soviet premier, Nikita Khrushchev, exchanged state visits, and the following year Nehru openly criticised Western 'imperialism' during the Suez crisis, an event that he condemned as an act of 'naked aggression' – though he failed to criticise the Soviet Union's brutal suppression of the Hungarian uprising in the same year. Nehru was also an admirer of Soviet advances in science and technology, particularly in atomic research. Meanwhile, the KGB was extraordinarily active in India, which became home to the greatest Soviet intelligence presence in any country in the developing world. India under Nehru's daughter and successor, Indira Gandhi, would also apparently be the arena of more KGB 'active measures' than anywhere else in the world. The result of India's closeness to the Soviet Union during the Cold War was a massive realignment of Western priorities. Broadly speaking, the US government supported Pakistan to act as a strategic firewall against Soviet influence in India.

Despite the chill between Western governments and India, relations between MI5 and the DIB remained remarkably close. At Mullik's request, in 1957 MI5 despatched a training officer to the DIB. MI5's SLO in New Delhi, John Allen, noted that 'with so many unfavourable winds blowing' between India and Britain, if Nehru realised how close their intelligence liaison was, he would probably cut it off. The good working relationship that successive SLOs enjoyed with the DIB provided Britain with key information at a time when the Soviet Union, through covert KGB measures, was attempting to build a special relationship with India. Following a visit to India in 1958, MI5's Director-General Sir Roger Hollis remarked that Mullik's views on communism were actually closer to those of MI5 than to those of his own government.[40]

Overall, Britain and its Western allies failed to prevent India from gravitating towards the Soviet Union in the Cold War. However, the situation for British policy-makers and Western governments more generally could have been considerably worse if British intelligence, particularly MI5, had not successfully maintained such close relations with the Indian intelligence services. MI5's liaison officers in New Delhi provided the British High Commission with a valuable, publicly deniable, back channel of communication to Indian government departments that was not officially available to the British government. In 1965, a year after Nehru's death, the British High Commissioner in New Delhi, John Freeman, wrote to MI5 in London to state how much he valued the role of MI5's SLO: 'his liaison is one that continues unaffected by changes in Indo–British relations'. In fact, Freeman rated the value of the SLO so highly that, when budget cuts in Whitehall threatened to close down the post that year, he told MI5 that he was willing to find extra work within the High Commission in order to keep him on his staff. MI5's SLO in Delhi remained in operation at least until 1967, working undercover as one of the High Commission's secretaries. The first female Director-General of MI5, Stella Rimington, was recruited to MI5 in 1967 while working in the High Commission in Delhi. She later recalled that the SLO who recruited her was 'best known for his Sunday curry lunches, which usually went on well into the evening, and for driving around Delhi in a snazzy Jaguar'.[41]

Equally remarkable as the intelligence liaison bonds that London established with Delhi after 1947 were the links British intelligence forged with other independent states that emerged out of Britain's former Indian empire. In Pakistan, unlike in India, MI5 did not maintain an SLO immediately after Partition and independence, but within a few years it had opened a station there. Contrary to what we might expect, it was actually the Pakistani government that requested an MI5 SLO to be posted to Pakistan, not the other way around. In April 1951 the first Prime Minister of Pakistan, Liaquat Ali Khan, personally wrote to Prime Minister Attlee and asked for a British security intelligence officer to be stationed in Karachi. Indian–Pakistani rivalry seems to have been partly behind his request, for as Khan noted to Attlee, he was aware that Britain already had an intelligence liaison officer in Delhi. MI5 duly posted an SLO to Karachi later that year, and the post operated until at least 1965. The head of the Intelligence Bureau (IB) in Pakistan, Sayid Kazim Raza, attended a Commonwealth Security Conference held in London in 1951.[42]

Although it was unusual, if not unique, for an intelligence liaison request to come from a former colony, as occurred with Pakistan, the spirit of intelligence cooperation between Britain and its former colonies was not. In the two decades after Indian independence a number of 'new' states entering the Commonwealth proved extraordinarily willing to liaise with British intelligence, attaching considerable importance to the connection, and apparently regarding it as a matter of pride to have an MI5 officer posted in their countries, illustrating that they were sitting at the High Table of international politics. MI5 established similar bonds as those in India and Pakistan with security authorities in Ceylon, which in February 1948 gained independence from Britain in a smooth transfer of power, without a shot being fired or any blood shed. The connections between MI5 and Ceylon's security agency, the Department of Public Security, established in 1955 on MI5's advice, are striking: in the late 1950s one-quarter of the officers working in its 'security section' were permanent members of MI5.[43]

INTELLIGENCE REFORM AT THE CENTRE

As well as instigating close links with intelligence agencies in the empire and Commonwealth, Britain's intelligence services, particularly MI5, also helped to restructure the central machinery of government in London to deal with anti-colonial 'Emergencies'. In fact, the intelligence services played a key role in the way Whitehall responded to anti-colonial movements in the empire in the post-war years. Above all, what was needed was to provide the Colonial Office in London with, to use its own words, an 'early warning' system for disturbances. The atmosphere of international politics in the late 1940s made it appear that communism was gaining ground in various parts of the empire, so Whitehall needed as much notice as possible of when revolts, likely to be sponsored by Moscow, might occur.

As we shall see in later chapters, the outbreak of a communist insurrection in Malaya in 1948 was followed by civil disturbances, with suspected Soviet involvement, in the Gold Coast in West Africa. In 1949 the communist revolutionary fighter Mao Tse-tung came to power in China after a protracted civil war in which nationalist forces were finally defeated on the Chinese mainland, and in June 1950 the Korean War broke out between rival camps supported by the United States and China. British policymakers needed as much information as possible on what appeared to be a new world order with the rise of communism. Newly available Colonial Office records reveal that, beginning in the late 1940s, a stream of correspondence commenced between MI5 and the Colonial Office discussing these alarming developments. In this correspondence, MI5 forcefully told leading civil servants, like Andrew Cohen, Assistant Undersecretary for African Affairs in the Colonial Office, that they were placing too much weight on 'political intelligence' (meaning diplomatic reporting) instead of actual security intelligence (relating to espionage, subversion and sabotage). In 1948 MI5 convinced the Colonial Secretary, Arthur Creech Jones, to rethink the entire system of colonial intelligence reporting and instigate a new arrangement whereby the colonial governors in each of the forty-two British dependencies across the empire would send reports to London focusing specifically on security intelligence. Furthermore, partly in response to MI5's recommendations, in 1948 the Colonial Office was for the first time admitted as a full member of the JIC in London. Thereafter, the Colonial Office representative was able to task the JIC to make assessments of specific threats.[44]

As part of its bid to help streamline colonial intelligence and provide the Colonial Office with an early warning of uprisings and communist plots in the empire, in June 1954 MI5 posted a permanent Security Intelligence Adviser (SIA) to the Colonial Office. The officer chosen for this new post was Alec MacDonald, a veteran of the Indian police whose CV boasted a term in the Bombay CID, a 'good working knowledge of Hindi and Marathi' and service under Major General Sir Gerald Templer in Malaya. MacDonald's role was invigorated in April 1955 when Templer, fresh from putting down the Emergency in Malaya (discussed in the next chapter), published his famous report on colonial security, which recommended a variety of reforms. Although the impact of the 'Templer report' should not be overstated, as several of its recommendations were never adopted, it did have the effect of focusing minds in Whitehall. Templer recommended that colonial administrations should attach much greater importance to intelligence matters if they were to deal effectively with future insurgencies:

> Whereas in the military world 'Intelligence' is a highly specialized field of its own, in the Colonial (and other civilian) services it naturally tends to be regarded as merely one aspect of the political 'knowledge' which permeates the whole business of administration. Nor is this aspect held to be a very important one: 'intelligence' is often considered to be a narrow, if sensational, function of the police. The administration is apt not to concern itself closely with the machinery for its collection and appreciation, nor with its relation to security in the broadest sense. As a result, security intelligence has I think come to be regarded as a kind of spicy condiment added to the Secretariat hot-pot by a supernumerary and possibly superfluous cook, instead of being an expertly planned and expertly served dish of its own.[45]

One of Templer's recommendations which was adopted was for two further MI5 SIAs to be posted to the Colonial Office to assist MacDonald. Upon Templer's recommendation, in 1955 the Colonial Office also established its own secret 'Intelligence Security Department' (ISD), the records of which were only released in 2008. They reveal that the ISD's remit was truly worldwide, dealing with security and intelligence issues in every major British territory, and liaising closely with all of Britain's secret services, MI5, SIS and GCHQ. The ISD was led by an experienced colonial administrator, Duncan Watson, and C.J.J.T. (Juxon) Barton, a veteran Colonial Office official, who among other previous appointments had served as a District Commissioner in East Africa. As we shall see, Juxon Barton had in fact already been liaising closely with MI5 since the late 1940s over questions relating to communist involvement in African colonies.[46]

INTELLIGENCE MISSIONARIES

The Gouzenko defection, combined with the unease MI5 felt about the Indian High Commission in London, soon drew it into reviewing the entire process of how Britain shared intelligence with colonial and Commonwealth countries. The more it looked at colonial security after 1947, the less it liked what it saw. In February 1948 MI5's Director-General, Percy Sillitoe, warned the JIC that security standards in some of the 'new' countries entering the Commonwealth, principally India and Pakistan, were so low as to be 'practically non-existent' – a breathtaking statement considering how poor Britain's own domestic security arrangements were at that time, as we have seen. Sillitoe said that 'leakages were taking place in all directions' in the Indian government. To meet this threat, MI5 recommended to the JIC a grading system of intelligence to limit sensitive information being passed to insecure states. The JIC accepted and implemented wholesale MI5's grading system for intelligence, dividing countries into three categories, A, B and C.[47]

Category A was the highest and most trusted level of security, which at first comprised the United States and the 'Old Dominion' (read: white/European) countries of Australia, New Zealand, Canada, Southern Rhodesia and South Africa. Britain freely shared top-secret and secret intelligence with countries in Category A, though as we shall see, the intelligence relationship between London and South Africa and Rhodesia would later become considerably more complicated.

Intelligence that Britain sent to category B countries, which included France, was restricted and sanitised, but was still classified top secret. At first India and Pakistan were placed in category B, not because their security standards were considered to be robust – far from it – but because it was essential for strategic purposes in the Cold War for Britain to be able to share classified intelligence with them. From 1949 onwards Britain had bases in Pakistan from which it could launch bombing raids on the Soviet Union. The JIC stressed that India and Pakistan should not under any circumstances be made aware that they were receiving doctored intelligence, a task that was made more difficult after 1952, when both governments sent delegates to Commonwealth Security Conferences in London. Meanwhile, countries placed in the lowest category, C – such as Burma – received hardly any classified intelligence from Britain.

A year after the JIC's first report, in 1949, the whole grading system was rearranged on a more permanent basis, this time allowing only the United States and Canada to accompany Britain in category A. Australia, New Zealand and South Africa were downgraded to category B. India, Pakistan and Ceylon were relegated to the lowly status of category C, because the JIC realised that whatever their strategic importance in the escalating Cold War, their security standards were so lax that they could not be trusted with top-secret intelligence.[48]

The real impetus behind MI5's reform of intelligence-sharing was the US government's passing of the McMahon Act, which prevented US authorities sharing atomic research with any foreign power. Washington exerted huge pressure on London to safeguard US intelligence that was forwarded to colonial and other governments, as is clearly revealed in the key JIC reports in 1948 and 1949 that devised Britain's grading system for the disclosure of intelligence, which stress that no US intelligence could be passed on to countries like India and Pakistan without specific permission from Washington. The US government's concerns over the insecurity of intelligence in the British empire and Commonwealth were, it seems, as much a blight on the 'special relationship' in the early Cold War as American political distaste for supporting the British empire and 'colonialism'. To safeguard its own secrets and calm American doubts, Britain would orchestrate its withdrawal from empire in the 1950s and 1960s by a process of careful information-management, just as it had done in India.[49]

As well as limiting intelligence to 'insecure' countries, the British secret state also began a much more positive process of overhauling the entire system of colonial and Commonwealth security, both at home and abroad.

By the end of the Second World War, as has already been noted, MI5 had twenty-seven DSOs permanently posted overseas. In the late 1940s, following the precedent set in India, MI5 began to replace its DSOs with SLOs. The key distinction between the two posts was that DSOs were attached to a British military garrison, while SLOs operated under civilian cover, usually from the offices of British colonial governors, or in Commonwealth countries from British high commissions. By the early 1950s MI5 had a total staff of approximately 840, which included nearly thirty SLOs in countries across the globe, from the West Indies to the Far East. At the peak of post-war decolonisation, Britain had forty-two SLOs abroad.[50]

The posting of SLOs to every major British colony and dependency in the two decades after 1945 is even more striking when the connections between British intelligence and the empire before then are considered. As we saw in Chapter 1, there were significant spillovers from the empire to Britain's intelligence services in the first half of the twentieth century, with many senior officers beginning their careers in colonial service. After 1945, exactly the opposite occurred: the posting of MI5 officers to the British empire in the two decades after the war, precisely as Britain began to withdraw from empire, was one way in which 'the empire struck back'.

Until recently, the activities of MI5's SLOs in the empire and Commonwealth in the early Cold War left few ripples in the vast sea of official British records. Before the release of MI5 records in the last few years, it was impossible to find anything more than a few scanty references to 'PO Box 500, London' (MI5's cover address), or perhaps to glimpse the word 'Subsided' (the cover cypher address used by SLOs in British colonies). Even when one did stumble across these subtle, cursory references, the actual correspondence between MI5 and colonial governments was invariably withheld. Using newly available MI5 and Colonial Office records, we are at last able to see that the SLOs played a significant role in the history of both British decolonisation and the Cold War, effectively working as intelligence missionaries in colonies as they approached independence.[51]

The responsibilities of the SLOs were many and varied, but first and foremost they provided colonial administrations with background intelligence on anti-colonial activists campaigning for independence. Often this intelligence on nationalist leaders-in-waiting was crucial for colonial administrations in preparing for the transfer of power. The secret of the SLOs' success was that they were able to pass intelligence to colonial governments at the highest level, enjoying personal meetings with colonial governors, local chiefs of police and other high-level civilian and military officials. Among their responsibilities was to provide a secure channel of communication, using cypher machines, between MI5's headquarters in London and colonial administrations, often directly to colonial governors themselves – one imagines information being passed on in hushed tones, at furtive meetings in the governors' official residencies. As MI5 proudly liked to emphasise, SLOs provided colonial governments with access to a worldwide pool of security intelligence, derived not only from MI5 sources in Britain, but also from its regional collection centres in the Middle East (SIME) and the Far East (SIFE). At the same time, flowing in the opposite direction, the SLOs provided colonial governments with a direct channel of communication back to London – a route that the Colonial Office frequently complained bypassed its own communications.

Other responsibilities of SLOs included performing 'personnel security measures', which involved the tiresome but important task of checking visa entry and exit applications, and 'physical security measures', such as sweeping for listening devices in government buildings. Fears in the early 1950s that Soviet intelligence was bugging British and other Western governments were well founded. In January 1952 a Soviet bug was discovered in the US embassy in London in a wooden model of the Great Seal of the United States, which had been given by the Soviet envoy in Britain as a present to the US ambassador. The bug was discovered in an alarming incident when the voice of the ambassador, who was in one room in the embassy, was heard being transmitted in another room entirely. This led to a bugging scare across British government departments, at home and in colonies overseas. The ensuing British investigation into the bug in the US embassy, conducted by the Ministry of Defence's chief scientist, Sir Frederick Brundrett, discovered that it was powered by short-range radio waves, which, the investigation concluded, could be effectively countered by fluorescent lighting. It is probably too much to suppose that this is the reason British government departments have so much ugly fluorescent lighting to this day.[52]

The value that the Colonial Office attached to MI5's SLOs was clearly expressed in a classified circular that Alan Lennox-Boyd, the Colonial Secretary from 1954 to 1959, sent to all colonial governors in April 1956:

> The role of the Security Service [MI5] in Colonial territories is to assist and advise, as implied in the designation of the Security Liaison Officer; executive responsibility for intelligence work rests entirely on the local

intelligence organisation. The Security Liaison Officer is however the link with a widespread security intelligence network, whose resources are at the disposal of Colonial territories and contribute a great deal to Colonial intelligence requirements ... There is close liaison between the Colonial Office and the Security Service in London, and it is essential that there should be in the field. It should also be borne in mind that where territories are moving forward to self government, the normal pattern of Commonwealth relationship in the security intelligence field is liaison on a professional basis between the United Kingdom Security Service and the security service of the country concerned through the person of a security Liaison Officer attached by the Security Service to the staff of the UK Government's representative in the country. Her Majesty's Government attach great importance to establishing and maintaining this relationship in former colonies which achieve Commonwealth status ...[53]

CREATING A COMMONWEALTH INTELLIGENCE CULTURE

As well as posting SLOs to colonies and Commonwealth countries, MI5 also instigated an enormous training scheme for colonial police forces. These programmes began in the late 1940s, but expanded rapidly following Templer's report on colonial security in April 1955. The report – only fully declassified in 2011 – noted that since 1950 MI5 had trained only 290 colonial police officers abroad and 140 on courses in Britain, numbers that were, in Templer's opinion, 'a drop in the ocean of what needs to be done'. On Templer's recommendation, MI5 dramatically increased its training schemes for colonial police forces, and officers visited every major British colony and dependency in the world to help give training in intelligence matters.

This enormous but secretive scheme was overseen by Alec MacDonald, MI5's first security adviser seconded to the Colonial Office, who between 1954 and 1957 made a staggering fifty-seven trips to twenty-seven different British dependencies overseas. His programmes helped to train a new generation of security intelligence officers. Between 1954 and 1958, MI5 helped to train an average of 250 colonial police and security officials per year, with the number jumping to 367 in 1959. Beginning in June 1956, MI5 also set up training courses for senior colonial officials at its headquarters at Leconfield House in London – before then they had merely participated in courses run by the police in Britain. Recruits were given lectures on 'The Threat' (Soviet intelligence and Sino-Soviet communism), 'methods of investigation' (interception, surveillance, defectors, agents and interrogation) and 'records' (having an accurate registry). The first course ended with a talk by MI5's Director-General, Roger Hollis, a visit from the Colonial Secretary, Alan Lennox-Boyd, and, as one of the lecture lists reveals, culminated in an evening 'MI5 cocktail party', at which guests were apparently invited to wear fake noses and moustaches.[54]

Alongside these schemes, MI5 also oversaw and ran a series of Commonwealth Security Conferences in London. The first, held in September 1948, was organised at the highest possible government level, with Prime Minister Clement Attlee writing personally to the Prime Ministers of the self-governing 'Old Dominions', Canada, Australia, New Zealand, Southern Rhodesia and South Africa, and asking for the heads of their security departments to accompany them in a forthcoming meeting of Prime Ministers in London. The resulting conference discussed how intelligence could be shared securely between the participating countries and vetting procedures enhanced for detecting communists in government departments.[55]

This first conference was so successful that it was followed by a second, in May 1951, which was attended by delegates from India (T.G. Sanjeevi Pillai), Pakistan (Sayid Kazim Raza) and Ceylon, much to the irritation of the Apartheid government of South Africa, which resented the idea of sharing intelligence with 'Asiatics', and threatened to boycott the whole conference – South Africa did not send representatives to the conferences after it left the Commonwealth in 1961. Evidence suggests that Commonwealth Security Conferences took place every two years after 1952, and probably continue to the present day.[56]

MI5's colonial intelligence-training courses, both in London and in the empire and Commonwealth, had a central tenet: that there was a fundamental difference between policing and intelligence work and that the two required completely different outlooks for officers. The courses stressed that, while policing was concerned with law enforcement and *actual* prosecutions, intelligence work involved the detection of merely *potential* threats. MI5 emphasised this principle, that there was a distinction between police and intelligence work, in its security reforms throughout the empire and Commonwealth during the Cold War.

The results of MI5's training schemes were profound. In the first place, as the imperial historian Philip Murphy has noted, they helped to establish an 'intelligence culture' which was successfully exported to police and security services across the empire and Commonwealth. While the key component of this culture was the separation of policing from intelligence, exactly how this was achieved depended on local circumstances in each country. In those that had a single unified police force, such as Canada, MI5 felt that intelligence matters could be handled by a dedicated Special Branch within the regular police force, operating within the Criminal Investigation Department (CID) but in practice functioning entirely separately from it. In other states, such as Australia, where separate federal police forces operated across the country, MI5 advised establishing an entirely new and separate agency, devoted to security intelligence, which could operate at a national level and coordinate intelligence matters among all of the regional police forces. In taking this line, MI5 was actually exporting Britain's own model for security intelligence: one of the reasons why it, MI5, had been established in 1909 as a separate security service operating at a national level was a fear in Whitehall that Britain's regional police forces and Special Branches were uncoordinated.[57]

CANADA AND AUSTRALIA

Canada and Australia clearly reveal the ways in which the British intelligence community had a major impact on Commonwealth security in the early Cold War. In Canada, before the defection of Igor Gouzenko, intelligence matters were handled by the CID of the Royal Canadian Mounted Police (RCMP). Following Gouzenko's defection, MI5 was brought in to advise the RCMP on how to establish a more efficient intelligence outfit. Its recommendation was that the RCMP should establish a separate Special Branch within the CID for dealing with intelligence. This was done in 1950, though in 1956 the Special Branch was renamed the Directorate of Security and Intelligence, or 'I Directorate', and subsequently the RCMP Security Service. In 1984 the Canadian parliament passed legislation establishing the Canadian Security Intelligence Service, in many ways the direct heir of MI5's early Cold War intelligence reforms in Canada.[58]

GCHQ brought a similar influence to bear on Canadian SIGINT, which in the post-war years was led by Lt. Col. Edward Drake, who unsurprisingly was a Canadian. From late 1946 he (more surprisingly) had as deputy a stalwart *British* code-breaker and expert on Russian coding systems, Geoffrey Stevens. Soon after, the Canadian Prime Minister, Mackenzie King, authorised the establishment of a small SIGINT agency, the Communications Branch of the National Research Council (CBNRC). Although it only had a small staff of about a hundred, a number of its senior personnel were seconded from GCHQ. In fact, it had so many GCHQ staff in its ranks that locals were prompted to observe that CBNRC stood for 'Communications Branch – No Room for Canadians'.[59]

The British intelligence community oversaw similar reforms in Australia. MI5 took a leading role in reforming security there in 1948, when Venona decrypts identified a high-level Soviet espionage network operating in Australian government circles in Canberra. The resulting counter-espionage investigations were among the few real-time ones produced by Venona decrypts, almost all of which revealed only retrospective information about Soviet agents. In the light of Venona's revelations, the US government placed a ban on all US intelligence going to Australia until security there was tightened. The responsibility to do so fell squarely on MI5, and in September 1948 Sir Percy Sillitoe and Roger Hollis travelled to Australia, accompanied by a senior officer from MI5's B-Division, Robert Hemblys-Scales. Realising that it would be impossible to obtain full cooperation from the Australian government without disclosing how they knew about the Soviet network, Sillitoe briefed the Australian Prime Minister, Ben Chifley, and the Ministers of Defence (John Dedman) and External Affairs (H.V. 'Bert' Evatt), in strictest confidence on the Venona secret. Thereafter, with full cooperation from the Australian government guaranteed, the MI5 delegation worked closely with the local police investigation, which eventually led to the successful prosecution of Soviet agents who had penetrated the Department of External Affairs. They also instigated a major overhaul of Australian security and intelligence.

On MI5's advice, the Australian government established an entirely new security agency which, because Australia had regional police forces like Britain, was modelled on MI5. From the outset of discussions between the Australian government and MI5's newly established SLO in Australia, Courtenay Young, who had served in the war as one of MI5's Far Eastern experts, it was agreed that the new security service would have an extremely close relationship with MI5: at one point during discussions the External Affairs Minister even described the planned agency as a 'proposed MI5 section'. Hollis returned to Australia in 1949 to help with the charter of the new agency, the Australian Security Intelligence Organisation (ASIO), founded in March that year, which exists to the present day.[60]

In 1952 SIS played a similarly prominent role in the establishment of Australia's first peacetime foreign intelligence service, the Australian Secret Intelligence Service (ASIS). The connections between the two services were so close that in the 1950s ASIS officers referred to SIS in London as 'headquarters'. To oversee these two new services, ASIO and ASIS, the Australian government also established a British-style JIC.[61]

One of ASIO's most significant early successes came with the defection of the Soviet intelligence (KGB) head of station in Canberra, Vladimir Petrov, in April 1954. Petrov first came to MI5's attention in 1950, when its SLO in Australia requested information on him, as he was due to be posted as a secretary to the Soviet embassy in Canberra. The only information MI5 and SIS had on file on him at that time was that he had previously been a secretary at the Soviet embassy in Stockholm. In late 1953, a source close to Petrov in Canberra reported to ASIO that Petrov was considering defecting. Although this source is not identified in MI5 records, it was almost certainly Mikhail Bialoguski, a Polish doctor and musician and part-time ASIO agent, who had cultivated Petrov for nearly two years, wining and dining him and taking him to visit prostitutes in Sydney's King's Cross area. In return for a guarantee of political asylum and protection, on 3 April 1954 Petrov defected. His reason for doing so, he later told his ASIO handlers, was that he liked living in Australia and did not want to return to the Soviet Union. Although he did not expressly state it as a reason for defecting, it is also likely that because he had been posted to Australia by the notorious Soviet intelligence chief Lavrenti Beria, who was subsequently purged and executed by the Soviet leadership in June 1953, Petrov may have feared being seen as a 'Beria man' if he returned to Moscow, where like Beria he may have been eliminated.[62]

Petrov did not tell his wife, Evdokia, of his planned defection, apparently wanting her to join him after he had made it safely into Australian custody. However, on 19 April, Mrs Petrov, it seems fearing that her husband was dead, was hustled by two armed Soviet hard men onto a BOAC Constellation aircraft at Sydney's Kingsford Smith airport, bound for Zurich. Amid frantic scenes, a crowd that had massed at the airport, apparently amounting to nearly a thousand people, shouted and booed to try to prevent her from being made to board the plane. Some of those present alleged that they heard her say, 'I don't want to go. Save me,' as she was marched on board. During the flight, the captain of the aircraft radioed ahead that Mrs Petrov seemed afraid of her Russian companions. When the plane touched down at Darwin airport for refuelling, she was met by a senior member of the Northern Territory administration, Mr R. Leydin, who asked her if she wanted to seek the protection of the Australian government. Other Australian officials engaged the two Soviet hard men in conversation so as to distract them from Mr Leydin's conversation with

Mrs Petrov. However, when they saw that she was talking with an Australian official, they attempted to brush past the police officers between them, one of the Russians reaching into his pocket for what appeared to be a weapon. A police officer immediately stopped him and, finding a loaded pistol in his inside pocket, disarmed him. The other Russian was found to have a holstered weapon under his jacket. Pandemonium ensued, as the police warned the two men that it was illegal to carry weapons on an aircraft. All of this gave Mrs Petrov time to make a long-distance phone call to her husband, who she now realised was still alive. After this, she formally asked Australian officials for political asylum, which she was granted. She was subsequently reunited with her husband, and they lived in Australia, under aliases, for the rest of their lives.[63]

The Petrovs provided their ASIO handlers with significant information on Soviet intelligence. It turned out that Mrs Petrov, far from being a mere consul at the Soviet embassy in Canberra, as MI5 and ASIO had believed, had in fact been a cypher clerk, as her husband had been during and after the Second World War. Although MI5 and SIS had not been aware of it, his position at the Soviet embassy in Stockholm had been cover for his real position as an intelligence cypher clerk. When he defected he had not been able to bring his cypher code books with him, as he had wanted, but he was able to provide ASIO with 'substantial information on personalities and code names' for the period from 1945 to 1948. He also brought with him documents, such as his instructions from Moscow for the coming year, and also, of particular interest to British intelligence, information on the Cambridge spies, Burgess and Maclean, who he revealed were living in the Russian city of Kubyishev. Vladimir Petrov was more than a cypher clerk in Canberra, however: he was actually responsible for identifying and running potential Soviet agents in the city. Ironically, his duties as head of Soviet station in Canberra also included preventing the defection of Soviet agents to the West.

It would take ASIO years to follow up all the leads produced by Vladimir Petrov into Soviet agents in Australia. The ramifications of the husband-and-wife defections also went far beyond the realm of counter-espionage, having dramatic political consequences. The Australian Prime Minister, Robert Menzies, opened an official inquiry into Soviet espionage in Australia, explaining to the House of Representatives that Australian nationals were involved in it – just as had been the case with the Gouzenko spy ring in Canada. Following the Petrov defections, the Australian and Soviet governments broke off diplomatic relations – the Soviet government expelled the Australian embassy staff in Moscow, and the Soviet embassy staff in Canberra were also recalled. The two countries did not re-establish diplomatic relations until March 1959.[64]

The Petrov defections were primarily an ASIO affair in which MI5 (and to a lesser degree SIS) played a supporting role. That said, MI5 records reveal that ASIO sought advice from MI5 at every major step. It was in the realm of SIGINT, however, that the most remarkable development in Anglo-Australian intelligence-sharing occurred. In 1947 the Australian government established a new SIGINT agency, the Defence Signals Branch (DSB), based in Melbourne. Amazingly, its first director was not an Australian, despite there being four Australian candidates, but a British officer from GCHQ, Teddy Poulden. The DSB soon became a shadow sister service of GCHQ. Poulden took over as its head in April 1947, commanding a staff of about two hundred, and filled twenty of the most senior posts with GCHQ staff on secondment. He communicated with GCHQ with his own special cypher, which guaranteed, to Washington's pleasure, the secure exchange of SIGINT between the Australian and British governments.[65]

The placement of a British officer as the head of Australia's first peace-time SIGINT agency demonstrates the impact that Britain's intelligence services had on Commonwealth security in the early Cold War. Safeguarding strategic security and intelligence in Australia became even more important for the British government after the testing of Britain's first nuclear weapon on the deserted Monte Bello Islands off the coast of Western Australia in 1952, and subsequently its first testing of an H-Bomb on Christmas Island in 1957 – both of which were accompanied by British deception ploys to disguise them from the Soviet Union.[66]

SIGINT: THE GREATEST SECRET OF BRITISH DECOLONISATION

The history of British decolonisation is currently in broadly the same position as that of the Second World War was before the disclosure of the Ultra secret. Put simply, until the role of SIGINT, which played a central part in the way British governments managed their retreat from empire, is fully revealed, there is a missing dimension in our understanding of that period. We have already seen how the Venona decrypts led in 1948 to massive security reforms in Commonwealth countries like Australia. However, the role of British SIGINT ran much deeper than this. After 1945

GCHQ presided over a vast system for intercepting colonial and Commonwealth communications. Its efforts were facilitated by a simple fact: the governments of many of these states relied on Enigma machines for their communications, just as Germany had done previously, and British code-breakers were able to intercept and read them in the same way as they had with German traffic. This was one of the reasons the British government did not disclose the Ultra secret sooner: the JIC knew that if Commonwealth governments discovered that Britain had successfully broken the wartime Enigma code, they would realise that it was probably still capable of doing so. GCHQ's interception activities were made easier by the fact that Britain was responsible for manufacturing the encrypting codes, known as one-time pads, theoretically impossible to break, which were used by many colonial and Commonwealth governments for their 'secure' traffic. As GCHQ had the keys for these pads, the colonial and Commonwealth communications for which they were used were effectively an open book.

The sheer volume of communications being read by GCHQ brought problems of its own. These were summarised by Sir William Jenkin, who until late 1947 had served as the Deputy Director of the IB in Delhi, but after that was catapulted into a new Whitehall department, the Commonwealth Relations Office (CRO), created in 1947 out of the former Dominions Office. From 1 March 1948 Jenkin became head of a new highly-secret section within the CRO that was responsible for receiving, circulating and recoding all intelligence relating to 'new' countries entering the Commonwealth, in order to provide Whitehall departments with regular 'live' intelligence reports. The section liaised closely with all of Britain's secret agencies, and received a flood of raw intelligence from MI5, SIS and GCHQ. Jenkin attached particular importance to that produced by GCHQ, which he (like other departments) received in files known as 'Blue Jackets' because of their distinctive blue covers. In fact, Jenkin was inundated with so much raw SIGINT from GCHQ that he complained he was unable to process and index it all, let alone analyse it and provide situation reports on it for his customers. As he explained:

In connection with Sigint particularly efforts have been made to increase the degree of security given to these reports and it is understood that those who provide reports in this category are satisfied that there is no good reason for anxiety. In connexion with Sigint and SIS reports, there is one aspect which is unsatisfactory, particularly in respect of the former which constitute most value intelligence material. It is that so far 'record-ing' has been little more than registering on receipt and 'putting away' on circulation. It is clear that if valuable information is not going to be lost sight of selected filing, sheet indexing and card indexing is necessary, and that this must be done by indoctrinated personnel.[67]

Jenkin's colleagues laconically noted that he was 'overworked'. He himself felt that as matters stood, GCHQ provided 'what they think and hope will be of interest rather than what they know will be of value'. He suggested that to make the avalanche of SIGINT more manageable, the tables should be turned, and his section should tell GCHQ 'what is wanted', and stated that a recent conference in India convened by Indonesian nationalists, which some saw as the trigger for the Malayan Emergency, was a good example of the kind of event that should be flagged up to GCHQ.

British SIGINT in the empire and Commonwealth was organised through a pact known as the UKUSA Agreement, first signed between the British and US governments in March 1946. The agreement was not a single document, as intelligence historians used to think, but in fact a series of agreements, with revisions made in 1948 and then periodically thereafter in the early 1950s. It codified the close SIGINT collaboration established between the British and US governments during the war, which had been organised through a previous treaty, known as BRUSA. The UKUSA Agreement became the fulcrum for the intelligence 'special relationship' between London and Washington in the Cold War. The text of the first UKUSA Agreement, which was only declassified in 2010 because it was considered too sensitive to release before then, makes clear that the British empire and Commonwealth played a prominent role in brokering the treaty between the two governments. A GCHQ outfit known as the London Signals Intelligence Board, representing the British govern-ment at the negotiations, bargained hard for Britain to have responsibility for SIGINT collection everywhere in the British empire, while the US government would be responsible for all other countries. However, the British delegation argued that although countries gaining 'Dominion' status would clearly no longer be part of the empire, they should not be thought of as 'third parties' and therefore outside Britain's SIGINT realm. The subtext of the negotations over the UKUSA Agreement was the loom-ing transfer of power in India.[68]

What the British government managed to do by reserving for itself the right to collect SIGINT in colonies gaining Dominion status was to guarantee its intelligence position in the post-war world, and to punch far above its weight despite its declining world power. When India and Pakistan achieved independence in 1947, they both gained what the authors of the UKUSA Agreement called 'Dominion status', though this was soon rechristened 'Commonwealth status', in a bid to make it sound less antiquated and patronising. Under the UKUSA Agreement, GCHQ retained the right to collect SIGINT in India. The UKUSA Agreement meant that Britain and its former colonies were therefore too important for Washington to ignore. A major role in brokering the agreement for the British government was played by F.H. 'Harry' Hinsley, then a young cryptanalyst who had worked at Bletchley Park, who would later write the official history of British intelligence in the Second World War.[69]

With GCHQ having secured the right to collect SIGINT in countries entering the Commonwealth, it thereafter became a recurrent theme in the 'special relationship' between London and Washington that the US government needed the vestiges of Britain's empire for intelligence collection, despite Washington's long history of anti-colonialism. Britain's colonial real estate across the world, and the deal struck in the UKUSA Agreement for GCHQ to collect SIGINT in colonial and new Commonwealth countries, guaranteed Britain's special status in the eyes of Washington, even as its imperial power and military 'hard power' influence decreased. In the 1950s and 1960s, in the pre-satellite era, when a great deal of communications were passed over long distances using high-frequency radio, Britain's remnants of empire performed an essential role by providing ground stations to collect those signals. In fact, in order to collect SIGINT, we can now see that Washington actually took over and bankrolled Britain's continued presence in some of its former colonial outposts, in the form of SIGINT outposts and intelligence agencies modelled on MI5, well after they gained independence. This confirms a thesis put forward by two influential historians of the British empire, Wm. Roger Louis and Ronald Robinson, in an article in 1994: as Washington took over parts of Britain's declining empire during the Cold War, there was effectively an 'imperialism of decolonisation'. Britain, propped up by the USA, maintained an informal empire in the Cold War, even after the demise of its formal empire. On the basis of the UKUSA Agreement, Britain's outposts of empire thus became as important for Washington for SIGINT collection as they had been for the British government itself.[70]

The UKUSA Agreement was revised in 1948 and the early 1950s to incorporate Canada, Australia and New Zealand, which divided the world into different SIGINT spheres, as covered by each signatory's listening posts, presided over by Washington and London. As Britain's formal empire began to disintegrate in the post-war years, London made huge efforts to secure strategic treaties allowing for a lasting British (and by extension American) presence in newly independent countries. Britain's old imperial bases dotted across the globe, from Cyprus to Singapore, became new homes to substantial SIGINT collection centres. In the 1950s Cyprus effectively became an enormous British SIGINT collection camp, with aerials and antennae springing up across the small island, many of them directly funded by the US government's new SIGINT agency, the NSA. In December 1963, when Prime Minister Sir Alec Douglas-Home asked whether Britain really needed to retain bases in Cyprus, the Defence Secretary, Peter Thorneycroft, replied with an emphatic 'yes', stating that the island 'houses the most important SIGINT stations and it also provided a base from which special reconnaissance flights are carried out'. In some instances, as we shall see, Britain was prepared to wage violent, dirty wars against equally violent insurgencies in order to secure its 'vital interests' in its last days of empire during the Cold War.

BRITISH GUIANA

The history of the colony of British Guiana, on the northern coast of South America, reveals just how confusing international relations could be in the Cold War. It is well known that intense pressure from the USA, steeped in its history of anti-colonialism, was one of the main reasons the British were forced to give up successive colonial holdings across the world after 1945. However, sometimes the US government's anti-colonial stance directly conflicted with its own requirements in the Cold War. When this was the case, Washington could prove itself even more colonialist than Britain.

Nowhere was this more clearly seen than in the small but geopolitically significant state of British Guiana, which from the late 1940s was campaigning for self-government and ultimately independence from Britain. Washington's attitude towards the colony was intensified by the rise to power of Fidel Castro in Cuba in 1959, and the Cuban Missile Crisis of October 1962, when the world came closer to nuclear Armageddon than at any time before or since.

As far as the US government was concerned, the main problem in British Guiana was its most prominent anti-colonial leader, Dr Cheddi

Jagan, an American-educated dentist descended from Indian sugar-plantation workers. Jagan was inspired by Nehru's anti-colonial writings, and both he and his American wife, Janet, held openly Marxist views. Jagan's politics clearly appealed to the ethnic Indian community in Guiana, who made up half of the colony's population. But the US State Department feared that if elected to power, Jagan's People's Progressive Party (PPP) would 'ruin' the colony and establish a Marxist-communist beach-head in America's back yard. Britain, for its part, made no secret of its desire to withdraw from Guiana, which had become a low strategic priority for London, as soon as possible.

Washington's fears were roused when in April 1953 Jagan was swept to power after winning a crushing victory in the colony's first ever general election for internal leadership, taking eighteen of the twenty-four newly-established constituent seats. Though Jagan had won at the polls, his electoral victory had to be ratified by London. Thereafter the USA went to extraordinary lengths to pressure Britain into postponing its planned withdrawal from the colony and ceding power to Jagan. In fact, it was apparently largely due to pressure from Washington that the British Governor, Sir Alfred Savage, took the remarkable step of overruling the general election and refusing to cede power to Jagan. This drastic measure was approved at the highest possible level in London, by Churchill himself, who on 27 September 1953 sanctioned Operation *Windsor*, the landing of British troops in British Guiana on 9 October, accompanied by the dismissal of the Jagan government and the suspension of the colony's new constitution, which for the first time included universal suffrage. After just 133 days as Chief Minister, Cheddi Jagan was ousted from office and Governor Sir Alfred Savage was given Emergency powers that remained in place for the next three years.[71]

Churchill's government justified Jagan's overthrow by claiming that 'the intrigues of Communists and their associates' in the PPP government had threatened to turn British Guiana into 'a Communist-dominated state'. London (and Washington) portrayed Jagan as an out-and-out communist. Oliver Lyttelton, the Colonial Secretary from October 1951 to July 1954, later claimed in his memoirs that he had decided to cancel Jagan's election and declare an Emergency after receiving reports from Britain's intelligence services that riots and bloodshed would soon break out, and the colony's mostly wooden capital, Georgetown, would be burned down. Lyttelton's initial reaction to Jagan's election was one of moderation, concluding that the electorate in British Guiana had spoken, and that

Jagan's manifesto included nothing more extreme than that of the opposition in Britain. However, that same month Churchill wrote to Lyttelton, venting his outrage about Jagan's election and urging that Britain 'ought surely get American support in doing all that we can to break Communist teeth in British Guiana'. He added dryly that perhaps the Americans 'would even send Senator McCarthy down there'. By September, Lyttelton's attitude had undergone a U-turn from his views in May, with him now informing the cabinet that Jagan was a dangerous communist. Something had clearly made him completely change his mind.

MI5's role in this astonishing affair was only clarified after the release in late 2011 of its numerous files on Jagan, which in total span over twenty volumes. There is nothing in them to indicate that MI5 was responsible for feeding London and Washington's fears about Jagan's communism. On the contrary, in 1951 MI5's SLO in Trinidad, whose responsibilities included British Guiana, reported that 'there is no evidence that the PPP is controlled or directed by any Communist organisation outside the Colony'. MI5's records show that Jagan first attracted the service's attention in May 1947, when the British embassy in Washington asked for information on him following a report from a 'highly confidential source' stating that Jagan had written to the Soviet embassy in Washington the previous year. MI5 and SIS had 'no trace' of Jagan in their records at the time. However, MI5's intensive surveillance of the British Communist Party revealed that from 1948 onwards he was in contact with the Party's London headquarters, which his wife Janet visited on a trip to Britain after the PPP's electoral victory in 1953. During a previous visit to Britain, in July 1951, MI5 had placed a HOW on Cheddi Jagan, intercepting his mail. The overall tenor of MI5's files on Jagan is that, although he was certainly a Marxist, and his wife was known to have been a member of a US Communist Party youth organisation in her native Chicago, beyond that there was little evidence of any political affiliation with communism. Unless MI5 provided Churchill's government with an assessment of Jagan wildly divergent from that in its own records, it is unlikely that it supported the pretext for cancelling the election in British Guiana – that Jagan was a communist. Furthermore, given its calming assessments of other leading anti-colonial figures like Kwame Nkrumah and Jomo Kenyatta, which will be discussed in Chapter 6, it seems unlikely that MI5 would have concluded that Jagan was a committed communist. In reality, as we can now see, Jagan was above all a nationalist, albeit one who spoke in Marxist language.

It appears that what really happened in 1953 was that the Colonial Office simply used 'communism' as an excuse to cancel Jagan's election. The real cause of London's alarm is more likely to have been the vast mineral wealth buried in the colony – it held huge aluminium and bauxite deposits, and in the early 1950s was providing about two-thirds of all bauxite imports to the US. From London and Washington's perspective, British Guiana was far too valuable to be handed over to a Marxist like Jagan, whose main electoral promise was to nationalise the colony's mineral reserves and redistribute its wealth. And so, having decided that Jagan would be styled a communist, it seems that London and Washington chose the version of the facts that best suited their needs – a classic intelligence failure.

This view is supported by records, currently tucked away in Oxford, which show that when making an assessment of Jagan's communism, the Colonial Office turned to one of its in-house experts, W.H. Ingrams. Ingrams had had a long colonial career, having served in various British colonies in Africa since the 1920s. In July 1953, two months after Jagan's election, he made a trip to the West Indies and British Guiana. In his ensuing report for the Colonial Office he painted a thoroughly bleak picture, describing Jagan as a committed communist and even advising that 'the Friends' (a euphemism for SIS) should be brought in to mount a counter-Soviet information campaign in the colony. We do not know what the results of Ingrams's proposals were, but they would have been music to the ears of hawks in the Colonial Office who already distrusted Jagan. It is most likely not a coincidence that it was Ingrams who, at approximately the same time, was the primary voice claiming that Jomo Kenyatta was a communist and the Mau Mau revolt in Kenya was a communist uprising, as we shall see in Chapter 6. As one contemporary in-house MI5 note complained, Ingrams and a group of his colleagues in the Colonial Office insisted on seeing a communist 'behind every gooseberry bush in every colony'.[72]

The Emergency powers in British Guiana remained in place until August 1957, when Jagan was returned to office after the PPP won another electoral victory for domestic party leadership, this time under a new constitution. As Jagan's hold on power strengthened, the British and American governments began to contemplate instigating covert action to destabilise his rule. In October 1961 Jagan again won a clear general election victory, and thereafter became Premier of British Guiana, with London still refusing to call him Prime Minister, apparently for symbolic reasons. By now, however, it was clear to London and Washington that unless covert action could produce a result to the contrary, Jagan would be the leader of independent Guiana.

In the normal course of events, MI5's background intelligence on Jagan would have played a crucial role in the transfer of power in the colony, as it did in other colonies. In British Guiana, however, MI5 was effectively sidelined. Unlike most other imperial trouble spots, it never had a resident SLO there. Instead, the SLO in Trinidad visited the colony about once a month between 1960 and 1963. Ironically, in 1963 Jagan's wife Janet was appointed Minister of Home Affairs, meaning that her duties involved liaising with MI5's SLO in Trinidad about security intelligence matters. The two people, the spy and the spied on, met on several occasions during the SLO's visits to the colony, and he provided her with extremely carefully vetted reports.

What MI5's SLO did not inform Janet Jagan was that the greatest threat to British Guiana actually came from Britain's main ally, the United States. In fact, after the October 1961 elections in British Guiana, the British government essentially gave Washington a free hand to instigate covert activities in the colony. As the imperial historian Richard Drayton has noted, the US government was given greater freedom to influence policy in British Guiana than in any other British colony. The State Department and the CIA launched a series of covert activities designed to destabilise Jagan. These involved rigging elections, paying off trade unions, and in February 1962 organising strikes and riots, and apparently even orchestrating bombing campaigns. Their main aim was to strengthen the position of Jagan's principal political rival, a supposedly 'anti-communist' black lawyer, Forbes Burnham, the leader of the People's National Congress (PNC). A moderate, a gifted orator, a graduate of the London School of Economics and a devout Methodist, who nevertheless had a taste for fast cars and women, Burnham was clearly Washington's man.[73]

Soon after his election victory in 1961, Jagan had visited President John F. Kennedy in the White House to seek US support for British Guiana's independence. Cheddi Jagan might be a Marxist, Kennedy said afterwards, 'but the United States doesn't object, because that choice was made by an honest election, which he won'. In private, JFK said the opposite. Washington feared that Jagan would turn British Guiana into another Cuba, to which he paid an official visit in 1960, as he also did to the USSR and China. The following year, as MI5 discovered, he also asked for help from the British Communist Party. After the humiliating failure to overthrow Castro by means of a CIA-backed coup, the Bay of Pigs fiasco in April 1961, Kennedy was determined not to allow a repeat with Jagan. The US Secretary of State, Dean Rusk, wrote to the British Foreign Secretary, Lord Home, in February 1962, stating: 'I must tell you now that I have reached the conclusion that it is not possible for us to put up with an independent British Guiana under Jagan.' Prime Minister Harold Macmillan told Home that Rusk's letter was 'pure Machiavellianism', exposing a 'degree of cynicism' which he found surprising in view of the fact that the Secretary of State was 'not an Irishman, nor a politician, nor a millionaire'. In his diary, Macmillan summarised the situation in British Guiana well when he noted that the Americans 'are ready to attack us as colonialists whenever it suits them', but 'are the first to squeal when "decolonisation" takes place uncomfortably near them'. Home replied sharply to Rusk:

> You say that it is not possible for you 'to put up with an independent British Guiana under Jagan' and that 'Jagan should not be allowed to accede to power again'. How would you suggest that this can be done in a democracy? And even if a device could be found, it would almost certainly be transparent ...[74]

Soon, however, Macmillan and Home gave way to US pressure. In August 1962 Kennedy authorised a covert $2 million CIA operation to drive Jagan from power before British Guiana became independent. In no other British colony was the United States ever allowed to take the lead in covert action. In October 1962, the month of the Cuban Missile Crisis, the Colonial Secretary, Duncan Sandys, agreed that the CIA should be allowed to approach Forbes Burnham, and his party, the PNC, duly received American funding. US covert action, which involved a staggering array of plots and subterfuge, began to make itself felt in the course of 1963. In April of that year the British Guiana Trades Union Congress, with American support, instigated a crippling general strike that was to last for ten weeks – longer than any general strike anywhere in the world before. US covert action was also responsible for instigating strikes and riots in Georgetown, in which as many as two hundred people may have died. In July 1963 Macmillan once again summarised the situation well, capturing the ironies of Washington's policies:

We shall not give B. Guiana 'independence' only to create a Cuba on the mainland. It is, however, rather fun making the Americans repeat over and over again their passionate plea to us to stick to 'Colonialism' and 'Imperialism' at any cost.[75]

Although Macmillan's government consented to US covert activities in British Guiana, between 1961 and 1964 a number of British officials nevertheless became increasingly exasperated by US attempts to subvert the democratic process there. In February 1962 President Kennedy's 'fixer', the Harvard historian Arthur Schlesinger Jnr, had what was apparently a heated meeting with Iain Macleod, the Colonial Secretary from October 1959 to October 1961, who told him that he disagreed with the American assessment of Jagan as a communist. Macleod warned Schlesinger that it would be impossible to 'dislodge a democratically elected party' – conveniently forgetting that this was precisely what Churchill and the Colonial Office had done in British Guiana in 1953. Although it cannot be proved conclusively, it seems highly likely that Macleod's moderate assessment of Jagan came from MI5.

It is also worth noting that US covert activities in British Guiana did not, as we might expect, originate solely with the CIA. Papers held in President Kennedy's personal archive reveal that it was the State Department, not the CIA, which was responsible for channelling funds, through American trade unions, to the British Guiana TUC.[76]

For its part, MI5 was strenuously against the use of covert action, or 'special political action' (SPA), in British Guiana. In April 1961, seven months before Jagan's election as Prime Minister, MI5's SLO in Trinidad warned that SPA would be unlikely to influence the outcome of the forthcoming elections, and 'the results of failure would probably be disastrous'. The most passionate opposition to the use of SPA against any colonial or Commonwealth government came from Alex Kellar, the Director of MI5's overseas department, E-Division:

Despite the political stresses and strains that occur between the countries of the Commonwealth, there are factors that continue to bind the individual members together to make the Commonwealth still a powerful force with which to be reckoned in world affairs. Among these factors, none is more important than the Commonwealth security complex in which the Security Service and its SLO play so dominant and influential a role. Our SLOs, in particular, have taken a leading part because, whatever the personal contributions they have made in the field as individuals, all have conducted themselves with a complete honesty of purpose and, by so doing, have gained and retained the trust, confidence and respect of the indigenous officials, administrative as well as police, that matter so much; and no more so than in the case of those new Commonwealth countries who, sensitive about their newly acquired independence, can so easily go sour on us should they identify us in, or even suspect us of, activity behind their backs.

This danger becomes more and more real as pressures ... for clandestine action within these emergent territories gain momentum with the inevitable, as it now seems, involvement of the SLO and consequent corruption of his position.

... I accept that there are recalcitrant members of our Commonwealth and that that they try our patience to the full but the UK, with its greater maturity, political experience and pivotal position, has a special responsibility for exercising patience.[77]

Despite America's covert backing of Forbes Burnham, he was unable to beat Jagan at the ballot box. But in December 1964 the US administration was able to achieve what President Kennedy described as 'a good result': although Jagan's PPP won the highest percentage of the vote, Burnham's PNC was able to form a coalition government and Burnham became Premier. In May 1966 British Guiana (renamed Guyana) gained independence, with Burnham as its first Prime Minister.

By hook or by crook, the US and British governments had achieved their aim: preventing a devoted Marxist from taking power. Ironically, however, they had created a monster. Washington's protégé, Burnham, had learned well from his American masters, slyly changing the electoral process and rigging elections after 1964. He went on to rule Guyana corruptly and incompetently for more than twenty years, wrecking the country's economy and encouraging hostility between its Afro-Caribbean and Indian communities. The story of Guyana is a perfect illustration of the theory of 'blowback' described by the American political scientist Chalmers Johnson: that US and British attempts to assert themselves in various parts of the world, and influence local policies, invariably have unintended and damaging consequences.[78]

5

Jungle Warfare:
British Intelligence and the
Malayan Emergency

Dear Lyttelton
  Malaya.
  We must have a plan.
  Secondly we must have a man.
  When we have a plan and a man, we shall succeed: not otherwise.
  Yours sincerely
  Montgomery (FM)

OLIVER LYTTELTON, *The Memoirs of Lord Chandos*[1]

'Watch out for the volcano ...'
  'What volcano?'

LEWIS CARROLL, *Alice's Adventures in Wonderland*[2]

Following the Japanese occupation during the Second World War, Britain reoccupied Malaya, its strategically vital colony in South-East Asia, which it had held since the eighteenth century, and attempted unsuccessfully to bring cohesion to it. The British ruled Malaya, but did not govern it. This was largely because of the disparate nature of the colony, which was a true melting pot of cultures. Two-thirds of the Malayan Peninsula, which separates the South China Sea from the Bay of Bengal, was comprised of thick, steamy jungle, and although the capital was Kuala Lumpur, a large amount of autonomy was devolved to the nine Malay states, each of which was a protectorate governed by its own sultan. Formal British rule was centred on the two 'Straits Settlements', or crown colonies, of Penang and Malacca, as well as Singapore. Britain attempted to bring unity to Malaya's autonomous states by creating the 'Union of Malaya'. However, the existence of the Union was vehemently opposed by the majority of the ethnic Malay population, particularly by the main vehicle for post-war nationalism, the United Malay National Organisation (UMNO). The UMNO resented concessions given to non-Malay ethnic groups in the Union, which in 1948 forced the British into replacing the Union with the 'Federation of Malaya' – the establishment of Federations became a favourite and mostly hopeless tactic on the part of Whitehall to wrap together and govern as a single entity colonies that were often totally divergent. The Malayan Federation was not very different from the Union that preceded it. It reconfirmed the privileged position of Malays in the colony's society, and likewise reinforced much of the self-governing rule of the sultans.[3]

One of the fundamental problems for the British in Malaya was that Malayan politics were divided along ethnic, racial and religious lines. A census taken in 1947 revealed that Malaya had a population of approximately five million, about half of whom were ethnically Malay and predominantly Muslim. Approximately 38 per cent of the population was ethnically Chinese, with two-thirds of that number born in mainland China, the largest single Chinese community anywhere outside China itself, while the remaining 12 per cent were Indian, with a variety of religions. The main instrument for communism there was the Malayan Communist Party (MCP), which in 1947 had about 11,800 members, the vast majority of whom (about 95 per cent) were ethnically Chinese. This meant that for many British officials in Malaya, the words 'Chinese' and 'communism' were justifiably synonymous. The British never properly understood the Chinese community in Malaya, and by extension communism in Malaya. Chinese-speakers were a rarity in the British administration: eighteen months into the Emergency, only twenty-three of the 256 Malayan Civil Service officers had passed the designated Chinese-language exams. The colony's police force was also predominantly Malay – in 1946 only 5 per cent of its members were ethnically Chinese. This inevitably caused misunderstandings and tensions between the two ethnic communities. By the middle of 1948 the British had approximately 12,000 police officials to govern the whole of the colony of Malaya, many of whom were extremely poorly equipped. Some district police forces relied on such outdated weapons as Lee Enfield rifles from 1917. However, the rewards of ruling the Malayan Peninsula, with its rich rubber plantations and tin mines, were too great for London to relinquish. Malaya was vital to Britain's Commonwealth exchange tariff area, the 'Sterling Area': in 1948 the dollar earnings of Malaya were worth more than the entire industrial output of Britain, while its rubber production represented about half of all rubber imports to the United States, and nearly all of US tin imports. The British 'Emergency' in Malaya was an old-fashioned colonial 'small war', or counter-insurgency, fought for control of rubber and tin, but at the same time a hot war fought for strategic purposes, to contain communism, in the Cold War.[4]

BRITAIN'S INTELLIGENCE FAILURE IN MALAYA

The outbreak of the Malayan 'Emergency' – or 'communist insurrection', as it was sometimes called – in June 1948 represented a dramatic intelligence failure for British intelligence in London and the British administration in Malaya. On 14 June the local Malayan Security Service (MSS) issued a report that later became notorious as a sign of its incompetence. The report assured its readers that there was 'no immediate threat to internal security in Malaya', though it conceded that 'the position is constantly changing and is potentially dangerous'. Exactly two days later, following the killing of two European estate managers and an assistant at rubber plantations in the Perak district, the colony's Governor declared an Emergency, and Britain embarked on what would become a twelve-year campaign against approximately 8,000 communist guerrillas in the jungles of Malaya. Britain's 'small but costly preoccupation' in Malaya, as Winston Churchill termed the counter-insurgency there, was to be the longest colonial Emergency that Britain faced in the post-war years, lasting from June 1948 until 1960. The Malayan Emergency soon became a war by another name: approximately 3,000 British service personnel were killed in action there, with the conflict claiming the lives of thousands of guerrilla fighters, or 'bandits' as the British first termed them, as well as probably several thousand innocent (non-combatant) people.[5]

Many of those who have studied modern intelligence failures, from Pearl Harbor to 11 September 2001, have attempted to explain them as arising from either a failure of intelligence collection, or a failure of intelligence analysis, or a combination of the two. In Malaya we can see that there was a failure of both. In fact, before the outbreak of the insurgency, Malaya's intelligence machinery was hardly worthy of the name. Its twin components were, at least in theory, the MSS and the Malayan Special Branch, but neither communicated effectively with the other. The MSS was led by John Dalley, a brave if eccentric man who had fought with the communists in the Malayan jungles against the Japanese during the war, leading a guerrilla resistance outfit called 'Dalforce'. After the war, his eccentricity expressed itself as a remarkable ability to alienate his colleagues. His irksome personality was apparently the main reason he was not allowed to sit on the Joint Intelligence Committee in the Far East (JICFE), Britain's highest overall intelligence-assessment agency in South-East Asia, established in Singapore after the war. The formal explanation given by the JICFE for Dalley's exclusion was that the MSS was 'too parochial', and was centred on Malaya. In fact, a good dose of 'parochialism' was probably precisely what the JICFE needed. Whichever way one looks at it, with the head of the local intelligence outfit absent from the JICFE, Britain's intelligence-assessment efforts in the region were inevitably going to be inefficient and uncoordinated. To make matters worse, under Dalley the MSS also produced intelligence reports that were full of contradictions and that provided their readers with no clear picture of threats. One of his colleagues remarked that Dalley sat on so many fences it was amazing he was not cut from splinters.[6]

The organisation of the MSS, which had been established in 1939, moreover did not facilitate the coordination of intelligence collection or assessment. Its Director, Dalley, was based in Singapore, while his deputy was based in Kuala Lumpur. To make matters worse, the resources the MSS had at its disposal were minuscule given the scale of its tasks. After the outbreak of the Emergency, Dalley attempted to respond to criticisms by lamenting that his service was 'desperately short of staff'. He was not wrong. In 1946 he had just four European officers on his staff, and was able to offer them only paltry pay. A translator working in the MSS was paid even less than one in the Chinese secretariat, which made employment there an unattractive prospect. As a result, noted Dalley, when the Emergency was declared, documents were 'piling up un-translated because there are not enough hours in the day for these few loyal and devoted men and women to complete their work'. Meanwhile, in 1948 the Special Branch of the Malayan police CID had just twelve officers, and they too were divided between Singapore and Kuala Lumpur – hardly a satisfactory situation for the effective coordination of intelligence.[7]

Although it is easy to ridicule the failures of Dalley's MSS, the genuine difficulties of gathering intelligence in Malaya need to be borne in mind. With its negligible resources, the MSS had to make assessments of a country in which there was no universal language, but instead a series of dialects, and an iconographic script of approximately 10,000 characters. As one MI5 officer based in Singapore later remarked: 'It is not difficult to imagine what a nightmare this makes of interpretation, translation and registry recoding in counter-intelligence work.' The MSS's failures before 1948 were also due to the extraordinary difficulties it confronted when attempting to gather intelligence on communism in the post-war years. Many of these difficulties stretched back to the war. The fall of Singapore to the Japanese in February 1942, described by Churchill as the worst defeat in British military history, was a humiliating failure for British intelligence. None of Britain's secret agencies (MI5, SIS, GCHQ) provided a warning of the Japanese land invasion, and British forces were so ill-prepared that there was not a single tank devoted to the defence of Singapore. The widespread belief that the colony's guns were facing the wrong way, pointing out to sea, is a later myth, but it is true that they were equipped with woefully insufficient shells to deal with a land invasion. SIS, in particular, devoted meagre resources in the pre-war years to gathering intelligence on the threat posed by imperial Japan, with its operations in the Far East effectively being run as a one-man show, centred on a single officer, Harry Steptoe, based in Singapore. Although Steptoe was probably more effective than his subsequent detractors like Philby gave him credit for, he did not provide the British administration in Singapore with any significant warning of Japanese invasion.[8]

One of the results of the Japanese occupation of Malaya was the loss of all significant Malayan Special Branch and MSS records on communism. The Japanese secret service, the *Kempeitai*, used these detailed records to perpetrate atrocities on the local population, especially communists. MI5's DSOs in Singapore and Hong Kong had both been interned by the Japanese, though luckily for them and the rest of British intelligence, their true identities and intelligence work remained undetected. If the Japanese had identified them, it is likely that under interrogation, which doubtless would have been brutal, they may have revealed high-level secrets, such as MI5's Double Cross System, the consequences of which would have been disastrous for Allied intelligence efforts.

The MSS and Malayan Special Branch also experienced a devastating decline in operational intelligence on communism because they lost their prize agent within the MCP. The case of Loi Tek, or Lai Tek, or 'Mr Wright', is one of the most extraordinary in the entire history of espionage, a true cloak-and-dagger story. In the course of his espionage career Loi Tek served as a triple agent, working at various times for the French, Japanese and British intelligence services. To this day, the lack of documentation about him makes it difficult to draw any definite conclusions. The outline of the story, however, can be established. It is known that Loi Tek was

Vietnamese, of mixed Sino-Vietnamese descent, the son of a bicycle-shop owner, who in the late 1920s joined the Communist Party in Indochina (the French colonial territories comprising modern Vietnam, Laos and Cambodia). He was recruited as an agent by the French security service, the Sûreté, who at some point in the early 1930s passed him over to the British in Singapore and Kuala Lumpur. In 1934 the Malayan Special Branch inserted him as a penetration agent into the Malayan Communist Party.

Loi Tek became a more successful agent than his early British handlers could have imagined. By a process of carefully arresting his immediate superiors, the British engineered his rapid rise through the Party's ranks. The breakthrough came in 1938, when he was appointed the Party's General Secretary. Due to his position, it is not an exaggeration to say that before the war the British effectively ran the Malayan Communist Party. The information provided by Loi Tek, complemented by meticulous mail interception, allowed the British to assert confidently that they had neutralised the Comintern in the Far East. Loi Tek's information led in 1931 to the arrest and imprisonment in Hong Kong of the Vietnamese communist leader Ho Chi Minh.[9]

After the fall of Singapore, as we have seen, Britain's Force 136 provided logistical support and training to the predominantly communist Malayan People's Anti-Japanese Army (MPAJA). The liaison officer between the MPAJA and Force 136 was a high-ranking Chinese member of the Malayan Communist Party, whose *nom de guerre* was Chin Peng. One of his colleagues in Force 136 later described him as 'Britain's most trusted guerrilla fighter'. As a reward for his valiant wartime efforts, five months after the end of hostilities Chin Peng was awarded an OBE, which he received from the Supreme Allied Military Commander in South-East Asia, Lord Louis Mountbatten, on the steps of the Municipal Building in Singapore. The British even treated him to a stay in Singapore's luxurious Raffles Hotel, the home of British colonial rule in South-East Asia. It is tempting to imagine Chin Peng sipping a Singapore Sling at Raffles, where that cocktail was invented. However, the post-war honeymoon between the British and Chin Peng (OBE) did not last long. The photographs that had been taken at the Victory Parade in Singapore, when he received his OBE, were soon being used to hunt down MCP members. Much like the Irgun in Palestine, who received wartime training from SOE and SIS, soon after the war Chin Peng turned on his former allies. Like many Malayan communists, he resented the replacement of one form of imperial rule (Japanese) with another (British). Furthermore, in the post-war years

Chin Peng and other high-ranking MCP officials began to suspect the activities of their leader, Loi Tek.[10]

Loi Tek's wartime intelligence subterfuge was built layer upon layer. As well as working for the British, he is known to have collaborated with the Japanese, apparently masterminding the Japanese massacre of the MCP's Central Committee in a notorious incident at the Batu caves in September 1942 – an event that conveniently eliminated most of his opponents within the Party. However, his true allegiances are undoubtedly revealed by the fact that only one British officer in Force 136 was ever betrayed and lost because of him, having apparently ignored Loi Tek's warnings that the Japanese were on to him. It is likely that intercepted communications (SIGINT) also showed his loyalty to the British, though at present a lack of documentation prevents this being substantiated.

The Malayan Communist Party grew increasingly suspicious about Loi Tek, especially about his alleged dealings with the Japanese. Although the exact sequence of events remains murky, it seems that in early 1947 he began to fear that the net was closing in on him, and in March that year he vanished, absconding with $130,000 of the Party's money. He remained in hiding in Singapore until August 1947, when he travelled to Hong Kong, and onwards to Siam (Thailand). The evidence suggests that sometime in late 1947 he was liquidated by a Chinese assassination squad in Siam. The involvement of British intelligence in Loi Tek's exfiltration from Malaya remains the missing piece in this mysterious drama. Given his wartime allegiances, and the fact that he fled to Singapore and then Hong Kong, it seems likely that the British were responsible for organising his escape. After his disappearance, Loi Tek's deputy, Chin Peng, was appointed as the new General Secretary of the Party, and attempted to regroup its ranks, shocked as they were by the treachery of their former leader.[11]

With such an extraordinarily valuable source as Loi Tek, the British had become complacent when it came to gathering intelligence on the Malayan Communist Party, and felt it unnecessary to recruit other communist agents. The problem was that when the light at the top of the stairs went out, there was total darkness. This, then, was the unfortunate situation facing the Malayan Special Branch and the MSS immediately before the outbreak of the insurgency in June 1948. Having lost all of their significant wartime records on the Party when they had been captured by the Japanese, they had now also lost their principal agent in the Party.

As well as this unenviable position regarding intelligence *collection*, there were also inherent problems that reduced accurate intelligence *assessment.* In the post-war years, Dalley's MSS was blindly fixated on Indonesian and Malay nationalism, rather than on the growing threat of communism in Malaya. It also attempted to address so many security issues, and produced so many detailed reports, that their readers were left unclear about what were genuine threats. Dalley subsequently claimed that he had issued a clear warning about the dangers posed by the MCP at a high-profile meeting in June 1947, chaired by the British Commissioner General in South-East Asia, Malcolm MacDonald. The problem, as can be seen from this meeting's minutes, was that Dalley sounded the klaxon so many times that it became meaningless. MSS cried wolf too many times.[12]

It is clear from existing British intelligence assessments of the Emergency that at the time no part of the British intelligence community, either in Malaya or in Whitehall, properly understood the nature of the insurgency. The outbreak of violence in June 1948 took Britain's secret agencies completely by surprise. Lacking any kind of firm intelligence, Dalley's MSS issued a stern report that an 'organised campaign of murder' was being waged by 'communist organisations' in the colony. The reality was completely different. The insurgency in Malaya was not an organised plot orchestrated by Chin Peng and the MCP, as British intelligence suspected, but a spontaneous rural revolt 'from below' against foreign domination and imperialism, designed to undermine British economic production in the colony. Ultimately, the reason the MSS so spectacularly failed to predict the revolt was because no plot had actually existed before 1948. In reality, the MCP's leadership was as surprised by the sudden outbreak of violence as the British. The subsequent arrest of several of the Party's cadres, including Chin Peng's deputy, Yeung Kuo, revealed how ill-prepared the Party was for the insurrection.[13]

Ironically, it was the colonial administration itself that gave shape to the insurgency. By declaring an Emergency on 18 June 1948, it provided Chin Peng and the MCP with a rallying point, a *casus belli*, which they exploited ruthlessly. British colonial authorities would repeat this same mistake in subsequent years, as one colonial Emergency after another was declared across the empire. In each there was a self-fulfilling – or self-defeating – cycle by which the declaration of an Emergency provided a rallying point for insurgents, and thus largely created otherwise non-existent coordinated insurgencies.

Chin Peng seized the opportunity presented by a spontaneous revolt, and turned it into overall insurgency. On the first day of the Emergency he escaped from the clutches of the British, leaping over a wall, and fled

into the jungle, where he took up what would become a twelve-year struggle. He soon regrouped about 3,000 former anti-Japanese (MPAJA) guerrilla fighters into their old formations. The humid jungle air had not
destroyed the munitions dumps they had left behind in 1945, as the British
hoped. However, they fought against the British with the same ferocity
with which they had previously fought the Japanese. The insurgency they
waged thereafter was not a war against the British as such, but against
'imperialism'. It was, above all, a war for 'national liberation'. Chin Peng's
establishment in February 1949 of the Malayan People's Liberation Army
(MPLA) was designed to symbolise the nationalist struggle of Malaya's
three principal ethnic groups, Malays, Chinese and Indians. For recruits,
the MPLA drew heavily on townsfolk and 'squatters' living at the edges of
the jungle, which indicates that the insurgency was fuelled by the massive
politicisation of previously disenfranchised social groups, like women,
peasants and workers, all of whom came together to fight British 'imperialism', as they had previously done against the Japanese.[14]

INTELLIGENCE: BRITAIN'S ACHILLES HEEL IN MALAYA

All of the British government departments concerned with Malaya, both
civilian and military, in Whitehall and in the colony itself, were spectacularly slow at applying what should have been learned from previous counter-insurgency campaigns. Although Britain's recent experiences in
Palestine provided clear lessons about how not to wage a successful counter-insurgency, the authorities in Malaya largely overlooked them, which
is even more surprising considering that about five hundred former
Palestine policemen were transferred to Malaya after Britain's evacuation
from Palestine in May 1948, including Nicol de Gray, the former
Commissioner of Police in Palestine.

In the early stages of the Emergency, MI5 was called in to advise. It
attempted, largely in vain, to reform the ways in which intelligence was
collected in the colony. MI5's Director-General, Sir Percy Sillitoe, visited
Malaya, where he was spotted by a number of local reporters – although
subsequent historians have largely failed to identify MI5's role in the
Emergency. Sillitoe and Dalley got off to a bad start when Dalley accused
the MI5 head of being a Glasgow street-corner boy – a reference to Sillitoe's
days as a policeman in Glasgow. Sillitoe took the insult badly, and it was
largely on his recommendation that Dalley's Service, the MSS, was
disbanded and replaced by the Special Branch of the Malayan police CID,

though by any reckoning the MSS was so incompetent that it deserved to be closed down.[15]

The Special Branch liaised closely with MI5's regional SLOs, based in Kuala Lumpur and Singapore, who in turn reported to Britain's inter-service agency in the Far East, Security Intelligence Far East (SIFE). The founding charter of SIFE in August 1946, only recently available in archives, reveals that it was closely modelled on Security Intelligence Middle East (SIME). Like its sister outfit, SIFE was a non-executive and purely advisory agency, not responsible for intelligence collection (espionage), but only for intelligence assessment and its dissemination. Although it was technically inter-service, it was predominantly an MI5 show. At its height it had over sixty officers reporting to it, a large number of whom were seconded from MI5. All of MI5's regional SLOs in the Far East, from New Delhi to Hong Kong, reported to SIFE's headquarters located at the offices of the Commissioner General of South-East Asia, Malcolm MacDonald, in the Cathay Building, Phoenix Park, Singapore, described by *The Times* as a 'tropical duplication of Whitehall', as did the regional SIS stations across Asia. SIFE was therefore responsible for the assessment of intelligence both from British colonial and Commonwealth countries (through MI5) and from foreign territories (through SIS).

The first head of SIFE was C.E. Dixon, who was replaced in 1947 by an experienced and well-respected MI5 officer, Malcolm Johnson, a veteran of the Indian police who had served in the IB in Delhi for seventeen years. Johnson was killed in an air crash soon after taking up his appointment, and was replaced by a succession of MI5 officers. Following his visit to Malaya, Sillitoe took the opportunity to appoint a new head of SIFE. He chose the eccentric MI5 officer Alex Kellar, a former head of SIME who had been one of the main MI5 officers dealing with Zionist terrorism. Sillitoe warned him not to push himself too hard and suffer another nervous breakdown, as he had experienced at SIME. He hoped that with Kellar at the helm and with Dalley now gone, Britain's intelligence-gathering efforts in Malaya would soon improve. His hopes were ill-founded: it took three years for them to start working properly.[16]

The reforms that MI5 instigated in Malaya after the declaration of the Emergency were a step in the right direction, but they were not nearly enough to cope with the intelligence requirements needed to defeat the insurgency. Malcolm MacDonald was particularly scathing about the level of intelligence with which he was presented. MacDonald, a former Colonial Secretary and the son of the former Prime Minister Ramsay

MacDonald, had a good deal of knowledge of intelligence matters, having served as British High Commissioner in Canada when the Gouzenko scandal broke. He was also responsible for chairing annual meetings of the JIC Far East.

Personality clashes within the Malayan administration were the root of many of the problems in the colony, and continued to beleaguer Britain's intelligence and security efforts there even after Dalley's departure. MacDonald had a visceral dislike of MI5's Alex Kellar, which undermined their effective cooperation. In an attempt to improve the situation, Kellar was replaced as head of SIFE by another MI5 officer, John Morton, a veteran of the Indian police. While Morton's appointment helped relations between SIFE and MacDonald, acrimonious disputes and turf wars arose between the new British High Commissioner in Malaya, appointed in September 1948, Sir Henry 'Jimmy' Gurney (formerly Chief Secretary in Palestine) and the new Police Commissioner, Nicol de Gray (formerly Commissioner of Police in Palestine). Relations between the two were so bad that by 1950 they were barely on speaking terms. Gurney was a slight fifty-year-old with a great deal of panache (even while stationed in Palestine he was a regular contributor to the satirical magazine *Punch*), while Gray was a much more no-nonsense character, who arrived in Malaya with a coterie of former Palestine police officers.

The Colonial Secretary, Arthur Creech Jones, initially thought the Palestine element was a good idea in Malaya, but it proved to be a major mistake. Many of the ex-Palestine servicemen had been thoroughly brutalised by their experiences there. They were totally ignorant of local conditions in Malaya, and on a number of occasions showed themselves to be a liability, resorting to violent, arbitrary behaviour. In the early stages of the conflict Britain's propaganda agencies tried hard to cover up unpleasant 'Palestinian' incidents.

Added to an already noxious mixture of personality clashes was the holder of the ill-defined position of Director of Intelligence in Malaya, Sir William Jenkin, who set himself up as a rival to Police Commissioner Gray. Jenkin was brought in from the IB in Delhi, and would later, as we have seen, head up a top-secret new intelligence department in the Commonwealth Relations Office. Partly as a result of the competing personalities and bureaucracies of Gurney, Gray and Jenkin, intelligence in Malaya was an uncoordinated mess. In fact, in April 1950 the talented Director of Military Operations in Malaya, General Sir Harold Briggs, who formulated the most influential blueprint for dealing with the Emergency, known as 'the Briggs Plan', lamented that intelligence was the 'Achilles' heel' of Britain's counter-insurgency efforts in Malaya, when it should have been the first line of attack.[17]

If Britain's experiences in Palestine had shown anything, it was that coordinated intelligence efforts were crucial to waging an effective counter-insurgency. However, the British authorities in Malaya failed to learn this lesson, which could have saved time, money and manpower. In the early stages of the Emergency the administration attached little weight to intelligence matters, failing to upgrade and overhaul its operations beyond the most basic reforms proposed by MI5. Instead, it preferred to attack its enemies in the jungles by launching special forces operations. Immediately after the declaration of the Emergency, the administration established a secret new group, 'Ferret Force', made up of six special units, mostly comprised of old Force 136 personnel, many of whom had only recently been demobilised. Force 136 had only been officially disbanded in 1946, so when Jenkin proposed the establishment of a 'Special Service Unit' for Malaya in June 1948, it was obvious where a pool of recruits could be found. Talent spotters scoured the Special Forces Club in London's Knightsbridge, where many old Force 136 men gathered to tell their war stories at the bar. Recruitment to 'Ferret Force' was mostly through word of mouth and letters of recommendation, some of which took on a comic air, such as one that proposed a twenty-seven-year-old veteran of Force 136 campaigns in South Siam who had 'just failed his Law Society Finals', and who, as his recruiter pointed out, was probably looking for another adventure. That is exactly what he got. Ferret Force attacked the MCP's training camps deep in the jungle and carried out raids to cut off its supply routes. It benefited from the experiences of old Force 136 hands like Richard Broome and John Davis, who advised the new unit and taught its officers how to penetrate the MCP by placing agents in its ranks.[18]

The creation of Ferret Force out of the remnants of Force 136, many of whose officers had only recently been demobilised, was parallel to Chin Peng's guerrillas, the overwhelming majority of whom had fought with Force 136 during the war. Despite the enormous sum of US$350 that the British administration offered wartime MCP fighters to come out of the jungle and demobilise after 1945, it is clear that some never laid down their weapons, either literally or psychologically. In many ways, warfare in Malaya never really stopped in September 1945. The MCP mobilised against the British where they had left off against the Japanese, while

Ferret Force was assembled out of Force 136. The result was that after June 1948 there were effectively two SOE-trained special forces units pitched against each other in the jungles of Malaya. One member of British special forces, Major 'Mad' Mike Calvert ('Mad' because of his bravery), a veteran of Orde Wingate's Chindit operations in India, recalled an amusing moment when he was ambushed by the MCP:

> ... my driver and I were moving at a fair pace along the road when a burst of machine-gun fire came from the thick bush, slightly ahead of us. We jerked to a halt and flung ourselves into a ditch by the side of the road. For the first time in more than five years I was under enemy fire when a grenade landed neatly beside me in the ditch. I thought it was for the last time. I snatched up the grenade, hoping to be able to throw it before it went off, and then I noticed that the pin was still in position. A piece of paper was attached to it and a scrawled message said; 'How do you do, Mr Calvert?' It could mean only one thing. Somebody I had known, and probably trained, in the old days in Hong Kong or in Burma, was now in the other side, fighting for the Communists.[19]

Ferret Force was not as successful as the British had hoped. It only survived for about a year, when animosity between it and conventional military forces in Malaya, which resented the encroachment of a 'private', largely civilian army into their realm, forced its closure. However, by 1952 special forces operations had once again become a priority in Malaya, heralded by the arrival of the Special Air Service (SAS). Despite its wartime successes, the SAS had been disbanded in 1945. But, in the face of mounting pressure from Britain's commitments overseas, coupled with budget cuts at home that ruled out expanding conventional military forces, in 1947 it was reformed as a territorial and volunteer regiment, known as 21 SAS (the Artists). It maintained itself as a force-in-waiting, ready to go whenever and wherever needed. General Templer would later attach considerable importance to the SAS in Malaya.[20]

When violence first erupted in Malaya, it was surprising that the British military authorities had failed to learn lessons from Palestine, but it was even more surprising that they also overlooked the British Army's own wartime experiences of irregular warfare in the jungles of Malaya and Burma. These had been set out in a British Army pamphlet commonly known as 'The Jungle Book', but British forces largely neglected it in the early stages of the Emergency, with the result that they were forced to relearn many of the combat lessons they had already established. To make matters worse, the Special Branch and other security forces in Malaya did not even have a reliable photograph of their new arch enemy, Chin Peng. As the MCP leader later explained, the photo of him that the Malayan police had on record happened to have been taken while he was suffering from a serious bout of malaria, with an extremely swollen face, and thus bore little resemblance to him. British security patrols were therefore scouring the countryside for a phantom. An indication of how confused they were about their new enemies was the fact that they could not even decide what to call them. At first they called Chin Peng's guerrilla fighters 'bandits', then 'terrorists', and eventually after 1952 settled on 'communist terrorists' (shortened to 'CTs'), a name that helped to reinforce the Emergency's Cold War credentials for sceptical US and UN audiences, who opposed anything that smacked of 'old colonialism'.[21]

MOSCOW GOLD

The outbreak of the Emergency produced an 'information panic' in Malaya, much like those British colonial authorities had frequently experienced in India in the past. SIGINT obtained by GCHQ, referred to by its wartime epithet as 'Most Secret Sources', provided some indications about guerrilla formations, derived from their intercepted radio communications. Security forces also scrambled to gather information by interrogating captured insurgents. Neither of these, however, produced any meaningful intelligence. Lacking significant information on how the 'campaign of violence' was being orchestrated, British authorities convinced themselves, and tried to convince others, that outside powers were to blame for it. Needing a scapegoat, all of the main components of British intelligence in Malaya – the Special Branch, MI5, SIFE and the JICFE – became obsessed with the idea that the insurgency was being orchestrated by communists abroad.[22]

The Malayan Emergency certainly had all the hallmarks of a Stalinist plot carried out by the Cominform, which under the leadership of Andrei Zhadanov aimed to 'liberate' colonies from the yoke of imperialism. Another plausible culprit was the looming spectre of communist China. After all, as has been noted, about two-thirds of the Chinese in Malaya were born in mainland China, and the vast majority of the MCP's membership were ethnically Chinese. It was only natural, argued British intelligence assessments, that communist guerrillas in Malaya should be taking their instructions from either the Soviet Union or China. Such assessments undoubtedly helped the British government when persuading Washington and the United Nations that it was not fighting a colonial war of yesteryear, but a valuable struggle within the Cold War. In 1950 the Colonial Office published a major appraisal of the British empire, designed to assuage US and UN criticism over 'colonialism', which alleged that the MCP was 'part of the Kremlin's worldwide campaign against western powers'. Some British officials claimed the insurrection was funded by Moscow gold, while Malcolm MacDonald was convinced that Chinese communism lurked behind Chin Peng's guerrillas.[23]

Despite Britain stressing the Cold War credentials of the conflict, relations between British intelligence and the newly established CIA, founded in 1947, were not close when it came to Malaya. By 1948 the CIA had opened stations in Singapore and Hong Kong, but as one MI5 report that year noted, little information was forthcoming from either. There was, complained MI5, essentially a one-way flow of information, with the CIA station in Singapore functioning as little more than a 'post-box'. This probably arose because of the CIA's nervousness about cooperating with other intelligence agencies, even Britain's, and not because of the strategic importance of Britain's struggle in Malaya. A CIA assessment of the situation there, compiled in November 1949, bluntly recognised its strategic importance, opening with the words: 'Primarily, Malaya is of importance to the US because it is the world's greatest producer of rubber and tin.'[24]

The smoking gun, as far as British intelligence was concerned, which proved outside communist control of the insurgency in Malaya, was a joint conference of the World Federation of Democratic Youth and the International Union of Students, both Moscow-controlled, held in Calcutta in February 1948. It was here, allegedly, that Moscow provided instructions for Malayan communists to start a revolt. Information reaching MI5 at the time, which has been repeated numerous times since, was that the leader of the Australian Communist Party, Laurence Sharkey, passed instructions to Chin Peng and the MCP on his stop-off in Singapore during his return trip to Australia in March 1948. However, according to the recently published account of the insurgency by Chin Peng, and also according to Soviet archives, this was not the case. While Chin Peng and the MCP were aware of 'outside' influences, and witnessed communist successes in China with admiration, they did not receive instructions from abroad to instigate guerrilla operations, nor did Soviet intelligence offer any specific instructions.[25]

British intelligence was so fixated on identifying outside communist influences that it never really understood the nature of the insurgency in Malaya, which in fact was largely spontaneous and fuelled by small town and village loyalties, which the MCP mobilised. While Chin Peng and his comrades were of course aware of the Soviet underground organisation Cominform, their principal reason for preparing an armed struggle was actually the fact that the MCP's main tool, the Pan-Malayan Federation of Trade Unions, was to be outlawed by the colonial administration. The resulting insurgency was caused by a social crisis within Malaya between different ethnic communities, both urban and rural, and was largely the result of opportunism. Organised crime gangs were particularly successful at fanning the flames of colonial grievances for their own purposes. In 1947 the Malaya CID had estimated that there were as many as 20,000 Chinese triads living in the colony, 2,000 of whom were thought to be actively leading criminal lives. The insurgency in Malaya became a catch-all revolt for anyone with a grievance against the status quo, from communists to organised crime gangs.[26]

THE MAN WITH THE PLAN

The year 1951 was a low point for Britain's counter-insurgency effort in Malaya. It seemed clear to British officials that they were losing the war. Weary of his bureaucratic battles with Gray, in October that year Jenkin resigned as Director of Intelligence. Moreover, the talented Director of Military Operations, Sir Harold Briggs, was terminally ill with cancer and retired in November, dying in Cyprus little more than a year later. Combined with these losses, Sir Henry Gurney, the High Commissioner, was killed in a bloody ambush by MCP guerrillas. Gurney was an easy target, usually travelling around the colony in a staff car flying a Union flag. On 7 October his escort vehicle broke down, but Gurney took the decision to press on. As his car rounded Fraser's Hill in Pahang, the MCP's guerrillas struck. Sir Henry's wife and private secretary took cover, but he himself made an attempt to reach a bank at the side of the road, where he was shot point-blank, execution style. The thirty or so guerrilla fighters who had carried out the ambush were hunted down, but only five were eventually incarcerated.[27]

In short, the situation for the British in 1951 could not have been worse. It was at that point, however, that the tide began to turn. The real turning point came with the appointment of General (later Field Marshal) Sir

Gerald Templer as High Commissioner in Malaya in January 1952. To enable him to carry out his mission, Churchill bestowed on Templer more power than any British military leader had held since the time of Oliver Cromwell, three centuries before. Templer was a hard-hitting, no-nonsense military man, a former Director of Military Intelligence and one of Montgomery's wartime protégés, who had earned a reputation for one of his hobbies, fire-eating, and also for sacking the Mayor of Cologne in occupied Germany, Konrad Adenauer, later the first Chancellor of West Germany. It is debatable to what extent he devised new strategies in Malaya, and to what extent he simply imposed existing ones, but his presence in the colony certainly had the effect of 'electrifying' British forces there, as one MI5 report put it. The 'Tiger of Malaya' enforced the Briggs Plan with an iron first. When he arrived in Kuala Lumpur in April 1952 he drove from the airport in the car, still riddled with bullet holes, in which Gurney had been ambushed.[28]

As a former Director of Military Intelligence, Templer 'knew his onions', as he put it, when it came to intelligence matters. From the start of his time in Malaya he placed intelligence at the forefront of operations. Soon after his arrival he told the journalist Harry Miller of the *Straits Times*: 'The Emergency will be won by our intelligence system – our Special Branch.' One of his earliest and most important intelligence reforms was to quash the bureaucratic in-fighting between the various agencies. He removed Police Commissioner Gray, and replaced him with a bright London Special Branch officer, Arthur Young, whom we shall encounter again in Kenya. He also overhauled the entire intelligence structure in the colony, ordering that from that point on a single agency, the Special Branch, would be responsible for all intelligence operations there, and giving it considerably more resources. In 1948 it had just twelve officers and forty-four inspectors, but in 1952 alone Special Branch inspectors and police lieutenants rose from 114 to 195, increasing to 297 the following year, with significantly more Chinese-speakers.[29]

To oversee these reforms Templer appointed a new Director of Intelligence, who sat on his staff, the Directorate of Operations, at the highest level and had direct access to Templer himself. Templer's first choice for the job was MI5's Dick White, who like Sillitoe had made a personal inspection of Malaya, but White turned it down, probably because he had his eye on becoming MI5's Director-General. Instead, Templer chose another highly recommended MI5 officer, Jack Morton, then serving as the head of SIFE. Morton became one of Templer's closest

advisers, seeing him most evenings, often over gin & tonic sundowners. As
with Sillitoe's visit to the colony, it is remarkable, given that Morton's
name and his MI5 position were publicised at the time, more historians
have not noticed the direct role performed by MI5 in the Malayan
Emergency.[30]

Under Templer and Morton a coordinated intelligence system was
established in Malaya. Even Chin Peng admitted that 'the enemy's intelligence efforts improved under Templer'. The task facing Templer and
Morton was to acquire operational intelligence that would be useful for
British forces fighting insurgents in the jungle. The Colonial Secretary,
Oliver Lyttelton, had grasped the value of this when he made a crisis visit
to the colony at the end of 1951:

> The importance of intelligence in the Malayan campaign cannot be exag-
> gerated. Every police operation is in a large measure an intelligence task
> and the Malayan campaign is in essence a police operation. In a country
> covered with dense jungle, where evasion is easy and contact with the
> enemy cannot be made without secret information, it is essential that
> intelligence should be gained from the Communist forces without their
> knowing. Intelligence, therefore, to use semi-technical language, must be
> 'live' as well as 'blown' or 'dead'.[31]

Templer ordered that more effort should be put into gathering 'live' intelligence, acquired primarily from human agents and SIGINT, but he also
acknowledged the continued need for obtaining 'dead' intelligence, from
sources such as captured documents or prisoners of war, which provided
valuable background information but was not usually directly
'actionable'.

Undoubtedly the most important reform that Templer and Morton
instigated, however, was to make the Special Branch solely responsible for
gathering 'live' intelligence. This put an end to the years of confusion and
duplication of duties that had hitherto undermined Britain's intelligence
efforts in Malaya. In Morton's words, after 1952 the Special Branch became
the 'sharp end of the intelligence machine', and was the colony's 'national
security and intelligence organisation'. Morton was served by a Combined
Intelligence Staff, which embraced (as its name suggests) all three armed
services, the police and civilian agencies. After the introduction of these
reforms, military intelligence officers were attached to the Special Branch,
and were made responsible for feeding operational intelligence to security

forces. This close coordination of intelligence-gathering transformed the British response to the Malayan Emergency into arguably the most successful counter-insurgency in modern times. Templer also recommended the establishment of what he termed 'killer squads', a rapid-deployment force at the disposal of the Special Branch who could track down and kill insurgents on the basis of intelligence received.

The newly appointed head of Special Branch, who served as Morton's right-hand man and oversaw all these reforms, was Guy Madoc, a career Malayan Special Branch officer. Madoc had previously been in charge of the Special Branch's communist section, and in his spare time was a keen ornithologist, the author of a book on the birds of Malaya, which he started writing on stolen paper while incarcerated by the Japanese in Singapore during the war.[32]

To help oversee the reforms, in 1952 Morton also brought in a talented Australian intelligence (ASIO) officer, a Cambridge-educated anthropologist and veteran of Force 136 in Malaya, Richard Noone – an appropriate name for a spook. Noone helped to lead a special SAS unit, the Malayan Scouts, made up of aboriginal forces including Gurkhas, Iban and Dyak trackers. The Malayan Scouts effectively served as the killer squads Templer had previously recommended. Their type of 'special action', as it was euphemistically termed, received considerable logistical support from Templer, who carried on the tradition of Force 136's wartime operations.

Templer was extremely well-versed in the value of guerrilla warfare, having spent six months on SOE's governing council at the invitation of its leader, Major General Colin Gubbins, after he had been wounded in April 1943 in Italy (by a grand piano blown out of a lorry in front of him). With Templer's overall leadership and Noone's day-to-day guidance, the Malayan Scouts and 21 SAS made use of increasingly daring tactics to find and eliminate insurgents. One of the greatest difficulties 21 SAS faced when carrying out deep-penetration patrols was the time and energy spent actually walking into the main operational theatre. Troop-carrying helicopters only became regularly used in 1953. Under the leadership of Mike Calvert, 21 SAS therefore developed what became known as 'tree jumping', a tactic by which operatives were parachuted directly into the jungle, in the hope that its thick trees would catch their canopies, and they could then safely lower themselves to ground. The SAS units operating in Malaya also maintained close liaison with Britain's secret agencies, which provided them with special equipment, including 'small wireless sets, silent pistols' and 'S-phones', an early form of walkie-talkie.

Templer also sanctioned the creation of a small special forces unit to track down and if possible eliminate the colonial administration's public enemy number one, Chin Peng himself. The unit, established in February 1953, was run from a small room at Templer's headquarters in Kuala Lumpur, with Morton's support. The mission to hunt down and kill Chin Peng was codenamed Operation *Profit*, but after six months, with few leads to go on, it was shut down. Today, nearly sixty years later, Chin Peng is still alive, proving how elusive an enemy he was for the British in the jungles of Malaya.[33]

Malaya holds an important place in the history of British special forces. It was there that the SAS found its form and function for the post-war world. In 1952 it established a full-time regiment, known as the 22 SAS, which grew out of the Malayan Scouts. Over subsequent decades, with the break-up of the empire, successive British governments found an increasing need for the SAS as a low-profile counter-insurgency outfit. Its functions from its earliest days in Malaya to the present have largely remained the same: it specialises in sabotage, ambush, covert liaison and intelligence collection. One of the most important SAS efforts in Malaya was Operation *Termite* in July 1954, which was the largest operation of combined British forces at that point in the Emergency. The target was two communist camps in the Kinta and Raia valleys east of Ipoh, in the state of Perak, which was one of the most communist-controlled areas in all of Malaya. More than fifty aircraft (Lincolns, Hornets and Valettas) and helicopters, two hundred SAS paratroopers and ground forces from the West Yorkshire Regiment and the 1/6th Gurkhas were deployed in a coordinated attack. Two sweeps of Lincolns made bombing attacks on the communist bases, thirty seconds apart, dropping 1,000-pound bombs. As soon as the bombing had finished, Valettas dropped two squadrons of the 22nd SAS Regiment. The operation was a success, with a considerable number of communists killed. However, the SAS also suffered casualties, largely during the parachute descent into the trees.

Jack Morton retired as Director of Intelligence in Malaya in 1954, and went on to serve as an MI5 Security Intelligence Adviser seconded to the Colonial Office, thereafter working in MI5's section for 'overseas affairs', E-Division, and ending his career in Northern Ireland. Guy Madoc remained as head of the Special Branch until Malaya's independence in 1957, and was retained by the new government as 'Deputy Director (Security and Intelligence)' in the Prime Minister's office until 1959. Morton was replaced as Director of Intelligence in Malaya by his old

colleague Richard Noone, who retained the job until Malaya's independence. In the early 1960s Noone became a special adviser on jungle warfare
to US forces, and was responsible for drawing up plans for counter-
subversion in Vietnam and Laos.[34]

BREAKING THE INSURGENCY

Some historians, such as Anthony Short, have argued that it was Templer
who broke the back of the insurgency in Malaya, while others, such as Karl
Hack, have suggested that the tide had already turned for the British before
his arrival, under his predecessor, Sir Harold Briggs. Briggs became
Director of Operations in Malaya in 1950, and was the architect of the
most influential counter-insurgency strategy in the colony. Evidence
seems to indicate that the so-called 'Briggs Plan' was causing communist
guerrilla forces considerable problems even before the arrival of Templer.
This has been acknowledged by Chin Peng himself, who later explained
that the Party's so-called October 1951 'Directives' meant that even at that
point the Party was facing a 'crisis of survival', and had been forced to
change its guerrilla combat tactics.

The cornerstone of the Briggs Plan, which after his arrival Templer
brutally enforced, was a massive system of population control, detention
and resettlement – a strategy that the British would repeat in subsequent
anti-colonial Emergencies, particularly in Kenya. In Malaya about 10 per
cent of the colony's entire population, that is over 500,000 people, were
forcibly resettled by British forces. As Jack Morton later noted in a lecture
he gave to MI5, the resettlement programme was 'a social experiment
without parallel anywhere in the history of British colonial administration'. Its aim was to separate jungle insurgents from the rest of the population, and particularly to break the link (called the *Min Yuen*) between the
urban populations and jungle fighters. The British military suspected
(with some justification) that the so-called 'squatter' populations at the
fringes of the jungle – which were predominantly Malay Chinese –
provided logistical support to the jungle fighters. British forces therefore
took the drastic step of rehousing this entire population in a total of 480
'New Villages', essentially detention compounds guarded by police and
dogs, floodlit at night, and surrounded by high barbed-wire fences. To
enforce the physical and psychological separation of the New Villages,
guards enforced strict curfews and identity checks at their entrances and
exits, with people searched and their movements recorded. There were

allegations that during entry to the New Villages, women were forced to strip and were roughly handled. In addition to the forced resettlement of 'squatters' into New Villages, the British also deported about 12,000 individuals from Malaya altogether, mostly to mainland China, the majority of whom were expelled between 1948 and 1952.[35]

It is not an exaggeration to say that during the Emergency, Malaya effectively became a police state. A series of Emergency Regulations provided the colonial administration and its security forces with widespread powers, which often led to arbitrary forms of 'justice'. The Emergency Regulations that British colonial administrations unleashed in Malaya and in subsequent colonial Emergencies had their origins in the 1939 Emergency Powers Order-in-Council, which allowed colonial administrations, as subsidiary legislatures, to implement Emergency Regulations as and when needed. The 1939 Order-in-Council was itself probably derived from British 'imperial policing' efforts in India in the nineteenth century and in Ireland in the 1920s. The Emergency Regulations that the British deployed also bear close resemblance to previous European colonial 'small war' practices in the late nineteenth and early twentieth centuries.

One of the most important points to appreciate about the Emergency Regulations let loose on Malaya was that, as in later British colonial insurgencies, the civilian administration continued to function after the declaration of the Emergency: martial law was not declared across the whole of the colony. That said, the Emergency Regulations provided the British in Malaya with widespread punitive powers that came close to martial law. Among other provisions, Articles 17C and 17D of the Regulations meant that anyone found carrying arms, ammunition or explosives without a licence could be hanged, while those caught with communist propaganda were liable to a sentence of ten years' imprisonment. The Regulations also stipulated that the colony's entire population had to be registered, with their fingerprints and photographs taken, and forced to carry identity cards at all times – a hallmark of a police state. They also allowed for resettlement, banishments, curfews and capital punishment, as well as detention without trial, with the administration deploying the tired old argument that the suspension of *habeas corpus* was necessary to prevent the intimidation of witnesses. By May 1950, 7,644 individuals were being held by the security forces under the Emergency Regulations, and another 3,076 were under collective detention orders. By mid-January 1952 the colonial administration had signed a total of 26,741 detention orders.

These figures tell only part of the story, however. As MI5's Morton recognised, before his appointment the policy of mass arrests was a blunt instrument that in many cases was counter-productive: 'The number [of those detained] was in fact 10,730 and the tragedy was that through ignorance or lack of good information in the first place, many of these prisoners were innocent but were now being converted into embittered communists'.[36]

To make matters worse, some security forces abused the widespread powers they had at their disposal. There were instances when the police would set people up, pushing communist literature through their letter-boxes, and five minutes later Special Branch teams would storm in and find the 'incriminating' evidence. The draconian Emergency Regulations, combined with the abuse of those powers by some security personnel, place Britain's anti-guerrilla campaigns in Malaya squarely alongside the notorious end-of-empire campaigns fought by other European powers, such as the French in Algeria and the Dutch in Indonesia. As two leading historians, Christopher Bayly and Timothy Harper, have recently noted, Britain's counter-insurgency efforts in Malaya are not pretty when looked at closely.[37]

An early example of the ferocious way in which Templer would enforce the Emergency Regulations was seen just a month after his arrival in the colony, in March 1952, at Tanjong Malim, a small town thirty miles north of Kuala Lumpur. Guerrilla forces cut off the water supply to the town, then ambushed the patrol party sent out to restore it, killing twelve, with five more injured. Following the ambush, Templer travelled to the town and imposed collective punishments on its inhabitants, denying them food and imposing a curfew for twenty-two hours per day until the culprits were handed over. He told the inhabitants that it was their duty to inform the authorities who the guerrillas were, and provided them with sealed boxes for anonymously naming insurgents, which led to twenty-four arrests. Templer's tactic of using anonymous questionnaires to encourage Chinese villagers to divulge information about guerrillas was subsequently replicated with success throughout the whole colony, code-named Operation *Letter-Box*.

The fundamental problem facing British forces in Malaya was the elusive nature of Chin Peng's guerrilla forces, who rarely risked fighting in the open. Instead of being able to engage their enemies in conventional ways, security forces and the Special Branch switched their attention to penetrating the courier system of the *Min Yuen*, literally translated as 'the organisation'. The *Min Yuen* was comprised of 'squatters' at the edge of the jungle who formed a kind of lifeline or umbilical cord for the 'bandits' in the jungle. They relayed messages between guerrilla forces and provided them with logistical support and supplies. Briggs realised that the insurgents drew all their support – food, intelligence and supplies – from local populations, so the logical way to defeat them was to attack and cut off their supply routes. However, identifying and penetrating *Min Yuen* operations was no easy task for the Special Branch, for the methods they used were, in Morton's words, 'almost fool-proof'. The method Briggs devised of bringing guerrilla fighters out into the open, where they could be attacked, was through a process of food denial. British forces imposed a strict system of rationing in the 'New Village' compounds, so that no extra food was available for *Min Yuen* operatives to smuggle out to insurgents in the jungle. No one could buy food without identity papers, and cooks in the New Villages were deliberately instructed to prepare meals that would quickly spoil in the jungle's humid air. These methods were remarkably successful. The tighter the food controls became, the more guerrillas were forced out of the jungle to search for food, enabling security forces to attack and either capture or kill them.

The Special Branch also penetrated the *Min Yuen*, and recruited some of its operatives as double agents. Some of the most valuable intelligence acquired by the British during the whole of the Emergency came from double agents, or 'surrendered enemy personnel' (SEPs). SEPs were usually *Min Yuen* couriers whom the Special Branch recruited and turned, then sent back into the jungle to make contact with the guerrilla forces they were supplying. The origin of using SEPs in this way is unclear. Although similar tactics had been used by British special forces in Palestine, in the so-called 'Q-Patrols', the British forces in Malaya seem to have devised the use of SEPs as double agents independently, albeit with a nod to practices in Palestine and to SOE's wartime tradition in Malaya itself. Whatever their exact origin, the Special Branch placed such a high value on SEPs, and imposed such tight security over their activities, that British officials were not even allowed to mention the existence of SEPs over telephone or radio for fear of interception.

Some details about how the Special Branch turned *Min Yuen* couriers and other SEPs into double agents remain mysterious, but the main elements of the story can now be pieced together. The usual method was that, through intensive surveillance within the New Villages and anonymous questionnaires, the Special Branch would monitor suspected *Min*

Yuen operatives and when possible, gather compromising material on their activities, including photographs, intercepted communications or captured documents. Usually an Asian Special Branch officer would then make an approach to the suspect, and present him or her with the compromising material. Suspects were then taken to a Combined Services Detailed Interrogation Centre, where interrogators set to work attempting to 'break' and 'turn' them. While they were being interrogated, their belongings were rifled through and scrutinised for messages between insurgent forces. Some of the messages discovered were written in minute Chinese characters on rice paper, rolled up in small containers thinner than matchsticks and hidden in household products like baby powder. A small, dedicated, Special Branch team would carefully unravel the tiny messages, photograph them and put them back together exactly as they were found. The product of these intercepts, known as source 'Dangle', was then distributed to British security forces in the field. By recruiting couriers as agents and intercepting communications in this way, the Special Branch discovered a number of the most important 'Directives' that Chin Peng issued to his fighters.

After their release, double agents were usually followed back into the jungle by special forces, typically Gurkhas and Malay trackers, who noted the location of guerrilla forces. Some of the most sophisticated methods for tracking insurgent forces were provided by SIGINT. When the Special Branch released double agents back into the jungle they were sometimes provided with radio sets specially modified to transmit direction-finding (D/F) signals. Using these signals, security forces could triangulate the exact location of insurgents, who were then captured or killed by security patrols, or targeted for heavy bombing by the RAF.[38]

The methods that security forces used to 'break' and 'turn' SEPs were harsh. Before Morton's arrival in Malaya there was no dedicated intelligence interrogation facility in the colony, only police (CID) interrogation facilities. On MI5's recommendation, in April 1949 a specialised intelligence interrogation centre was established for the Special Branch near Kuala Lumpur, modelled on MI5's successful wartime facility, Camp 020. It even had its own airfield, so prisoners could be flown in and rapidly interrogated. Interrogators at the new facility used many of the techniques that MI5 had developed at Camp 020: it was wired with microphones, and 'stool pigeons' (or undercover agents) were inserted into cells to get prisoners to talk. SEPs were often disorientated by being deprived of sleep for seventy-two hours, and were threatened and humiliated. Many were offered enormous amounts of money to work for the British – as much as 12,000 Malay dollars, equivalent to about ten years' wages for a rubber-tapper. Under Templer, Chin Peng had a staggering US$240,000 reward on his head, and SEPs were promised huge financial rewards for every insurgent captured or killed as a result of information they provided. The Special Branch also provided SEPs who provided information with sophisticated protection, relocating them and giving them new identities.

At the same time as promising these substantial rewards, Special Branch interrogators convinced SEPs that their only option was to collaborate with them: they threatened them with execution if they refused, or with an even worse fate (execution would at least be a quick death) – to release them in suspicious circumstances. It was well known that the MCP exacted brutal vengeance upon those suspected of being traitors, often forcing them to dig their own graves in the jungle and then slitting their throats. Another Special Branch tactic to turn SEPs was to blackmail them, usually by making threats to their families.[39]

There were incidents when British interrogators tortured detainees in Malaya, but there is no evidence that torture, either as it was understood at the time or as it is defined now in international law, was institutionalised there. It is not possible to come to any generalised conclusions about how and why torture occurred. As with other conflicts, before and since, there were probably as many reasons why prisoners were tortured in Malaya as there were interrogators. There also seems to have been a grey area between actions that were officially ordered and those that were unofficially condoned. This noxious mixture was compounded by often poor training of interrogation officers.

However, some matters are clear from the historical record. In Malaya, as in other colonial Emergencies, there were broadly two kinds of interrogations: front-line interrogations, often conducted by forces trailing double agents deep into the jungle; and those conducted later, usually by Special Branch or army interrogators. The first kind of interrogation aimed to achieve quick answers to specific questions, often while literally under fire. Usually the troops and police who interrogated insurgents at the front line in this way had no specialised training in interrogation methods. By contrast, the second kind of interrogations were genuinely intelligence-driven, aiming to build up a broad picture of what a prisoner actually knew in order to gather strategic intelligence on the MCP's plans. MI5 had the most direct control over these interrogations.

In keeping with the lessons learned at Camp 020 during the Second World War, MI5 recognised that using physical coercion, or 'third-degree' measures, would be futile when attempting to 'turn' double agents in Malaya. On the one hand, it acknowledged that an interrogation centre 'cannot be run as a welfare institution. It is a place where firm discipline needs to be maintained.' On the other hand, senior MI5 officers in London, along with Morton in Malaya, emphasised that any attempt to 'turn' an agent through the use of torture would inevitably backfire: the agent would simply resent his interrogators and not want to work with them. Contemporary MI5 guidelines on interrogations in Malaya and other counter-insurgencies were strongly opposed to the use of physical violence: 'Moral considerations alone should suffice to prohibit it. Further, it is the purpose of interrogation to elicit valid intelligence, whereas extorted confessions are likely to be unreliable.' The directions in Malaya also stated that particular care was needed when interrogating female prisoners: 'It is completely erroneous for the interrogator to threaten the removal of a female prisoner's clothing and to threaten to expose the prisoner in the nude.' Later guidelines that MI5 compiled in 1961, which drew on earlier lecture notes, stated:

> Physical violence or mental torture – apart from moral and legal considerations – opposed to – short sighted – like wilfully damaging engine of car wanted for long journey – under violence anyone will talk – you may get a confession to prevent torture but it will not be the truth – Intelligence gained usually useless.[40]

Some interrogators in Malaya seem to have heeded MI5's advice, or else came to similar conclusions on their own. In 1950 the commanding officer of 22 SAS, Michael Calvert, literally kicked a policeman out of his mess when he told Calvert that torture was the best way of extracting information from a prisoner. Guidelines issued by all of the British armed forces also expressly forbade the use of physical violence during interrogations:

> Prisoners will be treated according to the Geneva Convention at all times; interrogation by torture or ill-treatment is not, in any circumstances, permitted. Indeed, it is to be doubted whether such methods would prove fruitful as the prisoner might tend to say what he believed the interrogator wanted to hear, whether or not this accorded with the facts. Acts of violence or spite only tend to arouse the prisoner's animosity. Moreover,

such an approach really amounts to a confession of failure. The basic aim of the interrogator is to win the willing cooperation of the prisoner since only then is he likely to gain complete, reliable and accurate military information. This cooperation and respect is likely to gain by a blend of firmness, understanding and sympathy.[41]

Despite these guidelines, MI5 was not able to get its message across to all the security forces operating in the colony. Especially to those fighting at the front line, recommendations from MI5's comfy lectures, dealing with ethical questions more apt for airy philosophy seminars, were easily forgotten. The result was that some interrogators resorted to torture. There were incidents, particularly during resettlement programmes, but also during police interrogations, when detainees were beaten up and had their fingernails torn out. The Malaya Special Branch could be ruthless. Even Morton, who mostly comes across in his correspondence as a mild-mannered man, recalled instances where 'several penetration agents had to be sacrificed so that security force action could be taken to relieve guerrilla pressure in sensitive areas':

> I recall that in one district a succession of successful operations led to a full scale Communist inquisition into the security of the local Party organisation. Unfortunately, the Special Branch agent was among those who were liquidated in the ensuing purge. He was made to dig his own grave and two strong men then slowly strangled him to death. It was, however, some consolation to know that other comrades who were not agents were also executed. The Communists were taking no chances.[42]

During the trial in 1951 of an Australian rubber-planter on a charge of consorting with insurgents, evidence emerged that the Malayan police had resorted to techniques such as 'threats with revolver shots, kickings, punchings, and severe beatings with a rattan cane to the insertion of a needle under the fingernails'. When British interrogators used 'Gestapo methods' in Malaya, they seem to have occurred mostly at the front line, often in retribution-style interrogations designed to 'punish' prisoners, rather than in those that were genuinely intelligence-driven, which were mostly conducted by the Special Branch interrogators. It is fair to say that MI5 failed to implement its own lessons for effective interrogations in Malaya. However, it is equally fair to say, with only a few MI5 officers stationed in Malaya, and given the large number of security forces, civilian

and military, operating there, that it is not surprising MI5 failed to indoctrinate all of them with its 'good practices'. It nevertheless strove hard to
train local Special Branch officers on the best way to interrogate SEPs,
break them and turn them into double agents. Morton and Guy Madoc
set up a Combined Services Detailed Intelligence Centre (CSDIC) and a
training school for the Malayan Special Branch near Kuala Lumpur, set in
lush grounds with cows and elephants grazing in them. It essentially
served as an intelligence school, with Special Branch officers giving
lectures on the history of the MCP and the *Min Yuen*, how to penetrate
them with agents, and MI5 officers speaking on 'the science of intelligence
work'. By June 1954, MI5 and SIS had collaborated to produce a 'training
bible' for security officials in South-East Asia. This was devised by an MI5
training officer seconded to SIFE, a man named Sutcliffe, and by an influential SIS officer then stationed in Singapore, Maurice Oldfield, who
would later rise to become a Chief of SIS. In a single year, 1953, Sutcliffe
gave eleven training courses to security officials in Malaya, Singapore,
Burma, India and Indonesia. He attempted to convert his audiences to
MI5's views about the best way to run double agents, especially the futility
of using physical violence. It is no coincidence that Britain's intelligence
efforts in Malaya improved when, as one senior police officer put it in
1954, there was 'less beating up'. MI5 gave a further series of training
courses to Malaya Special Branch officers in Kuching in May 1956, this
time delivered by an MI5 officer named R.G.I. Elliott.[43]

Enforcing discipline during interrogations, especially those conducted
by personnel at the front line, with forces drawn from across the British
armed forces as well as a number of Commonwealth states, was easier said
than done. In fact, it was difficult even when MI5 had relatively direct
control over the interrogators. MI5 is known, for example, to have catastrophically failed to instil its interrogation guidelines at an inter-service
detention and interrogation centre run in the post-war years in occupied
Germany, led by none other than Lt. Col. Robin 'Tin Eye' Stephens, who
had run Camp 020 during the war so successfully, in large part because of
his strict rule of non-violence there. Unlike Camp 020, the detention
centre in Germany, located in the quiet and picturesque spa town of Bad
Nenndorf, was staffed by interrogation officials from a cross-section of
Allied military and civilian services, some of whom were extremely badly
trained. As a result of a breakdown in discipline, in the winter of 1946 a
horrific torture scandal erupted at the centre, where two prisoners were
killed and several others attempted suicide. One German prisoner was

subjected to such inhuman treatment at the hands of British interrogators that he attempted to commit suicide by swallowing a spoon, and after arriving at hospital had to have four of his toes amputated because of frostbite caused by exposure in his freezing cell. Although a subsequent court-martial cleared Stephens of personal responsibility for the prisoners' deaths and abuse, the scandal was a striking example of MI5 failing to enforce its own guidelines on interrogations. In fact, the lessons derived from MI5's wartime experiences have been confirmed by countless other examples from history which show that using physical violence produces unreliable intelligence.[44]

Part of the reason MI5 failed to enforce its interrogation guidelines across the board in Malaya, and cases of 'coercive' interrogations arose, seems to have been because of poor discipline among interrogation officials. Even when it came to the Special Branch in Malaya, over which MI5 had the most direct control, it was unable to safeguard every interrogation, to say nothing of those carried out by other branches of the security forces. Some interrogators may have resorted to 'third degree' simply because of sadism or vindictiveness, while others may have been influenced or 'conditioned' by their environment. Years later, two notorious experiments, conducted respectively by the American psychologists Stanley Milgram and Philip Zimbardo, would demonstrate that 'ordinary' people can be influenced to inflict violence when they consider it 'proper' to do so, and to administer extraordinarily tough forms of treatment against prisoners.

However, there were also deeper, more systemic reasons why torture occurred in Malaya. One of the fundamental problems was that despite the introduction of international human rights legislation from the 1940s onwards, in the Geneva Conventions and other agreements, at the time the British government did not uphold a uniform standard for interrogations within the empire. Opinions over how detainees should be interrogated in counter-insurgencies seem to have differed wildly between government departments, the military and colonial administrations. The British Army's official regulations, for example, strictly forbade the use of physical duress, yet forces on the ground seem to have taken a more relaxed attitude. The result of this lack of uniformity was that situations were created in Malaya, and in subsequent counter-insurgencies, that were ripe for abuses by British and local security officials.

Britain's unwillingness to standardise its interrogation practices persisted for a remarkably long time. A harrowing testimonial to the use

ABOVE: Sir Vernon Kell, the founding father of MI5. In 1909 Kell helped to establish the Secret Service Bureau, which during the First World War was renamed MI5.

TOP RIGHT: The original 'C', Sir Mansfield Cumming, was responsible for the Secret Service Bureau's foreign section, which during the First World War was renamed MI1C, and eventually MI6 or SIS. He remains a legendary figure within SIS, revered as its founding father.

RIGHT: Lawrence of Arabia. T.E. Lawrence, who helped wage campaigns against German and Turkish forces in the Middle East during the First World War, placed a high value on the role of intelligence in non-conventional warfare.

RFC plane with aerial reconnaissance camera, 1916. British campaigns in the Middle East during the First World War introduced modern intelligence warfare.

The 'Colossus' at Bletchley Park. Although missing from most history books of the post-war years, Bletchley Park's code-breakers continued to operate after 1945, breaking the codes of many colonial and Commonwealth countries.

Jasper Maskelyne, a former stage conjuror, was recruited by British forces in North Africa during the Second World War to assist with deception campaigns, creating illusions such as dummy tanks and planes to deceive the Axis powers about Allied military strategies.

Dudley Clarke, the founding father of modern strategic deception. In 1943 he was arrested in Madrid dressed as a woman. He told local police that he was taking the clothes to a friend, and decided to try them on as 'a prank' – but as one official at the British embassy in Madrid noted, this did not explain why the women's shoes and brassière he was wearing fitted him.

BELOW: The Hungarian Count László Almásy (left) before setting out to find the legenday oasis Zerzura, 1931. Almásy was the real-life 'English patient'. However, his MI5 files reveal that rather than the handsome hero portrayed in the novel and film, in reality he was an incompetent agent for German intelligence.

Long Range Desert Group, North
Africa. It was in the deserts of North
Africa that modern British special
forces were first established. The Special
Air Service (SAS), set up in Egypt
in July 1941, would go on to play a
significant role in Britain's violent end
of empire campaigns across the globe
after 1945.

Under the watch of Sir Percy Sillitoe,
appointed Director-General in 1946,
MI5 came to play a significant role
in colonial and Commonwealth
intelligence. Sillitoe tried to evade press
attention when leaving and arriving at
airports by wearing sunglasses, though
this usually attracted more attention
than it avoided.

Police use tear gas during a riot in Calcutta. Despite all the chaos, bloodshed and misadministration of Britain's transfer of power in India in 1947, British intelligence was able to maintain close liaisons with the new independent Indian government.

On 22 July 1946, one of the two terrorist groups fighting the British in Palestine, the Irgun, set off an enormous bomb at the King David Hotel in Jerusalem, killing ninety-one people. It was one of the worst terrorist attacks in British history, and a direct blow to British intelligence: both MI5 and SIS had offices in the hotel.

Menachem Begin wanted poster. Begin, the leader of the Irgun in the post-war years, and the mastermind of the King David Hotel bombing, later became the sixth Prime Minister of Israel and the joint winner of the Nobel Peace Prize.

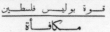

THE PALESTINE POLICE FORCE

REWARD

A REWARD OF L.P. 2000 WILL BE PAID BY THE PALESTINE GOVERNMENT TO ANY PERSON GIVING INFORMATION WHICH LEADS DIRECTLY TO THE APPREHENSION OF THE PERSON WHOSE NAME AND PHOTOGRAPH APPEAR HEREUNDER.

قوة بوليس فلسطين

مكافأة

تعطي حكومة فلسطين مكافأة قدرها ٢٠٠٠ جنيه فلسطيني لاي شخص يعطي اخبارية تؤدي مباشرة لالقاء القبض على الشخص الذين اسمه وصورته ادناه:—

משטרת פלשתינה (א״י).

גמול

פרס בסך 2000 לא״י ישולם ע״י הממשלה הא״י לכל אדם שימסור ידיעה שתוביל באופן ישר לידי מאסרו של האדם ששמו ותמונתו נקובים להלן.

MENACHEM BEGIN

מנחם ביגין

Age:	34 years
Height:	173 cms.
Build:	thin
Nose:	long, hooked
Teeth:	bad
Speaks:	Polish, English, Hebrew.
Peculiarities:	Appears to be badly shaved. Walks with a peculiar flat-footed stride.

ماخم بيچن

INFORMATION MAY BE GIVEN AT ANY TIME TO ANY POLICE OFFICER OR TO ANY POLICE STATION

Jerusalem,
July, 1945

J. M. RYMER JONES
Inspector-General.

Sir John Shaw, 'the flying pencil', Chief Secretary of the Palestine Mandate, narrowly escaped being killed in the King David Hotel bombing. He joined MI5 in 1948, becoming the head of its Overseas Section.

MI5 report warning that Victory in Europe (VE) Day would be a D-Day for Jewish terrorists in the Middle East.

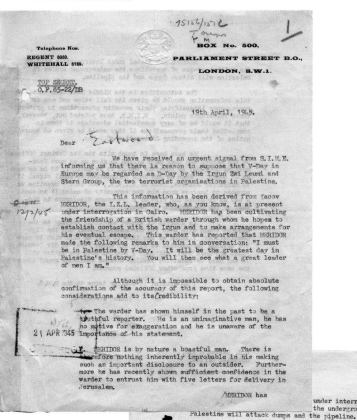

Telephone Nos.
REGENT 6050.
WHITEHALL 6789.

BOX No. 500,
PARLIAMENT STREET B.O.,
LONDON, S.W.1.

TOP SECRET.
O.F.85-22/DB

19th April, 1945.

Dear Eastwood

We have received an urgent signal from S.I.M.E. informing us that there is reason to suppose that V-Day in Europe may be regarded as D-Day by the Irgun Zwi Leumi and Stern Group, the two terrorist organisations in Palestine.

This information has been derived from Yacov MERIDOR, the I.Z.L. leader, who, as you know, is at present under interrogation in Cairo. MERIDOR has been cultivating the friendship of a British warder through whom he hopes to establish contact with the Irgun and to make arrangements for his eventual escape. This warder has reported that MERIDOR made the following remarks to him in conversation: "I must be in Palestine by V-Day. It will be the greatest day in Palestine's history. You will then see what a great leader of men I am."

Although it is impossible to obtain absolute confirmation of the accuracy of this report, the following considerations add to its credibility:

1. The warder has shown himself in the past to be a truthful reporter. He is an unimaginative man, he has no motive for exaggeration and he is unaware of the importance of his statement.

2. MERIDOR is by nature a boastful man. There is therefore nothing inherently improbable in his making such an important disclosure to an outsider. Furthermore he has recently shown sufficient confidence in the warder to entrust him with five letters for delivery in Jerusalem.

MERIDOR has

... under interrogation that in ... the underground armies in Palestine will attack dumps and the pipeline.

The Authorities in the Middle East feel that this information should be given its full value and are in consequence intensifying their security precautions to protect these vulnerable points. S.I.M.E. have pointed out, however, that it would be of very substantial advantage to them in completing their preparations if they could be given 48 hours' notice of the impending declaration of V-Day.

We have been in touch with the War Cabinet Offices on the matter and they have agreed to give us as much fore-warning of V-Day as possible though it is unlikely to be as much as 48 hours. When we get this information we shall signal it to Brigadier Roberts, Head of S.I.M.E., but in the meantime we propose to impress upon him the necessity of using it in such a way as to avoid the risk of a premature disclosure in Mid-East of the declaration of V-Day.

As Roberts is almost certainly keeping in the closest touch with both the Commander-in-Chief and the High Commissioner, I think we can take it that he will wish to pass the advance information we give him about V-Day to Sir Bernard Paget and Lord Gort, although I imagine both the latter will in any case be receiving similar advance knowledge round about the same time from other official sources.

I am writing in similar terms to the D.M.I.

Yours sincerely

C.G. Eastwood Esq.,
Colonial Office.

British soldiers question a group of schoolboys in Jerusalem, 1947. British police and security officials relied on outmoded tactics, such as mass arrests and curfews, which alienated the local Jewish population in Palestine, when it would have been better to try to win them over.

The war in Palestine brought home: Major Roy Farran at his brother's grave, St Nicholas' church, Codsall, 1948. Farran was involved in undercover paramilitary operations in Palestine, and the Stern Gang targeted him for assassination, sending a letter bomb to his home in England. His brother opened it and was killed in the ensuing explosion.

A British paratrooper after landing in the jungle, north Malaya, 1952. British special forces developed what became known as 'tree jumping', a tactic by which operatives were parachuted directly into the jungle, in the hope that its thick trees would catch their canopies, and they could then safely lower themselves to the ground.

The Duchess of Kent, Sir Charles Arden-Clarke and Kwame Nkrumah at Ghana's independence ceremony, 1957. The smooth transfer of power in Ghana (formerly the Gold Coast) owed much to the close relationship between the final Governor, Arden-Clarke, and Nkrumah, the first leader of the independent nation. However, behind the scenes, MI5 provided Arden-Clarke with a stream of intelligence on Nkrumah, which reassured him that Nkrumah was not a communist, as much of Whitehall and Washington feared.

Jomo Kenyatta became the leading anti-colonial politician in Kenya after 1945. MI5 had already assembled a large file on him, and used its intelligence to calm many of the fears in London about his supposed 'communism'. It was less successful in Nairobi, where the colonial administration viewed him as the leader of Mau Mau and imprisoned him.

Dead policeman, suspected Mau Mau victim. The British struggled to understand the Mau Mau revolt in Kenya, with many in London and Nairobi viewing it as a communist conspiracy. In reality it was an anti-colonial revolt, which also became a civil war. In the course of the insurgency, thirty-two colonial settlers lost their lives. By contrast, thousands of Africans were killed by Mau Mau insurgents and British forces.

Britain's response to the Mau Mau revolt was one of overwhelming force. According to evidence put before the High Court in London in 2012, but not yet conclusively proved, officials in Whitehall may have known more about instances of torture of Mau Mau suspects by security forces than was previously supposed

The empire comes home: the arrival of the *Empire Windrush* at Tilbury, 22 June 1948. MI5's remit included keeping a close watch on immigrant groups arriving in Britain in the 1940s and 1950s.

The Petrov affair. Evdokia Petrov is dramatically escorted across the tarmac at Sydney's Kingsford Smith airport by two armed Soviet couriers, 19 April 1954. The defection of the Soviet cypher clerk Vladimir Petrov was one of the flashpoints in the early Cold War, revealing Soviet penetration of Western governments.

British paratroopers embarking for operations in the Suez crisis, Cyprus, c. October 1956. The Suez crisis was an outward display to the world that Britain was no longer the global power it once was. Newly available intelligence records reveal that it was also a dramatic intelligence failure. British forces on the ground were let down by a flagrant abuse of intelligence by Eden's government. The intelligence dossier on Nasser provided by the Joint Intelligence Committee was 'sexed up' to suit political needs, in a manner with resonances closer to our own time.

Cheddi Jagan, democratically elected leader of British Guiana, with ousted ministers in Georgetown, 1953. Jagan's election was cancelled by the Colonial Office in London on the grounds that he was a 'communist'. It did not suit the US to have a Marxist sympathiser in America's backyard. In the early 1960s the US set about undermining Jagan's leadership with covert action, and pressured London to remain in British Guiana for longer than it wanted: when the Cold War necessitated it, anti-colonial America could show itself to be far more colonialist than Britain.

Archbishop Makarios visiting a British Army camp in Cyprus, 1960. The British counter-insurgency in Cyprus was another intelligence failure, with the Cyprus administration failing to learn lessons from Palestine, Malaya and Kenya.

British soldiers erect a barbed-wire barricade in a mountain village in Cyprus, c.1956. The British Army and security personnel in Cyprus failed to learn the lessons of the Malayan Emergency, namely that a 'hearts and minds' campaign was essential to winning a counter-insurgency.

A British soldier threatening Arab demonstrators, Crater, Aden, 1967. Britain's withdrawal from Aden was one of its most ignominious exits – a lamentable intelligence failure that repeated many of the mistakes of previous Emergencies.

The end of the line: Governor Chris Patten during the ceremony marking the handover of Hong Kong to China in July 1997. Intelligence records relating to the end of British rule in Hong Kong are still classified, but it is reasonable to assume that British intelligence was hard at work behind the scenes to secure a smooth transfer of power there, as it had been in previous British territories.

The small island of Diego Garcia in the Indian Ocean. In order to pave the way for an enormous US base on the island and its neighbouring archipelago, the British and US governments came to an agreement that local populations would be 'cleared'.

of torture was given in 1960 by a National Serviceman who recalled the intelligence corps training he had received in 1949:

> My platoon was taught, among other things, the way in which to inter-
> rogate a prisoner and we were told that, in certain cases, it would prob-
> ably be necessary for us to use various forms of physical torture. The
> tortures that were described to us had the advantage of leaving none of
> the visible traces which might be noticed by members of the International
> Red Cross and included beating the prisoner after his body had been
> wrapped in a wet blanket, filling his body with water and holding him
> against a hot stove. Our instructor, a Regular sergeant in the Intelligence
> Corps, told us that he had seen these tortures used against Japanese pris-
> oners in Burma. I have since been told by other National Servicemen that
> the same methods were being recommended as recently as three years
> ago, and there is, of course, every reason to believe that they are still
> being taught today.

As late as the 1970s, the British government came close to condoning torture when the JIC in London, which usually took an avuncular role, almost like an Oxbridge senior common room, agreed to the use of 'Five Techniques' for interrogations in Northern Ireland, including stress positions and sleep deprivation. The Five Techniques were only rescinded following a public outcry and a successful case against the British government at the European Court of Human Rights.[45]

The Special Branch in Malaya achieved some remarkable levels of penetration into rebel guerrilla forces, the most successful of such agents having been recruited using interrogation methods that fell short of physical violence. One case was disclosed in the summer of 1953, when Chin Peng, after 'slogging through thickest jungles in the world' to establish a new headquarters at Grik in northern Malaya, near the Thai border, was told that there must be a traitor among his men. He recalled that for the previous year, 'Intended guerrilla operations had been thwarted by the British before they could be launched. Weapons, ammunition and food supplies had been revealed to the enemy and seized. Key Party officials had been betrayed and arrested.' The traitor agent, a local Party secretary, was identified soon afterwards when a government cheque for $50,000 was found in his shirt pocket. It is unclear what happened to him, though he was probably executed by the MCP. Late in 1954 Chin Peng was forced to move his headquarters even deeper into the jungle, across the Thai border.

One Special Branch double agent, T.S. Sambantha Murthi, who 'surrendered' to the British in 1955 in a communist-infested area of Kluang, in Jahore, brought with him such vital information on communist forces that he was later awarded a George Medal at a secret ceremony held at the King's House in Kuala Lumpur.[46]

Templer developed a system of zones in Malaya, based upon areas where communists were active ('black' zones), somewhat active ('grey' zones), and not active ('white' zones). The success of his strategy can be seen by the fact that no white zone ever became a black one. Some contemporary Whitehall discussions, whose tenor has tended to be adopted by subsequent historians, suggested that there was a smooth progression from black zones to white zones, essentially a march towards peace and civilisation. This, however, belies the violent and authoritarian nature of British rule in Malaya during the Emergency. In reality, Templer's strategy was to make life in the black zones so harsh for the local population that they would never want to return to it, and would give up guerrilla fighters because of the collective punishments inflicted upon them. Black zones were a focus for killer squads, while living in a white zone had significant benefits for inhabitants, with curfews lifted, food shortages lessened, and a degree of normality restored. This, then, was a story not so much of an orderly march towards 'civilisation', but instead of complicity resulting from harsh measures exacted upon local populations.

The term 'low-intensity warfare' does not do justice to the extremely violent fighting in Malaya, which was effectively a war by another name. Records from the secret colonial archive kept at Hanslope Park reveal that British security personnel effectively operated a shoot-to-kill policy in Malaya. Monthly reports circulated by the Director of Intelligence on 'subversive activities' indicate that the 'elimination of terrorists' was a commonly discussed theme. One report from May 1957 shows that 'success' was measured in the number of dead insurgents:

> The total of terrorist eliminations for the month is a slight improvement on the figures for April, but, at an average of one C.T. per day, remains slightly below the average of 32 per month during the first five months of this year. (The monthly average for the whole of 1956 was 39 eliminations.) A heartening feature has been the elimination of 9 C.T. leaders, three of them of State Committee rank. Most C.T. leaders are men with pre-Emergency experience of Communist Subversion, and thus are the very men whom the present M.C.P. policy of Conservation of Strength is

designed to preserve for the fresh Political Campaign of Subversion which
is the principal aim of the Party.

In total, British forces killed 6,697 bandits or 'communist terrorists' in
Malaya, not all of whom were combatants, while 1,865 members of the
security forces and police lost their lives, and 2,473 civilians were killed.
These figures, however, do not do justice to the extraordinary social dislocation and upheaval that accompanied the shooting war, caused primarily
by arrests, detentions and forced relocations to the so-called 'New Villages'.
It is difficult to quantify the social trauma that such policies produced, but
clearly it was acute. As well as social dislocation, security forces on the
ground in Malaya are known to have committed atrocities, unleashing
arbitrary violence, killing some people but sparing others. Dead insurgents were decapitated, and their hands were chopped off, apparently
because foot patrols in the jungle found it 'too onerous' to drag whole
bodies back to headquarters for fingerprinting. Some of the acts of decapi-
tation were allegedly performed by Iban 'headhunters', though this hardly
explains the pictures that emerged of British soldiers posing with the
heads of decapitated enemies as trophies. It seems fair to say that on one
level these acts of barbarism arose because of the nature of warfare in
Malaya, which was both brutal and brutalising. Invariably, however, the
immediate cause of the atrocities there was the same as it had been in
Palestine: there was a vicious cycle of violence, in which incidents by and
against security forces were followed by reprisals. Added to this already
noxious mix, as in Palestine, the use of special forces units, often operating
deep behind enemy lines, cut off from communications lines and central
command and control, created situations where violence and reprisals
could easily escalate.[47]

One of the most notorious incidents occurred soon after the outbreak
of the Emergency, on 11–12 December 1948. A group of soldiers from 2
Battalion the Scots Guards Regiment killed twenty-five rubber-tappers in
Batang Kali, in Selangor, in extremely dubious circumstances. The soldiers
claimed the men were 'bandits', but they were killed suspiciously soon
after an ambush that had eliminated one of their comrades in the Scots
Guards. Many at the time described the incident as a retaliation killing, a
cold-blooded atrocity. Bizarrely, the British government decided not to
hold a public inquiry. The Attorney-General for Malaya, Sir Stafford
Doster-Sutton, carried out an investigation, but to this day it has never
been made public. The Scots Guards have persistently denied that their

soldiers acted illegally, though the killings have never been properly explained. The episode stinks of an official cover-up, as seems to have been confirmed by subsequent independent investigations. The British government launched an inquiry into it in 1970, with a Scotland Yard team led by Frank Williams, a detective who played a key role in investigating the Great Train Robbery. The investigation was shelved by the incoming Conservative government, ostensibly for lack of evidence. In the same year, the *People* newspaper quoted one of the soldiers involved as saying: 'Once we started firing we seemed to go mad ... I remember the water turning red with their blood.' The Malaysian police carried out an investigation in the 1990s, some of the results of which were obtained by Ian Ward and Norma Miraflor, authors of the book *Slaughter and Deception at Batang Kali*. In 1992 the BBC made a documentary, *In Cold Blood*, in which the sole surviving Scots Guards soldier involved in the incident was interviewed, which claimed that there had been a deliberate order for a mass killing, which was then hushed up.[48]

The incident at Batang Kali made the news once again in May 2011, when lawyers representing victims' families started proceedings to compel the British government to disclose all of the documents about the killings in its possession. In September 2012 the High Court in London ruled that the government should not be obliged to open an inquiry into Batang Kali, and at the time of writing the British government still refuses to acknowledge that it has any relevant records on the massacre in its possession. It is striking that there are no such records within the 'lost' Colonial Office records, until recently housed at the British government's top-secret facility at Hanslope Park in Buckinghamshire. Given that it took so long for the government to admit the existence of its 'lost' records at Hanslope Park, its claim that it does not have any further records on Batang Kali must be treated with scepticism. In 1949 the then High Commissioner, Sir Henry Gurney, admitted that the British Army was breaking the law 'almost every day' in Malaya. The attack at Batang Kali appears to have been shockingly similar to the massacre by US forces at My Lai in Vietnam in 1968. Chin Peng is probably correct to have called it a 'calculated massacre'. One British policeman who arrived at the scene of the killings soon after they occurred, and photographed the carnage, was clear that the dead bodies he saw were not terrorists, but innocent civilian rubber-tappers.[49]

Britain's violent counter-insurgency campaign in Malaya was ultimately successful, if success is measured solely in terms of eliminating an enemy, because of the massive intrusion of military power into the colony. At its height in 1951, the Malayan People's Liberation Army had about 7,000 fighters, while the British had three battalions, 10,000 police, six Gurkha battalions and two regiments of Malays, giving them a numerical superiority of about 5:1 over the guerrilla forces. British land operations were supported by the RAF, which by 1950 had Lincoln bombers stationed in Malaya capable of dropping heavy 10,000-pound bombs. RAF pilots later recalled watching their bombs drop onto the thick jungle foliage, scorching trees and obliterating anything in their path. The overall cost of operations in Malaya was enormous for the post-war British government that was essentially bankrupt and dependent on US loans. By the end of 1948 it was spending $300,000 per day on fighting in Malaya, and by the end of 1951 the cost of maintaining and running forces there had spiralled to £48.5 million. This vast expenditure was ultimately met by a boom in the rubber and tin industries which was fortuitously produced by the contemporary Korean War. Warfare thus paid for more warfare, with one military-industrial complex feeding off another.[50]

THE QUIET ENGLISHMAN

The violent shooting war was not the entire focus of Britain's counter-insurgency efforts in Malaya. Accompanying it was a pioneering 'hearts and minds' campaign (though the term was not coined till later), designed to win over the local population. Templer himself said that the shooting war was roughly 25 per cent of the battle, while 75 per cent was winning over the people. Behind the barbed-wire fences of the New Villages, British authorities attempted to rebuild and transform the lives of those who had been resettled in them, establishing sports halls, health services and village councils, and holding democratic elections at the council level for the first time in 1954. Accompanying these projects were massive road and electricity construction projects, which 'resulted in infrastructure that few countries in Asia could match'. In the words of one eminent historian of British decolonisation, Wm. Roger Louis, the result was one of the most ambitious state-building projects in the post-war era.[51]

In conjunction with 'rehabilitation' programmes within the New Villages, British authorities also devised 'hearts and minds' campaigns for the whole of Malaya. This top-secret propaganda campaign was coordinated by an experienced BBC journalist and later Director-General of the BBC, Hugh Carleton Greene, who from September 1950 led the Emergency

Information Services. Carleton Greene was well versed in propaganda work, having spent time during the war liaising between the BBC and Britain's wartime 'black propaganda' outfit, the Political Warfare Executive. He was a half-brother of the famous novelist Graham Greene, one of the best espionage writers of all time, who had worked for SIS in the war and who visited him in Malaya in 1951. Greene's novel *The Quiet American* (1955), about French and American attempts to stem the flow of communism in Indochina, was largely inspired by what he saw on his visit to Malaya. In the novel Greene accurately predicted that America would encounter many of the same problems and communist guerrilla tactics in South-East Asia that the French and British had already faced – just as he would accurately predict the rise of Fidel Castro in Cuba in his novel *Our Man in Havana* (1958).

In Malaya, Hugh Carleton Greene was as much a Quiet Englishman as Alden Pyle, Graham Greene's character, was a Quiet American. As head of the Emergency Information Services he liaised closely with all of Britain's secret agencies, and oversaw a massive expansion of psychological warfare ('psy-war') efforts in the colony. Soon after his arrival he realised how much work needed to be done. Interrogations of surrendered insurgents revealed that few of them had ever seen any government propaganda material. According to a later report, Carleton Greene recalled that he devised propaganda that aimed to help win the Emergency in three distinct ways: by intensifying the psy-war campaign against the insurgents, by boosting the morale of the local population, and by inducing them to provide the police with information on insurgents.[52]

Under Carleton Greene, the Emergency Information Services worked closely with Britain's Cold War covert propaganda outfit, the Information Research Department (IRD), one of the most secretive British agencies in the whole of the Cold War. The IRD was established in January 1948 under the auspices of the Foreign Office to direct and disseminate counter-Soviet propaganda in Britain, the empire and across the rest of the world. By the early 1950s it had grown to become one of the Foreign Office's largest departments. Christopher Warner, whose official title was Assistant Undersecretary for Information Activities, but who was really in charge of the IRD, explained: 'Our whole object is to enlighten those who have no idea how unpleasant the conditions in Communist-controlled countries are.' To do so the IRD employed an array of famous writers, including George Orwell, whose celebrated critiques of communism *Animal Farm* and *Nineteen Eighty-Four* were partly funded by the IRD, and Arthur

Koestler, whose IRD-sponsored attack on communism famously described it as 'the god that failed'.[53]

Sometimes the IRD had to struggle to link anti-colonial insurgencies to the Cold War (as in Cyprus, for example, where as we shall see, the guerrilla forces were in fact led by a near-fascist, not by a communist). This was not the case in Malaya, where Chin Peng's communist guerrillas provided rich material. By 1949 the IRD had a 'Regional Information Office' operating from Phoenix Park, Singapore, run by John Rayner. The IRD and the Emergency Information Services bombarded villages and the jungle with voluminous amounts of propaganda. The RAF equipped three Dakota and two Auster aircraft with large speaker equipment, and flew them over the colony's jungles broadcasting to insurgents that they would receive rewards and fair treatment if they gave themselves up. Similar messages were delivered by leaflets, some of them written by surrendered personnel, usually promising fair treatment at the hands of the British, rewards for information, and sometimes including photographs of dead or captured rebels to demoralise other insurgents. In 1953 some ninety-three million leaflets were distributed throughout the colony, fifty-four million of which were dropped by the RAF. In 1956, speaker-equipped RAF aircraft flew 2,000 sorties in Malaya and dropped a staggering one hundred million leaflets. Mobile cinema projectors, the number of which increased under Carleton Greene's leadership from twenty-three to fifty-three, hammered home the administration's message to audiences that were largely illiterate. The success of Britain's propaganda efforts can be seen in the fact that the total number of enemy personnel surrendering increased from seventy-four in the last eight months of 1950 to 136 in 1957. Many of those surrendering admitted they did so because of British propaganda, with some carrying propaganda leaflets when they gave themselves up.[54]

As well as propaganda directed against their enemies, which is known as 'white' or 'grey' propaganda, British officials in Malaya also made use of what is called 'black' propaganda. This is much more secretive, and is designed to deceive an enemy into thinking the information it has acquired arose from its own side. Black propaganda was pioneered by Dudley Clarke in Egypt during the Second World War, and as we have seen, was then adopted by the London Controlling Station (LCS). The way in which these deception operations rolled into the post-war years, led by the Hollis Committee, shows the extent to which warfare never really stopped in South-East Asia after 1945. For Britain's deception chiefs, the advent of the

Cold War and the Malayan Emergency meant a continuation of wartime practices, not something inherently new.

With the outbreak of the Korean War in June 1950, the Hollis Committee was once again reformed as the 'Directorate of Forward Plans', a truly Graham Greene-sounding outfit, which was run by a wartime MI5 officer, John Drew, under the auspices of the Ministry of Defence, created in 1946 from the old War Office. By 1950 the Directorate of Forward Plans had deception officers stationed at British military headquarters in both Kuala Lumpur and Singapore, and as records only made available in 2011 reveal, their highly sensitive missions involved the elaborate use of camouflage to hide the location of security forces, as well as using radio transmissions to deceive insurgent forces about the location of their fellow fighters. In 1950 an electronic-reconnaissance-equipped Lancaster bomber was sent out to Malaya from RAF 90 Group, which tracked and scrambled the radio communications of guerrillas, and provided their location to ground forces.[55]

BRITISH INTELLIGENCE AND MALAYAN INDEPENDENCE

At the same time as providing 'live', actionable intelligence to the security forces, Britain's intelligence services also played a vital, but largely undisclosed, role in constitutional advancements made in Malaya, which paved the way for the colony's independence in August 1957. In May 1954, immediately after Templer left Malaya, elections were held by his successor as High Commissioner, Donald MacGillivray. The politician who emerged victorious from these elections was Tunku Abdul Rahman, leader since 1951 of the United Malay National Organisation (UMNO), who would be a leading force in Malayan politics in subsequent years. The Tunku, or 'prince', as he was known, was a Malay aristocrat from Kedah, and was considered by the Colonial Office to be someone with whom the British could work. He was moderate and extremely Westernised, having studied law at Cambridge and practised as a barrister in London, where he developed a reputation as something of a playboy, spending more of his time racing cars than practising or studying law – which partly explained his gentleman's third class degree from Cambridge. In 1954 the Tunku formed a new 'Alliance' Party, which aimed for the first time in Malayan politics to create a party not divided along racial-ethnic-religious lines, but instead as a political consensus. The party tried to balance the rights of all the main groups in Malayan society (Malay, Chinese, Indian) and establish equal citizenship, but at the same time to retain the special privileges that Malays demanded for themselves as the largest ethnic group. The Tunku's critics claimed that he was nothing more than a British stooge; he lacked the scars of a freedom fighter or the years of prison service which other anti-colonial leaders could boast. The reality, however, was that he was a genuine consensus politician.[56]

The growth of the Tunku's Alliance Party after 1954, with its manifesto of unity and independence, forced the Malayan Communist Party to the sidelines. In 1955 John Davis, the former colonial policeman and veteran of SOE's Force 136, who had fought alongside Chin Peng during the war, was sent into the jungle to meet his old ally and attempt to negotiate a ceasefire. Davis greeted Chin Peng at the designated rendezvous, in a clearing in the jungle, with the words 'Long time no see' in Cantonese, then escorted him to the negotiations across the border in Thailand, although these initial talks were unsuccessful.

Throughout 1955 there were increasing demands in Malaya for self-government and independence (*Merdeka*). At the election in July the Alliance Party obtained a crushing victory, winning fifty-one of the fifty-two available seats in the parliament in Kuala Lumpur, and the following month the Colonial Office made a major concession of power when it officially recognised the Tunku as 'First Minister' of Malaya, effectively heralding self-government and recognising him as the Prime Minister-in-waiting.

As in India and Palestine, the devolution of power to the Federation of Malaya was not the result of a pre-formulated plan. The reality was that the Colonial Office and the Colonial Secretary, Alan Lennox-Boyd, were forced to respond to events that were largely beyond their control. Nonetheless, as the British empire in South-East Asia began to disintegrate, the Colonial Office was able to make the best of what for it was a bad situation. From August 1955 onwards it made major concessions in Malaya, on the grounds that devolution of power was necessary in order to retain the goodwill of the Tunku and the Malayan people, while delay would risk causing resentment and inspiring radical groups.

The British administration in Malaya watched with fear the French withdrawal from Indochina and the Dutch exit from empire in neighbouring Indonesia, the latter of which arose in 1947 largely in response to US pressure to avoid a lurch to the left in the colony. In both Indochina and Indonesia, relations between the new national governments and the former colonial powers were embittered by years of bloodshed. At the same time, Britain – and behind it, the United States – realised that a premature withdrawal from power in Malaya would cause a power vacuum which could allow Chin Peng's forces to regroup and rise again, or Soviet or Chinese communists to move in and take control. The same logic that forced the Dutch withdrawal from Indonesia required Britain to stay in Malaya until it was safe to leave – no sooner, no later. For strategic Cold War purposes, the task facing Britain was thus to provide the Tunku's government-in-waiting with sufficient tools to be able to withstand the communist challenge after independence.

During the period of 'shared rule' between Britain and the Tunku's government, a period known to end-of-empire historians as 'diarchy', the British government retained control over Malaya's defence and security. In February 1956 the Colonial Office transferred responsibility for them to local Malay ministers, a major concession of power which the Colonial Secretary, Lennox-Boyd, hoped and correctly predicted would help to retain the goodwill of the Tunku's government during discussions over independence being held at Lancaster House in London. Behind all the diplomatic negotiations relating to independence, Britain's covert agencies were hard at work trying to build and preserve the goodwill of the new Malayan government, just as they had done in India a decade earlier. They brokered and guided key defence and security discussions, and maintained close, but non-avowed, relations with the Malayan government after independence in August 1957.

In July 1956 the head of SIFE, an MI5 officer not named in declassified records, met the Tunku and brokered a crucial agreement between him and the British government. The Tunku agreed to follow the model MI5 proposed for security intelligence, which was the same for Malaya as it was for other parts of the British empire: that it should be kept entirely separate from policing. The Tunku agreed to MI5's proposals, and allowed the intelligence and police system to remain as it was, with the Special Branch responsible for security intelligence, but operating separately from the CID of the police. The Tunku said that he wanted a rapid 'Malayanisation' of the regular police force, but a much slower 'Malayanisation' of the Special Branch, with expatriate London Special Branch and MI5 staff to be retained after independence. Further details were worked out over the following months, during talks between the Colonial Secretary, Lennox-Boyd, the British High Commissioner in Malaya, MacGillivray, and the Tunku.

A potential sticking point in these talks – only revealed by records in 2011 – concerned the activities of the British barrister and Communist

Party member Neil Lawson QC, who was acting as legal adviser to the rulers of the Malay States, especially on constitutional matters. MI5 was alarmed about Lawson's connections with the British Communist Party, with which, as it discovered through intercepted correspondence and its surveillance on the Party's headquarters, Lawson continued to maintain covert contact, despite publicly distancing himself from it. MI5 considered that Lawson was a serious risk to the smooth transfer of power in Malaya, and proposed that the Malay rulers be informed about his communist affiliations. The Colonial Office, however, preferred to keep the matter quiet, judging that it could potentially jeopardise the talks.

As it was, they progressed smoothly, especially over the most sensitive matters, security and intelligence. It was agreed that MI5 would post a permanent SLO to the new Malayan government. The SLO arrived in Kuala Lumpur in April 1956, and with the Tunku's support continued to serve on the staff of the British High Commission after the Malayan Federation gained independence in August 1957. In fact, he developed such close relations with the Tunku in the run-up to independence that he was trusted with the numbers of the combination locks to the Tunku's safes. After independence two further MI5 officers were seconded to the Malayan government to help train a new generation of local officers. MI5 continued to have an SLO based in Kuala Lumpur until at least 1968, and probably even longer.[57]

The SLO worked closely with the local Special Branch and shared intelligence with the Tunku's new government. However, it is clear that, just as it did in India, MI5 carefully 'managed' the intelligence it passed to Malayan officials and ministers, with the SLO retaining sensitive information, described in reports as 'UK Eyes Only'. The Malayan government doubtless mirrored this practice and sanitised the flow of its own intelligence to the SLO. Even among the closest of allies, as the old intelligence saying goes, there is no such thing as a friendly secret service, only the secret service of a friendly country. Despite the inevitable reticence on both sides, just as the Tunku wanted, the Special Branch remained more 'Europeanised' than Malaya's regular police, the CID, and though there is little evidence at present, it seems likely that the Special Branch continued to monitor extremist groups in the Tunku's government, as had occurred previously in India.[58]

Records found in the Hanslope Park archive show that during the run-up to independence in Malaya, as in India previously, British officials deliberately destroyed 'sensitive' records, often relating to intelligence matters. In July 1956, on the eve of Malaya's independence, a junior colonial official in Kuala Lumpur, W.J. Watts, wrote to the governor's office at King's House:

> ... the strong room here is very overcrowded and the Secretary for external affairs has asked me to see if some of the older records in it cannot be cleared out. A number of them were obviously acquired during the period when the Deputy High Commissioner was in occupation of Carcosa House and presumably they are duplicated in King's House. If this is the case would you agree that they might be destroyed. A list is attached marked 'A'.
>
> The largest quantity of records consists of savingrams, telegrams to and from the Colonial Office etc. – I attach a list marked 'B'. I believe that these records are probably duplicated either in your office or that of the Secretary to Government ... Our suggestion is that they should be parcelled up and shipped back to the Colonial Office.
>
> List C deals with several bundles of old King's House files. I have been through them and it would seem that some contain items of historical interest in the event of anyone writing a history of the Emergency or a biography of the former High Commissioner. The others should be dealt with in detail but I have not had time to do this. Would you agree to their disposal as suggested against individual files in the list?

Thus, it seems that records in Malaya were destroyed without even being referred to senior officers.

One of the reasons MI5 carefully 'managed' – manipulated – intelligence as the new state of Malaya was born was because, as in India, many of its leading politicians were themselves previous targets of MI5 and Malayan Special Branch investigations. Both agencies are known to have maintained files on the Tunku himself, though at the time of writing his MI5 file has not been declassified. Nevertheless, an indication of the kind of information MI5 probably held on the Tunku is revealed by its multi-volume file on Anthony Brooke, the nephew of the last of the 'White Rajahs' to rule Sarawak (British Borneo), Vyner Brooke, who in 1946 ceded the territory to Britain. The public explanation for the cession, which brought an end to 'Brooke rule' in Sarawak, which had essentially been run as a private dynasty, steeped in eccentric tradition, was the growing communist threat in the principality, but conveniently for Vyner, it was made in exchange for a sizeable pension. Vyner was by any measure an eccentric, who described himself in *Who's Who* as having 'led several expeditions into the far interior of the country to punish head-hunters', and as understanding 'the management of natives', while his wife, Sylvia, Lady Brooke, described herself as the 'Queen of the headhunters' – a reference to the tradition practised by the Ibans of Sarawak of decapitating their victims. After Vyner's surprising cession, Anthony Brooke, as Heir Apparent, set himself up as a leading 'anti-cessionist' politician in the territory. Though he was extremely anglicised, having been educated at Trinity College, Cambridge, when it came to what he felt was 'his' dynasty in Sarawak, he was a diehard nationalist.[59]

Matters grew more complicated when, in December 1949, the British Governor of Sarawak, Duncan Stewart, was assassinated. It did not take long for suspicion to fall on Anthony Brooke. This sparked MI5's interest in him, and its wish to 'get wind of any other plots he and his associates might be hatching'. It opened a file on Brooke in January 1950, and began to scrutinise his activities in London, the base of his government-in-exile. MI5's interception of Brooke's mail, carried out by means of a HOW, was so effective that in October 1950 it was even able to tell the Colonial Office when and where he lost his wallet. Despite MI5's suspicions, Brooke was not in fact involved in Stewart's assassination, which was carried out by a lone 'anti-cessionist'. Stewart was stabbed during a trip to Sibu, while he was inspecting the guard of honour of the Sarawak Constabulary, by a young Malay opposed to the cession of Sarawak to Britain, and died soon thereafter. Even after the nature of his death was clear, however, MI5 maintained that while Brooke may not have been directly responsible for the murder, he was still 'indirectly responsible' for it as the head of the anti-cessionist struggle. Although MI5 started off by seeing Brooke as little more than a 'nuisance', in the course of its investigations it began to regard him as a serious security risk, the leader of illegal 'anti-British' activities in the region. It is unlikely that Brooke ever really was the security threat MI5 saw him to be, though he did provide the anti-cessionist movement with a figurehead. It was largely on MI5's advice that in late 1950 he was denied entry back into Sarawak, and had to make neighbouring Singapore his base of operations. Eventually he formally resigned his dynastic title. After Malayan independence, MI5's SLO in Kuala Lumpur shared some carefully vetted intelligence on Brooke with the Tunku's government. He did not tell the Tunku that MI5 also had a file on him, though the Tunku probably guessed that it did.[60]

The role performed by MI5 and Britain's other secret agencies in the transfer of power in Malaya was part of a much broader picture in which the British government preserved its interests and established close bonds with the government of the new country, which remained within the Commonwealth after independence. These bonds, sealed by defence treaties and economic ties, secured Britain's 'vital interests' in South-East Asia throughout the Cold War. Britain negotiated a series of defence treaties with the Malayan government that allowed, for example, naval right of passage through the Malayan Straits, which was valuable for Commonwealth defence requirements. It also agreed to assist with Malaya's internal and external security after independence, in return for the Malayan government remaining in the Sterling Area and agreeing to keep its gold reserves in London. Both governments upheld their sides of the agreement, and by 1965 some 65 per cent of all capital held in the country was British. Meanwhile, British and Commonwealth forces continued to help the new government to fight communist guerrillas, with the Emergency not finally being declared over until 1960, three years after independence.[61]

There was a similar story in Singapore. The fortress city state, the name of which means 'Lion City' in Sanskrit, was a 'crown colony', separate from Britain's other imperial possessions on the Malayan Peninsula. From the early 1950s there were increasing demands in Singapore for full self-government and independence. The British Chiefs of Staff, however, were vehemently opposed to any concession of power without guaranteeing Britain's strategic interests, which they regarded as vital for Commonwealth defence obligations in Australia, New Zealand, Fiji and Hong Kong. Some 10,000 British troops were stationed in Singapore, and there was no suitable alternative base for them in the region. One report from the Colonial Office's newly established Intelligence and Security Department (ISD) in August 1956 summarised Britain's strategic position bluntly: 'we wish to maintain, more or less on a permanent basis, certain defence interests and installations [in Singapore]', which as another of its reports noted, meant that Britain would have to 'insist on a firm agreement on certain aspects of intelligence and security' before the city state could be granted full independence.[62]

As in Malaya, MI5 played a significant but secret role in constitutional discussions over the future of Singapore, negotiating with successive First Ministers, first David Marshall and then Lim Yew Hock, in order to guarantee and preserve British strategic intelligence interests in Singapore. Marshall was a prominent Jewish-Iraqi lawyer, who despite his smooth talking failed in 1955 to obtain an agreement from Britain for the devolution of power and the establishment of internal self-government in the crown colony. As a result he was replaced as First Minister by Lim, a popular Chinese Singaporean politician. From 1955 Britain began to concede limited powers to Singapore, primarily to retain the goodwill of the Singaporean government, and partly because it wanted to avoid heightening grievances that already threatened a communist takeover of the city, whose population of 1.5 million was three-quarters ethnically Chinese.

Between September and October 1956 a series of meetings took place at the highest level, between the Governor of Singapore, Sir Robert Black, the First Minister, Lim, and MI5's SLO in Singapore, whose name is not revealed in the records. The result of these discussions was an agreement that the SLO would remain in Singapore after independence; that he would have access to the Chief Minister himself and the Minister for Internal Security; and that he would sit on the new Internal Security Council, based in Government House in Singapore. Lim, who was a staunch anti-communist, gave an assurance that 'UK officers and agencies would have the fullest access to security intelligence from Singapore sources'. At the same time, a highly secret deal was brokered between Lim and Lennox-Boyd, by which, during the transitional period when Britain shared rule with Singaporean ministers, Lim was allowed to arrest a number of 'subversives' in Singapore. It is now clear that this deal, which received cabinet approval in London, was designed not to attack genuine subversives, but Lim's political opponents. As we shall see, this tendency on the part of new national governments to use the security apparatus relinquished by the British for their own ends was a disturbing legacy that Britain left in a number of its former colonies.[63]

Singapore achieved full internal self-government in 1959, with Lee Kuan Yew as its first Prime Minister, and like Malaya, it remained in the Commonwealth. Unlike Malaya, however, the British government retained ultimate control over Singapore's defence and foreign policies – internal self-government did not include foreign policy. Singapore remained a firm ally of Britain and the West throughout the Cold War, and was ultimately protected by a coalition of British, Commonwealth and American forces. The city state joined the Federation of Malaya in 1963, but broke away in 1965 and thereafter became a fully independent city republic. As in Malaya, British intelligence established a close relationship with authorities in Singapore up to and beyond its full independence in 1965. In the mid-1960s Lee Kuan Yew, who held the Singaporean premiership for over three decades, thanked MI5 for the value of the work done by its SLO, Christopher Herbert, an old colonial sweat. A graduate of Trinity College, Dublin, with a first class degree in experimental science, Herbert had joined the Indian Civil Service in 1936, and in 1950 had been recruited to MI5, becoming a Security Intelligence Adviser at the Colonial Office in 1955. As SLO in Singapore in the early 1960s, Herbert took over all of MI5's local responsibilities when the position of the head of SIFE was closed down and its final head, Michael Serpell, retired in October 1962.[64]

Singapore is justifiably regarded, together with Hong Kong, as one of the main Cold War spy capitals of the Far East. The JICFE and SIFE both continued to be based there after it achieved internal self-government in 1959, and GCHQ likewise maintained a significant presence in the city republic throughout the 1960s and beyond, with listening posts and antennae springing up on a number of British installations there. SIS also came to play an increasingly important role in Singapore as it moved towards independence. SIS had maintained a station in Singapore since the 1930s, and with the coming of full independence it took over MI5's responsibilities there. At least one Chief of SIS, Sir Dick White, the only person ever to head both MI5 and SIS, is known to have visited Singapore (in 1956). However, the story of how SIS eventually took over British intelligence responsibilities in Singapore is one that unfortunately lies beyond the scope of this book, for there are simply not enough records available at present to tell it.[65]

Much of the story of the British in Malaya is clearly one of success. Traditional interpretations of the Malayan Emergency suggest that between 1948 and 1957, Britain secured an economically crucial part of its empire; defeated communist insurgents; insulated the colony from communist regimes elsewhere; and successfully established a unified political and economic administration, an impressive infrastructure and a strong state structure in the Malayan Peninsula. Unlike the outcome of America's struggle in Vietnam, Malaya was, to use President Eisenhower's analogy, the domino that stood. The British feared in Malaya, as the Americans would later do in Vietnam, that if one country fell to communism, others in the region would follow like dominoes. As we have seen, British intelligence played an important role in developing a successful counter-insurgency strategy in Malaya, which relied both on military operations and on 'hearts and minds' campaigns – and which can be considered a useful model for counter-insurgencies in our own time.

Clearly the British response to the Malayan Emergency was successful in its immediate aims: eliminating the communist threat in Malaya and isolating communists from power in the colony.

In 1963 the Federation of Malaya was successfully transformed into Malaysia, an expanded state including the territories of British North Borneo (Sabah), Sarawak and Singapore, the creation of which led to a violent confrontation (*Konfrontasi*) with the Indonesian government. Indonesia's president, Sukarno, believed that the establishment of the Federation was an attempt to re-establish colonial rule, and so decided to try to capture the pro-British state in Borneo, Brunei. Britain, upholding its defence treaties with the Malaysian Federation, supported it against Indonesia's onslaught. Sukarno's attempted revolt in Brunei was suppressed by Gurkhas, whom the British flew in from Singapore, but fighting soon spilled over into mainland Malaysia. SIGINT played an important role in the resulting successful combat operations. Commonwealth forces, comprised of troops from Britain, Australia and New Zealand, were assisted by decrypts obtained by GCHQ, which revealed both Sukarno's intentions and the location of fighters in jungles.[66]

These, then, are some of the successes Britain's secret agencies gained in the transfer of power in Malaya. However, it is debatable whether the British government's role in the birth of modern Malaysia was really as successful as most histories suggest. In reality, the Emergency in Malaya produced some sinister legacies. It is true that, thanks in large part to MI5's advice, security intelligence in Malaya was separated from policing, and thereby the establishment of a secret police force after independence in 1957 was avoided. However, the sovereign Malayan government adopted and retained a number of highly authoritarian instruments of power that the British had imposed during the Emergency, such as detention without trial. The Malayan Sedition Act (1960) allowed it to wield vast powers against anyone whom it labelled 'seditious'. Modern Malaysia was, in Macmillan's phrase, 'a shotgun wedding'. It was a loose collection of states born against a backdrop of war, occupation and Emergency, and it retained a number of the illiberal security procedures forged at that time. Some have argued that true independence will not be complete in Malaysia until those powers are abolished and more liberal forms of government are established.[67]

6

British Intelligence and the Setting Sun on Britain's African Empire

'He's dangerous; he's mad …'

'Wouldn't you feel like that if we'd been invaded by the continental invader?'

PETER ABRAHAMS, *A Wreath for Udomo*[1]

The only good Mau Mau is a very, very dead one.

WILLIAM BALDWIN, *Mau Mau Man Hunt*[2]

Britain had maintained trading links in West Africa for hundreds of years, but it was not until the nineteenth century that it, like other European powers, established proper colonies there. During the so-called 'scramble for Africa', beginning in the 1880s, competition among all of the major European colonial powers led them to claim vast tracts of land in the 'dark continent'. What was arrogantly termed the 'white man's burden' involved bringing 'civilisation' and 'education' to supposedly uncivilised and uneducated areas of Africa.

The Second World War transformed the nature of British rule in its West African colonies, chiefly the Gold Coast and Nigeria, the most populous colony in all of Africa. During the war, large numbers of African recruits fought for Britain and the Allies, with thousands losing their lives in the name of freedom and democracy, from the jungles of Burma to the beaches of northern France. When the survivors returned to their homelands, many of them were driven by a vehement sense of anti-colonialism, and were prepared to fight for freedom and democracy in their own countries. Although some historians have questioned the extent to which postwar anti-colonialism was rooted in the experiences of the Second World War, there can be little doubt that the spectacle of 'civilised' European peoples slaughtering each other forced many African recruits to question what was really meant by European 'civilisation'. When African soldiers returned to their countries of origin, Britain – like other European colonial powers – faced a juggernaut of anti-colonial nationalism.[3]

THE GOLD COAST

In February 1948 the capital of the Gold Coast, Accra, was the scene of an eruption of violent civil disturbances, with protesters demanding 'self-government now' from the British colonial administration. The riots resulted in twenty-nine killed and 237 injured, figures that may have been small by Indian – let alone Indonesian – standards, but were still alarming for the British authorities. Occurring at the same time as the outbreak of the Malayan Emergency, it seemed to many observers in Whitehall (and Washington) that the spectre of communism lay behind both outbreaks of violence. Even before these riots, Britain had been forced to address the question of increasing political representation for Africans in the Gold Coast. In 1946 the so-called Burns Constitution had favoured a gradualist approach to constitutional reform in the colony, with the establishment of an Executive Council (something like a cabinet) which would eventually have limited African representation. The riots forced the British government to look again at constitutional reform in the colony. In their aftermath, the colonial administration in the Gold Coast and the Colonial Office in London instigated two important commissions, the conclusions of which were groundbreaking.

The first was the so-called Watson Commission, named after its head, Aiken Watson, a retired left-leaning judge who questioned whether the gradualist approach advocated by the Burns Constitution was the right way forward. Instead, Watson concluded that Africans should be brought into local government more rapidly. This was a milestone in the history of British colonial rule in Africa, and for African nationalism more generally. The Watson Commission's final report was a remarkably forward-thinking document, which deliberately exceeded its brief: the eminent historians of British decolonisation, Richard Rathbone and Ronald Hyam, have termed it 'one of the most important documents in the end of empire'. It was followed by a second commission under Mr Justice Coussey, which again was pathbreaking, firstly because it was comprised entirely of African (albeit moderate) delegates, and secondly for its conclusions. In October 1949 the Coussey Commission advocated major constitutional reforms, concluding that it was necessary to establish a more representative form of government for Africans in the colony.[4]

It is crucial not to read the Watson and Coussey Commissions as advocating full independence for the Gold Coast: the word 'independence' does not appear once in either Commission's report. It is likewise revealing that a Colonial Office report compiled in 1950 predicted that it would take 'decades' for colonies like Nigeria to gain independence from Britain, and the Gold Coast was not even mentioned in the forecast. Nevertheless, the Watson and Burns Commissions do represent a substantial shift on the path towards self-government in the Gold Coast.

The conclusions of both commissions found a welcome audience back in London in the person of Andrew Cohen, one of the most talented officials in the Colonial Office. Cohen had made something of a name for himself with the so-called 'local government' despatch of February 1947, usually associated with the Secretary of State, Arthur Creech Jones, and commonly referred to as the 'Creech Jones Despatch', which urged colonial governors to instigate efficient, local, representative government as a priority wherever possible. He subsequently became a leading advocate of the devolution of power to moderate, well-disposed national governments in former British colonies. In May 1947 he helped to prepare an influential report, known as the 'Caine-Cohen report', which became the centrepiece of the Labour government's Africa policy. It recommended that colonies should be allowed to progress towards self-government in local affairs whenever and wherever possible, though it wrongly concluded that even in the most advanced territory, the Gold Coast, this was unlikely to occur 'in much less than a generation'. Although it has not been commonly acknowledged by historians, Cohen and other officials in the Colonial Office liaised closely with Britain's secret agencies, which informed and helped to shape their views about anti-colonial movements in the Gold Coast and other colonies. According to the renegade former MI5 officer Peter Wright, shortly before Cohen's death in 1968, he came under suspicion from Wright as possibly being linked to Soviet espionage. However, there is no evidence in the public domain to support this.

Soon after the riots in the Gold Coast in February 1948 a new Governor was appointed to the colony, Sir Charles Arden-Clarke, who was as English as they came: a clergyman's son, an ex-army officer and a dog lover. He was also an old Africa hand and a long-serving, moderate colonial official, who had most recently served in the kingdom of Sarawak. Arden-Clarke's experiences in the Far East, where he had witnessed the violent spread of communism at first hand, would shape his subsequent response to nation-alism and communism in West Africa. In the Gold Coast he would forge a close personal bond with Dr Kwame Nkrumah, the leader of the Convention People's Party (CPP), who went on to become the first leader of independent Ghana, as the Gold Coast became after 1957.

Nkrumah, more than anyone else, focused and led post-war anti-colonial nationalism in the Gold Coast. He was the son of a goldsmith, who through hard work had won a scholarship in 1935 to study in the United States. He helped to fund his studies at Lincoln University, Pennsylvania, by working variously in his spare time as a dishwasher, bellhop, soapmaker and fish peddler. He preached at black churches in New York, sometimes sleeping on the subway for lack of a bed. At the end of the war he moved to London, and in November 1945, along with many other aspiring anti-colonial politicians, he attended an influential Pan-African Congress held in Manchester. In London he was enrolled at various times at University College London and the London School of Economics, where he studied briefly under the philosopher A.J. Ayer. Most of his time, however, was spent associating with a group of left-wing African and West Indian students and intellectuals, including the Marxist-Leninist George Padmore and his fellow Trinidadian author C.L.R. James, one of the finest of all writers on cricket, to say nothing of his Marxist historical works.

In late 1947 Nkrumah returned to the Gold Coast, where he soon rose to prominence in the United Gold Coast Convention Party (UGCC), led by the liberal lawyer Joseph Danquah. Nkrumah's self-proclaimed mission was to 'throw the Europeans out of Africa'. He quickly grew tired of the UGCC, and set up his own party, the Convention People's Party (CPP), which with its slogan 'self-government now' would become the loudest voice demanding constitutional reform and advancement in the Gold Coast.[5]

Having studied in both America and Britain, Nkrumah was relatively Westernised, and his ideas about colonial emancipation were largely inspired by events in India, particularly Gandhi's theories of passive resist-ance and Nehru's influential anti-colonial tract *The Discovery of India*. Like many other national leaders in British colonies, before and after, his 'subversion' soon landed him in prison. In fact, like Nehru in India, who was his inspiration, Nkrumah earned his nationalist credentials by serving time in a British jail. In January 1950 the colonial administration arrested him for organising illegal strikes and sedition, which the CPP termed 'positive action'. He was sentenced to three years' imprisonment, but from his cell in the St James fort in Accra he smuggled out edicts, some of which were written on toilet paper, to his followers.

In a general election held in February 1951, while Nkrumah was still in prison, the CPP won a crushing victory, claiming thirty-four of the thirty-eight seats available. At this point Arden-Clarke took the momentous decision to release Nkrumah from jail and to work with him, to 'channel not check' the growing nationalism in the Gold Coast, as he told the Colonial Office, using 'batons not bullets'. Nkrumah became the 'leader of government business' in the Gold Coast, and from February 1952 was officially called 'Prime Minister'. A year later, in February 1953, the Gold Coast achieved internal self-government, meaning it gained control over its own domestic affairs – an unprecedented step for a black African colony – although the colonial administration reserved control over defence and foreign affairs. Nkrumah gained a further electoral victory in June 1954, winning seventy-two of the 102 available seats, with 55 per cent of the votes. The Gold Coast, or Ghana as it then became, went on to gain full independence from Britain in 1957, remaining within the Commonwealth.[6]

As the Gold Coast advanced towards self-government, MI5 played a significant role in reforming security and intelligence procedures in the colony. As we have seen in previous chapters, the year 1948 was pivotal for British imperial security in the context of the escalating Cold War between East and West. After the first riots in Accra and the declaration of the Malayan Emergency four months later, the Colonial Office ordered a review of all colonial police forces. In a circular despatched to all governors and police commissioners throughout the empire in August 1948, the Colonial Secretary, Arthur Creech Jones, warned:

> It is in my view essential that every possible means should be taken to prevent similar happenings in other Colonial territories, and there is much evidence that the sources which have inspired the outbreak in Malaya (and have some indirect responsibility for those in the Gold Coast) are on the look out for similar opportunities elsewhere.[7]

Shortly after the outbreak of riots in the Gold Coast, MI5's Alex Kellar travelled (under an alias) to the colony. Some historians have noted that a 'shadowy' figure named Kellar arrived there in February 1948, and was involved with security in some way, but hitherto it has been impossible to discover much more about his activities. In fact, during his trip to the Gold Coast in 1948 Kellar helped to reform and overhaul the entire system of security intelligence in the colony, bringing it in line with the needs of the Cold War. As with MI5's colonial reforms elsewhere, he recommended that there should be a distinction between police and intelligence. The fact that the colony had a single, unified police force meant that in MI5's judgement the existing Special Branch was sufficiently equipped to handle security intelligence, and there was no need to establish a new security service modelled on MI5. The Special Branch in the Gold Coast thereafter formed an intelligence unit separate from the CID of the regular colonial police. Kellar also recommended substantially increasing the number of Special Branch officers, and establishing a registry dedicated to security intelligence records, as opposed to law-enforcement police records. Again, his proposals were implemented.[8]

To help oversee these reforms, Kellar recommended that MI5 should have an officer permanently stationed in the Gold Coast. It had had a DSO in Accra during the Second World War, who ran an inter-service 'West African Intelligence Centre', but at the end of the war this position had been shut down. In 1948 MI5 opened a new post, an SLO, in the Gold Coast, who had direct access to the colonial administration at the highest level, including the Governor himself, the chief of police, the Colonial Secretary and representatives of the armed forces in the colony. The SLO was also in charge of a new 'Central Security Committee', which provided the Governor with periodic intelligence assessments. As elsewhere throughout the empire and Commonwealth, MI5's officers in the Gold Coast provided a two-way secure channel of communication between London and the local administration. Its first SLO in the Gold Coast was none other than Robin 'Tin Eye' Stephens, MI5's ace interrogator from Camp 020 during the Second World War.[9]

Stephens and his successors as SLO attended most of Nkrumah's political rallies, and reported political developments to MI5 and the Colonial Office in London. In June 1949, after attending one of the CPP's rallies, Stephens correctly forecast that the party would win a general election when it was called. Despite this accurate forecast, when we read MI5's SLOs' reports from the Gold Coast, it is clear that they never really understood the nature of tribal societies in the colony. They could not, for example, even decide on the correct spelling of Nkrumah's name. That said, it is equally clear from MI5's discussions with other Whitehall departments that it did not see the role of its SLOs in the Gold Coast as 'understanding' tribal societies, in the manner of information-gathering and ethnographic studies from the colonial past. Their entire focus was on detecting and assessing the threat of communism as the Gold Coast moved towards self-government in the early Cold War. The reforms that MI5 instigated in the Gold Coast, and other British territories in Africa, were summarised in a subsequent Colonial Office intelligence report:

> Following the Gold Coast disturbances [in February 1948] the head of MI5 Overseas Department [Kellar] recently paid a visit to three of the four West African Territories; as a result of his tour a Security Liaison Officer has been appointed with HQ at Accra to coordinate security intelligence in that region ... The Director-General of MI5 last year [1947] paid a visit to East Africa and held a conference of all the Intelligence and Security Officers of the East African Territories to review security arrangements. There is a Security Liaison Officer in Nairobi for East Africa, and a MI5 Officer will shortly be leaving for Salisbury [Rhodesia], where he will act as Security Liaison Officer for the Central African Territories and will coordinate with the Union [of South Africa] authorities.[10]

As many historians have recognised, the smooth transfer of power in the Gold Coast would have been impossible without the close personal bond between Sir Charles Arden-Clarke and Kwame Nkrumah. As Arden-Clarke later recalled, Nkrumah was the only realistic hope for stability that Britain had in the colony ('the only dog in the kennel'), so in many ways he had to get along with him. Behind the cordial personal relationship they established, however, was a stream of high-grade intelligence that MI5 provided Arden-Clarke with on Nkrumah, which helped to shape the response of the Colonial Office, and the British government more generally, to him.

Nkrumah had first come to the attention of British intelligence when he was residing in England after the war. His name had been forwarded to MI5 by the FBI, which had detected his involvement with several pan-African 'activist' groups in the United States while he was studying there. Nkrumah himself was not the direct target of MI5 enquiries at this time, but several of the anti-colonial groups he was associated with in London were under close surveillance, and his name appeared on MI5's radar through them.[11]

It is crucial to appreciate that MI5 did not monitor the activities of anti-colonial groups in Britain simply because they advocated 'colonial emancipation' or 'national liberation', or were 'pro-independence'. As MI5 internal reports repeatedly noted, these were legitimate political aspirations, albeit they were fraught with dangers for Britain during the Cold

War. Rather, MI5 monitored such groups because of their suspected or established links with communism. As we have seen, at the time MI5 also had the Communist Party of Great Britain under intensive surveillance, tapping the telephones of its offices, intercepting its written communications and installing 'special facilities' (bugs) in its headquarters. These microphone bugs provided voluminous amounts of diplomatic intelligence on Nkrumah and other anti-colonial leaders in the post-war years.

One of the specific functions of MI5's new 'Overseas Section' ('OS' Section), established in 1948 and led by Sir John Shaw, was to observe and study African students living in the United Kingdom, and to establish whether they had any connections with communism. In the post-war years colonial subjects like Nkrumah had the right to enter Britain without restriction, and one of the consequences of this was a dramatic increase in the number of immigrants from the empire and Commonwealth, many of whom came to the imperial heartland in the hope of finding a better life. In 1950 the entire immigrant population in Britain was about 25,000, but by 1955 this had increased to 43,000. In 1953 2,000 immigrants arrived from the West Indies alone, and in the single year of 1955 some 27,500 immigrants arrived in Britain. It is not an exaggeration to say that in the post-war years the empire effectively came back to Britain, permanently changing the composition of British society. This trend continued until 1962, when restrictions on immigration from the empire and Commonwealth were imposed with the passing of the controversial Commonwealth Immigration Act.[12]

At the time when Nkrumah was residing in Britain, in the immediate post-war years, colonial immigrants in London and other major British cities were faced with a foreign and often unwelcoming environment, and tended therefore to build up close-knit relationships among their own communities. This was brilliantly depicted by the South African writer Peter Abrahams in his novel *A Wreath for Udomo* (1956), which was loosely modelled on Nkrumah's life in England and in which both Nkrumah ('Udomo') and the first leader of independent Kenya, Jomo Kenyatta ('Mhendi'), appear as fictionalised versions of themselves.[13]

Close groups of colonial subjects living in Britain such as these were carefully monitored by MI5. It investigated a remarkable range of anti-colonial groups and individuals, for example the International Africa Bureau, which had been established in London by the noted Trinidadian activist for pan-Africanism, George Padmore, a self-proclaimed Marxist 'revolutionary' who had previously been something of a campus rebel in the United States. MI5 and the Special Branch also monitored the Pan-African Congress held in Manchester in 1945, which was attended by Nkrumah and several other future leaders of independent states in Africa, and at which the Special Branch deployed undercover officers. MI5 likewise investigated the activities of the West African National Secretariat (WANS), a 'pro-independence' group for West African students in London which Nkrumah and close associates like Bankole Awooner-Renner established in 1945. Nkrumah later recalled in his memoirs that the WANS office in Gray's Inn Road 'must have been the busiest little place of its size in the whole of London':

> It was rarely empty, for as soon as word went round of its whereabouts, it became the rendezvous of all African and West Indian students and their friends. It was there that we used to assemble to discuss our plans, to voice our opinions and air our grievances.[14]

Unknown to Nkrumah and his colleagues in WANS, MI5 was intercepting the mail and tapping the telephones of its offices.[15]

Although Nkrumah was not himself the subject of MI5 enquiries, MI5 desk officers and its Registry staff carefully noted and recorded every piece of information that came in to them on his activities, from surveillance of either the CPGB or of pan-African groups like WANS. This, more than anything else, reveals the fundamental difference between a law-enforcement police agency and an intelligence service: MI5 opened files on Nkrumah and other anti-colonial campaigners residing in Britain in a preventative and prophylactic manner, based on just a few scraps of information, in Nkrumah's case a tip-off from the FBI, an undercover Special Branch surveillance report at the Pan-African Congress in Manchester in November 1945, and an intercepted telephone call that Nkrumah made to the Communist Party in London. Nkrumah had not committed a crime, and MI5 had no intention of ever bringing legal proceedings against him, but nevertheless it opened a file on him.

Although it had no executive powers, and relied on other departments to carry out its recommendations, which prevented it from enforcing its own policies and thereby becoming a secret police, the nature of MI5's preventative enquiries into anti-colonial campaigners like Nkrumah is nevertheless both remarkable and alarming from the perspective of civil liberties – an issue to which we shall return. The result of MI5's pre-emptive enquiries into Nkrumah's political activities in England was that, when he decided to return to the Gold Coast in 1947, it had built up detailed records on him and his associates. This background intelligence dossier would become crucial for colonial authorities in Accra and London as the Gold Coast moved towards self-government and ultimately independence.

The surveillance of Nkrumah's political activities in England was so intensive that, on the basis of an intercepted telephone call to the Communist Party in November 1947, MI5 officers were able to inform port authorities in England and the Gold Coast when he was due to leave England. In his memoirs, Nkrumah alluded to the problems he faced when departing from Liverpool, which though he did not realise it at the time, were prompted by MI5's tip-off:

> At Liverpool I unexpectedly encountered difficulties with the authorities at the docks for, unknown to me, the police [MI5] had collected quite a file of information about my political activities in London. They were not at all happy about my presence at Communist meetings. In the end, after lengthy questioning, they grudgingly stamped my passport and I was allowed to embark. I had a feeling that whilst they were happy to see the back of me, they were a little worried about what I was going to do in the Gold Coast. I could have told them then, but they would never have understood.[16]

At face value, Nkrumah and many of his close associates had dangerously left-wing views, which were Marxist if not outright communist. The leaders of Nkrumah's new party in the Gold Coast, the CPP, referred to themselves as 'comrades', and he subsequently dedicated his memoirs to the notoriously assassinated first Prime Minister of the Congo, Patrice Lumumba, suspected by Washington of holding communist beliefs. When Nkrumah was arrested in March 1948 an unsigned membership card of the CPGB was found among his possessions, and a note on something called 'the Circle', the expressed aim of which was to establish a Union of African Socialist Republics in West Africa. Having no information on the Circle from either sources in Moscow or from US intelligence, MI5 desk officers admitted that they had never heard of it, but thought it could be receiving 'outside' (Soviet) guidance.[17]

To make an already alarming picture even worse, Nkrumah's closest ideological associate in London, George Padmore, had openly Marxist beliefs and had been a member of the French Communist Party in the 1920s, turning to communism primarily because he hoped it would help emancipate his native Trinidad from British 'imperialism'. Beginning in the late 1940s, MI5 had a letter and telephone HOW imposed on Padmore's house in Hampstead, in North London, which revealed that he was at the centre of a group of ambitious and highly capable West Indian and African campaigners, some of whom were in direct contact with the CPGB's 'colonial section'. This section of the Party was run by another West Indian, Peter Blackman, a former priest who had given up religion for the faith of communism.[18]

With associates like these, many officials in the Colonial Office in London, as well as in the Gold Coast itself, regarded Nkrumah as an out-and-out communist, and his CPP as a puppet run by Moscow. The leading historian of the end of British rule in West Africa, Richard Rathbone, has noted that it was almost a 'hallowed belief' in Whitehall in the late 1940s that Nkrumah was a communist, and consequently that if granted independence, the Gold Coast would become a Soviet state. To give just one example of the extent to which this belief shaped British attitudes, in 1950 the research department of the cabinet's Imperial Affairs Committee noted that Nkrumah maintained contact with communists in London, and described an unnamed one of these contacts, probably Padmore, as 'a Moscow trained communist'.[19]

These opinions filtered through and infected British press reporting on Nkrumah. In October 1950 the *Daily Telegraph* ran a story entitled 'Red Shadow over the Gold Coast', which claimed that Nkrumah's CPP was orchestrated from Moscow, 'using Ju Ju of darkest Africa'. Nkrumah's socialist-Marxist background sent many quarters of Whitehall – and Washington – into near hysteria. In short, it appeared to most British colonial officials a distinct probability that a communist was rising to power in the Gold Coast, the strategic consequences of which would have been disastrous for Britain's imperial security at the time when the Cold War was escalating.[20]

The key question to which colonial officials in London and the Gold Coast, as well as their Western allies, particularly the United States, needed an answer was whether Nkrumah was actually a communist. Because of its clandestine sources, to which no other British government department had access, MI5 was uniquely placed to answer this crucial question. Remarkably, given how much circumstantial evidence there was suggesting that Nkrumah was a communist, before 1957 MI5 and the rest of the British intelligence community persistently played down the communist threat posed by the leader of the Gold Coast and his 'comrades'.

For a number of reasons, this is the opposite of what we might have expected. The purpose of intelligence services is obviously to assess threats to national security, and it seems inherently logical that they would therefore have a vested interest in increasing the perceptions of such threats, 'sexing up' their dossiers if only cynically to obtain more resources: armies, of course, will always ask for more tanks. The reality, however, is that if an intelligence service is doing its job properly, then, as one former head of the JIC, Sir Percy Cradock, put it, one of its main responsibilities is to tell a government what it does not want to hear. That is exactly what MI5 did as Nkrumah grew steadily more powerful in the Gold Coast. Indeed, MI5's assessments of Nkrumah and many other anti-colonial leaders in British colonies in Africa had a calming effect in Whitehall.

The crucial evidence that MI5 obtained on Nkrumah's political allegiances came from its intensive surveillance of the British Communist Party: the bugs installed in the Party's headquarters revealed that in the late 1940s the Party's leadership was becoming increasingly disillusioned with the communist credentials of its African protégés like Nkrumah. By 1952 the CPGB was regularly complaining that Nkrumah was a 'lost job'. This information, combined with the interception of Nkrumah's mail, allowed MI5 to come to a much more sober and nuanced assessment of Nkrumah's political allegiances than other British government departments, and allowed it to argue persuasively against the received wisdom of Nkrumah's 'communism' within Whitehall.[21]

For two years before Nkrumah's arrest in the Gold Coast in March 1948, MI5 had been providing the Colonial Office with reports on the activities of the West African National Secretariat. As Nkrumah became a more powerful figure, especially after the CPP's general election victory in 1951, MI5 was tasked by the Colonial Office to make an overall assessment of his political views and affiliations. It assembled all of its intelligence into a background dossier which it circulated to the Colonial Office and selected other Whitehall departments, and through the new SLO in the Gold Coast, Robin Stephens, to the Governor himself. This clearly spelled out that, although Nkrumah held socialist and Marxist views, there was no evidence that he was a communist. His overriding ambition was independence for the Gold Coast, and just as he was dissatisfied with political control from London, it was unlikely he would ever be prepared to receive instructions from Moscow:

His interest in Communism may well be prompted only by his desire to enlist aid in the furtherance of his own aims in West Africa … Although an undoubted nationalist, N'KRUMAH's aims are probably tainted by his wishes for his own personal advancement.[22]

MI5 also assured the Colonial Office that even Nkrumah's association with ideologues such as George Padmore was less menacing than they at first seemed. On closer inspection, 'OS' Section explained, Padmore's communist credentials were far from orthodox. He had indeed been a member of the Party in the 1920s, but by the early 1930s he had become disillusioned with Moscow's commitment to colonial 'independence' movements, and in 1934 was expelled from the French Communist Party, thereafter becoming a heretical 'Trotskyist' from the perspective of Moscow, which denounced him as a 'former person'. MI5 stressed that the threat posed by Padmore was thus far less than it first appeared. Its 'personality note' on Nkrumah, which it again passed to the Colonial Office and to Governor Sir Charles Arden-Clarke in the Gold Coast, noted:

It would be unwise to base any too definite a conclusion about N'KRUMAH's evolution as a nationalist politician upon his early career. He has certainly received a thorough grounding in Marxism and has received moral support from the British Communist Party during its rise to power. He is politically immature, however, and there are indications of an individualism in him which may ultimately over-ride his communist training … Source TABLE [the bugs in the CPGB headquarters] indicates that the British Communist Party are no longer confident that their protégé will remain faithful to them. Source CHEST [Nkrumah's intercepted mail] assures us that their fears are justified, since the C.P.P., in announcements made since its accession to power, has taken its line direct from the free-lance 'Trotskyist', George PADMORE, in the UK.[23]

An extraordinary situation had thus arisen: MI5 mounted pre-emptive investigations into colonial subjects residing in Britain who had not committed any crime, which is alarming from the perspective of civil liberties, but the fact that MI5 acquired such detailed proactive intelligence on individuals like Nkrumah and Padmore meant that it was able to calm fears about their communist affiliations. Intensive and prophylactic investigations had led, counter-intuitively, to the reduction of a perceived threat. MI5's 'calming' assessments found a receptive audience within certain important quarters in the Colonial Office. One official in particular, Juxon Barton, who had served as a District Commissioner in East Africa in the 1930s, and who in 1954 would become head of the Colonial Office's new Intelligence and Security Department, used MI5's intelligence to placate his hawkish colleagues and ease their alarmist theories about Nkrumah's 'red communism'. By 1951 the Colonial Office, assisted by the information provided by MI5, had come to view Nkrumah as a moderate, albeit a mild Marxist.[24]

As it did in London, MI5's assessment of Nkrumah played a significant role in the Gold Coast itself. Following the elections in February 1951, in which the CPP won an overwhelming majority, Arden-Clarke was convinced that Nkrumah was a moderate with whom he could work. It has already been noted that Arden-Clarke was a pragmatist who paid little attention to allegations of Nkrumah's extremism. It is impossible to know whether MI5's assessments changed Arden-Clarke's mind about Nkrumah, or whether they merely confirmed what he already believed. Like other colonial governors, he was extremely guarded about intelligence matters, and never, it seems, committed them to paper – there is nothing about MI5 or intelligence-related affairs in his personal papers, now held at London's School of Oriental and African Studies. Undoubtedly, however, he would have welcomed the evidence provided by MI5's bugging of the CPGB's headquarters, which showed that Nkrumah had fallen out with the Party.

From MI5 records, we can now tell how close the connections between MI5 and the Governor were. On New Year's Eve 1951, with Nkrumah on the brink of gaining unprecedented power for a local politician in any British colony in Africa, Arden-Clarke stayed up until 2 a.m. talking on the telephone with the head of MI5's 'OS' Section, Sir John Shaw, in London. Among other subjects, they discussed Nkrumah and the groundbreaking constitutional advancements that were taking place in the Gold Coast. The next day, New Year's Day 1952, Shaw noted in Nkrumah's MI5 file that, provided Arden-Clarke and Nkrumah could continue to get along, there was cause for 'quiet optimism' about a smooth transfer of power.[25]

Shaw was not wrong. Historians have rightly described Arden-Clarke as having held one of the most important political positions in post-war Africa. The transfer of power in the Gold Coast, from self-government to independence, was a turning point in the history of modern Africa, heralding emancipation movements in European colonies across the continent. It would have been unthinkable without the extremely close working relationship that Arden-Clarke built up with Nkrumah. At one of their first meetings after he released Nkrumah from jail in 1951, Arden-Clarke had the idea of giving him a dog, called Topsy, whose love affairs would thereafter be a subject of friendly conversation between the two men. Arden-Clarke played a high-stakes game with Nkrumah, but his rationale was that if he did not collaborate with him, it could drive him into an even more radical position; likewise, if he did not act quickly and assuage his constitutional aspirations, Nkrumah's later demands could be even more extreme. As Arden-Clarke noted to the Colonial Office in late 1951, if he made concessions to Nkrumah, 'there is at least a chance of ordered progress by successive stages being successfully pursued'. Arden-Clarke's negotiations with Nkrumah were also driven by a pragmatic realisation that it made little material difference to British interests whether the Gold Coast was a colony or a self-governing state within the Commonwealth. As Nkrumah reassured Arden-Clarke in February 1952, when he officially became Prime Minister, all of the political parties in the Gold Coast desired self-government within the Commonwealth, not outside it.[26]

Fears about Nkrumah's communist affiliations, and especially about his associates like Padmore, continued to be felt as the Gold Coast advanced towards self-government and ultimately independence, as Ghana. The Colonial Office asked MI5 to make further assessments of Nkrumah at two important constitutional junctures: in February 1952, when Nkrumah became the Prime Minister and was proposing significant changes to the colony's constitution, establishing internal self-government; and then in May 1953, when he was pushing those constitutional changes through the colony's parliament. The Colonial Office remained deeply suspicious about Padmore's influence over Nkrumah, especially when it discovered that Nkrumah was periodically asking Padmore for advice about constitutional reforms. Again, however, MI5 argued against the idea that Nkrumah's association with Padmore was menacing. Intercepted communications in March 1952 told a far more reassuring story, showing Nkrumah's intention to follow the constitutional path. MI5's assessment was set out by one of its desk officers in 'OS' Section, Herbert Loftus-Brown, in a letter to the Colonial Office in July 1952:

> ... PADMORE has always been politically a doctrinaire. His influence over N'KRUMAH appeared to be greatest when N'KRUMAH, who had imbibed Marxism from his Communist contacts in England, was building up the Convention People's Party on Marxist ideological lines. Like

many other politicians who have passed from opposition to government, N'KRUMAH may have found himself driven off his ideological course by the compulsion of party politics, and may experience increasing difficulty in reconciling his preconceived theories with the tactical manoeuvres necessary to keep himself in office.[27]

Loftus-Brown repeated these arguments in another letter to the Colonial Office in June 1953, when intercepted correspondence again revealed that Nkrumah was seeking advice from Padmore:

> Without trying to read too much into occasional reports by SWIFT [mail interception] we cannot go beyond the conclusion at which we have already arrived, that NKRUMAH will pursue his demand for self government by constitutional methods, at least for some time to come, and that while he may listen to PADMORE's advice on political strategy, he may nevertheless turn a deaf ear to any encouragement to adopt revolutionary tactics.[28]

In the early 1950s, MI5's intelligence on African nationalist leaders like Nkrumah thus urged that what Harold Macmillan would later call the 'wind of change blowing through this continent' would not be as destructive as was feared. By calming the Colonial Office's anxieties about Nkrumah's links with international communism, MI5 helped to shape the British government's response to rapid constitutional changes in the Gold Coast. Its assessments were, judging from Soviet archives, remarkably accurate. In reality, the KGB, unlike the British Communist Party, took so little interest in sub-Saharan Africa that it did not even establish a department to specialise in the region until 1960.[29]

MI5's moderating assessments of Nkrumah, however, do raise an important question: what would have happened if it had produced an adverse report on him, heightening fears about his communist beliefs? Although such counter-factual questions are ultimately impossible to answer, nevertheless, as we saw with the example of British Guiana in Chapter 4, the Colonial Office and its Western allies, particularly Washington, could cancel constitutions and democratically elected leaders could be prevented from taking power if they were feared to be communists. In the Gold Coast, however, such drastic measures were never necessary. It is striking that contemporary CIA assessments of Nkrumah, doubtless made in collaboration with Britain's secret agencies, came to similarly dovish conclusions as MI5's. One CIA assessment in January 1951 concluded that Nkrumah was not a communist, but rather 'a nationalist and opportunist adapting Communist support to his own ends'.[30]

In 1953 the Deputy Director-General of MI5, Roger Hollis, submitted a key overall assessment about communism in British territories in Africa, including the Gold Coast, to the JIC, and thus to the Chiefs of Staff and key upper echelons of Whitehall, including select cabinet ministers in London. As with MI5's previous assessments on Nkrumah, Hollis reported that the threat was not significant. There was not, his report pointed out, a single organised communist party in any British territory in Africa. MI5 repeated this message over the coming years, emphasising that communism in Africa was 'not killed but scotched'.[31]

In February 1956, armed with MI5's non-alarmist assessments of Nkrumah, the Colonial Office's new Intelligence and Security Department (ISD) blocked a propaganda effort led by the Foreign Office's Information Research Department that attempted to style Nkrumah as a Soviet stooge. Juxon Barton of the ISD commented on the Foreign Office's paper about a new 'Soviet drive' in Africa:

> We have replied [to the Foreign Office] that, so far, we have had no reports from the African colonies to prove that any such thing is happening, and we have said at meetings that we would like to see the evidence ... A year or two ago we had much difficulty with that department of the Foreign Office [the IRD] which literally saw a Communist behind every gooseberry bush, and the paper now sent to us is yet another instance of 'crying wolf'. (Indeed I regard it as perilously near a fake.) I do not think that we should be in any way complacent about communism in any Colony, but the fact is that, if anything, there have been far fewer manifestations during 1955 than at any time in the last 5 years.[32]

The main buttress against communism in the Gold Coast, and an important factor in the colony's smooth transfer of power, was Arden-Clarke's working relationship with Nkrumah. It was so close that Arden-Clarke even helped Nkrumah to fight off a rival political party, the National Liberation Association (NLA), which was based in the predominantly Ashanti territories in the north of the colony. With Arden-Clarke's assistance, Nkrumah was able to fend off the challenge of the NLA in elections held in June 1954, thus proving the CPP's national legitimacy in the eyes of the electorate.

However, despite the ostensible goodwill and even friendship between the two men, there was a Machiavellian side to the Governor's relationship with the Prime Minister-in-waiting. Recently released MI5 records reveal that Arden-Clarke allowed highly controversial forms of intelligence-gathering to operate in the colony right up until the moment before its independence. Despite his personal assurances to Nkrumah in 1952 that the Gold Coast Special Branch was no longer investigating him, in fact it continued to read Nkrumah's mail and tap his phone. It did so against the recommendation of MI5, which felt it was too risky – 'The game is not worth the candle,' as Sir John Shaw put it. 'OS' Section noted that the interception of Nkrumah's mail was 'operated unofficially by the Special Branch, against the written orders of the Governor, who receives the product in a form which he is not obliged to recognise as the fruits of disobedience of his own orders'.[33]

At the same time as the Special Branch's continued and deceitful interception of Nkrumah's mail, the British secret state formulated a process of careful 'intelligence management' in the Gold Coast as it moved towards independence. The watershed moment came in 1952, when Nkrumah and other local politicians were elected to positions of power within the administration. Soon thereafter it became impossible for MI5, and Britain's other secret services, not to share intelligence with Nkrumah and his cabinet. In order not to arouse his suspicions, while not divulging overly sensitive information, from 1952 onwards Arden-Clarke began to pass highly sanitised intelligence reports to Nkrumah, just as had been done in India before its independence.

One of Nkrumah's ministers who proved to be a headache for the colonial administration and MI5 was Kojo Botsio, who had been Nkrumah's right-hand man and close confidant since their student days in England. Botsio was well educated, having received a diploma at Oxford, and was a former warden of the West African Students' Union. In 1947 he became the first General Secretary of the CPP, and after Nkrumah's election as Prime Minister in 1952 he became a cabinet minister. The problem for the colonial administration was that Botsio was known to hold extreme Marxist views, which possibly verged on being outright communist – in 1954 the Special Branch in Accra intercepted voluminous quantities of communist literature addressed to him. This troubling situation was compounded by the fact that, as Minister of State in the Gold Coast from 1954, Botsio became the legitimate recipient of intelligence reports.

In November 1955 the colonial government established a new Defence Committee, whose members included the predictable key figures in the colony's government – Arden-Clarke, Nkrumah, representatives of the armed forces, MI5's SLO and the Commissioner of Police – and also Botsio. MI5's Bill Magan noted in Botsio's MI5 file that 'We must either lump him or leave him,' but then added, 'Clearly we must lump him.' In light of Botsio's position in the Gold Coast's government, MI5's SLO in Accra passed only carefully vetted and sanitised intelligence reports to the Defence Committee. But as MI5's files reveal, before the colony gained independence its SLO and the Gold Coast Special Branch continued to monitor the activities of Botsio, so far as possible 'under the circumstances'. This careful, two-faced process of intelligence management, involving both intelligence-sharing with national leaders and continued investigations into them up until the last moment before independence, followed the model that MI5 had already established in India, and would be replicated in other British colonies across the world as they approached independence.[34]

One of the greatest challenges facing the Gold Coast Special Branch before the transfer of power in 1957 was the rapid recruitment and training of local African officers into its ranks – a process known within the Special Branch as 'Africanisation'. Constitutional advances took place so rapidly after Nkrumah was elected Prime Minister in 1952 that, as we can see with hindsight, neither MI5 nor the Colonial Office's new Intelligence and Security Department had made adequate preparations for the Special Branch's transition to independence. From May 1956 onwards, on the eve of the colony's independence, MI5 had a training officer posted to the Gold Coast, in addition to its SLO. Thereafter Special Branch officers undertook MI5 training programmes both in the colony and at MI5's headquarters in London, along the lines that we have discussed in previous chapters. This training, however, occurred far down the road to independence. The flood of local African recruits to the Special Branch, combined with the exodus of European officers after independence, made it impossible to train all the new recruits to the Special Branch effectively, or to safeguard and check their loyalties. In 1958 there were two African gazetted officers and 120 Europeans in the entire Ghanaian police force; by 1960 the proportions were almost exactly reversed.

MI5's training programmes in the Gold Coast were largely successful in their immediate aims: they prevented communist penetration into the colony's Special Branch, and helped to build it into an agency capable of withstanding the transition to independence. However, they were far less successful in their longer-term goal – to keep the Special Branch politically neutral after the transfer of power. They did not prevent it from being abused by Nkrumah after independence, when as we shall see he became increasingly megalomaniacal and dictatorial. There was a rapid evacuation, or 'scuttle', of intelligence training before Britain's handover of power. This is revealed by the fact that in MI5 and Colonial Office records from the period there is an almost total lack of discussion about whether Nkrumah might exploit the Special Branch and intelligence apparatus for his own purposes. In October 1955 MI5's Security Intelligence Advisers, seconded to the Colonial Office, did warn that the Special Branch could be used by Nkrumah as a political weapon after independence – MI5 had similar concerns in other colonies across the empire as they approached independence – but this seems to have been a solitary warning, and to have fallen on deaf ears in both Whitehall and Accra. By not providing sufficient training to Special Branch recruits, especially local Africans, and failing to instil in them the nature of independent and non-political intelligence work, MI5 and the Colonial Office unwittingly empowered Nkrumah's authoritarian rule after 1957.[35]

Britain's signals intelligence service, GCHQ, was also involved in 'intelligence management' in the Gold Coast. Again, this was essentially a process of duplicity: GCHQ both shared intelligence with Nkrumah's government-in-waiting and continued to spy on it. Put simply, GCHQ 'helped' Nkrumah's government-in-waiting to establish secure codes and cyphers for its communications. In September 1956 the London Communications Security Agency, a subsidiary branch of GCHQ and a public front for it, liaised with MI5 and its SLO in Accra, R.J.S. (John) Thomson, about ways of protecting the security of Ghana's cyphers after independence. The most reliable way to do this, said GCHQ, was for Nkrumah's government to use 'one-time pads' in special cypher 'Typex' machines, which at least in theory were impossible to break, for they continually changed sets of codes that were only used once. But GCHQ noted that one-time pads were difficult and costly to manufacture, and the Gold Coast did not have sufficient resources to do so. It therefore proposed that Thomson should ask Nkrumah's cabinet-in-waiting whether they would be prepared to accept one-time pads manufactured in Britain. Neither GCHQ nor MI5 held much hope that they would agree to such an offer, because it would be clear that if British officials had the keys to these one-time cyphers, they would obviously be able to read Ghanaian communications.

In December 1956 Thomson delicately raised the subject with Nkrumah, flattering him by stressing that it would be important for his new government to have one-time pads so the British government could communicate with it securely, and also so that Ghana could communicate safely with its own embassies across the world. In the event, Thomson's strategy of encouraging Nkrumah to be 'part of the club', and share intelligence with Britain, worked remarkably well. To MI5 and GCHQ's surprise, Nkrumah and his cabinet agreed to the proposal. As Thomson noted to MI5 in London:

> They [Nkrumah's cabinet] did not seem to take much interest in it and appeared to be satisfied that it was a system which completely safeguarded the security of their communications. The question of obtaining the pads from the United Kingdom was not raised [by them], and we are therefore proceeding on the assumption that the pads should be obtained from the London Communications Security Agency.[36]

Although no records are currently available, it is doubtless the case that, having manufactured the one-time pads and equipped them with their keys, after 1957 GCHQ was indeed able to intercept and read Ghanaian government communications.

As with India after 1947, the story of how MI5 brokered and maintained liaison contacts with Nkrumah's government after Ghana's independence is a neglected, but highly important, chapter in the history of both British decolonisation in West Africa and the Cold War more generally. In September 1956 MI5's SLO in Accra, John Thomson, formally identified himself to Nkrumah as an MI5 officer, and informed him of the advantages of maintaining a link with MI5 so as to keep informed of subversion sponsored by Egypt's new president, Gamal Abdel Nasser, of whom Nkrumah was increasingly suspicious. Nkrumah agreed that Thomson should be allowed to remain in Ghana after it gained independence in March 1957, and he continued to serve there until 1960, returning in 1962. Thomson is listed in *Who's Who* and in official Foreign Office despatches as serving as a First Counsellor at the British High Commission in Ghana from 1955 to 1960 (Recreations: 'singing, gardening'), but it is of course not noted that his official position was cover for his MI5 posting. During his time as SLO in Accra he was one of the most important channels of communication between the British and Ghanaian governments. On Nkrumah's personal request he agreed to extend his posting in Ghana from November 1959 until January 1960, and Nkrumah even sent a personal letter of thanks to MI5 in London for this. Ghana's Interior Minister, Ashford Emmanuel Inksumah, said that ideally they would have liked Thomson to stay 'forever'. Thomson's service as SLO was equally appreciated by the British High Commission in Accra. In 1963 the High Commissioner, Sir Arthur Snelling, wrote to the Foreign Office that Thomson's 'contact with his professional colleagues produced not only straight intelligence but very frequently a political dividend as well'. Thomson himself shared the view of one Colonial Office official who said of Nkrumah that 'We have turned an LSE communist into a progressive socialist.'[37]

Within a year of independence, Ghanaian security officers attended one of the Commonwealth security conferences held in London, and apparently continued to do so in subsequent years, much to the chagrin of the Apartheid South African government. However, the problem for MI5, and for Thomson in particular, about sharing intelligence with Ghana was Nkrumah's increasingly corrupt and intolerant behaviour. Even before independence, MI5 and SIS had reliable evidence that he was involved in diamond-smuggling from West Africa to Europe, which they feared was enabling him to buy political favours in Eastern Bloc countries.

MI5's investigations into Nkrumah's diamond-smuggling were assisted by the world-famous diamond firm De Beers, which ran its own 'Illicit Diamond Trafficking' unit. In 1955 this unit was run by none other than Sir Percy Sillitoe, and was staffed with a number of former MI5 and SIS officers. After leaving MI5 in 1952, Sillitoe had briefly opened an unsuccessful sweet shop in Eastbourne, but then found a much better use of his time when he joined De Beers. His career there was so successful that he even earned a walk-on role in Ian Fleming's *Diamonds are Forever* (1956) – one of the few real-life characters ever to appear in a James Bond novel. MI5 passed its evidence of Nkrumah's diamond-smuggling on to Sir Charles Arden-Clarke, but to everyone's relief, by 1956 it seemed that the Prime Minister elect was no longer involved in the illegal trade. However, much worse was to follow after Ghana's independence.[38]

Had it not been for MI5's accurate, non-alarmist reports about Nkrumah's supposed communism, and the bonds MI5 was able to establish with the government-in-waiting, the transfer of power in the Gold Coast would probably have been considerably more turbulent. That said, MI5 totally failed to foresee the pace of change in Ghana after 1960 – the year in which Nkrumah became the country's first President – and in particular Nkrumah's political 'lurch to the left'. With independence came the freedom for Nkrumah to make mistakes. In the early 1960s he became the target of sustained KGB deception plots, which purported to show that the CIA was mounting operations to overthrow his government. In reality it was the KGB, not the CIA, that was seeking to subvert Nkrumah's rule. KGB archives viewed by the Soviet defector Vasili Mitrokhin reveal that, following an unsuccessful attempt on Nkrumah's life by local dissidents, he was completely deceived by KGB forgeries, and became increasingly paranoid about Western influence in his country, over which his rule became more and more tyrannous. He ruined Ghana's economy, which relied on the banana industry, and became steadily more power-hungry, implementing his own form of socialism, which he inevitably termed 'Nkrumahism'. In private, he even compared himself to Christ. His newly established 'National Security Service' (NSS) was swollen with recruits from the KGB and Eastern Bloc security services, and became the vehicle by which he violently stamped out dissent. The NSS acted primarily as a kind of bodyguard service for the President, running vast networks of agents and informers, and reporting solely and sycophantically to him alone.[39]

The KGB's 'active measures' in Ghana increased to such an extent that the British High Commissioner in the early 1960s, Sir Arthur Snelling, was not mistaken when he described the country as 'the key battlefield of the Cold War'. The head of Special Branch in Ghana, J.K. Harley, was convinced that Nkrumah was turning the country into a Soviet satellite, and on 24 February 1966 instigated a successful *coup d'état* against him. The following day, Snelling, now at the Commonwealth Relations Office in London, rang MI5's Director-General, Sir Martin Furnival-Jones, and asked him to despatch Thomson urgently back to Ghana to make an assessment of the situation. Thomson arrived in Accra on 28 February, and on 2 March, after a favourable report from him about the post-Nkrumah 'National Liberation Council', the British government formally recognised the new regime. This episode captures the crucial, but covert, role that MI5 played in brokering relations with post-colonial governments. It was also the only occasion on which an MI5 officer was charged by the British government to make the first contact with a new government that had seized power by coup.[40]

NIGERIA

Britain's secret services were involved in the process of decolonisation in Nigeria in similar ways as they were in the Gold Coast. Nigeria was the largest and most populous British colony in Africa – in fact, after the transfer of power in India in 1947, it was the most populous colony anywhere in the British empire. With over thirty million inhabitants in 1950, it was home to one-third of all the people in the empire. Given its geographical location, Nigeria was historically a staging post for goods being transported from Europe to southern Africa. This continued in the years after 1945, but as well as goods and matériel, it became a hub for Commonwealth communications, a natural relay area for radio signals passing from Britain to southern parts of the continent. It played a valuable strategic Commonwealth role for Britain, to say nothing of its rich oil and other natural resources.

In the post-war years, however, the colony of Nigeria was actually little more than a geographical expression. It was comprised of three distinct, largely autonomous regions that were sharply divided along religious and ethnic lines, with over 250 tongues spoken between them, and with each region attempting to minimise the influence of the others. The Northern Region was predominantly Muslim and populated by the Fulani; the Eastern Region was mostly comprised of the Ibo (Igbo); and the Western Region was home to the Yoruba people. By 1950 MI5 had an SLO posted to Nigeria, but given the sheer size of the colony, he – and it seems all MI5 SLOs at this time were men – faced an almost insurmountable task in attempting to influence local security and intelligence matters in meaningful ways. In 1953, Nigeria's Special Branch had just five (white) officers and fifty (African) staff of other ranks to cover a territory of 360,000 square miles. The Northern Region had just a single Special Branch officer, and twenty-four other ranks, for an area larger than the whole of France.[41]

Despite the meagre resources MI5 and the Nigerian Special Branch had at their disposal, which were dwarfed by the scale of their responsibilities, they were able to provide the colonial administration with some valuable information. MI5 obtained crucial background intelligence on the colony's leading anti-colonial politician, Benjamin Nnamdi Azikiwe, who would become the first President of independent Nigeria in October 1960. Azikiwe, or 'Dr Zik' as he was known, was an Ibo and a former all-round athlete of international repute, 'powerful as an ox', who in 1945 was General Secretary of the National Council of Nigeria. The Colonial Office felt that he was sufficiently Westernised, having been educated in the United States, at Howard and Lincoln Universities, to be a moderate with whom it could work, and MI5 offered similarly non-alarmist reports. As with Nkrumah, MI5's intensive surveillance of the British Communist

Party, combined with its interception of mail between West Africa and Britain, revealed that although Zik held Marxist views, he was definitely not a communist. Following two visits he made to Britain, as leader of pan-African delegations in 1947 and 1949, MI5 compiled a background dossier on Zik, which it passed to the Colonial Office. It stated: 'He is not a communist, but he is very ready to accept the support of communists whenever he considers it likely to further his own interests.' In 1950, MI5's first SLO in Nigeria, M.T.E. Clayton, passed similar reports to the colonial Governor, Sir John MacPherson. The Nigeria Special Branch kept Zik and his party, the National Congress of Nigeria and the Cameroons, under close surveillance. According to John O'Sullivan, formerly of the Palestine CID, who was posted to the Special Branch in the Northern Region and later became Assistant Commissioner of Police in Nigeria, the Special Branch obtained valuable information on violent underground supporters of Zik ('Zikists') by seizing documents in house raids and sending plain-clothes policemen to political rallies.[42]

The greatest challenge facing MI5 and the Nigeria Special Branch lay in responding to the rapid pace of constitutional change in the colony beginning in the early 1950s. The speed at which power should be devolved to Nigeria was the source of a sharp dispute between the Colonial Secretary, Oliver Lyttelton, and the colonial Governor, MacPherson, in the early 1950s. MacPherson felt that it would be too risky for Nigeria to follow the Gold Coast and elect a 'Prime Minister', arguing that the colony, with its highly autonomous provinces, needed to develop at a slow pace constitutionally, allowing sufficient time for it to develop a centralised administration. Lyttelton, by contrast, influenced by events in the Gold Coast, felt that the devolution of power in Nigeria should be accelerated: better to act rapidly and secure goodwill than to delay and possibly cause ill-feeling.

Lyttelton's view, that decentralisation was the only way to prevent the disintegration of the colony, prevailed. In October 1954 a new constitution was enacted in Nigeria, which recognised the autonomy of the different regions and their administrations, including police and Special Branches. A visit by the young Queen Elizabeth II in early 1956 helped to establish bonds between Nigeria and the Commonwealth. The Eastern Region was granted internal self-government in 1957, and following a decision by the cabinet in London in October 1958, the Northern Region was also given internal self-government in the spring of 1959. Nigeria gained full independence from Britain in October 1960, under the leadership of Zik, and remained within the Commonwealth. The new constitution recognised the rights of minorities in each of the three regions, making it the first African country with a constitution embodying fundamental human rights, which would become almost mandatory for colonies gaining independence from Britain in the years thereafter.[43]

For MI5 and the Nigeria Special Branch, the rapid pace of constitutional change meant there was a scramble to train and prepare for independence. From 1954 onwards MI5 had a training officer stationed in Lagos, in addition to its SLO there, who offered training courses on security intelligence along the lines discussed previously. These training courses were, in the opinion of John O'Sullivan, so successful that 'thereafter the Special Branch developed as a professional and competent security intelligence organisation'. However, it was not until 1959, on the eve of independence, that Nigeria's Special Branch was formally divorced from the regular police (CID) and became a dedicated security intelligence outfit.

One of the most difficult tasks for MI5 was to assist the rapid 'Nigerianisation' of the Special Branch's ranks in the years preceding full independence. Ensuring the trustworthiness of the Special Branch's registry's staff was a particular concern, because they had access to highly sensitive records, including 'much secret information, breaches of which might very seriously affect UK, Commonwealth, Federal or Regional security'. The registry was staffed almost wholly by women, as was MI5's registry in London, but they came from various religious and tribal backgrounds in Nigeria. As MI5 noted, this meant they could be susceptible to local political pressures. In an attempt to counter this, MI5 and senior Special Branch officers devised a system of intensive 'mentoring': six wives of expatriate Special Branch officers were put in charge of training new recruits, and watched them closely for any sign of disloyalty.[44]

In the years before independence, MI5 and the colonial administration in Nigeria began a process of intelligence management, sharing highly sanitised and vetted intelligence with Zik and other locally elected ministers, just as happened in the Gold Coast. One of the most important sources of intelligence that the Special Branch shared with Zik was derived from SIGINT. From 1956 onwards a highly secretive 'Radio Monitoring Service' operated from a special 'technical section' within the Nigerian Special Branch, with equipment purchased for £800 and costing £1,000 a year to run – significant amounts of money at the time. This kept a round-the-clock watch on illicit radio broadcasts from Nigeria to other parts of West Africa, some of which concerned communism and opposition to Zik.

The Special Branch shared summaries of these reports with Zik, who found them 'extremely informative'.

At the same time, however, the Special Branch continued to spy on Zik even after he was elected as Nigeria's leader-in-waiting. The last British Governor in the colony, Sir James Robertson, freely employed dirty tricks in the run-up to independence. Zik's communications are known to have been intercepted, and although MI5 records – at least those currently declassified – are silent on the matter, given what we have seen in the Gold Coast, where the Special Branch intercepted Nkrumah's mail and gave it to the Governor, it seems likely that the Nigeria Special Branch did the same. There is also some existing, but inconclusive, evidence that senior British colonial officials engineered 'election rigging' to help secure victories for Zik. Given the lengths the Colonial Office went to in order to secure a 'good electoral result' in the colony of British Guiana in the early 1950s, it is not beyond belief that it resorted to similar measures in Nigeria.[45]

As in the Gold Coast and other colonies, MI5 obtained an agreement from Zik's government-in-waiting for its SLO to remain in Lagos after Nigeria gained independence in October 1960. The SLO continued to play an important role in the years that followed, as a succession of coups and counter-coups removed one government after another. By 1966 MI5's SLO in Lagos was in such a trusted position that he was given one of the twenty secret telephones allocated to senior Nigerian officials. In July that year, during a coup that brought General Yakubu Gowon to power, the British High Commissioner told MI5 that its SLO was a lifeline for information on day-to-day events through his contacts with the Nigerian police. Although there are not currently any records available, it seems likely that MI5's SLO continued to play a similarly important role after that in Nigeria, until its responsibilities were eventually, at a date not presently revealed in records, taken over by SIS.[46]

KENYA

British colonial rule in Kenya has typically been depicted as both benevolent and necessary, bringing culture and civilisation to a people presumed to have had neither. Much of this popular image is derived from Karen Blixen's classic memoir *Out of Africa*, published in 1937, at the height of British rule in the East African colony. The book is based on Blixen's experiences running a farm at the foot of the lush Ngong hills, a popular area for European settlers to set up plantation estates and a hunter's dream, with elephants, zebras and giraffes roaming the land. Blixen presents Kenya as a kind of colonial Utopia: not only is it fertile, accommodating and picturesque, it is also a place of racial harmony, where colonial settlers live happily and paternalistically with their Kikuyu labourers.[47]

The reality could not have been further from Blixen's depiction. During the 1950s Britain waged an extraordinarily violent counter-insurgency in Kenya after a rebellion broke out which seemed to threaten British rule in the colony. In the course of the so-called Mau Mau insurgency, which erupted in October 1952 and formally ended in 1956, although in fact it continued beyond that, British forces killed as many as 20,000 Africans. By contrast, just thirty-two colonial settlers lost their lives – fewer than the number of people killed in road traffic accidents in Nairobi alone in the same period. Furthermore, the violence was not confined to the shooting war. Over the course of the four years of the insurgency, it is estimated that the British incarcerated a staggering 80,000 indigenous Africans on account of their supposed involvement with Mau Mau, a greater number than were detained in any other colonial counter-insurgency in the post-war years, from Palestine to Malaya. They were held behind barbed-wire fences, in a series of camps up and down the colony known as 'the Pipeline', where they were subjected to a fierce process of what the British euphemistically termed 'rehabilitation'.[48]

The presumption of the British forces operating the 'Pipeline' camps was that Mau Mau detainees could be reformed through forced labour and harsh beatings. A recent study by the Harvard historian Caroline Elkins, based on research carried out over a ten-year period, has compared Britain's detention camps in Kenya to the Soviet Gulag system. While Elkins's study is not flawless – her use of statistical evidence is often unclear, and she overlooks violence inflicted by black African ethnic groups on each other – her central point is still valid: Britain fought an extremely dirty and violent war in Kenya. Police, troops and 'loyalist' Kikuyu Home Guards subjected entire villages to collective punishments, in which they showed an almost total disregard for human life. In a more careful recent study than Elkins's, the Oxford historian David Anderson has noted that the authorities in Kenya resorted to capital punishment – hanging – more frequently than at any other point in the history of British colonial rule. Despite notions to the contrary, Britain's dirty war in Kenya does not look too dissimilar to the notorious end-of-empire campaigns fought by other European powers, such as the French in Algeria.[49]

As explained in the introduction to this book, in 2011 the Foreign Office 'rediscovered' 1,500 previously classified files on Mau Mau, contained in almost three hundred boxes, which stretched to over one hundred linear feet of shelving in the secret facility at Hanslope Park. This book draws on the first tranche of these secret records, which was made available to the public in April 2012. Although unfortunately the records in the Hanslope Park archive relating to abuses allegedly committed by British security personnel during Mau Mau have not been released to the public at the time of writing, they were seen by the High Court and the expert witnesses in the Mau Mau case, including the hisorians David Anderson, Caroline Elkins and Huw Bennett, and some of their findings appear in the case's court reports. The still-retained documents, seen by the court and those historians, are said to detail the way suspected Mau Mau insurgents were beaten to death, burned alive, castrated and kept in manacles for years. The documents also apparently reveal that senior British officials were far more aware of abuses committed in Kenya than they themselves liked to reveal and than historians have supposed. In June 1957 Eric Griffiths-Jones, the Attorney General of the British administration in Kenya, wrote to the Governor, Sir Evelyn Baring, detailing ways in which the regime of abuse at the colony's detention camps was being subtly altered. From now on, Griffiths-Jones wrote, for the abuse to remain legal, Mau Mau suspects must be beaten mainly on their upper body – 'vulnerable parts of the body should not be struck, particularly the spleen, liver or kidneys' – and it was important that 'those who administer violence … should remain collected, balanced and dispassionate'. Almost as an afterthought, the Attorney-General reminded the Governor of the need for complete secrecy: 'If we are going to sin,' he wrote, 'we must sin quietly.'[50]

A SUNNY PLACE FOR SHADY PEOPLE

British settlers began moving to Kenya in the last decade of the nineteenth century, attracted by the fertile country's staggering potential for agriculture. Large numbers of them established coffee and tea plantations in the central highlands, which were soon nicknamed the 'white highlands'. After its use as a military base during the First World War, many upper-class young British officers remained in the colony, and much of the indigenous population, for the most part Kikuyu (pronounced 'Gikuyu'), was made landless by the white plantocracy. The British established a 999-year-lease rule for the land they had acquired, allowing white settlers more than thirty generations' worth of land ownership. Effectively alienated from ever owning land, many Kikuyu became tenant farmers on the European-owned plantations, given a patch of ground to farm in exchange for their labour.[51]

The British imposed a series of harsh regulations to ensure Kikuyu subservience to British rule – hut tax, coffee-growing bans and an ever-decreasing wage for native labourers. For all the injustices, however, there were instances of benevolent colonial rule of the kind Karen Blixen described. One does not have to trawl far through the histories of Kenya to find examples of British missionaries performing backbreaking work to bring education to children who had previously lacked any sort of formal schooling. That said, some of the most notorious European settlers in the colony, such as the Delameres, lived on vast estates on a peppery diet of alcohol, adultery and racism surpassing even the most extreme depictions of gin-swigging planters found in the works of Somerset Maugham. General 'Bobby' Erskine, who took over military operations in Kenya in 1952, even vented his fury about the colony's European settlers in a letter to his wife, noting that Kenya was 'a sunny place for shady people', and that he 'hated the guts of them all'.[52]

By the 1940s, 30,000 European farmers owned 12,000 square miles of the best land in the colony. By contrast, about a million so-called 'squatters' of the Kikuyu, Kenya's largest, best-educated and probably most Westernised tribe, owned just 2,000 square miles between them. This meant that 0.07 per cent of the population owned approximately a fifth of the colony's best land. Increasing levels of 'land hunger' and 'land encroachment' during the 1930s and 1940s caused fierce resentment among the colony's main tribes, the Kikuyu, Embu and Meru, some of whom fought for the British in the Second World War. This resentment was nothing new: its roots stretched back to the early 1900s, when the British had made land purchases that the Kikuyu had erroneously (though understandably) assumed were merely rental agreements. Following their 'purchase', the settlers of course refused to relinquish the land they had laboured hard to cultivate, but which the Kikuyu regarded as their own. Escalation in 'land hunger' and further alienation of the Kikuyu from their own territory led to increasing levels of poverty, starvation and a huge economic gulf between the indigenous and settler populations. Out of this was born a strong anti-colonial sentiment that would soon lead to an uprising against British rule.

THE MAU MAU REVOLT

Despite the fact that, in retrospect, the unrest in Kenya was not surprising given the blatant unfairness of land ownership, at the time it broke out in October 1952 it was both unexpected and underestimated by the British. As Graham Greene described it, it was as though 'Jeeves had taken to the jungle', with apparently faithful servants turning into guerrilla fighters. At first the British authorities passed off the revolt as little more than minor unrest, which did not need to be taken seriously. In the eyes of the British, indigenous Kenyan populations did not have the military capacity to start a serious dispute, but if anything significant were to happen, it could be easily quashed by Britain's overwhelming military force. Compared to the danger posed to the empire by the Malayan Emergency, the revolt in Kenya seemed to be nothing, a local dispute orchestrated by primitive peoples. Even Captain Frank Kitson, who was later to play an instrumental role in defeating the insurgency, and who later became one of the most influential architects of Britain's post-war counter-insurgency doctrine, dismissed the activities of the Mau Mau rebels as little more than 'the antics of naughty schoolboys'.[53]

This could not have been further from the truth: Mau Mau soon escalated into a war by another name. On 9 October 1952 a staunch Kikuyu supporter of the British, Senior Chief Waruhiu, was shot dead, an event that seems to have sparked wider violence in the colony. On 20 October, as violence in the colony grew, the British Governor Sir Evelyn Baring declared a State of Emergency. The proclamation was issued under the Emergency Powers Order-in-Council 1939. As a part of the process of proclaiming the Emergency, the Governor also promulgated the Emergency Regulations 1952, again made by powers conferred by the 1939 Order. Those regulations (like previous regulations passed in Malaya) included wide powers of arrest and detention of suspected persons. From about March 1953 detention camps were constructed in Kenya to accommodate large numbers of persons detained under the Emergency powers. That State of Emergency remained on the statute books in Kenya until 12 January 1960.[54]

Even as the Mau Mau revolt seemed to envelop Kenya, British intelligence – like the colonial administration there itself – completely misunderstood it. This is perhaps not altogether surprising, given that it was impossible for most observers at the time, just as it has been for historians since, to establish what the exact causes of the revolt were. Despite the volumes of ink that have been expended on studying the insurgency, historians still disagree about what the Mau Mau represented. Even the name itself is shrouded in confusion – 'Mau' is not a word in either Kikuyu or Swahili. Some have suggested that it might be an anagram of 'Uma uma', meaning 'Get out', while others have conjectured that it was actually made up by the British in order to discredit the movement's motives and deny it any legitimacy on the international stage. Propaganda and hysterical accounts written at the time affect perceptions of the uprising even to this day. The focal point of British popular reporting on Mau Mau was undoubtedly its oath-taking ceremonies, which took place deep in the jungle and supposedly involved acts of barbarity and fornication so extreme that, we are told, civilised European minds could scarcely imagine them. Of course, published accounts warning their readers along those lines would invariably then describe these acts in lurid and meticulous detail. An example is Robert Ruark's bloodcurdling and much reprinted contemporary novel *Something of Value*, which was loosely based on the author's safari visits to Kenya. Tom Askwith, the Municipal African Affairs Officer stationed in Nairobi, stated that the oathing 'represented everything evil in Mau Mau'. Reports forwarded on to the War Office in London described 'confessions' of oath-takers, which included hair-raising acts of fornication, though it is not clear in what circumstances these 'confessions' were obtained. British officials in London and Nairobi convinced themselves that, far from being a legitimate political movement, Mau Mau was barbaric and uncivilised.[55]

These accounts have led to confusion over the true nature of the uprising. It has been variously described as a nationalist struggle, a religious cult and a communist conspiracy. The colonial administration was so baffled that it even contracted a psychologist, Dr J.C. Carrothers, to investigate the phenomenon, which he concluded was the result of a form of mass hysteria or mania. For some contemporary observers Mau Mau was the work of no less than the Antichrist, and the Colonial Secretary at the time, Oliver Lyttelton, compared its supposed leader, Jomo Kenyatta, who would later become the first leader of independent Kenya, to Lucifer himself. Lyttelton recalled in his memoirs that when he read reports about Mau Mau and Kenyatta the horns of the Devil passed over the pages on his desk before him. Some European settlers preferred to see the rebellion as simply a throwback to atavistic, primitive barbarism, 'the yell from the swamp', as one of them, the writer Elspeth Huxley, described it. Another prominent settler in Kenya, and Minister without Portfolio in the colonial

administration, Michael Blundell, described Mau Mau as 'debased crea-
tures from the forest', with 'all the mumbo jumbo of tribal witchcraft'.
Such interpretations reinforced the fundamental idea underpinning
British colonial rule in Kenya – that the colony, and Africa as a whole,
benefited from Britain's 'civilising mission' there.

Despite attempts to theorise Mau Mau into a united rebellion fronted
by a strong leader and driven by a single cause, this was not the case: in
reality, the uprising was a multi-faceted and complex movement that had
many parochial agendas, passed through many stages, and influenced
various parts of Kenya in various ways. Mau Mau was a paradox, an
extraordinarily complex event, incapable of being reduced to simple or
simplistic explanations. It meant different things to different people. As
one of the most eminent scholars of Kenyan history, John Lonsdale, has
explained, there were many different Mau Maus of the mind. Though a
strict definition is near impossible, by intent Mau Mau *was* an anti-colonial struggle, often directed against European settlers. Soon after the
declaration of the Emergency, a number of British settlers were murdered,
often with sambas (machetes). Beginning on New Year's Day 1953, there
appeared to be a fully-blown murder campaign waged against white
settlers by Mau Mau rebels. The members of one British family, the Rusks,
were murdered and mutilated in their home. Horrific photos emerged
depicting the butchered body of Mr Rusk; Mrs Rusk managed to get a few
shots off at her attackers, but their six-year-old son was hacked to death in
his nursery. The stories of settler deaths struck a chord in the British
popular press back home; many of the settlers, like the Rusks, had been
killed on their own farms, in their dressing gowns, in front of their children, in the bath, even on golf courses.[56]

While it is impossible to draw a single overall conclusion about the
motives and agenda of the Mau Mau rebellion, the statistics of the insurgency are nevertheless clear: many more black Africans were killed than
Europeans. As has been noted, just thirty-two European settlers died, and
there were fewer than two hundred casualties among the British regiments and police who served in Kenya during the insurgency. By contrast,
more than 1,800 African civilians were killed by Mau Mau guerrillas, with
many more disappearing. Official British figures state that the number of
Mau Mau insurgents (as opposed to civilians) killed was 13,500, though
the figure generally accepted by historians is closer to 20,000.
Approximately 90 per cent of the Mau Mau killed were Kikuyu. These
figures, however, do not reflect the full scale of the violence unleashed in

Kenya. Local populations paid a terrible price for the rebellion, including immeasurable social dislocation. British forces eventually suppressed Mau Mau by instigating a process of mass detention and mass deportation by means of the Pipeline incarceration system, through which a staggering total of more than a million people were forcibly displaced. On a conservative estimate, one in four Kikuyu males were held in often brutal camps and prisons at some point during the Emergency. Many of the female detainees were raped. Under the Emergency Regulations, the regime was permitted to confiscate property of those suspected of being Mau Mau insurgents. Records from the Foreign and Commonwealth Office's secret archive at Hanslope Park reveal that British officials often gave few reasons for issuing collective punishments, confiscating property, land and goods.[57]

It must be stressed that not all of those who died lost their lives at the hands of the British military. Mau Mau was more than just an attack on a largely hated colonial system. With the participation of locally recruited 'loyalist' Kikuyu Home Guards – a coalition of tribal police and private armies, sanctioned by the colonial administration – and other moderates who cooperated with the British, the rebellion became something close to a civil war fought between ethnic groups in the colony. Graham Greene, who based his 1948 novel *The Heart of the Matter* on his experiences of working for SIS in West Africa during the Second World War, noted that the uprising was, above all, a private war. Violence came from all sides: the British, Mau Mau and Kikuyu were all responsible for varying degrees of bloodshed and brutality. The Kikuyu Home Guard killed more Mau Mau than any other military formation. Some Kikuyu used their membership of the Home Guard to settle old scores over land disputes, or took vengeance after friends had been killed by Mau Mau. Even Jomo Kenyatta, whom the colonial administration erroneously accused of leading the rebellion, was menaced by Mau Mau guerrillas.[58]

What the British termed Mau Mau was thus not a straightforward anti-colonial struggle. It grew out of internal factionalism and dissent among the Kikuyu people, as well as opposition to British rule. It was not a single movement born of primeval savagery, but a diverse and fragmented collection of individuals, organisations and ideas. It was a struggle about class, but it was not a class struggle, at least in the Marxist sense. Put simply, Mau Mau drew its support from a long series of grievances, both imagined and real, voiced by two generations of Kikuyu against the British colonial administration. The centre of these grievances lay with 'land hunger', but as it grew, Mau Mau unleashed a maelstrom of violence in Kenya.[59]

MI5 AND MAU MAU

MI5 had been pressing for much-needed reform of the security and intelligence machinery in Kenya since the end of the Second World War. In 1947 the head of Security Intelligence Middle East (SIME), Bill Magan, travelled to Nairobi for discussions with the Governor, Sir Philip Mitchell. It should come as no surprise that MI5's initial suggestions came to nothing: Mitchell explained to Magan that the little extra finance he could muster needed to be spent on health and education, not on policing or intelligence. Magan's position was understandable, but in hindsight we can see that it was short-sighted. Just as in Malaya, reforms of the intelligence machinery in Kenya did not take place until it was too late. MI5 did have an SLO stationed in Nairobi by 1948, but it would appear that the colonial administration paid little attention to the reports he produced. With intelligence thus having been largely neglected, when the Mau Mau insurgency broke out in October 1952, just six months after Kwame Nkrumah became Prime Minister in the Gold Coast, security forces in Kenya were as hopelessly unprepared as they had been at the outset of the Emergency in Malaya. Just as in Malaya, the outbreak of the insurgency in Kenya represented a spectacular intelligence failure for Britain.[60]

Shortly after Baring's declaration of a State of Emergency on 20 October 1952, MI5's Director-General, Sir Percy Sillitoe, wrote to the Colonial Office to offer MI5's assistance. The Permanent Undersecretary at the Colonial Office, Thomas Lloyd, politely declined the offer, replying that what was needed was 'a good man from some Special Branch'. The head of MI5's Overseas Section, Sir John Shaw, noted that in his opinion Lloyd's proposal would prove 'futile': 'Sooner or later, too late, we shall be asked for help.' The request came sooner than Shaw expected. A month after the declaration of the Emergency, on 20 November 1952, at the personal request of Baring, Sillitoe and one of his deputies, Alec MacDonald, flew to Nairobi, where they were joined by Alex Kellar, who arrived from the Middle East. 'So,' remarked Shaw to Lloyd, 'the first XI of MI5 is to play the Mau Mau.'[61]

The delegation arrived on a Friday, drafted their recommendations for intelligence reform in Kenya the following Tuesday, and they were accepted by Baring that same morning. The recommendations followed

MI5's usual model for imperial intelligence reform: intelligence should be separated from policing, and given that Kenya had a unified police force and not a regional one, it should be vested solely in the hands of the Special Branch. Sillitoe also recommended that the Kenya Special Branch should establish a dedicated registry for intelligence records, that more recruits should be found for it, and that its coverage should be extended throughout the colony, and not confined to the major cities of Nairobi and Mombasa, as it had been before then. The Kenyan administration accepted Sillitoe's recommendations wholesale, and furthermore, also on MI5's advice, it established a new Kenya Intelligence Committee (KIC). The KIC's members included the Governor, the SLO, the chief of police, representatives of the armed forces and the 'Director of Intelligence', a post that was given to John Prendergast, who had previously served in the Palestine and Gold Coast Special Branches, and in the Canal Zone in Egypt.[62]

As with other local intelligence committees, the KIC was designed to streamline reporting from the provincial level to the upper echelons of the Kenya administration, from where reports could be passed on to the JIC in London if necessary. To help oversee these reforms Sillitoe agreed for an MI5 officer, Alec MacDonald, who had served in the Indian police before 1947, to be seconded to the administration in Kenya. As we have seen, after spending nearly two years in Kenya, MacDonald went on to become MI5's first Security Intelligence Adviser (SIA) seconded to the Colonial Office in London, and would travel to colonies across the empire to help reform their intelligence machinery. In Kenya, his job was 'to concert the activities of all intelligence agencies operating in the colony and to promote collaboration with Special Branches in adjacent territories'. His first task was to reorganise the Special Branch, which he found 'grossly overworked, bogged down in paper, housed in offices which were alike impossible from the standpoint of security or normal working conditions'. Furthermore, he continued, 'the officers were largely untrained. Equipment was lacking and intelligence funds were meagre.'[63]

During the Emergency, the Kenya Special Branch was paranoid about the spectre of Mau Mau insurgents lurking everywhere. This paranoia stretched to MI5, all of whose staff in Kenya were issued with guns and given target practice. MI5's SLO in Nairobi, Robert Broadbent, even slept with a revolver under his pillow. His fears were not unfounded: unknown to him, a Mau Mau arms dump was hidden in his kitchen. Broadbent was only to discover this during a reception at his house when, after a waiter dropped a tray of drinks, he entered the kitchen and discovered Mau Mau guerrillas who had come to retrieve their arms threatening staff.[64]

MacDonald and Sillitoe's reforms were enacted so quickly that by 1955 MacDonald recommended that his own position be abolished. He wrote to MI5 head office in London, stating that 'Special Branch goes from strength to strength and we now have some excellent sources operating. I have no qualms at leaving this lusty infant to look after itself.' In the words of one Kenyan Special Branch officer, T.W. Jenkins, MacDonald's reforms were of 'enormous assistance' to the Special Branch, or as Michael Blundell later put it, MacDonald had almost single-handedly established a 'first class' Special Branch in Kenya. Despite the reforms that Sillitoe and MacDonald instigated in Kenya, things on the ground in the colony proved much different. As late as 1954, two years into the Mau Mau insurgency, the Kenya Special Branch was still extremely under-staffed, with just three European officers, one Asian officer and a handful of rank and file on its staff, all working from Nairobi. Sir Gerald Templer's report on the state of colonial security around the world in 1955 bluntly declared: 'it is possible that, had our intelligence been better, we might have been spared the emergency in Kenya'. It was not until 1955 that Kenya followed MI5's earlier recommendation, and the lesson from Malaya, and appointed a single Director of Intelligence who reported directly to the Director of Operations.[65]

THE BRITISH COUNTER-INSURGENCY IN KENYA

The British counter-insurgency effort in Kenya was ultimately successful, if – as in Malaya – success is measured in purely military terms, mostly due to a huge deployment of metropolitan military power. By 1956 the rebellion had effectively been quashed, although the State of Emergency remained in force until early 1960. In the course of the insurgency a full infantry division together with five British battalions and five battalions of the Kenya African Rifles (KAR) were deployed in the colony, together with armoured cars, artillery and two RAF squadrons equipped with heavy bombers. In addition to this, the Home Guard swelled to about 70,000 recruits, around 50,000 of whom were Kikuyu. The ranks of the Kenya Police Reserve (KPR), which had been created in 1948, also expanded rapidly. The KPR had a certain degree of autonomy throughout the insurgency, with some of its officers gaining notoriety for acting like vigilantes. A number of its recruits came from South Africa and Southern

Rhodesia, held white supremacist views and used the KPR to pursue personal racial vendettas. With such an enormous deployment of reservists and regular forces, it was difficult for either the British military or the colonial authorities to maintain discipline. 'Friendly fire' incidents were not uncommon, with one British regiment even managing to kill its own colonel.[66]

Much like Templer in Malaya, the man placed in charge of British forces in Kenya, General Sir George Erskine, was granted extraordinary powers. He was even given a written order from Winston Churchill that allowed him to declare martial law in the colony if necessary. It is said that he carried the order around folded up in his spectacles case, keeping it close at hand in case all hell should break loose. Though he stopped short of declaring martial law, the Emergency Regulations effectively turned the colony's central Kikuyu Reserve into a police state, just as had been the case in Palestine and Malaya. As in Malaya, the Emergency Regulations – which allowed for curfews, forced registration, detention without trial, collective punishment along with corporal and capital punishment – were blunt instruments that affected friends and foes alike. During the insurgency over 1,000 Mau Mau fighters were sentenced to hang for murder, which as the historian David Anderson has shown, is more than at any other point in the history of the British empire. Two hundred non-Mau Mau were sent to the gallows for murder during the same period.[67]

It is remarkable that the authorities in Kenya did not learn more lessons from previous and contemporary anti-colonial insurgencies, particularly in Malaya. Despite the transfer of British personnel from Palestine and Malaya, little appears to have been learned in Kenya about the importance of waging 'hearts and minds' campaigns alongside the shooting war. Typical of the military and civilian intelligence officers who were steeped in lessons from previous insurgencies was Richard Catling (later Sir Richard), who had served in the Palestine CID for thirteen years, between 1935 and 1948, then served in Malaya under Templer, and came to Kenya in 1954, where he was commissioner of police until 1963. Catling later remarked that almost his whole career had been spent in 'Emergency' conditions. Despite a pool of officers like Catling who had experience of effective counter-insurgencies, instead of learning from the past, British forces in Kenya largely attempted to reinvent the wheel – a sad tendency also repeated by militaries in counter-insurgencies closer to our own time. Alec MacDonald, the Colonial Office's first Security and Intelligence

Adviser, and architect of Kenya's Special Branch, later captured the failure of the Colonial Office to apply lessons from previous insurgencies to Kenya:

> I think in the past we have failed to make proper use of the previous experience. When the emergency was declared in Kenya, that Government set about problems of detention, propaganda, rehabilitation, etc as if they were new and strange phenomenons [sic]. Cyprus in turn did much the same thing. I do not think it was the fault of either Government. It was merely that the experience gained in Malaya was nowhere summarised in a form available for reference. Cyprus, in turn, suffered from a lack of any systematic collation of experience gained in Kenya.
>
> ... What I would really like to see would be a distillation of the experience gained in Malaya, Kenya and Cyprus on such matters as intelligence organisation, information machinery, internment and rehabilitation problems. I think that it is in this type of work we fall down badly in comparison to the Armed Services; they always analyse their experience and digest it for future use in similar situations. We allow it to become buried in dormant files and attack 'de novo' problems which should be old and familiar. It is true that the Colonial Office can draw on previous experience, but we seldom have the whole story and it is not in readily available form.[68]

Britain's counter-insurgency campaign in Kenya began with Operation *Jock Scott* on 20 October 1952, the very same day as the declaration of Emergency. One hundred and eighty of the supposed leaders of Mau Mau were arrested. Six of them, later to be known as the Kapenguria Six, including Jomo Kenyatta, were placed on trial and charged with involvement in Mau Mau and conspiracy to murder. All were convicted and given prison sentences. It was thought that *Jock Scott* would decapitate the rebellion, defuse the violence and quickly usher in the end of the Emergency. It has been suggested, however, that the violent tactics of the operation may only have served to alienate the Kikuyu further, driving them to Mau Mau. After *Jock Scott* the rebels turned from what had been a disorganised collection of scattered groups into a veritable guerrilla army. The declaration of Emergency had itself created the real Emergency. The guerrilla army consisted of around 15,000 Kenyans, mostly Kikuyu but also Embu and Meru, and small numbers of Kamba and Maasai. In a not wholly dissimilar scenario from that in Malaya, the Kenyan rebels found refuge in the Aberdares, a thick forest area in the central region of the colony, not far from Mount Kenya.

The watershed moment for the British counter-insurgency in Kenya came with Operation *Anvil* in April 1954 in which the military, led by Erskine, took the extraordinary step of blockading, detaining and removing the entire non-working Kikuyu population of Nairobi. This was an extreme step, going further than British forces had ever gone in a previous Emergency. *Anvil* was the result of a familiar chain of events: poor intelligence at the outset of an insurgency led the colonial and military authorities to take increasingly extreme action. The key principles underlying the operation were coercion and repression. Taking his cue from a similar tactic used in Tel Aviv before the Second World War, Erskine deployed 25,000 security forces into the capital, in an attempt to eliminate the Mau Mau presence in the city in one fell swoop. The operation dealt a crushing blow to the revolt. Around 45,000 men, women and children were forcibly removed from Nairobi, often amid scenes of violence. About 16,500 people were detained in centres outside Nairobi in the *Anvil* operation, and other operations were conducted elsewhere in the colony. This technique of mass deportation was not unique to Kenya: as we have already seen, the British authorities resorted to similar tactics in Malaya. For all the similarities, though, the scale of detention and forced relocation in Kenya was unprecedented in any British colonial Emergency – so much so that it astonished even hardened, veteran officials. When Richard Catling arrived in Kenya in 1954, he was shocked by the scale of detentions, noting that in Palestine approximately five hundred Irgun and Stern Gang activists had been detained, while in Malaya 1,200 individuals had been detained, compared to approximately 78,000 in Kenya. By the end of 1952, just three months into the Emergency, over 18,000 Kenyans were being held in custody in 176 different detention centres across the country.[69]

After Operation *Anvil*, the colonial regime is alleged to have introduced three new features to the detention process: 'screening', 'villagisation' and the 'dilution' technique, which taken together, increased and systematised the abuse of detainees. Screening was the process by which detainees were interrogated in order to obtain operational intelligence and to assess their level of indoctrination into Mau Mau. Villagisation was a process by which the regime mandated forced resettlement throughout the Kikuyu reserves (the Kimabu, Fort Hall, Nyeri and Embu districts). By the end of 1955, a total of 1,050,899 Kikuyu were removed from their scattered homesteads and forcibly relocated into one of 804 villages, comprising some 230,000 huts. As in Malaya, emergency villages were highly restrictive: they were surrounded by barbed wire and spiked trenches, and were under twenty-four-hour guard. Villagers were forced to labour on communal projects, and it is said that women detainees were frequently raped and subjected to other abusive behaviour.

It has been contended that the dilution technique was a deliberate policy by Baring and the Colonial Office to make the the detention-camp Pipeline more systematically brutal over time. It is thought to have been conceived at Gathigiriri Camp in December 1956 by John Cowan, senior Prisons Officer of the five camps on the Mwea Plain, which would be known as the Mwea camps. This technique involved isolating small numbers of detainees from the larger group, and using force, together with confessed detainees, to exact compliance and cooperation. In March 1957 the dilution technique was allegedly systematised in the Mwea camps and its methods disclosed to the Colonial Office. The Colonial Secretary apparently approved of the technique, along with the use of 'compelling force' – a carefully worded phrase, which the colonial administration distinguished from 'punitive force', though the difference between them was in reality meaningless. It is said that the dilution technique led to the murder of eleven inmates at Hola Camp in March 1959, discussed below.[70]

Given the scale of detentions in Kenya, it is not surprising that the penal detention system instigated by the British has been compared to the Soviet Gulag. Although the scale of detentions in Kenya is shocking, it is nevertheless misleading to describe them as equivalent to the Soviet system, which involved the incarceration of about 2.5 million people. Important as it is to acknowledge the atrocities and abuses that the British committed in Kenya, it is inappropriate to compare these two hugely differing penal detention systems.[71]

INTELLIGENCE, INTERROGATION AND TORTURE IN KENYA

It is difficult, if not impossible, given the incomplete documentation presently available, to come to any overall conclusions about British interrogation practices and the use of torture in Kenya. It is certainly the case that some security forces in Kenya tortured detainees during interrogations. This was bluntly revealed by General Erskine in a top-secret letter that he wrote to the Secretary of State for War in December 1953:

There is no doubt that in the early days, i.e. from Oct 1952 until last June there was a great deal of indiscriminate shooting by Army and Police. I am quite certain prisoners were beaten to extract information. It is a short step from beating to torture and I am now sure, although it has taken me some time to realise it, that torture was a feature of many police posts. I do not believe the regular police were heavily involved although some of them may have been. The real trouble came from the Kenya settler dressed as KPR or in the Kenya Regt ...

The method of deployment of the Army in the early days in small detachments working closely with Police and Administration tended to remove the Army from the close control of its senior officers. This may have been a necessary use of the Army in those days but it had evil results.

You ought to know about 'screening teams'. They work under the Administration and their object is to comb through labour and distinguish Mau Mau from the rest and the degree of Mau Mau. Some of these screening teams have used methods of torture ...[72]

Corroborating evidence pointing to the use of torture by British security forces in Kenya comes from the records of contemporary Church missionaries. In February 1953 a British missionary in Kenya is known to have received 'a constant stream of reports of brutalities by police, military and home guards'. Evidence of torture also featured in contemporary judgements of Kenyan courts, which, like Erskine's letter, reveal that abusive methods were used by security forces in the screening process. In Criminal Appeals 988 and 989 of 1954, it appears that the court was concerned with two accused who were tortured repeatedly in a screening camp in 1954. The judgement concluded with the following passage:

We cannot, however, conclude this judgment without drawing attention once more to the activities of the so-called 'screening teams' ... From this case and others that have come to our notice it seems that it may be a common practice when a person is arrested in the commission of a terrorist offence, or on suspicion of such offence, for the police to hand him over to the custody of one of these teams where, if the accounts given are true, he is subjected to a 'softening up' process, with the object of obtaining information from him. To judge by the same, the function of a 'screening team' is to sift the good Kikuyus from the bad; but if that was its only function, there could not have been, in the instant case, any reason to send the Appellant to such a team for he had been arrested in the actual commission of an offence carrying capital punishment. What legal powers of detention these teams have or under whose authority they act we do not know. The power to detain suspected persons given in Emergency Regulation No 3 would not seem to be exercisable in this case and the right of a police officer to detain in police custody pending trial … does not authorise the handing over of the person detained into some other custody. It has certainly been made clear to us by the disclaimer made to Mr Brookes for the Crown and Respondent that the Attorney General is not in any way responsible for screening teams and there are some indications that they are not under the control of the police but are under administration officers. But, whatever the authority responsible, it is difficult to believe that these teams could continue to use methods of unlawful violence without the knowledge and condonation of the authority. Such methods are the negation of the rule of law which it is the duty of courts to uphold, and when instances come before the courts of allegations that prisoners have been subjected to unlawful criminal violence, it is the duty of such courts to insist on the fullest enquiry with a view to their verification or refutation.[73]

Secondly, in Criminal Case No 240 of 1954 (*R v Muiru and others*, 10 December 1954), Acting Justice Cram said:

Looking at the evidence in this case that there exists a system of guard posts manned by headmen and chiefs and these are interrogation centres and prisons to which the Queen's subjects whether innocent or guilty are led by armed men without warrant and detained and as it seems tortured until they confess to the alleged crimes and are then led forth to trial on the sole evidence of those confessions, it is time that this court declared that any such system is constitutionally illegal and should come to an end and these dens emptied of their victims and those chiefs and headmen exercising arbitrary power checked and warned.[74]

However, as with Malaya, it is misleading to make generalisations about 'the British' torturing people in Kenya. When we look at the question of the abuse of prisoners in Kenya, it should be borne in mind that there was not a single security force in Kenya, and there was not a uniform standard for interrogations during the Emergency. In fact, this was precisely the problem. There was an enormous divergence between Whitehall recommendations for interrogation practices, written by deskbound soldiers safely thousands of miles away from the fighting, and the realities of interrogations that actually took place on the ground. It has been traditionally assumed that in Kenya the regular British Army stood aside and left interrogations to the police, the Home Guard and the settlers of the Kenya Regiment. It is usually thought that this was the case because they, unlike British soldiers, could speak Kikuyu. However, it has been claimed that the revelations of the secret archive at Hanslope Park suggest that the British Army may have been more involved in interrogations than was previously apparent. This is one of the major points of contention in the Mau Mau case that came before the High Court in London in 2012. Records before the court also apparently reveal that the Special Branch and British Army military intelligence officers (MIOs) may have been more involved in 'screening' interrogations than previously thought by historians.[75]

From the start of the Emergency until October 1956, when Mau Mau suspects were arrested, it has been testified that they were classified as 'white', 'grey' or 'black'. The classification system was then altered, with letters (e.g. 'Z', 'Y', 'YY' and 'XR') and numbers (e.g. 'Z1' and 'Z2') being used. Civilian and military personnel carried out screening interrogations in a variety of locations, including gazetted and ungazetted centres, police stations, detention camps and Home Guard posts. Detainees were required to labour while in the Pipeline. Those who refused were sent to a Special Detention Camp, where they could be forced to work.[76]

The reality was that there was a large number of civilian and military bodies in Kenya undertaking interrogations, all with their own priorities and methods. Despite the inherent problems in attempting to draw conclusions about this, nevertheless we can see that, as in Malaya, a crucial distinction existed between different kinds of interrogations in Kenya: some were intended to punish and 'rehabilitate' Mau Mau suspects, and these were often extremely violent; some were conducted at the front line of 'hot' combat, while others took place later, after a captured insurgent had been transported to a detention centre. The latter were more likely to be conducted by trained Special Branch officers, and had the aim of eliciting operational strategic intelligence. These seem to have involved less physical violence, for the simple reason that, as we have seen, the best interrogators understood that physical violence would not produce reliable intelligence or loyal agents.[77]

In January 1954, security forces captured one of the principal Mau Mau fighters, General Waruhiu Itote, also known as 'General China'. An experienced Kenya Special Branch officer, Ian Henderson, subjected Itote to about sixty-eight hours of interrogation, during which he skilfully elicited formerly unknown strategic intelligence about the Mau Mau formations and their order of battle in the Mount Kenya area. Most importantly, Itote revealed that Mau Mau forces were divided into regional commands and gangs. This was significant, because as the Commissioner of Police in Kenya, Richard Catling, noted, attempting to estimate the size of Mau Mau was akin to 'looking into a crystal ball and trying to recognise something sensible upon which to base estimates of numbers, ranks and duty posts'. Henderson managed to coax answers from Itote by playing on what he believed were his vulnerabilities. Itote had been severely wounded during his capture, and throughout his interrogation he believed he was going to die. Henderson played upon his boastfulness, ridiculing him and taunting him with his lack of importance in Mau Mau. By doing so, he managed to get Itote to tell him the location of numerous Mau Mau gangs. There is no evidence that Henderson used physical coercion during Itote's interrogation. Although it cannot be proved conclusively without further documentation, it seems likely that his interrogation tactics were derived from MI5's training programmes in Kenya, which were in turn derived from its experiences and lessons from the Second World War. MI5's SLO in Nairobi, whose name is not revealed in presently available records, and Alec MacDonald, the MI5 officer seconded to the Kenya administration, are known to have given training courses and instructions to the Kenya Special Branch about interrogation techniques. A former Kenya Special Branch officer has confirmed that MI5 played a guiding role over Special Branch interrogation practices at the time.[78]

One of the most important sources of operational intelligence for the authorities in Kenya came from double agents. Captain (later General Sir) Frank Kitson, a British military intelligence officer seconded to the Special Branch in Kiambu district, developed a pioneering technique to fight Mau Mau with what he termed 'counter-gangs' or 'pseudo gangs'. The breakthrough came for Kitson and the Special Branch when in 1953 they discovered, it seems by reconnaissance, that Mau Mau insurgents were not controlled by one operational centre, but were divided into regional commands and gangs. The recruitment and setting up of 'counter-gangs' to act as double agents was much like the use of 'Q-Patrols' in Palestine and 'surrendered enemy personnel' in Malaya, although once again, it is remarkable in hindsight that British forces in Kenya did not learn more lessons from Palestine and Malaya. Instead, they came up with 'new' ideas about counter-insurgencies, such as the best way to run double agents, which in fact was already well-trodden ground.

Kitson, who later became the father of Britain's counter-insurgency doctrine, and would spend time in Northern Ireland, where he applied lessons learned from Britain's end-of-empire insurgency campaigns, wrote in his account of his experiences in Kenya that information on Mau Mau gang members usually came first from an informer. British forces argued that such informers could not appear as witnesses in court due to fear of reprisals, so the administration controversially decreed that it was necessary to suspend legal due process and *habeas corpus* – an argument that continues to resurface during national security emergencies time and again, down to the present day. Once gang members had been identified as potential recruits, the Special Branch undertook intensive surveillance on them, gathered compromising material and then presented them with it. If successfully 'turned', they were sent back to the Mau Mau gangs as 'counter-gangs', and thereafter provided a flow of crucial intelligence for the military authorities, which led to Mau Mau fighters being arrested or killed. By the end of the counter-insurgency three to four hundred surrendered Mau Mau insurgents were employed in counter-gangs. Their identities are closely guarded to this day: they are still known colloquially as turncoats (*Miguru*). As Kitson observed, the success of counter-gangs could be seen in the fact that, once turned, none of them ever defected back to their old Mau Mau gangs. Moreover, he noted, even when counter-gangs did not provide pinpoint details of the location of Mau Mau gangs, which were able to escape security patrols, their intelligence nevertheless had the effect of keeping the gangs on the run.[79]

For the recruitment of counter-gangs Kitson did not rely on physical coercion, but rather on mental pressure, just as Henderson had done with Itote. Detainees were often threatened with being released under suspicious circumstances, with the unnerving knowledge of the vengeance that Mau Mau gangs exacted on turncoats. Financial rewards were also offered. According to Kitson, there was no single method for turning an agent: in fact, there were probably as many reasons for turning as there were counter-gang members. However, as Kitson recalled, one of the most successful techniques was the careful compilation of background intelligence, gathered through informers or surveillance and carefully compiled in Special Branch registries. When prisoners were presented with detailed dossiers of intelligence, they would often assume that the interrogator already knew everything about them. This was precisely the same method that MI5 used so successfully at Camp 020, which as we have seen was termed 'mental pressure' by 'Tin Eye' Stephens. After being presented with their supposedly secret dealings with Mau Mau gangs, prisoners could then be broken, at which point they were turned into double agents as counter-gang members.

None of this is to suggest that Special Branch interrogations in Kenya were not often extremely brutal. In some parts of the colony the Special Branch was compared to the Nazis, and even nicknamed the 'Kenya SS' on account of some of the third-degree interrogation methods it used. The Kenya police used techniques like placing an upturned bucket on a prisoner's head and beating it with a metal instrument, or forcing a prisoner to 'put his head between his knees, put his arms around the back of his knees and hold his ears, and stay in that position until he gave in'. An officer in the Kenya Police Reserve tried to frighten a prisoner into telling him the location of a Mau Mau gang by firing a shot over his head and threatening, 'Next one goes through your skull.' Part of the reason practices like these occurred was because of a lack of centralised control, either from Nairobi or London. Given the multitude of recruits to police and military forces in the colony, many of whom conducted their own style of interrogations and had their own local vendettas, it was difficult – if not impossible – for central authorities to maintain discipline.

But that is only half the explanation. It seems that some British soldiers knew perfectly well that the prisoners they handed over to the Kenya police, Home Guard and the Kenya Regiment were likely to be ill-treated. There appears to have been an indifference on their part about violence meted out to prisoners. One of the few, if not the only, American recruits to British forces during the Kenyan Emergency, William Baldwin, recalled that during the interrogation of one Mau Mau suspect a Special Branch interrogator left the room temporarily, but returned to find that in his absence his Kikuyu Home Guard assistant had killed the prisoner. Apparently the Special Branch officer reacted with indifference.[80]

Furthermore, there were aspects of the shooting war that increased the likelihood of the abuse of prisoners in Kenya. Though it was useful for achieving immediate results, the system of counter-gangs produced an environment in which abuses could easily occur. As in Palestine and Malaya, these turned agents operated deep undercover, cut off from their chain of command and from regular forces, in highly stressful and volatile circumstances, often deep in the jungle. The need to gain quick answers to questions about enemy forces created a fertile ground for malpractice and atrocities, and the lack of safeguards imposed by the administration to target only those who were genuinely involved in Mau Mau led to a huge number of wrongful detentions.

The most important reason detainees were tortured in Kenya was that the mechanisms devised by the British to crush the insurgency allowed it to occur. In fact, they institutionalised it. The Pipeline system and the 'dilution' technique were set up to rehabilitate prisoners by force; the physical coercion, or abuse, of detainees was a clear part of this. Torture seems to have been particularly prevalent in the screening teams, institutionalised by British authorities as a front line in the counter-insurgency. Part of the system of 'screening' was the use of informants, who were typically hooded to conceal their identities and placed in front of a row of Mau Mau suspects, from whom they would indicate those involved with Mau Mau. The system of hooded informants institutionalised personal vendettas. Those accused of Mau Mau crimes were unable to face their accusers – fundamental to any system of justice worth the name.

Another reason why the abuse of policing powers occurred in Kenya was because the administration – particularly the Governor himself, Baring – refused to give police forces in the colony the same legal standing they had in Britain. Far from being independent of government, as police officers in Britain were, those in Kenya were tools of the administration, often performing its dirty work. When Sir Arthur Young arrived in Kenya as the new Commissioner of Police in 1953, having previously served in the same position in Malaya, he was dismayed to discover the widespread mistreatment of Mau Mau suspects in police custody, especially by the Home Guard, who routinely beat prisoners, often on the basis of personal vendettas. As a result, Young, together with the Attorney-General in Kenya, John Whyatt, attempted to establish an impartial and fair police force in the colony. They proposed to reform the existing system and give police officers in Kenya the same standing as constables under English common law, which would effectively allow them to act independently. Young argued that fighting 'terrorism' with terror was counter-productive, and would ultimately alienate the local population. Baring opposed Young's proposed reforms, arguing that they were not 'suitable' to Kenya and the needs of the Emergency. This led to Young's resignation in 1954 and his public criticism of the Kenya administration. It was only after detailed exchanges with the Colonial Secretary, Alan Lennox-Boyd, that agreement was reached on the phrasing of his statement of resignation. In the end, it read that the 'administration of the law was seriously jeopardised by the activities of the Home Guard whose powers were liable to abuse owing to their lack of discipline'. In private, Young was much more critical – he described Kenya as a 'police state', and with hindsight we can see that he was correct. There was a bastardisation of independent police work in Kenya, which in turn prevented effective oversight and control, leading to an abundance of malpractice and abuse.[81]

MI5 AND DIPLOMATIC INTELLIGENCE ON KENYATTA

MI5 provided the Colonial Office and the colonial administration in Kenya with high-level diplomatic intelligence on Jomo Kenyatta, as it had done for Kwame Nkrumah in the Gold Coast. Kenyatta, the first leader of independent Kenya, was and remains probably the most misunderstood national leader in the history of British Africa. He aroused much greater fears among the colonial administration in Kenya and also in London than Nkrumah ever did. At the outbreak of the Mau Mau rebellion in 1952, the colonial administration was quick to depict him as the master of mayhem and the undisputed leader of Mau Mau, and these views permeated much of official British thinking. Even after his release from prison in 1960 – he had been found guilty on flagrantly rigged charges of 'leading' Mau Mau – the Governor of Kenya, Patrick Renison, persisted in claiming that Kenyatta was the leader of Mau Mau 'to darkness and death'. For many in Kenya and London, if Mau Mau was a manifestation of evil, Kenyatta was the personification of it.[82]

One eminent historian of Kenya, Bruce Berman, has suggested that if British intelligence had known more about Kenyatta's politics, much of the 'intense suspicion and hostility with which the British viewed him could well have been avoided'. In fact, this observation – made before the recent release of MI5 records – largely misses the point. In reality, British intelligence managed to allay some of the fears in London surrounding Kenyatta, particularly about his communist beliefs.[83]

Although Kenyatta's and Nkrumah's careers ended up very differently, the two men originally came to the attention of British intelligence in similar ways. Like Nkrumah, Kenyatta first appeared on MI5's radar when he travelled to England. Born into a peasant family and raised by Scottish missionaries, Kenyatta first came to England in 1929 as the leader of the Kikuyu Central Association and to study, like so many other post-war anti-colonial leaders, at the London School of Economics. The KCA was the main pressure group campaigning for land reform in Kenya, and

Kenyatta was also editor of its journal, *Muigwithania*, meaning 'understanding' in Kikuyu. His activities in London were monitored by the London Special Branch, which compiled a 'large file' on him. In 1930 it was reported that he was believed to have joined the Communist Party of Great Britain, and that a leading British communist, Robin Page Arnot, had called him 'the future revolutionary leader of Kenya'. MI5 opened a file on Kenyatta three months later, after receiving a report from SIS that he was going to Hamburg to attend a 'Negro conference'.[84]

Unknown to British intelligence at the time, after his trip to Germany Kenyatta travelled on to Moscow in order to study at the University of the Toilers of the East, which he attended under the alias 'James Joken'. MI5 learned of Kenyatta's time in Moscow soon after his return to Britain in late 1933 from a Special Branch informer, who reported that Kenyatta had received 'instructions' to become a Comintern agent. The Director-General of MI5, Sir Vernon Kell, personally relayed this information to the Colonial Office and the commissioner of police in Nairobi. For seven months MI5 imposed a letter-check (HOW) on Kenyatta, who was now living on Cambridge Street in London, but this was not as successful as hoped: so prompt was postal delivery in pre-war London that on two occasions Kenyatta complained to the Post Office that he believed his mail was being opened because there was a delay in receiving it – it is doubtful that suspicions would be aroused on similar grounds today. To calm his suspicions, MI5 suspended the HOW in July 1934.[85]

MI5 continued to gather whatever information it could on Kenyatta, who was now studying at the LSE under the renowned anthropologist Bronisław Malinowski. In 1936 the head of the Kenya Special Branch visited MI5 in London and reported: 'The Kenya Authorities view this person [Kenyatta] with a good deal of mistrust and feel that he is the sort of person whose affairs would well repay a certain amount of attention.' As soon as the Second World War broke out, at the behest of the Kenya administration MI5 again placed Kenyatta under active surveillance, imposing a HOW that allowed his mail and his telephone calls to be intercepted. The desk officer responsible for investigating Kenyatta during the war was Roger Hollis, who was in charge of MI5's wartime section on 'subversive activities', F-Division.

By 1940 Kenyatta had moved to West Sussex. His political ties seemed to be dwindling, and MI5 was reassured that any suspicions of communist links could be dismissed. MI5's intensive wartime surveillance of the CPGB, particularly through the microphones that Hollis's F-Division installed in the Party's headquarters, revealed that Kenyatta's relationship with British communists was cooling. MI5 was so relaxed about Kenyatta's politics that in September 1943 it allowed him to lecture British troops on the subject of Africa. In September 1944 MI5's Director-General, Sir David Petrie, sent an overall report on Kenyatta to the Director of Intelligence and Security (DIS) in Nairobi. Petrie said that MI5 had placed Kenyatta under prolonged observation at the start of the war, but this had produced little of security interest:

> KENYATTA continues to live at 'Highover', Heath Common, Storrington, Sussex, in a house in which several persons of extreme left wing or Trotskyist sympathies reside, but he does not attract attention in any way and can, I think, hardly be taking an active part in politics.[86]

O.J. Mason, later to become MI5's first SLO in East Africa, echoed these views when he reported to the Colonial Office about a speech Kenyatta gave at the Pan-African Congress held in Manchester in 1945:

> During the last few years, Kenyatta appears to have led a fairly quiet and non-political life, but previously he had been known as something of an anti-British agitator. It is believed that he was at one time a communist, but is thought to have quarrelled with the Party.[87]

Despite MI5's reports, when Kenyatta returned to Kenya after the war, in 1946, his long residence in England, and particularly the trip he had made to the Soviet Union in 1932, became the subject of much controversy and suspicion in London and Nairobi. After the declaration of the State of Emergency in Kenya in October 1952, the colonial administration alleged that he had been indoctrinated as a communist during his 'education' in Moscow; that he was a covert Soviet agent; and that the Mau Mau revolt was a communist plot. Britain's covert propaganda outfit, the Information Research Department (IRD), needed little persuasion to depict Kenyatta as a communist. The portrayal of Kenyatta and Mau Mau as communist was in fact a shrewd move on the part of London to gather American support for its operations in Kenya. This was not a colonial war, claimed British officials in Washington, but a valiant effort in the Cold War, much like Malaya. The problem was that, unlike Malaya, there was no significant evidence that either Kenyatta or Mau Mau had anything to do with communism.

Soon after the declaration of the Emergency, on 20 October 1952, the Colonial Office tasked MI5 to make an assessment of Kenyatta's communist credentials and of communist involvement in the Mau Mau revolt. Due to its pre-emptive investigations into Kenyatta and his associates in England beginning in the 1930s, MI5 had voluminous records on which to draw. On 10 November 1952 a high-level meeting was called between MI5's 'OS' Section and representatives from the Colonial Office, including two long-serving colonial officials, Juxon Barton and W.H. Ingrams. After the meeting, Herbert Loftus-Brown of 'OS' Section noted:

I am anxious to put on record a statement of our basic views on racial unrest in Kenya, for the benefit of the Colonial Office, as soon as possible, so that the Colonial Office may not make representations to the Government of Kenya which are at variance with information on our files.[88]

As had been the case with Nkrumah, MI5's intensive surveillance of the CPGB placed it in a unique position to comment on Kenyatta's communist affiliations, and on what British Communist Party leaders thought of Mau Mau. On 22 November MI5 sent a stinging letter to the Colonial Office:

… We have seen nothing to suggest Communist intervention in Mau Mau activities. By virtue of its own theories, the international Communist movement is bound to support any colonial group which can be fitted into the category of a 'National Liberation movement', but during the present emergency in Kenya the only signs of intervention or support of Communists are to be found in their propaganda, and even that does not appear exceptionally well informed … There seems to be little doubt, however, that KENYATTA, himself, is concerned solely with the furthering of the cause of the Kikuyu tribe and that he has interested himself in the affairs of the Soviet Union and of international communist organisations abroad only so far as the communists are prepared to help him.[89]

MI5's calming assessment of Kenyatta, much like its assessment of Nkrumah, was entirely correct. Records from former Soviet archives, only recently made available, reveal that during his trip to Moscow in 1932 the KGB did indeed attempt to recruit Kenyatta, but like many other anti-colonial leaders who visited Moscow in the 1930s, he was more horrified than inspired by his time there. In 1951 a report from MI5's SLO in Southern Rhodesia, Bob de Quehen, revealed Kenyatta's disillusioning experience in Moscow nearly twenty years earlier. Kenyatta had revealed to a South African police source that he had witnessed instances of racism during his stay in the Soviet Union – he had seen Albert Nzula, the first black Secretary General of the Communist Party of South Africa, dragged out of a meeting in Moscow by two OGPU officers, apparently never to be seen alive again. While Kenyatta was in Moscow a Politburo member is reported to have accused him of being a 'petty-bourgeois', to which Kenyatta supposedly responded: 'I don't like this "petty" thing. Why don't you say I'm a big bourgeois?' He left the Soviet Union unconvinced, unconverted and distinctly un-communist. By contrast, Kenyatta enjoyed his time in England, and by the time he left in 1946 had become something of an anglophile. He led a bohemian lifestyle in London, drinking literally inflammable Nubian gin and featuring as an extra in Alexander Korda's 1935 film *Sanders of the River*. Britain was a life-changing place for Kenyatta; it gave him a world-class education and the love of an English wife. He would not forget it.[90]

MI5 used the intelligence it had gained on Kenyatta to help shape the British response to the Mau Mau revolt. Some colonial officials, particularly Juxon Barton, used this intelligence to thwart attempts by their hawkish colleagues in the Colonial Office to allege that Kenyatta was a communist, and that consequently Mau Mau was a communist conspiracy. The exchanges between Ingrams, who continued to argue impulsively that Kenyatta was a communist, and Barton, who was backed up by MI5's intelligence, were heated, and still make startling reading. Ultimately, MI5 and Barton were able to lessen fears in London about Kenyatta's 'communism'. They managed, for example, to block an attempt by the propagandists in the IRD to claim that Mau Mau was part of an international plot organised by Moscow, and that Kenyatta was a Soviet agent. Sir John Shaw, the head of 'OS' Section, wrote to the Foreign Office on 23 December 1952 in unambiguous terms:

> We have not seen anything to suggest that Mau Mau is in any way inspired by Communism, or that it should be viewed in the perspective of the Communist 'colonial liberation' campaign … It is characteristic of those African 'nationalist' politicians who have received some early training in orthodox Communism that, when they return to their own territories, they adapt what they have learned to the needs of the local situation;

while they may retain some Marxist principles, they can in no sense be called Communists, since they are not responsive to Party line. They are concerned with their own 'nationalist' ambitions and are not instruments of international Communist strategy. Consequently, their activities must be viewed against the background of the local political situation. There is no indication that Jomo KENYATTA, or other suspected leaders of Mau Mau, are exceptions to this principle.[91]

In order to gather as much information as possible about Kenyatta's politics, MI5 investigated his known associates in England. In some instances this led it into practices that, from the perspective of civil liberties, were at best dubious. One of Kenyatta's closest contacts in London was Peter Koinange, the son of a Kikuyu chief implicated in Mau Mau. As soon as the Emergency was declared in Kenya, MI5 agreed to a request by the colonial administration to place Koinange under surveillance, imposing a HOW on his home address. Intercepted mail revealed that Koinange was a keen supporter of the Congress of Peoples Against Imperialism (COPAI), a left-leaning group whose mission was to campaign for colonial emancipation. MI5 was unwilling to commence investigations into COPAI itself, not least because its supporters included several Labour MPs, including Barbara Castle and Fenner Brockway.

However, at the end of October 1952, under intense pressure from the Colonial Office, MI5 reluctantly agreed to impose a HOW on COPAI's headquarters, though it was careful to make it clear that if this should ever be discovered, the Colonial Office would share responsibility with MI5 for it. As MI5 noted to the Colonial Office: 'It is not only the protection of our sources with which we are concerned. We share with you the responsibility of having to investigate an organisation whose methods are overt and legitimate, and which number among its supporters many members of Parliament, because of the impact of its activities upon matters which are of security interest.' Within a matter of weeks of imposing the HOW, MI5 reported to the Colonial Office that it had produced nothing of security interest, and would therefore be shut down. Clearly, however, in its investigations into COPAI, MI5 was sailing close to the wind in terms of what was permissible for an intelligence service in a liberal democracy. In fact, judging from some of the annotations in Koinange's MI5 file, MI5 even had files on Castle and Brockway, an alarming fact from a constitutional perspective, given the sanctity that is given to Members of the House of Commons under the British constitution.[92]

Ironically, these questionable investigations allowed MI5 to conclude with a degree of certainty that Kenyatta was not an ideologically committed communist, and that his trip to Moscow had been made out of curiosity rather than conviction. While MI5 successfully calmed fears in London about Kenyatta, it was less successful in Nairobi, where the colonial administration remained blindly convinced that he was the leader of Mau Mau, a communist, and an agent of Moscow. MI5's SLO in Nairobi when the Emergency was declared, C.R. Major, wrongly believed that Kenyatta had helped to organise some early Mau Mau incidents before October 1952, but that thereafter they had 'a snowball effect' which he was powerless to prevent. In reality, Kenyatta had never been involved with any Mau Mau incidents.

However, Major was correct when he bluntly reported to MI5 in London that the colonial administration's decision to put Kenyatta on trial was motivated by political expediency and a need to find a culprit to placate the European settlers in the colony – to which Major was strongly opposed. We now know just how low the colonial administration stooped to convict Kenyatta: so desperate was it to establish Kenyatta's guilt that it even alleged his studies in anthropology during his time in London had allowed him to conjure up the sorcery and black magic of Mau Mau. Crown witnesses were effectively bribed at his trial on wildly trumped-up charges. In April 1953 Kenyatta was found guilty of 'managing and being a member' of Mau Mau, and remained in prison until 1959, after which he was detained at Lodwar, in the arid remote north of the colony. When the official inquiry into Mau Mau, the Corfield Report, was published in 1960, it continued to allege that Kenyatta was a communist and the leader of Mau Mau. In reality, the colonial administration had confused the *symbol* of the revolt for its *leader*.[93]

During the Emergency in Kenya, MI5's efforts were focused on providing operational intelligence for the military forces. However, as the tide turned in the shooting war, especially after Operation *Anvil* in 1954, MI5 and the Kenya Special Branch provided the administration with increasing amounts of diplomatic and political intelligence. Governor Baring noted in 1956 that MI5's SLO in Kenya had a close relationship with the administration, with intelligence flowing in both directions between London and Nairobi.

Despite the protests of the European settlers in the colony, in 1957 the so-called 'Lyttelton constitution' was enacted in Kenya, bringing greater political representation to local populations, as had occurred in Nigeria just a few years before. This brought an elected black African minister to Kenya's Legislative Council for the first time. The minister was Tom Mboya, a brilliantly talented Oxford-educated politician from the 'white highlands'. His election forced MI5 and the Special Branch to address the question of sharing intelligence with local politicians, many of whom were themselves the subjects of MI5 and Special Branch inquiries.

As had happened in other colonies that moved towards internal self-government and ultimately independence, such as India and the Gold Coast, the Kenyan Special Branch destroyed compromising records it held on anti-colonial leaders, especially those relating to informers and agents. One British official noted in August 1963, on the eve of Kenyan independence, that the problem for the Kenya Special Branch was that it was 'saddled with a legacy of distrust'. To overcome this, it began to share intelligence with ministers in the government-in-waiting – at least outwardly. New light is thrown on this process by the records of the Colonial Office's Intelligence and Security Department, together with the personal papers of the Director of Intelligence in Kenya, Mervyn Manby. As constitutional advancements were made in Kenya, MI5 and the Kenya Special Branch developed a system by which 'clean' intelligence, that is vetted intelligence 'heavily slanted to define security threats and matters of law and order', was passed to local ministers like Mboya. This was called 'Legacy material'. These records reveal, however, that despite this gesture of goodwill, the Director of Intelligence in Kenya retained a small group of European Special Branch officers who continued to monitor the activities of the colonial administration's old foes, even if they had now been elected to the Legislative Council. This group reported its findings to the Director of Intelligence and the Governor himself, 'directly but covertly' and always orally, not in writing.[94]

Recently released records from the secret archive at Hanslope Park reveal that the colonial administration separated cypher codes into two categories: one that was 'safe' to hand over to the independent Kenyan government, and another that was 'unsafe', and was to be retained under strict secrecy by the colonial governor. As in India before it, the transfer of power in Kenya was a process of careful intelligence management and manipulation by the British. The Hanslope Park archive also confirms in greater detail than previously known that in the last days of British rule in Kenya, colonial officials were instructed to separate those papers to be left in place after independence, as mentioned above, the 'Legacy files', which contained 'clean' material, from those that were to be selected for destruction or removal to Britain, which contained 'dirty' material, such as intelligence reports and the names of agents. In Kenya, and it appears in other colonies, the unsafe 'dirty' records were known as 'Watch' files, and were stamped with a red letter 'W', alerting their readers not to show them to any non-Europeans. The precautions set up to prevent the eventual inheritors of records ever discovering that there were Watch files were remarkable. Officials scoured through archive files held in registries in colonial offices in Nairobi and removed any trace of Watch papers. When a single Watch file was to be removed from a group of safe Legacy files, colonial officials were instructed to create a 'twin file', or dummy, which was to be inserted in its place. This was intelligence manipulation on a remarkable scale.[95]

There is still a degree of debate about the exact connection between Mau Mau and Britain's decision to relinquish power in Kenya. Nationalist histories (predictably) have argued that Mau Mau was a war of 'national liberation', which was ultimately responsible for Kenyan independence. By contrast, other histories have argued that it may actually have delayed Britain's devolution of power in the colony. Whatever the case, the watershed moment for British rule in Kenya came in March 1959, after a notorious incident at a remote prison camp for Mau Mau suspects at Hola, in which eleven inmates were beaten to death by prison guards. Inmates at Hola were coerced into the British 'rehabilitation' process by being forced to work; the camp's brutal regime ensured that even the most reluctant prisoners would be 'rehabilitated' away from their wicked Mau Mau ways. The administration's attempts to explain away the eleven deaths as being caused by dysentery and malnutrition led to a vociferous attack by the British government's usual left-wing critics, such as Castle and Brockway. More surprising was the strong criticism from Conservative backbenchers such as Enoch Powell, who in July 1959 launched a stinging but eloquent attack in the House of Commons on British policies in Kenya. As Powell memorably put it:

> We cannot say, 'We will have African standards in Africa, Asian standards in Asia and perhaps British standards here at home.' We have not that choice to make. We must be consistent with ourselves everywhere. All Government, all influence of man upon man, rests upon opinion. What we can do in Africa, where we still govern and where we no longer govern, depends upon the opinion which is entertained of the way in which this country acts and the way in which Englishmen act. We cannot, we dare

not, in Africa of all places, fall below our own highest standards in the acceptance of responsibility.[96]

After the incident at Hola, Harold Macmillan's famous 'wind of change' speech, given in Cape Town on 3 February 1960, heralded the start of a new policy for Britain in Africa. Macmillan argued that the wind of African nationalism was blowing so hard that it could not be stopped. He said that the task facing Britain, and all Western governments, was to guide the juggernaut of nationalism in Africa, while steering clear of the threat of Soviet and Chinese communism. Although the speech is commonly acknowledged as a turning point in the history of Britain's end of empire, its Cold War message has often been forgotten, even though it is perfectly clear:

> The wind of change is blowing through this continent, and whether we like it or not, this growth of national consciousness is a fact. We must all accept it as a fact, and our national policies must take account of it ... As I see it the great issue in this second half of the twentieth century is whether the uncommitted peoples of Asia and Africa will swing to the East or to the West. Will they be drawn into the Communist camp? Or will the great experiments in self-government that are now being made in Asia and Africa, especially within the Commonwealth, prove so success-ful, and by their example so compelling, that the balance will come down in favour of freedom and order and justice?[97]

At the time, it certainly seemed that the wind of change was blowing away European colonies in Africa, whose dissolution acted as a sort of prophetic looking-glass for Britain about how not to manage a retreat from empire. The violent disintegration of the Belgian Congo in 1960, which produced a massive refugee crisis, with victims fleeing to British colonies in East Africa, including Kenya, highlighted the need for Britain and other colonial powers to find a quick and smooth exit from Africa. A few years later, in 1964, in an important article published in the *Spectator*, the Colonial Secretary, Iain Macleod, explained that one of the major reasons behind his decision to speed up the process of Britain's withdrawal from its colonies in Africa was the spectacle of the violent end of Belgian rule in the Congo.[98]

The first election for domestic party leadership had been held in Kenya in March 1957, but this had led to deadlock, with no clear electoral winner, as had a second election in March 1959. However, in January 1960 the British government agreed to hold constitutional talks in London about the future of Kenya. The talks, held while Kenyatta was still detained in Lodwar, took place in the ornate setting of Lancaster House, the 'dignity and splendour' of which were thought to exert a 'potent and helpful' influence on colonial delegations. In the course of the Lancaster House talks, Macmillan's government committed itself to African majority rule in Kenya.

However, rivalries were quick to emerge between the different Kenyan political groups, which, as was common in Kenya, were divided along ethnic lines. The strongest divisions were between the moderate Kenya African Democratic Union (KADU) and the more radical Kenya African National Union (KANU), which was established soon after the talks and was led by Kenyatta's great political rival and the future Deputy President of independent Kenya, Oginga Odinga, a Luo, not a Kikuyu, politician. Under Odinga's firebrand leadership, KANU's uncompromising platform called for the confiscation of all settler estates and property, the ending of foreign investment and the nationalisation of industry. Progress was made more complicated by the emergence of new political parties, such as the New Kenya Group, led by Michael Blundell, who tried to orchestrate politics in Kenya along a national line, rather than ethnic lines, hoping that this would protect the 30,000 or so European settlers.

However, KANU was by far the most popular party, and in February 1961 it won a sweeping victory in the general election. Nevertheless, the party, whose slogan was *Uhuru na Kenyatta* ('Freedom and Kenyatta'), refused to form a government until Kenyatta was freed. In August 1961 Kenyatta was finally released from detention, but far from emerging as a shadow of his former self, a decrepit and alcoholic old man, as his rival Odinga doubtless hoped, in fact he seemed stronger than ever – just as would happen with Nelson Mandela over thirty years later in South Africa. Kenyatta made use of his freedom to outmanoeuvre rivals like Odinga, and distance himself from KANU's radical platform.[99]

Kenya was granted full internal self-government in late 1962, and in October 1963 Kenyatta led a KANU delegation to another set of talks at Lancaster House, which paved the way for Kenya's full independence. As has been well documented, these talks ran into continual difficulties because of the opposing demands of KANU, for which Tom Mboya played a key role, and Michael Blundell's New Kenya Group. However, what has not been appreciated is that during both sets of constitutional talks at

Lancaster House, in 1962 and 1963, MI5 bugged the Kenyan delegations. Transcripts of bugged conversations proved extraordinarily useful for British officials in their negotiations with the various Kenyan delegates, and the intelligence they provided was valued highly by the Colonial Secretaries during the two rounds of talks, Iain Macleod and Duncan Sandys. As a former Minister of Defence, Sandys was well versed in the dark arts of espionage and the benefits intelligence-gathering could produce. He became an avid consumer of MI5's bugging transcripts when negotiating with the main Kenyan delegations, particularly KANU. In fact, he made so much use of them that, after one incident when he unsubtly quoted from a KANU discussion conducted in private, MI5 had to start limiting the number of transcripts he was given.[100]

It was widely suspected by the delegations that the 'secret service' was bugging their discussions. When the Rhodesian leader Ian Smith visited London in 1965 he insisted on having some of the more sensitive conversations with his delegation in the ladies' lavatories of Lancaster House, convinced that this was the one place British intelligence would not dare to place microphones. He was almost certainly wrong.[101]

MI5's use of 'special facilities' (microphones) at Lancaster House was first publicly revealed by the renegade MI5 officer Peter Wright in his book *Spycatcher*, published in 1987, which makes it even more surprising that subsequent historians have not identified their use before. Although Wright's conspiracy theories infect much of his book, particularly his allegation that MI5's Director-General Sir Roger Hollis was really a Soviet agent, the sections of *Spycatcher* dealing with MI5's technical capabilities are more reliable: Wright worked in MI5's technical section, responsible for installing microphones and other covert activities, and therefore knew what he was talking about. More recently, the use of microphones by British intelligence during independence negotiations in Africa has been depicted in John le Carré's novel *The Mission Song* (2006).

In fact, when MI5 installed microphones in Lancaster House in the early 1960s, Roger Hollis was nervous that his service might have stepped beyond its legitimate remit, which was to investigate threats to British national security, as informally established by the so-called 'Maxwell Fyfe Directive' of 1952, which made MI5 responsible to the Home Secretary. Hollis expressed his concerns to the Home Secretary, R.A. 'Rab' Butler, explaining that the African delegates posed little significant threat to British national security. Butler replied that given the importance of what was being discussed – negotiations that it was hoped would allow Britain to preserve its 'vital interests' in East Africa – it was advantageous for MI5 to bug the delegations, and he authorised it to do so.[102]

MI5 AND THE INDEPENDENT KENYAN GOVERNMENT

One of the most remarkable declassified intelligence documents in the entire history of Britain's end of empire concerns Jomo Kenyatta's personal involvement with MI5. After his release from detention in August 1961, Kenyatta's reputation underwent an extraordinary transformation in the eyes of the British. Having previously been regarded as the incarnation of evil, he soon became recast as loyal 'Old Jomo', the 'wise one' (*Mzee*) and 'the reconciler' (*Muigwithania*). Kenyatta did not harbour grudges against the British, as many people would have done: his public slogans were 'Together' (*Harambee*) and 'Forgive and forget'. After he was elected Prime Minister of Kenya in 1963, and President in 1964, his ability to cooperate, forgive and forget was often remarkable. When Baring showed Kenyatta the desk in Government House on which he had signed his arrest warrant, Kenyatta said that he would have done the same.

The 'mastermind of Mau Mau', as Baring had mistakenly called Kenyatta, in fact proved a master of magnanimity. When Kenya gained full independence in December 1963, he reached out to the remaining European settlers and urged them to stay. In a heartfelt broadcast speech, he told the settlers directly that 'many of you are as Kenyan as myself', and promised to put the atrocities of the Emergency behind him and his country: 'Let this be the day on which all of us commit ourselves to erase from our minds all the hatreds and difficulties of those years which now belong to history. Let us agree that we shall never refer to the past.' Most of the Europeans heeded his advice, and continued to farm in Kenya for years. Even Kenyatta's clothing symbolised the reconciliation that had been achieved between Britain and Kenya – he was often seen sporting an LSE tie and carrying a Kikuyu lion's-tail flywhisk. Under Kenyatta's leadership, Kenya remained in the Commonwealth after independence in December 1963, and stayed firmly in the Western camp during the Cold War.[103]

Unlike many of the former African colonies of other European powers, Kenya has remained under civilian government ever since independence – even if, as the civil unrest that erupted in 2008 revealed, ethnic tensions are never far from the surface. Intelligence played a crucial, but hitherto largely undisclosed, role in the continued friendly relations between Britain and Kenya. The intelligence-sharing between the two governments followed the same pattern as in India, Malaya and the Gold Coast before it. Just as in those countries, as it became clear that Kenyatta would be the leader of independent Kenya, he and other members of his cabinet-in-waiting were given access to carefully vetted British intelligence reports.

Then, in a major step, following Kenyatta's election as Prime Minister in August 1963 he was formally introduced by the Governor, Patrick Renison, to MI5's resident SLO in Nairobi, Walter Bell, who had previously served as an SLO in Delhi after Indian independence. According to a later report, Kenyatta and Bell got on extremely well – Bell lived next door to Kenyatta's daughter in Nairobi. It was doubtless partly due to the accord established between the two men that Kenyatta asked Bell to remain in place after Kenya's independence. Thereafter Bell was listed in *Who's Who* as a 'counsellor at the British High Commission in Nairobi' and an 'adviser to the government of Kenya'. Bell, and MI5's subsequent SLOs in Nairobi, passed over to the Kenyan Special Branch intelligence on subjects like contact between Kenyan politicians and the CPGB.[104]

It was not just through its SLOs that MI5 built up and maintained close relations with the security and intelligence authorities in independent Kenya. In recently declassified records of the Colonial Office's Intelligence and Security Department, an extraordinary transcript survives of a highly confidential meeting between Kenyatta and MI5's Director-General himself. In August 1963, while he was in London for constitutional talks at Lancaster House, Kenyatta and his conservative Attorney-General, Charles Njojo, called on MI5's headquarters at Leconfield House in Curzon Street, apparently at Kenyatta's request. During the course of the meeting, the Kenyan leader-in-waiting explained that he already knew MI5's representative in Nairobi, Walter Bell, that they got on well, and that he looked forward to working closely with him and with MI5 in the future. Kenyatta asked the Director-General for assistance with training the Special Branch in Kenya after independence. Njojo also took a particular interest in the model MI5 recommended: the separation of intelligence and police work. One well-placed observer, Richard Catling, remembered: 'We were fortunate, too, in having an African Attorney-General [Njojo] then who was an experienced and sophisticated lawyer who understood the impropriety and danger of politicians attempting to interfere with or influence the law enforcement authority in execution of their duties.'

The meeting between Kenyatta and the Director-General at MI5's headquarters perfectly encapsulates the close bonds, often on a personal level, that MI5 was able to establish with colonial states that gained independence from Britain. However, the truly remarkable twist in this tale is that the MI5 Director-General whom Kenyatta met was none other than Sir Roger Hollis, who as a junior desk officer had been responsible for investigating Kenyatta while he was living in England during the Second World War. Twenty years later, the two finally met face to face: Kenyatta as the leader-in-waiting of independent Kenya, and Hollis as the Director-General of MI5. Understandably, Hollis did not reveal to Kenyatta that he had previously read his mail.[105]

Soon after Kenya's independence, Kenyatta began using the security and intelligence machinery left by the British, especially the Special Branch, to monitor the activities of his political rivals. His main target was Oginga Odinga, the former leader of KANU, Kenyatta's own party, and independent Kenya's first Vice President. Odinga was known to hold extremist Marxist views, and to have strong links with both China and the Soviet Union: in July 1962 the Kenya Special Branch discovered that Odinga had received around £90,000 in cash, almost certainly from Eastern Bloc countries. The Soviet government provided scholarships for students from Kenya to study in the Eastern Bloc, and at the end of the Lancaster House conference in 1963 the Kenya Special Branch identified 159 such students, one of whom was Odinga's son, Raila, who himself went on to become a leading politician in Kenya – at the time of writing he is Prime Minister. In April 1965 Attorney-General Charles Njojo informed the British High Commissioner, Malcolm MacDonald, of reports that Odinga was planning a coup, and requested the intervention of British troops if necessary. The coup never materialised, but when the Special Branch searched Odinga's offices they found several crates of machine guns and grenades. In 1966 Odinga was replaced as Vice President, and left KANU to form a new opposition party, the Kenya People's Union (KPU). As well as obtaining intelligence on his political rivals, Kenyatta also used the new intelligence machinery bestowed by the British to thwart Somali incursions ('*shifta*' campaigns) in Kenya's North-Eastern Province.[106]

Just as Kenyatta had promised in 1963, the new Kenyan government continued to work closely with British intelligence after independence. In fact, the bonds were so close that in 1967 the Secretary of the new Kenyan National Security Executive, who reported directly to the President himself, was an MI5 officer and subsequently an SIS officer. Intelligence connections, along with formal military treaties, trade agreements and economic ties, were ways in which Britain managed to preserve its 'vital interests' in Kenya during the Cold War.[107]

Soon after Kenya gained independence, MI5 and SIS became increasingly concerned not just about Soviet and Chinese infiltration in the country, which was predictable, but also about the involvement of the intelligence services of Britain's Cold War allies, particularly the CIA and the Israeli Mossad. Colonial Office records reveal increasing levels of British alarm about CIA activities in Kenya in the mid-1960s. A serious headache arose for MI5 when, in 1965, it faced significant budget cuts within Whitehall, with about £100,000 having to be saved on the 'Secret Vote' (the hush-hush parliamentary procedure by which the intelligence services were funded) the following year. Hollis warned that slashing MI5's budget would have disastrous consequences, forcing it to close down some of its SLO stations abroad. In a letter to the Cabinet Secretary, Burke Trend, in November 1965 he said that if this occurred, both the Israelis and the Soviets would soon start offering training programmes for security officers in former British colonies like Kenya. The result would be that Britain would lose its influence over Commonwealth countries, which it could not afford in view of the Cold War.[108]

In the end, largely because of Hollis's campaigning within Whitehall, MI5's funding was not substantially reduced. It managed to find savings of £30,000 on its own budget, and as a result only had to shut down its SLO posts in Sierra Leone and Pakistan. One of the remarkable aspects of Hollis's letter to Trend is that he placed Israel before the Soviet Union as a threat to British influence in former colonies in Africa. He was not scaremongering: the Israeli intelligence services did indeed attempt to court the leaders of newly independent countries in Africa – they notoriously backed Colonel Idi Amin, who had served in the King's African Rifles and fought against the Mau Mau, during his rise to power in Uganda. One of Kenyatta's close advisers, the post-independence Minister for Agriculture Bruce MacKenzie, a former fighter pilot from South Africa with a handlebar moustache to match, was often reputed to have been an SIS agent (which he may well have been). Recent research has shown that he was also one of Mossad's longest-serving and most influential agents (codenamed 'the Duke') in the whole of Africa. As we have seen, this was not altogether unusual: the activities of Western intelligence services in the Cold War often cut across political alignments, with unexpected consequences.[109]

SOUTH AFRICA

One of the most difficult relationships for British intelligence during the Cold War proved to be with the South African government. MI5 had maintained relations with the South African police since the First World War, but these had become increasingly uncomfortable, with memories of the Boer War never far from minds in Pretoria. Before the election in 1948 of the white supremacist government of Daniel François Malan, the founder of Apartheid rule, South Africa relied almost entirely on British intelligence. In the years following 1945, as in other colonies, with the onset of the Cold War British intelligence was directly involved in reforming security intelligence in South Africa. However, as the Apartheid government entrenched itself, Britain's secret agencies, particularly MI5, resisted its efforts to develop its own autonomous intelligence capability. They did this out of concern that such a service could be used for domestic political purposes, which by the late 1940s meant the exploitation of black Africans.[110]

In 1946 MI5's Alex Kellar travelled to South Africa, where he followed the usual formula for security and intelligence in British territories established by MI5, recommending that a security service be set up that was entirely separate from the Criminal Investigation Department of the police. Kellar advised that the South African Special Branch be reorganised in order to 'be able to deal efficiently with the problems of a) counter espionage b) counter communism c) defensive security'. The South African government followed these recommendations to the letter, and the South African Police (SAP) Special Branch received counter-subversion training from MI5 officers.[111]

MI5's reforms and recommendations had a significant impact on the South African intelligence machinery, establishing the apparatus it would employ for years to come. One of the recommendations, which the government followed, was that the head of Special Branch should also become the *de facto* Chief Security and Intelligence Adviser to the government. Among the unfortunate consequences of this, we can see with hindsight, was the concentration of a large amount of power in the hands of a single individual.[112]

In 1948 the situation in South Africa was totally transformed by the election of Malan's white racist government and the subsequent development of its policy of Apartheid. This presented innumerable problems for Britain's intelligence liaison with the country. The same year, MI5's

Director-General Sir Percy Sillitoe, a veteran of the British South Africa Police, visited South Africa, but contrary to the wishes of the South African government, he refused to post an MI5 SLO to Pretoria, meaning that the nearest SLO was over 1,000 miles away in Salisbury, Southern Rhodesia. As he explained in December 1949:

> The improper use to which a Security Service might be put by the Nationalists might well include its use against the Parliamentary opposition and against those members of the British Community out of sympathy with the Nationalist political programme. It would certainly be used to keep down the black races. In these circumstances the part played by the Director-General in establishing any form of security organisation in the Union (more particularly if separate from the police) might therefore lay him open to the criticism that he had assisted Boer Nationalists in implementing their extremist political programme by actively helping in the creation of a Gestapo.[113]

Just a few years after the Second World War, the word 'Gestapo' carried a particularly powerful meaning.

Despite MI5's reluctance to have anything to do with enforcing Apartheid policies in South Africa, it did continue to pass intelligence on international communism to the South Africa Police (SAP). In some instances it was unable to control the way such intelligence was used by the SAP, who exploited it to persecute their political enemies. This was clearly the case with the anti-Apartheid cleric Rev. Michael Scott. In the early 1950s MI5 passed intelligence concerning Scott's links with the CPGB to the SAP, on the strict understanding that it would remain confidential. However, the SAP swiftly broke this agreement, using the information to vilify Scott publicly and to justify his expulsion from South Africa. Thereafter, MI5's policy on sharing intelligence with the SAP was amended, restricting the flow of intelligence between the two governments. An in-house MI5 circular noted:

> It is the more necessary to realise that, once we have passed information to the South African Government, we cannot put any restriction upon its political use, nor can we expect them to agree with our interpretation of discretion.[114]

In July 1956 the newly-established Cabinet Committee on Counter-Subversion in the Colonial Territories noted that 'it was difficult to exchange information with the South African authorities about security risks, since the South African definition of a Communist was often unusually broad and the action taken unacceptably drastic'. South African intelligence officers attended the Commonwealth Security Conference held in London in 1948, and reluctantly, due to the inclusion of Asian delegates, also the next conference in 1952. However, in the course of the 1950s Britain's secret agencies became increasingly unable to influence the politicisation of 'security' operations in South Africa, with disastrous consequences, as the bloody Sharpeville massacre in March 1960 revealed to the world.

Sillitoe's fears about the establishment of a racist Gestapo in South Africa unfortunately proved justified, and in 1961 South Africa unilaterally withdrew from the Commonwealth, largely in response to fierce criticism of its white supremacist rule. At this point MI5's intelligence liaison with the South African government effectively finished, although it did by 1961 have an SLO based in Pretoria. This fact was not lost on Jomo Kenyatta, when in October 1961 he had a confidential meeting with MI5's Director-General Roger Hollis at MI5's headquarters in London, and noticed on the wall of Hollis's office a map with red pins showing the locations of MI5's SLOs across the world. Seeing that Kenyatta was growing agitated about the pin placed on Pretoria, Hollis stressed that the SLO there was only responsible for liaising with the so-called British High Commission Territories (Basutoland, Bechuanaland and Swaziland), and not with South Africa itself.[115]

After South Africa's withdrawal from the Commonwealth, Britain's intelligence liaison with the South African government passed to SIS. However, it was not apparently an abrupt shift. Remarkably, it seems that MI5 continued to perform some vetting services for the South African government well into the 1970s. Although there is little documentary evidence currently in the public domain about SIS activities in relation to South Africa, it has been convincingly suggested that it maintained an effective, covert and deniable channel of communication between Britain and the Apartheid government. The activities of the South African intelligence services, especially the foreign intelligence agency, the Bureau of State Security (BOSS), are also known to have fed Labour Prime Minister Harold Wilson's paranoid conspiracy theories in the mid-1970s regarding the activities of British intelligence and its allies. As Christopher Andrew's official history of MI5 reveals, the so-called 'Wilson plot' was little more than a fantasy of the Prime Minister, who convinced himself that intelligence services around the world were attempting to destabilise his premiership.

Wilson's fantasies reached a climax in 1975, which became known as the 'Year of Intelligence', during which CIA plots to destabilise and assassinate the communist Cuban leader, Fidel Castro, became publicly known. The Prime Minister's belief that the CIA and other intelligence services were playing 'dirty tricks' on him was one of his main preoccupations during his last two months of office in 1976. His paranoia was heightened by a bizarre scandal that engulfed the Liberal leader Jeremy Thorpe, the facts of which are so peculiar that they would be considered fantasy if they were not real. The story involved the attempted murder in 1975 of Thorpe's former lover, an ex-male model named Norman Scott. The inexperienced would-be hitman, Andrew Newton, a former airline pilot, succeeded only in killing Scott's dog, a Great Dane named Rinka – on account of which the scandal became known as 'Rinkagate'.

Early in 1976, while on trial for benefit fraud, Scott publicly claimed that he had been 'hounded' due to his sexual relationship with Thorpe. To save face, Thorpe succeeded in persuading Wilson that he was being framed by an elaborate plot devised by BOSS. Wilson's acceptance of Thorpe's excuse only proves his intense fixation on intelligence plots and paranoia, particularly as the only 'evidence' of the plot came from a South African freelance journalist and BOSS agent, Gordon Winter. Winter had previously slept with Scott, and after learning of his affair with Thorpe, he made the story of the supposed plot public. Although the British intelligence services, including MI5, quickly concluded that this was a 'private initiative' of Winter, Wilson was unconvinced. Despite the fact that it was apparent that BOSS was not the most sophisticated of intelligence operations, Wilson (and parts of the media) persisted in his view until the end of his leadership in April 1976 and beyond. Wilson's mental stability started to decline in the months before his resignation, and he even planted his own parliamentary question in order to respond on the record: 'I have no doubt that there is a strong South African participation in recent activities relating to the leader of the Liberal Party.' The source of much of the information that gave rise to Wilson's conspiracy theories about BOSS was his private and political secretary Lady Falkender, or as he called her, 'Detective Inspector Falkender'.[116]

In sharp contrast to Wilson's paranoid imaginings, several former SIS officers have stated that SIS supplied the British government with valuable intelligence in the run-up to the end of Apartheid rule, and provided a back channel of communication between the white South African government and Nelson Mandela's African National Congress (ANC). It has even been alleged that Nelson Mandela himself was an SIS agent, though the person who made this allegation, a disaffected former SIS officer named Richard Tomlinson, is far from credible, and Mandela has strenuously denied it.[117]

THE CENTRAL AFRICAN FEDERATION

British intelligence maintained no less awkward relations with the so-called Central African Federation, an illogical confederation devised by Britain that included three vastly different states north of the Limpopo River: Nyasaland (later Malawi), Northern Rhodesia (Zambia) and Southern Rhodesia (Zimbabwe). Together the Federation, stretching over 1,000 miles from near the mouth of the Zambezi River all the way up to Lake Tanganyika, bordered on seven other countries. The Colonial Office favoured the establishment of Federations wherever possible – as in Malaya, the West Indies and South Arabia – even if the states comprising them had little in common.

This was certainly the case with the Central African Federation; even a cursory examination of the populations of the three territories involved would have revealed how dissimilar they were, and how ill-suited to being lumped together. Nyasaland and Northern Rhodesia were British colonies, while for over forty years Southern Rhodesia had been a self-governing Dominion. Colonial history aside, the demographics of the three states were reason enough to keep them separate. In Southern Rhodesia there was a considerably higher proportion of white settlers (one white for every thirteen black Africans) than in Northern Rhodesia (one white for every thirty-one black Africans), while in Nyasaland the ratio was much more extreme (one white for every 328 black Africans). Put simply, white rule was much more entrenched in Southern Rhodesia, which had been ruled by a white supremacist government since 1945. This caused strong tensions with the other two states of the Federation. Nevertheless, London fought to keep the Federation alive and functional, if only because it was a symbol of Britain's commitment to multi-racialism in Africa. In private, however, some British officials acknowledged that the Federation would be 'a garden of flowers for the European settlers, and a deep grave for the natives'.[118]

As the Cold War set in, MI5 helped to maintain security in the hotch-potch Central African Federation, with varying degrees of success. In 1953 it played a guiding role in the establishment of the Federal Security Intelligence Bureau (FSIB) – its first head, Maurice 'Bob' de Quehen, had previously served as an MI5 SLO in Central Africa. The FSIB was responsible for security intelligence in the whole of the Federation, but was based in Salisbury, Southern Rhodesia, and was unsurprisingly dominated by members of the Southern Rhodesian government. The position of Bob de Quehen placed London in an awkward position. An MI5 officer was in charge of an intelligence agency of a government that was increasingly at odds with Britain itself.

The most notorious episode the FSIB had to deal with was the declaration of States of Emergency in all three of the states in the Federation in 1959, following the apparent discovery by the Nyasaland Special Branch of a 'murder plot' intended to assassinate prominent British officials. The authorities responded in as ham-fisted and ill-conceived a way as other colonial rulers reacted to similar unrest. In early March 1959 the Governor of Nyasaland, Sir Robert Armitage, declared a State of Emergency, which brought into force draconian legislation and was soon extended to the other states of the Federation.

As with the Mau Mau revolt in Kenya, events in Nyasaland confirmed the fears of those in Whitehall and the Federation who saw the machinations of Moscow behind all anti-colonial plots. When disturbances had arisen in the Federation six years earlier, in 1953, the then Governor of Nyasaland, Sir Geoffrey Colby, had requested MI5's advice on the 'dangerous anti-British organisation inspired from outside'. The local Special Branch in Nyasaland was ill-equipped to deal with assessing the nature of the threat it apparently faced. It had meagre resources at its disposal: although it had typewriters, it was so short of funds that the previous year, 1952, its senior officers had to do their own typing. However, the head of MI5's overseas section, Sir John Shaw, reassured the Colonial Office of the improbability of the 'dangerous anti-British organisation' actually being inspired from abroad, and recommended that Bob de Quehen, MI5's SLO for Central Africa, should be called in to advise. De Quehen's non-alarmist report attempted to put matters into perspective for colonial officials who tended to see sinister communist influence everywhere:

To those unaccustomed to reading political and security intelligence summaries, there is a natural tendency to feel that the security situation is gloomy. Whereas, to those who are used to this sort of thing it is probably no worse than usual. Such reports obviously highlight bad spots, and so one tends to forget that 95 per cent or so of the population are perfectly content and law abiding.[119]

The only real evidence of the existence of the murder plot came from a Nyasaland Special Branch report, dated 13 February 1959, which recounted apparently secret meetings that had taken place the month before, concerning a date, known as 'R-Day', on which leading British officials would be killed. After Armitage declared a State of Emergency in Nyasaland on 3 March 1959, the British government published a White Paper on 29 March which sought to vindicate its stance in the colony. It is now clear that behind the scenes in Whitehall, the existence of the murder plot had been regarded with scepticism by some of Britain's secret departments. The head of the newly-created Intelligence and Security Department (ISD) in the Colonial Office, Duncan Watson, responded to the report of the Nyasaland Special Branch with a large degree of caution, particularly because the information it contained about the murder plot came from second-hand informants.

However, MI5 was less sceptical. One of its Security Intelligence Advisers posted to the Colonial Office, G.R.H. Gribble, was sent to Nyasaland to oversee the evidence given for the declaration of Emergency. Gribble and MI5's SLO in Salisbury were convinced that there was indeed a murder plot, and even after the idea had been debunked by the British government's official inquiry into the disturbances in Nyasaland, the Devlin Report, MI5 remained convinced that it existed. Apparently MI5 was in possession of tape recordings of speeches given in February 1959 by two of the alleged plotters, H.B. Chipembere and Y.K. Chisiza, which left 'no doubt' about their intentions. Nothing more about these tape recordings can presently be established. Despite this 'evidence', MI5 did not, however, believe that the main anti-colonial leader in Nyasaland, Dr Hastings Banda, was directly involved in the plot, although, it noted, the disturbances suited his aims.

It is also now clear that MI5 and Duncan Watson of the ISD did not want to make intelligence on the murder plot public. Watson's objections appear to have been overruled following an intervention on 10 March by the Minister of State at the Commonwealth Relations Office, Cuthbert Alport, who warned that in order to counter allegations in the House of Commons that it had been 'cooked up', 'it was vital to procure quickly as much evidence of the "plot" as possible'. It was in this context that 'intelligence' on the plot was published in the White Paper, although the 13

February Nyasaland Special Branch report in which the details were given was not named. At this point several Conservative ministers, especially the Undersecretary of State for the Colonies, Julian Amery, 'sexed up' the idea of a murderous anti-colonial plot.[120]

Unlike in the Gold Coast and Kenya, MI5 failed to restrain the far-fetched ideas about the murder plot in Nyasaland. On 3 March 1959 Banda was arrested along with 250 other members of the main political party in the colony, the Nyasaland African Congress, as part of Operation *Sunrise* – the name was a snide attack on Banda's rhetoric about the 'dawn' of freedom coming to Nyasaland. On the same day, in a separate police operation, the leading anti-colonial figure in Northern Rhodesia, Kenneth Kaunda, was also arrested. In total the administration rounded up and detained 1,322 people suspected of being involved in the alleged plot. The Nyasaland Special Branch took Banda from his home in such a hurry that he was hustled out still wearing his pyjamas. Thereafter he was flown to Southern Rhodesia, where, judging from existing FSIB reports, his confidential conversations with his lawyer in his prison cell were bugged – an act flagrantly in violation of lawyer–client privilege. Following the arrests, the colonial administration banned all nationalist parties in the Federation.

The reality was that there never really was a murder plot. By overreacting and declaring an Emergency as they did, the British ironically actually created a situation of unrest – just as in Malaya and Kenya. Protesters gathered in Nyasaland's main cities, and in one incident, at Nkata Bay, a crowd tried to rush to a jetty to release detainees who were being transferred by boat. Soldiers opened fire, killing twenty people and wounding another twenty-five. Coincidentally, this occurred on the very same day, 3 March 1959, as the Hola Camp massacre several thousand miles away in Kenya – a fateful day for the British empire.

The worst excesses of the Nyasaland administration during the State of Emergency were exposed by the Devlin Report, published in July 1959, which flatly contradicted the previous White Paper. The report, compiled by a retired High Court judge, Mr Justice Devlin, famously concluded that Nyasaland had become a 'police state, albeit temporarily', and described a number of gross abuses committed on those arrested, including beatings. The government's reaction to the report was one of exasperation. Prime Minister Harold Macmillan noted in his diary that the report was 'dynamite', and that it might well blow his government out of office. In fact, Macmillan considered resigning over the Devlin Report, cruelly adding in his diary that Devlin was nothing more than a lapsed Catholic Irish hunchback, bitterly disappointed that he had not been made Lord Chief Justice and 'no doubt with that Fenian blood that make Irishmen anti-government on principle'.[121]

After the State of Emergency in Nyasaland was declared over in August 1960, but possibly even before then, MI5 provided Whitehall and the Federation administrations with valuable background intelligence on anti-colonial leaders, just as it had done with Nkrumah in the Gold Coast and Kenyatta in Kenya. Like Nkrumah and Kenyatta, Banda had first come to MI5's attention when he was living in England. He prac-tised as a GP in North Shields, near Newcastle upon Tyne, and at some point, probably in the immediate post-war years, MI5 opened a file on him on account of his anti-colonial politics and association with communism. After Banda's return to Nyasaland in 1958, almost unable to speak his native tongue after more than thirty years abroad, in the United States and Britain, MI5 continued to provide intelligence on him, particularly on his association with the British Communist Party. Yet, just a few years after Banda was detained in March 1959 as a leader of the non-existent murder plot, MI5 came to view him as a moderate, Westernised politician (he often dressed in a Homburg hat and a three-piece suit) with whom it was safe to work. Nevertheless, rumours about him continued to circulate within the Nyasaland administration – for example, that he wanted to poison the colony's 8,000 white settlers with forty tons of arsenic.

It seems that MI5 also provided background intelligence on Northern Rhodesia's Kenneth Kaunda, the son of a Church of Scotland minister who in 1979 would famously dance with Margaret Thatcher at a Commonwealth conference in Zambia's capital Lusaka. It was said that Kaunda's Zambian African National Congress resembled the American criminal organisation Murder, Inc., and that his goal was to establish a campaign of civil disobedience that would make Kenya's Mau Mau look like a 'child's picnic'.[122]

After the end of the State of Emergency in the Federation, MI5 was able to establish close bonds with both Banda and Kaunda as Nyasaland and Northern Rhodesia moved towards self-government and eventual inde-pendence. In November 1962, just two and a half years after the two men had been detained, MI5 and the Colonial Office were in high-level discus-sions about how and when MI5's local SLO could be identified to them. The head of the Colonial Office's ISD, Duncan Watson, noted that consti-tutional advancement in Nyasaland 'brings us to the stage where the SLO ought normally to be disclosed at least to the Prime Minister [Banda]'. The Governor of Nyasaland, Sir Glyn Jones, 'did not think that he would have any problem in introducing the SLO as such to Dr Banda'. MI5's Alex Kellar explained the procedure to be followed:

> The normal presentation of a SLO to local Ministers is on the basis of his being a link in a well-established and mutually advantageous Commonwealth Security network. Dr Banda will certainly not be opposed to any normal Commonwealth link, but he will very likely be suspicious of a link of this nature including the Federal Government and Southern Rhodesia.
>
> As you know, it is our custom to declare the role of the Security Service, and that in particular of its SLOs, when the office of the Chief Minister is first held by an indigenous politician. It is our normal practice to do this at the same time as indigenous ministers are officially informed of the Special Branch and the local intelligence community as a whole. Such was the procedure followed in the case of both Dr NYERERE [future PM of Tanganyika] and Mr OBOTE [future PM of Uganda] and you may recall that in each case I went out personally to assist the Governor in this over-all declaration.[123]

In Nyasaland and Northern Rhodesia MI5 followed this procedure, which had been established by Kellar in 1961 and 1962 when he met the leaders-in-waiting of Tanganyika and Uganda, Julius Nyere and Milton Obote. During trips he made to Nyasaland in January 1963 and Northern Rhodesia in March 1964, Kellar personally brokered deals with Banda and Kaunda for their countries to maintain liaisons with MI5 after independence. However, as MI5 had predicted, both Banda and Kaunda made it clear that they refused to accept any intelligence coming from an SLO based in the white supremacist government of Southern Rhodesia. Following a trip by MI5's Deputy Director-General, Sir Martin Furnival-Jones, to southern Africa in February 1964, MI5 therefore agreed to establish a separate SLO for the newly independent Malawi (formerly Nyasaland) and Zambia (formerly Northern Rhodesia), who would be based not in Salisbury, but instead in Lusaka, and would be responsible for liaising with Malawi and Zambia, but not Rhodesia (formerly Southern Rhodesia). According to a Colonial Office report, Kaunda 'welcomed' this arrangement. The first SLO in Lusaka was an experienced MI5 officer, Eric Leighton.[124]

As well as maintaining security intelligence links with Malawi and Zambia, MI5 was also able to exert some control over the conspiratorial views of the pugnacious Rhodesian politician Sir Roy Welensky, a former prize-fighter and an 'ox of a man', as the British Prime Minister Harold Macmillan noted. It has often been said, probably with justification, that Welensky was the driving force behind the declaration of the State of Emergency in Nyasaland in March 1959. As Prime Minister of the Federation of Rhodesia and Nyasaland from 1957 onwards, Welensky attempted to portray his government as a bulwark against communism, in the hope that Britain would turn a blind eye to its racist policies. However, Macmillan had a strong personal dislike for Welensky, and was far from prepared to turn a blind eye. Macmillan's suspicions about Welensky were so great that he permitted his room at the Savoy to be bugged when he was in London in 1963.[125]

One of the frequent and tiresome wild claims made by Welensky was that communism was a cancer growing all over the African continent, and that he and his government were the cure. However, as MI5 pointed out, the reality was quite different. MI5's Director-General, Sir Roger Hollis, personally challenged Welensky's scaremongering when the two met in September 1962. According to Hollis's report of the meeting, he put in blunt terms to Welensky what he had already reported to the JIC: that communism was not as much a threat in Africa as it first appeared. He said that although the Soviets' efforts were likely to increase as they gained experience of the continent, they were currently 'newcomers in Africa and had a lot to learn'. He acknowledged the increasing flow of African students to the Patrice Lumumba University in Moscow and other Eastern Bloc institutions, but suggested that these students were far less numerous and able than those going to British and American universities. The most remarkable aspect of Hollis's account of his meeting with Welensky, however, related to the subject of African ministers travelling to the Eastern Bloc:

Sir Roy asked me whether I did not think it significant that so many Ministers of the newly independent countries were visiting the Soviet Union. I said this seemed to be natural: the Soviet Union had shown a fantastic development from the backwardness of Russia in 1917 to the present, and obviously African countries wanted to develop very quickly. They wanted to see how this had been done. Furthermore, in colonial times Russia and communism had been forbidden fruit; it was not surprising that with independence they wanted to have a look. I said that

I thought a number of the Ministers who went to Russia were well aware that there were dangers in communism and were alert to this, and that this came from the briefing they had had from us and from their own security authorities over the years.[126]

MI5 did not maintain an SLO in Salisbury after the Central African Federation was disbanded in late 1963, largely as a result of the electoral victory of the white nationalist Rhodesian Front in Southern Rhodesia (later renamed Rhodesia), which sealed the Federation's fate. Instead, its SLO was moved to Pretoria, where he had responsibility for liaising and sharing intelligence with the British High Commission Territories, Basutoland, Bechuanaland and Swaziland. Meanwhile, the FSIB, which MI5 had helped to set up, was replaced by the Rhodesian Central Intelligence Organisation (CIO), established in 1963. Its first head, Ken Flower, attempted to maintain links with MI5, but as he noted in his memoirs, the CIO's relationship with British intelligence was never close. After the white supremacist Rhodesian government of Ian Smith unilaterally declared independence from Britain in November 1965, Rhodesia, like South Africa, dropped out of the Commonwealth. Thereafter, SIS, which is known to have had an officer stationed in Salisbury from at least 1960, became responsible for intelligence relations between Britain and the Rhodesian government. Some insiders have noted that SIS maintained unofficial links with Ian Smith's extremist government throughout the violent guerrilla war that was waged in Rhodesia in the 1970s.

Ken Flower, who stayed on to work for Smith after Rhodesia's declaration of independence, unsuccessfully attempted to open a formal liaison between the CIO, MI5 and SIS. Although little is publicly known about the covert channels it maintained with the Rhodesian government, it is clear that one of SIS's greatest failures in post-colonial Africa was its failure to recognise that the real destabilising threats in Rhodesia did not come from black nationalism, but from white extremism – 'the failures of Surbiton', as Macmillan described Smith and his followers. It seems likely that, as it had done with previous similar negotiations, MI5 bugged the Rhodesian independence talks that were held at Lancaster House in London between 1979 and 1980. In many ways it was these talks that led SIS and the rest of the British government, disastrously, to assess the highly educated and brutally clever Robert Mugabe as the best bet for Zimbabwe, which Rhodesia became after independence in 1980.[127]

* * *

British intelligence thus influenced the way the sun set on Britain's colonial empire in Africa in a number of ways, ending with both success and failure. MI5 provided the British government with top-secret diplomatic background intelligence on a number of African national leaders before and after colonies gained independence from Britain. Its intelligence assessments helped to calm fears within Whitehall about the communist beliefs of some anti-colonial leaders, such as Nkrumah and Kenyatta. MI5 also helped to reform local intelligence practices when anti-colonial insurgencies broke out and Emergencies were declared, as in Kenya and Nyasaland. However, intelligence reforms were enacted in Kenya too late, after the Mau Mau revolt had broken out, with the result that British officials in London and Nairobi had little reliable intelligence with which to work. This, more than anything else, explains much of the confusion experienced by the British, and then their subsequent overreaction and the shocking levels of violence they unleashed in the colony. This was a story repeated time and again, as Britain experienced anti-colonial insurgencies in Cyprus and Aden. It was in the Middle East that British intelligence experienced some of its greatest difficulties as Britain's influence in the region declined, but at the same time London tried to cling on to what it termed its 'vital interests' in the area.

7

British Intelligence, Covert Action and Counter-Insurgency in the Middle East

I think we should ask if there has been a failure of our intelligence in Egypt – manifestly something has gone wrong.

INTELLIGENCE AND SECURITY DEPARTMENT,
COLONIAL OFFICE (1 August 1956)[1]

I am troubled about the legal basis for the action taken by Her Majesty's Government in relation to Egypt and I am worried about the consequences for Her Majesty's Government should it become known that the Law Officers are not able to support the main legal contentions so far advanced ... It is not true to say that we are entitled under the Charter [of the UN] to take any measures open to us 'to stop the fighting'. Nor would it be true to say that under international law apart from the Charter we are entitled to do so. Further, it is not true to say that under international law we are entitled to take any measure open to us 'to protect our interests which are threatened by hostilities' ... States can intervene to protect their nationals so long as force is proportional ... It is quite a different proposition that armed intervention is justified by the need to secure a right or interest.

ATTORNEY-GENERAL REGINALD MANNINGHAM-BULLER
to Foreign Secretary Selwyn Lloyd (1 November 1956)[2]

In the post-war years, Britain maintained formal control and informal influence over a number of territories across the Middle East, from Gibraltar at the western end of the Mediterranean to Aden at the southern tip of the Arabian Peninsula, which controlled the strategically important gateway to the Arabian Sea. As the Cold War set in, but at the same time Britain's overt control of colonies in the region weakened, due to anti-colonial nationalism, the role performed by British intelligence became increasingly important for London. In order to try to maintain Britain's influence in the region, Britain's spy chiefs deployed a host of dirty tricks, some of the consequences of which can be seen down to the present day.

REGIME CHANGE: IRAN

As well as its formal colonies such as the Gold Coast and Kenya, in the post-war years Britain also maintained informal influence over other territories. Two such places were Iran and Egypt, where in the 1950s the British government attempted, with varying degrees of success, to overthrow regimes hostile to it and to install more pliant governments. It tried to do this by what was known within Whitehall as 'special political action' (SPA), a euphemism for 'covert action', as it was more commonly known in Washington and elsewhere.

Britain had occupied Iran during the Second World War, and continued to maintain a strong influence in the country thereafter, particularly through the oil industry. The enormous Anglo-Iranian Oil Company (AIOC) dominated oil production in the region, boasting one of the largest refineries in the world, at Abadan. AIOC was half-owned by the British government, and was crucial for Britain's failing balance of payments and for maintaining sterling as a world currency in the post-war years – in 1951 alone it returned £100 million in profits. It was therefore a potential disaster for Britain when, in May 1951, the new Iranian Prime Minister, Dr Mohammed Mossadeq, announced the nationalisation of AIOC. Mossadeq, a wealthy landowner, had come to power following the convenient assassination two months earlier of his rival and predecessor as Prime Minister, General Ali Razmara, who had opposed AIOC's nationalisation. As with the profitable rubber industry in Malaya, Britain was determined to keep control of AIOC and the vast revenues flowing from its pipelines into Whitehall's coffers.[3]

Iran was a constitutional monarchy, with power shared between the Shah, or king, and the Prime Minister. The Shah was responsible for appointing prime ministers, but he did not have the right to dismiss them. Although his powers were limited, the Shah was a powerful figurehead, and as the new SIS head of station in Iran, Christopher 'Monty' Woodhouse, realised, he would be key to any attempted regime change. Soon after his arrival in Iran in 1951, Woodhouse began to plot for the overthrow of Mossadeq and the return of the Shah with direct rule. Woodhouse appreciated that in order to succeed, any plot seeking to overthrow Mossadeq would have to involve Washington: though the CIA had only been established in 1947, even by 1951 the resources available to it dwarfed those of Britain's secret agencies. The problem was that it would be difficult, if not impossible, to sign up the US government to a plot to overthrow Mossadeq if it were seen as old-fashioned British imperialism. The fact that in 1951 AIOC was paying more in taxes in London than in Tehran certainly stank of an old-style colonial venture. Woodhouse therefore decided that when discussing 'special political action' in Iran with Washington, the way forward was to stress the Cold War credentials of such a plot. Although in reality Britain viewed the Iranian problem essentially as a sterling crisis and an empire question, in SIS's discussions with the CIA, Woodhouse and his colleagues in London emphasised the growing communist threat in the country.[4]

There was plenty of evidence that in 1951 communism was on the rise in Iran. The pro-communist Tudeh Party was extending its grip, and was advocating worrying things like removing pictures of Mossadeq and the Shah from public buildings. The genuine threat posed by the Tudeh Party, which SIS seized upon in its discussions with the CIA, was that Mossadeq, the Shah and the Iranian constitution could be ousted and overturned, communists installed in their place, and Iran could become a Soviet satellite state. This confirmed the CIA's own reporting on the situation, and SIS's arguments worked remarkably well in Washington: the US Secretary of State, Dean Acheson, commented that Iran was 'a bad spot', and in April 1953 Allen Dulles, the Director of Central Intelligence, made $1 million available to American agents to be used 'in any way that would bring about the fall of Mossadegh'.

Nevertheless, President Truman remained unconvinced of the benefit of covert action in Iran. The turning point occurred in January 1953, when Dwight D. 'Ike' Eisenhower took up office as President, following his election in November 1952. As the former wartime Supreme Allied Commander in Europe, Eisenhower was a thorough convert to the value of intelligence and special operations. In July 1953 he gave the green light for what the British codenamed Operation *Boot* and the Americans Operation *Ajax*: the overthrow of Mossadeq and the reinstallation of the Shah on the Peacock Throne.[5]

The planning of Operation *Boot* had begun in earnest in late 1952 in a series of meetings between leading SIS and CIA officers concerned with the Middle East. The SIS liaison officer in Washington, John Bruce Lockhart, met his opposite numbers in the CIA, particularly the Director of Operations, Frank Wisner, but it was in Cyprus that the main plans for the operation were drawn up. In early 1953 SIS's man in Iran, Woodhouse, travelled to the island where he met the SIS head of station, John Collins, and another SIS officer stationed there, Norman Darbyshire (a former MI5 officer), as well as the SIS Controller for the Middle East, George Kennedy Young (whose views on the Middle East and on Arabs can only be described as racist, and later made him an embarrassment to his service). They were joined by a leading CIA officer specialising in the Middle East, Donald Wilbur, author of the now declassified CIA history of the coup in Iran, and the CIA's head of the Near East and Africa section, the wonderfully named Kermit Roosevelt, grandson of former US President Theodore Roosevelt. The plotters also received input from General Norman Schwarzkopf, father of the future 'Desert Storm' commander, who during the war had overseen the Iranian police force and in 1952 was appointed US military liaison officer in Tehran. According to the CIA history of the coup, its aim was remarkably simple: to 'bring to power a government which would reach an equitable oil settlement'. The plot, put simply, was to gather mass support for the Shah within Iran through street demonstrations and other public protests, and then to depose Mossadeq and install the Shah along with a pliant Prime Minister.[6]

In the spring of 1953 SIS maintained contact with its main assets in Iran through wireless communications three times a week – though the CIA was forced to concede that as it had supplied the Iranian military with wireless direction-finding equipment, its communications were probably being traced. Actual liaison with the Shah, Mohammed Reza Pahlavi, a timid and suspicious figure who was unconvinced that the British and Americans would really support him, was conducted through his twin sister, Princess Ashraf (codenamed 'Boy Scout'). To help with logistics for subversive activities on the ground, SIS brought in one of the world's leading experts on Iran, Robert Zaehner, an Oxford scholar who had worked for SIS in Iran during the war. Though initially doubtful about the plot, Zaehner travelled back to Tehran and set to work. SIS's main agents there, cultivated through Zaehner, were the Rashidian brothers, two of Iran's most loyal royalists, who along with Zaehner had countered German influence in Iran during the war. SIS and the CIA decided that they would be the main point of contact in Iran, responsible for distributing funds to rent-a-crowd mobs on the streets, and organising popular demonstrations against communists.[7]

The plot to oust Mossadeq went from planning to the operational stage in July 1953 when, after President Eisenhower gave the official go-ahead,

Kermit Roosevelt made an epic drive across the desert from Damascus in Syria to Tehran carrying $100,000 in small-denomination Iranian bank-notes. The CIA money was used to fund a host of covert activities, including a series of bombs that were set off in the capital and blamed on the pro-communist Tudeh Party, as well as anti-Mossadeq cartoons planted in local newspapers. To help convince the Shah that Eisenhower and Churchill supported him, and that they meant business, he was told to listen for specific phrases that would be used on the BBC Persian Channel.[8]

The CIA-SIS plot, however, did not get off to a good start. Unfortunately for the plotters, the Tudeh Party actually came out in support of the Shah, who in August was forced to flee for safety in Baghdad and then to Rome. But the tide soon began to turn. There were increasing levels of violence on the streets of Tehran, as pro-communist gangs pitted themselves against pro-Shah groups. The British- and American-backed demonstrations got out of control, with over three hundred people killed, but they served their immediate purpose: on 22 August 1953 the Shah made a triumphant return from his exile in Rome. Using 'popular' dissent and the results of a (doubtless rigged) referendum as a pretext, the Shah dismissed Mossadeq and appointed Fazlollah Zahedi, a retired General in the Iranian army and Mossadeq's former Interior Minister, as Prime Minister. Mossadeq was placed under house arrest in Ahmadabad, where he lived out the rest of his days. The CIA immediately funnelled $5 million to the Shah to help him consolidate his rule. The Shah told Kermit Roosevelt: 'I owe my throne to God, my people, my army and to you!'[9]

Roosevelt left Iran at the end of August, and arrived to a hero's welcome at SIS headquarters (the Broadway Buildings) in London. As the now-declassified CIA history of the coup makes clear, SIS was grateful not only for Roosevelt's involvement in the plot, but also for the enhanced standing it gave SIS with the CIA and in the rest of Whitehall. This was, after all, a time when SIS's reputation on both sides of the Atlantic was at an all-time low, following the exposure of Kim Philby and the other Cambridge spies. The CIA history of the coup noted that when Roosevelt visited SIS headquarters, many of the old colonial policemen who had previously staffed it no longer appeared to be there – though this was perhaps a deliberate attempt on the part of SIS, often dismissed as an 'old boys' club', to appear more modern than it really was.

Roosevelt was given a personal meeting with an ailing Churchill, who conducted it in his typically eccentric style, from his bed. Churchill told Roosevelt that if he had been younger he would have liked nothing more than to have accompanied him on this mission. Although Churchill did not know what the initials 'CIA' stood for, he believed it had something to do with its forerunner, the wartime US Office of Strategic Studies (OSS), run by a legendary figure in US intelligence history, 'Wild Bill' Stephenson. It would not take much imagination to see this encounter between Churchill, hunched in bed, talking in flattering tones to a resourceful young American, as personifying the trajectory of their two countries in the post-war world. Perhaps more than any other single episode, the coup in Iran demonstrated the eclipse of Britain's intelligence resources compared to those of the United States. At the end of the war in 1945 Britain's secret agencies were the undisputed leaders in the intelligence world, with many American intelligence officials regarding their British counterparts with something approaching reverence. However, just eight years later, the students had become the masters: as the CIA history noted, SIS was prepared to act as the 'junior partner' in the coup, and looked to the CIA with a 'degree of envy'.[10]

For the plotters, the overthrow of Mossadeq appeared at the time to be an unambiguous success: it achieved its aim, preventing a communist takeover in Iran. With hindsight, nearly sixty years later, we can see that it was in fact a disaster. As the Shah told SIS's George Kennedy Young when they met for the first time in 1955, he had tried democracy, 'but ended up on the run in Rome, with a few thousand lire and a republic declared in Tehran', and from then on, he decided, he was going to 'rule myself'. The Shah was true to his word. He grew increasingly intolerant of dissent and used his new security service (SAVAK), to stamp out opposition – the first chief of SAVAK was alleged to use a wild bear during his interrogation of victims. The Shah's dictatorial rule ultimately led to his overthrow by the Islamic Revolution of 1979.

The sad reality was that Mossadeq was never really a communist, nor were there ever any significant connections between him and the Tudeh Party. Behind all of the machinations of the 1953 coup was not so much a genuine fear about the rise of communism, but a desire to secure Iranian oil supplies. Even in this, the British government was not as successful as it initially hoped. After the Shah's return from exile, Britain secured only 40 per cent of the share of the oil it had previously held under AIOC, with the rest being taken by US oil companies. AIOC was disbanded and refor-mulated into a new company, British Petroleum. To this day, BP, which was effectively born from SIS's subversive activities in Iran, continues to main-tain a close relationship with SIS, often being used as cover for its officers posted overseas. The connections between Iran, oil and Anglo-American intelligence ran deeper still. Kermit Roosevelt continued to work for the CIA until 1958, when he found employment in Gulf Oil, serving for six years as its Director of Government Affairs.[11]

We can now see the coup in Iran as an early example of what the British and American governments would repeatedly encounter over subsequent decades when they launched special operations in various parts of the developing world: blowback. That is, their schemes often produced short-term successes, but in the longer term they invariably had – and continue to have – harmful, counter-productive consequences. Even more counter-productive than Britain's efforts to launch covert action alongside the USA was its attempt to do so on its own, without Washington's support, as it disastrously did during the Suez crisis in 1956.

INTELLIGENCE FAILURE: THE SUEZ CRISIS

At the same time that Britain was preparing for the transfer of power in its colonies in West Africa, and following the apparent success of special operations in the 1953 coup in Iran, the new Conservative government of Anthony Eden, who replaced a bedridden Churchill in April 1955, embarked on one of the most disastrous overseas interventions that any British government would undertake in the whole of the twentieth century: the Suez invasion of October 1956. The Suez crisis was one of the worst British foreign-policy decisions of modern times, eclipsed perhaps only by the Munich Agreement of 1938. In fact, it was remarkably similar to the Blair government's use, and apparent abuse, of intelligence before the invasion of Iraq in 2003. We can now see that, as with the recent invasion of Iraq, the Suez crisis was a catastrophic intelligence failure. A small coterie within the British government, centred on the Prime Minister, sexed up the intelligence brief they were given beyond all recognition in pursuit of an obsession to overthrow an unwanted Middle Eastern dictator. Like those other two notorious events, 'Suez' has rightly become a byword for controversy and failure. The consequences of the debacle were widespread and profound: it caused the most serious rift between Britain and the United States of the post-war years, and it also painfully revealed the extent to which Britain was no longer a great imperial power. The Suez crisis broke Britain's imperial grip and the French cultural hold over the Middle East, and at the same time led to the massive redeployment of British troops away from Egypt, with consequences for self-government in the British territories of Cyprus and Malta. Suez also had the effect of making Britain public enemy number one at the United Nations. In 1960 the UN passed a key Resolution, number 1514 (XV), which demanded a 'speedy and unconditional end to colonialism'. Despite the best spin that Colonial Office mandarins in Whitehall could offer, Resolution 1514 (XV) effectively made Britain's colonial empire a repugnant anachronism in the modern world.[12]

Anthony Eden was, as the historian and political commentator Peter Hennessy has noted, one of the most tragic figures to hold the office of Prime Minister in the post-war years. Behind his dapper exterior, Eden was a weak, paranoid, sickly and vain figure who always wanted things his own way. Throughout the Suez crisis he was in intense pain, suffering from a botched bile-duct operation, for which he was heavily medicated on a cocktail of drugs, including powerful 'uppers' and 'downers', benzedrine and pethidine. This is important because it may explain some of the bizarre decisions regarding intelligence that Eden took during the crisis. At its height, some of his close cabinet advisers reported to their wives that Eden had 'gone mad' or 'potty'. He chaired one cabinet meeting, at the height of the conflict, with a temperature of 105 degrees. Eden's mindset throughout the crisis was also, it seems, coloured by painful memories of the British government's appeasement of fascism in Europe before 1939. For Eden, the Egyptian President, Colonel Gamal Abdel Nasser, was a latterday Hitler or Mussolini (albeit wearing a fez), and needed to be shown a kind of toughness that had been missing from Britain's dealings with fascist leaders in the 1930s. Again, this mindset probably explains some of the bizarre decisions Eden took during the crisis.

Eden's nemesis, Nasser, the son of a former post office worker, had come to power in a military coup in 1952, becoming Prime Minister of Egypt in 1954 and President in 1956. Nasser, the first ethnic Egyptian to rule the nation in over 2,000 years, was the figurehead of an extraordinary nationalist platform in Egypt, the largest country in the Middle East. One of his great aims, which was designed to demonstrate both his own prowess and that of Egypt as a nation, was to construct a dam on the River Nile at Aswan. However, to do so he desperately needed money. An obvious source for this was the Suez Canal, which had been under effective British control since Britain's military occupation of Egypt in 1882.[13]

Although Egypt had been granted formal independence from Britain through a treaty negotiated in 1935, the British government retained control over the Suez Canal Zone, holding about 44 per cent of the shares in the Suez Canal Company. In the post-war years, however, Britain's treaty with Egypt over the canal was strained by a sharp spike in Egyptian nationalism, led by the radical Muslim Brotherhood, whose principal aim was to force the British out of Egypt. To make matters worse for Britain, the 1935 treaty was due to expire in 1956.

London was desperate to retain control of the canal, the strategic importance of which for Commonwealth security in the 1950s is hard to overstate. At the time, the Canal Zone, comprising 750 square miles carved out of the desert between Suez and the Nile, was home to a massive British military industrial complex, with 80,000 British troops stationed there, and was equipped with ports, seaplane docks, ten airfields, a railway system and a road network. The canal played a vital role in British imperial security and Commonwealth defence: it was the geopolitical pivot for power in the Middle East, a gateway between the Middle East and Far East, a shield against Soviet intrusion and the safeguard of Britain's supply of oil, most of which passed through it. By 1956 one-third of all ships using the canal were British.

In 1954 an agreement was reached between Nasser and the British government that British troops would be gradually withdrawn from the Canal Zone over the next seven years, but Britain would retain essential access rights. However, this agreement was shattered on 26 July 1956, when Nasser, who by this time was President of Egypt, used the US government's decision to stop financing his treasured Aswan Dam Project as a pretext to do what he had almost certainly been meaning to do for a long time: he announced the nationalisation – strictly the de-internationalisation – of the Suez Canal.

The announcement caused consternation in London. Eden became obsessed with overthrowing Nasser, and tasked SIS to instigate a coup to depose or even assassinate him. For the new Chief of SIS, Sir Dick White, formerly a Director-General of MI5, the crisis was a baptism of fire. Britain's Minister of State for Foreign Affairs, Sir Anthony Nutting, revealed in an interview in 1985 that after the nationalisation of the canal Eden rang him up, over an open telephone line, and told him unambiguously that he wanted Nasser 'destroyed' or 'murdered'. Following the success of covert action in Iran, some SIS officers, led by the Deputy Chief of SIS and Controller for the Middle East, George Kennedy Young, apparently devised elaborate ways of carrying this out. SIS's section responsible for creating gadgets for the field, Q-Ops section, led by Major Francis Quinn (hence 'Quinn-Ops'), attempted to inject poison into some popular Egyptian chocolates, which it was hoped could be given to Nasser, but this proved too difficult a task. The renegade MI5 officer Peter Wright recalled that, next, two officers from the SIS's 'Technical Services' asked him about ways to eliminate the Egyptian President. On Wright's advice they all went to Porton Down, the British government's chemical and biological weapons establishment, where they came up with a plot to introduce nerve gas into the ventilation system of Nasser's headquarters in Cairo. However, this plan was shelved when it was concluded that too many innocent people would be killed in the process. Refusing to accept failure, the team then set about devising other assassination methods, some of which involved weapons that could be straight from the pages of a James Bond novel. One of their ideas was a deadly cigarette packet modified by the Research and Development Establishment at Porton Down to fire a dart tipped with poison. Whether the SIS team were aware of it or not, these types of 'toys' were similar to those feared to be used by the Nazi intelligence services at the end of the war, as we have seen in Chapter 3, and the equipment found in the hands of KGB assassin Nikolai Khokholov a few years earlier. They were also similar to the exploding cigar that the CIA developed in the early 1960s in a plot to assassinate the Cuban leader, Fidel Castro. It is possible that Wright's account was embellished, but it is still not beyond the bounds of credibility that in some quarter of Britain's secret state officers were devising these types of assassination methods to be used against Nasser.[14]

Dick White told his biographer that it fell to him, as the new Chief of SIS, to put the brake on these increasingly unrealistic plots to kill Nasser. White told Eden that even if SIS devised some ingenious mechanism to assassinate Nasser, and even if it judged it profitable to carry out the act, which it did not, it did not have an agent in Cairo with close enough access to the President to do so. In the end, all these plots came to nothing, because in the summer of 1956 Eden devised an even more elaborate and ill-fated plan to oust Nasser.[15]

It is unclear who first used the term 'collusion' in relation to Suez, but we know that the essential components for the 'collusion' plot hatched between the British, French and Israeli governments were finalised at a now-notorious meeting that took place at Sèvres, near Paris, on 24 October 1956. The meeting was so secret that, according to the French description of it, the British representative, Foreign Secretary Selwyn Lloyd, arrived wearing a false moustache. After the Suez crisis the British government denied that the meeting ever took place, but unfortunately for the British, the Israelis did not destroy one of their copies of the agreement reached at the meeting, which was duly released to Israeli archives. The so-called 'Sèvres Protocol' stated that the British, French and Israeli governments would collude together to overthrow Nasser. The plan was that Israel would launch an attack on Egypt across the Sinai desert, which would then give Britain and France a pretext to intervene militarily. Following a black pantomime of sorts at the United Nations, the three governments would install a pliant new leader in Egypt, and thereby secure Western strategic interests in the region, particularly Egypt's oil supplies.[16]

This would have been an ambitious deception campaign even at the best of times. The number of people in Britain who knew of the plot was restricted to a handful of Eden's closest advisers in the cabinet's so-called 'Egypt Committee'. When Selwyn Lloyd eventually briefed Dick White, who had been deliberately excluded from the collusion plot, the SIS chief is reported to have remarked, 'That's a pretty tall order.' Eden did not just deceive members of his own government, but he also excluded Britain's closest ally, the United States, from the plot – an act of deception that has no parallel in the history of the 'special relationship'. The main reason the USA was excluded was that Allen Dulles, the Director of Central Intelligence, was much more sympathetic to Nasser than was Eden's government. Dulles felt that, for all his faults, Nasser was the safest bet for US interests in Egypt and the wider Middle East. Ever since Nasser had come to power in Egypt following the overthrow of King Farouk in 1952, successive CIA heads of station in Cairo, first James Eichelberger and then Miles Copeland, had maintained covert channels of communication between Washington and Nasser. In fact, the ubiquitous CIA operative Kermit Roosevelt had provided the Free Officers Movement, which had led the coup against King Farouk, with $3 million, some of which Nasser later used to build the Cairo Tower, a large granite landmark he called 'Roosevelt's erection'. It is little wonder that, given American funding for him, the Egyptian ruler referred in private to the Americans and the British respectively as 'the coming and the going' (*el gayin wa el rayin*).[17]

As an ultimate sign of hubris, the British-French-Israeli conspirators hoped that, although Washington had been excluded from the collusion plot, Nasser's engagement with communist states like Czechoslovakia meant that it would be willing to provide financial assistance with reconstruction after the military intervention was complete. The overall aims of the plot devised at Sèvres were to retake the Suez Canal, topple Nasser, and construct a new regime in Egypt that would safeguard British oil, shipping and other interests in the region, as well as prevent Soviet penetration of the Middle East. The plan failed on almost all counts. In little more than three months, the British government alienated most of the Arab world, as well as the US government, much of the Commonwealth and the United Nations. Eden managed not to topple Nasser, but to topple himself.

In accordance with the collusion plan, Israel embarked on military operations in Egypt on 29 October (Operation *Kadesh*), which were duly followed on 31 October by Britain's supposed 'peacekeeping' intervention (Operation *Musketeer*). British troops, ships and aircraft were deployed from Malta and Cyprus, but the RAF and Royal Navy were so under-equipped that merchant ships and commercial aircraft had to be chartered, while RAF bases in Cyprus were so congested and ill-prepared that British and French planes could barely take off. A JIC report warned the Chiefs of Staff in London before the outbreak of hostilities that so little preparation had been made for secure communications that messages between British ships were often being passed *en clair*. One Royal Navy ship nearly entered into a skirmish with a US frigate off the Egyptian coast. During the airborne assault on Port Said in the Canal Zone, involving the world's first assault from helicopters, only one battalion (about five hundred men) was successfully dropped on target. Despite these setbacks, on 5 November British and French paratroopers and commandos successfully took Port Said.

In the wider world, pandemonium ensued. There was condemnation of Britain's actions by the USA and Commonwealth governments, and at a special emergency session called by the UN General Assembly. The Canadian Foreign Minister, Lester Pearson, later lamented that Suez brought the Commonwealth to 'the verge of dissolution', and described his response to the Suez plot as 'tearful … like finding a beloved uncle arrested for rape'. For most Commonwealth countries, even the ever-faithful New Zealand, Britain's intervention in Egypt stank of a kind of old-fashioned colonialism, anathema to the modern world. US President Dwight D. Eisenhower was so incensed that he threatened to sell part of the American government's holdings in sterling. The result would have been a sharp devaluation of the pound, the economic consequences of which would have been disastrous for Britain, warned the Chancellor of the Exchequer, Harold Macmillan. Eisenhower's fury did not arise because Britain wanted to intervene in Egypt, but rather because of the manner in which Eden chose to do so. It does not seem likely that Ike would have been alarmed by *covert* British action in Egypt – after all, he had a long history of involvement in CIA-sponsored covert activities, including the coup in Iran in 1953, and a similar intervention in Guatemala in 1954. Covert action would have given the USA plausible deniability, but overt military action was politically impossible for him to support, given Washington's anti-colonial stance. On 4 November Ike telephoned Eden and simply asked him, 'What the hell is going on?' The huge pressure imposed by the US government forced Eden to seek a ceasefire, which was duly enacted at midnight on 6 November. The British government was left alienated and humiliated, its international reputation in tatters.[18]

All of this raises an obvious and fundamental question, which has not been fully answered by historians: what intelligence was Eden provided with during the Suez crisis? Unfortunately we do not have Eden's personal copies of JIC papers, which he presumably annotated, as he did with many of his cabinet papers during the crisis. Furthermore, at a key cabinet meeting on Suez in early October, Eden ordered that no notes or minutes should be taken. Although we do not have Eden's own JIC papers, we do have the JIC papers that were passed to him and to select members of the cabinet Egypt Committee, the Chiefs of Staff and other high-ranking members of the military, the civil service and the diplomatic corps in the summer and autumn of 1956. It is clear from reading these that the JIC was not responsible for feeding Eden's demons about Nasser. The CIA liaison officer who sat on the JIC in London, Chester Cooper, recalled in his memoirs that JIC officials were not above joking that Nasser was a 'Mussolini' or a 'petty Hitler'. However, none of this nonsense – Nasser's intellectual inspiration was not *Mein Kampf* but the writings of Ahmed Hussein, theorist of 'Young Egypt' – fed into JIC papers themselves, which provided a sober and no-nonsense assessment of Nasser and his intentions. Soon after Nasser's nationalisation of the canal, the JIC issued one of its most important papers in the entire post-war period. Prepared on 3 August 1956 and circulated on 10 August, it described Nasser as follows:

> As a demagogue he is liable to be carried away by the violence of passions which he himself has whipped up. As a dictator, his actions over the past three years show subtlety and calculation and have so far all resulted in gain to Egypt. We should be prepared for any action that may enhance his prestige and maintain him in power.

It then issued a warning that could not have been clearer:

We do not believe that threats of armed intervention or preliminary build up of forces would bring about the downfall of the Nasser regime or cause it to cancel the nationalisation of the canal.

In fact, the JIC warned that military intervention in Egypt could be counter-productive:

Should Western military action be insufficient to ensure early and decisive victory, the international consequences both in the Arab states and elsewhere might give rise to extreme embarrassment and cannot be forecast.[19]

It is clear from this key paper, and from the subsequent papers the JIC issued during the crisis, that it was unaware of the collusion plans formulated with the French and the Israelis. A degree of suspicion has arisen over the JIC's role in the crisis because its chairman at the time, Sir Patrick Dean, a career Foreign Office official and previous British representative at the United Nations, is known to have been present at the notorious Sèvres meeting. No documentary evidence is available about his contribution to the meeting, and he refused ever to discuss it publicly. However, we know that after the meeting he told his friend, the CIA liaison officer Chester Cooper, that he felt certain Britain was in for trouble. Although its chairman knew of the collusion plans hatched at Sèvres, this did not influence the JIC's clear warnings to Eden's government before the outbreak of hostilities. The JIC performed its primary duty during the crisis: it conveyed unwelcome news to its customers.[20]

The problem was that these reports were apparently not heeded by Eden, who instead seems to have set about cherry-picking the intelligence that suited his aims. Some dubious intelligence on Nasser was definitely provided to Eden by SIS, which had a source codenamed 'Lucky Break'. In March 1956 Eden despatched a secret telegram to Eisenhower stating that, based on intelligence, almost certainly provided by Lucky Break, the British government believed that Nasser was attempting to establish hegemony in the Middle East. One of the main revelations provided by Lucky Break, which was music to Eden's ears, was the close relationship Nasser was establishing with Soviet Bloc countries, especially Czechoslovakia.

However, there was a major flaw with the single-source intelligence provided by Lucky Break. SIS's agent was not in fact a member of Nasser's government, as Eden led others to believe, but a member of the Czech intelligence service. His understanding of Nasser's intentions was therefore peripheral, at best. Nevertheless, his warnings about Nasser's association with communist countries were not without foundation. Before the crisis, Nasser had refused to join the British-sponsored Baghdad Pact, designed to provide a buttress against Soviet intrusion in the Middle East. At the same time, there were alarming indications of growing Soviet aggression. During the visit of the Soviet Premier Nikita Khrushchev to London in April 1956, an SIS frogman named Lionel 'Buster' Crabb was killed – decapitated – in suspicious circumstances while attempting to install a listening device on the Soviet ship in Portsmouth that had brought Khrushchev to England. The affair caused a meltdown within SIS, as the story hit the headlines and led to the resignation of SIS's Chief, Sir John Sinclair, and his replacement by Dick White. Then, in October 1956, just as the Suez crisis was unfolding, Soviet tanks rolled into Hungary, revealing to the world that despite Stalin's death in 1953, Moscow was still intent on imposing its will across Eastern Europe.

However, while circumstantial evidence is one matter, deliberately distorting facts to fit an argument is quite another. It is unclear whether SIS erroneously let Eden believe that Lucky Break was close to Nasser, or whether he himself deliberately distorted the picture in his own mind, but the result was the same: there was a flagrant abuse of intelligence during Suez. Indeed, Eisenhower was quick to point out to Eden that the portrait he was painting of Nasser was inaccurate: 'You are making Nasser a much more important figure than he is ... a picture too dark and severely distorted.'[21]

MI5 also played a role in the Suez crisis, but at present few records on the matter are available. The head of MI5's outfit in the Middle East, SIME, David Stewart, is known to have issued strong warnings about the possible outcomes of military intervention, but beyond this little can be established about MI5's role.[22]

One of the most bizarre twists in this entire sad story relates to SIGINT. After the crisis, Selwyn Lloyd – not unfairly described as the monkey to Eden's organ-grinder – wrote to GCHQ to congratulate it on the 'volume' and 'excellence' of the Middle East decrypts it had provided, and stated how valuable they had been. However, among the Egypt Committee's papers is a copy of a warning sent to the French government, annotated in Eden's own hand, stating that some of the French codes were insecure. The inference that must be drawn from this is that GCHQ was successfully intercepting and reading French traffic, which presumably means that US

and Soviet code-breakers were also doing so. In fact, as recently declassified US intelligence records reveal, the CIA had discovered the existence
of negotiations between Britain, France and Israel, but not what was being
discussed. In September and October 1956 the US SIGINT agency, the
NSA, reported a vast build-up of traffic between France and Israel. Several
American intelligence officers had actually already figured out the collusion plot. The American military attaché in Tel Aviv realised something
was up when his civilian driver, a reservist in the Israeli army who had one
leg and was blind in one eye, was suddenly recalled to duty. He deduced,
quite correctly, that this could only mean one thing: imminent war.
Despite Eden's acknowledgement that French codes had been broken, and
that therefore the deception game was up, the Prime Minister nevertheless
persisted with the charade arranged at Sèvres. His persistence with this
ploy is utterly inexplicable. One former Chairman of the JIC, Sir Percy
Cradock, is surely correct to describe the Suez affair as a low point in the
history of responsible government.[23]

Apart from the JIC intelligence assessments that reached his desk, Eden
also ignored clear warnings from the government's law officers that there
was no legal justification for intervention in Egypt. One of the most poign-
ant legal warnings came from the Attorney-General, Reginald
Manningham-Buller ('Bullying Manner', as Churchill called him), father of
the future Director-General of MI5, Eliza Manningham-Buller, who wrote
to Lloyd on 1 November stating that there was no basis in international law
for attacking a sovereign nation in order merely to secure 'rights' or 'interests', as Britain was attempting to do. Manningham-Buller and the Foreign
Office's own legal adviser, Sir Gerald Fitzmaurice, concluded that there was
an 'absence of any legal justification for our present actions in Egypt'. Again,
the parallels with the invasion of Iraq in 2003 are striking.[24]

In the immediate aftermath of the fiasco, Anthony Eden played his
most bizarre hand of all: in December 1956, apparently suffering from a
complete mental and physical breakdown, he took himself off to the West
Indies, finding refuge in Ian Fleming's villa in Jamaica, 'Goldeneye'. Even
his closest advisers were shocked by his behaviour. Eden's personal secretary, Evelyn Shuckburgh, later noted in his diary:

> Meanwhile A.E. had broken down and gone to Jamaica. This is the most
> extraordinary feature of the whole thing. Is he on his way out, has he had
> a nervous breakdown, is he mad? The captain leaves the sinking ship
> which he had steered personally on to the rocks.[25]

Eden was indeed on his way out: Suez cost him his premiership. He formally resigned when he returned from Jamaica in January 1957, and was replaced as Prime Minister by Harold Macmillan. Under Macmillan, Britain soon repaired its relationship with the USA; and the process of Britain's withdrawal from empire rapidly accelerated. Two-thirds of Britain's possessions in Africa gained independence under Macmillan (it had fifteen territories in Africa in 1957 but only four by 1964).

The fallout from the Suez affair did not only affect the political arena: it also had a direct impact on the British intelligence establishment, and led to a massive reorientation and overhaul of the way intelligence was conducted in Whitehall. In the aftermath of the debacle, the JIC was taken away from the Chiefs of Staff and placed in an entirely new committee of the Cabinet Office, where it remains to this day. From 1957 the JIC therefore had a different set of customers – cabinet ministers, who for the first time could set requirements for it and task it for reports and assessments. If more ministers had been given access to JIC reports, it was assumed, undoubtedly correctly, the Suez fiasco would never have been able to gain such momentum.

Suez also led the government to reassess Britain's position in the world. One of Macmillan's first actions after taking office in January 1957 was to ask for an audit of empire, 'something akin to a profit and loss' account. It is surprising that it took Britain so long to carry out an analysis of this kind – 1857 would perhaps have been a more appropriate year in which to do so, not 1957. The conclusion of this 'balance sheet of empire', chaired by the skilful Cabinet Secretary, Sir Norman Brook, was that the economic costs and benefits of the empire were evenly matched: economic damage could be done to Britain by the premature grant of independence to a colony, but equally dangerous would be its delay for 'selfish reasons'. The most important point, argued the report, was that independence should be negotiated in the spirit of goodwill.

Macmillan's review of Britain's position in the world came to a sober realisation: Britain's future did not lie with conventional military power, or 'hard' power, which had been proved so desperately lacking during Suez, nor even with economic power; instead, it lay with power by proxy, or 'soft' power, which meant power by persuasion rather than coercion. Equally important as Brook's 'profit and loss' study, in 1957 the Minister of Defence, Duncan Sandys, conducted a crucial review of Britain's defence policy, published in a so-called White Paper, which fundamentally changed Britain's defence strategy in the post-war world. The reason for

the White Paper was that in the early 1950s Britain's armed forces, strug-
gling with commitments in three colonial Emergencies (Malaya, Kenya
and Cyprus), plus the war in Korea and the Suez debacle, had shown
themselves unable to cope. The advent of the H-bomb also, it seemed,
rendered conventional military forces obsolete. From 1957, as a result of
Sandys' review, Whitehall's defence policy was geared less towards a large
standing army – compulsory National Service had been introduced a
decade earlier, in 1947 – and more towards nuclear deterrent and highly
mobile, specialised military forces. This is the broad strategy that marks
Britain's defence policy to the present day. Beginning with Templer's
review of colonial security, and confirmed by Sandys' review of British
defence policy, there would also be a greater emphasis on recruiting local
soldiers to fight colonial Emergencies, rather than Britain's metropolitan
army being deployed. British troops were to be summoned to colonial
crisis zones as a last, not a first, resort.[26]

One of the ways in which Whitehall officials concluded that Britain
could continue to assert influence on the world stage was through the 'soft'
power of intelligence, which thereafter became a surrogate for Britain's
fading military and economic 'hard' power. The intelligence provided by
Britain's secret services allowed London to punch far above its weight in
the years after 1957, for the rest of the Cold War.[27]

CYPRUS

The small Mediterranean island of Cyprus was a colony fraught with
geographical and political contradictions. Straddling East and West, it was
a beautiful conflict zone, a tourist's idyll. Located on a key Mediterranean
shipping route, for centuries it has been a trading post for luxuries such as
gold, silver, ivory and silk. It is no wonder, then, that Cyprus has been
subjected to millennia of conflict, seeing fighting among its Byzantine
monasteries, the rugged Troodos mountains and the narrow limestone
ridge of Kyrenia. From the Assyrian Empire to the Ottoman Turks, Cyprus
was ruled by a succession of foreign powers. It was ceded to the British in
1878.

Given the colony's strategic position as the gateway to Suez, Britain
wanted to keep it squarely under its control. In the early 1950s SIS's
regional headquarters was moved from the Canal Zone in Egypt to
Nicosia, Cyprus's capital, and in July 1954 Britain's main military headquarters in the region, British Middle East Command, was moved from

Egypt to Episkopi on Cyprus. After a series of evacuations in the post-war period that saw Britain lose bases in the Middle East – in Palestine, Iraq and most notoriously the Canal Zone in Egypt after the Suez debacle in 1956 – Cyprus became a key strategic staging post, home to a Very Heavy Bomber base and a prime location for both American and British atomic weapons. It was also the base for covert British and American 'black' propaganda broadcasting, particularly during Eden's premiership. Throughout the Suez crisis the 'Voice of Britain' was broadcast from the SIS station in Cyprus, Sharq el Adna, apparently with the assistance of Britain's top-secret propaganda outfit, the IRD. With a transmitter that could reach thousands of supposedly impressionable listeners as far away as Lebanon, Syria, Jordan and even parts of Saudi Arabia, Sharq el Adna provided an alternative to Radio Cairo.[28]

Cyprus was also an obvious location for Anglo-American SIGINT operations, especially in the pre-satellite era when it was necessary to have listening posts within physical range of the Soviet Union. Cyprus was 1,000 miles closer to the USSR than US and British bases in Libya, and in the early 1950s US Air Force SIGINT units in Cyprus could reach deep inside southern Russia, the heart of the missile and aircraft testing area. Soviet tests produced radio waves that bounced off the upper atmosphere, and could be captured by receivers in Cyprus. Neither London nor Washington was prepared to lose Cyprus as a base for SIGINT collection.[29]

However, as in many other imperial trouble spots in the post-war years, a growing number of Cyprus's inhabitants grew weary of British rule, and looked to form a union, or *enosis*, with their spiritual counterpart, Greece. Eighty per cent of the island's population were ethnic Greeks; the remaining 20 per cent were ethnic Turks, and were vehemently opposed to *enosis*. Ethnic tensions were already rife even before tax increases in the 1930s which furthered a sense of discontent with British rule. In 1931 the centre of British government in Cyprus, Government House in Nicosia, was burnt down in Greek Cypriot riots, and by 1950 around 96 per cent of the adult Greek Cypriot population were pro-*enosis*. After talks in the early 1950s between Britain, Greece and Turkey proved fruitless, Nicosia erupted in violence, with protests engulfing Metaxas Square and the British Institute going up in flames. By 1953, if not earlier, Athens was covertly providing dissident Greeks in Cyprus with arms. Supplied with these weapons, in the mid-1950s a violent insurgency against British rule began, led by a small group of nationalist guerrilla fighters known by the Greek acronym EOKA (National Organisation of Cypriot Fighters). With the slogan 'Death to traitors', EOKA targeted anyone who resisted union with Greece – namely the British government, its representatives, and the island's Turkish population.[30]

EOKA launched a series of bombings and assassinations on British targets. It placed bombs under diplomatic and military vehicles, sent letter bombs, blew up aircraft, shot off-duty personnel while they were bathing, murdered picnicking civilians and mined drinking fountains used by British soldiers after their customary Sunday-afternoon football matches. Between April 1955 and November 1956 there were 638 major explosions in Cyprus, and 517 minor ones. Over the same period EOKA killed seventy-one British personnel.[31]

The leading advocate of *enosis* was Archbishop Michail Christodoriou Makarios III, head of the Greek Orthodox Church on the island. A charismatic and inspiring figure, with a black beard, stovepipe hat and long robes, he was one of the few (if not the only) episcopal guerrillas ever to become a national leader. By contrast, the logistical head of EOKA was the ruthless Georgios Grivas, who went by the *nom de guerre* 'Dighenis', a mythological Byzantine hero. Grivas was a former general in the Greek army, a near-fascist who had gained notoriety for massacring communists in the Second World War and was inspired by the IRA and the Irgun. He instilled fierce discipline among his EOKA fighters, establishing 'execution groups' to carry out horrific reprisals against traitors. Grivas landed secretly in Cyprus from Greece on 10 November 1954, and began to organise small groups of EOKA fighters in Nicosia and neighbouring villages. His mission was, in his own words, 'a crusade for a greater Greece'. He soon found himself with a £500 British bounty on his head.[32]

Behind the campaign of bombings and assassinations led by Grivas, and supported by Makarios, lay a lamentable intelligence failure on the part of the British. Cyprus fits squarely into a pattern that we have seen in the post-war years: despite MI5's protests, the colonial administration devoted insufficient resources to intelligence matters until it was too late, after an insurgency had broken out, at which point intelligence reform became simply a process of crisis management. As in Palestine, Malaya and Kenya, British authorities failed to learn lessons from the past, and repeated the same mistakes previous colonial administrations had made. The Cyprus Special Branch had only been set up at the end of 1954, largely as a result of the efforts of Alec MacDonald, the MI5 officer seconded to the Colonial Office as the first Security Intelligence Adviser. In November that year the SIS station in Athens received a tip-off that allowed the Royal Navy to intercept an arms shipment from Athens to Cyprus. In January 1955, HMS *Comet* likewise intercepted a gun-running vessel, the *Ayios Georghios* (St George), and 10,000 sticks of dynamite were found close to shore, where its crew had dumped them. The British also picked up the receiving party on shore, and soon afterwards captured the EOKA activist Socrates Loizides, who was sentenced to twelve years' imprisonment.[33]

Despite these clear indications of what was likely to come, the administration remained complacently unaware of the impending revolt against it, with the Governor even retreating to his holiday house on the terraced slopes of the Troodos mountains. In the spring of 1955 EOKA launched its wave of bombings, using, in Grivas's own words, 'powerful and deadly bombs filled with shrapnel placed as to cause maximum damage'. On 16 March alone, sixteen bombs went off across the island, targeting power plants and police stations. Bombs were left in bags on bicycles, and grenades were thrown into pubs. In his memoirs Grivas described the objectives of his terror campaign:

> ... my chief objective would be to paralyse the police, so that the army would be drawn deeper into the terrain of my choosing and their strength dissipated ... My town groups would execute police who were too zealous on the British behalf, while my countryside groups would attack police stations, kill isolated policemen and ambush local police.[34]

The British response to the wave of bombings and killings was one of desperation, and predictably, because of a lack of intelligence on their enemies, overreaction. MI5's reforms in late 1954, led by MacDonald, had introduced the basic intelligence requirements for the Cyprus Special Branch – an MI5 officer, Philip Ray, ex-Punjab Special Branch and a former DSO in Iraq, was seconded to the Special Branch for six months; a proper registry was established with the help of an MI5 registry clerk; and its secret funds were quadrupled. But beyond this, though, little was achieved. When EOKA's onslaught stepped up a gear on April Fool's Day 1955, the British authorities in Cyprus had a shocking lack of intelligence on their enemies. According to Field Marshal Harding, who became Governor of the colony in October 1955, the embryonic Special Branch relied on what 'I call gossip sources – cafés, coffee houses and so on, which is totally inadequate. And anyway, there was no clear information about EOKA, its strength, its armament, its tactics or anything.'[35]

The fledgling Cyprus Special Branch had been aware that a mysterious organisation it called 'X' (in reality EOKA) had been planning anti-British attacks on the island since the early 1950s, but they did not know who its head was. In fact, they believed it was a communist group, while in reality EOKA was an extremist right-wing organisation – it was not until 1956 that they realised that Grivas actually had bad relations with the Cypriot Communist Party (AKEL). At the outbreak of EOKA's terror campaign the Special Branch was even unsure whether 'Dighenis' was a committee or an individual. Its language skills were so poor that, in desperation, it was forced to recruit British officers who had studied classical Greek at school and give them a crash course in modern Greek.

As in Palestine and in Malaya before Templer, intelligence coordination between the different intelligence agencies in Cyprus (military intelligence, the Special Branch and MI5) was poor. In April 1955 the Special Branch had only twenty-one gazetted officers, and the various police districts on the island did not have secure scrambler telephones with which to communicate with each other. Although Grivas had a vested interest in accentuating the failures of the British, he was not entirely wrong when he wrote:

> The cream of British intelligence was sent to Cyprus to smash this system, yet during four years of fighting they captured only a few letters; and the information they did obtain was followed by deplorable slowness.[36]

The British did not formally declare a State of Emergency in Cyprus until November 1956, at which point, it might be thought, they would look to previous Emergencies for guidance. The reality was that they repeated many of the mistakes their predecessors had made in Palestine, Malaya and Kenya. As in these previous insurgencies, the British in Cyprus wrongly believed they could prevail with minimal force and by using out-of-date tactics such as cordons and searches. These were ineffective against EOKA, which not only fought in the mountains and villages, but had terror cells conducting murder campaigns in the towns. The initial tactics that the British security forces deployed, such as arrests without warrants and the imposition of curfews and collective punishments, served only to alienate the island's local population.

Furthermore, the authorities failed to take a decisive step to deal with EOKA's terror campaign, either by declaring an Emergency outright or by employing traditional policing methods. Instead, they attempted to combine these strategies; but ended up getting the worst of both. They initially tried to solve the problem on the cheap, with police forces supported by a military presence, but as they soon discovered, this produced unsatisfactory results and blunted the efficiency of both the police and the army. Just as in Palestine, Malaya and Kenya, the British soon realised that they required much more military manpower. By 1956 the British had mustered 12,000 troops and 2,000 police in Cyprus to deal with approximately 1,000 EOKA fighters. By January 1958 the security forces had swollen to such an extent that there was one armed man per Greek Cypriot household. This surge came far too late, however: EOKA had already achieved an essential foothold. Unlike the insurgents in Malaya and Kenya, EOKA had the support of the majority of the local population, and with every attack on the British its fighters gained support and momentum, making it even more difficult for the British to acquire intelligence from the local population and to recruit agents.

As EOKA's terror campaign heightened in the spring of 1955 its fighters meted out horrific reprisals on their enemies, including slitting the throats of traitors in their own ranks. In May 1955 an experienced MI5 officer, Donald Stephens, was seconded to the Cyprus government to take up the newly created post of Director of Intelligence, a position analogous to that of Jack Morton in Malaya. In September 1955 a new Governor and commander in chief was appointed, Field Marshal Sir John Harding, a Malayan veteran whose position – like that of Templer in Malaya – bridged the political–military divide. The fact that political and military power was vested in one person, Harding, greatly strengthened Stephens's position: like Morton in Malaya, it meant that he had only one boss to whom to report.

MI5's recommendations for intelligence in Cyprus followed its usual formula. The Special Branch was made entirely separate from the regular police, and more Greek Cypriots were recruited to it, as before then it was predominantly (about 70 per cent) Turkish. However, these reforms were again too little too late, and only produced meagre results. Although EOKA's organisation was not as sophisticated as Grivas liked to portray it, it was brutally effective, and the Cyprus Emergency is a classic example of how difficult it is for a major power to defeat an insurgency supported by the majority of a local population. It was difficult, if not impossible, for the Cyprus Special Branch to recruit agents and gather intelligence on EOKA's fighters – in fact, Grivas probably achieved greater penetration of the Special Branch than it ever did of EOKA: he claimed that in 1956 he planted agents in Special Branch who were able to obtain recordings of high-level security conferences.

With swelling support from the local population, EOKA became more and more daring. In August 1955 EOKA hitmen killed a Special Branch officer, PC Michael Poullis, in broad daylight in the centre of Nicosia. EOKA fighters even targeted Harding himself, who on at least one occasion had a lucky escape. In April 1956 one of his aides, a secret EOKA agent, left a bomb under his bed, but it failed to go off, with Harding sleeping peacefully through the night on top of it.[37]

In December 1955 the British launched Operation *Foxhunter*, which involved searching all Greek Orthodox monasteries in Cyprus. They uncovered a cache of EOKA documents, including some of Grivas's remarkably verbose diaries, and almost succeeded in capturing Grivas himself, who at one point was hiding behind a tree within an arm's length of a British soldier. Operation *Lucky Alphonse* in June 1956 captured seven members of Grivas's entourage, his favourite Sam Browne belt and a further 250,000 words of his diary, stuffed into a jam jar in a field near Lyssi. Once again, Grivas had the closest of shaves, escaping just in time after being alerted to the arrival of British forces by a barking patrol dog. As he made his way through a succession of British cordons, a forest fire – allegedly started by the British Army – swept through the Troodos mountains, killing nineteen British soldiers, but allowing Grivas to escape.

The British found it so unbelievable that the secretive EOKA leader would have written a diary, let alone left it behind, that they had it checked by a graphologist who was specially flown in from London. Grivas's compulsive diary-keeping probably arose from his desire to have a detailed record of his dealings with Archbishop Makarios, whom he distrusted. Despite the initial incredulity of the British, the diaries, which contained a host of EOKA addresses and other information, proved genuine. Sections of them, which were read out at a London press conference and then published, provided damning evidence of the links between Makarios and EOKA, and helped to justify Harding's decision in March 1956, after peace negotiations broke down in December 1955, to deport the Archbishop to Mahe, a far-away island in the Seychelles, where he was housed in the agreeable surroundings of the Governor's summer house. Records from the secret colonial archive at Hanslope Park reveal that Britain was planning the deportation of Makarios in September 1955, before the talks failed, which suggests either that London never intended the talks to succeed, or that it was planning for the worst. Among the Hanslope Park records is a message written by the Governor of the Seychelles, Sir William Addis, in verse. He had previously advised that the government lodge, named *Sans Souci* ('No Worries'), might be too small to house Makarios, and that he be placed instead in another residence, named *La Bastille*. The Colonial Office evidently objected on the grounds that it would be unwise to use a house that shared the name of the famous French prison, prompting Sir William to draft a calypso: 'Well in Sans Souci so let it be/Thus denying opposition opportunity/Of stating Archbishop ne peut pas rester tranquille/In a house with the name La Bastille.'[38]

Despite the remarkable discovery of Grivas's diary, the Cyprus Special Branch was still unable to catch the EOKA leader – a fifty-eight-year-old man on an island less than half the size of Wales. In fact, in the summer of 1956 things seemed to be going from bad to worse for the British. In Operation *Lucky Alphonse* more British soldiers died in one day than in any other action conducted during the four-year-long conflict. The violence reached its climax in 'Black November' 1956, with 2,500 violent acts and over two hundred deaths reported. It led to a new intelligence-led offence against EOKA, which finally achieved a number of successes for the British. Among the tactics employed were 'Q-Patrols', composed of turned EOKA guerrillas and anti-EOKA Greek Cypriots, who would arrive in a village pretending to be guerrillas fleeing from British forces and ask to be put in touch with those who could shelter them. As we have seen, the British used Q-Patrols in Palestine, and they were similar to the SEPs used in Malaya and the counter-gangs in Kenya, yet the British security forces in Cyprus appear to have overlooked these precedents, and instead (re)discovered the tactic on their own initiative. Over six months, the Q-Patrols in Cyprus obtained intelligence that led to the death or capture of around thirty-five EOKA personnel and uncovered sixty weapons. Among the EOKA members they identified were twenty priests and six policemen. In March 1957 alone, thirty EOKA bases were uncovered and twenty-two senior guerrillas captured or killed – among them Grivas's second in command, Gregory Afxentiou, who was killed after an eight-hour firefight.[39]

Yet the elusive Grivas himself was still nowhere to be found. As a result of increasingly desperate attempts to locate him, some British interrogators resorted to physical torture, thrashing prisoners with metal chains, for which they became known as Her Majesty's Torturers (or HMTs for short). Although exact figures are impossible to establish, at least six people are known to have been killed during interrogations by British personnel in

Cyprus, and others were shot while 'trying to escape'. Masked informants, unflatteringly known as 'hooded toads', were used to identify EOKA guerrillas when suspects had been rounded up. As in Kenya, this system had obvious flaws, allowing informants to avenge personal grievances, while the accused were not able to face their accusers. Makarios was not mistaken when he said that Cyprus should dedicate a statue to Governor Harding, for he, more than anyone else, had kept alive the spirit of Hellenic resistance. When asked later about the way prisoners were treated after their capture, Harding replied in blunt terms:

> As far as ill-treatment, rough treatment on capture, I think that it is something which inevitably does happen. After all if you've got troops or police who are engaged in an anti-terrorist operation and they've seen some of their comrades killed in action, well then they capture some of the enemy responsible, naturally they are liable to be rough handled, and that is a perfectly natural thing to happen, and not something which you can regulate against. I don't think it happened to any serious extent in Cyprus, but certainly there were occasions when a captured EOKA man was pretty roughly handled in the course of his arrest. And that's something which is perfectly natural, and to my mind, acceptable.[40]

Revelations of torture were just part of a much larger picture of the way in which the British forces alienated the island's inhabitants. Stories (probably true) circulated of soldiers pointlessly emptying villagers' bags of grain, pouring out oil and tipping out fruit and vegetables. There was a remarkable failure to learn lessons from Malaya about how important effective 'hearts and minds' campaigns are in a counter-insurgency. News of British torture in Cyprus soon attracted the attention of the tireless Labour MPs Barbara Castle and Fenner Brockway, both outspoken advocates of colonial independence movements and influential human rights campaigners. The two travelled to Cyprus in 1958, where Castle met Makarios himself (who by then had been released from exile). Apparently, however, she was the target of a 'black bag' operation: the material she had collected on her trip, and notes she had compiled, were extracted from her luggage by unidentified individuals, photographed and then telegraphed to London before she arrived back, providing Macmillan's government with forewarning of the criticisms she was to make.[41]

Following the killing of his second in command, Gregory Afxentiou, Grivas agreed to a ceasefire, in return for which Makarios was released from captivity in the Seychelles. He made his way back to Cyprus on an appropriately named British vessel, the *Olympic Thunderer*, and travelled via Athens, where he was forced (probably deliberately) to stay in the Hotel Grand Bretagne. The need to reconcile the conflicting demands of Greek and Turkish Cypriots meant that the negotiations between the British government, Makarios and Turkish representatives dragged on at a torturous pace. The biography of Dick White states that during the negotiations Makarios was blackmailed by the British using information from SIS about his homosexuality. However, there is no evidence in available British intelligence records, or in any other source, to support this.

In December 1957 a new Governor, Sir Hugh Foot, was appointed. Known as 'M' among his friends, Foot was the brother of the left-wing Labour MP Michael Foot, and was apparently left-leaning himself. He had had a long and distinguished career as a colonial administrator, and appeared better suited to finding a political solution in Cyprus than Field Marshal Harding. The task, however, was daunting even for him. His wife, Lady Sylvia, later recalled that when they arrived in Cyprus they were shocked to discover the beleaguered state of British civilian life there. They were forced to live behind the protection of barbed wire and sandbags, patrolled by sentries and overseen by guard towers.[42]

After his arrival, Foot declared: 'We have always been weakest on the intelligence side and our effort against EOKA cannot be fully effective until all intelligence work is pulled together and given better central direction.' To help remedy the situation, in October 1958 he sent a personal request to MI5's Director-General, Roger Hollis – Foot had become well-versed in MI5's colonial operations while serving as Governor of Jamaica – to despatch a 'high grade research officer' to collate and assess all available intelligence, with the aim of capturing Grivas and the rest of the EOKA leadership. Hollis responded by sending Bill Magan, who had risen to become Director of MI5's overseas E-Division, to Cyprus on secondment for six months.[43]

Magan set about profiling Grivas in a way no previous British intelligence officer had done hitherto, and his efforts were soon producing results. In Operation *Sunshine*, in February 1959, Grivas was tracked down to an area in Nicosia where security forces thought he could be seized by a snatch squad. This breakthrough was largely due to Magan and MI5's new SLO in Cyprus, Philip Kirby Greene, joined by a young officer from MI5's technical section, Peter Wright, who helped to track down Grivas using radio signals. The new Director of Intelligence, John Prendergast, fresh from Kenya – he later moved on to Aden and Hong Kong – also made it his personal mission to locate and eliminate Grivas.

Just as the British intelligence officers' net was closing in on Grivas, however, events overtook them. That same month, tense negotiations on the future of Cyprus opened at Lancaster House in London. Over dinner one night Harold Macmillan asked the Greek Foreign Minister, Angelos Averoff, how he thought the capture of Grivas would affect the situation on the island. Averoff replied that the negotiations would collapse and a bloodbath would follow. Later that same evening, Macmillan therefore instructed that Grivas was to be left undisturbed in his hiding place. Eventually, in March 1959, he was found by a British patrol in a monastery in the Troodos mountains with an elaborate complex of secret rooms and annexes. He had been sleeping in a cell constructed below a kitchen sink, and two female couriers were the only people who knew his location.[44]

With Macmillan having ordered that Grivas was to be left untouched, and the guerrilla leader's skin thus effectively saved, in February 1959 the Lancaster House conference agreed on the establishment of an independent Cyprus with a Greek President (Makarios), a Turkish Vice President and a House of Representatives with 70 per cent Greek and 30 per cent Turkish membership. The minority rights of Turkish Cypriots were at least theoretically safeguarded by the new republic's constitution – though later events on the island would show this was not the case. As with other newly independent colonies, the Cypriot government agreed that an MI5 liaison officer would be stationed in Cyprus after independence, attached to the British military garrison in Episkopi (and therefore a DSO, not an SLO). One of the bitterest ironies about Britain's counter-insurgency in Cyprus was that the vicious guerrilla war instigated from Athens for *enosis* actually ended up with Cyprus's independence not only from Britain, but from Greece as well. Makarios preferred international to provincial status for Cyprus. The result was that many lives were lost for what was really a mirage of Greek *enosis*.[45]

In 1954 the Minister of State for Colonial Affairs, Henry Hopkinson, had caused consternation when he let slip in the House of Commons that there were some territories, like Cyprus, that would 'never' be granted independence from Britain. On one level his statement was wildly off the mark: Britain gave up control of Cyprus just six years later. On another level, however, Hopkinson was not as far from the truth as might be thought. During the independence talks at Lancaster House in early 1959, the British government bargained hard until it achieved the result it wanted: to retain strategic rights over two bases in Cyprus which would go on to become crucial outposts throughout the rest of the Cold War. The British delegation at the talks, led by Julian Amery, Undersecretary of State for the Colonies, started with an extravagant bid for four hundred square miles of territory, though they eventually settled for ninety-nine square miles, housing two so-called Sovereign Base Areas – which exist to the present day. The first of these was RAF Pergamos, a forty-three-acre site which effectively became a vast GCHQ camp. Its large tented encampment was home to over 1,000 SIGINT personnel drawn from British bases at Sarafand in Palestine, Heliopolis in Egypt and Habbaniya in Iraq, all of which Britain had been forced to withdraw from in the post-war years. The second was the largest British SIGINT base on Cyprus, Ayios Nikolaos, which was so big that it had begun to encroach on the municipal area of Famagusta itself. When Makarios protested, GCHQ agreed that it could retreat a little without serious damage to its operations.[46]

Washington found Cyprus just as useful as London did, and the NSA and the CIA bankrolled many of the most important SIGINT operations on the island. As with British Guiana, this was a striking example of the United States propping up the vestiges of the British empire when it suited its Cold War needs to do so. In fact, SIGINT collection was so important to the West that it helped to shape international relations concerning Cyprus – the SIGINT tail wagged the policy dog. In 1963, faced with rising levels of inter-communal violence between the Greek and Turkish populations on the island, the new British Prime Minister, Sir Alec Douglas-Home, questioned whether Britain really needed bases there. The Defence Secretary, Peter Thorneycroft, responded with an emphatic 'yes', explaining that Cyprus 'houses the most important SIGINT stations and it also provides a base from which special reconnaissance flights are carried out'. Thorneycroft said that while most other activities could be relocated, it was 'not considered that SIGINT facilities could be adequately replaced elsewhere'.

A decade later, in 1974, when faced with a financial crisis, the British government formally decided to withdraw from its bases in Cyprus in order to save money. Within days Washington told London that this decision was not acceptable, and they must stay. The reason was simple: the SIGINT bases in Cyprus that allowed America to listen in to the Middle East were indispensable. In 2013, nearly forty years after the British government's decision to withdraw from the bases, they are still there, and have grown considerably in size.[47]

THE FEDERATION OF SOUTH ARABIA

Aden was one of the first, and was also one of the last, territories in Queen Victoria's empire, a crown colony claimed by the British in 1839 and abandoned over a century later, in 1967. Along with British Guiana, it proved to be one of the most difficult and disorderly transfers of power: Britain was forced to evacuate Aden ingloriously, with service personnel effectively having to shoot their way out of the state.

When the British first came to Aden it had been colonised for over five centuries by various powers, including the Portuguese and the Ottoman Empire. Aden, located in the region known to the ancient Romans as Arabia Felix, had been ruled by the same line of priest-kings for eight centuries. To the north and east of the colony were the two dozen separate states of the Eastern and Western Aden Protectorates. They covered an inhospitable and undeveloped region of about 112,000 square miles, inhabited by a population of about 800,000, ruled by their own emirs and sheiks. The Protectorates were effectively closed to visitors – it was said that most of the populations in the hinterland had never seen a white man – and had no economic interest for the British. Apart from a few urban areas they had no infrastructure whatsoever, but they did provide a kind of buffer for the Aden colony.

For the British, as for the colonial powers before them, the value of Aden was its location, a seaport on the southern tip of the Arabian Peninsula, at the neck of the Red Sea and with easy access to the Persian Gulf. It was also conveniently located between Bombay, the Suez Canal and Zanzibar, all of which were important British holdings. For hundreds of years it had acted as a stopover for sailors, and the British continued this tradition, using it primarily as a coaling station for ships on the trade routes between East and West. As the twentieth century dawned, the piles of coal were joined by a cluster of oil refineries. In the first half of the twentieth century, Aden grew from a village with a population of about six hundred to a thriving international port, much like Singapore.[48]

For the British, Aden's primary importance lay in its strategic position as a gateway to India. It was effectively run as an adjunct to the Indian empire, and was ruled from Bombay for almost a hundred years, until the British withdrew from India in 1947. After that the city colony became something of a backwater in the eyes of numerous colonial officials: it was described by one Governor as the station 'on the route to nowhere'. Apart from its fine natural harbour and useful position, Aden had little by way of natural assets. Set in the sunburnt crater of an extinct volcano, it was described by Rudyard Kipling as 'the cinder heap of the world', a harsh landscape that was home to a mixed bag of badly-behaved officers and disgraced regiments.

It may, therefore, be wondered why the British desperately clung on to Aden until 1967, even though the colony's primary strategic role had been lost twenty years earlier with Indian independence. The answer lies in the fact that its strategic importance, like that of Cyprus, was heightened after the Suez fiasco in October 1956, following which the headquarters of the British Middle Eastern Command moved from Egypt to Aden. Between 1957 and 1959 the total number of British service personnel stationed in Aden quadrupled. Following the financial and military cutbacks of the late 1950s, Aden was the linchpin of Britain's policy 'East of Suez', a vital link between the enclaves of Gibraltar and Hong Kong.[49]

The aim of the Macmillan government following Suez was to consolidate British influence in the Arab world by maintaining a base in Aden and setting up a federation of protectorates in South Arabia, ruled by traditional tribal chiefs. Although Macmillan had been relatively quick to acknowledge the 'wind of change' blowing through Africa, he greatly underestimated the rising Arab nationalism in the Middle East, inspired by the charismatic Egyptian leader Gamal Abdel Nasser, who was widely believed in the region to have humiliated the British and French 'imperialists' during the Suez crisis, and whose image seemed to smile down from posters on every wall in Aden.

In 1959 six states of the Western Aden Protectorate were persuaded to form a Federation of Arab Emirates of the South, and sign a mutual cooperation agreement with Britain. By the end of 1962 the total number of states in the Federation had grown to eleven. In January 1963 the Aden colony joined the Federation as the State of Aden, much to the displeasure of many of its inhabitants, who regarded the neighbouring hinterland as 'backward', and the Federation was renamed the Federation of South Arabia.[50]

Much like the hotchpotch Central African Federation, there was never any realistic chance that the Federation of South Arabia could unite its disparate elements. Its government was never going to be able to stem the rising tide of Arab nationalism, sponsored by Nasser. In pursuit of his dream of uniting the Arab world, Nasser saw that controlling Yemen, the state neighbouring Aden, would provide a base from which he could proceed effortlessly up through Saudi Arabia and on to attack his main enemy, Israel. In September 1962 he sponsored a coup by the leader of Yemen's republican faction, Colonel Abdullah as-Sallal – who not long previously had been a street charcoal-seller – which overthrew the newly crowned Imam, Muhammad al-Badr. Macmillan noted in his diary that this was 'very dangerous' for the Aden Protectorate.[51]

He was not mistaken. The overthrow of the Imamate in Yemen triggered a bitter civil war that spilled over the country's borders into surrounding states, including Aden, with Nasser doing all he could to support opposition to British rule in Aden and its neighbouring Protectorates. As he later declared during a visit to Yemen: 'We swear by Allah to expel the British from all parts of the Arab Peninsula.' In June 1962 he sponsored the foundation in Aden of the People's Socialist Party (PSP), led by Abdullah al-Asnag, as an offshoot of the Aden Trades Union Congress. Its aim was to cause labour unrest, provoke a government crackdown and radicalise Adeni opinion. This was relatively easy to do, as social conditions in Aden had generally not improved during British rule, with locals benefiting little from heavy taxes such as the levy on *qat* – a narcotic leaf that turns addicts' teeth green – which raised over half a million pounds a year. The following year Nasser provided support for the newly founded National Liberation Front (NLF), which from its base in Yemen began to plan a nationalist rebellion in Aden through a network of secret operational cells. So, from 1962 onwards Britain faced internal opposition in the Federation that was receiving active aid from a foreign power (Egypt) operating in a neighbouring country (Yemen).[52]

In 1963 the NLF launched a series of violent attacks on British targets in Aden. The home for most of the NLF fighters was the mountainous Radfan region, about sixty miles north of Aden. This was close to the porous Yemeni border, across which Soviet bazookas and machine guns obtained by Nasser were shipped to NLF forces. It was reported that in 1967, 60,000 people and 20,000 vehicles, as well as three hundred camels, passed through security checkpoints between Aden and its hinterland every day, but that only 5.5 per cent of those people, and an even smaller percentage of vehicles, were stopped and searched.[53]

The NLF's attacks culminated on 10 December 1963 in the attempted assassination of the British High Commissioner, Sir Kennedy Trevaskis, at Aden's Khormaksar airport as he was waiting for a flight to London. Trevaskis survived the attack with only a minor injury to his hand, but the Deputy High Commissioner, George Henderson, was killed while attempting to shield him from the grenade thrown by an assailant. An Indian woman was also killed, and twenty-four other people, including the Federal Minister of the Interior, were injured. Trevaskis's immediate response, doubtless as the PSP and NLF had hoped, was to declare a State of Emergency. Over 140 local nationalist and trade union leaders were arrested, even though there was no real evidence that they were connected with the attack, and a number of Yemenis living in Aden were deported.[54]

Lying behind the assassination attempt was a humiliating intelligence failure on the part of the Federation government, just as there had been in Palestine, Malaya, Kenya, Cyprus and Nyasaland. Local security officials had failed to warn Trevaskis about the outbreak of violence in Aden generally, and the threat to him in particular. The outfits responsible for collating and assessing such information, the Local Intelligence Committee (LIC) and the Aden Intelligence Centre, were aware of the 'possibility of the resort to terrorism and sabotage', but had failed to give a specific warning about the likelihood of an attack on the High Commissioner, who at any rate was doubtful about the value of the raw intelligence produced by the LIC. Astonishingly, despite his narrow escape from death, Trevaskis reported that he was 'satisfied' with the supply of intelligence, and refused to implement a reform of the intelligence machinery in the Federation, as the LIC urged. He preferred to regard the NLF as an irritant rather than a serious threat. They were 'military tiddlywinks', in the phrase of one report sent to London.[55]

It was Trevaskis's attitude towards intelligence matters that lay at the heart of the failure of security measures in Aden. The fundamental problem was that he had little faith in the intelligence services. As one of the chief architects of the Federation, he was clearly of the opinion that when it came to intelligence assessments about it, he knew best. He was convinced that the mounting unrest in the region was due to the manipulation of the tribal chieftaincies in the Protectorates surrounding Aden in the struggles between the Yemeni Imamate and Britain on the one hand, and between Egypt and Britain on another. Trevaskis's interpretation of events, which was reminiscent of the nineteenth-century 'Great Game', had little room for the popularity of 'Nasserism' in South Arabia. With his mind firmly made up, the High Commissioner acted as his own intelligence assessor, grafting his version of the security situation onto reports rather than letting briefings from the LIC, whose members included MI5 and SIS officers, inform his judgement. It was a classic intelligence failure, an example of an official editing intelligence reports to fit what he wanted to hear. By overlooking and manipulating the reports of the LIC, Trevaskis bypassed the objective assessments available to him from the British intelligence community, especially the JIC in London. The fact is that, even if the LIC had produced a clear warning about an attempt on his life, it is likely that Trevaskis would have ignored it.[56]

Matters were even worse than this, though. The normal practice was that when a Governor disagreed with a report from a Local Intelligence Committee, he would note his disagreement on the report sent to London. This did not happen in the Federation of South Arabia. Whenever Trevaskis was 'at variance' with LIC assessments, he altered them unilaterally and without notification. The result was that the readers of the LIC reports in London, including the JIC, were seeing Trevaskis's interpretation of events, rather than the LIC's. The Colonial Office vented its growing exasperation in April 1964: 'There does seem a tendency on his part to regard the volume of evidence as being more important than the sifted evidence.' At that point Trevaskis was altering LIC reports to such an extent that, in the eyes of one Colonial Office official, they lacked 'objectivity' and were 'very dangerous'. Given the lack of reliable intelligence coming from Aden, it was unsurprising that the JIC had wrongly concluded at the beginning of 1962: 'On the whole, however, there seems no reason to expect any serious trouble in either the Colony [of Aden] or Protectorate.'[57]

With little leadership from Trevaskis, intelligence in the Federation of South Arabia was splintered and uncoordinated. The High Commissioner persistently overruled any attempt to create a unified intelligence outfit across the Federation. One security official in the Colonial Office, William Formoy, noted in April 1963 that 'Sir Kennedy Trevaskis has no enthusiasm' for establishing a formal Federal intelligence apparatus under British tutelage. Instead, Trevaskis's overriding belief was that for Britain to retain a long-term presence in South Arabia, it was vital to work towards independence as soon as possible. The establishment of an intelligence outfit on a Federation-wide level was, he felt, anathema to this.

Unsurprisingly, the advice coming from the British intelligence community was the opposite. Britain's senior spies urged that the most important legacy Britain could leave in the Federation, whenever independence came, would be a coordinated and efficient Special Branch, so the newly independent states could protect themselves. As early as 1956, as part of its colonial intelligence reforms, MI5 had recommended in the strongest terms that a professional Special Branch should be established in Aden, dedicated to intelligence matters. This proposal effectively came to nothing. Although a Special Branch was set up, it was crippled by a lack of support and funding from Trevaskis, as well as by poor leadership. Much as had happened in Malaya before the declaration of the Emergency there, the head of the Aden Special Branch, Bob Waggitt, was heavily criticised for failing to place agents within the PSP or the NLF in the run-up to violence in 1963. William Formoy bluntly concluded in early 1964: 'I do not think we can yet be satisfied with the local coverage of the Aden TUC and PSP.'[58]

In Aden, as in previous colonial Emergencies, the Special Branch found itself at the front line. In January 1964 Radio Cairo began to threaten senior Arab Special Branch officers by name, and on Christmas Day that year the NLF started to assassinate them. Chief Inspector Fadhle Khalil was slain 'sitting in his car while parked near the municipal market Crater' by fire from an automatic weapon from a passing car. In September 1965 the corpse of an Arab Special Branch constable, bound, gagged and shot, was discovered with 'a white turban on the head of the body bearing the words in Arabic, "this execution was carried out by the Front"'. Special Branch informers were liable to meet the same grisly fate.

The NLF's assassination tactics, particularly against Arab personnel, effectively crippled Special Branch. The High Commissioner reported in June 1965 that 'Aden Special Branch has now virtually no Arab element and will take considerable time to re-establish on an Arab basis even if Arabs can be found to serve in it. There is no likelihood of this happening in the foreseeable future.' Four months later an experienced colonial Special Branch officer, John Prendergast, reported that 'Special Branch was in a particularly bad state'. The Federal government's response to the task of rebuilding the Special Branch was to import expatriate British officers. However, in a remarkably short-sighted manner, the Special Branch made matters worse for itself by reserving key positions, with the best pay, for these officials. This attracted the scorn of MI5's John Morton, who in April 1964 had conducted an overall review of intelligence in South Arabia. Morton made his views clear in his report: 'It's all very well to talk about "rebuilding Special Branch on an expatriate basis" but one still must have the Arabs.'[59]

The lack of coordination of intelligence in South Arabia was shown in the fact that the overall intelligence assessment body, the LIC, was based not in the Federation's capital, al-Ittihad, but in Aden. This might have made sense if Aden had been just another state within the Federation, but when the city had been acrimoniously admitted to it in February 1963, its citizens had hung black flags to show their disagreement. The fact that the LIC was based in Aden, and not in the hinterland, inevitably coloured its assessments and made them less than reliable. Furthermore, because the Federation included both British colonial territory (the Aden state) and states that were only loosely attached to Britain through a series of treaties (the Protectorates), and were therefore essentially foreign territories, the roles of MI5 and SIS in the Federation were also confused.

However, by far the clearest illustration of the lack of intelligence coordination in the Federation was the fact that for most of the Emergency it did not have an overall Director of Intelligence. Following the declaration of the State of Emergency, a senior MI5 officer, Jack Morton, the former Director of Intelligence under Templer in Malaya, was seconded to the Federation government. In a major report he compiled in April 1964, he advised that if intelligence matters were to improve in the Federation, an intelligence 'overlord' would have to be established. Despite Morton's pleading, Trevaskis persistently resisted establishing a Director of Intelligence, which would have streamlined the overall intelligence efforts in Aden, bringing them under the control of a single professional intelligence officer, as had occurred in Malaya under Templer and in Cyprus under Harding. British officials in Aden once again failed to learn the lesson from previous Emergencies about the need to provide a unified response to insurgencies. There was no equivalent in Aden of the 'Briggs Plan' in Malaya. In fact, there seems to have been general apathy in London towards the security problems posed in the Federation. South Arabia remained firmly delegated to the Colonial Office and the JIC, whereas policy in Malaya had been dictated from April 1950 by a cabinet-level committee led by the Minister of Defence, Emmanuel Shinwell. A report from the Political Adviser Middle East Command in December 1965 made the failures of intelligence abundantly clear:

> There is no Intelligence Service, properly speaking, covering and targeting the Protectorate. The nearest thing to an Intelligence Service is the Special Branch, which is confined to Aden State, which has been gravely weakened by assassinations and which, because of these assassinations and through intimidation of the population, is receiving far less than the normal flow of information.[60]

The Federation of South Arabia did not actually acquire a Director of Intelligence until July 1966, when Trevaskis finally relented to pressure from Morton. The first Director, John Prendergast, came to the Federation with a long pedigree, having served in the Special Branches of Kenya, Cyprus and Hong Kong. In the same year a Federal Intelligence Staff was also created, with three Arabic-speaking officers, which brought a degree of cohesion to the intelligence machinery in Aden. However, it was too late. By the time Prendergast arrived the British had already lost the insurgency, and all he could achieve was short-term damage limitation before Britain withdrew from the Federation altogether. In February 1966 the British government had announced that it was to withdraw from South Arabia. Ironically, the intelligence community in the Federation of South Arabia thus achieved the cohesion that it desperately needed *after* Britain announced its decision to withdraw.

Rather than using intelligence briefings to inform his assessment of the security situation in the Federation, Trevaskis favoured the extensive use of covert action, which he believed would 'bring about a clash between the PSP and the SPL [the rival South Arabian League] which will encourage them to slit each other's throats'. Back in 1964 he had been authorised by the Secretary of State for the Colonies, Duncan Sandys, to spend £15,000 'penetrating their organisations, suborning their key figures, stimulating rivalries and jealousies between them, encouraging dissension and the emergence of splinter groups and harassing them generally, for example by breaking up public meetings'. In Trevaskis's view, the only (extremely limited) role for intelligence in South Arabia was to support this kind of covert action, the overall aim of which was to 'retaliate' against NLF attacks. The emphasis he placed on covert action was similar to French campaigns during the Algerian war for independence. France's 'Service Action', a covert group like something out of the pages of Frederick Forsyth's *The Day of the Jackal*, carried out assassination campaigns in Europe against arms dealers and others directly supporting the Front de Libération Nationale (FLN), the main militant group fighting for Algerian independence. However, just as the French use of covert action failed in Algeria, so did the British in South Arabia. Both failed to address the underlying political problems.[61]

In the autumn of 1965 the intelligence picture in Aden slightly improved. The interrogation of NLF suspects began to yield results, and between September and November the security forces were able to build up a picture of what they termed the NLF's order of battle, the names of its cells and the codenames of its active members. These numbered about a hundred, and half of them were promptly arrested. However, reports that spoke of the NLF's 'order of battle' were slightly disingenuous. In reality, the NLF was not a tightly structured group of Egyptian- and Yemeni-trained cadres, as the Aden Special Branch liked to claim. Rather, it was a relatively open political movement that used Arab nationalist rhetoric to maximise its membership. Consequently, it had access to an almost unlimited pool of poorly trained but eager recruits. The British did little to stem the flow of such recruits, utterly failing to win Adeni hearts and minds. Some British military officials claimed that intelligence dried up when Britain announced that it would withdraw from Aden in February 1966, but it is clear that the flow had already been reduced to a trickle even before then, as the local population hedged its bets over Nasser's probable victory in the surrounding hinterland. In a manner that was depressingly familiar, the Aden Special Branch's total failure to obtain useful intelligence on its enemies led some of its officers to take matters into their own hands. Just as in previous colonial Emergencies, and in the contemporary French campaign in Algeria, some British interrogators in Aden resorted to torture in a desperate bid to produce intelligence.[62]

Then as now, torture was the last refuge of the ineffectual. As in every other colonial Emergency in the British empire, the use of torture in Aden was really the result of systemic failures on the part of the local intelligence officials to carry out what should have been their normal function: to place human agents among their enemies. Lacking such agents, officials attempted to gather whatever information they could by whatever means. British military forces adopted the same 'Q-Squad' tactics that had previously been used in Palestine, and more recently Cyprus – which were themselves similar to Surrendered Enemy Personnel in Malaya and counter-gangs in Kenya. The essential purpose of Q-Squads was to cajole captured enemy fighters into working as double agents. Just as in all previous colonial Emergencies, interrogation methods at the front line in Aden, either to co-opt agents or to get information out of them, sometimes involved harsh 'third degree' methods, which constituted torture – by our standards and theirs. The Q-Squad tactics in Aden bore a striking resemblance to French tactics in Algeria, where similarly cajoled Arab agents, the *Bleus de chauffe*, were used, principally during the battle of Algiers in 1957.

After his arrival in July 1966, John Prendergast attempted to reform the Aden Special Branch interrogation methods, putting greater emphasis on the recruitment of agents. Prendergast was 'not at all convinced' about the use of torture to produce intelligence or recruit agents, a view he seems to have gained from MI5. Nevertheless, it is clear that some British forces in

Aden continued to mete out tough punishments to prisoners. In 1967 the 1st Argyll and Sutherland Highlanders reoccupied the Crater district in Aden, after their temporary evacuation following the killing of a number of their comrades. Upon their return they imposed what the media termed 'Argylls' law' – even sympathetic reporters called the actions of the battalion 'rough justice'. One soldier later recalled that his battalion had established a special interrogation centre, from where he could hear sticks cracking skulls, rifle-butts striking chins, and screams in Arabic. Allegations of torture at Fort Morbut in Aden, the headquarters of British Middle East Command, were so rampant that the Aden government's own legal adviser recommended a judicial inquiry. The colonial Governor, Sir Richard Turnbull, rejected the idea because of the tired old arguments that it would harm morale and the effectiveness of interrogators.[63]

As part of its covert action against the NLF, the British government was also drawn into a shadowy secret war against Nasser's forces in Yemen, predicated on the understanding that the conflict in South Arabia was a proxy war against Egypt. Prime Minister Harold Macmillan wrote in his memoirs that Aden had attracted 'the envious hostility both of Nasser and of those countries of the Arab world which had fallen under his baneful influence'. Nasser sent perhaps as many as 70,000 Egyptian 'volunteers' to Yemen to support republican factions led by as-Sallal. In order to check them, and in response to requests for aid from King Hussein of Jordan, Britain unofficially did all it could to support anti-Nasser royalist forces in Yemen. Julian Amery, Minister for War, and Neil 'Billy' McLean, the so-called 'MP for royalist Yemen', headed an elaborate secret network that supplied matériel and mercenaries to the royalist cause. Apparently with the tacit support of SIS's Chief, Dick White, they recruited a group of British mercenaries, largely comprised of SAS and former SOE types, to fight Nasser's forces and train local Yemeni militias. Most were approached over whisky and sodas in White's and the Special Forces Club in London. Their leader, Jim Johnson, was a former territorial SAS officer. In the run-up to the mercenaries' deployment in 1964, intercepts provided by GCHQ gave a detailed picture of Egyptian troop formations in Yemen, and also revealed tensions between the republican ministers and the Egyptian chiefs of staff. GCHQ's intercepts seem also to have been particularly important in October 1962, informing the JIC, and later the British cabinet, about the flagging morale of the Egyptian forces.[64]

As always, the 'special relationship' between London and Washington played a guiding role in Britain's secret war against Nasser in Yemen – 'the war that never was', as it has been called. The difficulty for Britain was that the US government distrusted the Yemeni royalists, and favoured conciliation with Nasser. At least outwardly, the British government therefore dared not admit that it was supporting Yemeni royalists against the wishes of Washington. Prime Minister Sir Alec Douglas-Home was less than truthful when he told the House of Commons in May 1964: 'Our policy towards the Yemen is one of non-intervention. It is not our policy to supply arms to the royalists in Yemen.' In fact, he lied outright. The benefit for Britain of using unofficial mercenaries in Yemen, supported by SIS channels, was that they were officially deniable. Although the mercenaries' mission had something of a Boy's Own adventure about it – it was run from a basement in Sloane Square – it was remarkably successful. After they arrived in Yemen in 1964 they lived in flea-infested caves, where they were routinely bombed with high explosives and gas. Despite these hardships they managed to galvanise local Yemeni tribal militias to fight the occupying Egyptian forces. Britain's proxy war in Yemen dragged on until 1970, with Nasser losing over 20,000 men. The Egyptian leader remarked that Yemen was his Vietnam.[65]

In February 1966 Harold Wilson's Labour government announced that South Arabia was to be fully independent by 1968 at the latest, and that Britain would withdraw from its Aden military base and end its defence commitment to the Federation. It was expected that this announcement would diminish the insurgency, but in fact it served only to intensify it. By September 1967, amid scenes of increasing violence in the Federation, the British Foreign Secretary, George Brown, had washed his hands of South Arabia. 'It can't be helped,' he said privately. 'Anyway, we want to be out of the whole of the Middle East as far and as fast as we possibly can.' The Leader of the House of Commons, Richard Crossman, cynically noted in his diary that the fact that 'the regime ... should have been overthrown by terrorists and has forced our speedy withdrawal, is nothing but good fortune'.[66]

Already by 1966 all pretence had disappeared, and British officials in the Federation government and intelligence agencies had begun winding down their affairs in preparation for withdrawal. Despite it being a 'cardinal policy' to 'organise effective Special Branches before handing over', no such provision was made in South Arabia. In April 1966 a JIC working group concluded that the Federal rulers would have to rely upon their 'traditional sources' of intelligence. Even before that, the political adviser to the Federation concluded that there would be a 'special relationship' that would 'provide automatically for close intelligence cooperation' between Britain and South Arabia after independence. All in all, the British made few preparations for the transfer of power, and totally failed to relinquish control to an effective or stable government. Aden was a classic 'scuttle' from empire. Britain withdrew from South Arabia in November 1967 in a shameful manner, handing power over to a homicidal Marxist regime, the People's Republic of South Yemen. The consequences are still with us today, in particular the extremist groups that were allowed to flourish due to the lack of an effective Yemeni government.[67]

Conclusion

British Intelligence:
The Last Penumbra of Empire

Britain has lost an empire but has not yet found a role.
US SECRETARY OF STATE DEAN ACHESON (1962)[1]

We cannot hope to fight Russia and Egypt mounted on an anti-colonial war chariot if the Americans insist on driving about the world on a similar model.
Colonial Office minute (13 February 1958)[2]

An intelligence service ought to act as a kind of agency operating in the interests of the various formations which are in effect its customers ... It should be the business of Intelligence to anticipate their needs, and to provide the required facts even before they are demanded. It should circulate to each all relevant facts even before they are demanded.
MARC BLOCH, *Strange Defeat*[3]

The British empire was an empire of secrets. On the one hand, this was because of the clandestine activities of Britain's intelligence services (MI5, SIS and GCHQ), which worked behind the scenes during the twilight of empire, striving to maintain what was termed Britain's 'vital interests' in every major British colony that gained independence across the world after 1945. However, the British empire was also an empire of secrets in another way: the records relating to British intelligence at the end of empire have remained secret, locked away by Whitehall departments for much longer than they need to have been. The result has been that, until recently, the role performed by Britain's intelligence services in the end of empire has remained a closed chapter in history. Intelligence is the missing dimension of the history of British decolonisation.

This is the first book devoted to British intelligence during the twilight of empire that has been based on declassified intelligence records. Some historians have argued that instead of understanding decolonisation from a British or European 'metropolitan' perspective, it is better to use the records of anti-colonial movements themselves to understand colonial retreat. Such arguments overlook the simple point that intelligence is a metropolitan offering that provides a new chapter on Britain's end of empire. Drawing on a wealth of intelligence records that have only become available in the past few years – some of them only in 2012 – it has revealed how, and why, Britain's intelligence services were involved in the end of empire. However, the British secret state almost certainly played a role in a number of armed conflicts during the demise of empire, from Oman to Borneo, which have not featured in this book. The reason they are missing is that the intelligence archive relating to them is still classified. Readers will have noticed that this book covers the period, broadly, up to the mid-1960s. This is not a cut-off date that has been chosen arbitrarily by me. It is the moment at which the intelligence records presently available on British decolonisation begin to dry up; and, because this book is primarily based on records, it is the moment at which it has to finish. Unfortunately, Whitehall still regards it as too sensitive to release intelligence records on the end of empire after the mid-1960s.

Despite the noose put on historians in this way, it is not difficult to conclude that Britain's secret services were involved in end-of-empire conflicts after the mid-1960s, in just the same way as they were before, even if official records are not presently available. At the time of writing, for example, there are almost no declassified intelligence records on the Falklands conflict of 1982. Nevertheless, it is known, both from insiders and from an official history written by Sir Lawrence Freedman, published in 2005, that British intelligence played a role in the Falklands War. The JIC was responsible for briefing ministers on the situation, apparently drawing on SIGINT and SIS sources in Argentina, in just the same way that it briefed ministers and the Chiefs of Staff before then – and as it continues to do. We shall have to wait for the intelligence records finally to become available for the full clandestine story of the Falklands conflict to be told.[4]

* * *

That said, even from the scanty records currently declassified and available, it is possible to piece together at least some of the intelligence story relating to the later chapters of Britain's end of empire. This is particularly the case with Hong Kong. Hong Kong island became a British colony in 1842, after China's defeat in the First Opium War. Britain acquired the neighbouring territory of Kowloon in 1860 and leased the New Territories from China in 1898. Over subsequent decades, particularly in the years after 1945 when the Cold War set in, Hong Kong was to become one of the world's great espionage capitals. As we have seen, senior MI5 officers such as Sir Eric Holt-Wilson had travelled there as early as the 1920s, and on the eve of the Second World War it was one of the first places where MI5 stationed a permanent liaison officer. The decision of the British government to take Hong Kong back in 1946 after the wartime Japanese occupation, instead of relinquishing control of it altogether, meant that during the Cold War the colony became a focal point for Western powers in an otherwise communist-dominated region, a 'Berlin of the East'. As the imperial historian Wm. Roger Louis has noted, Clement Attlee's decision to hold on to Hong Kong was one of the most courageous he ever made. After Mao Tse-tung came to power in China in 1949, Hong Kong found itself at the front line of the Cold War. In fact, it was as important to the United States as it was to Britain, as the USA did not even have an embassy in mainland China. 'Hong Kong became a watchtower on China,' recalled Jack Smith, who looked after the Far East in the CIA's Office of National Estimates. Although the vast majority of Britain's intelligence archive relating to it is still classified, it is nevertheless clear that one issue, above all, dominated all British (and apparently US) intelligence assessments of Hong Kong: its relationship with the 'motherland', China.[5]

MI5's first post-war Director-General, Sir Percy Sillitoe, visited Hong Kong in 1948 and recommended reforming security there to bring it in line with MI5's security overhauls elsewhere in the empire. However, despite the pressure put on it, the Hong Kong Special Branch was reluctant to accept MI5-seconded officers until 1956, after the first 'confrontation' between China and Hong Kong. At this stage it seemed that China might well take over Hong Kong – or take it back, depending on how one viewed the manner in which the British acquired it. The confrontation in 1955 did not, in the end, lead to hostilities, but there was a much more serious flashpoint in 1967, during Mao's so-called 'Cultural Revolution', when it seemed that the Red Army was poised to attack. Hong Kong's 8,000 British troops would have been no match for the 41,000 Chinese troops standing by, ready to launch an offensive, and MI5 began to draw up emergency plans to evacuate senior British officials and their families from the colony. The situation was all the more alarming because, as the JIC in London frankly admitted, SIS was hardly able to gather any reliable intelligence on Chinese intentions. Given the nature of Mao's highly policed state, it was impossible for SIS to get agents into positions of influence within the Chinese government and learn anything about its strategic intentions. By contrast, as JIC reports show, it was comparatively easy to gather reliable intelligence on the Chinese nationalist party (the Kuomintang, or KMT), based on Taiwan.[6]

Despite the alarming nature of the situation in Hong Kong, the JIC in London nevertheless provided the British Chiefs of Staff and cabinet ministers with sober and realistic assessments of the threat posed by Mao's China. Beginning in 1949, JIC reports repeatedly explained to their readers that, strategically, it made no sense for China to take over Hong Kong. As the JIC correctly reasoned, the Chinese government relied on Hong Kong as a base for its espionage operations against the West just as much as the West relied on Hong Kong for its operations against China. In a major review of British policy in the Far East in 1953, the JIC stated:

> We still believe that, on balance, the Chinese find it to their advantage to preserve the status quo in Hong Kong, and that they realise that an unprovoked direct attack on Hong Kong would seriously increase the risk of Anglo-American attack on China.[7]

Even when tensions between Britain and China heightened to unprecedented levels during the confrontation in 1967, the JIC made similarly non-alarmist assessments. Thanks in large part to these JIC briefings, British ministers did not push for urgent military action or risk inflaming the situation by overreacting.[8]

Although not expressly stated in the JIC reports, it seems that the best source of British intelligence on China during the confrontation came from SIGINT. HCHQ had opened a listening base in Little Sai Wan, on the eastern end of Hong Kong Island, particularly focusing on Russian traffic, most importantly on KGB messages. In 1954 Britain used its SIGINT capabilities to launch Operation *Debenture*, a covert radio project described as 'the first UK operations of any magnitude for the penetration of mainland China'. Its aim was to provide an undercover 'black' broadcasting station that would increase the desire among the Chinese middle classes for contacts with Hong Kong, and increase the number of defections across the border. Originally Hong Kong was earmarked for this 'black station', but it was eventually located in Singapore, hidden in one of the military bases there.

In Hong Kong, as in Cyprus, the British also experimented with intelligence-gathering radar. In fact, after the outbreak of the Korean War in June 1950 the massive expansion of SIGINT requirements in Hong Kong presented problems of its own. A stream of British National Servicemen who had learned Chinese on RAF language courses provided GCHQ units in Hong Kong with linguists, but by 1957 there was such demand that GCHQ was forced to start using civilian Chinese-speakers. As civilians could not be used for some of the menial duties carried out by National Service personnel, GCHQ resorted to employing deaf-and-dumb locals in its more sensitive sites in Hong Kong.[9]

There were so many intelligence activities taking place in Hong Kong in the 1950s and 1960s that some British diplomats resented the position they were put in, being continually forced to deny covert operations. One Governor of Hong Kong, Sir Alexander Grantham, detested the way in which his territory had become home to a myriad of espionage activities. The specific event that sparked Grantham's resentment was when, in July 1952, the US Communications Intelligence Board tried to convince their British opposite numbers of the need to send an eight-hundred-strong US Air Force SIGINT unit to Hong Kong. The fact of the matter was that, despite Grantham's protests, Hong Kong was too important *not* to be used in the Cold War by both Britain and the United States. During the 1950s and 1960s the US State Department and the Pentagon considered Hong Kong to be the single most vital British overseas territory from the point of view of intelligence-gathering. The NSA opened substantial facilities on Hong Kong and its surrounding islands, while GCHQ's main radar site was located 3,000 feet up the precipitous cliffs of Tai Mo Shan in Hong Kong's New Territories on the Chinese mainland. Staring straight into Chinese airspace, it provided intelligence on China for London, Washington and Canberra. It appears that one of the major success stories of joint UK–US SIGINT efforts in Hong Kong was the prediction of China's detonation of its first nuclear weapon in 1964.[10]

Hong Kong remained a major centre for British intelligence in the Far East until Britain finally handed over the colony to China on the expiry of its ninety-nine-year lease in July 1997. A former high-ranking SIS officer has stated that SIS provided the final British Governor of Hong Kong, Chris Patten, with crucial intelligence on how to manage the handover, right up until the final curtain call. The lowering of the British flag in Hong Kong was a symbolic moment for Britain, unambiguously marking its final endgame of empire.[11]

Britain's rapid exit from empire, largely in the two decades after 1945, was in general relatively smooth and successful, especially when compared to the disorderly withdrawals of other European colonial powers, France, Holland and Belgium, from their empires. Although in some instances Britain relinquished power to what became failed states, such as Pakistan, and to others that turned to dictatorship and dropped out of the Commonwealth, such as Burma and Zimbabwe, it was usually able to maintain reasonably close and friendly relations with its former colonies, especially when compared to other European colonial powers. As this book has shown, Britain's intelligence services helped to smooth the process of colonial retreat, providing the fancy footwork of end of empire.

The Cold War was the context in which Britain exited its colonial empire in the years after 1945, so that the red that once proudly covered British imperial maps was reduced, by the mid-1960s, to a small scattering of dependencies across the globe. As we have seen, it was the Cold War that shaped and dictated how British intelligence and British policy-makers responded to anti-colonial movements in the post-war years. In fact, the Cold War meant that Britain's intelligence services were not just tangentially involved with decolonisation: they were actually at its front line. The assumption made by governments on both sides of the Atlantic was that the Soviet Union and communist China were intent on turning Britain's former colonies into new satellite states of their own. This was not fanciful. The KGB deployed a host of measures to court governments across the world that had gained independence from Britain. Yet Malaya was the only colonial state where Britain actually experienced an insurgency activated along communist lines. All of the other colonial Emergencies in the post-war years – including Palestine, Kenya, Cyprus and Aden – were fought by radical nationalists, not communists.

It is possible to identify a number of areas in which the activities of British intelligence paid direct dividends for the British government (and by extension, thanks to the 'special relationship', also the American government) during the retreat from empire. One of the most striking of these

areas was SIGINT. Even though it has not been recognised by most historians, the phenomenal successes that British code-breakers gained during the
Second World War with Ultra continued throughout the Cold War. The
UKUSA Agreement brokered in 1946 between GCHQ and US SIGINT
authorities (the text of which was only publicly disclosed in 2011) guaranteed that Britain held an important place for Washington, because under its
terms it was agreed that GCHQ would be responsible for SIGINT collection
in new states entering the Commonwealth. GCHQ provided the British and
American governments with valuable information on Britain's declining
colonial empire, comprising much of what is now called the developing
world. The fact that many colonial and Commonwealth governments used
Enigma machines, just as the Germans had during the war, meant their
communications were easy for GCHQ to break in the post-war years.

Britain's intelligence services also helped to smooth the end of empire
by providing background intelligence on anti-colonial leaders, many of
whom, like Jomo Kenyatta in Kenya, became the first leaders of new independent states. As we have seen, contrary to what one might assume, many
of the assessments that British intelligence made of leaders like Kenyatta
were sober and non-alarmist, dispelling fears of their communist beliefs,
rather than heightening them. Furthermore, although it is a story missing
from nearly all histories of British decolonisation, the secret services
helped the British government to establish and then maintain close liaisons with former colonies. The transfer of power in India in 1947 set a
precedent that was followed in every major British colonial state that
gained independence thereafter. During the period before colonies gained
full independence, MI5 built close relationships with them – so close that
they remained intact after independence. In many instances, as we have
seen, MI5's Security Liaison Officers (SLOs) provided a secret channel of
communication between London and newly independent national
governments. In fact, as was demonstrated in India, intelligence liaison
between Britain and its former colonies remained close even when diplomatic relations were strained.

By the mid-1950s MI5 had established a formula for presenting its
SLOs to the elected leaders of new national governments, usually on the
eve of independence. Typically, at a certain point during the transition
period of internal self-government, before a colony reached full independence, when Britain was sharing rule with local ministers, colonial governors would formally present MI5's resident SLO to national
leaders-in-waiting and a select group of other high-ranking local

ministers. We are told from MI5 records that, in order to dispel any fears ministers might have had about the role of MI5 and local Special Branches, the governor would usually stress that MI5's role was not to 'spy' on colonial or Commonwealth countries, but to support them. Sometimes the presentation of SLOs was done with 'pomp and circumstance', to quote one MI5 report, while at other times they were low-key affairs. It is tempting to suppose that they took place in smoke-filled rooms, behind closed doors, or maybe over gin & tonics at a colonial governor's official residence, Government House. Whatever the exact situation, these meetings were delicate affairs because, as both sides doubtless would have appreciated, the ministers-in-waiting who were being indoctrinated into the secrets of British intelligence would invariably have been the targets of previous MI5 and Special Branch investigations. It seems that, in order to help sugar-coat these meetings, colonial governors would often appeal to local ministers' vanity, stressing that cooperating with British intelligence signified the importance Britain attached to their countries. Apparently they would also emphasise that if they retained MI5's services for their new governments, there would be no financial cost to them: SLOs were paid for by the British government. The formula that MI5 devised for brokering these agreements was highly successful: without significant exception, new national governments retained MI5's SLOs after they gained independence from Britain. The anti-colonial poachers rapidly turned into gamekeepers.[12]

However, the story was not quite as trouble-free as the discussion above suggests. During the period of internal self-government in colonies, especially after the colonial governor had disclosed MI5's SLO to local ministers, the situation would inevitably arise when MI5, and other parts of the British secret state, had to begin sharing intelligence with those ministers. After all, taking control of security and defence matters was one of the clearest expressions of independence for governments-in-waiting. Furthermore, on the eve of independence local ministers were often already sitting on security councils at which intelligence matters were discussed. However, as we have seen, during the period of self-government in British colonies there was actually a two-tier system of intelligence in place: while MI5's SLOs shared some intelligence with local ministers, there was another entirely separate stream of intelligence that went only to the Governor himself and his immediate advisers, marked 'UK Eyes Only'. MI5's SLOs provided ministers-in-waiting only with carefully vetted 'clean' intelligence, termed 'Legacy' material, which was judged safe to leave behind after the British had departed. It was usually primarily concerned with law-and-order matters, and hardly ever discussed issues like communism. Meanwhile, 'dirty' or 'non-Legacy' material, which contained information that was judged not safe to be distributed to non-Europeans, was stamped with a 'W', meaning 'Watch', or 'Guard'. In some instances papers were removed and files reordered to avoid any trace of 'Watch' records being found by their inheritors after handover, while dummy files were created so as to not arouse suspicion about missing records on handover.[13]

The situation, however, was even more Machiavellian than this. As we have seen, MI5's SLOs and colonial Special Branches continued to monitor the activities of some democratically elected ministers until the last possible moment before a colony's independence, and perhaps even beyond – in some instances, such as in the Gold Coast, in contradiction to promises that a colonial governor had made face-to-face to those ministers. Britain's need to be sure of the trustworthiness of ministers who were about to take power meant they were regarded as legitimate targets for investigation, even if that meant going back on promises. In order to negotiate an orderly transfer of power, MI5 and colonial governments were willing to employ dirty tricks, giving with one hand but taking with the other. This process of continued surveillance on elected ministers is one of the most closely guarded secrets of Britain's last days of empire, known only to a select number of British colonial officials and carried out by a small, secret team of trusted (European) colonial Special Branch officers. However, the truly extraordinary end to this tale is that, as we have discovered, once national governments had gained full independence from Britain, many of them adopted and deployed the same black arts of intelligence that they had inherited from the British, but now against their own enemies.

Britain's intelligence services, particularly MI5, trained large numbers of colonial intelligence officials in the last days of empire. This was one of the ways that, as the imperial historian Philip Murphy has pointed out, Britain successfully managed to export an 'intelligence culture' to the empire and the Commonwealth. Overall, it can be said that Britain's intelligence services helped to transform the empire into the Commonwealth, a loose confederation of like-minded states, reinvigorated within the geopolitical context of the Cold War. Alex Kellar, the head of MI5's Overseas Division between 1958 and 1962, summarised the successes of MI5's SLOs in winning the confidence of newly independent governments:

In the case of the African Commonwealth countries, I have felt – profoundly so – that the contributions that we as a Security Service have been making to their own security by our training facilities, by our service of information, and by the close links which we are building up in running joint agent operations, together constitute a record of which we can be legitimately proud ... We have built up in these new emergent territories cadres of indigenous officials who admire, respect and trust us and who can do much to influence their political masters in the right direction ... We shall never be able to make any African country pro-West but, by this kind of support, we can at least assist them to sit on the fence and not fall over on the wrong side.[14]

The reforms that British intelligence instigated, driven by the politics of the Cold War, produced liaisons between London and colonies so robust that, in the overwhelming majority of cases, they remained intact even after those colonies gained independence. In November 1957 the JIC summarised Britain's imperial intelligence reforms in the following way:

An experienced and efficient intelligence organisation, manned by officers of the requisite professional calibre and integrity, and with close ties with the Security Service [MI5], is a legacy of particular value to Colonies moving into independent status within the Commonwealth, as well as a safeguard of H.M.G.'s long-term intelligence interests ... the aim is to build an indigenous intelligence service, able to stand on its own two feet when self-government is attained ... The links thus formed have proved capable of surviving the transition to independence and are reinforced by Security Liaison Officers who continue to provide advice and a secure exchange of intelligence in the many Colonial and Commonwealth territories to which they are accredited.[15]

Some of Britain's imperial intelligence reforms in the early Cold War produced legacies that still shape intelligence and security matters in the present day. The colonial and Commonwealth intelligence network that MI5 established was inherited by SIS in the 1960s, providing SIS with a truly global intelligence network, which it continues to exploit today. As late as the 1990s, the Queen's Personal Secretary, Sir Robert Fellowes, asked the Deputy Chief of SIS, Sir Gerry Warner, how he might describe the role of the secret intelligence service to Her Majesty. The Deputy Chief replied: 'Tell her that we are the last penumbra of empire.'

One of the most striking measures of MI5's success in building up a colonial and Commonwealth intelligence network is the fact that Britain managed to maintain intelligence liaisons even with some British dependencies that did not remain in the Commonwealth, often amid scenes of intense anti-British violence. This was the case with the state of Israel. By October 1949, just eighteen months after the Israeli state had come into being amid anti-British violence, relations between SIS and Israeli intelligence had become largely normalised, with SIS operating a station in Tel Aviv. This was undoubtedly assisted by the fact that some of the key figures in early Israeli intelligence, such as Reuven Zislani, the first head of Israel's foreign intelligence service, the Mossad, had previously worked with British intelligence in Palestine against the Irgun and the Stern Gang. In 1953 the JIC in London noted that 'standards of security of the Israeli police and security service are high and are based on the British methods of training and practice'.[16]

However, the success of the Commonwealth as an idea, supported by intelligence liaisons, should not be exaggerated. The Commonwealth has certainly managed to promote links between nations, through means that include sport and education, and anyone who has seen the words 'Imperial Standard', found in bathrooms from Singapore to the West Indies, will be aware of at least one manifestation of the continuing legacy of the British empire. Nevertheless, beyond the realms of urinals and weights and measures, many of the plans most keenly advocated for the Commonwealth – from which the word 'British' was politely dropped in 1948 after Indian independence – never got off the ground. There was never a Commonwealth court, as some had hoped, and the idea of a universal declaration of rights for the Commonwealth was vetoed. That said, with MI5 presiding over a Commonwealth-wide intelligence network, it was a valuable tool in the Cold War, providing an ideological bulwark against anti-Western propaganda spewed out by the Sino-Soviet Bloc. Without the intelligence network developed by MI5, it is likely that the Soviet Union would have been more successful in its Cold War efforts in the former British empire than it was.[17]

Along with these positive contributions by British intelligence to the way Britain managed its retreat from empire – the use of SIGINT, providing background intelligence on nationalist leaders, building and maintaining close liaisons with national governments after independence – it would be misleading to suggest that all of MI5's imperial and Commonwealth reforms were successful. The minimal resources that MI5 had at its disposal in the 1950s meant that its impact on the ground was inevitably limited. In the early 1950s MI5 had a grand total of just three officers stationed on the whole of the continent of Africa. When it was investigating communist involvement in the Mau Mau insurgency, it did not have any officers who spoke Kikuyu, and it was so strapped for cash that it could not afford to hire a translator. Its proposals for security reforms in colonial and Commonwealth countries were also not always adopted straight away. One of Britain's closest Commonwealth partners, New Zealand, did not establish a separate security service until 1956, even though MI5 had recommended it as early as 1948. Some of MI5's SLOs in former colonies were also unable to achieve their main task: to establish close and lasting relations with post-independence countries. The SLO in Uganda reported in 1962 that ministers there were 'unwilling or unready to absorb our advice'. The SLO in post-independence Tanganyika failed to establish a productive working relationship with the government, and was withdrawn in 1964. Likewise, the SLO in Zambia found himself frozen out when an African head of the Special Branch took over from a British expatriate, and the posts there and in Uganda were closed down in 1967.[18]

Similar failures occurred in Burma. Britain's transfer of power there in January 1948 was an abject failure, and a lesson in how not to exit a colony. The British government's hopes for Burmese independence had been pinned on General Aung San, an acclaimed military leader who during the war had first collaborated with the Japanese and then switched sides to support the Allies. Unfortunately, San – father of the current Burmese pro-democracy leader Aung San Suu Kyi – was assassinated in July 1947, six months before Burma was due to gain independence. Thereafter British officials lost control of the transfer of power, and 'scuttled' from Burma. After 1948 Burma developed as a dictatorial siege economy, outside the Commonwealth. It appears from the diary of MI5's Guy Liddell that, following the murder of Aung San, Britain's plans for establishing an intelligence liaison with Burma were scuppered. Contemporary JIC papers reveal that immediately after independence, no section of British intelligence maintained a liaison with the new Burmese national government. Colonial Office records show that it was only by the early 1950s that MI5 had opened an SLO post in the Burmese capital, Rangoon, as it had during the Second World War. This station was unique in that, although it was on non-British territory, it was run by MI5, and in fact doubled as both an MI5 and an SIS station. It is known to have existed until at least 1954.

Judging from JIC reports, the MI5 station in Rangoon does not appear to have produced significant intelligence in the early Cold War, when the intelligence relations between Britain and Burma were effectively frozen.[19]

Britain faced similar complications in its liaison with the Republic of Ireland, which left the Commonwealth in 1948. MI5 and SIS almost certainly maintained 'links' with the Irish police and military intelligence (G2) in the years after 1945, as they had done immediately before and during the war. At the time, however, Irish security issues were not the responsibility of British intelligence. In the decades after 1945, British and Irish authorities regarded the threat of IRA and 'Loyalist' paramilitary groups as primarily a law-and-order issue, and responsibility for dealing with them therefore fell to the police on both sides of the border, in both the Republic of Ireland and Northern Ireland. During the later period of the so-called 'Troubles' in Northern Ireland, beginning in the 1970s, Irish security increasingly became the responsibility of the British Army. MI5 is known to have stationed an SLO in Belfast in the early 1970s, but it did not take a lead in Irish-related security issues, including terrorism, in mainland Britain or in Northern Ireland until the 1990s – a story that lies far beyond the scope of this book.[20]

As well as these failures, the strict demarcation between MI5 and SIS's operations, within the empire and in 'foreign' territories respectively, meant that when SIS took over from MI5 in Commonwealth countries, it was less prepared than it would have been if it had been allowed to operate in those countries previously: according to one former high-level SIS officer, it had to start agent-running operations from scratch when it was finally allowed to start work in a Commonwealth territory, albeit often using the same registry of files that MI5 and local Special Branches had previously accumulated. It appears, however, that SIS was at least partly to blame for its own slow start in Commonwealth countries, as it devoted few resources to setting up operations in them. One SIS recruit recalled that the section in London dealing with the whole of Africa in the early 1960s, precisely the time when SIS was starting to move into former British colonies there, was a small affair, consisting of only a few officers. Its head, the 'Controller for Africa', was the eccentric John Bruce Lockhart ('JBL'), the nephew of Robert Bruce Lockhart, the famous British representative in Moscow after the 1917 Bolshevik revolution. Despite his pedigree, JBL was apparently a man with whom it was difficult to get along.[21]

The decline of Britain's empire, combined with the scramble for SIS to take over from MI5 in former colonies, also led to a boom in what remains a growth area to the present day: independent security contractors. As the empire disintegrated, a proliferation of private security consultants offered a range of services to states that had recently won their freedom from Britain. A group of such security experts, mostly comprised of former colonial Special Branch officers, travelled from one crisis zone to another, offering private security services. Typical of these men was Ian Henderson, who as we have seen worked in the Kenya Special Branch, but after that moved to Rhodesia and then became a security consultant in the Gulf States. The origins of notorious private security firms such as Blackwater, which operated in the recent war in Iraq, lie in this period.

At the outset of the Cold War in the early 1950s, Winston Churchill popularised the idea that Britain's future lay in straddling three interlocking circles: the Commonwealth, the United States (the 'special relationship'), and Europe. However, a decade later, in the early 1960s, one of the main ideas behind the Commonwealth, as an economic trading zone known as the Sterling Area, had crumbled; Britain's relationship with Washington was one of dependence; and Western Europe had been transformed by the creation of the European Economic Community (EEC), without British participation. Britain had initially refused to join the EEC in 1957, but in 1961 Harold Macmillan's Conservative government, realising that it was being left behind, attempted to gain entry, only to be emphatically vetoed by the French President Charles de Gaulle. It was at this point that, to use the phrase of the historian David Reynolds, it could be said that Britain's status as a world power was overruled, compared to what it used to be.[22]

Despite its dwindling status in terms of 'hard' power, Britain's former colonial holdings – its imperial real estate – meant that it continued to have an important role to play in the eyes of Washington. Britain's scattering of former colonial dependencies, from Cyprus to Hong Kong, acted as staging posts for intelligence operations during the Cold War, especially in the pre-satellite era, which was as useful for Washington as it was for London. With US funds far outstripping anything that the British Exchequer could provide, the US SIGINT agency, the NSA, took over and bankrolled some of the most important British Cold War SIGINT operations in places like Cyprus. As we have seen with the small colony of British Guiana, in some instances the US government was more colonial in its outlook and actions, more desperate to prop up imperial rule, than was the British government itself. This was also the case with the tiny island of Diego Garcia, the largest atoll in the chain known as the Chagos Islands in the Indian Ocean, located roughly halfway between Africa and Indonesia. Recently available records from the secret colonial archive at Hanslope Park reveal the extent to which the British and American governments hoodwinked the public on both sides of the Atlantic about their plans for Diego Garcia, which was important for Washington within the geopolitics of the Cold War because it did not have any bases in the region.

In November 1965 the British and American governments started drafting an agreement under which Diego Garcia and its surrounding islands would be separated from Mauritius and the Seychelles (which administered the Chagos Islands at the time) and reconstituted as the 'British Indian Ocean Territories', or BIOT. The purpose of the agreement, formally signed by the two governments in December 1966, was to provide London and Washington with the use of the islands for fifty years, and the 'construction of defence facilities' there. According to the agreement, however, the islands were to be acquired without a resident population. In private, American officials made it clear to their British counterparts that they wanted the islands 'cleared' of people. The problem was that the islands were in fact inhabited by about 1,200 people, who had no interest in making way for an Anglo-American military base.[23]

The original intention was that Britain would meet the cost of resettling the island's inhabitants and 'buying the agreement of Mauritius and the Seychelles', while America would pay for the installations. However, as time when on, it became clear that the 'sweetener' demanded by Mauritius and the Seychelles was larger than expected – in the region of £10 million. British ministers decided that Washington should contribute to this, and American defence officials reluctantly agreed, on condition that this neo-colonial activity would be hidden from the public. The arrangement was carried out secretly, and the American contribution was paid, according to an agreement in 1967, by deducting that sum from money Britain owed for buying Polaris missiles. American officials knew that Congress in Washington would disapprove of America subsidising the 'separation of the Chagos archipelago' to create a new British colony, and in the opinion of one Foreign Office official, Richard Sykes, in April 1967, the Americans were increasingly nervous about telling what was 'frankly an outright lie'.[24]

Over the following years the Colonial Office, under pressure from Washington, set about depopulating the Chagos Islands. The British Commissioner for BIOT in the Seychelles declared an ordinance that allowed him to purchase plantations from residents of the Chagos Islands for what (it has been later claimed) was insufficient compensation. The Colonial Office deliberately avoided using words like 'permanent residents' to describe the Chagos Islanders at the UN, in order to avoid the impression that they had any right to remain there. In private, however, British officials exposed their true feelings. In August 1966 the Permanent Undersecretary at the Foreign Office, Sir Paul Gore Booth, wrote to Dennis Greenhill, a British diplomat at the UN, about the implications of the purchase of the islands from Mauritius:

> We must surely be very tough about this. The object of the exercise was to get some rocks which will remain ours; there will be no indigenous population except seagulls who have not yet got a committee (the Status of Women Committee does not cover the rights of birds) ... The United States Government will require the removal of the entire population of the atoll by July.

This led Dennis Greenhill (later Baron Greenhill of Harrow) to reply in the following terms:

> Unfortunately along with the birds go some few Tarzans or Men Fridays whose origins are obscure, and who are being hopefully wished on to Mauritius etc. When this has been done I agree we must be very tough and a submission is being done accordingly.[25]

The shocking language used by Greenhill is more similar to that we would expect from a British official at the height of the Victorian era, when colonial populations were arrogantly dismissed as 'inferior', than from a Foreign Office official in the mid-1960s, when Britain was attempting to prove to the world that its remaining colonial holdings were not a repugnant anachronism. In order to 'sell' the depopulation of the Chagos Islands to sceptics at the UN, the Colonial Office deliberately misconstrued the reason why the Chagossians were being removed, stating that it was primarily for commercial reasons: they had good jobs to go to in Mauritius, it was claimed – though British officials at the UN chose not to emphasise that Mauritius was over 1,000 miles away from the Chagos Islands, making it difficult to portray their resettlement as a simple process of 'rehousing'. The Colonial Office pressured a company, Moulinie & Co. (Seychelles) Ltd, which operated a coconut plantation on the Chagos Islands, to ship the islanders to Mauritius and the Seychelles. Unfortunately, however, the jobs they had been promised there never materialised, with many of the exiled Chagossians being forced to live in poverty. The issue of their resettlement remains a live one to the present day. They have already brought legal proceedings against the British government for one aspect of their depopulation, and have intimated that they will do so again for broader compensation.[26]

Meanwhile, the British and American governments got exactly what they wanted. They built an enormous airfield, with a runway 3,500 feet long, on the depopulated island of Diego Garcia, which in 1970 also became home to a large SIGINT station, as well as a base for about 250 service personnel, mostly paid for with US dollars. The British Defence Secretary, Lord Carrington, told his opposite numbers in Washington in November 1970 frankly that 'while the [British] government is prepared to partner the US in setting up a defence communications base on the island of Diego Garcia in the Indian Ocean, the US will have to bear the bulk of the cost'. The most remarkable twist in this story, however, was an agreement that Britain and America reached in 1974. In January of that year the Cabinet Secretary, Sir John Hunt, was sent on a delicate mission to the White House to discuss the thorny issue of whether America would be given 'unrestricted access' to the base on Diego Garcia in a time of crisis. The results of Hunt's mission are extraordinary. Publicly, it was stated on both sides of the Atlantic that this would be a 'joint decision', seemingly with a British veto. However, behind the scenes there was a highly secret agreement between Hunt and the US President, Richard Nixon, which effectively changed this to mere consultation. The result was that Britain allowed America to use the Chagos Islands effectively as its own colony. In the Indian Ocean, as in British Guiana, the anti-colonialist Americans proved themselves to be considerably more colonialist than the British.[27]

On one level, the story set out in this book is one of overwhelming failure, in particular a failure to learn lessons from the past. Despite the warnings of Britain's intelligence services, colonial administrations generally paid little attention to intelligence matters until it was too late, after unrest had broken out in their colonies. This problem was compounded by the fact that, when they faced anti-colonial violence, the colonial administrations, as well as the Colonial Office in London and the British Army, were all extremely bad at learning lessons from previous Emergencies. The army attempted to codify a doctrine of low-intensity warfare, but continued to make the same basic mistakes, first in the sands of Palestine, then in the jungles of Malaya and Kenya, and then in the rocky hilltops of Cyprus and the deserts of Southern Arabia. Despite the lessons Palestine could have provided, the British Army and government departments across Whitehall proved to be remarkably poor at transferring experiences from there to later Emergencies. Britain's failure to learn lessons from Palestine is all the more remarkable considering that, after it withdrew from the Mandate in May 1948, there was an exodus of Palestine police, civil servants and security advisers to other parts of the empire. Rather than learning lessons from Palestine, they repeated old mistakes, attempting to reinvent the wheel each time a new Emergency was declared, first scrambling to gather intelligence on their enemies, then attempting to put down insurgencies on the cheap, by use of minimal necessary force. After a period, they would invariably realise that this could not be done, so they would resort to the use of overwhelming force, coercion and repression, often at huge loss of life. This was ultimately counter-productive, as it sowed the seeds of the colonial administration's own destruction. Sir Hugh Foot, who had served as a senior official in Palestine during the pre-war Arab Revolt, and who in 1957 became Governor of Cyprus, recalled that:

> ... action against a subversive or terrorist movement ... must be selective and not indiscriminate. That sounds obvious, but in Palestine and then in Cyprus there was often a tendency to attempt to make up for a lack of Intelligence by using the sledgehammer – mass arrests, mass detentions, big cordons and searches and collective punishments. Such operations can do more harm than good and usually play into the hands of the terrorists by alienating general opinion from the forces of authority. It is not by making the life of ordinary people intolerable that a nationalist movement is destroyed – it is by a selective drive against the terrorist leadership undertaken by small numbers of skilled forces acting intelligently on good information.[28]

MI5's experience during the Second World War was that the use of torture in interrogations could never produce reliable intelligence – a lesson as important then as it is today. MI5 officers tried to instil this view among colonial Special Branches in the post-war years, but they often failed to do so. One does not have to look far in the pages of the history of British campaigns in Palestine, Malaya, Kenya and Aden to find gruesome instances of British security personnel torturing detainees, both as the term was legally understood then and as it is now. In Palestine British soldiers are understood to have forced the heads of Irgun and Stern Gang suspects into buckets of water until they came close to drowning. In Kenya there were instances of what can only be called sadism during interrogations, as security personnel treated detained Mau Mau suspects to 'rough justice', with beatings commonplace. In Cyprus and Aden, interrogators are known to have resorted to practices like placing metal buckets over the heads of prisoners and banging them with rifle barrels until they confessed. Other stories emerged of interrogators inserting pins under the fingernails of prisoners, as well as other techniques that were designed to inflict pain but leave no traces on their victims. In Aden, the intelligence corps of the British Army apparently ran a secret torture facility in Fort Morbut in the 1960s, the horrors of which have not yet been revealed. Set against this, it must be remembered that those fighting the British in places like Palestine, Malaya, Kenya and Aden were also ruthless, often torturing captured British soldiers as well as killing members of the local populations for whom they professed to be fighting – sadly, the tendency for paramilitary groups to kill their own brethren is one that persists to the present day.

It is probably impossible to draw any overall conclusions about why British security personnel tortured prisoners in colonial Emergencies in the twilight of empire. There are probably as many different reasons as there were interrogators. Man's inhumanity to man is capable of infinite explanations, especially in the heat of battle: from desperation to gather information, to the settling of old scores or taking vengeance for an injured friend, to the workings of a deranged mind. However, the failure of senior British military and civilian officials, including the intelligence services, to set up adequate safeguards to prevent torture occurring in the first place, especially at the front line of battle, is part of the reason torture occurred in Britain's dirty end-of-empire conflicts.

The resort to torture seems to have occurred less often in interrogations designed to elicit strategic intelligence, or to turn a prisoner into a double agent – interrogations that were often carried out in specialist facilities, away from the front line of fighting, and conducted by colonial Special Branch officers with MI5 oversight. Torture seems to have been used more frequently in interrogations conducted at the front line, or when interrogators combined gathering intelligence with the 'rehabilitation' of prisoners. As we have seen, the 'screening' process in Kenya, when prisoners were interrogated to gather intelligence and to assess how radicalised they were into Mau Mau, appears to have been one occasion when security forces committed a large number of abuses.[29]

The history of British decolonisation is a story of deception. Thanks to the release of previously classified records, we can now see that the British government deliberately doctored the historical record of its end of empire. In the last days of colonial rule, in territories across the world, British officials deliberately destroyed 'sensitive' records, while others were shipped back to Britain for safekeeping, ending up at the top-secret Foreign Office facility at Hanslope Park. The result was that historians have been deceived about important aspects of British decolonisation. It is difficult, at this early stage, to draw any definite conclusions about the secret colonial-era archive at Hanslope Park, as the first tranche of records was only made available in April 2012. Early indications suggest that these records will add new details to our understanding, but are unlikely to change fundamentally the existing historical narrative. Details of the manipulation of intelligence in the last days of the British empire into 'Legacy' and 'non-Legacy' records could already be found in other records, if one looked carefully, even before the disclosure of the Hanslope Park archive. However, it appears that these new records do reveal that British ministers and officials in London knew more about the worst crimes and abuses committed by British security personnel in colonial Emergencies than historians previously thought, and were not as innocent about colonial crimes as they liked to portray themselves.[30]

The reason colonial officials destroyed records, or transferred them back to Britain, was often on the grounds of national security. It is easy to have some sympathy with this. It is not hard to understand why records relating, for example, to informants in the colonial period would have to be guarded closely: their disclosure would be awkward for the British government, and potentially life-threatening to the informants themselves after the transfer of power. However, judging from the first tranche of the Hanslope Park archive, many of the records that were kept secret were suppressed not for reasons of national security, but because of a fear of 'embarrassing' Her Majesty's Government. Embarrassment seems to have been used as an excuse to withhold records that, by any reasonable measure, should have been disclosed long ago.

The release of records from the Hanslope Park archive leads us inevitably to ask another question: what is still being withheld, even now, either on national security grounds or because it may embarrass the British government? It is undoubtedly the case that there are many more skeletons in the cupboard relating to the history of Britain's end of empire. It has come out, for example, that at least one official in the Foreign and Commonwealth Office was advocating in 1960 that the leader of the Congo, Patrice Lumumba, should be killed. The official who made these remarks, Howard Smith, went on to become a Director-General of MI5 – though at the time he wrote them he was completely unconnected with MI5. Still, the question remains whether British plots to assassinate Lumumba, or other troublesome leaders who died in suspicious circumstances, ever amounted to anything. At present, we do not know. It is, of course, the case that history never repeats itself exactly. That said, history can provide a guide to the present – and a warning for the future. It is only when all the secret records on the bloody wars that Britain fought in its twilight of empire are released that the historical record will be put straight and we will be able properly to learn lessons from the past.

Acknowledgements

In the course of writing this book I have incurred more debts to people than I could ever repay. First and foremost, my thanks are due to my PhD supervisor, Christopher Andrew, who first sparked my interest in the history of British intelligence and without whose continual support this book would not have been possible. I am greatly indebted to him for giving me the exciting opportunity to work as a research assistant on his unprecedented official history of the Security Service (MI5). I also owe thanks to a number of British intelligence officers, serving and retired. Their identities must remain secret, but they know who they are.

During seven years of research at Cambridge University, between 2002 and 2009, it was a privilege for me to teach on (and help organise) the specialist undergraduate paper on intelligence history. One of the benefits of teaching at Cambridge is that one can test out new ideas on exceptionally bright minds. The Cambridge University Intelligence Seminar, which I helped to organise between 2006 and 2009, is arguably the most active academic intelligence seminar in the world, and it has been a pleasure to present papers at it over the years on many of the subjects that appear in this book. I also tested many of the ideas it contains at an international conference on intelligence and empire, which I helped to organise, held at King's College Cambridge, in April 2009. My own college at Cambridge, Trinity, was a particularly appropriate place at which to study the history of British intelligence (and the KGB). Trinity is as generous as it is wealthy, and I owe particular thanks to its bursaries. My doctoral work was funded by the UK Arts and Humanities Research Council, to which I am extremely grateful, and my post-doctoral Junior Research Fellowship at Darwin College Cambridge was funded in part by a generous grant from the Isaac Newton Trust.

I would like to thank, in particular, the following people who kindly read drafts of this book at various stages: Peter Martland, Bruce Hoffman,

Philip Murphy, Richard Aldrich and Peter Hennessy. Terry Barry has been a stalwart support ever since I met him at Trinity College, Dublin, years ago. Will Leslie, of the Cambridge University intelligence seminar, assisted me with photographing records at the National Archives, and Sophie Webb assisted me with an earlier draft. My editors at HarperCollins, Martin Redfern and Robert Lacey, have been exceptionally helpful throughout, as has my literary agent, Jon Elek at A.P. Watt.

Along the way, friends have provided me with more support than they probably ever knew. At Cambridge there were several people who kept me (relatively) sane after long days of research: Kevin Quinlan, Adam Shelley, Jonathan Chavkin, Jochen Schenk, Jonathan Masters and Giles Kingsley-Pallant. I am lucky to be able to call Ian Russell a friend, and I have bene-fited greatly from talking with him about our respective research over the years. Friends in London provided good company and welcome breaks from hours hunched at a desk in the National Archives: Tom Bruxner and Juliet McDermott for their discussions about the British military; Kunal Patel and Ali Al-Rufaie for helping me to understand more about medi-cine; and in particular Tim Persson, whose home in Swaziland was an inspiration for me to start thinking about colonial history.

I would also like to thank several people who, accidentally, I failed to name in the UK hardback edition of this book, whose friendship means a great deal to me: Andy Hui, Seb Davison, and Mark Hamilton. I am also grateful to a number of people who have contacted me since the publica-tion of the UK hardback version pointing out errors in the text: in particu-lar, Chris Hale, Michael Henderson, Michael Nelson, Brian Haigh, Nigel West, and Chikara Hashimotio. This edition is updated to correct the errors they identified.

Although it barely needs to be said, my sincere thanks go to my imme-diate family (my father Michael, my mother Lila, and sister Lia, and her partner, Chris), who in recent times have gone through more than any family should have to. Without the support of my father, who grew up in colonial Kenya, this book would have foundered long ago, and I hope that he will be able to enjoy seeing it in print. Above all, my deepest gratitude goes to my partner, Jennifer, who has sustained me throughout, and to whom this book is dedicated. I could not have done it without her.

CALDER WALTON
September 2013

Note on Sources and Methodology

This book is based on a vast number of previously classified records. The research for it took, in total, nearly ten years to complete. The primary research was conducted at the National Archives (formerly the Public Record Office) in Kew, in London.

The main intelligence records currently available at the National Archives are from the Security Service (MI5), which can be found under the series 'KV', and the Joint Intelligence Committee (JIC), which for the post-war years can be found in the records of the Cabinet Office under the series 'CAB'. The records of the Colonial Office's Intelligence and Security Department can be found under the series 'CO 1035', and recently released records of the Colonial Office's 'migrated archive' can be found under the series 'FCO 141'.

In addition to these records, the book draws on a multitude of files from other British government departments now held at the National Archives, such as the Foreign Office (under the series 'FO'), the Prime Minister's Office ('PREM') and the War Office ('WO').

One of the methodological problems facing anyone wanting to study intelligence history is that while – like anyone conducting a historical enquiry – we are dependent upon the sources available to us, unlike other areas of historical research, with intelligence history we have to rely on the subjects under examination (intelligence services) themselves to reveal their history. This inevitably leads to a question about the extent to which we can trust the hand that feeds us, or whether we are being presented merely with a version of the past as the intelligence services want us to see it. That may be the case, but there are many reasons to suppose otherwise. For one thing, the records released by the intelligence services reveal a surprising number of failures on their own part, the episode of the 'Cambridge spies' being the most obvious. If there was a desire on their part to present their past through rose-tinted glasses, they have done a remarkably poor job.

In my experience, one way to alleviate the problem of relying solely on intelligence services to declassify their own records, and to give their activities the historical place they deserve, is to combine intelligence records with those of other government departments. After all, it is the job of intelligence services to *service* other government departments with classified information (or intelligence), and it is therefore only natural that records from the intelligence services should be found in the files of other departments. One way to obtain such records is to use the Freedom of Information Act 2000 (FOIA 2000). Unfortunately FOIA 2000 does not apply to Britain's intelligence services: it is not possible to use it to apply for the release of records held by them. However, it does apply to other government departments, and this book has benefited from several applications for records made under FOIA 2000.

Another way in which we can place Britain's intelligence services in their proper historical context is to use records from other archives. Records in private collections of papers have sometimes managed to avoid Whitehall record 'weeders', whose job it is to extract sensitive information from records being declassified. This book therefore draws on a number of collections of private papers held at other archives, such as India Office papers held at the British Library in London; papers held at the Imperial War Museum in London; various papers of former colonial officers now at Rhodes House Library in Oxford; and papers at Cambridge University Library. In addition to these sources, this book has also benefited from an examination of contemporary newspapers, which sometimes contain clues to the activities of British intelligence when they bubbled up into the public domain. Often old newspaper reports contain new ideas. The *Times* digital archive, which is word searchable, has been particularly useful in this regard.

In addition to researching written records, I conducted a number of interviews (twelve in total) with former intelligence officers. However, the general methodology for this book has been based on written records, rather than interviews. This is because, in my experience, it is better to attach weight to written records, especially when their authors never thought they would be declassified, as was the case with all the MI5 and JIC records from the time, than to interviews. Anyone acquainted with courtrooms can confirm that the testimony of even the most well-meaning witness can be unreliable – memory is easily capable of playing tricks.

References to endnotes have been placed at the end of paragraphs, rather than within them. This has been done with the intention of making the text easier to read, without it being cluttered with references. Although some readers may find this objectionable from a scholarly point of view, those wishing to follow up citations should be able to find them easily in the endnotes. The author is happy to respond to questions and can be contacted at www.calderwalton.com.

Notes

Introduction

1 Le Carré, *The Honourable Schoolboy* p.35
2 'Terrorist Bomb in Whitehall', *The Times* (17 Apr 1946); Burt, *Commander Burt of Scotland Yard* pp.126–7; The National Archives London [TNA] CO 537/1723 'Terrorist outrages: extension to UK'
3 Ferguson, *Colossus* p.112
4 Walton and Andrew, 'Still the missing dimension' in Major and Moran (eds), *Spooked*; the classic description of intelligence as the 'missing dimension' is in Andrew and Noakes (eds), *The Missing Dimension: Governments and Intelligence Communities in the Twentieth Century*
5 Bennett, 'Declassification and release policies of the UK's intelligence agencies'; Gill, 'Reasserting control: recent changes in the oversight of the UK intelligence community'; Wark, 'In Never Never Land? The British archives on intelligence'; Aldrich, *The Hidden Hand* pp.1–16
6 Examples of older studies that ignore British intelligence include the momentous Mansergh (ed.), *Transfer of Power in India* series; more recent studies that still overlook the subject include Clayton, '"Deceptive might": imperial defence and security, 1900–1968' in Louis (ed.), *The Oxford History of the British Empire*; Bayly and Harper, *Forgotten Wars*; Heinlein, *British Government Policy and Decolonisation*; Hyam, *Britain's Declining Empire*. The minority of studies that do include British intelligence include Bloch and Fitzgerald, *British Intelligence and Covert Action: Africa, the Middle East and Europe Since 1945*; French, *Liberty or Death: India's Journey to Independence and Division*; French, *The British Way in Counter-Insurgency*
7 Clarke, *The Last Thousand Days of the British Empire*; Hennessy, *Never Again: Britain 1945–1951* p.215
8 Hyam, *Britain's Declining Empire* pp.xiii–xv
9 Whitehall's attitude in 1957 that few colonies would gain independence can be seen in Hyam and Louis (eds), *British Documents on the End of Empire Project* [*BDEEP*]: *The Conservative Government and the End of Empire* doc [3], Sir Norman Brook, 'Future constitutional development in the colonies' (6 Sept 1957); Herman, *Intelligence Power in Peace and War*; Macleod, 'Trouble in Africa', *Spectator* (31 Jan 1964)
10 Hyam, *Britain's Declining Empire* pp.xiv, 261, 262; Herman, *Intelligence Power in Peace and War*
11 Ben Macintyre, 'The Truth Will Out', *The Times* (10 May 2011); Ben Macintyre, 'Mau Mau and So Much More', *The Times* (16 Apr 2011); Ben Macintyre, 'Brutal Beatings and the "Roasting Alive" of a Suspect: What Secret Mau Mau Files Reveal' (13 Apr 2011); Banton, '"Destroy?", "Migrate?", "Conceal?": British strategies for the disposal of sensitive records of colonial administrations at independence'

12 Ian Cobain and Richard Norton-Taylor, 'The Secrets that Shamed the Last Days of Empire', *Guardian* (18 Apr 2012); Ben Macintyre, 'A Mistake or Mmurder in Cold Blood?' *The Times* (28 Apr 2012); *Mutua and others v Foreign and Commonwealth Office* [2011] EWHC 1913 (QB)

Chapter 1: Victoria's Secrets

1 Kipling, *Kim* pp.194–5
2 Nielson and McKercher, *Go Spy the Land*; Johnson, *Spying for Empire*
3 Bayly, *Empire and Information*; Satia, *Spies in Arabia*; Brendon, *The Decline and Fall of the British Empire* p.328; Hyam, *Britain's Declining Empire* p.10
4 Ferris, 'Before "Room 40": The British Empire and Signals Intelligence 1898–1914'; Jeffries, *The Colonial Office* pp.29–31
5 Edney, *Mapping an Empire*; Anderson, *Imagined Communities* Ch 10, 'Census, Map, Museum'; Scott, *Seeing Like a State* (1998); Brendon, *Decline and Fall* p.525; Thomas, *Empires of Intelligence*
6 Callwell, *Small Wars*; Andrew, *Secret Service* pp.30–4; Boot, *The Savage Wars of Peace* p.112
7 Andrew, *Defence of the Realm* pp.21–8
8 The National Archives London [TNA] CAB 16/232 The setting up of a Secret Service Bureau (28 Apr 1909); WO 106/6292 'Memorandum re. formation of a S.S. Bureau' (26 Aug 1909); Jeffery, *MI6* pp.13–15, 42–5
9 Raeff, 'The Well Ordered Police State'; Andrew, *Secret Service* pp.21–65
10 Curry, *The Security Service* p.41; TNA WO 106/6292 'Memorandum re. formation of a S.S. Bureau' (26 Aug 1909); *The 9/11 Commission: Final Report of the National Commission on the Terrorist Attacks upon the United States*
11 Andrew, *Defence of the Realm* pp.3–4; Jeffery, *MI6* pp.12–15
12 Holquist, 'Information is the Alpha and the Omega of our Work'; Curry, *The Security Service* p.98; TNA INF 4/9 General Staff Paper: 'The Organization of the Services of Military Secrecy, Security and Publicity' (Oct 1917) p.44; WO 32/10776 Historical Sketch of the Directorate of Military Intelligence in the Great War of 1914–1918; KV 1/73 MI9 Testing Department
13 Ellis, *Eye Deep in Hell*; Ferguson, *Empire* pp.301–3; Fussell, *The Great War and Modern Memory*
14 Ferguson, *Empire* pp.298–303; Buchan, *Greenmantle* p.12: 'We have laughed at the Holy war, the Jehad that old von der Goltz [German military mission to Turkey] prophesied. But I believe that stupid old man with spectacles was right. There is a Jehad preparing.'
15 'The German Emperor in the East', *The Times* (23 Nov 1898); Pipes, *A Concise History of the Russian Revolution* pp.115–18; Boghardt, *Spies of the Kaiser* pp.12–13
16 Popplewell, *Intelligence and Imperial Defence* pp.178–9; Ferguson, *Empire* p.303
17 Popplewell, *Intelligence and Imperial Defence* pp.219–21; Barooah, *Chatto: The Life and Times of an Anti-Imperialist in Europe*; Andrew, *Defence of the Realm* pp.90–1
18 TNA KV 1/19 'D-Branch Report' p.13; Basil Thomson, *Queer People* p.103; Andrew, *Defence of the Realm* pp.92–3
19 Andrew, *Defence of the Realm* p.93; Lowes, 'British intelligence in India from the First World War to Independence'
20 TNA KV 1/19 D-Branch Report p.13; Popplewell, *Intelligence and Imperial Defence* p.221
21 Mohs, *Military Intelligence and the Arab Revolt: The First Modern Intelligence War* pp.2, 68–73, 120–3, 125–9
22 Ibid. pp.88–91
23 Aldrich, *GCHQ* p.15; Andrew, *Secret Service*
24 Andrew, *Defence of the Realm* pp.86–90; Dudgen, *Roger Casement – The Black Diaries* pp.481–5; O'Halpin, 'British Intelligence in Ireland' in Andrew and Dilks (eds), *The Missing Dimension* pp.59–61

25 Curry, *The Security Service* pp.38, 80; TNA KV 1/65 'Control of Aliens'; Panayi, *The Enemy in Our Midst*; Panayi (ed.), *Minorities in Wartime*; Fitzpatrick, 'The Civil War as a Formative Experience' in Gleason, Kenez and Stites (eds), *Bolshevik Culture* pp.57–76; Mommsen, 'Militär und zivile Militisierung in Deutschland, 1914 bis 1938' in Frevert, *Militär und Gesellschaft im 19. und 20. Jahrhundert* pp.265–76; Holquist, *Making War and Forging Revolution*; Nicolai, *The German Secret Service* pp.265–7; KV 4/222 'Policy and procedure for imposition of Home Office Warrants' s.22a: H.R. Scott, Home Office, to V.G.W. Kell (29 Jun 1926); Ibid. s.25a: Major Ball to H.R. Scott, Home Office (16 Jul 1926)

26 Curry, *The Security Service* p.80; Lenin, *Essential Works of Lenin* pp.237, 239; Petrie, *Communism in India 1924–27*; Andrew and Mitrokhin, *The Mitrokhin Archive* vol. II passim

27 British Library [BL] London IOR L/P&J/12/34 IPI Financial Arrangements s.2 IPI letter (13 Jan 1926); IOR L/P&J/12/38 IPI's Office Accommodation s.3 IPI to Sir A. Hirtzel, India Office (13 Jun 1924); Ibid. IPI's Office Accommodation s.28 IPI to Peel [IO] (14.12.28); 'Sir Philip Vickery', *Who Was Who* (online edition accessed 1 Jun 2011)

28 TNA KV 4/222 'Policy and procedure for imposition of Home Office Warrants'; KV 4/19 'Report on the Operations of A.D.A, in connection with the Administrative Services of the Security Service during the war 1939–1945', Appendix IV 'Technical Equipment'; Curry *The Security Service* p.23; cf. Wright, *Spycatcher* p.54: 'For five years we bugged and burgled our way across London at the state's bequest, while pompous bowler-hatted civil servants in Whitehall pretended to look the other way'

29 Masters, *The Man Who Was M*; TNA KV 4/227 'History of the operations of M.S. (agents) during the war 1939–1945' p.32; KV 2/1022 'Statement of "X" the statement of the informant in this case' (25 Jan 1938) pp.1–2

30 'Official Secrets Case', *The Times* (8 Feb 1938); Quinlan, 'Human intelligence operations and MI5 tradecraft in Britain' pp.178–9

31 West, *MASK: MI5's Penetration of the Communist Party of Great Britain* passim

32 IOR L/P&J/12/348 'Meerut Conspiracy Case: Scotland Yard officers proceeding to India as witnesses' s.27a: 'List of original telegrams' and passim; Andrew, *Defence of the Realm* pp.137–8

33 Curry, *The Security Service* p.54; 'Sir Eric Holt-Wilson', *Who Was Who* (online edition accessed 1 Jun 2011); Imperial War Museum London [IWML] Kell Mss. Holt-Wilson 'Security Intelligence in War' (1934); Andrew, *Defence of the Realm* p.138

34 Cambridge University Library [CUL] Add 9794/2/72 Eric Holt-Wilson to Audrey Holt-Wilson, Bombay (1 Apr 1938); 'Sir Eric Holt-Wilson', *Who Was Who* (online edition accessed 1 Jun 2011)

35 CUL Add 9794/2/75 Eric Holt-Wilson to Audrey Holt-Wilson, Singapore (10 Apr 1938); Ibid. Eric Holt-Wilson to Audrey Holt-Wilson, Government House, Hong Kong (28 Apr 1938)

36 Gwynn, *Imperial Policing*; Anderson and Killingray, 'An orderly retreat?' in Anderson and Killingray, *Policing and Decolonisation* pp.1–21

37 Jeffery, *MI6* p.236; Andrew, *Defence of the Realm* p.129; TNA KV 4/206 'Visit of Mr. G.C. Denham to USA to investigate need for permanent Security Service representative in western hemisphere' s.70c: G.C. Denham to Sir David Petrie (8 Jul 1943) p.3

38 BL IOR l/P&J/12/293 Jawaharlal Nehru s.11 IPI report to DIB, MI5 and SIS (12 Feb 1936); BL IOR L/P&J/12/30 Rajani Palme Dutt; TNA KV 2/1807–1809 Rajani Palme Dutt; BL L/P&J/12/28 Clemens Palme Dutt; TNA KV 2/2504–2505 Clemens Palme Dutt

39 See TNA KV 4/19 'Report on the operations of A.D.A., in connection with the Administrative Services of the Security Service during the war 1939–1945' s.6a: 'MI5 officers' (n.d.); Curry, *The Security Service* pp.396–7

40 Curry, *The Security Service* pp.396–7; IWML 80/30/1 Brigadier R.J. Maunsell Ms. 'Security Intelligence in Middle East 1914–1918 and 1934–1944' pp.2–4

41 Hinsley, *British Intelligence in the Second World War* vol. IV p.141

42 'Sir Vernon Kell','Sir Eric Holt-Wilson', 'Sir David Petrie', 'Sir Percy Sillitoe', entries in *Oxford Dictionary of National Biography* [*DNB*] (online edition accessed 1 Jun 2011); Sillitoe, *Cloak Without Dagger* pp.1–47; Curry, *The Security Service*; Curry, *The Indian Police* (1932); Hoare (ed.), *Camp 020* p.8; Philby, *My Silent War*

43 'Valentine Vivian' and 'Felix Cowgill', *DNB* (online edition accessed 1 Jun 2011); Jeffery, *MI6* pp.167, 486; Philby, *My Silent War* pp.46, 48, 66

44 Aldrich, *GCHQ* p.19; Thomson, *Scene Changes*; Thomson, *Queer People*; Andrew, *Defence of the Realm* p.82

45 Aldrich, *GCHQ* p.19; Cole, *Suspect Identities* pp.63–73; Singha, 'Settle, Mobilise, Verify'; TNA KV 4/267 'Policy on control of communists' Minute 176a: Sir David Petrie (31 Jan 1945)

46 Kelly, 'Papon's transition after World War II. A prefect's road from Bordeaux, through Algeria, and beyond, August 1944–October 1961' in Golsan (ed.), *The Papon Affair: Memory and Justice on Trial* pp.35–72; Thomas, *Empires of Intelligence*; Arendt, *The Origins of Totalitarianism* pp.158–221; Holquist, 'To count, extract, to exterminate' in Suny and Martin (eds), *A State of Nations* pp.111–44

47 Richards, *A Time of Silence: Civil War and the Culture of Repression in Franco's Spain, 1936–1945* pp.26–34; Holquist, 'To count, extract, to exterminate' passim; Hull, *Absolute Destruction*; Moses, *Empire, Colony, Genocide*; Zimmerer et al., *Genocide in German Southwest Africa*

48 Andrew, *Defence of the Realm* p.842

Chapter 2: Strategic Deception

1 Ondaatje, *The English Patient* pp.34–5

2 TNA KV 4/87 s.2a: Sir David Petrie to Sir Anthony Eden (26 Jun 1944) p.7; Emily Wilson, 'The War in the Dark: The Security Service and the Abwehr, 1940–1944' p.213

3 Hinsley, *British Intelligence in the Second World War* vol. IV *Security and Counter-Intelligence* pp.11–12; Curry, *The Security Service* pp.22–5, 148

4 TNA KV 4/170 'D.G. White's lecture notes regarding counterespionage investigations and organisation of RSS and GC&CS', s.1a: Mr. Dick White's lecture for new Regional Security Liaison Officers (9 Jan 1943)

5 Wark, *The Ultimate Enemy: British Intelligence and Nazi Germany*; TNA KV 4/290 'Measures to counter activities of German Nazi & Italian Fascist groups in the UK – pre 1939 with particular reference to sabotage, subversion in the forces etc', s.2a: Sir Vernon Kell to Lord Hankey, CID (6 Jul 1936), forwarding [Curry] 'Memorandum on the possibilities of sabotage by the organisations set up in British countries by the totalitarian governments of Germany and Italy'; Andrew, *Secret Service* p.644; Reynolds, *Britannia Overruled* pp.119–26

6 TNA KV4/195 Diaries of Guy Liddell (6 Sept 1944)

7 Curry, *The Security Service* pp.145–6, 160; Hinsley, *British Intelligence in the Second World War* vol. IV *Security and Counter-Intelligence* p.66; TNA CAB 63/193 Hankey, 'The Secret Services. Inquiry by the Minister without Portfolio. Second report dealing with the Security Service (MI5) (May 1940) p.52; CAB 81/97 JIC (40) 73 'Invasion of the United Kingdom' (17 May 1940); Ibid. JIC (40) 101, 'Summary of likely forms and scales of attack that Germany could bring to bear on the British Isles in the near future' (5 Jun 1940); Schellenberg, *Invasion 1940: The Nazi Invasion Plan for Britain* pp.122–37; 'Sir Vernon George Waldegrave Kell', *Who's Who* (London, 1920) p.1412

8 Aldrich, *GCHQ* p.31; Aldrich, *The Hidden Hand* p.25; Trotter, *The Winter War: The Russo-Finnish War of 1939–1940*

9 TNA KV 4/85 'The Enemy Alien population in the UK by Mr. Aiken-Sneath' (Jul 1943) pp.27–8, 36; Grant, 'Desperate Measures: Britain's internment of fascists during the Second World War'; Thurlow, 'Internment in the Second World War'

10 Curry, *The Security Service* p.373; Jeffery, *MI6* pp.382–9

11 Burleigh, *Blood and Rage*; Winter, 'British Intelligence, Adolf Hitler and the German High Command, 1939–1945'

12 Kershaw, *Nazi Dictatorship: Problems and Perspectives of Interpretation*; Adam Sisman, *Hugh Trevor-Roper: The Biography* p.92; Curry, *The Security Service* pp.48, 146–8

13 Winter, 'Libra Rising: Hitler, Astrology and British Intelligence, 1940–43'

14 Andrew, 'Churchill and Intelligence'

15 Aldrich, *GCHQ* pp.5, 25–7; Hinsley, 'British Intelligence in the Second World War' in Andrew and Noakes (eds), *Intelligence and International Relations* p.210; However, Smith, 'Bletchley Park and the Holocaust' shows that the original argument put forward by Breitman, *Official Secrets: What the Nazis Planned, What the British and Americans Knew*, has to be doubted

16 Hinsley, 'The influence of Ultra' in Hinsley and Stripp (eds), *Codebreakers*; see Aldrich, *GCHQ* p.59 for a summary

17 Masterman, *The Double-Cross System* p.3

18 Shelley, 'Empire of Shadows' pp.131–2. I would like to thank Dr Adam Shelley for his pioneering research on strategic deception and the Middle East.

19 Maskelyne, *Magic – Top Secret* pp.31–6; Howard, *British Intelligence in the Second World War* vol. V *Strategic Deception* p.38

20 Howard, *British Intelligence in the Second World War* vol. V pp.xii, 23–5; Foot, *Memories of an SOE Historian* p.172

21 Holt, *The Deceivers* pp.218, 270; Howard, *British Intelligence in the Second World War* vol. V pp.37, 62–3; TNA KV 4/197 'Organisation and functions of SIME special section, 1942–45', s.3a: Douglas Roberts, 'Report on Cheese' (19 Feb 1943

22 Montagu, *The Man Who Never Was*; Macintyre, *Operation Mincemeat*

23 TNA KV 4/87 s.2a: Sir David Petrie to Sir Anthony Eden (26 Jun 1944); Hesketh, *Fortitude: The D-Day Deception Campaign*; Pujol with West, *Garbo*; Harris, *Garbo: The Spy Who Saved D-Day*

24 Jeffery, *MI6* pp.406–7

25 Masterman, *Double-Cross System* pp.8–9 suggests that strategic deception was not a priority for MI5 at the start of the war

26 Wilson, 'War in the Dark' p.126; IWML David Mure papers 67/312/1 T.A. Robertson to David Mure (28 Feb 1979)

27 'Obituary: Sir John Masterman', *The Times* (7 Jun 1977); Andrew, *Secret Service* p.471

28 Curry, *The Security Service* p.254; Harris, *GARBO: The Spy Who Saved D-Day*

29 Bristow, *A Game of Moles* p.28

30 TNA KV 4/18 'Report on the operation of overseas control in connection with the establishment of DSO's in the British colonies & liaison with the security authorities in the Dominions during the war of 1939–1945' pp.2–3; TNA KV 4/169 'Functions of overseas control'; KV 4/234 'Intelligence organisation in the Middle East (SIME)', s.1a: T.A. Robertson's visit to Egypt (20 Mar 1942–17 Apr 1942); KV 4/240 'Report by D.G. White on visit to the Middle East in 1943'; Curry, *The Security Service*

31 Aldrich, *GCHQ* p.153; E.D.R. Harrison, 'British Radio Security and Intelligence', *English Historical Review* (2009)

32 O'Halpin (ed.), *MI5 and Ireland* pp.46–7; Hull, 'The Irish interlude: German intelligence in Ireland' pp.702–3; Buchheit, *Der Deutsche Geheimdienst* pp.241–2; Curry, *The Security Service* p.125

33 Trevor-Roper, *The Last Days of Hitler* p.23; R.A. Ratcliff, *Delusions of Intelligence*

34 Jeffery, *MI6* p.381

35 TNA KV 2/86 Dr Norbert von Rantzau [Nikolaus Ritter], s.144a: Major Gwyer, F.2.c (15 May 1946)

36 TNA KV 2/1163 Ernst Paul Fackenheim; Bar-Zohar, *Hitler's Jewish Spy* pp.212–13; KV 2/400 Kurt Wieland s.17a: SIME Report (30 Oct 1944); Burleigh, *Blood and Rage* pp.96–8

37 TNA KV 2/1463 Mohsen Fadl s.22a: RJ Maunsell, SIME, to DG White, MI5 London, 'PYRAMID organisation' (20 Jun 1943); KV 2/1468 Hans Eppler s.22a: EB Stamp, B1B (5 Jan 1943); KV 3/74 German espionage in North Africa s.3a: Enemy W/T communications in the Sahara and Libyan desert (19 Dec 1941); Matthias Schulz, 'The Gay "English Patient"', *Der Spiegel* (online edition 4 Feb 2010, accessed 22 Oct 2012)

38 BL IOR L/P&J/12/218 Bose conspiracy case s.33 IPI to Mr Silver, India Office, copied to SIS (24 Mar 1942) Ibid. s.63 IPI to Mr Silver, India Office (26 Jan 1943), forwarding arrest notes 'Bhagat Ram's story'; Ram, *The Talwars of Pathan Land and Subhas Chandra's Great Escape*

39 TNA KV 4/332 Liaison with D.I.B. India in handling special agents s.102a: JH Marriott, B1a (1 Sept 1943); Hauner, *India in Axis Strategy* p.338

40 Howard, *British Intelligence in the Second World War* vol. V *Strategic Deception* p.208; TNA KV4/191 Diaries of Guy Liddell (15 Jun 1943); Ibid. KV4/192 (19 Aug 1943)

41 TNA KV 4/332 Liaison with DIB India in handling special agents s.26c Marriott New Delhi to DG MI5 (28 Mar 1943) p.2

42 Magan, *Middle Eastern Approaches* pp.16–19; Bose, *The Indian Struggle* pp.434–7

43 Foot, *Special Operations Executive*; TNA HS1; TNA HS3

44 Aldrich, *Intelligence and the War Against Japan* pp.65–6

45 Bayly and Harper, *Forgotten Wars: The End of Britain's Asian Empire* pp.30–1; Cross, *Red Jungle* pp.19–37; Chapman, *The Jungle is Neutral* p.34

46 Cruickshank, *SOE in the Far East* p.27

47 Chapman, *The Jungle is Neutral* Ch 4; Shelley, 'Empire of Shadows' pp.120, 122

48 Cruickshank, *SOE in the Far East* pp.14, 27, 196–209; Hudson, *Undercover Operator* p.131

49 Aldrich, *Intelligence and the War Against Japan* p.66

50 Foot, *SOE in the Low Countries*

51 Foot, 'Was SOE Any Good?' in Laqueur (ed.), *The Second World War* pp.241, 248

52 TNA KV 4/132 Powers of detention, interrogation and deportation to UK of enemy aliens and alien suspects apprehended in the Dominions and colonies (including non-enemy aliens removed from ships) Minute 11 D.G. White to SLA [legal adviser] (9 Jun 1942)

53 TNA KV 2/2116–2118 Roger Lannoy. I am grateful to Sarah Miller (Cambridge University and Harvard Law School) for drawing this case to my attention; *Liversidge v Anderson* [1942] AC 206; private information

54 TNA KV 4/132 Minute 13: SLA (11 Jun 1942)

55 Hart, *The Concept of Law*

56 Hoare (ed.), *Camp 020* p.270; KV 2/1722 Osmar Hellmuth Minute 18 H.L.A. Hart, B.1.b (20 Oct 1943); Schellenberg, *The Memoirs of Hitler's Spy Chief*

57 TNA KV2/2946 De Freitas; *Camp 020* pp.206, 213–14; Philby, *My Silent War* pp.50–1

58 KV 2/1107 Alfredo Manna s.19a: Alfredo Manna SIS to Courtenay Young, MI5 (17 Jun 1943); Muggeridge, *The Infernal Grove* pp.170–1. Again, I would like to thank Sarah Miller for sharing with me her detailed research on the Manna case

59 Moen, *John Moe: Double Agent*; *Camp 020* pp.57–8; TNA FO 1005/1744 'Detailed interrogation centre 10, Bad Nenndorf. Court of inquiry reports', statement Lt. Col. R.G.W. Stephens (7 Apr 1947) pp.3–4

60 *Camp 020* p.270

61 Curry, *The Security Service* p.229

62 TNA KV 4/190 Diaries of Guy Liddell (27 Oct 1942)

63 TNA KV 4/191 Diaries of Guy Liddell (16 Mar 1943); Andrew and Mitrokhin, *The Mitrokhin Archive*

64 Aldrich, *GCHQ* pp.30–1; Aldrich, *The Hidden Hand* p.38; TNA HW 171–3 'Decrypts of communist international (COMINTERN) messages, 1934–1945'; HW 17/53–66 'Iscott'

65 TNA KV 4/54 'Report on the operations of F-Division in connection with subversive

activities during the War 1939–1945' p.3; Curry, *The Security Service* p.350

66 TNA KV 4/21 'Report on the operations of the Registry during the war 1939–1945', s.1a: Roger Hollis (12 Dec 1945); Robert Cecil, 'The Cambridge Comintern' in Andrew and Dilks (eds), *The Missing Dimension* p.179; TNA KV4/473 Diaries of Guy Liddell

67 Dilks (ed.), *The Diaries of Sir Alexander Cadogan* p.586

68 TNA KV 4/224 'KISS' s.10a: Alan Roger, MI5 DSO Tehran, 'Cooperation with Russian security' (28 Dec 1944); Ibid. s.14a: 'Information about Russian intelligence gained from cooperation between DSO and Russian security authorities' (7 Mar 1945); KV 4/225, s.18a: Alex Kellar to Roger Hollis (7 Apr 1945)

69 TNA KV 4/223, s.68a: H.K. Dawson-Shepherd, CICI Baghdad (14 Jul 1945)

70 TNA KV 4/267 Minute 189a: Sir David Petrie (29 Aug 1945); Ibid. Minute 52a: Roger Hollis (5 Sept 1945); Andrew and Walton, 'The Gouzenko Case and British Secret Intelligence' in Black and Rudner (eds), *The Gouzenko Affair*

Chapter 3: 'The Red Light is Definitely Showing'

1 Conrad, *The Secret Agent* p.46

2 IWM Montgomery papers 211/18 Cunningham to Colonial Office (13 Nov 1946)

3 TNA CAB 81/121 JIC (44) 464 (0) Final, 'Soviet strategic interests and intentions after the war' (18 Dec 1944); CAB 81/132 JIC 81/123 JIC (46) 1 (0) (Final), 'Russia's strategic interests and intentions' (1 Mar 1946); CAB 81/133 JIC (46) 70 (0) Final, 'The spread of communism throughout the world and the extent of its direction from Moscow' (23 Sept 1946); Hennessy, *The Secret State* pp.2–3

4 Gaddis, *We Now Know*; Barrass, *Great Cold War*

5 Hennessy, *Having it so Good* p.313; Hennessy, *The Secret State* pp.2–3

6 KV 4/158 'Brief notes on the Security Service and its work prepared for Permanent Under Secretaries, service intelligence departments etc.' Minute 14a: John Curry (1 Oct 1946)

7 TNA KV 3/414 'Use of poisons by German Sabotage Service' s.1a 'Note by Lord Rothschild' (20 Feb 1945); Ibid. s.3a Supreme Allied Headquarters report 'German terrorist methods' (2 Apr 1945); Ibid. s.16b 'Belt buckle pistols' (XX US Corps, n.d.)

8 TNA KV 2/271 'Ernst Kaltenbrunner', s.65a: U.S. 12 Army Group to War Room, London, through OSS (13 Jun 1945) s.74a: Robert Stephens to Helenus Milmo (18 Jun 1945); no mention is made, for example, of Kaltenbrunner's interrogation at Camp 020 in Overy, *Interrogations: The Nazi Elite in Allied Hands, 1945*; Trevor-Roper, *The Last Days of Hitler*

9 Bennett, *The Zinoviev Affair*

10 Simpson, *In the Highest Degree Odious: British Internment in the Second World War*: Grant, 'Desperate Measures'

11 TNA KV 4/158, s.13a: 'A short note on the Security Service and its responsibilities' (Oct 1946) p.3

12 TNA KV 5/30 'Stern Group', s.111z: Alex Kellar to Trafford Smith, Colonial Office (16 Aug 1946); Ibid. James Robertson to Leonard Burt, Special Branch (26 Aug 1946); CO 733/457/13 'Terrorist outrages. Extension to the United Kingdom', s.4: Sir David Petrie to Sir Alexander Maxwell, Home Office (2 Apr 1945); KV 5/4 'United Zionist "Revisionist" youth organisation' Minute 24a: Sir David Petrie (30 Mar 1946)

13 Aldrich, *The Hidden Hand* p.258

14 Burleigh, *Blood and Rage* pp.101–4

15 TNA KV 2/2252 'Menachem Begin', Minute 131: John Shaw (5 Aug 1953); TNA KV4/467 Diaries of Guy Liddell (2 Aug 1946); Clarke, *By Blood and Fire* p.252; Letters to the Editor, *The Times* (24 Jul 2006); Brendon, *Decline and Fall* p.475

16 TNA FO 371/67796 'Italy': E. Irdell, British embassy, Rome (23 Jan 1947); CO 537/1723 'Terrorist outrages: extension to UK'; EF 5/12 'Outrages 1947–1948: letter bombs', H.E. Watts, Chief Inspector of Explosives (24 Jun 1947); Cesarani, *Major Farran's Hat* p.85; 'Terrorist Bomb in Whitehall', *The Times* (17 Apr 1946); 'Letter Bombs from Turin', *The Times* (7 Jun 1947); Burt, *Commander Burt of Scotland Yard* pp.126–7; 'Avner', *Memoirs of*

an Assassin pp.18–20

17 Walton, 'British Intelligence and the Mandate of Palestine'

18 Clarke, *The Last Thousand Days of the British Empire* p.84

19 Hyam, *Britain's Declining Empire* pp.125, 130; Burleigh, *Blood and Rage* pp.91–5, 100

20 Cohen, 'Appeasement in the Middle East: the British White Paper on Palestine'

21 Burleigh, *Blood and Rage* p.100; Andrew, *Defence of the Realm* p.354; Hyam, *Britain's Declining Empire* pp.57, 129; Shepherd, *Ploughing Sand*; Ritchie Ovendale, *Britain, the United States and the end of the Palestine Mandate*

22 Hyam, *Britain's Declining Empire* pp.123–30; Andrew, *Defence of the Realm* pp.352, 448; Brendon, *Decline and Fall* p.476

23 Brendon, *Decline and Fall* p.476

24 Burleigh, *Blood and Rage* p.99; Brendon, *Decline and Fall* p.475; Sprinzak, *Brother Against Brother*; Pedahzur, *The Israeli Response to Jewish Extremism and Violence: Defending Democracy*; Hyam, *Britain's Declining Empire* pp.57–8; Cohen, *Woman of Violence: Memoirs of a Young Terrorist*; Hoffman, *Inside Terrorism* p.29; 'British Anger at Terror Celebration', *The Times* (20 Jul 2006); Begin, *The Revolt* pp.59–60; Shamir, *Summing Up: An Autobiography* pp.32–50

25 Andrew, *Defence of the Realm* pp.352, 448; Freeman and Penrose, *Rinkagate: The Rise and Fall of Jeremy Thorpe* pp.72–4

26 Rathbone, 'Political intelligence and policing in Ghana' in Anderson and Killingray (eds), *Policing and Decolonisation* p.86; 'A.J. Kellar' entry in *Who's Who*

27 TNA KV 3/41, s.7a: 'Director-General's lecture' (16 Mar 1948) p.1

28 Sillitoe, *Cloak Without Dagger* p.xvi

29 Koestler, *Thieves in the Night: Chronicle of an Experiment*; TNA KV 2/1273 'Arthur Koestler'; TNA KV 2/132 'Joel Brandt'

30 TNA KV 3/41, s.2a: Alex Kellar notes for Sir Percy Sillitoe, 'Present trends in Zionism' (2 Sept 1946) p.7

31 TNA KV 5/38, s.171z: Richard Thistlethwaite, DSO Palestine, to MI5 London (6 Dec 1946)

32 TNA KV 5/29, 'Stern Group', s.75a: Alex Kellar to Trafford Smith, Colonial Office (19 Feb 1946); Cohen, *Woman of Violence* p.1

33 TNA KV 2/2251 Menachem Begin s.40a: cutting from *News Chronicle* (18 Mar 1947); TNA KV 2/2251 s.38a: SIS [name withheld] to H.J. Seager, MI5 (13 Feb 1947); Andrew, *Defence of the Realm* p.355

34 TNA CO 733/457/13, s.7: 'Policy regarding suspected Jewish terrorists in H.M. Forces', MI5 [unnamed] report sent to J.M. Martin, Colonial Office (21 Aug 1945); CAB 81/93 JIC sub-committee 'Probable reaction of Jewish personnel in His Majesty's Forces and Polish units to Jewish disturbances in Palestine', 13th meeting (20 Feb 1945)

35 TNA KV 2/196 Diaries of Guy Liddell (15 May 1945); CO 733/457/1, s.7: 'Policy regarding suspected Jewish terrorists in H.M. Forces', MI5 report [unsigned] copied to J.M. Martin, Colonial Office (21 Aug 1945); RHLO J.J. O'Sullivan papers Diary entry (17 Sept 1947); KV 3/41, s.7a: 'Director-General's lecture' (16 Mar 1948) pp.13–14; KV 3/41, s.1a: 'Notes for the Director-General's meeting with the Prime Minister' (28 Aug 1946) p.1

36 TNA KV 2/1435 'Jewish Agency for Palestine'; KV 5/10 'Jewish-Arab league'; KV 5/11 'The Jewish Legion'; KV 5/4 'United Zionist "Revisionist" youth movement'; KV 5/16 'Hisraduth (Zionist federation of Jewish labour)'. Others include: KV 5/14 'Middle East society'; TNA KV 5/4 Minute 88a: Bernard A. Hill (19 Nov 1946); Ibid. Minute 90a: Herbert Loftus-Brown (12 Dec 1946)

37 TNA KV 5/4 s.115a: Sir Percy Sillitoe to E.W. Jones, Special Branch (24 Apr 1946); KV 5/4 Minute 20a: James Robertson (29 Mar 1946)

38 Burleigh, *Blood and Rage* p.95; TNA FO 371/24085 'Situation of Jewish refugees in Danzig (January 1939)', s.87: British Consul-General Danzig to Foreign Office, London (13 Feb 1939); FO 371/23251 'Palestine', 'Palestine Labour Party's political summary' (7 Sept

1939); Heller, *The Stern Gang* pp.85–9

39　Cohen, *Woman of Violence* pp.4–5

40　TNA KV 3/41, s.7a: 'Director-General's lecture' (16 Mar 1948) pp.13–19

41　TNA KV3/41, s.2a: Alex Kellar notes for Sir Percy Sillitoe, 'Present trends in Zionism' (2 Sept 1946) p.4

42　Burt, *Commander Burt of Scotland Yard* p.129; '7 years' Sentence in Explosives Case', *The Times* (15 Oct 1948); private information

43　TNA KV 4/190 Diaries of Guy Liddell (23 Sept 1942); TNA KV 5/38 'Irgun Zvi Leumi', s.187b: 'IZL activities in Palestine' (31 Jul 1947); KV 3/41, s.2a: CREAM CX [number withheld] SIS [name withheld] to Dick White, MI5 (31 Mar 1947); Cohen, *Woman of Violence* p.121

44　TNA KV 2/1435, 'Jewish Agency for Palestine' Minute 86a: Alex Kellar (30 Apr 1945)

45　TNA KV 5/31 s.157a: David Scherr, 'Information from Reuven Zaslani' (19 Feb 1948); Eshed, *Reuven Shiloah: The Man Behind the Mossad*; Chavkin, 'British intelligence and the Zionist, South African, and Australian intelligence communities during and after the Second World War'

46　TNA KV2/2261–2264 Theodor Kollek; KV 5/34 'Extract from report on interview with Teddy Kollek, forwarded by DSO Palestine' (18 Aug1945). The author is grateful to Dr Jonathan Chavkin of the Cambridge University Intelligence Seminar for this reference

47　TNA KV 4/216 'Policy and procedure for contacting Jewish Agency intelligence representatives in London, 1946–1947' Minute 8a: T.A. Robertson (19 Sept 1946); Ibid. s.14b: C.A.G. Simkins (3 Feb 1947); Minute 31a: James Robertson (14 Mar 1947); Kollek, *For Jerusalem* pp.57–66

48　Yaacov Eliav, *Wanted* p.246

49　Ibid. p.244; Cesarani, *Major Farran's Hat* p.85

50　Eliav, *Wanted* p.245; Cesarani, *Major Farran's Hat* pp.86–7

51　Eliav, *Wanted* p.249; Andrew, *Defence of the Realm* p.357

52　Yaakov Heruti, *One Truth not Two* pp.132–6, 140. I would like to thank Yisrael Meded for kindly providing me with extracts of Heruti's book, and Tamar Drukker of SOAS for translating them

53　Interview by author with former Stern Gang member (13 Apr 2008)

54　Heruti, *One Truth not Two* pp.141–2; 'Avner', *Memoirs of an Assassin* pp.130–1

55　RHLO J.J. O'Sullivan papers, diary entry (4 Oct 1947); Briscoe, *For the Life of Me* pp.262, 264, 295

56　Herzog, *Living History: A Memoir* pp.46–53, 75; TNA KV 3/41, s.7a: 'Director-General's lecture' (16 Mar 1948) p.14

57　Rose, *A Senseless Squalid War* pp.123–4

58　Aldrich, *GCHQ* p.97

59　TNA KV 2/1390 'Moshe Sneh', s.191a: MI5 dossier on Sneh for the CIA (25 Aug 1948); KV 5/31, s.149a: T.A. Robertson to Winston M. Scott, American embassy, London (1 Oct 1947); Heller, *The Stern Gang* pp.145–7, 170–3

60　TNA KV 4/36, s.108b: H.A.R. Philby to T.E. Bromley, Foreign Office, J.D.S. Bates, Colonial Office, copied to Alex Kellar, MI5 (9 Jul 1945); Ro'i, 'Soviet policy towards Jewish emigration: an overview' in Lewin-Epstein, Ro'i and Ritterband (eds), *Russian Jews on Three Continents: Migration and Resettlement* pp.51–6

61　'Refugee Ship Boarded', *The Times* (19 Jul 1947); Marrus, *The Unwanted. European Refugees in the Twentieth Century* pp.338–9; Brendon, *Decline and Fall* p.476

62　TNA KV 3/56 s.69b: 'Report on tour of MI5 liaison officer in France, Germany, Austria and Italy'; Burleigh, *Blood and Rage* p.101

63　TNA CO 537/1825 Min. Trafford Smith (10 Dec 1946)

64　TNA CAB 158/1 JIC (47) 31 (0) Final, 'Organisation of illegal immigration' (24 Jul 1947); CAB 104/279 'Illegal immigration: action to stop traffic at source'; CAB 158/1 JIC (47) 28 (0) (Final), 'Illegal immigration to Palestine–complicity of certain organisations' (11 Jun

1947); CO 733/490/3 'Detention of illegal immigrants in Cyprus'; CAB 104/270 'Palestine: strategic aspects': COS (46) 221 (0), 'Accommodation for illegal Jewish immigrants' (25 Aug 1946)

65 Jeffery, *MI6* pp.691–2

66 Ibid. pp.693–5

67 TNA CAB 81/133 JIC (46) 45 (0) (Final), 'The Anglo-American committee of enquiry into Palestine and the condition of Jews in Europe' (1 May 1946); CAB 158/2 JIC (47) 52 (0) (Final), 'Possible future of Palestine' (9 Sept 1947); Ibid. JIC (47) 61 (0) (Terms of reference), 'Repercussions and implementation of the proposal for the partition of Palestine' (1 Nov 1947); Ibid. JIC (47) 60 (0) (Final), 'Threat of Arab Intervention in Palestine' (18 Oct 1947); Crossman, *Palestine Mission* p.131

68 Hoffman, *The Failure of British Military Strategy in Palestine* p.34

69 Begin, *The Revolt* pp.99–100; 'Avner', *Memoirs of an Assassin* p.16; Charters, 'British Intelligence in the Palestine Campaign' p.134; Aldrich, *The Hidden Hand* p.258

70 Dorril, *MI6* p.546; Deacon, *'C': A Biography of Sir Maurice Oldfield*

71 Farran, *Winged Dagger* p.321; Cesarani, *Major Farran's Hat*

72 Cesarani, *Major Farran's Hat* pp.208–18

73 'British Sergeants Found Murdered', *The Times* (1 Aug 1947); Carruthers, *Winning Hearts and Minds* p.53; Burleigh, *Blood and Rage* p.105; Aldrich, *Hidden Hand* p.261

74 Peter Hennessy, *Never Again* p.242; Hyam and Louis (eds), *BDEEP: The Labour Government and the End of Empire* doc [21] CAB 129/16 CP (47) 49 Cabinet memorandum by Bevin and Creech Jones (6 Feb 1947)

75 Begin, *The Revolt* p.133; Morris, *The Birth of the Palestinian Refugee Problem Revisited*; Brendon, *Decline and Fall* p.480

76 TNA KV 5/32, s.203a: G.A. Carey-Foster to H. Ashley, British embassy, Paris (15 Oct 1948); Luke Harding, 'Menachem Begin "Plotted to Kill German Chancellor"', *Guardian* (15 Jun 2006); Hyam, *Britain's Declining Empire* p.58

Chapter 4: The Empire Strikes Back

1 Quoted in TNA CAB 21/2925 General Sir Gerald Templer, 'Report on colonial security' (Apr 1955)

2 Mansergh (ed.), *Transfer of Power in India* vol. VIII no 26, Chiefs of Staff (India) Committee (Jul 1946) pp.56–7; vol. VII pp.930–3; *BDEEP* part 3 pp.207–8 (no 273) CAB 129/1 CP (45) 144 memo by Attlee (1 Sept 1945)

3 TNA KV 2/804 'Walter J. Krivitsky' s.29a: Jane Archer, 'Report' (3 Feb 1940)

4 'Leakages in Canada', *The Times* (5 Feb 1946); 'Soviet Spy Ring in Canada', *The Times* (16 Mar 1946); Sillitoe, *Cloak Without Dagger*

5 TNA KV 2/2213 s.289a: 'Statement of Alan Nunn May' (20 Feb 1946); TNA KV 2/2215 s.456a: H.A.R. Philby to R.H. Hollis (10 Dec 1946); 'Atomic Secrets Charge', *The Times* (20 Mar 1946)

6 Andrew, 'The Venona Secret' in Robertson (ed.), *War, Resistance and Intelligence: Essays in Honour of M.R.D. Foot* pp.203–25; Haynes and Klehr, *Venona: Decoding Soviet Espionage in America*; West, *Venona*

7 West, *Venona*

8 TNA KV 2/1245, s.1b: C-Division note, 'Emil Julius Klaus Fuchs' (2 Jun 1942); TNA KV 2/1245 Minute 55: Roger Hollis (4 Dec 1946); KV 2/1245 Minute 57: Diaries of Guy Liddell (20 Dec 1947); Moss, *Klaus Fuchs: The Man Who Stole the Atom Bomb*; Holloway, *Stalin and the Bomb* pp.222–3

9 TNA KV 2/2080 'Herbert Skinner and Erna Skinner'; KV 2/1246, s.177b: David Storrier (27 Sept 1949)

10 TNA KV 2/1263 'Klaus Fuchs', prosecution volume; KV 2/1264 'Klaus Fuchs', prosecution volume and papers on denaturalisation; KV 2/1246, s.177b: David Storrier (27 Sept 1949)

11 British Library ADD Ms. 88902/1 Anthony Blunt Manuscript p.26; TNA KV 2/186

Diaries of Guy Liddell (7 Jun 1940); Curry, *The Security Service* pp.259–60

12 Philby, *My Silent War* p.199; Andrew and Gordievsky, *KGB: The Inside Story of its Foreign Operations*; Andrew and Mitrokhin, *The Mitrokhin Archive* vol. I *The KGB in the West* pp.127, 156; Wright, *Spycatcher*; Pincher, *Their Trade is Treachery*

13 Roosevelt Archive, Hyde Park, NY, Ernest Cuneo papers Box 107 'CIA' file; TNA KV 4/242 'Security Service action in the case of Pontecorvo', s.52b: Michael Serpell, 'Note on meeting with Prime Minister' (2 Nov 1950); Reynolds, *From World War to Cold War* pp.320–1

14 TNA AB 16/202 'Comparison of UK and US Atomic Energy Acts, 1946'; FO 371/93198–93204 'Proposed co-operation between US and UK on development of atomic energy'; Reynolds, *In Command of History: Churchill Fighting and Winning the Second World War* pp.160–3

15 TNA CAB 130/20 GEN 183/1 'Cabinet committee on subversive activities', 'The employment of civil servants etc., exposed to communist influence' (29 May 1947); Hennessy, *The Secret State* p.87; Hennessy and Brownfeld, 'Britain's Cold War Security Purge' pp.965–73

16 Clarke, *The Last Thousand Days of the British Empire* pp.xiv–xv

17 Sillitoe, *Cloak Without Dagger* p.191

18 Ibid. pp.160–1, 191–3; 'New Director at the War Office', *The Times* (18 Jan 1946); TNA CO 1035/187 Organisation of intelligence services in the colonies; Andrew, *Defence of the Realm* p.462

19 TNA KV 4/162 'Organisation and function of B-Division from 1941–1953', s.76a: 'Meeting in DG's office' (1 Nov 1948); Sir John Shaw RHLO Mss. Brit. Emp. s.456; 'Obituary: Sir John Shaw', *The Times* (22 Jan 1983)

20 TNA CAB 158/3 JIC (48) 35 (0) (Final) 'Scale and nature of initial attack on the British Isles – 1957' (27 Aug 1948) p.4; Goodman, 'British Intelligence and the Soviet Atomic Bomb'

21 TNA CAB 81/133 JIC (46) 70 (0) (Final), 'The spread of communism throughout the world and the extent of its direction from Moscow' (23 Sept 1946); CAB 158/1 JIC (47) 12 (0) (Final Revised), 'Role of colonies in war' (8 Apr 1947); CAB 158/2 JIC (47) 65 (0) (Final), 'Summary of principal factors affecting Commonwealth security' (29 Oct 1947)

22 The following paragraphs owe much to Hyam, *Britain's Declining Empire* pp.104–16

23 Hodson, *The Great Divide* p.125; the first major work to realise the omission of British intelligence in the history of the end of the Raj was French, *Liberty or Death*

24 BL IOR L/P&J/12/662 Reorganisation of IPI and the future of the DIB s.5 IPI letter to Silver [IO] (19 Dec 1944)

25 Ibid. s.66 Top Secret and Personal IPI (12 Apr 1945)

26 Ibid. s.114 IPI note (n.d.)

27 Aldrich, *Intelligence and the War Against Japan* p.386; Hinsley and Alan Stripp (eds), *Codebreakers*

28 BL IOR L/P&J/12/662 Reorganisation of IPI and the future of the DIB s.162 DIB telegram to Secretary of State for India (5 Apr 1947); Nehru, *The Discovery of India* pp.378–9; TNA KV/468 Diaries of Guy Liddell

29 BL IOR L/P&J/12/662 Reorganisation of IPI and the future of the DIB

30 Ibid. s.127 Top secret IPI note (21 Nov 1946)

31 Ibid. s.140 IPI note (n.d.); Bayly and Harper, *Forgotten Wars* p.456; Andrew and Mitrokhin, *The Mitrokhin Archive* vol. II

32 BL IOR L/P&J/12/662 Reorganisation of IPI s.147 IPI note (27 Feb 1947); Andrew, *Defence of the Realm* p.442

33 TNA DO 142/363 Political intelligence India: disclosure of information Minute Mr Rumbold (19 Jan 1949); PREM 11/349 Proposal for a Commonwealth security conference (1953) Whittick, HO, to Montague Brown, PM's office (27 Apr 1953); description of MI5's SLO in New Delhi in CO 1035/10 'Intelligence and Security Aspects

of constitutional developments in the West Indies Colonies' s.10a: Eric Battersby, SLO Jamaica, to Sir Hugh Foot, governor (9 Jun 1956); Mullik, *My Years with Nehru* pp.88, 208; Andrew, *Defence of the Realm* p.445

34 KV 4/278 'Arrangements for absorption within the Security Service of IPI records of Indians and Pakistanis' s.1a: Sir Philip Vickery, Extract on paper of the work of OS4 (16 Aug 1950); Andrew, *Defence of the Realm* p.443 and Jeffery, *MI6* pp.638–9 suggest that the 'Attlee Directive' dates from 1948, not 1946 as is sometimes thought

35 TNA KV 2/2509 Krishna Menon; KV 2/2511 Krishna Menon; KV 2/2512 Krishna Menon s.199a: Percy Sillitoe 'Note' (17 Apr 1951)

36 TNA KV 2/2512 Krishna Menon Minute 147 Guy Liddell (31 May 1949)

37 TNA KV 2/2512 Krishna Menon s.146a Statement made by DG at JIC meeting (1 Aug 1947); Ibid. s.197a MI5 note 'V.K. Krishna Menon'

38 TNA KV 2/2512 Krishna Menon Minute 203 C.W.E. U'ren (24 Apr 1951)

39 Andrew, *Defence of the Realm* p.443; Andrew and Mitrokhin, *The Mitrokhin Archive* vol. II p.315

40 Andrew, *Defence of the Realm* p.444; Andrew and Mitrokhin, *The Mitrokhin Archive* vol. II pp.312–30

41 TNA CO 1035/171 Security Liaison Officers – Policy s.E/4 Sir Roger Hollis, DG MI5, to Sir Burke Trend, Cabinet Office (13 Nov 1965); Rimington, *Open Secret* pp.68–70; Andrew, *Defence of the Realm* p.446

42 TNA PREM 8/1343 Letters from Prime Minister to Prime Ministers of Canada, Australia, New Zealand and S Africa on discussion of security at autumn conference (May 1951); Liaquat Khan, Karachi, to CVR Attlee, London (27 Mar 1951); Ibid. Eleanor J Emery to DSW Hunt, CRO (9 Apr 1951)

43 Described in TNA CO 1035/6 Problems of intelligence organisation in the Federation of Malaya in connection with constitutional development s.32a: 'Report on the intelligence and security organisation required by the Federation of Malaya' (31 Oct 1956) p.9

44 TNA CO 1035/31 Organisation of intelligence services in the colonies. Tanganyika CO Circular no 458/56 'Organisation of Intelligence' (28 Apr 1956); Percy Cradock, *Know Your Enemy*; Sinclair, *End of the Line* p.196

45 TNA CAB 129/76/CP (55) 89 Templer Report (23 Apr 1955)

46 TNA CAB 158/20 Joint Intelligence Committee JIC (55) 28 'Colonial intelligence and security' (23 Mar 1955)

47 TNA CAB 158/3 JIC (48) 17 (0) 'Disclosure of information to India and Pakistan' (16 Feb 1948); 'Disclosure of Anglo-American classified information to third parties' (5 Oct 1949)

48 TNA CAB 158/3 JIC (48) 17 (0) 'Disclosure of information to India and Pakistan' (16 Feb 1948); JIC (48) 22 (0) Final, 'Disclosure of information to India, Pakistan and Ceylon' (13 Apr 1948); CAB 158/8 JIC (49) 91 (Final), 'Supply of classified information to the new Commonwealth countries' (12 Oct 1949)

49 TNA CAB 158/8 JIC (49) 89, 'Disclosure of Anglo-American classified information to third parties' (5 Oct 1949); Ibid. JIC (49) 90 'Disclosure of classified US military information to Western Union' (29 Sept 1949)

50 TNA KV 4/18 'Report on the operation of overseas control in connection with the establishment of DSO's in the British colonies & liaison with the security authorities in the Dominions during the war of 1939–1945' pp.2–3; https://www.mi5.gov.uk/home/mi5-history/the-cold-war/the-british-empire-and-commonwealth.html

51 Murphy, 'Creating a Commonwealth Intelligence Culture'

52 TNA CO1035/2 Vulnerability of Buildings to eavesdropping devices; PREM 11/760 'Russian Eavesdropping'; CO 537/4287 'Functions of Security Liaison Officers in the Colonies'

53 TNA CO 1035/31 Organisation of intelligence services in the colonies: Tanganyika CO Circular no 458/56 'Organisation of Intelligence' (28 Apr 1956)

54 TNA CO 885/119 Record of the conference of colonial Commissioners of Police at the

Police College, Ryton-on-Dunsmore (Apr 1951) p.2; CO 1035/55 Course for senior police officers on intelligence and security subjects; private information. For the Templer Report, see Cormac, 'Organizing intelligence'

55 TNA PREM 11/349 'Commonwealth security conference (Jun 1953)'
56 Murphy, 'Creating a Commonwealth Intelligence Culture' p.142; Rimington, *Open Secret* p.261
57 Outlined in CO 1035/6 Problems of intelligence organisation in the Federation of Malaya in connection with constitutional development s.32a: 'Report on the intelligence and security organisation required by the Federation of Malaya' (31 Oct 1956)
58 Richelson and Ball, *The Ties that Bind* p.83
59 Aldrich, *GCHQ* p.94
60 Andrew, 'The Growth of the Australian Intelligence Community and the Anglo-American Connection'; Andrew, *Defence of the Realm* p.371
61 TNA CAB 158/6 JIC (49) 17 'Joint intelligence bureau, Melbourne: priorities for Australian intelligence survey' (25 Feb 1949)
62 TNA KV2/3439 Vladimir Petrov; private information
63 TNA KV2/3440 Vladimir Petrov s.79a: R.T. Reed MI5 (8 Apr 1954); 'Soviet Espionage in Australia', *The Times* (14 Apr 1954); 'Struggle for Mrs Petrova', *The Times* (20 Apr 1954); 'Mrs Petrova Flying Back to Join Her Husband', *The Times* (21 Apr 1954)
64 TNA KV2/3440 Vladimir Petrov s.79a: RT Reed MI5 (8 Apr 1954)
65 Aldrich, *GCHQ* pp.93–4; Hennessy, *The Secret State*
66 TNA FCO 19/23 Diplomatic Service Administration: supply of cryptographic material to Commonwealth countries s.1 M.B. Eaden, Communications Department (5 Jan 1968)
67 BL IOR L/WS/1/1200 s.11 'Note by Sir W. Jenkin on "Charter" of his appointment'. The author is grateful to Richard Aldrich for drawing this file to his attention
68 TNA HW80/2 'Draft British–US Communication Intelligence Agreement' (1 Nov 1945)
69 Ibid.
70 Louis and Robinson, 'The Imperialism of Decolonisation'
71 Drayton, 'Anglo-American "Liberal" Imperialism' in Louis (ed.), *Yet More Adventures with Britannia*; National Archives, Washington DC, CREST files 'CIA Current Intelligence Digest' (13 May 1952)
72 Lyttelton, *The Memoirs of Lord Chandos* pp.427–30; Drayton, 'Anglo-American "Liberal" Imperialism'; Gallagher, 'Intelligence and decolonisation in British Guiana'; RHLO Mss. Brit. Emp. s.429, W.H. Ingrams papers 5.5, Prevention of communism in West Indies (13 Jul 1953); PREM 11/827 Suspension of Constitution in British Guiana and declaration of a state of emergency
73 TNA CO 1035/41 Organisation of intelligence services in the colonies – British Guiana s.4: N.D. Watson to Sir Patrick Renison, British Guiana (n.d.); CO 1035/173 'Visits by SLO Trinidad to British Guiana' s.1a: JL Jones, MI5, to JR Downie, CO (2 Sept 1963); Drayton, 'Anglo-American "Liberal" Imperialism'
74 TNA PREM 11/3666 Home to Rusk (26 Feb 1962); Andrew, *Defence of the Realm* pp.477–8; Drayton, 'Anglo-American "Liberal" Imperialism' pp.334–5; *Foreign Relations of the United States* vol. XII Doc 267 memorandum from the president's special envoy (Schlesinger) to the ambassador to the United Kingdom (27 Feb 1962); Gallagher, 'Intelligence and Decolonisation in British Guiana'
75 Catterall (ed.), *The Macmillan Diaries* vol. II (27 Sept 1962) pp.500, 578
76 Gallagher, 'British intelligence and decolonisation in British Guiana'
77 Andrew, *Defence of the Realm* pp.478–9
78 Johnson, *Blowback: The Costs and Consequences of American Empire*; Drayton, 'Anglo-American "Liberal" Imperialism' p.342

Chapter 5: Jungle Warfare

1 Lyttelton, *The Memoirs of Lord Chandos* p.379
2 Quoted in TNA CAB 21/2925, Templer, 'Report on Colonial Security' (23 Apr 1955)
3 Lyttelton, *The Memoirs of Lord Chandos* pp.359–66; Hyam, *Britain's Declining Empire*
4 Bayly and Harper, *Forgotten Wars* pp.408–9, 437; TNA KV 4/408 The Malayan Emergency Lecture Material s.1a: JP Morton's Lecture Notes (n.d.)
5 TNA CO 537/6006 Law and Order – Malaya. Internal Security; Stockwell (ed.), *BDEEP: Malaya* doc [148] CO 717/167/52849/2/1948 Creech Jones 'Declaration of emergency' (17 Jun 1948)
6 TNA KV 4/422 Organisation and function of Security Intelligence Organisation in the Far East (SIFE) s.94a: SIFE Representation on JIC(FE) (7 Aug 1948); RHLO, John Dalley, 'The Malayan Security Service' (1 Jul 1948); for a classic discussion of how intelligence failures can arise, see Wohlstetter, *Pearl Harbor: Warning and Decision*
7 Hack, 'British Intelligence and Counter-Insurgency in the Era of Decolonisation: The Example of Malaya'; RHLO, John Dalley, 'The Malayan Security Service' (1 Jul 1948)
8 TNA KV 4/408 The Malayan Emergency Lecture Material s.3: J.P. Morton, 'The problems we faced in Malaya and how they were solved' (Jul 1954) p.4; Aldrich, *Intelligence and the War Against Japan* p.65; Philby, *My Silent War*; Millar, 'British Intelligence in the Far East'
9 Aldrich, *The Hidden Hand* p.495; Bayly and Harper, *Forgotten Wars* pp.32–3
10 Peng, *My Side of History* p.163; Short, *The Communist Insurrection in Malaya* pp.39 –40
11 Peng, *My Side of History* p.190; Harper, *The End of Empire and the Making of Malaya* pp.50, 142–3; Short, *The Communist Insurrection in Malaya* p.38; Bayly and Harper, *Forgotten Wars* pp.342–50
12 Short, *The Communist Insurrection in Malaya*; RHLO Mss. Ind. Ocn. s.254 Special Conference. Conference held under the chairmanship of HE the Governor-General, Singapore (26 Jun 1947); Comber, 'The Malayan Security Service (1945–1948)'
13 Bayly and Harper, *Forgotten Wars* p.430
14 Harper, *The End of Empire and the Making of Malaya* pp.142–9
15 Comber, 'The Malayan Security Service (1945–1948)'
16 TNA KV 4/421 Organisation and function of Security Intelligence Organisation in the Far East (SIFE) s.3a: Sir Percy Sillitoe, Charter for Security Intelligence Far East (6 Aug 1946); KV 4/422 Organisation and function of Security Intelligence Organisation in the Far East (SIFE) s.98a: Telegram Sillitoe to Kellar (18 Aug 1948); Elwell, *An Autobiography* pp.91–3
17 Hack, 'Corpses, Prisoners of War and Captured Documents'; Brendon, *Decline and Fall* p.442; Aldrich, *The Hidden Hand* p.497; Miller, *Jungle War in Malaya* p.91; Stockwell (ed.), *BDEEP: Malaya* doc [216] CAB 21/1681 MAL C (50)23 Chief of Staff report for Cabinet Malaya Committee (24 May 1950)
18 TNA CO 537/4757 Special Service Unit for Malaya; CO 537/4239B Special Forces: Malaya s.10 O.H. Morris (17 Aug 1948); FCO 141/12407 Sarawak: Dayak units to police the jungle
19 MacKenzie, *Special Force* p.296
20 Aldrich, *The Hidden Hand* p.498
21 Peng, *My Side of History* p.300; Marston, 'Lost and Found in the Jungle: The Indian and British Army Jungle Warfare Doctrines for Burma, 1943–5, and the Malayan Emergency, 1948–60' in Strachan (ed.), *Big Wars and Small Wars*
22 For the formulation of 'information panics', see Bayly, *Empire of Information*; TNA CO 537/2662 Intelligence reports from DSO, Federation of Malaya and Singapore s.2: DIA Hamblen, MI5, to Sir Marston Logan, CO (20 Jul 1948); Ibid. s.3a: Monthly report of DSO Federation of Malaya and Singapore (Jul 1948); KV 4/408 The Malayan Emergency Lecture Material s.3: Morton, 'The problems we faced in Malaya' p.11; RHLO Mss. Ind. Ocn. S. 254 Special Conference. Conference held under the chairmanship of HE the Governor-General, Singapore (26 Jun 1947)

23 Hyam (ed.), *BDEEP: The Labour Government and the End of Empire* CO 537/5698 'The colonial empire today' (May 1950) [doc 72] p.342

24 KV 4/426 Organisation and function of Security Intelligence Organisation in the Far East (SIFE) s.272a: JA Harrison 'SIFE liaison with foreign intelligence services' (20 Jan 1954); National Archives Washington DC Digital National Security Archive CIA assessment 'Current situation in Malaya' (17 Nov 1949)

25 TNA KV 4/408 The Malayan Emergency s.3: Morton, 'The problems we faced in Malaya' p.8; Harper, *The End of Empire and the Making of Malaya* pp.96–103

26 KV 4/408 The Malayan Emergency Lecture Material s.1a: JP Morton's Lecture Notes (n.d.)

27 Aldrich, *The Hidden Hand* pp.502–3; KV 4/408 The Malayan Emergency s.3: Morton, 'The problems we faced in Malaya' p.4

28 Short, *Communist Insurrection in Malaya* p.386; Cloake, *Templer: Tiger of Malaya*; Smith, 'General Templer and counter-insurgency in Malaya: hearts and minds, intelligence, and propaganda'; Hack, 'Corpses, prisoners of war and captured documents'; TNA KV 4/408 The Malayan Emergency Lecture Material s.1a: JP Morton's Lecture Notes (n.d.) p.6

29 Hack, 'Corpses, prisoners of war and captured documents' pp.215, 219; Miller, *Jungle War in Malaya* p.90

30 Miller, *Jungle War in Malaya* p.92; TNA CO 1022/51 The organisation and function of the intelligence service in Malaya s.4 General Sir Gerald Templer to S of S for the colonies (13 Feb 1952)

31 Lyttelton, *The Memoirs of Lord Chandos* pp.366–7; CAB 129/48 Lyttelton, 'Malaya' cabinet memorandum (21 Dec 1951) in Stockwell (ed.), *BDEEP: Malaya* vol. II doc 257 p.344

32 Aldrich, *The Hidden Hand* p.509; Comber, *Malaya's Secret Police* p.180; Madoc, *An Introduction to the Birds of Malaya*

33 Aldrich, *The Hidden Hand* pp.498, 505; Comber, *Malaya's Secret Police* p.188

34 Bayly and Harper, *Forgotten Wars* p.486; Aldrich, *The Hidden Hand* p.506; MacKenzie, *Special Force* p.69

35 TNA FCO 141/7475 Malaya: Commission of Enquiry into the Semenyih incident; allegations concerning searches; KV 4/408 The Malayan Emergency s.3: Morton, 'The problems we faced in Malaya' pp.11, 14, 15

36 TNA KV 4/408 The Malayan Emergency s.3: Morton, 'The problems we faced in Malaya' pp.11, 14, 15; Bayly and Harper, *Forgotten Wars* p.482

37 Bayly and Harper, *Forgotten Wars* p.532

38 The preceding paragraphs owe much to Aldrich, *The Hidden Hand* p.507; Aldrich, *GCHQ* p.150; Clutterbuck, *The Long Long War* p.97; Miller, *Jungle War in Malaya* pp.101–2; TNA CO 1035/7 Periodic Reports of the Malayan Holding Centre; KV4/426 Organisation and function of Security Intelligence Organisation in the Far East (SIFE) s.273 Director General's final instructions to SIFE (16 Feb 1954)

39 TNA KV 4/408 The Malayan Emergency Lecture Material s.3: Morton, 'The problems we faced in Malaya'; KV4/244 Organisation and function of Security Intelligence Organisation in the Far East (SIFE) s.172a: Rough Notes on SB Organisation (28 Apr 1949)

40 Andrew, *Defence of the Realm* pp.451, 938; TNA WO 32/19064 War Office Intelligence in internal security (28 Aug 1963); French, *The British Way* p.161

41 TNA KV 4/408 Morton, 'The problems we faced in Malaya'; WO 33/2335 Joint Services pamphlet, 'Interrogation in War' p.18; French, *The British Way* p.157

42 TNA KV 4/408 Morton, 'The problems we faced in Malaya' p.19

43 TNA KV 4/254 Organisation and function of Security Intelligence Organisation in the Far East (SIFE) S.254A: Courtenay Young to Sir John Shaw (23 Jun 1954); FCO 141/12625 Security/intelligence courses – Kuching; Miller, *Jungle War in Malaya* p.94; Comber, *Malaya's Secret Police* pp.83–4; French, *The British Way* p.157

44 TNA FO 371/70828 'Germany: Bad Nenndorf', 'The value of a detailed interrogation centre' (17 Dec 1947); TNA FO 1005/1744, Statement Lt. Col. R.G.W. Stephens (7 Apr 1947)

45 Quote taken from French, *The British Way* p.162; see also O'Halpin, 'A poor thing but our own'; TNA WO 33/2335 Joint Services pamphlet, 'Interrogation in War'

46 Andrew, *Defence of the Realm* p.450; Chin Peng, *My Side of History* pp.342–6; Miller, *Jungle War in Malaya* p.100

47 FCO 141/7429 s.6 Director of Intelligence The Monthly report on subversive activities (May 1957); French, *The British Way* pp.152–3

48 Ben Macintyre, 'Lawyers Seek Hidden Documents Linked to British Massacre of 24 Malayan Villagers – Colonial Cover-Up', *The Times* (9 Apr 2011)

49 Peng, *My Side of History* p.195; Bayly and Harper, *Forgotten Wars* pp.449–51; Hatton, *Tock Tok Birds* p.138

50 Bayly and Harper, *Forgotten Wars* pp.458, 524

51 Louis, *Ends of British Imperialism* p.563; KV 4/408 The Malayan Emergency s.1a: JP Morton's Lecture Notes (n.d.) p.3; Nagl, *Learning to Eat Soup With a Knife*; Hoffman, 'Insurgency and counterinsurgency in Iraq'

52 TNA KV 4/408 The Malayan Emergency s.5 H Carleton Greene, head Emergency Information Services, 'Report on emergency information services, Sept 1950–Sept 1951' (14 Sept 1951)

53 TNA FO1110/28 Warner Minute (16 Jun 1948); FCO 141/7460 Counter-propaganda: a Basic Analysis, extract from a lecture given by head of Information Research Department (Sept 1952), distributed in a FO circular; Koestler, *The God that Failed*

54 Carruthers, *Winning Hearts and Minds* pp.90–5; TNA KV 4/408 The Malayan Emergency s.5 H Carleton Greene, head Emergency Information Services, 'Report on emergency information services' (14 Sept 1951)

55 TNA DEFE 28/71 Directorate of Forward Plans (23 Jul 1951)

56 Brendon, *Decline and Fall* pp.458–9

57 TNA CO 1035/38 Organisation of intelligence services in the colonies. Federation of Malaya Sir Donald MacGillivray to Alan Lennox-Boyd (1 Aug 1956); CO 1035/6 Problems of intelligence organisation in the Federation of Malaya, in connection with constitutional development Minute ND Watson (6 Dec 1956); KV 2/3593 Neil Lawson Minute D.L Haldane Porter (4 Feb 1957); KV 2/3594 Neil Lawson s.253a: Note on Neil Lawson (20 Feb 1958); Andrew, *Defence of the Realm* p.451

58 TNA FCO 24/513 Malaysia: Defence. Intelligence cooperation with UK

59 Hyam, *Britain's Declining Empire* pp.6–7; Lady Brooke, *Queen of the Head-Hunters*; TNA FCO 141/7524 Disposal of surplus signals s.2 W.J. Watts to private secretary to His Excellency, King's House, Kuala Lumpur (Jul 1956)

60 TNA KV 2/1855 Anthony Brooke minute 10: CJL Elwell, OS2 (4 Feb 1950); Ibid. s.9a: H/ SIFE to DG MI5 London (25 Jan 1950); FCO 141/1241 'Murderous assault on His Excellency the Governor', Roskams, 'British intelligence, imperial defence ...'

61 TNA FCO 141/7234 Malaya: Defence Agreement between UK and Federation of Malaya; Working Party on the Agreement on External Defence and Mutual Assistance; Reynolds, *Britannia Overruled* p.210

62 TNA CO 1035/8 Intelligence and Security aspects of Singapore constitutional talks Minute ND Watson (14 Aug 1956); Ibid. Minute ND Watson (5 Dec 1956)

63 TNA FCO 141/12907 Security Intelligence Far East ISD 55/68/104 (24 May 1964); CO 1035/8 Intelligence and Security aspects of Singapore constitutional talks, Minute JB Johnson (28 Aug 1956); Lee Kuan Yew also seems to have been a party to the secret deal between Lennox-Boyd and Lim: see Murphy, *Lennox-Boyd* pp.177–8

64 TNA FCO 141/12907 Security Intelligence Far East ISD 55/68/104 (24 May 1964); Andrew, *Defence of the Realm* p.469

65 Stockwell, *BDEEP*

66 Mackay, *The Malayan Emergency 1948–60: The Domino That Stood*; Harper, *The End of Empire and the Making of Malaya* p.58; Aldrich, *GCHQ* p.165

67 Bayly and Harper, *Forgotten Wars* p.532; Harper, *The End of Empire and the Making of Malaya* pp.357–82; Laws of Malaysia Act 82 Internal Security Act 1960; TNA DO 35/9937 H. Ellsley to D.R.E. Hopkins (19 Nov 1959)

Chapter 6: British Intelligence and the Setting Sun on Britain's African Empire

1 Abrahams, *A Wreath for Udomo* p.76

2 Baldwin, *Mau Mau Man Hunt* p.63

3 For a different view, see Jackson, *The British Empire and the Second World War*

4 The preceding and following paragraphs owe much to Hyam, *Britain's Declining Empire* pp.146–8; Hyam and Louis (eds), *BDEEP: The Labour Government and the End of Empire* doc [59] CO 847/36/1 Report of the committee on the conference of African Governors (22 May 1947)

5 Brendon, *Decline and Fall* p.517; for Wright's allegation that Cohen came under suspicion, see *Spycatcher* pp.264–5

6 Hyam, *Britain's Declining Empire* pp.148–50, 182–4; Goldsworthy (ed.), *BDEEP: The Conservative Government and the End of Empire* doc [275] CAB 129/62 C(53) 244 Cabinet memorandum by Lyttelton, 'Constitutional developments in the Gold Coast' (4 Sept 1953)

7 TNA CO 537/2788 'Review of police and security forces in relation to communist infiltration, Gold Coast' (1948), s.1: Arthur Creech Jones, 'Circular to all Governors and colonial Police Commissioners' (5 Aug 1948)

8 Rathbone, 'Political intelligence and policing in Ghana'; TNA CO 537/3653 'Political intelligence reports, West Africa, reports on communism' (1948), 'Secret. Communist influence in West Africa' (14 Jul 1948)

9 TNA KV 4/308–312 'West African intelligence centre and general security'; FO 371/80614–80617 'Political intelligence reports for Colonel Stephens, Security Liaison Officer Accra'

10 TNA CO 537/3653 'Political intelligence reports, West Africa, reports on communism' (1948), 'Secret. Communist influence in West Africa' (14 Jul 1948)

11 TNA KV 2/1847 'Francis Kwame Nkrumah', s.1a: British Security Co-ordination, Washington DC, to Security Executive, London, forwarded to MI5 (31 Dec 1942); KV 2/1847, s.2a: Special Branch report cross-reference (9 Oct 1945); Hyam and Louis (eds), *BDEEP: The Labour Government and the End of Empire* doc [226] CO 537/7181 Minute A.B. Cohen (11 Jun 1951)

12 Hansen, *Citizenship and Immigration in Post-War Britain* p.19 and passim

13 Abrahams, *A Wreath for Udomo*

14 Nkrumah, *The Autobiography of Kwame Nkrumah* pp.45–6

15 TNA CO 537/3566 'West African national secretariat', s.2: MI5 [name withheld] to D. Bates, Colonial Office (31 Oct 1946); Ibid. s.6: MI5 [name withheld] to Sir Marston Logan, Colonial Office (3 Dec 1946)

16 Nkrumah, *Autobiography* p.63; TNA KV 2/1847, s.33ab: 'Tele-check CPGB headquarters' (1 Jan 1948); Ibid. TNA KV 2/1847, s.39a: Sir Percy Sillitoe to R.W.H. Ballantine, Commissioner of Police, Gold Coast (28 Jan 1948)

17 TNA KV 2/1847 Minute 50: G.T.D. Patterson (1 Apr 1948); Ibid. Minute 58: M.J.E. Bagot (30 Apr 1948)

18 TNA KV 2/1838 Peter Blackman, Minute 14: D.G. White (6 Jul 1938); no MI5 files on Padmore have been declassified at the time of writing, but information on him can be gleaned from files on Nkrumah, for example NA KV2/1849, s.128a: R. Stephens, SLO West Africa, to Director-General (26 Jul 1950)

19 Rathbone, 'Political intelligence and policing in Ghana' p.87; Rooney, *Sir Charles Arden-Clarke* p.113

20 Rathbone, 'Political intelligence and policing in Ghana' p.87

21 TNA KV 2/1849, s.128a: R. Stephens, SLO West Africa, to Director-General (26 Jul 1950)

22 TNA KV 2/1849, s.144a, 'Personality note' (Mar 1948); KV 2/1849, s.160b: source TABLE (11 Jun 1951); Ibid. s.174c: source TABLE (1 Jul 1951)

23 TNA KV 2/1847s.61b: 'Personality note' (Jun 1948); KV 2/1848, s.115a: 'Extract from SLO West Africa report on meeting with the new Governor of the Gold Coast' (13 Sept 1949); see also Rathbone (ed.), *BDEEP: Ghana* doc [85] CO 537/5263 FO Research Department 'A survey of communism in Africa' (Jun 1950)

24 TNA KV 2/1849, s.144a: MI5 [name withheld] to Juxon Barton, Colonial Office (20 Mar 1951); Ibid. s.146a: receipt for Top Secret document, Juxon Barton (20 Mar 1953); Hyam and Louis (eds), *BDEEP: The Labour Government and the End of Empire* doc [224] CO 537/7181 Sir Charles Arden-Clarke to A.B. Cohen (5 Mar 1951); Hyam, *Britain's Declining Empire* p.149; School of Oriental and African Studies (SOAS), University of London, Papers of Sir Charles Arden-Clarke

25 TNA KV 2/1850 Minute 209: Sir John Shaw (1 Jan 1952); KV 2/1850, s.245a: SLO West Africa to Director-General (24 Sept 1952)

26 Hyam, *Britain's Declining Empire* p.149; Pearce, *The Turning Point in Africa: British Colonial Policy, 1938–1948*; Rathbone (ed.), *BDEEP: Ghana* doc [115] Lyttelton cabinet memorandum 'Amendment of the Gold Coast constitution' (9 Feb 1952)

27 TNA KV 2/1850, s.226b: H. Loftus-Brown to Trafford Smith, Colonial Office (5 Jul 1952)

28 TNA KV 2/1851, s.285a: H. Loftus-Brown to Juxon Barton, Colonial Office (3 Jun 1953)

29 Andrew, *Defence of the Realm* p.452

30 National Archives, Washington DC, CREST system CIA Report 'Communism in Africa' (24 Jan 1951) p.19; see also TNA CO 1035/132 Commonwealth Prime Ministers' meeting. Probable attitudes of potential new Commonwealth members to the Soviet Union

31 TNA CAB 158/16 Chiefs of Staff. Joint Intelligence Committee JIC (53) 75 'Situation in Central African Colonies' (7 Aug 1953); JIC (53) 75 'Situation in East African Colonies' (7 Aug 1953); JIC (53) 75 'Situation in West African Colonies' (7 Aug 1953); CO 1035/132 Commonwealth Prime Ministers' meeting. Probable attitudes of potential new commonwealth members to the Soviet Union

32 TNA CO 1035/17 Communist influence in Africa, Minute Juxon Barton (14 Feb 1956)

33 TNA KV 2/1850, s.247a: 'Note for file', H. Loftus-Brown (15 Oct 1952); KV 2/1850, Minute 261: Sir John Shaw (1 Dec 1952); for Arden-Clarke, Nkrumah and the NLA, see Rathbone, *Nkrumah and the Chiefs: The Politics of Chieftaincy in Ghana, 1951–60*

34 TNA KV 2/1916 Kojo Botsio Minute 86 WMT Magan (27 Aug 1954); Ibid. s.82z: SLO West Africa, P.M. Kirby Green, to MI5 London (17 Aug 1954) including letter SLO to Sir Charles Arden-Clarke (5 Aug 1954); CO 1035/36 'Organisation of intelligence services in the colonies – Gold Coast'; s.2 Sir Charles Arden-Clarke to Alan Lennox-Boyd (27 Jun 1956)

35 TNA CO 1035/36 Organisation of intelligence services in the colonies – Gold Coast; CO 1035/95 Security Intelligence Advisers – Mr MacDonald's report the Gold Coast (Oct 1955)

36 TNA CO 1035/13 'Communications Security Problems' PH Canham Accra to JS Bennett CO London (18 Dec 1956); Ibid. s.34 Anthony Crane, LCSA, to ND Watson, CO (21 Sept 1956)

37 Andrew, *Defence of the Realm* p.454

38 TNA KV 2/1849 'Kwame Nkrumah' s.176a: 'Note', H. Loftus-Brown (13 Jul 1951); Sillitoe, *Cloak Without Dagger* pp.196–7; Fleming, *Diamonds are Forever*; CO 544/795 'Supply of information to Sir Percy Sillitoe concerning illicit diamond buying in West Africa'; Bristow, *A Game of Moles* pp.249–50

39 Andrew and Mitrokhin, *The Mitrokhin Archive* vol. II *The KGB and the World* pp.428–35; Baynham, 'Quis Custodiet Ipsos Custodes?: The Case of Nkrumah's National Security Service'

40 Andrew, *Defence of the Realm* p.460
41 TNA CO 1035/96 Reports by Security Intelligence Advisers – Mr MacDonald's report on Nigeria (Feb 1955) s.1a AM MacDonald, SIA, to Secretary of State for Colonies (1 Mar 1955)
42 TNA CO 1035/96 Reports by Security Intelligence Advisers – Mr MacDonald's report on Nigeria (Feb 1955) s.1a AM MacDonald, SIA, to Secretary of State for Colonies (1 Mar 1955); MSS Afr. s.1784 (14) JJ O'Sullivan, handwritten MS, 'Papers relating to service with Nigerian Special Branch' (23 Apr 1982); Brendon, *Decline and Fall* pp.525–6
43 Hyam, *Britain's Declining Empire* p.275
44 RHLO Mss. Afr. s.1784 (14) J.J. O'Sullivan, handwritten MS, 'Papers relating to service with Nigerian Special Branch' (23 Apr 1982) pp.34–6
45 Brendon, *Decline and Fall* p.538
46 Andrew, *Defence of the Realm* p.473
47 Blixen, *Out of Africa*; Anderson, *Histories of the Hanged*
48 Lapping, *End of Empire* p.425; Elkins, *Britain's Gulag*
49 Elkins, *Britain's Gulag*; Anderson, *Histories of the Hanged*; for criticism of Elkins, see David Elstein letter, *London Review of Books* (5 Jun 2005); Blacker, 'The Demography of Mau Mau'
50 Ian Cobain and Richard Norton-Taylor, 'Sins of Colonialists Lay Concealed in Secret Archive for Decades', *Guardian* (18 Apr 2012)
51 Berman and Lonsdale, *Unhappy Valley*
52 Lonsdale, 'British Colonial Officials and the Kikuyu People' in Smith (ed.), *Administering Empire: The British Colonial Service in Retrospect* pp.95–7
53 Kitson, *Gangs and Counter-Gangs* p.131
54 *Ndiku Mutua, Paulo Nzili, Wambugu Nyingi, Jane Muthoni Mara & Susan Ngondi v The Foreign and Commonwealth Office* [2011] EWHC 1913 (QB) at [20]
55 Ruark, *Something of Value*; Elkins, *Britain's Gulag*; Kyle, *The Politics of the Independence of Kenya* p.48; TNA WO 32/15834 Court of Enquiry in Kenya s.12a: George Erskine to Antony Head, Secretary of State for War (10 Dec 1953)
56 Lyttelton, *The Memoirs of Lord Chandos* pp.394–5; Lonsdale, 'Mau Maus of the Mind'; Hyam, *Britain's Declining Empire* pp.188–92; Sillitoe, *Cloak Without Dagger* pp. 191–3
57 Elkins, *Britain's Gulag*; Anderson, *Histories of the Hanged*; official figures given in Corfield, *Historical Survey of the Origins and Growth of Mau Mau*; TNA WO 236/18 General Sir George Erskine, 'The Kenya Emergency'; FCO 141/6086 Mau Mau unrest; collective punishment under Emergency Regulations 1952
58 Brendon, *Decline and Fall* p.555; Hyam, *Britain's Declining Empire* p.191
59 Lonsdale, 'Mau Maus of the Mind'
60 Magan, *Middle Eastern Approaches* p.126; TNA WO 276/10 'Security conference, Nairobi, August 18–29' (1947); Sillitoe, *Cloak Without Dagger* pp.10–58
61 Andrew, *Defence of the Realm* p.456
62 TNA CO 822/445, s.20: 'Note of meeting held in the Secretary of State's room' (15 Dec 1952); TNA CO 822/445, s.21 Sir Evelyn Baring to Sir Thomas Lloyd (10 Dec 1952); Ibid. s.22: Sir Thomas Lloyd to Sir Evelyn Baring (9 Jan 1953)
63 TNA CO 822/445, s.14: Sir Thomas Lloyd to Sir Evelyn Baring (15 Nov 1952); 'Kikuyu Base Surprised', *The Times* (22 Nov 1952); Heather, 'Intelligence and counter-insurgency in Kenya' p.61
64 Andrew, *Defence of the Realm* p.457
65 RHLO Mss. Afr. s.1784 (23) T.W. Jenkins, 'Memoire' (28 Aug 1982) p.30; Blundell, *So Rough a Wind* p.187; TNA WO 236/20 Lt Gen Lathbury, 'The Kenya Emergency' (3 May 1955–17 Nov 1956), Andrew, *Defence of the Realm* p.457
66 Brendon, *Decline and Fall* p.555
67 Anderson, *Histories of the Hanged*
68 TNA CO 926/1076 MacDonald to Neale (4 Jan 1957); French, *The British Way* p.216

69 TNA WO 236/18 Gen. Sir George Erskine, 'The Kenya emergency', Jun 1953–May 1955; Sir Richard Catling RHLO Mss. Afr. s.1784 (21) Paper delivered at University of New Brunswick, Canada (13 Feb 1979) p.55

70 TNA WO 236/18 Gen. Sir George Erskine, 'The Kenya emergency', Jun 1953–May 1955; Sir Richard Catling Mss. Afr. s.1784 (21) Paper delivered at University of New Brunswick, Canada (13 Feb 1979) p.55; for the 'dilution' technique, see Elkins, *Britain's Gulag* pp.319–32

71 Hyam, *Britain's Declining Empire* p.190

72 TNA WO 32/15834 Court of Enquiry in Kenya letter Erskine to Secretary of State for War (10 Dec 1953)

73 *Mutua v The Foreign and Commonwealth Office* [2011] EWHC 1913 (QB) at paragraph 126

74 Ibid.

75 Ibid. at paragraph 46

76 Ibid. at paragraph 43; Elkins, *Britain's Gulag*

77 French, *The British Way* pp.145, 157–8; WO 33/2335 Joint Services pamphlet, 'Interrogation in War'; author's interview with former Security Service officer (Sept 2011)

78 RHLO Sir Richard Catling Mss. Afr. s.1784 (21) 'Law Enforcement, Kenya' (Ms. written 10 May 1982) p.11; interview author's interview with former Security Service officer (Sept 2011)

79 Kitson, *Gangs and Counter-Gangs* p.74 and passim

80 Baldwin, *Mau Mau Man Hunt* p.83; French, *The British Way* p.158

81 RHLO Mss. Brit. Emp. s.486 6/4 s.10 Arthur Young Papers, 'Agreed public statement with Lennox-Boyd, colonial secretary, following resignation' (1955)

82 TNA FCO 141/6769 Statement by his Excellency the Governor (31 Mar 1960); Hyam, *Britain's Declining Empire* p.190

83 Berman, 'Jomo Kenyatta', *DNB* (online edition accessed 4 Jan 2010)

84 TNA KV 2/1787 Jomo Kenyatta s.13a: Sir Vernon Kell to D.C.J. McSweeney, Colonial Office (16 Dec 1933); Ibid. Sir Vernon Kell to Commissioner of Police, Kenya (18 Jan 1934); Ibid. s.23a: Home Office Warrant (3 Jan 1934)

85 TNA KV 2/1787 Jomo Kenyatta s.96b: Jane Archer (8 Jan 1936)

86 TNA KV 2/1788 Jomo Kenyatta s.233a: Sir David Petrie to A.W. Riggs, DIS Kenya (13 Sept 1944)

87 TNA KV 2/1788 Jomo Kenyatta s.248a: O.J. Mason, MI5, to J.D. Bates, Colonial Office (29 Dec 1945)

88 TNA KV 2/1788 Jomo Kenyatta Minute 357: H. Loftus-Brown (20 Nov 1953)

89 TNA KV 2/1788 Jomo Kenyatta s.357b: H. Loftus-Brown to Juxon Barton (22 Nov 1952)

90 TNA KV 2/1788 Jomo Kenyatta s.333b: B.M. de Quehen, SLO Central Africa, to Director-General MI5 (23 Jul 1951); Pegushev, 'Afrikanski v komminterne' pp.37–49; Pegushev, 'The Unknown Kenyatta' pp.172–198; Suchkov, 'Dzhomo Keniata v Mosckve' pp.106–21; McClellan, 'Africans and Black Americans in the Comintern Schools, 1925–1934' pp.371–90

91 TNA CO 968/261, s.1a: Sir John Shaw to T.S. Tull, IRD, Foreign Office, copied to Juxon Barton, Colonial Office (23 Dec 1952)

92 Revealed by TNA KV 2/2541 Peter Mbui Koinange, in particular s.334a: H. Loftus Brown to CJJT Barton, CO (31 Oct 1952)

93 TNA KV2/1788 Jomo Kenyatta s.357b: SLO East Africa Quarterly Review (20 Oct 1952); Lonsdale, 'Kenyatta's trials: breaking and making of an African nationalist' in Cross (ed.), *The Moral World of the Law* pp.196–239; Hyam, *Britain's Declining Empire* pp.190–1

94 RHLO Mss. Afr. s.1784 (24) M.C. Manby, 'Law Enforcement – Kenya' 'Law enforcement in former British African territories. A memoir by MC Manby' (Feb 1982); CO 1035/187 Organisation of intelligence services in the colonies – Kenya s.2: E.N. Griffith Jones, Governor's Office, Nairobi, to F.D. Webber, Colonial Office (18 Jun 1963)

95 TNA FCO 141/6957 Security of official correspondence s.38 'Measure for the protection of official documents. Protection of Special Branch Material. Use of the marking "Watch"' (Mar 1961); Ibid. s.43 Governor of Uganda to S of S for colonies (22 Mar 1961); Ibid. s.46/1 The Kenya Police Special Branch; FCO 141/6960 Kenya: cypher telegram traffic

96 Collings, *Reflections on a Statesman: The Writings and Speeches of Enoch Powell* p.207

97 Macmillan, *Pointing the Way* Appendix One: 'Address by Harold Macmillan to members of both Houses of the Parliament of the Union of South Africa, Cape Town, 3 February 1960'; Hyam and Louis (eds), *BDEEP: The Conservative Government and the End of Empire* doc [32] DO 35/10570 no 3 Address by Mr Macmillan (3 Feb 1960)

98 Macleod, 'Trouble in Africa', *Spectator* (31 Jan 1964)

99 Andrew, *Defence of the Realm* p.464

100 Wright, *Spycatcher* p.58; Andrew, *Defence of the Realm* pp.467, 852

101 Aldrich, *GCHQ* p.3

102 Andrew, *Defence of the Realm* p.852; le Carré, *Mission Song*

103 Andrew, *Defence of the Realm* p.464; RHLO MSS Brit Emp s.533 Macolm MacDonald, transcripts of interviews (1970) pp.10–11

104 TNA CO 1035/187 Organisation of intelligence services in the colonies – Kenya s.3: FD Webber to Sir Eric Griffith-Jones (6 Aug 1963); CAB 158/43 Joint Intelligence Committee JIC (61) 23 (Final) 'Background to the political situation in British territories in East and Central Africa' (23 Mar 1961); private information

105 TNA CO 1035/187 Organisation of intelligence services in the colonies – Kenya s.8 J.A. Harrison, SIA, to J.N.A. Armitage Smith (17 Oct 1963) with note RH Hollis DG 'Note' (11 Oct 1963); Sir Richard Catling RHLO Mss. Afr. s.1784 (21) 'Law Enforcement, Kenya' (Ms. written 10 May 1982) p.42

106 TNA FCO 141/7094 Oginga Odinga; RHLO Mss. Afr. s.2159 Box 2 'Miscellaneous reports' s.110 M.C. Manby, Director of Security and Intelligence, 'The present security scene in Kenya', copied to SLO Mr WF Bell (4 Jul 1962) pp.19–21

107 Andrew, *Defence of the Realm* p.475; Hyam and Louis (eds), *BDEEP: The Conservative Government and the End of Empire* doc [178] CAB 128/37 CC 41(63) Cabinet conclusions (24 Jun 1964); author's interview with former SIS officer (20 Apr 2009)

108 TNA CO 1035/171 Security Liaison Officers – Policy s.E/4 Sir Roger Hollis, DG MI5, to Sir Burke Trend, Cabinet Office (13 Nov 1965)

109 Bergman, 'Israel and Africa: military and intelligence liaisons' pp.119–21, 176–9; TNA CAB 158/51 Joint Intelligence Committee JIC (64) 8 (Final) 'Israeli activities in Africa' (29 Jul 1964)

110 TNA KV 1/19 'D-Branch Report'; PREM 8/1283 Security in South Africa: visit of Sir Percy Sillitoe 'Visit by the Director-General of the Security Service to South Africa' (Dec 1949)

111 Chavkin, 'British Intelligence and the Zionist, South African, and Australian intelligence communities'

112 O'Brien, *South African Intelligence Services* pp.19–21; Chavkin, 'British Intelligence and the Zionist, South African, and Australian intelligence communities'

113 TNA PREM 8/1283 Security in South Africa: visit of Sir Percy Sillitoe 'Visit by the Director-General of the Security Service to South Africa' (Dec 1949)

114 TNA KV 2/2502 Michael Scott

115 TNA PREM 8/1283 Memorandum for the Prime Minister from the Director General of the Security Service (18 Oct 1949); CO 1035/187 Organisation of intelligence services in the colonies – Kenya s.8 J.A. Harrison, SIA, to J.N.A. Armitage Smith (17 Oct 1963) with note RH Hollis DG 'Note' (11 Oct 1963); DO 183/480 The Security Liaison Officer Service and intelligence organisation in Central Africa s.11 JNA Armitage Smith to Sir Hugh Stephenson, British Embassy Cape Town (4 Jun 1963); Murphy, 'South African intelligence, the Wilson Plot and post-Imperial trauma' in Major and Moran (eds), *Spooked: Britain, Empire and Intelligence Since 1945* pp.97–118

116 Andrew, *Defence of the Realm* pp.635–7; Freeman and Penrose, *Rinkagate*

117 Tomlinson, *The Big Breach* pp.140–2

118 Hyam, *Britain's Declining Empire* pp.282–8; Brendon, *Decline and Fall* p.580; Reynolds, *Britannia Overruled* p.210

119 Murphy (ed.), *BDEEP: Central Africa* doc 102 Intelligence in central Africa, letter from I.M.R. Maclennan to R.W.D. Fowler, enclosing letter from B.M. de Quehen to Maclennan (15 Jun 1954)

120 Murphy, 'A Police State? The Nyasaland Emergency and Colonial Intelligence'; TNA CO 1035/143 Security Situation – Nyasaland s.10 J.E. Day [MI5] to N.D. Watson (3 Mar 1959)

121 Catterall (ed.), *The Macmillan Diaries* p.235 (13 Jul 1959); for the bugging of Banda in prison, see Murphy (ed.), *British Documents on the End of Empire: Central Africa* Doc 219 'Future of Hastings Banda' FISB summary of conversations between D Foot and H Banda [CO 1015/2442] (23–24 Jan 1960); Ibid. Doc 300 Activities of Lord Lambton: note for the record by TJ Bligh of a meeting between Mr Macmillan and Lord Lambton [PREM 11/3496] (2 Aug 1961)

122 TNA KV 2/1916 Kojo Botsio Minute 70a: MI5 DG to SLO Central Africa and West Africa (20 Mar 1953); Brendon, *Decline and Fall* pp.582, 584; private information

123 TNA DO 183/480 The Security Liaison Officer Service and intelligence organisation in Central Africa Minute N.D. Watson (30 Nov 1962); Ibid. s.1a A.J. Kellar to W.S. Bates, Central African Office, CO (5 Sept 1962)

124 TNA DO 183/480 s.18: Evelyn Detone, Government House, Lusaka, to S.P. Whitby, Central African Office, CO (14 Mar 1964)

125 Andrew, *Defence of the Realm* p.468

126 TNA DO 183/214 R.H. Hollis 'Memorandum' (21 Sept 1962)

127 Flower, *Serving Secretly* pp.11, 14–15, 81; Verrier, *The Road to Zimbabwe* pp.112–13

Chapter 7: British Intelligence, Covert Action and Counter-Insurgency in the Middle East

1 TNA CO 1035/24 Egyptian nationalisation of the Suez Canal Juxon Barton (1 Aug 1956)

2 TNA FO 800/749 Suez records s. Attorney General, Reginald Manningham-Buller, to Selwyn Lloyd (1 Nov 1956)

3 Brendon, *Decline and Fall* p.487

4 Woodhouse, *Something Ventured* p.110; Aldrich, *The Hidden Hand* p.480

5 Aldrich, *The Hidden Hand* p.470; Smith, *Ending Empire in the Middle East: Britain, the United States and Post-War Decolonization*

6 CIA Clandestine service history, 'Overthrow of premier Mossadeq of Iran, November 1952–August 1953' (Mar 1954) p.4, available; Verrier, *Through the Looking Glass*; Dorril, *MI6* p.569. The CIA history was first published by the *New York Times* in April 2000, and is available at http://www.nytimes.com/library/world/mideast/041600iran-cia-index.html

7 Woodhouse, *Something Ventured* p.101; CIA Clandestine service history, 'Overthrow of premier Mossadeq of Iran'

8 Aldrich, *The Hidden Hand* p.474

9 Woodhouse, *Something Ventured* p.130

10 CIA Clandestine service history, 'Overthrow of premier Mossadeq of Iran' pp.78–81

11 Young, *Who is My Liege?* p.7; Smith, *The Spying Game*; private information

12 Hennessy, *Having it so Good* pp.419–22; Louis, 'Public Enemy Number One: Britain and the United Nations in the aftermath of Suez' in Lynn (ed.), *The British Empire in the 1950s: Retreat or Revival?*

13 The following paragraphs owe much to Hyam, *Britain's Declining Empire* pp.226–40; see also Brendon, *Decline and Fall* p.488; Shuckburgh, *Descent to Suez* p. 341

14 Aldrich, *The Hidden Hand* p.480; Wright, *Spycatcher* p.160

15 Bower, *Perfect English Spy* p.192

16 Churchill College Archives Centre Misc 30 'Suez meeting at Sevres, 22–25 Oct 1956', narrative by Donald Logan (24 Oct 1956)

17 TNA CAB158/25 Joint Intelligence Committee JIC (56) 96 (Final) 'Operation Musketeer – security of signal traffic' (6 Sept 1956)

18 Andrew, *For the President's Eyes Only* p.227

19 TNA CAB158/25 JIC (56) 80 (Final) 'Egyptian Nationalisation of the Suez Canal Company' (10 August 1956)

20 Lucas, 'The missing link? Patrick Dean, chairman of the Joint Intelligence Committee' in Kelly and Gorst (eds), *Whitehall and the Suez Crisis* pp.117–25; Cradock, *Know Your Enemy: How the Joint Intelligence Committee Saw the World* p.134; Hennessy, *Having it so Good* pp.419–21; Cooper, *The Lion's Last Roar* p.170

21 Hennessy, *The Prime Minister* p.227; Kyle, *Suez* pp.84–5; Lucas, *Divided we Stand*

22 Private information

23 Cradock, *Know Your Enemy* p.134; Aldrich, *GCHQ* pp.156–9

24 TNA FO 800/747 Suez Canal GG Fitzmaurice to Sir Ivone Kirkpatrick (5 Nov 1956); FO 800/749 Suez records s.2 Attorney General, Reginald Manningham-Buller, to Selwyn Lloyd (1 Nov 1956); Hennessy, *Having it so Good* pp.427–9

25 Shuckburgh, *Descent to Suez* p.365

26 Hyam and Louis (eds), *BDEEP: The Conservative Government and the End of Empire* doc [1] CAB 134/1555 CPC (57)6 (28 Jan 1957); Ibid. doc [2] CAB 134/1551 CPC (57)27 Sir N. Brook, 'Future constitutional development in the colonies' (May 1957); Ibid. doc [3] Sir Norman Brook, 'Future constitutional development in the colonies' (6 Sept 1957); French, *The British Way* p.229

27 TNA PREM11/2321 Arrangement by Cabinet Secretary for small group of officials to carry out re-assessment of UK interests abroad s.9 'The Position of the United Kingdom in World Affairs' (5 Jun 1958)

28 CO 1035/22 Joint Intelligence Committee aspects: activities of Cairo radio and its impact on British territories in Africa

29 Aldrich, *The Hidden Hand* p.568; Aldrich, *GCHQ* pp.159–62

30 These paragraphs owe much to Brendon, *Decline and Fall* pp.615–20

31 Aldrich, *The Hidden Hand* p.574

32 Brendon, *Decline and Fall* p.620

33 TNA CO 1035/98 Reports by Security Intelligence Advisers – Mr MacDonald's report on Cyprus, December 1955 AM MacDonald Minute 8 Dec 1954; Ibid. s1a AM MacDonald, SIA, to Governor of Cyprus (21 Aug 1954)

34 Foley (ed.), *The Memoirs of General Grivas* p.40

35 French, *The British Way* p.22; TNA CO 1035/98 s.6: 'Final Report by the Security Service Adviser to the Cyprus Police Special Branch' (Nicosia, Apr 1955); CAB 158/30 Joint Intelligence Committee JIC (58) 49 'The situation in Cyprus' (28 Apr 1958)

36 Foley (ed.), *The Memoirs of General Grivas* p.28

37 Ibid. p.69; Aldrich, *The Hidden Hand* p.571; Andrew, *Defence of the Realm* p.464; Brendon, *Decline and Fall* p.620

38 Jack Malvern, 'Secret Plan to Deport Troublesome Cypriot' *The Times* (18 Apr 2012)

39 Aldrich, *The Hidden Hand* p.573; Andrew, *Defence of the Realm* p.463

40 French, *The British Way* p.159

41 Aldrich, *The Hidden Hand* p.577; Foley (ed.), *The Memoirs of General Grivas* p.69

42 Foot, *Emergency Exit* pp.19–22; Bower, *Perfect English Spy* p.231

43 Aldrich, *The Hidden Hand* p.577; Andrew, *Defence of the Realm* p.464

44 Andrew, *Defence of the Realm* p.465; Horne, *Macmillan* vol. II p.100

45 CAB 158/38 Joint Intelligence Committee JIC (59) 92 'Cyprus intelligence organisation' (30 Nov 1959)

46 Aldrich, *GCHQ* pp.162–3

47 Ibid. pp.7, 163

48 The following owes much to a pioneering Cambridge MPhil dissertation by Will Leslie, 'British intelligence in Aden and South Arabia, 1963–1967'; see also Vital, *The Making of British Foreign Policy* pp.89–103; Mawby, *British Policy in Aden and the Protectorate*; French, *The British Way* p.13

49 Brendon, *Decline and Fall* p.500

50 Andrew, *Defence of the Realm* p.473

51 Macmillan, *At the End of the Day: 1961–1963* p.267

52 TNA CO 1055/196 Trevaskis to Colonial Office (10 Dec 1963)

53 French, *The British Way* pp.26–7

54 TNA CO 1035/181/6 Colonial Office, Organisation of Intelligence 14 Jan 1964; CO 1055/62/9 Aden intelligence summary no.4 for the month of April 1963; Mawby, *British Policy in the Aden Protectorates* pp.25–6, 71–3, 78–9

55 TNA CO 1055/196 Trevaskis to Colonial Office (10 Dec 1963)

56 Leslie, 'British Intelligence in Aden' pp.30–3; cf. Trevaskis, *Shades of Amber* p.211

57 Leslie, 'British Intelligence in Aden' pp.30–3; TNA CO 1035/181/44 D Russell Minute (9 Apr 1964); CO 1035/181 s.7 'Note of a meeting between Secretary for Defence and the High Commissioner' (9 Jan 1964)

58 TNA CO 1035/178 s.1 W Formoy to D Russell (3 Apr 1963); CO 1035/86 Reports by Security Intelligence Advisers – Aden s.49a GRH Gribble, SIA, to Sir William Luce, Governor, Aden (17 Sept 1956)

59 TNA CO 1035/180 s.259, Report by J. Prendergast, Director of Special Branch, Hong Kong, on visit to Aden (18 Nov 1965); CO 1035/178/89 J. Morton (11 Feb 1965); CO 1035/178 s.82E Chairman JIC 1 Feb 1965; CO 1055/202 Acting High Commissioner to Colonial Office (25 Dec 1964); CO 1055/221 Turnbull to Colonial Office (14 Sept 1965); for the murder of Special Branch officers in above paragraph, see French, *The British Way* pp.24–6

60 Andrew, *Defence of the Realm* p.474; TNA FO 371/185233 J. Prendergast, 'A Note on Terrorism in Aden' (6 Dec 1966)

61 Andrew, *Defence of the Realm* p.474; Leslie, 'British Intelligence in Aden' p.54; TNA FO 371/185233 J. Prendergast, 'A Note on Terrorism in Aden' (6 Dec 1966); von Bulow, 'The Foreign Policy of the Federal Republic of Germany: Franco–German Relations, and the Algerian War 1954 –62'; Trevelyan, *Middle East in Revolution* p.222

62 French, *The British Way* p.242

63 Ibid. pp.149, 159, 170, 242; Horne, *A Savage War of Peace* p.212; TNA CO 1035/180 Prendergast to Turnbull, Aden Intelligence Centre, report by Prendergast on visit to Aden (18 Nov 1965); CO 1055/266 Petition by 27 detainees held at Fort Morbut to the minister of state for colonial affairs (27 Nov 1964)

64 Macmillan, *At the End of the Day 1961–1963* p.263; Hart-Davis, *The War that Never Was*; Smiley, *Arabian Assignment*; Hinchcliffe and Holt, *Without Glory in Arabia*; Aldrich, *GCHQ* p.164

65 Hart-Davis, *The War that Never Was*

66 Andrew, *Defence of the Realm* pp.476–7

67 TNA CAB 182/55/1 Joint Intelligence Committee Aden working party (15 Apr 1966); CAB 182/55/2 'Joint Intelligence Committee Aden working party (27 Apr 1966)

Conclusion

1 Hyam, *Britain's Declining Empire* p.326

2 TNA CO 1035/139 Survey of subversive activities in the colonies (1957) Minute ND Watson (13 Feb 1958)

3 Bloch, *Strange Defeat* p.83

4 Freedman, *The Official History of the Falklands*; Bicheno, *Razor's Edge: The Unofficial History of the Falklands War*

5 Aldrich, *GCHQ* p.151; TNA FCO 141/12635 Hong Kong Local Intelligence Committee;

FCO 141/7463 Papers of the Joint Intelligence Committee (Far East) JIC (FE) (55) 8 (Final) 'The probable attitude of the Chinese population of South East Asia and Hong Kong in the event of war' (7 Jun 1955); Louis, 'Hong Kong: the critical years 1945–49'

6 TNA FCO 21/199 'Long Term Study' OPDC (DR) (67) 52 (18 Aug 1967); Shibuya, 'British intelligence in Hong Kong in the era of the Cultural Revolution', passim

7 TNA CAB 158/7 JIC (49) 44/10 (Final) A Review of the threat to Hong Kong as of 19 September 1949; CAB 158/7 JIC 949) 44/11 (Final) A Review of the threat to Hong Kong as of 4 October 1949; CAB 158/15 JIC (53) 13 (Final) Radical Review – Consequences of reduction of garrison in Hong Kong (3 Feb 1953)

8 Shibuya, 'British intelligence in Hong Kong in the era of the Cultural Revolution' passim

9 Aldrich, GCHQ p.152

10 Ibid. p.154

11 Patten, East and West: The Last Governor of Hong Kong on Power, Freedom and the Future pp.38–9, 65; private information

12 TNA CO 1035/187 Organisation of intelligence services in the colonies – Kenya s.6: EN Griffith-Jones to FD Webber (14 Aug 1963)

13 TNA CO 1035/39 Organisation of intelligence services in the colonies s.2 Sir Robin Black to Alan Lennox-Boyd 'Organisation of intelligence' (3 Aug 1956); CO 1035/187 Organisation of intelligence services in the colonies – Kenya s.2: EN Griffith-Jones, Governor's Office, Nairobi, to FD Webber, CO (18 Jun 1963); FCO 141/6957 Security of official correspondence

14 Andrew, Defence of the Realm p.468

15 TNA CAB 158/30 JIC (57) 115 (Final) 'Intelligence organisation in the colonial territories' (8 Nov 1957) pp.1, 5, and p.4 for numbers of officers trained

16 Jeffery, MI6 pp.696–7; CAB 158/15 JIC 58 (53) 49 'Standards of security in Israel' (2 May 1953); Hennessy, Having it so Good p.299 for the quote by Sir Gerry Warner

17 BDEEP part 1 pp.190–251 (no 59) CO 847/36/1 no 9 (22 May 1947)

18 TNA FO 371/80617 'Political intelligence reports on West Africa for Colonel Stephens, Security Liaison Officer Accra', Juxon Barton, Colonial Office, to governor of Gold Coast (13 Nov 1950); KV2/1788 Jomo Kenyatta; Andrew, Defence of the Realm p.470; TNA kv4/469 Diaries of Guy Liddell (10 Sept 1947)

19 Craig, Crisis of Confidence; Andrew, Defence of the Realm pp.600–26

20 Frankland, Child of My Time p.89; private information

21 Private information

22 Reynolds, Britannia Overruled pp.203–8

23 FCO 141/1355 British Indian Ocean Territory (BIOT)

24 Pilger, Freedom Next Time p.38; Aldrich, GCHQ p.339

25 Bancoult v Secretary of State for Foreign and Commonwealth Affairs [2006] EWHC 1038 (Admin); FCO 141/1355 British Indian Ocean Territory (BIOT) s.13 BIOT 157/172 (17 Oct 1968)

26 Aldrich, GCHQ p.337; TNA FCO 141/1355 British Indian Ocean Territory (BIOT) FCO telegram to Washington (24 Nov1970); FCO 141/1431 BIOT radio traffic

27 French, The British Way p.33

28 TNA WO 32/15834 Court of Enquiry in Kenya letter Erskine to Secretary of State for War (10 Dec 1953); Lazreg, Torture and the Twilight of Empire from Algiers to Baghdad

29 Ian Cobain and Richard Norton-Taylor, 'Sins of Colonialists Lay Concealed in Secret Archive for Decades', Guardian (18 Apr 2012)

30 Murphy (ed.), BDEEP: Central Africa Doc 257 Belgian Congo FO Minutes by HFT Smith, ADM Ross, and Sir R Stevens on proposal to remove Patrice Lumumba [FO 371/146650] (28 and 29 Sept 1960)

Bibliography

Abrahams, Peter, *A Wreath for Udomo* (London: Faber & Faber, 1956)

Adi, Hakim, *West Africans in Britain, 1900–1960: Nationalism, Pan-Africanism and Communism* (London: Lawrence & Wishart, 1998)

Aldrich, Richard J. (ed.), *British Intelligence, Strategy and the Cold War 1945–51* (London: Routledge, 1992)

Aldrich, Richard J., *Intelligence and the War Against Japan: Britain, America and the Politics of Secret Service* (Cambridge: Cambridge University Press, 2000)

Aldrich, Richard J., *The Hidden Hand: Britain, America and Cold War Secret Intelligence* (London: John Murray, 2001)

Aldrich, Richard, *GCHQ: The Uncensored History of Britain's Most Secret Intelligence Agency* (London: HarperPress, 2010)

Aldrich, Richard J., 'GCHQ and sigint in the early Cold War, 1945–70', in Aid, Matthew M., and Wiebes, Cees, *Secrets of Signals Intelligence During the Cold War and Beyond* (London, 2001), pp.67–96

Anderson, Benedict, *Imagined Communities: Reflections on the Origin and Spread of Nationalism*, new edn (London: Verso, 2006)

Anderson, David, *Histories of the Hanged: Britain's Dirty War in Kenya and the End of Empire* (London: Weidenfeld & Nicolson, 2005)

Andrew, Christopher, *Secret Service: The Making of the British Intelligence Community* (London: Sceptre, 1985)

Andrew, Christopher, *For the President's Eyes Only: Secret Intelligence and the American Presidency from Washington to Bush* (London: HarperCollins, 1995)

Andrew, Christopher, *Defence of the Realm: The Authorized History of MI5* (London: Penguin, 2009)

Andrew, Christopher, 'The Venona Secret', in Robertson, K.G. (ed.), *War, Resistance and Intelligence: Collected Essays in Honour of M.R.D. Foot* (London: Leo Cooper, 1999), pp.203–25

Andrew, Christopher, 'Intelligence in the Cold War: lessons and learning', in Shukman, Harold (ed.), *Agents for Change: Intelligence Services in the Twenty-First Century* (London: St Ermin's Press, 2000), pp.1–22

Andrew, Christopher, 'Churchill and intelligence', *Intelligence and National Security* 3 (1988), pp.181–93

Andrew, Christopher, 'The growth of the Australian intelligence community and the Anglo-American connection', *Intelligence and National Security* 4 (1989), pp.213–56

Andrew, Christopher, and Dilks, David (eds), *The Missing Dimension: Governments and Intelligence Communities in the Twentieth Century* (London: Macmillan, 1984)

Andrew, Christopher, and Gordievsky, Oleg, *KGB: The Inside Story of its Foreign Operations from Lenin to Gorbachev* (London: Sceptre, 1991)

Andrew, Christopher, and Mitrokhin, Vasili, *The Mitrokhin Archive* vol. I *The KGB in Europe and the West* (London: Penguin, 1999); vol. II *The KGB and the World* (London: Penguin, 2005)

Andrew, Christopher, and Noakes, Jeremy (eds), *Intelligence and International Relations, 1900–1945* (Exeter: Exeter University Press, 1987)

Andrew, Christopher, and Walton, Calder, 'The Gouzenko case and British secret intelligence', in J.L. Black and Martin Rudner (eds), *The Gouzenko Affair: Canada and the Beginnings of Cold War Counter-Espionage* (Manotick, Ontario: Penumbra Press, 2006), pp.38–56

Arendt, Hannah, *The Origins of Totalitarianism* (London: Allen & Unwin, 1973)

Ashton, S.R., and Murray, D.J. (general eds), *British Documents on the End of Empire*, 14 vols (London: HMSO,1992–2005)

'Avner', *Memoirs of an Assassin*, English translation (London: A. Blond, 1959)

Baldwin, William W., *Mau Mau Man Hunt: The Adventures of the Only American who has Fought the Terrorists in Kenya* (New York: Dutton, 1957)

Banton, Mandy, ' "Destroy"? "Migrate"? "Conceal"? British Strategies for the Disposal of Sensitive Records of Colonial Administrations at Independence', *Journal of Imperial and Commonwealth History* 40 (2012), pp.321–35

Bar-Zohar, Michael, *Hitler's Jewish Spy: The Most Extraordinary True Spy Story of World War II* (London: Sidgwick & Jackson, 1985)

Bar-Zohar, Michael, *Yaacov Herzog: A Biography*, English translation (London: Barker, 1968)

Barooah, Nirode K., *Chatto: The Life and Times of an Indian Anti-Imperialist in Europe* (Delhi: Oxford University Press India, 2004)

Barrass, Gordon S., *The Great Cold War: A Journey Through the Hall of Mirrors* (Stanford, Ca: Stanford General, 2009)

Bayly, C.A., *Empire and Information: Intelligence Gathering and Social Communication in India, 1780–1870* (Cambridge: Cambridge University Press, 1996)

Bayly, Christopher, and Harper, Tim, *Forgotten Wars: The End of Britain's Asian Empire* (London: Allen Lane, 2007)

Baynham, Simon, 'Quis Custodiet Ipsos Custodes?: The Case of Nkrumah's National Security Service', *Journal of Modern African Studies* 23 (1985), pp.87–103

Begin, Menachem, *The Revolt*, English translation (London: W.H. Allen, 1951)

Bell, J. Bowyer, *Terror Out of Zion: Irgun Zvai Leumi, LEHI and the Palestine Underground, 1929–1949* (New York: St Martin's Press, 1977)

Bennett, Gill, *'A Most Extraordinary and Mysterious Incident': The Zinoviev Letter of 1924*, FCO History Note no 14 (London: FCO, 1999)

Bennett, Gill, 'Declassification and release policies of the UK's intelligence agencies', *Intelligence and National Security* 17 (2002), pp.21–32

Bergman, Ronen, 'Israel and Africa: military and intelligence liaisons' (PhD dissertation, University of Cambridge, 2007)

Berman, Bruce, and Lonsdale, John, *Unhappy Valley: Conflict in Kenya and Africa*, 2 vols (London: J. Currey, 1992)

Bicheno, Hugh, *Razor's Edge: The Unofficial History of the Falklands War* (London: Weidenfeld & Nicolson, 2006)

Blacker, John, 'The Demography of Mau Mau: Fertility and Mortality in Kenya in the 1950s: A Demographer's Viewpoint', *African Affairs* 106 (2007), pp.205–27

Bloch, Jonathan, and Fitzgerald, Patrick, *British Intelligence and Covert Action: Africa, the Middle East and Europe since 1945* (Dingle: Brandon, 1983)

Blundell, Michael, *So Rough a Wind: The Kenya Memoirs of Sir Michael Blundell* (London: Weidenfeld & Nicolson, 1964)

Boot, Max, *The Savage Wars of Peace: Small Wars and the Rise of American Power* (New York: Basic Books, 2002)

Bose, Subhas Chandra, *The Indian Struggle 1920–1942* (London: Asia, 1964)

Bower, Tom, *The Perfect English Spy: Sir Dick White and the Secret War, 1935–90* (London: Heinemann, 1995)

Boyle, Andrew, *The Climate of Treason* (London: Hutchinson, 1982)

Bozeman, Adda, *Strategic Intelligence and Statecraft: Selected Essays* (Washington: Brassey's, 1992)

Brendon, Piers, *The Decline and Fall of the British Empire 1781–1997* (London: Jonathan Cape, 2007)

Briscoe, Robert, *For the Life of Me* (London: Longman, 1959)

Bristow, Desmond, *A Game of Moles: The Deceptions of an MI6 Officer* (London: Little, Brown, 1993)

Brooke, Lady Sylvia, *Queen of the Head-Hunters: The Autobiography of H.H. the Hon. Sylvia Lady Brooke* (London: Sidgwick & Jackson, 1970)

Brown, Judith M., Louis, Wm. Roger, and Low, Alaine M. (eds), *The Oxford History of the British Empire: The Twentieth Century* (Oxford: Oxford University Press, 2001)

Buchan, John, *Greenmantle*, new edn (Oxford: Oxford University Press, 1993)

Buchheit, Gert, *Der Deutsche Geheimdienst: Geschichte der militärischen Abwehr* (Munich: Paul List, 1966)

Burleigh, Michael, *Blood and Rage: A Cultural History of Terrorism* (London: HarperPress, 2008)

Burt, Leonard, *Commander Burt of Scotland Yard* (London: Heinemann, 1959)

Callwell, Charles Edward, *Small Wars: A Tactical Textbook for Imperial Soldiers* (London: Greenhill Books/Lionel Leventhal, 1990)

Carruthers, Susan L., *Winning Hearts and Minds: British Governments, the Media and Colonial Counter-Insurgency 1944–1960* (London: Leicester University Press, 1995)

Cecil, Robert, 'The Cambridge Comintern', in Andrew, Christopher, and Dilks, David (eds), *The Missing Dimension: Governments and Intelligence Communities in the Twentieth Century* (London: Macmillan, 1984), pp.169–98

Cesarani, David, *Major Farran's Hat: Murder, Scandal and Britain's War Against Jewish Terrorism 1945–1948* (London: Heinemann, 2009)

Chapman, F. Spencer, *The Jungle is Neutral* (London: Chatto & Windus, 2006)

Charters, David A., *The British Army and Jewish Insurgency in Palestine, 1945–47* (Basingstoke: Palgrave Macmillan, 1989)

Chavkin, Jonathan, 'British intelligence and the Zionst, South African and Australian intelligence communities during and after the Second World War (PhD dissertation, University of Cambridge, 2009)

Chin Peng, *My Side of History* (Singapore: Media Masters, 2003)

Clarke, Peter, *The Last Thousand Days of the British Empire* (London: Allen Lane, 2007)

Clarke, Thurston, *By Blood and Fire: The Attack on the King David Hotel* (London: Hutchinson, 1981)

Clayton, Anthony, '"Deceptive might": imperial defence and security, 1900–1968', in Louis, Wm. Roger (ed.), *The Oxford History of the British Empire* vol. IV *The Twentieth Century* (Oxford: Oxford University Press, 1999), pp.280–305

Cloake, John, *Templer: Tiger of Malaya: The Life of Field Marshal Sir Gerald Templer* (London: Harrap, 1985)

Clutterbuck, Richard, *The Long Long War: The Emergency in Malaya, 1948–1960* (London: Cassell, 1967)

Cockerill, A.W., *Sir Percy Sillitoe* (London: W.H. Allen, 1975)

Cohen, Geulah, *Woman of Violence: Memoirs of a Young Terrorist, 1943–1948* (London: Hart-Davis, 1966)

Cohen, Michael J., 'Appeasement in the Middle East: The British White Paper on Palestine, May 1939', *Historical Journal* 16 (1973), pp.571–96

Cohen, Michael J., 'The British White Paper on Palestine, May 1939. Part II: The Testing of a Policy, 1942–1945', *Historical Journal* 19 (1976), pp.727–58

Cole, Simon A., *Suspect Identities: A History of Fingerprinting and Criminal Identification* (Cambridge, M.: Harvard University Press, 2001)

Collings, Rex, *Reflections of a Statesman: The Writings and Speeches of Enoch Powell* (London: Bellew, 1991)

Comber, Leon, 'The Malayan Security Service (1945–1948)', *Intelligence and National Security* 18 (2003), pp.128–53

Comber, Leon, *Malaya's Secret Police, 1945–60: The Role of the Special Branch in the Malayan Emergency* (Clayton: Monash Asia Institute, 2008)

Conrad, Joseph, *The Secret Agent: A Simple Tale*, revised edn (Oxford and Santa Barbara: Clio, 1988)

Cooper, Chester, *The Lion's Last Roar: Suez, 1956* (New York: Harper & Row, 1978)

Corfield, F.D., *Historical Survey of the Origins and Growth of Mau Mau* (London: Colonial Office, 1960)

Cradock, Percy, *Know Your Enemy: How the Joint Intelligence Committee Saw the World* (London: John Murray, 2002)

Craig, Anthony, *Crisis of Confidence: Anglo-Irish Relations in the Early Troubles, 1966–1974* (Dublin: Irish Academic Press, 2010)

Cross, John, *Red Jungle* (London: Hale, 1975)

Cruickshank, Charles, *SOE in the Far East* (Oxford: Oxford University Press, 1983)

Curry, John C., *The Security Service, 1908–1945: The Official History*, with an introduction by Christopher Andrew (London: PRO, 1999)

Darby, Phillip, *British Defence Policy East of Suez, 1947–1968* (London: Oxford University Press for the Royal Institute of International Affairs, 1973)

Darwin, John, *Britain and Decolonisation: The Retreat from Empire in the Post-War World* (Basingstoke: Macmillan, 1988)

Deacon, Richard, *'C': A Biography of Sir Maurice Oldfield* (London: Futura, 1985)

Dilks, David (ed.), *The Diaries of Sir Alexander Cadogan, O.M., 1938–1945* (London: Cassell, 1971)

Dorril, Stephen, *MI6: Fifty Years of Special Operations* (London: Fourth Estate, 2000)

Drayton, Richard, 'Anglo-American "Liberal" Imperialism, British Guiana, 1953–64, and the world since September 11', in Louis, Wm. Roger (ed.), *Yet More Adventures in Britannia: Personalities, Politics and Culture in Britain* (London: I.B. Taurus, 2005)

Dudgen, Jeffrey, *Roger Casement – The Black Diaries: With a Study of His Background, Sexuality and Irish Political Life* (Belfast: Belfast Press, 2002)

Edney, Matthew, *Mapping an Empire: The Geographical Construction of British India, 1765–1843* (Chicago and London: University of Chicago Press, 1997)

Eliav, Ya'akov, *Wanted*, English translation (New York: Shengold, 1984)

Elkins, Caroline, *Britain's Gulag: The Brutal End of Empire in Kenya* (London: Jonathan Cape, 2005)

Ellis, John, *Eye Deep in Hell: The Western Front 1914–1918* (London: Fontana, 1977)

Eshed, Haggai, *Reuven Shiloah: The Man Behind the Mossad. Secret Diplomacy in the Creation of Israel*, English translation (London: Frank Cass, 1997)

Farran, Roy, *Winged Dagger: Adventures on Special Service* (London: Collins, 1948)

Ferguson, Niall, *Empire: How Britain Made the Modern World* (London: Penguin, 2004)

Fergusson, Niall, *Colossus: The Price of America's Empire* (New York: Penguin, 2004)

Ferris, John, 'Before "Room 40": The British Empire and Signals Intelligence 1898–1914', *Journal of Strategic Studies* 12 (1989), pp.431–57

Fitzpatrick, Sheila, 'The Civil War as a Formative Experience', in Gleason, Abbott, Kenez, Peter, and Stites, Richard (eds), *Bolshevik Culture: Experiment and Order in the Russian Revolution* (Bloomington, Ind: Indiana University Press, 1985), pp.57–76

Flower, Ken, *Serving Secretly: An Intelligence Chief on Record, Rhodesia into Zimbabwe, 1964–1981* (London: John Murray, 1987)

Foley, Charles (ed.), *The Memoirs of General Grivas* (London: Longman, 1964)

Foot, M.R.D., *S.O.E. in France: An Account of the British Special Operations Executive, 1940–1944* (London: HMSO, 1966)

Foot, M.R.D., *SOE in the Low Countries* (London: St Ermin's Press, 2001)

Foot, M.R.D., *Memories of an SOE Historian* (Barnsley: Pen & Sword Military, 2008)

Foot, M.R.D. 'Was SOE Any Good?', in Laqueur, Walter (ed.), *The Second World War: Essays in Military and Political History* (London: Sage, 1982)

Foot, Sylvia, *Emergency Exit* (London: Chatto &Windus, 1960)

Frankland, Mark, *Child of my Time* (London: Chatto & Windus, 1999)

Freedman, Lawrence, *The Official History of the Falklands Campaign* (London: Routledge, 2005)

Freeman, Simon, and Penrose, Barrie, *Rinkagate: The Rise and Fall of Jeremy Thorpe* (London: Bloomsbury, 1996)

French, David, *The British Way in Counter-Insurgency 1945–1967* (Oxford and New York: Oxford University Press, 2011)

French, Patrick, *Liberty or Death: India's Journey to Independence and Division* (London: HarperCollins, 1997)

Fussell, Paul, *The Great War and Modern Memory* (Oxford: Oxford University Press, 1975)

Gaddis, John Lewis, *We Now Know: Rethinking Cold War History* (Oxford: Clarendon Press, 1997)

Gallagher, Pete, 'Intelligence and decolonisation in British Guiana' (Undergraduate dissertation, University of Cambridge, 2009)

Gill, Peter, 'Reasserting control: recent changes in the oversight of the UK intelligence community', *Intelligence and National Security* 11 (1996), pp.313–31

Grant, Jennifer, 'Desperate Measures: Britain's internment of fascists during the Second World War' (PhD dissertation, University of Cambridge, 2009)

Gwynn, Charles W., *Imperial Policing* (London: Macmillan, 1984)

Hack, Karl, 'British intelligence and counter-insurgency in the era of decolonisation: the example of Malaya', *Intelligence and National Security* 14 (1999), pp.124–55

Hack, Karl, 'Corpses, Prisoners of War and Captured Documents: British and Communist Narratives of the Malayan Emergency, and the Dynamics of Intelligence Transformation', *Intelligence and National Security* 14 (1999), pp.211–41

Hansen, Randall, *Citizenship and Immigration in Post-War Britain: The Institutional Origins of a Multicultural Nation* (Oxford: Oxford University Press, 2000)

Harper, Timothy N., *The End of Empire and the Making of Malaya* (Cambridge: Cambridge University Press, 1998)

Harris, Tomás, *Garbo: The Spy who Saved D-Day*, with an introduction by Mark Seaman (London: PRO, 2000)

Harrison, E.D.R., 'British Radio Security and Intelligence', *English Historical Review* 506 (2009), pp.53–93

Hart, Herbert, *The Concept of Law*, 2nd edn (Oxford: Clarendon, 1994)

Hart-Davis, Duff, *The War that Never Was: The True Story of the Men Who Fought Britain's Most Secret Battle* (London: Century, 2011)

Haynes, John Earl, and Klehr, Harvey, *Venona: Decoding Soviet Espionage in America* (New Haven, Conn, and London: Yale University Press, 1999)

Heather, Randall W., 'Intelligence and counter-insurgency in Kenya, 1952–56', *Intelligence and National Security* 5 (1990), p.57–83

Heinlein, Frank, *British Government Policy and Decolonisation, 1945–1963: Scrutinising the Official Mind* (London: Frank Cass, 2002)

Heller, Joseph, *The Stern Gang: Ideology, Politics and Terror, 1940–49* (London: Frank Cass, 1995)

Hennessy, Peter, *Never Again: Britain 1945–1951* (London: Jonathan Cape, 1992)

Hennessy, Peter, *The Prime Minister: The Office and its Holders Since 1945* (London: Penguin, 2001)

Hennessy, Peter, *The Secret State: Whitehall and the Cold War* (London: Penguin, 2002); revised edn (London: Penguin, 2010)

Hennessy, Peter, and Brownfeld, Gail, 'Britain's Cold War Security Purge: The Origins of Positive Vetting', *Historical Journal* 25 (1982), pp.965–74

Herman, Michael, *Intelligence Power in Peace and War* (Cambridge: Cambridge University Press, 1996)

Herzog, Chaim, *Living History: A Memoir* (London: Phoenix, 1998)

Hesketh, Roger, *Fortitude: The D-Day Deception Campaign* (London: St Ermin's Press, 1999)

Hinchcliffe, Peter, Ducker, John T., and Holt, Maria, *Without Glory in Arabia: The British Retreat from Aden* (London: I.B. Taurus, 2006)

Hinsley, F.H., *British Intelligence in the Second World War* vols 1–3 *Its Influence on Strategy and Operations* (London: HMSO, 1979–88); Hinsley, F.H., with Simkins, C.A.G., *British Intelligence in the Second World War* vol. IV *Security and Counter-Intelligence* (London: HMSO, 1990); Howard, Michael, *British Intelligence in the Second World War* vol. V *Strategic Deception* (London: HMSO, 1992)

Hinsley, F.H., and Stripp, Alan (eds), *Codebreakers: The Inside Story of Bletchley Park* (Oxford: Oxford University Press, 2001)

Hinsley, F.H., 'British Intelligence in the Second World War', in Andrew, Christopher, and Noakes, Jeremy (eds), *Intelligence and International Relations 1900–1945* (Exeter: Exeter University Press, 1987)

Hoare, Oliver (ed.), *Camp 020: MI5 and the Nazi Spies* (London: PRO, 2000)

Hodson, Henry V., *The Great Divide: Britain, India, Pakistan* (London: Hutchinson, 1969)

Hoffman, Bruce, *The Failure of British Military Strategy Within Palestine, 1939–1947* (Ramat-Gan, Israel: Bar-Ilan University Press, 1983)

Hoffman, Bruce, *Inside Terrorism*, 2nd edn (New York: Columbia University Press, 2006)

Holquist, Peter, *Making War, Forging Revolution: Russia's Continuum of Crisis 1914–1921* (Cambridge, Mass, and London: Harvard University Press, 2002)

Holquist, Peter, '"Information is the Alpha and the Omega of our work": Bolshevik surveillance in its pan-European context', *Journal of Modern History* 69 (1997), pp.415–50

Holquist, Peter, 'To count, extract, to exterminate: population statistics and population politics in late imperial and Soviet Russia', in Suny, Ronald G., and Martin, Terry (eds), *A State of Nations: Empire and Nation-Making in the Age of Lenin and Stalin* (Oxford: Oxford University Press, 2001), pp.111–44

Holt, Thaddeus, *The Deceivers: Allied Military Deception in the Second World War* (London and New York: Scribner's, 2004)

Horne, Alastair, *Macmillan* vol. 2 (London: Macmillan, 1989)

Horne, Alastair *A Savage War of Peace: Algeria 1954–1962* (London: Papermac, 1987)

Hudson, Sydney, *Undercover Operator: Wartime Experiences with SOE in France and the Far East* (Oxford: ISIS, 2005)

Hull, Isabel, *Absolute Destruction: Military Culture and the Practices of War in Imperial Germany* (Ithaca: Cornell University Press, 2005)

Hull, Mark M., 'The Irish interlude: German intelligence in Ireland, 1939–1943', *Journal of Military History* 66 (July 2002), pp.702–3

Hyam, Ronald, *Britain's Declining Empire: The Road to Decolonisation, 1918–1968* (Cambridge: Cambridge University Press, 2006)

Jackson, Ashley, *The British Empire and the Second World War* (London: Hambledon Continuum, 2005)

Jeffery, Keith, *MI6: The History of the Secret Intelligence Service* (London: Bloomsbury, 2010)

Jeffries, Charles, *The Colonial Office* (London: Allen & Unwin, 1956)

Johnson, Chalmers, *Blowback: The Costs and Consequences of American Empire* (New York: Metropolitan Books, 2000)

Johnson, Robert, *Spying for Empire: The Great Game in Central and South Asia, 1757–1947* (London: Greenhill Books, 2006)

Kelly, Vann, 'Papon's transition after World War II: A prefect's road from Bordeaux, through Algeria, and beyond, August 1944–October 1961', in Golsan, Richard J. (ed.), *The Papon Affair: Memory and Justice on Trial* (London and New York: Routledge, 2000), pp.35–72

Kershaw, Ian, *Nazi Dictatorship: Problems and Perspectives of Interpretation*, 4th edn (London: Arnold, 2000)

Kipling, Rudyard, *Kim* (London: Macmillan, 1901)

Kitson, Frank, *Gangs and Counter-Gangs* (London: Barrie and Rockliffe, 1960)

Koestler, Arthur (et al.), *The God that Failed: Six Studies in Communism* (London: Hamish Hamilton, 1950)

Koestler, Arthur, *Thieves in the Night: Chronicle of an Experiment* (London: Hutchinson, 1965)

Kollek, Teddy, *For Jerusalem: A Life* (London: Weidenfeld & Nicolson, 1978)

Kyle, Keith, *The Politics of the Independence of Kenya* (Basingstoke: Macmillan, 1999)

Lapping, Brian, *End of Empire* (London: Paladin, 1989)

Lazreg, Marina, *Torture and the Twilight of Empire: From Algiers to Baghdad* (Princeton, NJ, and Woodstock: Princeton University Press, 2008)

le Carré, John, *The Honourable Schoolboy* (London: Sceptre, 2006)

Lenin, V.I., *Essential Works of Lenin: 'What is to be Done?' and Other Works*, new edn (New York: Dover Books, 1987)

Leslie, Will, 'British intelligence in Aden and South Arabia, 1963–1967' (MPhil dissertation, University of Cambridge, 2008)

Lewin-Epstein, Noah, Ro'i, Yaacov, and Ritterband, Paul (eds), *Russian Jews on Three Continents: Migration and Resettlement* (London: Frank Cass, 1997)

Lonsdale, John, 'Mau Maus of the mind: making Mau Mau and remaking Kenya', *Journal of African History* 31 (1990), pp.393–421

Lonsdale, John, 'British colonial officials and the Kikuyu people', in Smith, John (ed.), *Administering Empire: The British Colonial Service in Rretrospect* (London: University of London Press, 1999), pp.95–102

Lonsdale, John, 'Kenyatta's trials: breaking and making of an African nationalist', in Peter Cross (ed.), *The Moral World of the Law* (Cambridge: Cambridge University Press, 2000), pp.196–239

Louis, Wm. Roger, *The Ends of British Imperialism: The Scramble for Empire, Suez and Decolonisation* (London: I.B. Tauris, 2006)

Louis, Wm. Roger, 'Public Enemy Number One: The British empire in the dock at the United Nations 1957–71', in Lynn, Martin (ed.), *The British Empire in the 1950s: Retreat or Revival?* (Basingstoke: Palgrave Macmillan, 2006), pp.186–213

Louis, Wm. Roger, and Robinson, Ronald, 'The imperialism of decolonisation', *Journal of Imperial and Commonwealth History* 22 (1994), pp.462–511

Lowes, Andrew, 'British intelligence in India from the First World War to Independence' (MPhil dissertation, University of Cambridge, 2003)

Lucas, W. Scott, 'The missing link? Patrick Dean, chairman of the Joint Intelligence Committee', in Kelly, Saul, and Gorst, Anthony (eds), *Whitehall and the Suez Crisis* (London and Portland, Or: Frank Cass, 2000), pp.117–25

Lyttelton, Oliver, *The Memoirs of Lord Chandos* (London: Bodley Head, 1962)

McClellan, Woodford, 'Africans and black Americans in the Comintern schools, 1925–1934', *International Journal of African Historical Studies* 26 (1993), pp.371–90

Macintyre, Ben, *Operation Mincemeat: The True Spy Story that Changed the Course of World War Two* (London: Bloomsbury, 2007)

Mackay, Donald *The Malayan Emergency 1948–60: The Domino That Stood* (London: Brassey's, 1997)

McKenzie, Alastair, *Special Force: The Untold Story of 22nd Special Air Service Regiment (SAS)* (London: I.B. Taurus, 2011)

Macmillan, Harold, *Riding the Storm, 1956–1959* (London: Macmillan, 1971)

Macmillan, Harold, *Pointing the Way, 1959–61* (London: Macmillan, 1972)

Magan, William, *Middle Eastern Approaches: Experiences and Travels of an Intelligence Officer, 1939–1945* (Norwich: Michael Russell, 2001)

Mansergh, Nicholas (ed.), *Constitutional Relations Between Britain and India: The Transfer of Power in India*, 12 vols (London, 1970–83)

Marrus, Michael, *The Unwanted: European Refugees from the First World War Through the Cold War* (New York and Oxford: Oxford University Press, 1985)

Marston, Daniel, 'Lost and Found in the Jungle: The Indian and British Army Jungle Warfare Doctrines for Burma, 1943–5, and the Malayan Emergency, 1948–60', in Strachan, Hew (ed.), *Big Wars and Small Wars: The British Army and the Lessons of War in the Twentieth Century* (London: Routledge, 2006), pp.84–114

Maskelyne, Jasper, *Magic – Top Secret* (London: Stanley Paul, 1949)

Masterman, John C., *The Double-Cross System in the War of 1939 to 1945* (New Haven and London: Yale University Press, 1972)

Masters, Anthony, *The Man Who Was M: The Life of Maxwell Knight* (Oxford: Basil Blackwell, 1984)

Mawby, Spenser, *British Policy in Aden and the Protectorates 1955–67: Last Outpost of a Middle East Empire* (London: Routledge, 2005)

Millar, Alexander, 'British intelligence and the Comintern in Shanghai, 1927–37' (PhD dissertation, University of Cambridge, 2010)

Miller, Harry, *Jungle War in Malaya: The Campaign Against Communism, 1948–60* (London: Barker, 1972)

Moen, Jan, *John Moe: Double Agent* (Edinburgh: Mainstream, 1986)

Mohs, Polly A., *Military Intelligence and the Arab Revolt: The First Modern Intelligence War* (London: Routledge, 2008)

Mommsen, Hans, 'Militär und zivile Militisierung in Deutschland, 1914 bis 1938', in Frevert, Ute (ed.), *Militär und Gesellschaft im 19. und 20. Jahrhundert* (Stuttgart: Klett-Cotta, 1997), pp.265–76

Montagu, Ewen, *The Man Who Never Was*, revised paperback edn (Oxford: Oxford University Press, 1996)

Morris, Benny, *The Birth of the Palestinian Refugee Problem Revisited* (Cambridge: Cambridge University Press, 2004)

Moses, A. Dirk, *Empire, Colony, Genocide: Conquest, Occupation, and Subaltern Resistance in World History* (New York and Oxford: Berghahn Books, 2008)

Muggeridge, Malcolm, *Chronicles of Wasted Time* vol. II *The Infernal Grove* (London: Fontana, 1975)

Mullik, B.N., *My Years with Nehru 1948–1964* (Bombay: Allied, 1972)

Murphy, Philip, *Alan Lennox-Boyd: A Biography* (London: I.B. Tauris, 1999)

Murphy, Philip, 'South African intelligence, the Wilson Plot and post-Imperial trauma', in Major, Patrick, and Moran, Christopher R (eds), *Spooked: Britain, Empire and Intelligence Since 1945* (Cambridge: Cambridge Scholars Press, 2010), pp.97–118

Murphy, Philip, 'Intelligence and Decolonization: The Life and Death of the Federal Intelligence and Security Bureau, 1954–63', *Journal of Imperial and Commonwealth History* 29 (2001), pp.101–30

Murphy, Philip, 'Creating a commonwealth intelligence culture: The view from central Africa, 1945–1965', *Intelligence and National Security* 17 (2002), pp.131–62

Murphy, Philip, 'A Police State? The Nyasaland Emergency and Colonial Intelligence', *Journal of Southern African Studies* 36 (2010), pp.765–80

Nagler, Jörg, 'Victims of the Home Front: Aliens in the United States During the First World War', in Panayi, Panikos (ed.), *Minorities in Wartime: National and Racial Groupings in Europe, North America and Australia During the Two World Wars* (Oxford: Berg, 1993), pp.191–215

Nehru, Jawaharlal, *The Discovery of India*, new edn (Delhi: Oxford University Press, 1985)

Neilson, Keith, and McKercher, B.J.C. (eds), *Go Spy the Land: Military Intelligence in History* (Westport, Conn: Praeger, 1992)

Nicolai, Walter, *The German Secret Service*, English translation (London: Stanley Paul, 1924)

Nkrumah, Kwame, *The Autobiography of Kwame Nkrumah* (Edinburgh and London: T. Nelson, 1957)

O'Brien, Kevin A., *The South African Intelligence Services* (London: Routledge, 2011)

O'Halpin, Eunan (ed.), *MI5 and Ireland 1939–1945: The Official History* (London: PRO, 2003)

O'Halpin, Eunan, 'British Intelligence in Ireland', in Andrew, Christopher, and Dilks, David (eds), *The Missing Dimension: Governments and Intelligence Communities in the Twentieth Century* (London: Macmillan, 1984), pp.59–61

O'Halpin, Eunan, '"A poor thing but our own": The Joint Intelligence Committee and Ireland 1965–71', *Intelligence and National Security* 23 (2008), pp.658–80

Ondaatje, Michael, *The English Patient* (London: Bloomsbury, 1992)

Ovendale, Ritchie, *Britain, the United States, and the End of the Palestine Mandate 1942–1948* (Woodbridge: Boydell Press, 1989)

Overy, Richard J., *Interrogations: The Nazi Elite in Allied Hands, 1945* (London: Allen Lane, 2001)

Panayi, Panikos, *The Enemy in Our Midst: Germans in Britain During the First World War* (New York and Oxford: Berg, 1991)

Panayi, Panikos (ed.), *Minorities in Wartime: National and Racial Groupings in Europe, North America and Australia During the Two World Wars* (Oxford: Berg, 1993)

Patten, Chris, *East and West: The Last Governor of Hong Kong on Power, Freedom and the Future* (London: Pan 1998)

Pearce, Robert, *The Turning Point in Africa: British Colonial Policy, 1938–1948* (London: Frank Cass, 1982)

Pedahzur, Ami, *The Israeli Response to Jewish Extremism and Violence: Defending Democracy* (Manchester and New York: Manchester University Press, 2002)

Pegushev, Andrei M., 'The Unknown Kenyatta', *Egerton Journal* 2 (1996), pp.172–98

Pegushev, Andrei M., 'Afrikanski v komminterne', *Vostok* 7 (1997), pp.37–49

Petrie, David, *Communism in India 1924–27* (Calcutta: Editions Indian, 1972)

Philby, H.A.R., *My Silent War: The Autobiography of a Spy* (London: MacGibbon & Kee, 1968); new paperback edn (London: Arrow, 2003)

Pilger, John, *Freedom Next Time* (London: Black Swan, 2007)

Pincher, Chapman, *Their Trade is Treachery: The Full, Unexpurgated Truth About the Russian Penetration of the Free World's Secret Defences* (London: Sidgwick & Jackson, 1981)

Pipes, Richard, *A Concise History of the Russian Revolution* (London: Harvill, 1995)

Popplewell, Richard J., *Intelligence and Imperial Defence: British Intelligence and the Defence of the Indian Empire, 1904–1924* (London: Frank Cass, 1995)

Pujol, Juan, with West, Nigel, *Garbo* (London: Grafton, 1986)

Quinlan, Kevin, 'Human intelligence operations and MI5 tradecraft in Britain' (PhD dissertation, University of Cambridge, 2008)

Raeff, Marc, 'The well ordered police state and the development of modernity in seventeenth- and eighteenth-century Europe: an attempt at a comparative approach', *American Historical Review* 80 (1975), pp.1221–43

Ram, Bhagat, *The Talwars of Pathan Land and Subhas Chandra's Great Escape* (New Delhi: People's Pub. House, 1976)

Ratcliff, R.A., *Delusions of Intelligence: Enigma, Ultra and the End of Secure Ciphers* (Cambridge: Cambridge University Press, 2006)

Rathbone, Richard, 'Political intelligence and policing in Ghana in the late 1940s and 1950s', in Anderson, David M., and Killingray, David (eds), *Policing and Decolonisation: Nationalism and the Police, 1917–1965* (Manchester: Manchester University Press, 1992), pp.84–104

Rathbone, Richard, *Nkrumah and the Chiefs: The Politics of Chieftaincy in Ghana, 1951–60* (Accra: F. Reimmer; Oxford: James Currey, 2000)

Reynolds, David, *Britannia Overruled: British Policy and World Power in the Twentieth Century*, 2nd edn (Harlow: Longman, 2000)

Reynolds, David, *In Command of History: Churchill Fighting and Winning the Second World War* (London: Allen Lane, 2004)

Richards, Michael, *A Time of Silence: Civil War and the Culture of Repression in Franco's Spain, 1936–1945* (Cambridge: Cambridge University Press, 1998)

Richelson, Jeffrey T., and Ball, Desmond, *The Ties that Bind: Intelligence Cooperation between UKUSA Countries – the United Kingdom, the United States of America, Canada, Australia and New Zealand*, 2nd edn (Boston: Hyman, 1985)

Rimington, Stella, *Open Secret: The Autobiography of the Former Director-General of MI5* (London: Hutchinson, 2001)

Rooney, David, *Sir Charles Arden-Clarke* (London: Collings, 1982)

Rose, Norman, *'A Senseless, Squalid War': Voices From Palestine, 1890s to 1948* (London: Pimlico, 2010)

Roskams, Samuel, 'British intelligence, imperial defence and the early Cold War in the Far East' (MPhil dissertation, University of Cambridge, 2007)

Ruark, Robert, *Something of Value* (London: New English Library, 1964)

Satia, Pryia, *Spies in Arabia: The Great War and the Foundations of Britain's Covert Empire in the Middle East* (Oxford: Oxford University Press, 2007)

Schellenberg, Walter, *The Schellenberg Memoirs* (London: André Deutsch, 1956)

Scott, James C., *Seeing Like a State: How Certain Schemes to Improve the Human Condition Have Failed* (New Haven and London: Yale University Press, 1998)

Shamir, Yitzhak, *Summing Up: An Autobiography* (London: Weidenfeld & Nicolson, 1994)

Shelley, Adam, 'Empire of Shadows: British Intelligence in the Middle East 1939-1945' (PhD dissertation, University of Cambridge, 2007)

Shepherd, Naomi, *Ploughing Sand: British Rule in Palestine 1917–1948* (London: John Murray, 1999)

Sherman, A.J., *Mandate Days: British Lives in Palestine 1918–1948* (London: Thames & Hudson, 1997)

Shibuya, Nao, 'British intelligence in Hong Kong in the era of the Cultural Revolution' (MPhil dissertation, University of Cambridge, 2008)

Short, Anthony, *The Communist Insurrection in Malaya, 1948–60* (London: Muller, 1975)

Shuckburgh, Evelyn, *Descent to Suez: Diaries 1951–56* (London: Weidenfeld & Nicolson, 1986)

Sillitoe, Percy, *Cloak Without Dagger* (London: Cassell, 1955)

Simpson, A.W.B., *In the Highest Degree Odious: Detention without Trial in Wartime Britain* (Oxford: Clarendon, 1975)

Sinclair, Georgina, *At the End of the Line: Colonial Policing and the Imperial Endgame, 1945–80* (Manchester: Manchester University Press, 2006)

Singha, Radhika, 'Settle, Mobilise, Verify: Identification Practices in Colonial India', *Studies in History* 16 (2000), pp.153–98

Sisman, Adam, *Hugh Trevor-Roper: The Biography* (London: Weidenfeld & Nicolson, 2010)

Smiley, David, *Arabian Assignment* (London: Cooper, 1975)

Smith, Michael, 'Bletchley Park and the Holocaust', *Intelligence and National Security* 19 (2004), pp.262–74

Smith, Simon C., 'General Templer and counter-insurgency in Malaya: hearts and minds, intelligence, and propaganda', *Intelligence and National Security* 16 (2001), pp.60–78

Smith, Simon C., *Ending Empire in the Middle East: Britain, the United States and Post-War Decolonization* (London: Routledge, 2012)

Sprinzak, Ehud, *Brother Against Brother: Violence and Extremism in Israeli Politics from Altalena to the Rabin Assassination* (New York: Free Press, 1999)

Strachan, Hew (ed.), *Big Wars and Small Wars: The British Army and the Lessons of War in the Twentieth Century* (London: Routledge, 2006)

Suckhov, D.I., 'Dzhomo Keniata v Mosckve', *Vostok* 4 (1993), pp.106–21

Thomas, Martin, *Empires of Intelligence: Security Services and Colonial Disorder After 1914* (Berkeley, Ca, and London: University of California Press, 2008)

Thomson, Basil, *Queer People* (London: Hodder & Stoughton, 1922)

Thomson, Basil, *The Scene Changes* (London: Collins, 1939)

Thurlow, Richard, 'Internment in the Second World War', *Intelligence and National Security* 9 (1994), pp.123–27

Tomlinson, Richard, *The Big Breach: From Top Secret to Maximum Security* (London: Cutting Edge, 2001)

Trevaskis, Kennedy, *Shades of Amber: A South Arabian Episode* (London: Hutchinson, 1968)

Trevelyan, Humphrey, *The Middle East in Revolution* (London and Basingstoke: Macmillan, 1970)

Trevor-Roper, Hugh, *The Last Days of Hitler*, new edn (London: Pan Books, 1952)

Trotter, William R., *The Winter War: The Russo-Finnish War of 1939–1940* (London: Aurum, 2002)

Verrier, Anthony, *Through the Looking Glass: British Foreign Policy in an Age of Illusions* (London: Jonathan Cape, 1983)

von Bülow, Mathilde, 'The Foreign Policy of the Federal Republic of Germany: Franco–German Relations, and the Algerian War 1954–62' (PhD dissertation, University of Cambridge, 2006)

Walton, Calder, 'British intelligence, the Mandate of Palestine and threats to national security immediately after the Second World War', *Intelligence and National Security* 23 (2008), pp.435–62

Walton, Calder, and Andrew, Christopher, 'Still the "Missing Dimension": British intelligence and the historiography of British decolonisation', in Major, Patrick, and Moran, Christopher R. (eds), *Spooked: Britain, Empire and Intelligence Since 1945* (Cambridge: Cambridge Scholars, 2009), pp.73–96

Walzer, Michael, *Just and Unjust Wars: A Moral Argument with Historical Illustrations*, 3rd edn (New York: Basic Books, 2006)

Wark, Wesley K., *The Ultimate Enemy: British Intelligence and Nazi Germany 1933–1939* (Ithaca: Cornell University Press, 1985)

Wark, Wesley K., 'In Never-Never Land? The British archives on intelligence', *Historical Journal* 35 (1992), pp.195–203

West, Nigel, *Mask: MI5's Penetration of the Communist Party of Great Britain* (London: Routledge, 2005)

West, Nigel, *Venona: The Greatest Secret of the Cold War* (London: HarperCollins, 1999)

Wilson, Emily, 'The War in the Dark: The Security Service and the Abwehr 1939–1945' (PhD dissertation, University of Cambridge, 2003)

Winter, J.M., *Sites of Memory, Sites of Mourning: The Great War in European Cultural History* (Cambridge: Cambridge University Press, 1995)

Winter, Paul, 'British Intelligence, Adolf Hitler and the German High Command, 1939–1945' (PhD dissertation, University of Cambridge, 2009)

Winter, P.R.J., 'Libra Rising: Hitler, Astrology and British Intelligence, 1940–43', *Intelligence and National Security* 21 (2006), pp.394–415

Winterbotham, Frederick, *The Ultra Secret: The Inside Story of Operation Ultra, Bletchley Park and Enigma* (London: Orion, 2000)

Wohlstetter, Roberta, *Pearl Harbor: Warning and Decision* (Stanford, Ca: Stanford University Press, 1963)

Woodhouse, C.M., *Something Ventured* (London: Granada, 1982)

Wright, Peter, *Spycatcher: The Candid Autobiography of a Senior Intelligence Officer* (Richmond, Victoria: William Heinemann Australia, 1987)

Young, George Kennedy, *Who is my Liege? A Study of Loyalty and Betrayal in Our Time* (London: Gentry, 1972)

Zimmerer, Juergen (et al., eds), *Genocide in German South-West Africa: The Colonial War (1904–1908) in Namibia and its Aftermath* (Monmouth: Merlin, 2008)

Index